Welcome to

The Official Guide to the GRE® General Test

The book you're holding is a one-of-a-kind resource: the only GRE guide created by the ETS team that produces the actual exam. This book is uniquely suited to help you do your best on this challenging test.

Here's what you'll find inside:

- **Two real, full-length GRE practice tests.** Use actual tests to sharpen your skills and build your confidence.

- **Three new Verbal Reasoning practice sets and three new Quantitative Reasoning practice sets** that you can take to see how you perform.

- **Authentic GRE questions with answers and explanations.** Practice with real test questions created by the test makers.

- **ETS's own test-taking strategies.** Learn valuable hints and tips that can help you get your best score.

- **Official information on the GRE General Test.** Get the facts about the test content and structure—straight from ETS.

About ETS

We believe in the life-changing power of learning. For the last 75 years, we've been driven by a vision of what's possible when all people can improve their lives through education. It's why our uncompromising commitment to equity and fairness is behind everything we do. ETS serves learners, educators and government agencies by providing measurement solutions and conducting research, analysis and policy studies. ETS develops, administers and scores tens of millions of tests annually—including the TOEFL® and TOEIC® tests, the GRE tests and The Praxis Series® assessments—in more than 200 countries, at over 9,000 locations worldwide. **www.ets.org**.

IMPORTANT

ETS makes available free test preparation materials for individuals planning to take a GRE test, including timed practice tests that simulate what you'll experience on test day. The information about how to prepare for the General Test, test-taking strategies, question strategies, etc., that is included in the free test preparation is also included in this *Guide*. The *Guide* also provides you with additional practice questions, additional practice sets and two additional full-length practice tests with explanatory materials.

For more information about the GRE General Test, free and low-cost GRE test preparation materials, and other GRE products and services, please visit the GRE website at

www.ets.org/gre

Inquiries concerning the practice test questions in this book should be sent to the GRE testing program at

GRETestQuestionInquiries@ets.org

*gre®

The Official
Guide to the
GRE® General Test

4th Edition

McGraw Hill

1 2 3 4 5 LBC 28 27 26 25 24

ISBN   978-1-266-79564-0
MHID   1-266-79564-2

e-ISBN   978-1-259-86242-7
e-MHID   1-266-05336-0

McGraw Hill products are available at special quantity discounts to use as premiums and sales promotions or for use in corporate training programs. To contact a representative, please visit the Contact Us pages at www.mhprofessional.com.

Interior Designer: Jane Tenenbaum

Contents

1 About the GRE General Test   1

2 GRE Analytical Writing   9

3 GRE Verbal Reasoning: Overview   27

4

GRE Verbal Reasoning: Practice Questions 37

5

GRE Verbal Reasoning: Mixed Practice Sets 91

6

GRE Quantitative Reasoning: Overview
175

7

GRE Quantitative Reasoning: Practice Questions
221

8

GRE Quantitative Reasoning: Mixed Practice Sets
285

9 GRE Math Review 373

10 GRE Practice Test 1 483

11 GRE Practice Test 2   579

How to Use This Book

This book provides a large amount of important information about the GRE General Test, the types of questions it includes, and the knowledge and skills that it measures. The book will help you:

- Familiarize yourself with the test format and question types
- Learn valuable test-taking strategies for each question type
- Review the math topics you need to know for the test
- Check your progress with Verbal Reasoning and Quantitative Reasoning practice questions presented by question type and difficulty level
- Continue to evaluate your progress with timed Verbal Reasoning and Quantitative Reasoning practice sections
- Take two full-length paper GRE General Tests, which provide scores on the Verbal Reasoning and Quantitative Reasoning measures as well as information to help you gauge your performance on the Analytical Writing measure

The following six-step program has been designed to help you make the best use of this book.

STEP 1 Learn About the GRE General Test Format

Chapter 1 of this book provides official information about the structure of the GRE General Test. Read this chapter to learn about the different test sections, the number of questions in each section, and the section time limits. You'll also find valuable test-taking strategies from ETS and important information about how the test is scored.

STEP 2 Study the Different GRE Question Types

Chapters 2, 3, and 6 of this book describe the types of questions you'll encounter in the three sections of the GRE General Test. Chapter 2 describes the Analytical Writing section, which requires you to write one essay in response to a prompt that you will be given. Chapter 3 describes the Verbal Reasoning question types. Chapter 6 describes the Quantitative Reasoning question types. In each case, you will learn what the questions are designed to measure, and you will get tips for answering each question type. You will also see samples of each question type, with helpful explanations.

STEP 3 Practice Answering GRE Verbal and Quantitative Reasoning Questions

Chapters 4 and 7 offer Verbal Reasoning and Quantitative Reasoning practice questions in the format of the GRE General Test. The question sets are arranged in order of increasing difficulty, from easy through medium to hard. Answer the questions in each set, then read through the explanations to see which test topics you found most challenging. Look for patterns. Did specific question formats give you trouble? When did you need to guess at the answer? Use your results to identify your weaknesses and to sharpen your test-taking skills.

STEP 4 Take GRE Verbal and Quantitative Reasoning Practice Sets

Chapters 5 and 8 contain five Verbal Reasoning and five Quantitative Reasoning mixed practice sets, respectively. The sections include a mix of question types and difficulty levels just like the Verbal Reasoning and Quantitative Reasoning sections on the actual GRE General Test. Take a practice set and then review your answers to the questions. Read through the explanations to see which questions you found most challenging. Use your results to help identify where you need to focus the remainder of your test preparation time.

STEP 5 Review GRE Math Topics

Chapter 9 provides a review of math topics tested in the GRE General Test Quantitative Reasoning sections. You do not necessarily need to tackle every topic in the review or to work through the review in the order in which it is presented. Skip around if you like, but remember to focus on the topics that you know give you trouble. Each section of the review ends with practice problems that you can use to see how well you have mastered the material. If you get a problem wrong, go back into the review section and reread the corresponding instructional text.

STEP 6 Take the Practice Tests

Once you have completed your review, get ready for a full-length practice exam by taking the authentic GRE practice tests in Chapters 10 and 11 of this book. When you take each practice test, try to simulate actual testing conditions. Sit in a quiet space, time yourself, and work through as much of the test as time allows. After you finish each test, follow the instructions for calculating your Verbal Reasoning and Quantitative Reasoning scores and evaluating your Analytical Writing performance.

Additional Practice with Official GRE Resources

Get even more practice with Official GRE Resources, including the free Test Preview Tool and practice tests, which you can access when you create an ETS account at www.ets.org/mygre.

These tools are designed to help you familiarize yourself with each of the question types, formatted as they would be on the actual test. Using these resources is also an opportunity for you to become familiar with all of the features of the computer-delivered GRE General Test, such as Help screens, the Review screen, word-processing software for the Analytical Writing section, and the on-screen calculator.

For information on how to access the abundance of Official GRE prep resources available to you, visit **www.ets.org/gre/prepare**.

1 About the GRE General Test

Your goal for this chapter

📖 Review basic information on the structure of the test, test preparation, and scoring

Introduction

The GRE General Test—the most widely accepted graduate admissions test worldwide—measures verbal reasoning, quantitative reasoning, critical thinking, and analytical writing skills that are necessary for success in graduate, business and law school.

Prospective graduate, business and law school applicants from all around the world take the GRE General Test. Applicants come from varying educational and cultural backgrounds, and the GRE General Test provides a common measure for comparing candidates' qualifications.

GRE scores are used by admissions committees and fellowship panels to supplement your undergraduate records, recommendation letters, and other qualifications for graduate-level study.

The GRE General Test is administered on computers at about 1,000 test centers in more than 160 countries. In most regions of the world, the test is available on a continuous basis throughout the year.

The GRE General Test can also be taken at home in most locations around the world. The at-home test is identical in content, format and on-screen experience to the GRE General Test taken at a test center. It is taken on your own computer and is monitored by a human proctor. Additional information about the at-home test, including equipment and environment requirements, is available at **www.ets.org/gre**.

For the most up-to-date information about the GRE General Test, visit the GRE website at **www.ets.org/gre**.

Content and Structure of the Test

Content

The GRE General Test is composed of three measures — Analytical Writing, Verbal Reasoning, and Quantitative Reasoning.

- **The Analytical Writing measure** assesses your ability to articulate and support complex ideas, sustain a focused and coherent discussion, and control the elements of standard written English. The Analytical Writing section requires you to provide a focused response to the task presented, so you can accurately demonstrate your skill in directly responding to a task.

- **The Verbal Reasoning measure** assesses your ability to analyze and evaluate written material and synthesize information obtained from it; understand the meanings of words, sentences, and entire texts; and understand relationships among words and among concepts. The Verbal Reasoning section measures your ability to understand what you read and how you apply your reasoning skills.

- **The Quantitative Reasoning measure** assesses your basic mathematical skills and your understanding of the elementary mathematical concepts of arithmetic, algebra, geometry, and data analysis. The Quantitative Reasoning section measures your ability to understand, interpret, and analyze quantitative information and to solve problems using mathematical models.

Test Structure

Measure	*Number of Questions*	*Allotted Time*
Analytical Writing (One section)	One essay task	30 minutes
Verbal Reasoning (Two sections)	Section 1: 12 questions Section 2: 15 questions	Section 1: 18 minutes Section 2: 23 minutes
Quantitative Reasoning (Two sections)	Section 1: 12 questions Section 2: 15 questions	Section 1: 21 minutes Section 2: 26 minutes
Total Testing Time		1 hour and 58 minutes

The Analytical Writing section will always come first in the test. The Verbal Reasoning and Quantitative Reasoning sections may appear in any order after the Analytical Writing section.

Total testing time is 1 hour and 58 minutes. The directions at the beginning of each Verbal Reasoning and Quantitative Reasoning section specify the total number of questions in the section and the time allowed for the section. For the Analytical Writing section, the timing for the task is shown when the task is presented.

Test Design Features

The Verbal Reasoning and Quantitative Reasoning measures of the GRE General Test are section-level adaptive. This means the computer selects the second section of a measure based on your performance on the first section.

The advanced adaptive design also means you can freely move forward and backward throughout an entire section. Specific features include:

- Preview and review capabilities within a section
- A "mark and review" feature to tag questions, so you can skip them and return later if you have time remaining in the section
- The ability to change/edit answers within a section
- An on-screen calculator for the Quantitative Reasoning measure

Preparing for the Test

Preparation for the test will depend on the amount of time you have available and your personal preferences for how to prepare. At a minimum, before you take the GRE General Test, you should know what to expect from the test, including the administrative procedures, types of questions and directions, approximate number of questions, and amount of time for each section.

The administrative procedures include registration and appointment scheduling, date, time, test center location, cost, score-reporting procedures, and availability of special testing arrangements. You can find out about the administrative procedures for the General Test in the *GRE Information Bulletin*, which is available at **www.ets.org/gre/bulletinandforms**.

Before taking the General Test, it is important to become familiar with the content of each of the measures. In this publication, you'll find information specific to each measure of the test. You can use this information to understand the type of material on which you'll be tested and the question types within each measure.

It is also important to spend some time preparing for the Analytical Writing section by reviewing the skills measured, scoring guide and score level descriptions, sample topics, scored sample essay responses, and reader commentary.

Test-Taking Strategies

Analytical Writing Section

The Analytical Writing measure of the General Test uses an elementary word processor developed by ETS so that individuals familiar with a specific commercial word processing software do not have an advantage or disadvantage. This software contains the following functionality: insert text, delete text, cut and paste, and undo the previous action. Tools such as a spelling checker and grammar checker are not available in the ETS software.

It is important to budget your time. Within the 30-minute time limit for the task, you'll need to allow sufficient time to think about the topic, plan a response, and compose your essay. Although you are under time constraints during the section, you will still want to produce the best possible example of your writing.

Save a few minutes at the end of the timed task to check for obvious errors. Although an occasional typographical, spelling, or grammatical error will not affect your score, severe or persistent errors will detract from the overall effectiveness of your writing and lower your score.

Verbal Reasoning and Quantitative Reasoning Sections

The questions in the Verbal Reasoning and Quantitative Reasoning measures are presented in a variety of formats. Some require you to select a single answer choice; others require you to select one or more answer choices, and yet others require you to enter a numeric answer. Make sure when answering a question that you understand what response is required. An on-screen calculator will be provided at the test center for use during the Quantitative Reasoning sections.

When taking the GRE General Test, you are free to skip questions that you might have difficulty answering within a section. The testing software has a "mark and review" feature that enables you to mark questions you would like to revisit during the time provided to work on that section. The testing software also lets you view a complete list of all the questions in the section on which you're working, indicates whether you've answered each question, and identifies the questions you've marked for review. Additionally, you can review questions you've already answered and change your answers, provided you still have time remaining to work on that section.

A sample review screen appears at the top of the page. The review screen is intended to help you keep track of your progress on the test. Do not spend too much time on the review screen, as this will take away from the time allotted to read and answer the questions on the test.

Your Verbal Reasoning and Quantitative Reasoning scores will be determined by the number of questions you answer correctly. Nothing is subtracted from a score if you answer a question incorrectly. Therefore, to maximize your scores on the Verbal Reasoning and Quantitative Reasoning measures, it is best to answer every question. Work as rapidly as you can without being careless. Since no question carries greater weight than any other, do not waste time pondering individual questions you find extremely difficult or unfamiliar.

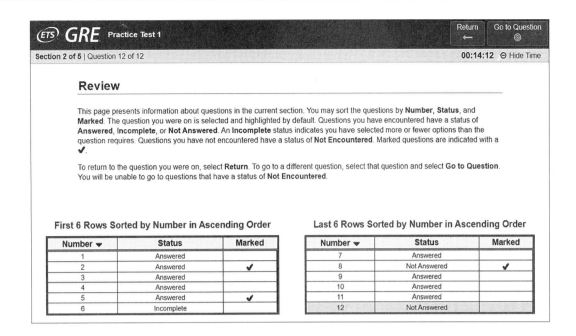

During the actual administration of the General Test, you may work only on one section at a time and only for the time allowed. Once you have completed a section, you may not go back to it.

Note-Taking Materials

If you test at a test center, you will receive a supply of scratch paper before you begin the test. You can replenish your supply of scratch paper as necessary throughout the test by asking the test administrator.

Acceptable note-taking materials for the at-home test include a small whiteboard or plastic transparency sheet that can be erased in view of the proctor.

Breaks

There are no breaks between test sections. If you are taking the test at a test center, section timing will not stop if you take an unscheduled break, so you should proceed with your test without interruption once it begins.

Unscheduled breaks are not permitted during the at-home test.

Understanding GRE Scoring

Analytical Writing Measure

Your essay response will be evaluated for its overall quality based on how well you:

● Respond to the specific task instructions

● Consider the complexities of the issue

- Organize, develop and express your ideas

- Support your ideas with relevant reasons and/or examples

- Control the elements of standard written English

The primary emphasis in scoring the Analytical Writing section is on your critical thinking and analytical writing skills. A scoring guide for the essay task is included in this publication, and it is also available on the GRE website at **https://www.ets.org/gre/ test-takers/general-test/prepare/content/analytical-writing/scoring.html**.

Independent Intellectual Activity

During the scoring process for the General Test, your essay response on the Analytical Writing section will be reviewed by ETS essay-similarity-detection software and by experienced raters. In light of the high value placed on independent intellectual activity within graduate schools and universities, your essay response should represent your original work. ETS reserves the right to cancel test scores of any test taker when an essay response includes any of the following:

- Text that is unusually similar to that found in one or more other GRE test essay responses

- Quoting or paraphrasing, without attribution, language that appears in any published or unpublished sources, including sources from the Internet and/or sources provided by any third party

- Unacknowledged use of work that has been produced through collaboration with others without citation of the contribution of others

- Essays submitted as work of the test taker that appear to have been borrowed in whole or in part from elsewhere or prepared by another person

When one or more of the preceding circumstances occurs, ETS may conclude, in its professional judgment, that the essay response does not reflect the independent writing skills that this test seeks to measure. When ETS reaches that conclusion, it cancels the Analytical Writing score, and because the Analytical Writing is score is an integral part of GRE General Test scores, ETS cancels those scores as well.

Verbal Reasoning and Quantitative Reasoning Measures

For the Verbal Reasoning and Quantitative Reasoning measures of the GRE General Test, the reported scores are based on the number of correct responses to the questions included in the actual sections of the measure.

The Verbal Reasoning and Quantitative Reasoning measures are section-level adaptive. This means the computer selects the second section of a measure based on your performance on the first section. Within each section, all questions contribute equally to the final score. For each of the two measures, a raw score is computed. The raw score is the number of questions you answered correctly.

The raw score is then converted to a scaled score through a process known as equating. The equating process accounts for minor variations in difficulty from test to test as well as the differences introduced by the section-level adaptation. Thus a given scaled score for a particular measure reflects the same level of performance regardless of which second section was selected and when the test was taken.

Score Reporting

Three scores are reported on the General Test:

- a Verbal Reasoning score reported on a 130–170 score scale, in 1-point increments

- a Quantitative Reasoning score reported on a 130–170 score scale, in 1-point increments

- an Analytical Writing score reported on a 0–6 score scale, in half-point increments

If you do not answer any questions at all for a measure (Verbal Reasoning, Quantitative Reasoning, or Analytical Writing), you will receive a No Score (NS) for that measure.

Descriptions of the analytical writing abilities characteristic of particular score levels are available in this publication on page 25, and on the GRE website at **www.ets.org/gre/awscoredescriptions**.

The *ScoreSelect*® Option

The *ScoreSelect*® option, available for both the GRE General Test and GRE Subject Tests, lets you decide which test scores to send to the institutions you designate. You can send scores from your most recent test administration or scores for all of the times you've taken a GRE test as part of your four free score reports. After test day, you can send scores from your *Most Recent, All,* or *Any* specific test administration(s) for a fee when ordering additional score reports. Just remember, scores for a test administration must be reported in their entirety. For more information, visit **www.ets.org/gre/scoreselect**.

Score Reporting Time Frames

Scores from computer-delivered GRE General Test administrations are reported approximately 8 to 10 days after the test date. Be sure to review the appropriate admissions deadlines and plan to take the test in time for your scores to reach the institution.

For more information on score reporting, visit the GRE website at **www.ets.org/gre/scores/get**.

2 GRE Analytical Writing

Your goals for this chapter

- Recognize the Analytical Writing task type
- Study examples of the task
- Learn strategies for responding to the writing tasks
- Review actual student responses and ETS reader commentary

Overview of the Analytical Writing Measure

The Analytical Writing measure assesses your critical thinking and analytical writing skills. It assesses your ability to articulate and support complex ideas, construct and evaluate arguments, and sustain a focused and coherent discussion. It does not assess specific content knowledge.

The Analytical Writing measure consists of one 30-minute timed analytical writing task. The task presents an opinion on an issue of broad interest followed by specific instructions on how to respond to that issue. You are required to evaluate the issue, consider its complexities, and develop an argument with reasons and examples to support your views.

Preparing for the Analytical Writing Measure

Everyone—even the most practiced and confident of writers—should spend some time preparing for the Analytical Writing measure before arriving at the test center. It is important to review the skills measured and how the section is scored. It is also useful to review the scoring guide and score level descriptions, sample topics, scored sample essay responses, and reader commentary for the task.

The task in the Analytical Writing measure relates to a broad range of subjects—from the fine arts and humanities to the social and physical sciences—but it does not require specific content knowledge. In fact, each task has been field-tested to ensure that it possesses several important characteristics, including the following:

- GRE test takers, regardless of their field of study or special interests, understood the task and could easily respond to it.

- The task elicited the kinds of complex thinking and persuasive writing that university faculty consider important for success at the graduate level.

- The responses were varied in content and in the way the writers developed their ideas.

To help you prepare for the Analytical Writing measure, the GRE Program has published the entire pool of tasks from which your test task will be selected. You might find it helpful to review the pool, which is available at **www.ets.org/gre/awtopics**.

General Strategies

- **It is important to budget your time.** Within the 30-minute time limit for the task, you will need to allow sufficient time to consider the issue and the specific instructions, plan a response, and compose your essay. You will want your essay response to be the best possible example of your writing that you can produce under the testing conditions.

- **Save a few minutes at the end of the timed task to check for obvious errors.** Although an occasional spelling or grammatical error will not affect your score, severe and persistent errors will detract from the overall effectiveness of your writing and thus lower your score.

Analytical Writing Task

Understanding the Task

The Analytical Writing task assesses your ability to think critically about a topic of general interest according to specific instructions and to clearly express your thoughts about it in writing. Each topic makes a claim that test takers can discuss from various perspectives and apply to many different situations or conditions. The topic statement is followed by specific instructions. Your task is to present a compelling case for your own position on the topic according to the specific instructions. Before beginning your written response, be sure to read the topic and instructions carefully and think about the topic from several points of view, considering the complexity of ideas associated with those views. Then, make notes about the position you want to develop and list the main reasons and examples that you could use to support that position.

It is important that you address the assigned topic according to the specific instructions. Each task is accompanied by one of the following sets of instructions.

- Write a response in which you discuss the extent to which you agree or disagree with the statement and explain your reasoning for the position you take. In developing and supporting your position, you should consider ways in which the statement might or might not hold true and explain how these considerations shape your position.

- Write a response in which you discuss the extent to which you agree or disagree with the recommendation and explain your reasoning for the position you take. In developing and supporting your position, describe specific circumstances in which adopting the recommendation would or would not be advantageous and explain how these examples shape your position.

- Write a response in which you discuss the extent to which you agree or disagree with the claim. In developing and supporting your position, be sure to address the most compelling reasons and/or examples that could be used to challenge your position.

- Write a response in which you discuss which view more closely aligns with your own position and explain your reasoning for the position you take. In developing and supporting your position, you should address both of the views presented.

- Write a response in which you discuss the extent to which you agree or disagree with the claim and the reason on which that claim is based.

- Write a response in which you discuss your views on the policy and explain your reasoning for the position you take. In developing and supporting your position, you should consider the possible consequences of implementing the policy and explain how these consequences shape your position.

Note that there is no "right" answer—in fact, there is no correct position to take. Instead, your response will be evaluated based on the skill with which you address the specific instructions and articulate and develop an argument to support your evaluation of the issue.

Understanding the Context for Writing: Purpose and Audience

The Analytical Writing task is an exercise in critical thinking and persuasive writing. The purpose of this task is to determine how well you can develop a compelling argument supporting your own evaluation of an issue and communicate that argument in writing to an academic audience. The scoring criteria are identified in the scoring guide for the Analytical Writing task (see pages 23–24).

To get a clearer idea of how actual essay responses are scored, you should review scored sample essay responses and reader commentary. The sample responses, particularly at the 5 and 6 score levels, will show you a variety of successful strategies for organizing, developing, and communicating a persuasive argument. The reader commentary discusses specific aspects of evaluation and writing, such as the use of examples, development and support, organization, language fluency, and word choice. For each response, the reader commentary points out aspects that are particularly persuasive as well as any that detract from the overall effectiveness of the essay.

Preparing for the Task

Because the task is meant to assess the persuasive writing skills that you have developed throughout your education, it has been designed neither to require any particular course of study nor to advantage students with a particular type of training.

Many college textbooks on composition offer advice on persuasive writing and argumentation that you might find useful, but even this advice might be more technical and specialized than you need for the Issue task. You will not be expected to know specific critical thinking or writing terms or strategies; instead, you should be able to respond to the specific instructions and use reasons, evidence, and examples to support your position on an issue. Suppose, for instance, that a topic asks you to consider a policy that would require government financial support for art museums and the implications of implementing the policy. If your position is that governments should fund art museums, you might support your position by discussing the reasons art is important and explaining that government funding would make access to museums available to everyone. On the other hand, if your position is that governments should not support museums, you might point out that, given limited governmental funds, art museums are not as deserving of governmental funding as are other, more socially important, institutions, which would suffer if the policy were implemented. Or, if you are in favor of government funding for art museums only under certain conditions, you might focus on the artistic criteria, cultural concerns, or political conditions that you think should determine how—or whether—art museums receive government funds. It is not your position that matters so much as the critical thinking skills you display in developing your position.

An excellent way to prepare for the Analytical Writing task is to practice writing on some of the published topics. There is no "best" approach: some people prefer to start practicing without regard to the 30-minute time limit; others prefer to take a "timed test" first and practice within the time limit. No matter which approach you take when you practice the task, you should review the task directions, then

- carefully read the claim and the specific instructions and make sure you understand them; if they seem unclear, discuss them with a friend or teacher

- think about the claim and instructions in relation to your own ideas and experiences, to events you have read about or observed, and to people you have known; this is the knowledge base from which you will develop compelling reasons and examples in your argument that reinforce, negate, or qualify the claim in some way

- decide what position on the issue you want to take and defend

- decide what compelling evidence (reasons and examples) you can use to support your position

Remember that this is a task in critical thinking and persuasive writing. The most successful responses will explore the complexity of the claim and instructions. As you prepare for the task, you might find it helpful to ask yourself the following questions:

- What precisely is the central issue?

- What precisely are the instructions asking me to do?

- Do I agree with all or with any part of the claim? Why or why not?

- Does the claim make certain assumptions? If so, are they reasonable?

- Is the claim valid only under certain conditions? If so, what are they?

- Do I need to explain how I interpret certain terms or concepts used in the claim?

- If I take a certain position on the issue, what reasons support my position?

- What examples—either real or hypothetical—could I use to illustrate those reasons and advance my point of view? Which examples are most compelling?

Once you have decided on a position to defend, consider the perspective of others who might not agree with your position. Ask yourself:

- What reasons might someone use to refute or undermine my position?

- How should I acknowledge or defend against those views in my essay?

To plan your response, you might want to summarize your position and make brief notes about how you will support the position you're going to take. When you've done this, look over your notes and decide how you will organize your response. Then write a response developing your position on the issue. Even if you don't write a full response, you should find it helpful to practice with a few of the topics and to sketch out your possible responses. After you have practiced with some of the topics, try writing responses to some of the topics within the 30-minute time limit so that you have a good idea of how to use your time in the actual test.

It may be helpful to get some feedback on your response from an instructor who teaches critical thinking or writing or to trade papers on the same topic with other students and discuss one another's responses in relation to the scoring guide. Try to determine how each paper meets or misses the criteria for each score point in the guide. Comparing your own response to the scoring guide will help you see how and where you might need to improve.

The Form of Your Response

You are free to organize and develop your response in any way that you think will effectively communicate your ideas about the issue and the instructions. Your response may, but need not, incorporate particular writing strategies learned in English composition or writing-intensive college courses. GRE raters will not be looking for a particular developmental strategy or mode of writing; in fact, when GRE raters are trained, they review hundreds of responses that, although highly diverse in content and form, display similar levels of critical thinking and persuasive writing. Raters will see, for example, some responses at the 6 score level that begin by briefly summarizing the writer's position on the issue and then explicitly announcing the main points to be argued. They will see others that lead into the writer's position by making a prediction, asking a series of questions, describing a scenario, or defining critical terms in the quotation. The raters know that a writer can earn a high score by giving multiple examples or by presenting a single, extended example. Look at the sample responses, particularly at the 5 and 6 score levels, to see how other writers have successfully developed and organized their arguments.

You should use as many or as few paragraphs as you consider appropriate for your argument—for example, you will probably need to create a new paragraph whenever your discussion shifts to a new cluster of ideas. What matters is not the number of examples, the number of paragraphs, or the form your argument takes but, rather, the cogency of your ideas about the issue and the clarity and skill with which you communicate those ideas to academic readers.

Sample Task

> As people rely more and more on technology to solve problems, the ability of humans to think for themselves will surely deteriorate.
>
> Discuss the extent to which you agree or disagree with the statement and explain your reasoning for the position you take. In developing and supporting your position, you should consider ways in which the statement might or might not hold true and explain how these considerations shape your position.

Strategies for This Topic

In this task, you are asked to discuss the extent to which you agree or disagree with the statement. Thus, responses may range from strong agreement or strong disagreement, to qualified agreement or qualified disagreement. You are also instructed to explain your reasoning and consider ways in which the statement might or might not hold true. A successful response need not comment on all or any one of the points listed below and may well discuss other reasons or examples not mentioned here in support of its position.

Although this topic is accessible to respondents of all levels of ability, for any response to receive a top score, it is particularly important that you remain focused on the task and provide clearly relevant examples and/or reasons to support the point of view you are expressing. Lower-level responses may be long and full of examples of modern technology, but those examples may not be clearly related to a particular position. For example, a respondent who strongly disagrees with the statement may choose to use computer technology as proof that thinking ability is not deteriorating. The mere existence of computer technology, however, does not adequately prove this point (perhaps the ease of computer use inhibits our thinking ability). To receive a higher-level score, the respondent should explain in what ways computer technology may call for or require thinking ability.

This topic could elicit a wide variety of approaches, especially considering the different possible interpretations of the phrase "the ability of humans to think for themselves." Although most respondents may take it to mean problem solving, others, with equal effectiveness, could interpret it as emotional and social intelligence (i.e., the ability to communicate/connect with others). With any approach, it is possible to discuss examples such as calculators, word processing tools such as spelling and grammar checks, tax return software, Internet research, and a variety of other common household and business technologies.

You may agree with the prompt and argue that:

- reliance on technology leads to dependency; we come to rely on problem-solving technologies to such a degree that when they fail, we are in worse shape than if we didn't have them in the first place

- everyday technologies such as calculators and cash registers have decreased our ability to perform simple calculations, a "use it or lose it" approach to thinking ability

Or you may take issue with the prompt and argue that technology facilitates and improves our thinking skills, arguing that:

- developing, implementing, and using technology requires problem solving

- technology frees us from mundane problem solving (e.g., calculations) and allows us to engage in more complex thinking

- technology provides access to information otherwise unavailable

- technology connects people at a distance and allows them to share ideas

- technology is dependent on the human ability to think and make choices (every implementation of and advance in technology is driven by human intelligence and decision making)

On the other hand, you could decide to explore the middle ground in the debate and point out that while technology may diminish some mental skill sets, it enables other (perhaps more important) types of thinking to thrive. Such a response might distinguish between complex problem solving and simple "data maintenance" (i.e., performing calculations and organizing information). Other approaches could include taking a historical, philosophical, or sociological stance, or, with equal effectiveness, using personal examples to illustrate a position. One could argue that the value or detriment of relying on technology is determined by the individual (or society) using it or that only those who develop technology (i.e., technical specialists) are maintaining their problem-solving skills, while the rest of us are losing them.

Again, it is important for you to avoid overly general examples or lists of examples without expansion. It is also essential to do more than paraphrase the prompt. Please keep in mind that what counts is the ability to clearly express a particular point of view in relation to the issue and specific task instructions and to support that position with relevant reasons and/or examples.

Essay Responses and Rater Commentary

Score 6 Response *

The statement linking technology negatively with free thinking plays on recent human experience over the past century. Surely there has been no time in history where the lived lives of people have changed more dramatically. A quick reflection on a typical day reveals how technology has revolutionized the world. Most people commute to work in an automobile that runs on an internal combustion engine. During the workday, chances are high that the employee will interact with a computer that processes information on silicon bridges that are .09 microns wide. Upon leaving home, family members will be reached through wireless networks that utilize satellites orbiting the earth. Each of these common occurences would have been inconceivable at the turn of the 19th century.

The statement attempts to bridge these dramatic changes to a reduction in the ability for humans to think for themselves. The assumption is that an increased reliance on technology negates the need for people to think creatively to solve previous quandaries. Looking back at the introduction, one could argue that without a car, computer, or mobile phone, the hypothetical worker would need to find alternate methods of transport, information processing, and communication. Technology short circuits this thinking by making the problems obsolete.

However, this reliance on technology does not necessarily preclude the creativity that marks the human species. The prior examples reveal that technology allows for convenience. The car, computer, and phone all release additional time for people to live more efficiently. This efficiency does not preclude the need for humans to think for themselves. In fact, technology frees humanity to not only tackle new problems, but may itself create new issues that did not exist without technology. For example, the proliferation of automobiles has introduced a need for fuel conservation on a global scale. With increasing energy demands from emerging markets, global warming becomes a concern inconceivable to the horse-and-buggy generation. Likewise dependence on oil has created nation-states that are not dependent on taxation, allowing ruling parties to oppress minority groups such as women. Solutions to these complex problems require the unfettered imaginations of maverick scientists and politicians.

In contrast to the statement, we can even see how technology frees the human imagination. Consider how the digital revolution and the advent of the internet has allowed for an unprecedented exchange of ideas. WebMD, a popular internet portal for medical information, permits patients to self research symptoms for a more informed doctor visit. This exercise opens pathways of thinking that were previously closed off to the medical layman. With increased interdisciplinary interactions, inspiration can arrive from the most surprising corners. Jeffrey Sachs, one of the architects of the UN Millenium Development Goals, based his ideas on emergency care triage techniques. The unlikely marriage of economics and medicine has healed tense, hyperinflation environments from South America to Eastern Europe.

This last example provides the most hope in how technology actually provides hope to the future of humanity. By increasing our reliance on technology, impossible goals can now be achieved. Consider how the late 20th century witnessed the complete elimination of smallpox. This disease had ravaged the human race since prehistorical days, and yet with the technology of vaccines, free thinking humans dared to imagine a

---

*All responses in this publication are reproduced exactly as written, including errors, misspellings, etc., if any.

world free of smallpox. Using technology, battle plans were drawn out, and smallpox was systematically targeted and eradicated.

Technology will always mark the human experience, from the discovery of fire to the implementation of nanotechnology. Given the history of the human race, there will be no limit to the number of problems, both new and old, for us to tackle. There is no need to retreat to a Luddite attitude to new things, but rather embrace a hopeful posture to the possibilities that technology provides for new avenues of human imagination.

Rater Commentary

The author of this essay stakes out a clear and insightful position on the issue and follows the specific instructions by discussing ways in which the statement might or might not hold true, using specific reasons and examples to support that position. The essay cogently argues that technology does not decrease our ability to think for ourselves. It merely provides "additional time for people to live more efficiently." In fact, the problems that have developed alongside the growth of technology (pollution, political unrest in oil-producing nations) actually call for more creative thinking, not less. In further examples, the essay shows how technology allows for the linking of ideas that may never have been connected in the past (like medicine and economic models), pushing people to think in new ways. Examples are persuasive and fully developed; reasoning is logically sound and well supported.

Ideas in the essay are connected logically, with effective transitions used both between paragraphs ("However," or "In contrast to the statement") and within paragraphs. Sentence structure is varied and complex, and the essay clearly demonstrates facility with the "conventions of standard written English (i.e., grammar, usage, and mechanics)" (see Issue Scoring Guide, pages 23–24), with only minor errors appearing. Thus, this essay meets all the requirements for receiving a top score, a 6.

Score 5 Response

Surely many of us have expressed the following sentiment, or some variation on it, during our daily commutes to work: "People are getting so stupid these days!" Surrounded as we are by striding and strident automatons with cell phones glued to their ears, PDA's gripped in their palms, and omniscient, omnipresent CNN gleaming in their eyeballs, it's tempting to believe that technology has isolated and infantilized us, essentially transforming us into dependent, conformist morons best equipped to sideswip one another in our SUV's.

Furthermore, hanging around with the younger, pre-commute generation, whom tech-savviness seems to have rendered lethal, is even less reassuring. With "Teen People" style trends shooting through the air from tiger-striped PDA to zebra-striped PDA, and with the latest starlet gossip zipping from juicy Blackberry to teeny, turbo-charged cell phone, technology seems to support young people's worst tendencies to follow the crowd. Indeed, they have seemingly evolved into intergalactic conformity police. After all, today's tech-aided teens are, courtesy of authentic, hands-on video games, literally trained to kill; courtesy of chat and instant text messaging, they have their own language; they even have tiny cameras to efficiently photodocument your fashion blunders! Is this adolescence, or paparazzi terrorist training camp?

With all this evidence, it's easy to believe that tech trends and the incorporation of technological wizardry into our everyday lives have served mostly to enforce conformity, promote dependence, heighten comsumerism and materialism, and generally create a culture that values self-absorption and personal entitlement over cooperation and collaboration. However, I argue that we are merely in the inchoate stages of learning to live with technology while still loving one another. After all, even given the examples provided earlier in this essay, it seems clear that technology hasn't impaired our thinking and problem-solving capacities. Certainly it has incapacitated our behavior and manners; certainly our values have taken a severe blow. However, we are inarguably more efficient in our badness these days. We're effective worker bees of ineffectiveness!

If technology has so increased our senses of self-efficacy that we can become veritable agents of the awful, virtual CEO's of selfishness, certainly it can be beneficial. Harnessed correctly, technology can improve our ability to think and act for ourselves. The first challenge is to figure out how to provide technology users with some direly-needed direction.

Rater Commentary

The language of this essay clearly illustrates both its strengths and weaknesses. The flowery and sometimes uncannily keen descriptions are often used to powerful effect, but at other times the writing is awkward and the comparisons somewhat strained. See, for example, the ungainly sequence of independent clauses in the second to last sentence of paragraph 2 ("After all, today's tech-aided teens . . . ").

There is consistent evidence of facility with syntax and complex vocabulary ("Surrounded as we are by striding and strident automatons with cell phones glued to their ears, PDA's gripped in their palms, and omniscient, omnipresent CNN gleaming in their eyeballs, it's tempting to believe . . . "). Such lucid prose, however, is often countered with an over-reliance upon abstractions and tangential reasoning (what does the fact that video games "literally train [teens] to kill" have to do with the use or deterioration of thinking abilities, for example?).

Because this essay takes a complex approach to the issue (arguing, in effect, that technology neither enhances nor reduces our ability to think for ourselves, but can be used to do one or the other depending on the user) and because the author makes use of "appropriate vocabulary and sentence variety" (see Issue Scoring Guide, pages 23–24), a score of 5 is appropriate.

Score 4 Response

In all actuality, I think it is more probable that our bodies will surely deteriorate long before our minds do in any significant amount. Who can't say that technology has made us lazier, but that's the key word, lazy, not stupid. The ever increasing amount of technology that we incorporate into our daily lives makes people think and learn every day, possibly more than ever before. Our abilities to think, learn, philosophize, etc. may even reach limits never dreamed of before by average people. Using technology to solve problems will continue to help us realize our potential as a human race.

If you think about it, using technology to solve more complicating problems gives humans a chance to expand their thinking and learning, opening up whole new worlds for many people. Many of these people are glad for the chance to expand their horizons by learning more, going to new places, and trying new things. If it wasn't for the invention of new technological devices, I wouldn't be sitting at this computer trying to philosophize about technology. It would be extremely hard for children in much poorer countries to learn and think for themselves with out the invention of the internet. Think what an impact the printing press, a technologically superior mackine at the time, had on the ability of the human race to learn and think.

Right now we are seeing a golden age of technology, using it all the time during our every day lives. When we get up there's instant coffee and the microwave and all these great things that help us get ready for our day. But we aren't allowing our minds to deteriorate by using them, we are only making things easier for ourselves and saving time for other important things in our days. Going off to school or work in our cars instead of a horse and buggy. Think of the brain power and genius that was used to come up with that single invention that has changed the way we move across this globe.

Using technology to solve our continually more complicated problems as a human race is definately a good thing. Our ability to think for ourselves isn't deteriorating, it's continuing to grow, moving on to higher though functions and more ingenious ideas. The ability to use what technology we have is an example

Rater Commentary

This essay meets all the criteria of a 4-level essay. The writer develops a clear position ("Using technology to solve problems will continue to help us realize our potential as a human race"). The position is then developed with relevant reasons ("using technology to solve more complicat[ed] problems gives humans a chance to expand their thinking and learning . . . " and "we are seeing a golden age of technology"). Point 1, "Using technology," is supported with the simple, but relevant notions that technology allows us access to information and abilities to which we would not normally have access. Similarly, point 2, "the golden age," is supported by the basic description of our technologically saturated social condition. Though the development and organization of the essay does suffer from an occasional misstep (see paragraph 3's abrupt progression from coffeepots to the benefits of technology to cars), the essay as a whole flows smoothly and logically from one idea to the next.

It is useful to compare this essay to the 3-level essay presented next. Though they both utilize some very superficial discussion and often fail to probe deeply into the issue, this writer does, however, take the analysis a step further. In paragraph 2, the distinction between this essay and the next one (the 3-level response) can most clearly be seen. To support the notion that advances in technology actually help increase thinking ability, the writer draws a clever parallel between the promise of modern, sophisticated technology (computer) and the equally substantial/pervasive technology of the past (printing press).

Like the analysis, the language in this essay clearly meets the requirements for a score of 4. The writer displays sufficient control of language and the conventions of standard written English. The preponderance of mistakes are of a cosmetic nature ("using technology to solve more complicating problems"). There is a sentence fragment ("Going off . . . ") along with a comma splice ("Our ability . . . isn't deteriorating, it's continuing to grow . . . ") in paragraph 4. These errors, though, are minor and do not interfere with the clarity of the ideas being presented.

Score 3 Response

> There is no current proof that advancing technology will deteriorate the ability of humans to think. On the contrary, advancements in technology had advanced our vast knowledge in many fields, opening opportunities for further understanding and achievement. For example, the problem of dibilitating illnesses and diseases such as alzheimer's disease is slowing being solved by the technological advancements in stem cell research. The future ability of growing new brain cells and the possibility to reverse the onset of alzheimer's is now becoming a reality. This shows our initiative as humans to better our health demonstrates greater ability of humans to think.
>
> One aspect where the ability of humans may initially be seen as an example of deteriorating minds is the use of internet and cell phones. In the past humans had to seek out information in many different enviroments and aspects of life. Now humans can sit in a chair and type anything into a computer and get an answer. Our reliance on this type of technology can be detrimental if not regulated and regularly substituted for other information sources such as human interactions and hands on learning. I think if humans understand that we should not have such a reliance on computer technology, that we as a species will advance further by utilizing the opportunity of computer technology as well as the other sources of information outside of a computer. Supplementing our knowledge with internet access is surely a way for technology to solve problems while continually advancing the human race.

Rater Commentary

This essay never moves beyond a superficial discussion of the issue. The writer attempts to develop two points: that advancements in technology have progressed our knowledge in many fields and that supplementing rather than relying on technology is "surely a way for technology to solve problems while continually advancing the human race." Each point, then, is developed with relevant but insufficient evidence. In discussing the ability of technology to advance knowledge in many fields (a broad subject rife with possible examples), the writer uses only one limited and very brief example from a specific field (medicine and stem-cell research).

Development of the second point is hindered by a lack of specificity and organization. The writer creates what might most be comparable to an outline. The writer cites a need for regulation/supplementation and warns of the detriment of over-reliance upon technology. However, the explanation of both the problem and the solution is vague and limited ("Our reliance . . . can be detrimental . . . If humans understand that we should not have such a reliance . . . we will advance further"). There is neither explanation of consequences nor clarification of what is meant by "supplementing." This second paragraph is a series of generalizations, which are loosely connected and lack a much-needed grounding.

In the essay, there are some minor language errors and a few more serious flaws (e.g., "The future ability of growing new brain cells" or "One aspect where the ability of humans may initially be seen as an example of deteriorating minds…"). Despite the accumulation of such flaws, though, meaning is generally clear. This essay earns a score of 3, then, primarily for its limited development.

Score 2 Response

In recent centuries, humans have developed the technology very rapidly, and you may accept some merit of it, and you may see a distortion in society occured by it. To be lazy for human in some meaning is one of the fashion issues in thesedays. There are many symptoms and resons of it. However, I can not agree with the statement that the technology make humans to be reluctant to thinkng thoroughly.

Of course, you can see the phenomena of human laziness along with developed technology in some place. However, they would happen in specific condition, not general. What makes human to be laze of thinking is not merely technology, but the the tendency of human that they treat them as a magic stick and a black box. Not understanding the aims and theory of them couses the disapproval problems.

The most important thing to use the thechnology, regardless the new or old, is to comprehend the fundamental idea of them, and to adapt suit tech to tasks in need. Even if you recognize a method as a all-mighty and it is extremely over-spec to your needs, you can not see the result you want. In this procedure, humans have to consider as long as possible to acquire adequate functions. Therefore, humans can not escape from using their brain.

In addition, the technology as it is do not vain automatically, the is created by humans. Thus, the more developed tech and the more you want a convenient life, the more you think and emmit your creativity to breakthrough some banal method sarcastically.

Consequently, if you are not passive to the new tech, but offensive to it, you would not lose your ability to think deeply. Furthermore, you may improve the ability by adopting it.

Rater Commentary

The language of this essay is what most clearly links it to the score point of 2. Amidst sporadic moments of clarity, this essay is marred by serious errors in grammar, usage, and mechanics that often interfere with meaning. It is unclear what the writer means when he/she states, "To be lazy for human in some meaning is one of the fashion issues in these-days," or " . . . to adapt suit tech to tasks in need." Despite such severe flaws, the writer has made an obvious attempt to respond to the prompt ("I can not agree with the statement that the technology make humans to be reluctant to thinking thoroughly") as well as an unclear attempt to support such an assertion ("Not understanding the aims and theory of them [technology] couses the disapproval problems" and "The most important thing to use the thechnology . . . is to comprehend the fundamental idea of them"). Holistically, the essay displays a seriously flawed but not fundamentally deficient attempt to develop and support its claims.

(Note: In this SPECIFIC case, the analysis is tied directly to the language. As the language falters, so too does the analysis.)

Score 1 Response

> Humans have invented machines but they have forgot it and have started everything technically so clearly their thinking process is deterioating.

Rater Commentary

The essay is clearly on topic, as evidenced by the writer's usage of the more significant terms from the prompt: "technically" (technologically), "humans", "thinking" (think) and "deterioating" (deteriorate). Such usage is the only clear evidence of understanding. Meaning aside, the brevity of the essay (one sentence) clearly indicates the writer's inability to develop a response that addresses the specific instructions given ("Discuss the extent to which you agree or disagree with the statement above and explain your reasoning for the position you take").

The language, too, is clearly one-level, as the sentence fails to achieve coherence. The coherent phrases in this one-sentence response are those tied to the prompt: "Humans have invented machines" and "their thinking process is deterioating." Otherwise, the point being made is unclear.

GRE Scoring Guide

Score 6

In addressing the specific task directions, a 6 response presents a cogent, well-articulated analysis of the issue and conveys meaning skillfully.

A typical response in this category
- articulates a clear and insightful position on the issue in accordance with the assigned task
- develops the position fully with compelling reasons and/or persuasive examples
- sustains a well-focused, well-organized analysis, connecting ideas logically
- conveys ideas fluently and precisely, using effective vocabulary and sentence variety
- demonstrates superior facility with the conventions of standard written English (i.e., grammar, usage, and mechanics) but may have minor errors

Score 5

In addressing the specific task directions, a 5 response presents a generally thoughtful, well-developed analysis of the issue and conveys meaning clearly.

A typical response in this category
- presents a clear and well-considered position on the issue in accordance with the assigned task
- develops the position with logically sound reasons and/or well-chosen examples
- is focused and generally well organized, connecting ideas appropriately
- conveys ideas clearly and well, using appropriate vocabulary and sentence variety
- demonstrates facility with the conventions of standard written English but may have minor errors

Score 4

In addressing the specific task directions, a 4 response presents a competent analysis of the issue and conveys meaning with acceptable clarity.

A typical response in this category
- presents a clear position on the issue in accordance with the assigned task
- develops the position with relevant reasons and/or examples
- is adequately focused and organized
- demonstrates sufficient control of language to express ideas with acceptable clarity
- generally demonstrates control of the conventions of standard written English but may have some errors

Score 3

A 3 response demonstrates some competence in addressing the specific task directions, in analyzing the issue, and in conveying meaning but is obviously flawed.

A typical response in this category exhibits ONE OR MORE of the following characteristics:
- is vague or limited in addressing the specific task directions and/or in presenting or developing a position on the issue
- is weak in the use of relevant reasons or examples or relies largely on unsupported claims
- is limited in focus and/or organization
- has problems in language and sentence structure that result in a lack of clarity
- contains occasional major errors or frequent minor errors in grammar, usage, or mechanics that can interfere with meaning

Score 2

A 2 response largely disregards the specific task directions and/or demonstrates serious weaknesses in analytical writing.

A typical response in this category exhibits ONE OR MORE of the following characteristics:
- is unclear or seriously limited in addressing the specific task directions and/or in presenting or developing a position on the issue
- provides few, if any, relevant reasons or examples in support of its claims
- is poorly focused and/or poorly organized
- has serious problems in language and sentence structure that frequently interfere with meaning
- contains serious errors in grammar, usage, or mechanics that frequently obscure meaning

Score 1

A 1 response demonstrates fundamental deficiencies in analytical writing.

A typical response in this category exhibits ONE OR MORE of the following characteristics:
- provides little or no evidence of understanding the issue
- provides little evidence of the ability to develop an organized response (e.g., is disorganized and/or extremely brief)
- has severe problems in language and sentence structure that persistently interfere with meaning
- contains pervasive errors in grammar, usage, or mechanics that result in incoherence

Score 0

Off topic (i.e., provides no evidence of an attempt to respond to the assigned topic), is in a foreign language, merely copies the topic, consists of only keystroke characters, or is illegible or nonverbal.

Score Level Descriptions

The reported score ranges from 0 to 6, in half-point increments. The statements below describe, for each score level, the overall quality of critical thinking and analytical writing demonstrated. The Analytical Writing section assesses your critical thinking and analytical writing skills (the ability to reason, assemble evidence to develop a position and communicate complex ideas) along with your control of grammar and the mechanics of writing.

Scores 6 and 5.5: Sustains insightful, in-depth analysis of complex ideas; develops and supports main points with logically compelling reasons and/or highly persuasive examples; is well focused and well organized; skillfully uses sentence variety and precise vocabulary to convey meaning effectively; demonstrates superior facility with sentence structure and language usage but may have minor errors that do not interfere with meaning.

Scores 5 and 4.5: Provides generally thoughtful analysis of complex ideas; develops and supports main points with logically sound reasons and/or well-chosen examples; is generally focused and well organized; uses sentence variety and vocabulary to convey meaning clearly; demonstrates good control of sentence structure and language usage but may have minor errors that do not interfere with meaning.

Scores 4 and 3.5: Provides competent analysis of ideas; develops and supports main points with relevant reasons and/or examples; is adequately organized; conveys meaning with reasonable clarity; demonstrates satisfactory control of sentence structure and language usage but may have some errors that affect clarity.

Scores 3 and 2.5: Displays some competence in analytical writing, although the writing is flawed in at least one of the following ways: limited analysis or development; weak organization; weak control of sentence structure or language usage, with errors that often result in vagueness or lack of clarity.

Scores 2 and 1.5: Displays serious weaknesses in analytical writing. The writing is seriously flawed in at least one of the following ways: serious lack of analysis or development; lack of organization; serious and frequent problems in sentence structure or language usage, with errors that obscure meaning.

Scores 1 and 0.5: Displays fundamental deficiencies in analytical writing. The writing is fundamentally flawed in at least one of the following ways: content that is extremely confusing or mostly irrelevant to the assigned task: little or no development; severe and pervasive errors that result in incoherence.

Score 0: The test taker's analytical writing skills cannot be evaluated because the response does not address any part of the assigned task, is merely an attempt to copy the assignment, is in a language other than English, or displays only indecipherable text.

Score NS: The test taker produced no text whatsoever.

3 GRE Verbal Reasoning: Overview

Your goals for this chapter	❧ Learn about the different GRE Verbal Reasoning question types ❧ Get tips for answering each question type ❧ Study examples of GRE Verbal Reasoning questions

Overview of the Verbal Reasoning Measure

The Verbal Reasoning measure assesses your ability to analyze and evaluate written material and synthesize information obtained from it, to analyze relationships among component parts of sentences, and to recognize relationships among words and concepts.

Verbal Reasoning questions appear in several formats, each of which is discussed in detail below. About half of the measure requires you to read passages and answer questions on those passages. The other half requires you to read, interpret, and complete existing sentences, groups of sentences, or paragraphs. Many, but not all, of the questions are standard multiple-choice questions, in which you are required to select a single correct answer; others ask you to select multiple correct answers; and still others ask you to select a sentence from the passage. The number of choices varies depending on the type of question.

Verbal Reasoning Question Types

The Verbal Reasoning measure contains three types of questions:

- Reading Comprehension
- Text Completion
- Sentence Equivalence

In this section you will study each of these question types one by one, and you'll learn valuable strategies for answering each type. Turn the page to begin.

Reading Comprehension Questions

Reading Comprehension questions are designed to test a wide range of abilities required to read and understand the kinds of prose commonly encountered in graduate school. Those abilities include

- understanding the meaning of individual words
- understanding the meaning of individual sentences
- understanding the meaning of paragraphs and larger bodies of text
- distinguishing between minor and major points
- summarizing a passage
- drawing conclusions from the information provided
- reasoning from incomplete data and inferring missing information
- understanding the structure of a text and how the parts relate to one another
- identifying the author's perspective
- identifying the author's assumptions
- analyzing a text and reaching conclusions about it
- identifying strengths and weaknesses
- developing and considering alternative explanations

As this list implies, reading and understanding a piece of text requires far more than a passive understanding of the words and sentences it contains—it requires active engagement with the text, asking questions, formulating and evaluating hypotheses, and reflecting on the relationship of the particular text to other texts and information.

Each Reading Comprehension question is based on a passage, which may range in length from one paragraph to four or five paragraphs. Each passage has anywhere from one to six questions associated with it. In any given test, most passages are one paragraph long, and one or two may be more than one paragraph. Passages are based on material found in books and periodicals, both academic and nonacademic, and are drawn from physical sciences, biological sciences, social sciences, business, arts and humanities, and everyday topics.

Questions can cover any of the abilities listed above, from recognizing the meaning of a particular word to assessing evidence that might support or weaken points made in the passage. Many, but not all, of the questions are standard multiple-choice questions, in which you are required to select a single correct answer; others ask you to select multiple correct answers, and still others ask you to select a sentence from the passage. These question types are presented in more detail below, and you should make sure that you are familiar with the differences among them.

General Advice

Reading passages are drawn from many different disciplines and sources, so you may encounter material with which you are not familiar. Do not be discouraged when this happens; all the questions can be answered on the basis of the information provided in the passage, and you are not expected to rely on any outside knowledge. If, however, you encounter a passage that seems particularly hard or unfamiliar, you may want to save it for last.

- Read and analyze the passage carefully before trying to answer any of the questions and pay attention to clues that help you understand less-explicit aspects of the passage.

  - Try to distinguish main ideas from supporting ideas or evidence.
  - Try to distinguish ideas that the author is advancing from those they are merely reporting.
  - Similarly, try to distinguish ideas that the author is strongly committed to from those they advance as hypothetical or speculative.
  - Try to identify the main transitions from one idea to the next.
  - Try to identify the relationship between different ideas. For example:

    — Are they contrasting? Are they consistent?
    — Does one support the other?
    — Does one spell another out in greater detail?
    — Is one an application of another to a particular circumstance?

- Read each question carefully and be certain that you understand exactly what is being asked.

- Answer each question on the basis of the information provided in the passage and do not rely on outside knowledge. Sometimes your own views or opinions may conflict with those presented in a passage; if this happens, take special care to work within the context provided by the passage. You should not expect to agree with everything you encounter in the reading passages.

Reading Comprehension Multiple-Choice Questions: Select One Answer Choice

Description

These are the traditional multiple-choice questions with five answer choices, of which you must select one.

Tips for Answering

- Read *all* the answer choices before making your selection, even if you think you know what the answer is in advance.
- Don't be misled by answer choices that are only partially true or only partially answer the question. The correct answer is the one that most accurately and most completely answers the question posed. Be careful also not to pick an answer choice simply because it is a true statement.
- Pay attention to context. When the question asks about the meaning of a word in the passage, be sure that the answer choice you select correctly represents the way the word is being used in the passage. Many words have quite different meanings in different contexts.

Reading Comprehension Multiple-choice Questions: Select One or More Answer Choices

Description

These provide three answer choices and ask you to select all that are correct; one, two, or all three of the answer choices may be correct. To gain credit for these questions, you must select all the correct answers, and only those; there is no credit for partially correct answers. These questions are marked with square boxes beside the answer choices, not circles or ovals.

Tips for Answering

- Evaluate each answer choice separately on its own merits. When evaluating one answer choice, do not take the others into account.
- Make sure the answer choice you pick accurately and completely answers the question posed. Be careful not to be misled by answer choices that are only partially true or only partially answer the question. Be careful also not to pick an answer choice simply because it is a true statement.
- Do not be disturbed if you think all three answer choices are correct. Questions of this type can have three correct answer choices.

Reading Comprehension Questions: Select-in-Passage

Description

These questions ask you to select the sentence in the passage that meets a certain description. To select a sentence, click on any word in the sentence or select the sentence with the keyboard. In longer passages, the question will usually apply to only one or two specified paragraphs; you will not be able to select a sentence elsewhere in the passage.

Tips for Answering

- Be careful to evaluate each of the relevant sentences in the passage separately before selecting your answer. Do not evaluate any sentences that are outside the paragraphs under consideration.
- Do not select a sentence if the description given in the question only partially applies. A correct answer choice must accurately match the description in the question. Note, however, that the description need not be complete; that is, there may be aspects of the sentence that are not fully described in the question.

Sample Questions

Reviving the practice of using elements of popular music in classical composition, an approach that had been in hibernation in the United States during the 1960s, composer Philip Glass (born 1937) embraced the ethos of popular music in his compositions. Glass based two symphonies on music by rock musicians David Bowie and Brian Eno, but the symphonies' sound is distinctively his. Popular elements do not appear out of place in Glass's classical music, which from its early days has shared certain harmonies and rhythms with rock music. Yet this use of popular elements has not made Glass a composer of popular music. His music is not a version of popular music packaged to attract classical listeners; it is high art for listeners steeped in rock rather than the classics.

Select only one answer choice.

1.   The passage addresses which of the following issues related to Glass's use of popular elements in his classical compositions?
   (A) How it is regarded by listeners who prefer rock to the classics
   (B) How it has affected the commercial success of Glass's music
   (C) Whether it has contributed to a revival of interest among other composers in using popular elements in their compositions
   (D) Whether it has had a detrimental effect on Glass's reputation as a composer of classical music
   (E) Whether it has caused certain of Glass's works to be derivative in quality

Consider each of the three choices separately and select all that apply.

2.   The passage suggests that Glass's work displays which of the following qualities?
   [A] A return to the use of popular music in classical compositions
   [B] An attempt to elevate rock music to an artistic status more closely approximating that of classical music
   [C] A long-standing tendency to incorporate elements from two apparently disparate musical styles

3.   Select the sentence that distinguishes two ways of integrating rock and classical music.

Explanations

The passage describes in general terms how Philip Glass uses popular music in his classical compositions and explores how Glass can do this without being imitative. Note that there are no opposing views discussed; the author is simply presenting their views.

   Question 1: One of the important points that the passage makes is that when Glass uses popular elements in his music, the result is very much his own creation (it is "distinctively his"). In other words, the music is far from being derivative. Thus one issue that the passage addresses is the one referred to in answer **Choice E**—it answers it in the negative. The passage does not discuss the impact of Glass's use of popular elements on listeners, on the commercial success of his music, on other composers, nor on Glass's reputation, so none of Choices A through D is correct.

The correct answer is **Choice E.**

Question 2: To answer this question, it is important to assess each answer choice independently. Since the passage says that Glass revived the use of popular music in classical compositions, answer **Choice A** is clearly correct. On the other hand, the passage also denies that Glass composes popular music or packages it in a way to elevate its status, so answer Choice B is incorrect. Finally, since Glass's style has always mixed elements of rock with classical elements, **Choice C** is correct.

Thus the correct answer is **Choice A** and **Choice C.**

Question 3: Almost every sentence in the passage refers to incorporating rock music in classical compositions, but only the last sentence distinguishes two ways of doing so. It distinguishes between writing rock music in a way that will make it attractive to classical listeners and writing classical music that will be attractive to listeners familiar with rock.

Thus the correct answer is **the last sentence of the passage.**

Text Completion Questions

Description

As mentioned above, skilled readers do not simply absorb the information presented on the page; instead, they maintain a constant attitude of interpretation and evaluation, reasoning from what they have read so far to create a picture of the whole and revising that picture as they go. Text Completion questions test this ability by omitting crucial words from short passages and asking the test taker to use the remaining information in the passage as a basis for selecting words or short phrases to fill the blanks and create a coherent, meaningful whole.

Question Structure

- Passage composed of one to five sentences

- One to three blanks

- Three answer choices per blank (five answer choices in the case of a single blank)

- The answer choices for different blanks function independently; that is, selecting one answer choice for one blank does not affect what answer choices you can select for another blank

- Single correct answer, consisting of one choice for each blank; no credit for partially correct answers

Tips for Answering

Do not merely try to consider each possible combination of answers; doing so will take too long and is open to error. Instead, try to analyze the passage in the following way:

- Read through the passage to get an overall sense of it.
- Identify words or phrases that seem particularly significant, either because they emphasize the structure of the passage (words like *although* or *moreover*) or because they are central to understanding what the passage is about.
- Think up your own words for the blanks. Try to fill in the blanks with words or phrases that seem to you to fit and then see if similar words are offered among the answer choices.
- Do not assume that the first blank is the one that should be filled first. Perhaps one of the other blanks is easier to fill first. Select your choice for that blank, and then see whether you can complete another blank. If none of the choices for the other blank seems to make sense, go back and reconsider your first selection.
- Double-check your answers. When you have made your selection for each blank, check to make sure that the passage is logically, grammatically, and stylistically coherent.

Sample Questions

> For each blank, select one entry from the corresponding column of choices. Fill all blanks in the way that best completes the text.

1. It is refreshing to read a book about our planet by an author who does not allow facts to be (i)_____ by politics: well aware of the political disputes about the effects of human activities on climate and biodiversity, this author does not permit them to (ii)_____ his comprehensive description of what we know about our biosphere. He emphasizes the enormous gaps in our knowledge, the sparseness of our observations, and the (iii)_____, calling attention to the many aspects of planetary evolution that must be better understood before we can accurately diagnose the condition of our planet.

Blank (i)	Blank (ii)	Blank (iii)
(A) overshadowed	(D) enhance	(G) plausibility of our hypotheses
(B) invalidated	(E) obscure	(H) certainty of our entitlement
(C) illuminated	(F) underscore	(I) superficiality of our theories

Explanation

The overall tone of the passage is clearly complimentary. To understand what the author of the book is being complimented on, it is useful to focus on the second blank. Here, we must determine what word would indicate something that the author is praised for not permitting. The only answer choice that fits the case is "obscure," since enhancing and underscoring are generally good things to do, not things one should refrain from doing. Choosing "obscure" clarifies the choice for the first blank; the only choice that fits well with "obscure" is "overshadowed." Notice that trying to fill blank (i) without filling blank (ii) first is very hard—each choice has at least some initial plausibility. Since the third blank requires a phrase that matches "enormous gaps" and "sparseness of our observations," the best choice is "superficiality of our theories."

Thus the correct answer is **overshadowed** (Choice A), **obscure** (Choice E), and **superficiality of our theories** (Choice I).

2. Vain and prone to violence, Caravaggio could not handle success: the more his (i)_____ as an artist increased, the more (ii)_____ his life became.

Blank (i)	Blank (ii)
Ⓐ temperance	Ⓓ tumultuous
Ⓑ notoriety	Ⓔ providential
Ⓒ eminence	Ⓕ dispassionate

Explanation

In this sentence, what follows the colon must explain or spell out what precedes it. So roughly what the second part must say is that as Caravaggio became more successful, his life got more out of control. When one looks for words to fill the blanks, it becomes clear that "tumultuous" is the best fit for blank (ii), since neither of the other choices suggests being out of control. And for blank (i), the best choice is "eminence," since to increase in eminence is a consequence of becoming more successful. It is true that Caravaggio might also increase in notoriety, but an increase in notoriety as an artist is not as clear a sign of success as an increase in eminence.

Thus the correct answer is **eminence** (Choice C) and **tumultuous** (Choice D).

3. In parts of the Arctic, the land grades into the landfast ice so _____ that you can walk off the coast and not know you are over the hidden sea.

Ⓐ permanently
Ⓑ imperceptibly
Ⓒ irregularly
Ⓓ precariously
Ⓔ relentlessly

Explanation

The word that fills the blank has to characterize how the land grades into the ice in a way that explains how you can walk off the coast and over the sea without knowing it. The word that does that is "imperceptibly"; if the land grades imperceptibly into the ice, you might well not know that you had left the land. Describing the shift from land to ice as permanent, irregular, precarious, or relentless would not help to explain how you would fail to know.

Thus the correct answer is **imperceptibly** (Choice B).

Sentence Equivalence Questions

Description

Like Text Completion questions, Sentence Equivalence questions test the ability to reach a conclusion about how a passage should be completed on the basis of partial information, but to a greater extent they focus on the meaning of the completed whole. Sentence Equivalence questions consist of a single sentence with just one blank, and they ask you to find two choices that both lead to a complete, coherent sentence and that produce sentences that are alike in meaning.

Question Structure

- Consists of:
  - a single sentence
  - one blank
  - six answer choices

- Requires you to select exactly two of the answer choices; no credit for partially correct answers.

These questions are marked with square boxes beside the answer choices, not circles or ovals.

> ### Tips for Answering
>
> Do not simply look among the answer choices for two words that mean the same thing. This can be misleading for two reasons. First, the answer choices may contain pairs of words that mean the same thing but do not fit coherently into the sentence, and thus do not constitute a correct answer. Second, the pair of words that do constitute the correct answer may not mean exactly the same thing, since all that matters is that the resultant sentences are alike in meaning.
>
> - **Read the sentence to get an overall sense of it.**
> - **Identify words or phrases that seem particularly significant,** either because they emphasize the structure of the sentence (words like *although* or *moreover*) or because they are central to understanding what the sentence is about.
> - **Think up your own words for the blanks.** Try to fill in the blank with a word that seems to you to fit and then see if two similar words are offered among the answer choices. If you find some word that is similar to what you are expecting but cannot find a second one, do not become fixated on your interpretation; instead, see whether there are other words among the answer choices that can be used to fill the blank coherently.
> - **Double-check your answers.** When you have selected your pair of answer choices for the blank, check to make sure that each one produces a sentence that is logically, grammatically, and stylistically coherent, and that the two sentences are alike in meaning.

Sample Questions

> Select the <u>two</u> answer choices that, when used to complete the sentence, fit the meaning of the sentence as a whole <u>and</u> produce completed sentences that are alike in meaning.

1. Although it does contain some pioneering ideas, one would hardly characterize the work as _____.
   - A orthodox
   - B eccentric
   - C original
   - D trifling
   - E conventional
   - F innovative

Explanation

The word "Although" is a crucial signpost here. The work contains some pioneering ideas, but apparently it is not overall a pioneering work. Thus the two words that could fill the blank appropriately are "original" and "innovative." Note that "orthodox" and "conventional" are two words that are very similar in meaning, but neither one completes the sentence sensibly.

Thus the correct answer is **original** (Choice C) and **innovative** (Choice F).

2. It was her view that the country's problems had been _____ by foreign technocrats, so that to ask for such assistance again would be counterproductive.
   - A ameliorated
   - B ascertained
   - C diagnosed
   - D exacerbated
   - E overlooked
   - F worsened

Explanation

The sentence relates a piece of reasoning, as indicated by the presence of "so that": asking for the assistance of foreign technocrats would be counterproductive because of the effects such technocrats have had already. This means that the technocrats must have had bad effects; that is, they must have "exacerbated" or "worsened" the country's problems.

Thus the correct answer is **exacerbated** (Choice D) and **worsened** (Choice F).

4 GRE Verbal Reasoning: Practice Questions

This chapter contains six sets of GRE Verbal Reasoning practice questions. Three of the practice sets consist of examples of Text Completion and Sentence Equivalence questions; the other three sets consist of Reading Comprehension questions. The sets are arranged in order of increasing difficulty. The first two are easy, the next two are medium, and the final two are hard.

Following the last set is an answer key for quick reference. At the end of the chapter, you will find complete explanations for every question. Each explanation is presented with the corresponding question, so that you can easily see what was asked and what the various answer choices were.

Sharpen your GRE Verbal Reasoning skills by working your way through these question sets. Begin with the easy sets and then move on to the medium-difficulty and hard sets. Review the answer explanations carefully, paying particular attention to the explanations for questions that you answered incorrectly. Turn the page to begin.

SET 1. Text Completion and Sentence Equivalence Questions: Easy

For Questions 1 to 5, select one entry for each blank from the corresponding column of choices. Fill all blanks in the way that best completes the text.

1. Dominant interests often benefit most from _____ of governmental interference in business, since they are able to take care of themselves if left alone.

    - Ⓐ intensification
    - Ⓑ authorization
    - Ⓒ centralization
    - Ⓓ improvisation
    - Ⓔ elimination

2. Kagan maintains that an infant's reactions to its first stressful experiences are part of a natural process of development, not harbingers of childhood unhappiness or _____ signs of adolescent anxiety.

    - Ⓐ prophetic
    - Ⓑ normal
    - Ⓒ monotonous
    - Ⓓ virtual
    - Ⓔ typical

3. An investigation that is _____ can occasionally yield new facts, even notable ones, but typically the appearance of such facts is the result of a search in a definite direction.

    - Ⓐ timely
    - Ⓑ unguided
    - Ⓒ consistent
    - Ⓓ uncomplicated
    - Ⓔ subjective

4. It is (i)_____ that so many portrait paintings hang in art museums, since the subject matter seems to dictate a status closer to pictures in the family photograph album than to high art. But perhaps it is the artistic skill with which the portraits are painted that (ii)_____ their presence in art museums.

Blank (i)	Blank (ii)
Ⓐ surprising	Ⓓ challenges
Ⓑ understandable	Ⓔ justifies
Ⓒ irrelevant	Ⓕ changes

5. In stark contrast to his later (i)_____, Simpson was largely (ii)_____ politics during his college years, despite the fact that the campus he attended was rife with political activity.

Blank (i)	Blank (ii)
Ⓐ activism	Ⓓ devoted to
Ⓑ apathy	Ⓔ indifferent to
Ⓒ affability	Ⓕ shaped by

For Questions 6 to 8, select the <u>two</u> answer choices that, when used to complete the sentence, fit the meaning of the sentence as a whole <u>and</u> produce completed sentences that are alike in meaning.

---

6. As my eyesight began to _____, I spent a lot of time writing about it — both poems and "eye journals" — describing what I saw as I looked out through damaged eyes.
    - Ⓐ deteriorate
    - Ⓑ sharpen
    - Ⓒ improve
    - Ⓓ decline
    - Ⓔ recover
    - Ⓕ adjust

7. The judge's standing in the legal community, though shaken by phony allegations of wrongdoing, emerged, at long last, _____ .
    - Ⓐ unqualified
    - Ⓑ undiminished
    - Ⓒ undecided
    - Ⓓ undamaged
    - Ⓔ unresolved
    - Ⓕ unprincipled

8. Modern agricultural practices have been extremely successful in increasing the productivity of major food crops, yet despite heavy use of pesticides, _____ losses to diseases and insect pests are sustained each year.
    - Ⓐ incongruous
    - Ⓑ reasonable
    - Ⓒ significant
    - Ⓓ considerable
    - Ⓔ equitable
    - Ⓕ fortuitous

SET 2. Reading Comprehension Questions: Easy

For each of Questions 1 to 9, select <u>one</u> answer choice unless otherwise instructed.

1. A person who agrees to serve as mediator between two warring factions at the request of both abandons by so agreeing the right to take sides later. To take sides at a later point would be to suggest that the earlier presumptive impartiality was a sham.

    The passage above emphasizes which of the following points about mediators?

    Ⓐ They should try to form no opinions of their own about any issue that is related to the dispute.

    Ⓑ They should not agree to serve unless they are committed to maintaining a stance of impartiality.

    Ⓒ They should not agree to serve unless they are equally acceptable to all parties to a dispute.

    Ⓓ They should feel free to take sides in the dispute right from the start, provided that they make their biases publicly known.

    Ⓔ They should reserve the right to abandon their impartiality so as not to be open to the charge of having been deceitful.

Was Felix Mendelssohn (1809–1847) a great composer? On its face, the question seems absurd. One of the most gifted prodigies in the history of music, he produced his first masterpiece at sixteen. From then on, he was recognized as an artist of preternatural abilities, not only as a composer but also as a pianist and conductor. But Mendelssohn's enduring popularity has often been at odds — sometimes quite sharply — with his critical standing. Despite general acknowledgment of his genius, there has been a noticeable reluctance to rank him with, say, Schumann or Brahms. As Haggin put it, Mendelssohn, as a composer, was a "minor master . . . working on a small scale of emotion and texture."

2.   Select a sentence in the passage whose function is to indicate the range of Mendelssohn's musical talents.

3.   The passage suggests that anyone attempting to evaluate Mendelssohn's career must confront which of the following dichotomies?

   Ⓐ The tension between Mendelssohn's career as a composer and his career as a pianist and conductor

   Ⓑ The contrast between Mendelssohn's popularity and that of Schumann and Brahms

   Ⓒ The discrepancy between Mendelssohn's popularity and his standing among critics

   Ⓓ The inconsistency between Mendelssohn's reputation during his lifetime and his reputation since his death

   Ⓔ The gap between Mendelssohn's prodigious musical beginnings and his decline in later years

4.   It can be inferred that the "reluctance" mentioned in the passage is being ascribed to

   Ⓐ most composers since Mendelssohn

   Ⓑ Schumann and Brahms

   Ⓒ the music-listening public

   Ⓓ music critics generally

   Ⓔ Haggin exclusively

5.   The author mentions Schumann and Brahms primarily in order to

   Ⓐ provide examples of composers who are often compared with Mendelssohn

   Ⓑ identify certain composers who are more popular than Mendelssohn

   Ⓒ identify composers whom Mendelssohn influenced

   Ⓓ establish the milieu in which Mendelssohn worked

   Ⓔ establish a standard of comparison for Mendelssohn as a composer

While most scholarship on women's employment in the United States recognizes that the Second World War (1939–1945) dramatically changed the role of women in the workforce, these studies also acknowledge that few women remained in manufacturing jobs once men returned from the war. But in agriculture, unlike other industries where women were viewed as temporary workers, women's employment did not end with the war. Instead, the expansion of agriculture and a steady decrease in the number of male farmworkers combined to cause the industry to hire more women in the postwar years. Consequently, the 1950s saw a growing number of women engaged in farm labor, even though rhetoric in the popular media called for the return of women to domestic life.

6. It can be inferred from the passage that the manufacturing and agricultural sectors in the United States following the Second World War differed in which of the following respects?

   (A) The rate of expansion in each sector

   (B) The percentage of employees in each sector who were men

   (C) The trend in the wages of men employed in each sector

   (D) The attitude of the popular media toward the employment of women in each sector

   (E) The extent to which women in each sector were satisfied with their jobs

7. Which of the following statements about women's employment in the United States during and after the Second World War is most clearly supported by the passage?

   (A) Most women who joined the workforce during the Second World War wanted to return to domestic life when the war ended.

   (B) The great majority of women who joined the workforce during the Second World War were employed in manufacturing jobs.

   (C) The end of the Second World War was followed by a large-scale transfer of women workers from manufacturing to agriculture.

   (D) The increase in women's employment that accompanied the Second World War was longer lasting in agriculture than it was in manufacturing.

   (E) The popular media were more forceful in calling for women to join the workforce during the Second World War than in calling for women to return to domestic life after the war.

Since the Hawaiian Islands have never been connected to other land masses, the great variety of plants in Hawaii must be a result of the long-distance dispersal of seeds, a process that requires both a method of transport and an equivalence between the ecology of the source area and that of the recipient area.

line
5   There is some dispute about the method of transport involved. Some biologists argue that ocean and air currents are responsible for the transport of plant seeds to Hawaii. Yet the results of flotation experiments and the low temperatures of air currents cast doubt on these hypotheses. More probable is bird transport, either externally, by accidental attachment of the seeds to feathers, or internally, by the swallowing of fruit and subsequent
10   excretion of the seeds. While it is likely that fewer varieties of plant seeds have reached Hawaii externally than internally, more varieties are known to be adapted to external than to internal transport.

8.   The author of the passage is primarily concerned with

Ⓐ   discussing different approaches biologists have taken to testing theories about the distribution of plants in Hawaii

Ⓑ   discussing different theories about the transport of plant seeds to Hawaii

Ⓒ   discussing the extent to which air currents are responsible for the dispersal of plant seeds to Hawaii

Ⓓ   resolving a dispute about the adaptability of plant seeds to bird transport

Ⓔ   resolving a dispute about the ability of birds to carry plant seeds long distances

9.   The author mentions the results of flotation experiments on plant seeds (lines 7–8) most probably in order to

Ⓐ   support the claim that the distribution of plants in Hawaii is the result of the long-distance dispersal of seeds

Ⓑ   lend credibility to the thesis that air currents provide a method of transport for plant seeds to Hawaii

Ⓒ   suggest that the long-distance dispersal of seeds is a process that requires long periods of time

Ⓓ   challenge the claim that ocean currents are responsible for the transport of plant seeds to Hawaii

Ⓔ   refute the claim that Hawaiian flora evolved independently from flora in other parts of the world

SET 3. Text Completion and Sentence Equivalence Questions: Medium

> **For Questions 1 to 5, select one entry for each blank from the corresponding column of choices. Fill all blanks in the way that best completes the text.**

1. It comes as no surprise that societies have codes of behavior; the character of the codes, on the other hand, can often be _____ .

Ⓐ predictable
Ⓑ unexpected
Ⓒ admirable
Ⓓ explicit
Ⓔ confusing

2. Like Béla Bartók, Ruth Crawford not only brought a composer's acumen to the notation of folk music, she also had a marked (i)_____ the task. This was clear in her agonizing over how far to try to represent the minute details of a performance in a written text, and this (ii)_____ makes her work a landmark in ethnomusicology.

Blank (i)	Blank (ii)
Ⓐ reverence for	Ⓓ fastidiousness
Ⓑ detachment from	Ⓔ didacticism
Ⓒ curiosity about	Ⓕ iconoclasm

3. Political advertising may well be the most (i)_____ kind of advertising: political candidates are usually quite (ii)_____ , yet their campaign advertisements often hide important differences behind smoke screens of smiles and empty slogans.

Blank (i)	Blank (ii)
Ⓐ polemical	Ⓓ interchangeable
Ⓑ effective	Ⓔ dissimilar
Ⓒ deceptive	Ⓕ vocal

4. Richard M. Russell said 52 percent of the nation's growth since the Second World War had (i)_____ invention. He said, (ii)_____ research, the government's greatest role in assuring continuing innovation is promoting a strong, modern patent office. "Unless we can (iii)_____ original ideas, we will not have invention," Mr. Russell said. Speculating on the state of innovation over the next century, several inventors agreed that the future lay in giving children the tools to think creatively and the motivation to invent.

Blank (i)	Blank (ii)	Blank (iii)
Ⓐ been at the expense of	Ⓓ in addition to restricting	Ⓖ evaluate
Ⓑ no bearing on	Ⓔ aside from supporting	Ⓗ protect
Ⓒ come through	Ⓕ far from exaggerating	Ⓘ disseminate

5. Statements presented as fact in a patent application are (i) _____ unless a good reason for doubt is found. The invention has only to be deemed "more likely than not" to work in order to receive initial approval. And, although thousands of patents are challenged in court for other reasons, no incentive exists for anyone to expend effort (ii) _____ the science of an erroneous patent. For this reason the endless stream of (iii) _____ devices will continue to yield occasional patents.

Blank (i)	Blank (ii)	Blank (iii)
Ⓐ presumed verifiable	Ⓓ corroborating	Ⓖ novel
Ⓑ carefully scrutinized	Ⓔ advancing	Ⓗ bogus
Ⓒ considered capricious	Ⓕ debunking	Ⓘ obsolete

> **For Questions 6 to 8, select the <u>two</u> answer choices that, when used to complete the sentence, fit the meaning of the sentence as a whole <u>and</u> produce completed sentences that are alike in meaning.**

6. Ever a demanding reader of the fiction of others, the novelist Chase was likewise often the object of _____ analyses by his contemporaries.

   A exacting

   B copious

   C respectful

   D acerbic

   E scathing

   F meticulous

7. Her _____ should not be confused with miserliness; as long as I have known her, she has always been willing to assist those who are in need.

   A stinginess

   B diffidence

   C frugality

   D illiberality

   E intolerance

   F thrift

8. A misconception frequently held by novice writers is that sentence structure mirrors thought: the more convoluted the structure, the more _____ the ideas.

   A complicated

   B engaged

   C essential

   D fanciful

   E inconsequential

   F involved

SET 4. Reading Comprehension Questions: Medium

For each of Questions 1 to 9, select <u>one</u> answer choice unless otherwise instructed.

Questions 1 and 2 are based on the following reading passage.

I enjoyed *A Dream of Light & Shadow: Portraits of Latin American Women Writers* for the same reasons that, as a child, I avidly consumed women's biographies: the fascination with how the biographical details of another female's life are represented and interpreted.

    A Dream offers a rich read, varied in both the lives and texts of the women portrayed, and the perspectives and styles of the sixteen essayists. Yet, as an adult, I have come to demand of any really "great" book a self-consciousness about the tenuous nature of representations of reality, a critical contextualization of florid detail, and a self-awareness of the role of ideology in our lives. In these critical senses, *A Dream* is inadequate.

For the following question, consider each of the choices separately and select all that apply.

1.   The author of the passage suggests that *A Dream* falls short in which of the following respects?

        [A] It does not appear to recognize that representations of reality can be unreliable.

        [B] It seems to focus on stylistic variety at the expense of accuracy of detail.

        [C] It offers a wealth of detail without sufficient critical examination of that detail.

2.   Which of the following best describes the function of the second sentence ("*A Dream* . . . essayists") in the context of the passage as a whole?

        (A) To give examples of how *A Dream* presents fascinating portraits that display awareness of the tenuous nature of representations of reality

        (B) To elaborate on how *A Dream* fulfills the author's childhood criteria for a pleasurable book

        (C) To suggest that the author enjoyed *A Dream* for reasons more sophisticated than the reasons she enjoyed certain books as a child

        (D) To illustrate ways in which the author finds *A Dream* to be inadequate in certain critical senses

        (E) To imply that *A Dream* is too varied in focus to provide a proper contextualization of the biographical details it offers

3. During the day in Lake Constance, the zooplankton *D. hyalina* departs for the depths where food is scarce and the water cold. *D. galeata* remains near the warm surface where food is abundant. Even though *D. galeata* grows and reproduces much faster, its population is often outnumbered by *D. hyalina*.

Which of the following, if true, would help resolve the apparent paradox presented above?

Ⓐ The number of species of zooplankton living at the bottom of the lake is twice that of species living at the surface.

Ⓑ Predators of zooplankton, such as whitefish and perch, live and feed near the surface of the lake during the day.

Ⓒ In order to make the most of scarce food resources, *D. hyalina* matures more slowly than *D. galeata*.

Ⓓ *D. galeata* clusters under vegetation during the hottest part of the day to avoid the Sun's rays.

Ⓔ *D. galeata* produces twice as many offspring per individual in any given period of time as does *D. hyalina*.

Tocqueville, apparently, was wrong. Jacksonian America was not a fluid, egalitarian society where individual wealth and poverty were ephemeral conditions. At least so argues E. Pessen in his iconoclastic study of the very rich in the United States between 1825 and 1850.

Pessen does present a quantity of examples, together with some refreshingly intelligible statistics, to establish the existence of an inordinately wealthy class. Though active in commerce or the professions, most of the wealthy were not self-made but had inherited family fortunes. In no sense mercurial, these great fortunes survived the financial panics that destroyed lesser ones. Indeed, in several cities the wealthiest one percent constantly increased its share until by 1850 it owned half of the community's wealth. Although these observations are true, Pessen overestimates their importance by concluding from them that the undoubted progress toward inequality in the late eighteenth century continued in the Jacksonian period and that the United States was a class-ridden, plutocratic society even before industrialization.

4. According to the passage, Pessen indicates that all of the following were true of the very wealthy in the United States between 1825 and 1850 EXCEPT:

    Ⓐ They formed a distinct upper class.

    Ⓑ Many of them were able to increase their holdings.

    Ⓒ Some of them worked as professionals or in business.

    Ⓓ Most of them accumulated their own fortunes.

    Ⓔ Many of them retained their wealth in spite of financial upheavals.

5. Which of the following best states the author's main point?

    Ⓐ Pessen's study has overturned the previously established view of the social and economic structure of early-nineteenth-century America.

    Ⓑ Tocqueville's analysis of the United States in the Jacksonian era remains the definitive account of this period.

    Ⓒ Pessen's study is valuable primarily because it shows the continuity of the social system in the United States throughout the nineteenth century.

    Ⓓ The social patterns and political power of the extremely wealthy in the United States between 1825 and 1850 are well documented.

    Ⓔ Pessen challenges a view of the social and economic systems in the United States from 1825 to 1850, but he draws conclusions that are incorrect.

The evolution of intelligence among early large mammals of the grasslands was due in great measure to the interaction between two ecologically synchronized groups of these animals, the hunting carnivores and the herbivores that they hunted. The interaction *line* resulting from the differences between predator and prey led to a general improvement 5 in brain functions; however, certain components of intelligence were improved far more than others.

The kind of intelligence favored by the interplay of increasingly smarter catchers and increasingly keener escapers is defined by attention — that aspect of mind carrying consciousness forward from one moment to the next. It ranges from a passive, free-floating 10 awareness to a highly focused, active fixation. The range through these states is mediated by the arousal system, a network of tracts converging from sensory systems to integrating centers in the brain stem. From the more relaxed to the more vigorous levels, sensitivity to novelty is increased. The organism is more awake, more vigilant; this increased vigilance results in the apprehension of ever more subtle signals as the organism becomes more 15 sensitive to its surroundings. The processes of arousal and concentration give attention its direction. Arousal is at first general, with a flooding of impulses in the brain stem; then gradually the activation is channeled. Thus begins concentration, the holding of consistent images. One meaning of intelligence is the way in which these images and other alertly searched information are used in the context of previous experience. Consciousness links 20 past attention to the present and permits the integration of details with perceived ends and purposes.

The elements of intelligence and consciousness come together marvelously to produce different styles in predator and prey. Herbivores and carnivores develop different kinds of attention related to escaping or chasing. Although in both kinds of animal, arousal stimu- 25 lates the production of adrenaline and norepinephrine by the adrenal glands, the effect in herbivores is primarily fear, whereas in carnivores the effect is primarily aggression. For both, arousal attunes the animal to what is ahead. Perhaps it does not experience forethought as we know it, but the animal does experience something like it. The predator is searchingly aggressive, inner-directed, tuned by the nervous system and the adrenal hor- 30 mones, but aware in a sense closer to human consciousness than, say, a hungry lizard's instinctive snap at a passing beetle. Using past events as a framework, the large mammal predator is working out a relationship between movement and food, sensitive to possibilities in cold trails and distant sounds — and yesterday's unforgotten lessons. The herbivore prey is of a different mind. Its mood of wariness rather than searching and its attitude of 35 general expectancy instead of anticipating are silk-thin veils of tranquillity over an explosive endocrine system.

6. The author refers to a hungry lizard (line 30) primarily in order to
    Ⓐ demonstrate the similarity between the hunting methods of mammals and those of nonmammals
    Ⓑ broaden the application of the argument by including an insectivore as an example
    Ⓒ make a distinction between higher and lower levels of consciousness
    Ⓓ provide an additional illustration of the brutality characteristic of predators
    Ⓔ offer an objection to suggestions that all animals lack consciousness

7. It can be inferred from the passage that in animals less intelligent than the mammals discussed in the passage

Ⓐ past experience is less helpful in ensuring survival

Ⓑ attention is more highly focused

Ⓒ muscular coordination is less highly developed

Ⓓ there is less need for competition among species

Ⓔ environment is more important in establishing the proper ratio of prey to predator

8. According to the passage, improvement in brain function among early large mammals resulted primarily from which of the following?

Ⓐ Interplay of predator and prey

Ⓑ Persistence of free-floating awareness in animals of the grasslands

Ⓒ Gradual dominance of warm-blooded mammals over cold-blooded reptiles

Ⓓ Interaction of early large mammals with less intelligent species

Ⓔ Improvement of the capacity for memory among herbivores and carnivores

9. According to the passage, as the process of arousal in an organism continues, all of the following may occur EXCEPT

Ⓐ the production of adrenaline

Ⓑ the production of norepinephrine

Ⓒ a heightening of sensitivity to stimuli

Ⓓ an increase in selectivity with respect to stimuli

Ⓔ an expansion of the range of states mediated by the brain stem

SET 5. Text Completion and Sentence Equivalence Questions: Hard

> For Questions 1 to 6, select one entry for each blank from the corresponding column of choices. Fill all blanks in the way that best completes the text.

1. For some time now, _____ has been presumed not to exist: the cynical conviction that everybody has an angle is considered wisdom.

(A) rationality
(B) flexibility
(C) diffidence
(D) disinterestedness
(E) insincerity

2. Human nature and long distances have made exceeding the speed limit a (i) _____ in the state, so the legislators surprised no one when, acceding to public demand, they (ii) _____ increased penalties for speeding.

Blank (i)	Blank (ii)
(A) controversial habit	(D) endorsed
(B) cherished tradition	(E) considered
(C) disquieting ritual	(F) rejected

3. Serling's account of his employer's reckless decision making (i)_____ that company's image as (ii)_____ bureaucracy full of wary managers.

Blank (i)	Blank (ii)
(A) belies	(D) an injudicious
(B) exposes	(E) a disorganized
(C) overshadows	(F) a cautious

4. No other contemporary poet's work has such a well-earned reputation for (i)_____, and there are few whose moral vision is so imperiously unsparing. Of late, however, the almost belligerent demands of his severe and densely forbidding poetry have taken an improbable turn. This new collection is the poet's fourth book in six years — an ample output even for poets of sunny disposition, let alone for one of such (ii)_____ over the previous 50 years. Yet for all his newfound (iii)_____, his poetry is as thorny as ever.

Blank (i)	Blank (ii)	Blank (iii)
Ⓐ patent accessibility	Ⓓ penitential austerity	Ⓖ taciturnity
Ⓑ intrinsic frivolity	Ⓔ intractable prolixity	Ⓗ volubility
Ⓒ near impenetrability	Ⓕ impetuous prodigality	Ⓘ pellucidity

5. Managers who think that strong environmental performance will (i)_____ their company's financial performance often (ii)_____ claims that systems designed to help them manage environmental concerns are valuable tools. By contrast, managers who perceive environmental performance to be (iii)_____ to financial success may view an environmental management system as extraneous. In either situation, and whatever their perceptions, it is a manager's commitment to achieving environmental improvement rather than the mere presence of a system that determines environmental performance.

Blank (i)	Blank (ii)	Blank (iii)
Ⓐ eclipse	Ⓓ uncritically accept	Ⓖ complementary
Ⓑ bolster	Ⓔ appropriately acknowledge	Ⓗ intrinsic
Ⓒ degrade	Ⓕ hotly dispute	Ⓘ peripheral

6. Philosophy, unlike most other subjects, does not try to extend our knowledge by discovering new information about the world. Instead it tries to deepen our understanding through (i)_____ what is already closest to us — the experiences, thoughts, concepts, and activities that make up our lives but that ordinarily escape our notice precisely because they are so familiar. Philosophy begins by finding (ii)_____ the things that are (iii)_____.

Blank (i)	Blank (ii)	Blank (iii)
Ⓐ attainment of	Ⓓ essentially irrelevant	Ⓖ most prosaic
Ⓑ rumination on	Ⓔ utterly mysterious	Ⓗ somewhat hackneyed
Ⓒ detachment from	Ⓕ thoroughly commonplace	Ⓘ refreshingly novel

For Questions 7 to 9, select the **two** answer choices that, when used to complete the sentence, fit the meaning of the sentence as a whole **and** produce completed sentences that are alike in meaning.

7. The government's implementation of a new code of ethics appeared intended to shore up the ruling party's standing with an increasingly _____ electorate at a time when the party is besieged by charges that it trades favors for campaign money.

   A aloof
   B placid
   C restive
   D skittish
   E tranquil
   F vociferous

8. Overlarge, uneven, and ultimately disappointing, the retrospective exhibition seems too much like special pleading for a forgotten painter of real but _____ talents.

   A limited
   B partial
   C undiscovered
   D circumscribed
   E prosaic
   F hidden

9. Newspapers report that the former executive has been trying to keep a low profile since his _____ exit from the company.

   A celebrated
   B mysterious
   C long-awaited
   D fortuitous
   E indecorous
   F unseemly

SET 6. Reading Comprehension Questions: Hard

> **For each of Questions 1 to 8, select <u>one</u> answer choice unless otherwise instructed.**

1. In the United States between 1850 and 1880, the number of farmers continued to increase, but at a rate lower than that of the general population.

    Which of the following statements directly contradicts the information presented above?

    Ⓐ The number of farmers in the general population increased slightly in the 30 years between 1850 and 1880.

    Ⓑ The rate of growth of the United States labor force and the rate of growth of the general population rose simultaneously in the 30 years between 1850 and 1880.

    Ⓒ The proportion of farmers in the United States labor force remained constant in the 30 years between 1850 and 1880.

    Ⓓ The proportion of farmers in the United States labor force decreased from 64 percent in 1850 to 49 percent in 1880.

    Ⓔ The proportion of farmers in the general population increased from 68 percent in 1850 to 72 percent in 1880.

2. A ten-year comparison between the United States and the Soviet Union in terms of crop yields per acre revealed that when only planted acreage is compared, Soviet yields were equal to 68 percent of United States yields. When total agricultural acreage (planted acreage plus fallow acreage) is compared, however, Soviet yield was 114 percent of United States yield.

    From the information above, which of the following can be most reliably inferred about United States and Soviet agriculture during the ten-year period?

    Ⓐ A higher percentage of total agricultural acreage was fallow in the United States than in the Soviet Union.

    Ⓑ The United States had more fallow acreage than planted acreage.

    Ⓒ Fewer total acres of available agricultural land were fallow in the Soviet Union than in the United States.

    Ⓓ The Soviet Union had more planted acreage than fallow acreage.

    Ⓔ The Soviet Union produced a greater volume of crops than the United States produced.

For hot desert locations with access to seawater, a new greenhouse design generates fresh-water and cool air. Oriented to the prevailing wind, the front wall of perforated cardboard, moistened by a trickle of seawater pumped in, cools and moistens hot air blowing in. This cool, humidified air accelerates plant growth; little water evaporates from leaves. Though greenhouses normally capture the heat of sunlight, a double-layered roof, the inner layer coated to reflect infrared light outward, allows visible sunlight in but traps solar heat between the two layers. This heated air, drawn down from the roof, then mixes with the greenhouse air as it reaches a second seawater-moistened cardboard wall at the back of the greenhouse. There the air absorbs more moisture before being cooled off again when it meets a seawater-cooled metal wall, which causes moisture in the air to condense. Thus distilled water for irrigating the plants collects.

For the following question, consider each of the choices separately and select all that apply.

3. It can be inferred that the process described in the passage makes use of which of the following?

    A The tendency of hot air to rise

    B The directional movement of wind

    C Variation in the moisture capacity of air

For the following question, consider each of the choices separately and select all that apply.

4. It can be inferred that the greenhouse roof is designed to allow for which of the following?

    A The avoidance of intense solar heat inside the greenhouse

    B The entry of sunlight into the greenhouse to make the plants grow

    C The mixture of heated air with greenhouse air to enhance the collection of moisture

Many critics of Emily Brontë's novel *Wuthering Heights* see its second part as a counterpoint that comments on, if it does not reverse, the first part, where a romantic reading receives more confirmation. Seeing the two parts as a whole is encouraged by the novel's sophisticated structure, revealed in its complex use of narrators and time shifts. Granted that the presence of these elements need not argue for an authorial awareness of novelistic construction comparable to that of Henry James, their presence does encourage attempts to unify the novel's heterogeneous parts. However, any interpretation that seeks to unify all of the novel's diverse elements is bound to be somewhat unconvincing. This is not because such an interpretation necessarily stiffens into a thesis (although rigidity in any interpretation of this or of any novel is always a danger), but because *Wuthering Heights* has recalcitrant elements of undeniable power that, ultimately, resist inclusion in an all-encompassing interpretation. In this respect, *Wuthering Heights* shares a feature of *Hamlet*.

5.   According to the passage, which of the following is a true statement about the first and second parts of *Wuthering Heights*?

    Ⓐ The second part has received more attention from critics.

    Ⓑ The second part has little relation to the first part.

    Ⓒ The second part annuls the force of the first part.

    Ⓓ The second part provides less substantiation for a romantic reading.

    Ⓔ The second part is better because it is more realistic.

6.   Which of the following inferences about Henry James's awareness of novelistic construction is best supported by the passage?

    Ⓐ **James, more than any other novelist, was aware of the difficulties of novelistic construction.**

    Ⓑ James was very aware of the details of novelistic construction.

    Ⓒ James's awareness of novelistic construction derived from his reading of Brontë.

    Ⓓ James's awareness of novelistic construction has led most commentators to see unity in his individual novels.

    Ⓔ James's awareness of novelistic construction precluded him from violating the unity of his novels.

7.   The author of the passage would be most likely to agree that an interpretation of a novel should

    Ⓐ not try to unite heterogeneous elements in the novel

    Ⓑ not be inflexible in its treatment of the elements in the novel

    Ⓒ not argue that the complex use of narrators or of time shifts indicates a sophisticated structure

    Ⓓ concentrate on those recalcitrant elements of the novel that are outside the novel's main structure

    Ⓔ primarily consider those elements of novelistic construction of which the author of the novel was aware

For the following question, consider each of the choices separately and select all that apply.

8. The author of the passage suggests which of the following about *Hamlet*?

   A. *Hamlet* has usually attracted critical interpretations that tend to stiffen into theses.

   B. *Hamlet* has elements that are not amenable to an all-encompassing critical interpretation.

   C. *Hamlet* is less open to an all-encompassing critical interpretation than is *Wuthering Heights*.

ANSWER KEY

SET 1. Text Completion and Sentence Equivalence Questions: Easy

1. **Choice E**: elimination
2. **Choice A**: prophetic
3. **Choice B**: unguided
4. **Choice A**: surprising; **Choice E**: justifies
5. **Choice A**: activism; **Choice E**: indifferent to
6. **Choice A**: deteriorate; AND **Choice D**: decline
7. **Choice B**: undiminished; AND **Choice D**: undamaged
8. **Choice C**: significant; AND **Choice D**: considerable

SET 2. Reading Comprehension Questions: Easy

1. **Choice B**: They should not agree to serve unless they are committed to maintaining a stance of impartiality.
2. **Sentence 4**: From then on, he was recognized as an artist of preternatural abilities, not only as a composer but also as a pianist and conductor.
3. **Choice C**: The discrepancy between Mendelssohn's popularity and his standing among critics
4. **Choice D**: music critics generally
5. **Choice E**: establish a standard of comparison for Mendelssohn as a composer
6. **Choice B**: The percentage of employees in each sector who were men
7. **Choice D**: The increase in women's employment that accompanied the Second World War was longer lasting in agriculture than it was in manufacturing.
8. **Choice B**: discussing different theories about the transport of plant seeds to Hawaii
9. **Choice D**: challenge the claim that ocean currents are responsible for the transport of plant seeds to Hawaii

SET 3. Text Completion and Sentence Equivalence Questions: Medium

1. **Choice B**: unexpected
2. **Choice A**: reverence for; **Choice D**: fastidiousness
3. **Choice C**: deceptive; **Choice E**: dissimilar
4. **Choice C**: come through; **Choice E**: aside from supporting; **Choice H**: protect
5. **Choice A**: presumed verifiable; **Choice F**: debunking; **Choice H**: bogus
6. **Choice A**: exacting; AND **Choice F**: meticulous
7. **Choice C**: frugality; AND **Choice F**: thrift
8. **Choice A**: complicated; AND **Choice F**: involved

SET 4. Reading Comprehension Questions: Medium

1. **Choice A**: It does not appear to recognize that representations of reality can be unreliable; AND **Choice C**: It offers a wealth of detail without sufficient critical examination of that detail.
2. **Choice B**: To elaborate on how *A Dream* fulfills the author's childhood criteria for a pleasurable book
3. **Choice B**: Predators of zooplankton, such as whitefish and perch, live and feed near the surface of the lake during the day.
4. **Choice D**: Most of them accumulated their own fortunes.
5. **Choice E**: Pessen challenges a view of the social and economic systems in the United States from 1825 to 1850, but he draws conclusions that are incorrect.
6. **Choice C**: make a distinction between higher and lower levels of consciousness
7. **Choice A**: past experience is less helpful in ensuring survival
8. **Choice A**: Interplay of predator and prey
9. **Choice E**: an expansion of the range of states mediated by the brain stem

SET 5. Text Completion and Sentence Equivalence Questions: Hard

1. **Choice D**: disinterestedness
2. **Choice B**: cherished tradition; **Choice F**: rejected
3. **Choice A**: belies; **Choice F**: a cautious
4. **Choice C**: near impenetrability; **Choice D**: penitential austerity; **Choice H**: volubility
5. **Choice B**: bolster; **Choice D**: uncritically accept; **Choice I**: peripheral
6. **Choice B**: rumination on; **Choice E:** utterly mysterious; **Choice G**: most prosaic
7. **Choice C**: restive; AND **Choice D**: skittish
8. **Choice A**: limited; AND **Choice D**: circumscribed
9. **Choice E**: indecorous; AND **Choice F**: unseemly

SET 6. Reading Comprehension Questions: Hard

1. **Choice E**: The proportion of farmers in the general population increased from 68 percent in 1850 to 72 percent in 1880.
2. **Choice A**: A higher percentage of total agricultural acreage was fallow in the United States than in the Soviet Union.
3. **Choice B**: The directional movement of wind; AND **Choice C**: Variation in the moisture capacity of air.
4. **Choice A**: The avoidance of intense solar heat inside the greenhouse; AND **Choice B**: The entry of sunlight into the greenhouse to make the plants grow; AND **Choice C**: The mixture of heated air with greenhouse air to enhance the collection of moisture.
5. **Choice D**: The second part provides less substantiation for a romantic reading.
6. **Choice B**: James was very aware of the details of novelistic construction.
7. **Choice B**: not be inflexible in its treatment of the elements in the novel
8. **Choice B**: *Hamlet* has elements that are not amenable to an all-encompassing critical interpretation.

Answers and Explanations

SET 1. Text Completion and Sentence Equivalence Questions: Easy

> **For Questions 1 to 5, select one entry for each blank from the corresponding column of choices. Fill all blanks in the way that best completes the text.**

1. Dominant interests often benefit most from _____ of governmental interference in business, since they are able to take care of themselves if left alone.

Ⓐ	intensification
Ⓑ	authorization
Ⓒ	centralization
Ⓓ	improvisation
Ⓔ	elimination

Explanation

The sentence explains why dominant interests often benefit from a certain condition. Since the explanation is that they are able to take care of themselves if left alone, it follows that the condition is one in which interference is absent. Thus the best answer is "elimination." None of the other answer choices suggests an absence of interference — indeed "intensification," "authorization," and "centralization" suggest quite the opposite.

　　Thus the correct answer is **elimination** (Choice E).

2. Kagan maintains that an infant's reactions to its first stressful experiences are part of a natural process of development, not harbingers of childhood unhappiness or _____ signs of adolescent anxiety.

Ⓐ	prophetic
Ⓑ	normal
Ⓒ	monotonous
Ⓓ	virtual
Ⓔ	typical

Explanation

The sentence contrasts the infant's reactions, part of a normal developmental process, with future unhappiness and anxiety. The missing word describes signs of adolescent anxiety as they relate to the infant. Choice A is correct: "prophetic" signs, like harbingers, foretell future occurrences, and for the infant, adolescent anxiety is a future occurrence. Since an infant cannot literally display signs of adolescent anxiety, "normal," "monotonous," and "typical" are all incorrect. And "virtual" is incorrect, because virtual signs are not real signs, and what Kagan is denying is that the infant's reactions are not real signs of later unhappiness.

　　Thus the correct answer is **prophetic** (Choice A).

3. An investigation that is _____ can occasionally yield new facts, even notable ones, but typically the appearance of such facts is the result of a search in a definite direction.

Ⓐ	timely
Ⓑ	unguided
Ⓒ	consistent
Ⓓ	uncomplicated
Ⓔ	subjective

Explanation

As the words "can occasionally" and "but typically" indicate, the missing word describes an investigation that contrasts with a "search in a definite direction." Among the answer choices, only "unguided" provides a contrasting description; none of the other choices suggests an appropriate contrast.

Thus the correct answer is **unguided** (Choice B).

4. It is (i)_____ that so many portrait paintings hang in art museums, since the subject matter seems to dictate a status closer to pictures in the family photograph album than to high art. But perhaps it is the artistic skill with which the portraits are painted that (ii)_____ their presence in art museums.

Blank (i)		Blank (ii)	
Ⓐ	surprising	Ⓓ	challenges
Ⓑ	understandable	Ⓔ	justifies
Ⓒ	irrelevant	Ⓕ	changes

Explanation

In the part following "since," the first sentence of the paragraph suggests that the subject matter of portraits might not seem to fit with the idea of "high art." So the suggestion is that the presence of portrait paintings in art museums is in that sense odd or unfitting. Of the choices available for Blank (i), "surprising" is the one that expresses this sense. The second sentence, in contrast to the first, offers a point in favor of portraits — "artistic skill." So the second sentence is offering a reason why portraits should be in art museums. Of the choices for Blank (ii), "justifies" is the one that completes that thought.

Thus the correct answer is **surprising** (Choice A) and **justifies** (Choice E).

5. In stark contrast to his later (i)_____, Simpson was largely (ii)_____ politics during his college years, despite the fact that the campus he attended was rife with political activity.

Blank (i)		Blank (ii)	
Ⓐ	activism	Ⓓ	devoted to
Ⓑ	apathy	Ⓔ	indifferent to
Ⓒ	affability	Ⓕ	shaped by

Explanation

The sentence tells us that there is a contrast between the way Simpson related to politics in his college years and how he related to politics later in life. So the choices that complete the blanks must contrast with each other. The part of the sentence beginning with "despite" indicates that Simpson's relation to politics in his college years did not involve engagement in the political activity that was "rife." Of the choices for Blank (ii), only "indifferent to" conveys that nonengagement. And of the choices for Blank (i), only "activism" supplies the required contrast with "indifferent to."

Thus the correct answer is **activism** (Choice A) and **indifferent to** (Choice E).

> For Questions 6 to 8, select the <u>two</u> answer choices that, when used to complete the sentence, fit the meaning of the sentence as a whole <u>and</u> produce completed sentences that are alike in meaning.

6. As my eyesight began to _____, I spent a lot of time writing about it — both poems and "eye journals" — describing what I saw as I looked out through damaged eyes.

   A deteriorate
   B sharpen
   C improve
   D decline
   E recover
   F adjust

Explanation

The author has "damaged" eyes, and any word that fills the blank must reflect that fact. The words that best do so are "deteriorate" and "decline" (Choices A and D), which generate sentences alike in meaning. "Sharpen" and "improve" produce sentences alike in meaning, but neither word makes sense when inserted into the blank. Though "adjust" makes some sense when inserted into the blank, no other option produces a sentence similar in meaning.

Thus the correct answer is **deteriorate** (Choice A) and **decline** (Choice D).

7. The judge's standing in the legal community, though shaken by phony allegations of wrongdoing, emerged, at long last, _____ .

   A unqualified
   B undiminished
   C undecided
   D undamaged
   E unresolved
   F unprincipled

Explanation

The use of the word "though" establishes a contrast between the blank, which requires a description of the judge's standing, and "phony allegations of wrongdoing." Thus the words that best complete the blank must indicate that the judge's reputation was not adversely affected by these allegations. The only words that do so are "undiminished" and "undamaged" (Choices B and D), which produce sentences alike in meaning. "Undecided" and "unresolved" also produce sentences alike in meaning, but neither word makes sense when inserted into the blank.

Thus the correct answer is **undiminished** (Choice B) and **undamaged** (Choice D).

8. Modern agricultural practices have been extremely successful in increasing the productivity of major food crops, yet despite heavy use of pesticides, _____ losses to diseases and insect pests are sustained each year.

    A   incongruous

    B   reasonable

    C   significant

    D   considerable

    E   equitable

    F   fortuitous

Explanation

The word "despite" suggests the level of losses is somehow surprising given the heavy use of pesticides. The only words that describe an appropriate level of losses are "significant" and "considerable" (Choices C and D), which produce sentences alike in meaning. "Reasonable" and "equitable" also produce sentences alike in meaning, but neither word generates the contrast necessary for the sentence to make sense.

Thus the correct answer is **significant** (Choice C) and **considerable** (Choice D).

SET 2. Reading Comprehension Questions: Easy

> **For each of Questions 1 to 9, select <u>one</u> answer choice unless otherwise instructed.**

1. A person who agrees to serve as mediator between two warring factions at the request of both abandons by so agreeing the right to take sides later. To take sides at a later point would be to suggest that the earlier presumptive impartiality was a sham.

The passage above emphasizes which of the following points about mediators?

  (A) They should try to form no opinions of their own about any issue that is related to the dispute.

  (B) They should not agree to serve unless they are committed to maintaining a stance of impartiality.

  (C) They should not agree to serve unless they are equally acceptable to all parties to a dispute.

  (D) They should feel free to take sides in the dispute right from the start, provided that they make their biases publicly known.

  (E) They should reserve the right to abandon their impartiality so as not to be open to the charge of having been deceitful.

Explanation

By pointing out the consequences of abandoning impartiality, the paragraph underscores the importance for mediators of maintaining impartiality at all times. This is the point made in **Choice B**, which is therefore the correct answer. Choice A is incorrect, because it goes further than anything asserted in the passage. The passage does not rule out the possibility that one can have an opinion about issues related to a dispute without taking sides in the actual dispute. Choice C is incorrect because it is a presupposition on which the passage is based rather than the point of the passage; that is, the fact that the mediator is acceptable to both parties is a given, since they both ask the mediator to serve. Choices D and E are both inconsistent with the main point of the passage, the importance of impartiality at all times, so both are incorrect.

Questions 2 to 5 are based on the following reading passage.

Was Felix Mendelssohn (1809–1847) a great composer? On its face, the question seems absurd. One of the most gifted prodigies in the history of music, he produced his first masterpiece at sixteen. From then on, he was recognized as an artist of preternatural abilities, not only as a composer but also as a pianist and conductor. But Mendelssohn's enduring popularity has often been at odds — sometimes quite sharply — with his critical standing. Despite general acknowledgment of his genius, there has been a noticeable reluctance to rank him with, say, Schumann or Brahms. As Haggin put it, Mendelssohn, as a composer, was a "minor master . . . working on a small scale of emotion and texture."

Description

The passage starts by outlining the popular view that Mendelssohn was a great composer and then points out that critics do not generally accord him that status.

2. Select a sentence in the passage whose function is to indicate the range of Mendelssohn's musical talents.

Explanation

This question asks which sentence in the passage serves to indicate the range of Mendelssohn's musical talents. The correct answer is the **fourth sentence** ("From then . . . conductor"), the only sentence in the passage that mentions Mendelssohn's achievements across three different realms: composing, piano performance, and conducting. All the other sentences can be eliminated because, while they consider the question of Mendelssohn's claim to greatness, they do not specifically discuss the broad range of his musical talents.

3. The passage suggests that anyone attempting to evaluate Mendelssohn's career must confront which of the following dichotomies?

    (A) The tension between Mendelssohn's career as a composer and his career as a pianist and conductor

    (B) The contrast between Mendelssohn's popularity and that of Schumann and Brahms

    (C) The discrepancy between Mendelssohn's popularity and his standing among critics

    (D) The inconsistency between Mendelssohn's reputation during his lifetime and his reputation since his death

    (E) The gap between Mendelssohn's prodigious musical beginnings and his decline in later years

Explanation

The passage clearly presents the discrepancy between Mendelssohn's popularity and his critical standing as an interpretive problem. Therefore, **Choice C** is correct. The other answer choices are incorrect because the passage never indicates that there was any conflict among the different aspects of Mendelssohn's professional life; never discusses Schumann's and Brahms's popularity; does not discuss any differences between Mendelssohn's reputation during his lifetime and after his death; and makes no mention of a decline in Mendelssohn's later life.

4. It can be inferred that the "reluctance" mentioned in the passage is being ascribed to

    (A) most composers since Mendelssohn

    (B) Schumann and Brahms

    (C) the music-listening public

    (D) music critics generally

    (E) Haggin exclusively

Explanation

Choice D is correct. The "reluctance" is mentioned in the context of a discussion about Mendelssohn's critical standing and thus is being ascribed to music critics generally. Choices A and B can be eliminated because the passage does not discuss any composer's views of Mendelssohn. Choice C is incorrect because the word "reluctance" is mentioned only after the passage turns from discussing the popular view of Mendelssohn to the critical view. Choice E is incorrect because the words "As Haggin put it" indicate that Haggin is only one example of critics who have this reluctance.

5. The author mentions Schumann and Brahms primarily in order to

    (A) provide examples of composers who are often compared with Mendelssohn

    (B) identify certain composers who are more popular than Mendelssohn

    (C) identify composers whom Mendelssohn influenced

    (D) establish the milieu in which Mendelssohn worked

    (E) establish a standard of comparison for Mendelssohn as a composer

Explanation

Schumann and Brahms are mentioned as a way of explaining how critics rank Mendelssohn — that is, as less accomplished than some other composers who are widely acknowledged as major. Therefore, **Choice E** is correct. Choice A might look like a correct answer at first glance. However, careful consideration reveals that the point the author is making when Schumann and Brahms are mentioned is not the frequency of that comparison but the results of it. Therefore, Choice A can be eliminated. Choices B, C, and D are incorrect because the passage does not discuss Schumann's and Brahms's popularity, Mendelssohn's influence on other composers, or the milieu in which Mendelssohn worked.

Questions 6 and 7 are based on the following reading passage.

While most scholarship on women's employment in the United States recognizes that the Second World War (1939–1945) dramatically changed the role of women in the workforce, these studies also acknowledge that few women remained in manufacturing jobs once men returned from the war. But in agriculture, unlike other industries where women were viewed as temporary workers, women's employment did not end with the war. Instead, the expansion of agriculture and a steady decrease in the number of male farmworkers combined to cause the industry to hire more women in the postwar years. Consequently, the 1950s saw a growing number of women engaged in farm labor, even though rhetoric in the popular media called for the return of women to domestic life.

Description

The first sentence states that the Second World War led to significant changes in women's employment, but that these changes were largely reversed in manufacturing after the war. The second sentence discusses the fact that unlike in other industries, employment of women in agriculture was more permanent; the third provides more detail regarding the trend in agriculture and the reasons for it; and the fourth summarizes the consequences of the trend.

6. It can be inferred from the passage that the manufacturing and agricultural sectors in the United States following the Second World War differed in which of the following respects?

   (A) The rate of expansion in each sector

   (B) The percentage of employees in each sector who were men

   (C) The trend in the wages of men employed in each sector

   (D) The attitude of the popular media toward the employment of women in each sector

   (E) The extent to which women in each sector were satisfied with their jobs

Explanation

The correct choice for this question is **Choice B**. We are told that few women remained in the manufacturing sector once men returned from the war, while the number of women who worked in agriculture increased after the war as the number of men in agriculture decreased. It is therefore inferable that the percentage of employees working in manufacturing who were men increased while the percentage of employees working in agriculture who were men decreased. Choices A, C, and E are incorrect because the passage provides no information about rates of expansion, wage trends, or women's job satisfaction. Choice D is incorrect because the only mention of the popular media occurs in the final sentence, and no distinction is made between the sectors there.

7.   Which of the following statements about women's employment in the United States during and after the Second World War is most clearly supported by the passage?

Ⓐ   Most women who joined the workforce during the Second World War wanted to return to domestic life when the war ended.

Ⓑ   The great majority of women who joined the workforce during the Second World War were employed in manufacturing jobs.

Ⓒ   The end of the Second World War was followed by a large-scale transfer of women workers from manufacturing to agriculture.

Ⓓ   The increase in women's employment that accompanied the Second World War was longer lasting in agriculture than it was in manufacturing.

Ⓔ   The popular media were more forceful in calling for women to join the workforce during the Second World War than in calling for women to return to domestic life after the war.

Explanation

The correct choice for this question is **Choice D**. We are told in the passage that women's employment in manufacturing fell quickly after men returned from the war. However, not only did women's employment in agriculture not decline after the end of the war, it actually increased. The other choices are incorrect because the passage provides no information about what women who joined the workforce wanted to do; about the distribution of women across industries; about what happened to women who left manufacturing; nor about media appeals for women to join the wartime workforce.

Questions 8 and 9 are based on the following reading passage.

Since the Hawaiian Islands have never been connected to other land masses, the great variety of plants in Hawaii must be a result of the long-distance dispersal of seeds, a process that requires both a method of transport and an equivalence between the ecology of the source area and that of the recipient area.

line

5   There is some dispute about the method of transport involved. Some biologists argue that ocean and air currents are responsible for the transport of plant seeds to Hawaii. Yet the results of flotation experiments and the low temperatures of air currents cast doubt on these hypotheses. More probable is bird transport, either externally, by accidental attachment of the seeds to feathers, or internally, by the swallowing of fruit and subsequent

10   excretion of the seeds. While it is likely that fewer varieties of plant seeds have reached Hawaii externally than internally, more varieties are known to be adapted to external than to internal transport.

Description

The passage raises the question of how seeds reached the Hawaiian Islands. It introduces one possible method — ocean and air currents — but refers to evidence that casts doubt on that method. It then introduces a second method — bird transport — and discusses two ways in which that might occur.

8.   The author of the passage is primarily concerned with

    (A)   discussing different approaches biologists have taken to testing theories about the distribution of plants in Hawaii

    (B)   discussing different theories about the transport of plant seeds to Hawaii

    (C)   discussing the extent to which air currents are responsible for the dispersal of plant seeds to Hawaii

    (D)   resolving a dispute about the adaptability of plant seeds to bird transport

    (E)   resolving a dispute about the ability of birds to carry plant seeds long distances

Explanation

Given the description of the preceding passage, it is clear that **Choice B** is correct: the passage focuses on "different theories about the transport of plant seeds to Hawaii." Choice A can be eliminated: while the passage does refer to flotation experiments, it does not elaborate on experimental methods. Choice C identifies an idea that is part of the passage's main concern, but since this is only one of the competing theories discussed in the passage, not the primary focus, Choice C is incorrect. Choices D and E are incorrect because the passage does not resolve any disputes.

9.   The author mentions the results of flotation experiments on plant seeds (lines 7–8) most probably in order to

    (A)   support the claim that the distribution of plants in Hawaii is the result of the long-distance dispersal of seeds

    (B)   lend credibility to the thesis that air currents provide a method of transport for plant seeds to Hawaii

    (C)   suggest that the long-distance dispersal of seeds is a process that requires long periods of time

    (D)   challenge the claim that ocean currents are responsible for the transport of plant seeds to Hawaii

    (E)   refute the claim that Hawaiian flora evolved independently from flora in other parts of the world

Explanation

This question asks why the author mentions flotation experiments. Flotation experiments are mentioned in the passage in order to show that some evidence casts doubt on the claim that ocean currents were the means by which seeds were transported to Hawaii. Thus, **Choice D** is correct. Choice A is incorrect since the claim that plant distribution in Hawaii is the result of long-distance dispersal of seeds is a given in the passage, not an idea that the author feels a need to substantiate. Choice B is eliminable since the flotation experiments are introduced at a point where the author is challenging, rather than lending credibility to, the air current hypothesis and because flotation experiments would more likely reflect on ocean currents than air currents. Choice C is eliminable since the passage does not address the length of time required for long-distance seed dispersal. Finally, Choice E is eliminable since it too describes an idea that is not discussed in the passage.

SET 3. Text Completion and Sentence Equivalence Questions: Medium

> For Questions 1 to 5, select one entry for each blank from the corresponding column of choices. Fill all blanks in the way that best completes the text.

1. It comes as no surprise that societies have codes of behavior; the character of the codes, on the other hand, can often be _____ .

Ⓐ	predictable
Ⓑ	unexpected
Ⓒ	admirable
Ⓓ	explicit
Ⓔ	confusing

Explanation

The words "on the other hand" indicate that while the existence of societal codes of behavior is no surprise, their character may be quite surprising. Thus the correct answer is Choice B, **unexpected**, which means the same as surprising. "Predictable" is the very opposite of surprising, and none of the other answer choices means "surprising."

Thus the correct answer is **unexpected** (Choice B).

2. Like Béla Bartók, Ruth Crawford not only brought a composer's acumen to the notation of folk music, she also had a marked (i)_____ the task. This was clear in her agonizing over how far to try to represent the minute details of a performance in a written text, and this (ii)_____ makes her work a landmark in ethnomusicology.

Blank (i)		Blank (ii)	
Ⓐ	reverence for	Ⓓ	fastidiousness
Ⓑ	detachment from	Ⓔ	didacticism
Ⓒ	curiosity about	Ⓕ	iconoclasm

Explanation

In this example, both blanks can be filled by focusing on the statement that Crawford agonized over the details in her representations of folk music performances. The only choice for blank (ii) that matches this description is "fastidiousness"; neither "didacticism" nor "iconoclasm" reflects the notion of agonizing over details. Similarly, only "reverence for" fits in Blank (i), since neither "detachment from" nor "curiosity about" reflects the degree of care Crawford took.

Thus the correct answer is **reverence for** (Choice A) and **fastidiousness** (Choice D).

3. Political advertising may well be the most (i)_____ kind of advertising: political candidates are usually quite (ii)_____, yet their campaign advertisements often hide important differences behind smoke screens of smiles and empty slogans.

Blank (i)	Blank (ii)
Ⓐ polemical	Ⓓ interchangeable
Ⓑ effective	Ⓔ dissimilar
Ⓒ deceptive	Ⓕ vocal

Explanation

Looking at Blank (i), it is hard to select a correct answer, since all three answer choices fit the immediate context well. Looking to the second part of the sentence, however, we can see such expressions as "hide" and "smoke screens," both of which suggest that the correct answer for Blank (i) is "deceptive." Making that assumption, we can go on to see that the answer for Blank (ii) is "dissimilar," since what is deceptive about political advertisements is that they hide important differences. Reading the sentence again with "deceptive" and "dissimilar" in place confirms those choices.

    Thus the correct answer is **deceptive** (Choice C) and **dissimilar** (Choice E).

4. Richard M. Russell said 52 percent of the nation's growth since the Second World War had (i)_____ invention. He said, (ii)_____ research, the government's greatest role in assuring continuing innovation is promoting a strong, modern patent office. "Unless we can (iii)_____ original ideas, we will not have invention," Mr. Russell said. Speculating on the state of innovation over the next century, several inventors agreed that the future lay in giving children the tools to think creatively and the motivation to invent.

Blank (i)	Blank (ii)	Blank (iii)
Ⓐ been at the expense of	Ⓓ in addition to restricting	Ⓖ evaluate
Ⓑ no bearing on	Ⓔ aside from supporting	Ⓗ protect
Ⓒ come through	Ⓕ far from exaggerating	Ⓘ disseminate

Explanation

A quick overview of the paragraph shows that its topic is the encouragement of invention and innovation. This implies that Blank (i) should be filled with "come through," which emphasizes the importance of invention; the other choices suggest that invention is irrelevant or somehow harmed by growth. Again, the only one of the choices for Blank (ii) that continues the theme of encouraging invention is "aside from supporting." Finally, the second sentence emphasizes the importance for innovation of a strong patent office, and this thought is reaffirmed in the following quotation from Mr. Russell, which requires "protect" in Blank (iii).

    Thus the correct answer is **come through** (Choice C), **aside from supporting** (Choice E), and **protect** (Choice H).

5. Statements presented as fact in a patent application are (i)_____ unless a good reason for doubt is found. The invention has only to be deemed "more likely than not" to work in order to receive initial approval. And, although thousands of patents are challenged in court for other reasons, no incentive exists for anyone to expend effort (ii) _____ the science of an erroneous patent. For this reason the endless stream of (iii)_____ devices will continue to yield occasional patents.

Blank (i)	Blank (ii)	Blank (iii)
Ⓐ presumed verifiable	Ⓓ corroborating	Ⓖ novel
Ⓑ carefully scrutinized	Ⓔ advancing	Ⓗ bogus
Ⓒ considered capricious	Ⓕ debunking	Ⓘ obsolete

Explanation

The paragraph appears to be explaining some odd or unexpected aspect of the patent process. The third sentence helps to clarify what this aspect is — it discusses challenges to patents. The only choice for Blank (ii) that is concerned with challenging a patent is "debunking," since "corroborating" and "advancing" suggest support instead. This in turn provides the answer for the third blank, since the preceding sentence does explain how "bogus" devices may nonetheless get a patent. And we can also now better understand the first sentence — it too must help explain how bogus devices get patents, which it can do only if the blank is filled with "presumed verifiable," suggesting that patent applications are taken at face value and not dismissed out of hand nor subjected to careful scrutiny.

Thus the correct answer is **presumed verifiable** (Choice A), **debunking** (Choice F), and **bogus** (Choice H).

> **For Questions 6 to 8, select the <u>two</u> answer choices that, when used to complete the sentence, fit the meaning of the sentence as a whole <u>and</u> produce completed sentences that are alike in meaning.**

6. Ever a demanding reader of the fiction of others, the novelist Chase was likewise often the object of _____ analyses by his contemporaries.

    A exacting
    B copious
    C respectful
    D acerbic
    E scathing
    F meticulous

Explanation

The use of the word "likewise" indicates that the analyses of Chase's work by contemporaries were similar to his analyses of the fiction of others. Since he is described as a "demanding reader," the words that best fit the blank will be similar in meaning to "demanding." The words that meet this requirement are "exacting" (Choice A) and "meticulous" (Choice F), and they produce sentences that are alike in meaning. Although "acerbic analyses" means close to the same thing as "scathing analyses," both "acerbic" and "scathing" have meanings that are quite different from "demanding," so neither fits well in the blank.

Thus the correct answer is **exacting** (Choice A) and **meticulous** (Choice F).

7. Her _____ should not be confused with miserliness; as long as I have known her, she has always been willing to assist those who are in need.

- [A] stinginess
- [B] diffidence
- [C] frugality
- [D] illiberality
- [E] intolerance
- [F] thrift

Explanation

The sentence explains that the person spoken of is not miserly, since she is quite prepared to be generous. So for the sentence to make sense, the word filling the blank has to be something that is consistent with generosity and yet might, by those without a full understanding of her behavior, be mistaken for miserliness. The words "frugality" and "thrift" fulfill this requirement and yield two sentences that are alike in meaning, so that pair forms the correct answer. Neither "stinginess" nor "illiberality" makes sense in the sentence, since they are synonymous with "miserliness" and inconsistent with generosity. Other choices, such as "diffidence," might perhaps make a sensible sentence if placed in the blank but do not form part of the correct answer since they have no companion word that would make a sentence of similar meaning.

Thus the correct answer is **frugality** (Choice C) and **thrift** (Choice F).

8. A misconception frequently held by novice writers is that sentence structure mirrors thought: the more convoluted the structure, the more _____ the ideas.

- [A] complicated
- [B] engaged
- [C] essential
- [D] fanciful
- [E] inconsequential
- [F] involved

Explanation

Because the second half of the sentence illustrates the idea that "structure mirrors thought," any word that fills the blank must be similar in meaning to "convoluted." The two words that are similar to "convoluted" are "complicated" and "involved" (Choices A and F), which produce sentences alike in meaning. "Fanciful," while somewhat similar in meaning to "convoluted," is not as similar to either "complicated" or "involved" as those words are to each other. The other answer choices are not similar in meaning to "convoluted," and thus do not produce coherent sentences.

Thus the correct answer is **complicated** (Choice A) and **involved** (Choice F).

SET 4. Reading Comprehension Questions: Medium

For each of Questions 1 to 9, select __one__ answer choice unless otherwise instructed.

Questions 1 and 2 are based on the following reading passage.

I enjoyed *A Dream of Light & Shadow: Portraits of Latin American Women Writers* for the same reason that, as a child, I avidly consumed women's biographies: the fascination with how the biographical details of another female's life are represented and interpreted.

A Dream offers a rich read, varied in both the lives and texts of the women portrayed and the perspectives and styles of the sixteen essayists. Yet, as an adult, I have come to demand of any really "great" book a self-consciousness about the tenuous nature of representations of reality, a critical contextualization of florid detail, and a self-awareness of the role of ideology in our lives. In these critical senses, *A Dream* is inadequate.

Description

The passage follows the following structure: the first sentence discusses a collection of biographical sketches and what the author found particularly appealing about similar works as a child; the second sentence describes several positive aspects of this particular collection and how it satisfies the author's early interests; the third sentence describes a demanding set of criteria that the author now applies when assessing such work; and in the fourth sentence the author says the collection being discussed does not meet those criteria.

For the following question, consider each of the choices separately and select all that apply.

1. The author of the passage suggests that *A Dream* falls short in which of the following respects?

    [A] It does not appear to recognize that representations of reality can be unreliable.

    [B] It seems to focus on stylistic variety at the expense of accuracy of detail.

    [C] It offers a wealth of detail without sufficient critical examination of that detail.

Explanation

Choices A and C are correct. We know from the final sentence that the collection falls short of several criteria established by the author.

Choice A is correct: the book does not demonstrate sufficient awareness of the "tenuous nature of representations of reality."

Choice B is incorrect: there is no mention in the passage of any concern on the part of the author about the accuracy of detail.

Choice C is correct: the book does not offer an adequate "critical contextualization of florid detail."

2. Which of the following best describes the function of the second sentence ("*A Dream* . . . essayists") in the context of the passage as a whole?

   Ⓐ To give examples of how *A Dream* presents fascinating portraits that display awareness of the tenuous nature of representations of reality

   Ⓑ To elaborate on how *A Dream* fulfills the author's childhood criteria for a pleasurable book

   Ⓒ To suggest that the author enjoyed *A Dream* for reasons more sophisticated than the reasons she enjoyed certain books as a child

   Ⓓ To illustrate ways in which the author finds *A Dream* to be inadequate in certain critical senses

   Ⓔ To imply that *A Dream* is too varied in focus to provide a proper contextualization of the biographical details it offers

Explanation

This question asks about the function of the second sentence. The correct choice is **Choice B**. As discussed in the description of the passage, that sentence describes what is appealing about the collection in the context of the author's childhood tastes. Choice A is incorrect both because the sentence does not provide examples and because the collection does not display an awareness of the tenuous nature of representations of reality. Choice C is not correct: although one might suspect that the author's enjoyment of collections as an adult would be on a more sophisticated level than when she was young, there is no discussion or even suggestion of that in the passage. Choice D is incorrect because the sentence describes the virtues of the collection. The aspects of the collection that the author finds inadequate are not addressed until later. Choice E is incorrect because, according to the passage, the fact that the collection is varied makes it a "rich" read. There is no suggestion that the variety hinders proper contextualization.

3. During the day in Lake Constance, the zooplankton *D. hyalina* departs for the depths where food is scarce and the water cold. *D. galeata* remains near the warm surface where food is abundant. Even though *D. galeata* grows and reproduces much faster, its population is often outnumbered by *D. hyalina*.

   Which of the following, if true, would help resolve the apparent paradox presented?

   Ⓐ The number of species of zooplankton living at the bottom of the lake is twice that of species living at the surface.

   Ⓑ Predators of zooplankton, such as whitefish and perch, live and feed near the surface of the lake during the day.

   Ⓒ In order to make the most of scarce food resources, *D. hyalina* matures more slowly than *D. galeata*.

   Ⓓ *D. galeata* clusters under vegetation during the hottest part of the day to avoid the Sun's rays.

   Ⓔ *D. galeata* produces twice as many offspring per individual in any given period of time as does *D. hyalina*.

Description

The paragraph presents an apparent paradox: the zooplankton that spends the day in less hospitable conditions often outnumbers the one that stays in more hospitable conditions.

Explanation

The presence of predators of zooplankton feeding near the surface during the day would suggest that *D. galeata* is consumed at a higher rate than *D. hyalina*: this would explain why *D. hyalina* is often more numerous, so **Choice B** is correct. Choices C and E are incorrect because although they help to explain why the two zooplankton reproduce at different rates, they do not help to resolve the apparent paradox. Choices A and D are incorrect because nothing is said in the paragraph to show the relevance of the presence of other species of zooplankton, nor of the habit of clustering under vegetation, to the relative population size of the two species.

Questions 4 and 5 are based on the following reading passage.

Tocqueville, apparently, was wrong. Jacksonian America was not a fluid, egalitarian society where individual wealth and poverty were ephemeral conditions. At least so argues E. Pessen in his iconoclastic study of the very rich in the United States between 1825 and 1850.

Pessen does present a quantity of examples, together with some refreshingly intelligible statistics, to establish the existence of an inordinately wealthy class. Though active in commerce or the professions, most of the wealthy were not self-made but had inherited family fortunes. In no sense mercurial, these great fortunes survived the financial panics that destroyed lesser ones. Indeed, in several cities the wealthiest one percent constantly increased its share until by 1850 it owned half of the community's wealth. Although these observations are true, Pessen overestimates their importance by concluding from them that the undoubted progress toward inequality in the late eighteenth century continued in the Jacksonian period and that the United States was a class-ridden, plutocratic society even before industrialization.

Description

The passage describes Pessen's argument that Jacksonian America was not fluid and egalitarian but class-ridden and plutocratic, and criticizes it for leaping to an unjustified conclusion.

4. According to the passage, Pessen indicates that all of the following were true of the very wealthy in the United States between 1825 and 1850 EXCEPT:
   - (A) They formed a distinct upper class.
   - (B) Many of them were able to increase their holdings.
   - (C) Some of them worked as professionals or in business.
   - (D) Most of them accumulated their own fortunes.
   - (E) Many of them retained their wealth in spite of financial upheavals.

Explanation

For this question, you are to identify the one statement that CANNOT be correctly attributed to Pessen. Therefore, you must first determine which of the statements given can be attributed to Pessen. According to the passage, Pessen maintains all of the following: there was a class of "inordinately wealthy" Americans (Choice A); in some places that class "constantly increased its share" (Choice B); its members were "active in commerce or the professions" (Choice C); and "these great fortunes survived the financial panics that destroyed lesser ones" (Choice E). However, Pessen also maintains, in contradiction to Choice D, that "most of the wealthy were not self-made but had inherited family fortunes." Therefore, **Choice D** is correct.

5. Which of the following best states the author's main point?

   (A) Pessen's study has overturned the previously established view of the social and economic structure of early-nineteenth-century America.

   (B) Tocqueville's analysis of the United States in the Jacksonian era remains the definitive account of this period.

   (C) Pessen's study is valuable primarily because it shows the continuity of the social system in the United States throughout the nineteenth century.

   (D) The social patterns and political power of the extremely wealthy in the United States between 1825 and 1850 are well documented.

   (E) Pessen challenges a view of the social and economic systems in the United States from 1825 to 1850, but he draws conclusions that are incorrect.

Explanation

It is important to realize that although most of the passage is devoted to describing Pessen's study, the author's main point is to criticize the conclusion Pessen draws. Choices A, C, and D omit any reference to the author's critical evaluation of Pessen's study, and hence are not statements of the author's main point. Choice B is also incorrect. Because Pessen criticizes Tocqueville and the author criticizes Pessen, it might seem that the author's main point is to defend Tocqueville's analysis. However, the passage does not indicate that Tocqueville's analysis is definitive. **Choice E** is correct. According to the first paragraph, Pessen challenges Tocqueville's view, but according to the second paragraph, Pessen's conclusions are incorrect.

Questions 6 to 9 are based on the following reading passage.

The evolution of intelligence among early large mammals of the grasslands was due in great measure to the interaction between two ecologically synchronized groups of these animals, the hunting carnivores and the herbivores that they hunted. The interaction resulting from the differences between predator and prey led to a general improvement in brain functions; however, certain components of intelligence were improved far more than others.

The kind of intelligence favored by the interplay of increasingly smarter catchers and increasingly keener escapers is defined by attention — that aspect of mind carrying consciousness forward from one moment to the next. It ranges from a passive, free-floating awareness to a highly focused, active fixation. The range through these states is mediated by the arousal system, a network of tracts converging from sensory systems to integrating centers in the brain stem. From the more relaxed to the more vigorous levels, sensitivity to novelty is increased. The organism is more awake, more vigilant; this increased vigilance results in the apprehension of ever more subtle signals as the organism becomes more sensitive to its surroundings. The processes of arousal and concentration give attention its direction. Arousal is at first general, with a flooding of impulses in the brain stem; then gradually the activation is channeled. Thus begins concentration, the holding of consistent images. One meaning of intelligence is the way in which these images and other alertly searched information are used in the context of previous experience. Consciousness links past attention to the present and permits the integration of details with perceived ends and purposes.

The elements of intelligence and consciousness come together marvelously to produce different styles in predator and prey. Herbivores and carnivores develop different kinds of attention related to escaping or chasing. Although in both kinds of animals, arousal stimulates the production of adrenaline and norepinephrine by the adrenal glands, the effect in herbivores is primarily fear, whereas in carnivores the effect is primarily aggression. For both, arousal attunes the animal to what is ahead. Perhaps it does not experience forethought as we know it, but the animal does experience something like it. The predator is searchingly aggressive, inner-directed, tuned by the nervous system and the adrenal hormones, but aware in a sense closer to human consciousness than, say, a hungry lizard's instinctive snap at a passing beetle. Using past events as a framework, the large mammal predator is working out a relationship between movement and food, sensitive to possibilities in cold trails and distant sounds — and yesterday's unforgotten lessons. The herbivore prey is of a different mind. Its mood of wariness rather than searching and its attitude of general expectancy instead of anticipating are silk-thin veils of tranquillity over an explosive endocrine system.

line

30

35

Description

The passage describes improvements in certain components of intelligence among early large mammals of the grasslands. The second paragraph focuses on attention as a primary area of improvement, and the third paragraph outlines how attention differs in predator and prey species.

6. The author refers to a hungry lizard (line 30) primarily in order to

   (A) demonstrate the similarity between the hunting methods of mammals and those of nonmammals

   (B) broaden the application of the argument by including an insectivore as an example

   (C) make a distinction between higher and lower levels of consciousness

   (D) provide an additional illustration of the brutality characteristic of predators

   (E) offer an objection to suggestions that all animals lack consciousness

Explanation

Choice C is correct. The "hungry lizard's instinctive snap" is contrasted with the mammal's higher level of awareness. Choices A and B are incorrect. The example of the hungry lizard provides a contrast; it does not demonstrate a similarity or extend the author's argument. Choices D and E are incorrect. Brutality is not mentioned in the passage as a characteristic of predators, and there is no suggestion that all animals lack consciousness.

7. It can be inferred from the passage that in animals less intelligent than the mammals discussed in the passage

   (A) past experience is less helpful in ensuring survival

   (B) attention is more highly focused

   (C) muscular coordination is less highly developed

   (D) there is less need for competition among species

   (E) environment is more important in establishing the proper ratio of prey to predator

Explanation

Choice A is correct. In lines 18–19, the author defines intelligence in terms of an animal's use of past experience. In the context of the entire passage, it can be inferred that more intelligent animals, such as the grassland mammals discussed, are better able to use past experience to help them survive than less intelligent animals are. Choice B is incorrect. The second paragraph of the passage indicates that attention is more highly focused in animals of greater, rather than lesser, intelligence. Choices C, D, and E are incorrect. The author does not discuss muscular coordination as an element in intelligence, gives no indication that in less intelligent species there is less need for competition, and does not discuss how a proper ratio of prey to predator is established.

8. According to the passage, improvement in brain function among early large mammals resulted primarily from which of the following?

 Ⓐ Interplay of predator and prey

 Ⓑ Persistence of free-floating awareness in animals of the grasslands

 Ⓒ Gradual dominance of warm-blooded mammals over cold-blooded reptiles

 Ⓓ Interaction of early large mammals with less intelligent species

 Ⓔ Improvement of the capacity for memory among herbivores and carnivores

Explanation

Choice A is correct. It directly paraphrases the statement in lines 3–5, which describes the author's view of the development of improved brain function in early mammals. Choice B is incorrect. It is likely that the persistence of "free-floating awareness" played a part in the animals' survival, but there is no indication in the passage that brain function improved because of it. Choices C and D are incorrect: the passage does not discuss the relationship between mammals and reptiles or the interaction between large mammals and less intelligent species. Choice E is incorrect. Improved capacity for memory is an improvement in brain function, rather than a reason for improved brain function.

9. According to the passage, as the process of arousal in an organism continues, all of the following may occur EXCEPT

 Ⓐ the production of adrenaline

 Ⓑ the production of norepinephrine

 Ⓒ a heightening of sensitivity to stimuli

 Ⓓ an increase in selectivity with respect to stimuli

 Ⓔ an expansion of the range of states mediated by the brain stem

Explanation

This question asks you what does NOT occur during arousal. To answer the question, you must first determine what does occur. According to the passage, arousal does stimulate the production of adrenaline and norepinephrine (lines 24–25); does increase sensitivity to stimuli (lines 12–13); and does increase concentration on specific stimuli (lines 15–17). Thus Choices A through D all describe consequences of arousal. Only **Choice E** is correct. There is no indication in the passage that the range of states mediated by the brain stem expands during arousal.

SET 5. Text Completion and Sentence Equivalence Questions: Hard

> For Questions 1 to 6, select one entry for each blank from the corresponding column of choices. Fill all blanks in the way that best completes the text.

1. For some time now, _____ has been presumed not to exist: the cynical conviction that everybody has an angle is considered wisdom.

Ⓐ	rationality
Ⓑ	flexibility
Ⓒ	diffidence
Ⓓ	disinterestedness
Ⓔ	insincerity

Explanation

The colon indicates that the second part of the sentence will explain the first part. The missing word will describe the opposite of the cynical conviction that "everybody has an angle," that is, that each person is concerned primarily with their own interests. Since "disinterestedness" means lack of self-interest, Choice D is correct. None of the other answer choices means something that is contrasted with or opposed to being primarily concerned with one's own interests.

   Thus the correct answer is **disinterestedness** (Choice D).

2. Human nature and long distances have made exceeding the speed limit a (i)_____ in the state, so the legislators surprised no one when, acceding to public demand, they (ii)_____ increased penalties for speeding.

Blank (i)	Blank (ii)
Ⓐ controversial habit	Ⓓ endorsed
Ⓑ cherished tradition	Ⓔ considered
Ⓒ disquieting ritual	Ⓕ rejected

Explanation

The reference to human nature and long distances suggest that it is rather routine for drivers to exceed the speed limit in this state. "Cherished tradition" best fits this context for Blank (i), since there is nothing in the sentence to suggest that speeding here is "controversial" or "disquieting." In Blank (ii) we need to consider what the legislature would do that would surprise no one with regard to increased penalties for speeding. Given what we have learned so far, "rejected" is the best answer; it would be surprising if the legislature "endorsed" or even "considered" increased penalties for speeding.

   Thus the correct answer is **cherished tradition** (Choice B) and **rejected** (Choice F).

3. Serling's account of his employer's reckless decision making (i)_____ that company's image as (ii)_____ bureaucracy full of wary managers.

Blank (i)	Blank (ii)
(A) belies	(D) an injudicious
(B) exposes	(E) a disorganized
(C) overshadows	(F) a cautious

Explanation

The correct answer for Blank (i) must support, or at least be consistent with, the contrast between Serling's account, which emphasizes the recklessness of the company's decision making, and the company's image, that of a bureaucracy full of wary managers. For Blank (i), "belies" is the best choice since Serling's account would certainly belie or contradict the company's image. "Exposes" makes little sense since the image presumably is already out in the open, and there is nothing in the sentence that suggests Serling's account "overshadows" the company's image. As for Blank (ii), "a cautious" is the most logical choice. Neither "an injudicious" nor "a disorganized" makes sense in Blank (ii) as they both go against the notion of wariness.

   Thus the correct answer is **belies** (Choice A) and **a cautious** (Choice F).

4. No other contemporary poet's work has such a well-earned reputation for (i)_____, and there are few whose moral vision is so imperiously unsparing. Of late, however, the almost belligerent demands of his severe and densely forbidding poetry have taken an improbable turn. This new collection is the poet's fourth book in six years—an ample output even for poets of sunny disposition, let alone for one of such (ii)_____ over the previous 50 years. Yet for all his newfound (iii)_____, his poetry is as thorny as ever.

Blank (i)	Blank (ii)	Blank (iii)
(A) patent accessibility	(D) penitential austerity	(G) taciturnity
(B) intrinsic frivolity	(E) intractable prolixity	(H) volubility
(C) near impenetrability	(F) impetuous prodigality	(I) pellucidity

Explanation

Since the author of the paragraph has described the poet's reputation as "well-earned," the correct completion for Blank (i) must be something that is consistent with what the rest of the passage says about the poet's work. Only "near impenetrability" fulfills this requirement, since the next sentence tells us that the poet's work is "severe" and "densely forbidding," which rule out both accessibility and frivolity. The Blank (ii) completion must contrast with "ample output," and of the available options, only "penitential austerity" does so. Finally, the word in Blank (iii), since it is preceded by "newfound," must refer to the change that has occurred in the poet's work. The change the paragraph has described is an increase in output, so "volubility" is the correct choice.

Thus the correct answer is **near impenetrability** (Choice C), **penitential austerity** (Choice D), and **volubility** (Choice H).

5. Managers who think that strong environmental performance will (i)_____ their company's financial performance often (ii)_____ claims that systems designed to help them manage environmental concerns are valuable tools. By contrast, managers who perceive environmental performance to be (iii)_____ to financial success may view an environmental management system as extraneous. In either situation, and whatever their perceptions, it is a manager's commitment to achieving environmental improvement rather than the mere presence of a system that determines environmental performance.

Blank (i)	Blank (ii)	Blank (iii)
Ⓐ eclipse	Ⓓ uncritically accept	Ⓖ complementary
Ⓑ bolster	Ⓔ appropriately acknowledge	Ⓗ intrinsic
Ⓒ degrade	Ⓕ hotly dispute	Ⓘ peripheral

Explanation

The first two sentences introduce two contrasting sets of managers. The managers identified in the second sentence view systems designed to help manage environmental concerns as "extraneous," suggesting that they would view environmental performance to be "peripheral" (Choice I) to financial performance. The other options for Blank (iii)— "complementary" and "intrinsic"—are not consistent with the idea that environmental management systems are extraneous. With Blank (iii) filled in, we can go back to Blanks (i) and (ii) with greater confidence: "bolster" works best in Blank (i), since the two sets of managers have contrasting views. Blank (ii) is not straightforward—clearly these managers would not "hotly dispute" this claim, but "appropriately acknowledge" is less easily ruled out. "Uncritically accept" makes sense and is confirmed when we look at the final sentence in which the author warns that, in either situation, "the mere presence of a system" is not enough to achieve environmental improvement. In fact, a system is not even necessary. Thus the author of the paragraph does not regard the systems as particularly valuable, ruling out "appropriately acknowledge."

Thus the correct answer is **bolster** (Choice B), **uncritically accept** (Choice D), and **peripheral** (Choice I).

6. Philosophy, unlike most other subjects, does not try to extend our knowledge by discovering new information about the world. Instead it tries to deepen our understanding through (i)_____ what is already closest to us—the experiences, thoughts, concepts, and activities that make up our lives but that ordinarily escape our notice precisely because they are so familiar. Philosophy begins by finding (ii)_____ the things that are (iii) _____.

Blank (i)	Blank (ii)	Blank (iii)
Ⓐ attainment of	Ⓓ essentially irrelevant	Ⓖ most prosaic
Ⓑ rumination on	Ⓔ utterly mysterious	Ⓗ somewhat hackneyed
Ⓒ detachment from	Ⓕ thoroughly commonplace	Ⓘ refreshingly novel

Explanation

The first two sentences present a contrast between extending our knowledge by discovering "new information about the world"—which we are told philosophy does not do—and extending knowledge through some activity involving "things that are closest to us." The first blank asks us to identify that activity, and although "attainment" makes little sense in context, both "rumination on" and "detachment from" have some appeal. However, the clear implication that philosophy attends to things that ordinarily escape our notice eliminates "detachment from" as a correct answer. Blank (ii) requires something that suggests the importance of familiar things as subjects of philosophical rumination, and "utterly mysterious" does just that. "Essentially irrelevant" and "thoroughly commonplace" do not fit logically since they suggest that these "familiar" things are unimportant. Similarly, Blank (iii) needs to be consistent with the description of those things as familiar and close. "Most prosaic" fits that idea while "refreshingly novel" goes in the other direction. "Somewhat hackneyed" has some plausibility but is too negative given the overall tone of the sentence; there is no indication that those things are in any way trite.

Thus the correct answer is **rumination on** (Choice B), **utterly mysterious** (Choice E), and **most prosaic** (Choice G).

> For Questions 7 to 9, select the <u>two</u> answer choices that, when used to complete the sentence, fit the meaning of the sentence as a whole <u>and</u> produce completed sentences that are alike in meaning.

7. The government's implementation of a new code of ethics appeared intended to shore up the ruling party's standing with an increasingly _____ electorate at a time when the party is besieged by charges that it trades favors for campaign money.

    A aloof
    B placid
    C restive
    D skittish
    E tranquil
    F vociferous

Explanation

The words filling the blank must be consistent with the idea that the ruling party needs to "shore up" its standing with the electorate. In their own way, Choices A, C, D, and F are consistent with that idea, but only two of these when taken together—"restive" and "skittish"—produce sentences that are alike in meaning. "Aloof" fits the blank reasonably well, but there is no other word offered that is nearly alike in meaning. The same holds for "vociferous." "Placid" and "tranquil" are similar in meaning but do not fit the context of the sentence.

Thus the correct answer is **restive** (Choice C) and **skittish** (Choice D).

8.   Overlarge, uneven, and ultimately disappointing, the retrospective exhibition seems too much like special pleading for a forgotten painter of real but _____ talents.

- A   limited
- B   partial
- C   undiscovered
- D   circumscribed
- E   prosaic
- F   hidden

Explanation

The sentence is explaining why the exhibition of the painter's work was unsatisfactory, and since it says that the painter's talents were real, the word in the blank has to indicate why those talents were not, in the opinion of the author of the sentence, good enough. The words "limited" and "circumscribed" do so and also produce sentences that are alike in meaning, so this pair forms the correct answer. Although "undiscovered" and "hidden" are similar in meaning, they do not make sense in the context of the sentence, since they do not indicate why the painter's talents were not adequate. Other choices, such as "partial" and "prosaic" might make sense in context, but none of the other choices that meets that criterion also has a companion choice that would produce another sentence alike in meaning.

Thus the correct answer is **limited** (Choice A) and **circumscribed** (Choice D).

9.   Newspapers report that the former executive has been trying to keep a low profile since his _____ exit from the company.

- A   celebrated
- B   mysterious
- C   long-awaited
- D   fortuitous
- E   indecorous
- F   unseemly

Explanation

The sentence needs to be completed with a word that suggests a reason for the executive to wish to keep a low profile. The words "indecorous" and "unseemly" both suggest such a reason, and the sentences completed with those two choices are alike in meaning. Therefore, that pair forms the correct answer. Although one might get a sensible sentence by filling the blank with another choice, such as "long-awaited," none of the other choices that meets that criterion also has a companion choice that would produce another sentence alike in meaning.

Thus the correct answer is **indecorous** (Choice E) and **unseemly** (Choice F).

SET 6. Reading Comprehension Questions: Hard

For each of Questions 1 to 8, select <u>one</u> answer choice unless otherwise instructed.

1.   In the United States between 1850 and 1880, the number of farmers continued to increase, but at a rate lower than that of the general population.

   Which of the following statements directly contradicts the information presented?

   Ⓐ   The number of farmers in the general population increased slightly in the 30 years between 1850 and 1880.

   Ⓑ   The rate of growth of the United States labor force and the rate of growth of the general population rose simultaneously in the 30 years between 1850 and 1880.

   Ⓒ   The proportion of farmers in the United States labor force remained constant in the 30 years between 1850 and 1880.

   Ⓓ   The proportion of farmers in the United States labor force decreased from 64 percent in 1850 to 49 percent in 1880.

   Ⓔ   The proportion of farmers in the general population increased from 68 percent in 1850 to 72 percent in 1880.

Explanation

The given sentence indicates that the proportion of farmers in the general population decreased from 1850 to 1880. **Choice E** says exactly the opposite — that this proportion increased — and therefore it contradicts the passage and is the correct response. Choice A is incorrect because it agrees with the given sentence, and Choices B, C, and D are all incorrect because they refer to the labor force, about which the given sentence says nothing.

2. A ten-year comparison between the United States and the Soviet Union in terms of crop yields per acre revealed that when only planted acreage is compared, Soviet yields were equal to 68 percent of United States yields. When total agricultural acreage (planted acreage plus fallow acreage) is compared, however, Soviet yield was 114 percent of United States yield.

From the information presented, which of the following can be most reliably inferred about United States and Soviet agriculture during the ten-year period?

(A) A higher percentage of total agricultural acreage was fallow in the United States than in the Soviet Union.

(B) The United States had more fallow acreage than planted acreage.

(C) Fewer total acres of available agricultural land were fallow in the Soviet Union than in the United States.

(D) The Soviet Union had more planted acreage than fallow acreage.

(E) The Soviet Union produced a greater volume of crops than the United States produced.

Explanation

If crop yield per planted acre was less in the Soviet Union than it was in the United States, yet crop yield per total (planted plus fallow) agricultural acreage was greater in the Soviet Union than it was in the United States, the percentage of the total acreage that was left fallow must have been lower in the Soviet Union than in the United States. Therefore, **Choice A** is the correct answer. Since the information provided in the paragraph is given in terms of yield per acre, no conclusion can be drawn about actual acreage, so Choices B, C, and D are all incorrect. Similarly, it is impossible to determine the total volume of crops produced in the Soviet Union, so Choice E is incorrect.

Questions 3 and 4 are based on the following reading passage.

For hot desert locations with access to seawater, a new greenhouse design generates fresh water and cool air. Oriented to the prevailing wind, the front wall of perforated cardboard, moistened by a trickle of seawater pumped in, cools and moistens hot air blowing in. This cool, humidified air accelerates plant growth; little water evaporates from leaves. Though greenhouses normally capture the heat of sunlight, a double-layered roof, the inner layer coated to reflect infrared light outward, allows visible sunlight in but traps solar heat between the two layers. This heated air, drawn down from the roof, then mixes with the greenhouse air as it reaches a second seawater-moistened cardboard wall at the back of the greenhouse. There the air absorbs more moisture before being cooled off again when it meets a seawater-cooled metal wall, which causes moisture in the air to condense. Thus distilled water for irrigating the plants collects.

Description

The passage describes a greenhouse design and the process by which the design generates fresh water and cool air in a desert environment lacking in these things.

For the following question, consider each of the choices separately and select all that apply.

3. It can be inferred that the process described in the passage makes use of which of the following?

   A   The tendency of hot air to rise
   B   The directional movement of wind
   C   Variation in the moisture capacity of air

Explanation

Choices B and C are correct. This question asks the reader which of the three phenomena listed in the answer choices is used in the process described in the passage.

   Choice A is incorrect: the passage does not indicate that the tendency of hot air to rise is used in the process, and in fact says that heated air is drawn down, not up, as part of the greenhouse design.

   Choice B is correct: the second sentence describes the orientation of a perforated cardboard wall toward the prevailing wind so that hot air blows in and is moistened.

   Choice C is correct: the process depends on the ability of hot air to contain moisture that is then deposited when the air cools.

For the following question, consider each of the choices separately and select all that apply.

4. It can be inferred that the greenhouse roof is designed to allow for which of the following?

   A   The avoidance of intense solar heat inside the greenhouse
   B   The entry of sunlight into the greenhouse to make the plants grow
   C   The mixture of heated air with greenhouse air to enhance the collection of moisture

Explanation

All three choices are correct. This question asks the reader which of the three effects listed in the answer choices are intended as part of the design of the greenhouse roof.

   Choice A is correct: the purpose of the double-layered roof is to trap solar heat before it gets inside the greenhouse proper.

   Choice B is correct: the coating on the inner layer of the roof allows visible sunlight into the greenhouse.

   Choice C is correct: the last two sentences of the passage describe how heated air from the roof is drawn down to mix with greenhouse air, resulting in the collection of distilled water for irrigation purposes.

Many critics of Emily Brontë's novel *Wuthering Heights* see its second part as a counterpoint that comments on, if it does not reverse, the first part, where a romantic reading receives more confirmation. Seeing the two parts as a whole is encouraged by the novel's sophisticated structure, revealed in its complex use of narrators and time shifts. Granted that the presence of these elements need not argue for an authorial awareness of novelistic construction comparable to that of Henry James, their presence does encourage attempts to unify the novel's heterogeneous parts. However, any interpretation that seeks to unify all of the novel's diverse elements is bound to be somewhat unconvincing. This is not because such an interpretation necessarily stiffens into a thesis (although rigidity in any interpretation of this or of any novel is always a danger), but because *Wuthering Heights* has recalcitrant elements of undeniable power that, ultimately, resist inclusion in an all-encompassing interpretation. In this respect, *Wuthering Heights* shares a feature of *Hamlet*.

Description

The passage discusses a critical view concerning the unity of structure of *Wuthering Heights*, then, following the use of "However," expresses a reservation about that view.

5. According to the passage, which of the following is a true statement about the first and second parts of *Wuthering Heights*?

   Ⓐ The second part has received more attention from critics.
   Ⓑ The second part has little relation to the first part.
   Ⓒ The second part annuls the force of the first part.
   Ⓓ The second part provides less substantiation for a romantic reading.
   Ⓔ The second part is better because it is more realistic.

Explanation

This question requires the reader to identify which of the given relationships between the novel's first and second parts is one that is described in the passage. According to the first sentence, the first part of the novel tends to confirm the "romantic" reading more strongly than the second. Therefore, **Choice D** is correct. Nothing in the passage suggests that critics have paid more attention to the second part, that the two parts have little relation, or that the second part is better. Therefore, Choices A, B, and E are incorrect. Choice C is a more extreme statement than any found in the passage, and therefore it is incorrect.

6. Which of the following inferences about Henry James's awareness of novelistic construction is best supported by the passage?

   Ⓐ James, more than any other novelist, was aware of the difficulties of novelistic construction.
   Ⓑ James was very aware of the details of novelistic construction.
   Ⓒ James's awareness of novelistic construction derived from his reading of Brontë.
   Ⓓ James's awareness of novelistic construction has led most commentators to see unity in his individual novels.
   Ⓔ James's awareness of novelistic construction precluded him from violating the unity of his novels.

Explanation

This question focuses on the passage's mention of Henry James and asks what can be inferred from it. The third sentence implies that James represents a very high degree of authorial awareness of novelistic construction and that no such claim is necessarily being made for Brontë. Thus, **Choice B** is the correct answer. Choice A is incorrect, since the passage does not imply that there are particular difficulties that James understood uniquely among novelists. Choice C is incorrect because the passage does not state or imply that James read Brontë. The passage also does not say anything about commentators' opinions of the unity of James's works; therefore Choice D is incorrect. Choice E is incorrect because the passage itself offers no information about the unity of James's novels.

7.   The author of the passage would be most likely to agree that an interpretation of a novel should

    Ⓐ not try to unite heterogeneous elements in the novel

    Ⓑ not be inflexible in its treatment of the elements in the novel

    Ⓒ not argue that the complex use of narrators or of time shifts indicates a sophisticated structure

    Ⓓ concentrate on those recalcitrant elements of the novel that are outside the novel's main structure

    Ⓔ primarily consider those elements of novelistic construction of which the author of the novel was aware

Explanation

This question requires the reader to determine what can be inferred from the passage about its author's view of the interpretation of novels. Choice A may seem attractive because in the passage the author says that *Wuthering Heights* has heterogeneous elements that resist inclusion in a unifying interpretive scheme. Choice A is incorrect, however, because the author does not indicate that the unification of different elements is to be avoided in interpretation generally. By contrast, the author's parenthetical statement about rigidity does present a general warning against inflexibility of interpretation, and it is this that supports **Choice B** as the correct answer. Choice C is incorrect, as the author actually suggests the contrary of this view in the second sentence of the passage. Although the author mentions recalcitrant elements of *Wuthering Heights*, there is no suggestion by the author that such elements deserve a special focus in interpretation. Therefore Choice D is incorrect. The author of the passage does not indicate which elements, if any, of novelistic construction are most worthy of consideration. Therefore Choice E is incorrect.

For the following question, consider each of the choices separately and select all that apply.

8.   The author of the passage suggests which of the following about *Hamlet*?

   A   *Hamlet* has usually attracted critical interpretations that tend to stiffen into theses.

   B   *Hamlet* has elements that are not amenable to an all-encompassing critical interpretation.

   C   *Hamlet* is less open to an all-encompassing critical interpretation than is *Wuthering Heights*.

Explanation

Choice B is correct. This question asks the reader which of the three statements about *Hamlet* listed in the answer choices are suggested by the author of the passage.

   Choice A is incorrect: the passage does not provide information about the characteristics of the usual critical interpretations of *Hamlet*.

   Choice B is correct: *Hamlet* is mentioned only in the final sentence of the passage, which refers to "this respect" in which *Hamlet* and *Wuthering Heights* are similar. The previous sentence reveals the point of similarity referred to: *Wuthering Heights* has elements that resist inclusion in an all-encompassing interpretive framework.

   Choice C is incorrect: the passage mentions only a feature shared between *Hamlet* and *Wuthering Heights*. It does not suggest anything about a difference in their openness to a particular critical interpretation.

5 GRE® Verbal Reasoning: Mixed Practice Sets

Your goals for this chapter

🔺 Practice answering *GRE*® Verbal Reasoning questions on your own

🔺 Review answers and explanations, particularly for questions you answered incorrectly

This chapter contains five GRE Verbal Reasoning practice sets. Each practice set contains a mixture of Verbal Reasoning question types and difficulty levels, similar to the mixture of questions on the actual GRE Verbal Reasoning measure.

Each practice set is followed by an answer key and explanations for the questions in the set. As in Chapter 4, each explanation is presented with the corresponding question so that you can easily see what is being asked and what the various answer choices are.

Review the answer explanations carefully, paying particular attention to the explanations for questions that you answered incorrectly. Begin the first Verbal Reasoning practice set on the next page.

Verbal Practice Set 1
15 Questions

> **For Questions 1 to 5, select one entry for each blank from the corresponding column of choices. Fill all blanks in the way that best completes the text.**

1. Analysis of the structural features that were thought to _____ kinship between the two species prompted an investigation that dispelled that presumption by revealing that they share an evolutionary history.

Ⓐ	establish
Ⓑ	preclude
Ⓒ	magnify
Ⓓ	disguise
Ⓔ	predict

2. Although posthumous biographies of the Nobel Prize winner often characterize him as a person of great _____, while alive he had a reputation for being quite reticent.

Ⓐ	aloofness
Ⓑ	self-absorption
Ⓒ	reclusiveness
Ⓓ	creativity
Ⓔ	effusiveness

3. Some social and political theorists are (i)_____ the idea and practice of civility. For those theorists, civility represents civic virtues such as tolerance, nondiscrimination, and public reasonableness that have the potential to (ii)_____ the tensions that abound in pluralistic societies.

Blank (i)		Blank (ii)	
Ⓐ	inured to	Ⓓ	exacerbate
Ⓑ	invested in	Ⓔ	enliven
Ⓒ	ignorant of	Ⓕ	ameliorate

4. When artist Faith Ringgold began to use fabric as a medium, many art critics, bound to conventional views about what constitutes high art, (i)_____ her textile works as mere crafts. Not everyone, fortunately, was so (ii)_____. Indeed a vast segment of the art-going public was surprisingly less (iii)_____ than the critics and received Ringgold's work enthusiastically.

Blank (i)	Blank (ii)	Blank (iii)
Ⓐ disparaged	Ⓓ detached	Ⓖ magnanimous
Ⓑ revered	Ⓔ intransigent	Ⓗ perspicacious
Ⓒ defended	Ⓕ negligent	Ⓘ parochial

5. People who have never worked in physics tend to describe it with words like "dry," "exact," and "precise." But physics is, in important respects, an art. Few real physics problems (i)_____ a precise, determinate solution. Therefore, to a physicist, solving a problem almost always involves judging which aspects of a phenomenon are (ii)_____ and which can be ignored, what parts of the mathematics to be faithful to and what parts to (iii)_____.

Blank (i)	Blank (ii)	Blank (iii)
Ⓐ dispense with	Ⓓ unknowable	Ⓖ maintain
Ⓑ account for	Ⓔ visible	Ⓗ alter
Ⓒ admit of	Ⓕ essential	Ⓘ calculate

Questions 6 and 7 are based on the following reading passage.

Although exotic, or introduced, plant species are often considered destructive agents, their impact may depend on the degree and type of habitat modification these invaders produce. Indeed, it has been shown that habitat modification by exotics can benefit resident fauna. A case in point is the introduced sea grass *Zostera japonica*. In a 1988 experiment, Posey observed that sedimentary and faunal changes caused by introducing *Z. japonica* into unvegetated areas were similar to those associated with the introduction of native sea grass. Moreover, local faunal richness and abundance within both naturally invaded and transplanted *Z. japonica* patches were higher than in adjacent unvegetated control areas, and no negative effects of *Z. japonica* on resident species were observed.

6. According to the passage, which of the following was true of *Zostera japonica* in Posey's experiment?

   Ⓐ Areas where *Z. japonica* was introduced had wider varieties of animals living in them than did those with no vegetation.

   Ⓑ Introducing *Z. japonica* created vegetated patches that were more durable than those composed of native sea grass.

   Ⓒ Some animal species that were present in unvegetated control areas were absent from areas where *Z. japonica* grew.

   Ⓓ Patches where *Z. japonica* had invaded naturally were observed to have more animal life than did those where *Z. japonica* had been introduced.

   Ⓔ *Z. japonica* created habitats that were significantly more beneficial for native animal species than were those created by native sea grass.

For the following question, consider each of the choices separately and select all that apply.

7. The author of the passage would be likely to agree with which of the following statements about exotic plant species?

   Ⓐ They can produce important modifications to the structure of habitats into which they are introduced.

   Ⓑ They sometimes produce effects that are detrimental to native organisms.

   Ⓒ They rarely thrive when introduced into areas that previously had no vegetation.

Recognizing that the issue of alcohol reform led many women in the United States to become politically active, historians have generally depicted women as a united force behind Prohibition (legislation banning alcoholic beverages, adopted in 1919 and repealed in 1933). In fact, however, women were divided over Prohibition. The Women's Christian Temperance Union (WCTU), claiming to speak for all women's interests, argued that Prohibition protected family life, but the Women's Organization for National Prohibition Reform (WONPR), while advocating temperance, objected to government regulation of private behavior and argued that the widespread disregard for law fostered by Prohibition undermined social order. By opposing the WCTU's position, WONPR members demonstrated that women were independent in their political thinking, yet even those historians who have discussed the WONPR have failed to recognize this fact. Early studies represented WONPR members as puppets of male brewers, while more recent studies have concluded that the WONPR was a satellite of the similarly minded all-male Association Against the Prohibition Amendment (AAPA), with which the WONPR did work closely, but by no means in a subordinate role.

line
5

10

15

8. The passage is primarily concerned with

   Ⓐ clarifying the reasons for a divergence of scholarly views

   Ⓑ questioning the accuracy of evidence on which a conclusion was based

   Ⓒ correcting a view that the author regards as inaccurate

   Ⓓ explaining why recent studies of a subject have departed from earlier ones

   Ⓔ discussing the forces that have shaped a particular historical view

9. The author of the passage indicates which of the following about the "historians" mentioned in line 2?

   Ⓐ They hold a view of women's reasons for becoming politically active that has been challenged by recent studies.

   Ⓑ They exaggerate the extent to which the issue of alcohol reform mobilized women politically.

   Ⓒ They fail to recognize the extent to which women in the Prohibition era were independent in their political thinking.

   Ⓓ They misrepresent the members of the WCTU as having claimed to speak for the interests of all women.

   Ⓔ They assume that women who held the views espoused by the WONPR were not independent political agents.

10. The author mentions "male brewers" (line 12) primarily in order to

    Ⓐ point out an unexpected finding

    Ⓑ illustrate a point made in the previous sentence

    Ⓒ cast doubt on a point made at the beginning of the passage

    Ⓓ refute a widely held view

    Ⓔ suggest that a certain piece of evidence is ambiguous

11. It can be inferred from the passage that members of the WONPR differed with members of the WCTU over which of the following?

   Ⓐ Whether women's interests lay primarily in the protection of family life
   Ⓑ Whether temperance was beneficial to families
   Ⓒ The extent to which the government's interests were compatible with those of families
   Ⓓ The way in which temperance could best be promoted
   Ⓔ The kinds of issues on which women should be politically active

---

For Questions 12 to 14, select the <u>two</u> answer choices that, when used to complete the sentence, fit the meaning of the sentence as a whole <u>and</u> produce completed sentences that are alike in meaning.

---

12. The company may soon have some legal issues to address, given that some of its new policies appear to _____ recently passed legislation.

   A demarcate
   B contravene
   C buttress
   D infringe
   E demand
   F underlie

13. In this instance, aesthetics _____ structure, and the unconventional design of the long, slender-decked bridge allowed its deck to move sideways excessively.

   A prevailed over
   B harmonized with
   C bowed to
   D dominated
   E invigorated
   F complemented

14. During the opera's most famous aria, the tempo chosen by the orchestra's conductor seemed _____ , without necessary relation to what had gone before.

   A arbitrary
   B capricious
   C cautious
   D compelling
   E exacting
   F meticulous

For Question 15, select <u>one</u> answer choice.

Question 15 is based on the following reading passage.

Numerous fragments of Greek household pottery have been unearthed at Gela, the site of an ancient city on the island of Sicily. Those fragments cannot be directly dated. However, the Greeks conquered and then colonized Gela in 689 B.C., and the colonists surely brought their everyday household pottery with them. Since household pottery typically does not last long, the earliest of the Greek household pottery present at Gela is unlikely to have been manufactured much before 689 B.C.

15. Which of the following, if true, most seriously weakens the argument?

    Ⓐ There is no record of Gela's having been attacked by the Greeks prior to 689 B.C.

    Ⓑ Greek household pottery that has been securely dated to 300 B.C. is strikingly different from the Greek household pottery unearthed at Gela.

    Ⓒ The Greek colony at Gela survived for almost 300 years.

    Ⓓ Gela is not the only city on the island of Sicily colonized by the Greeks for which a precise date of colonization is known.

    Ⓔ The Greeks engaged in commerce with the inhabitants of Sicily prior to the Greek colonization of the island.

Answer Key

Practice Set 1. Verbal Reasoning

Question Number	P+	Correct Answer
1	46	**Choice B:** preclude
2	45	**Choice E:** effusiveness
3	56	**Choice B:** invested in; **Choice F:** ameliorate
4	25	**Choice A:** disparaged; **Choice E:** intransigent; **Choice I:** parochial
5	15	**Choice C:** admit of; **Choice F:** essential; **Choice H:** alter
6	57	**Choice A:** Areas where Z. *japonica* was introduced had wider varieties of animals living in them than did those with no vegetation.
7	48	**Choice A:** They can produce important modifications to the structure of habitats into which they are introduced. AND **Choice B:** They sometimes produce effects that are detrimental to native organisms.
8	65	**Choice C:** correcting a view that the author regards as inaccurate
9	62	**Choice C:** They fail to recognize the extent to which women in the Prohibition era were independent in their political thinking.
10	42	**Choice B:** illustrate a point made in the previous sentence
11	39	**Choice D:** The way in which temperance could best be promoted
12	57	**Choice B:** contravene AND **Choice D:** infringe
13	61	**Choice A:** prevailed over AND **Choice D:** dominated
14	67	**Choice A:** arbitrary AND **Choice B:** capricious
15	54	**Choice E:** The Greeks engaged in commerce with the inhabitants of Sicily prior to the Greek colonization of the island.

Verbal Practice Set 1
15 Questions with Explanations

> **For Questions 1 to 5, select one entry for each blank from the corresponding column of choices. Fill all blanks in the way that best completes the text.**

1. Analysis of the structural features that were thought to _____ kinship between the two species prompted an investigation that dispelled that presumption by revealing that they share an evolutionary history.

Ⓐ	establish
Ⓑ	preclude
Ⓒ	magnify
Ⓓ	disguise
Ⓔ	predict

Explanation

The sentence describes a situation in which new research ("analysis") led to a reexamination of the presumed relationship between two species: the word "dispelled" indicates that what was previously believed ("that presumption") was completely invalidated by the revelation that the two species "share an evolutionary history." The nature of this revelation indicates that the earlier assumption was that the two species were *not* related, so the blank must be filled by a word that would deny their relatedness, or kinship. The only choice that negates the possibility of this kinship is "preclude." "Establish," "magnify," and "predict" all affirm the possibility of kinship between the species. While "disguise" suggests that the structural features conceal the species' kinship, it presupposes that they are—in spite of appearances—actually akin to one another.

   Thus the correct answer is **preclude** (Choice B).

2. Although posthumous biographies of the Nobel Prize winner often characterize him as a person of great _____, while alive he had a reputation for being quite reticent.

Ⓐ	aloofness
Ⓑ	self-absorption
Ⓒ	reclusiveness
Ⓓ	creativity
Ⓔ	effusiveness

Explanation

The word "although" suggests a contradiction between how posthumous biographies often characterize the Nobel Prize winner and how people thought of him while he was alive. Since he was known for "being quite reticent" while alive, the correct answer, which indicates his posthumous characterization, should describe him in the opposite way. Of the answer choices, only "effusiveness" satisfies that criterion: the opposite of a reticent or reserved person is someone who expresses their feelings liberally, even excessively.

   Thus the correct answer is **effusiveness** (Choice E).

3. Some social and political theorists are (i)_____ the idea and practice of civility. For those theorists, civility represents civic virtues such as tolerance, nondiscrimination, and public reasonableness that have the potential to (ii)_____ the tensions that abound in pluralistic societies.

Blank (i)	Blank (ii)
Ⓐ inured to	Ⓓ exacerbate
Ⓑ invested in	Ⓔ enliven
Ⓒ ignorant of	Ⓕ ameliorate

Explanation

The paragraph describes the relationship that some theorists have with "the idea and practice of civility"; the correct answer for Blank (i) helps describe that relationship. However, it is hard to select the correct answer for the first blank without first considering the second sentence. The second sentence says that civility, according to the theorists, represents virtues like "tolerance, nondiscrimination, and public reasonableness" that can have a particular effect on "the tensions that abound in pluralistic societies." It is reasonable to infer that the practice of such virtues will ameliorate, rather than exacerbate or enliven, the tensions; therefore, "ameliorate" is the best answer for Blank (ii). Returning to the first sentence, we can select "invested in" as the best answer for Blank (i): assuming that theorists believe that civility can ameliorate the tensions, it makes sense to conclude that they would care very much for, rather than be inured to or ignorant of, the idea and practice of civility.

Thus the correct answer is **invested in** (Choice B) and **ameliorate** (Choice F).

4. When artist Faith Ringgold began to use fabric as a medium, many art critics, bound to conventional views about what constitutes high art, (i)_____ her textile works as mere crafts. Not everyone, fortunately, was so (ii)_____. Indeed a vast segment of the art-going public was surprisingly less (iii)_____ than the critics and received Ringgold's work enthusiastically.

Blank (i)	Blank (ii)	Blank (iii)
Ⓐ disparaged	Ⓓ detached	Ⓖ magnanimous
Ⓑ revered	Ⓔ intransigent	Ⓗ perspicacious
Ⓒ defended	Ⓕ negligent	Ⓘ parochial

Explanation

This passage describes reactions to Faith Ringgold's textile art by critics and by the art-going public. In the first sentence, the adjective "mere" in the phrase "mere crafts" indicates that many art critics viewed her creations as something less than high art. The first blank, then, calls for a word that conveys this dismissiveness, and "disparaged" does that. The first sentence also indicates that this dismissive view came from critics who were "bound to conventional views"; the second blank calls for an adjective that describes such critics. "Intransigent," which means unwilling to change one's views, aptly characterizes critics who refuse to consider untraditional viewpoints. The third blank calls for a word that differentiates these critics from those in the art-going public who appreciated Ringgold's work. Nothing in the passage supports the idea that the critics were "magnanimous" (generous) or "perspicacious" (discerning). However, their adherence to tradition could be described as "parochial" (narrow-minded).

Thus the correct answer is **disparaged** (Choice A), **intransigent** (Choice E), and **parochial** (Choice I).

5.   People who have never worked in physics tend to describe it with words like "dry," "exact," and "precise." But physics is, in important respects, an art. Few real physics problems (i)_____ a precise, determinate solution. Therefore, to a physicist, solving a problem almost always involves judging which aspects of a phenomenon are (ii)_____ and which can be ignored, what parts of the mathematics to be faithful to and what parts to (iii)_____ .

Blank (i)	Blank (ii)	Blank (iii)
Ⓐ dispense with	Ⓓ unknowable	Ⓖ maintain
Ⓑ account for	Ⓔ visible	Ⓗ alter
Ⓒ admit of	Ⓕ essential	Ⓘ calculate

Explanation

The first sentence of this passage describes an outsider's view of physics as being an "exact" science; the "but" that begins the second sentence indicates that the rest of the passage presents a contrasting viewpoint. If one maintains that physics is often *inexact*, and if physics is as much an art as it is a science, then "admit of" (allow for) must be the correct choice for the first blank. There would be "few" real-life physics problems that would "admit of" precise and determinate solutions. The remainder of the passage elaborates on the notion of physics as an art form by outlining the choices that physicists make between two extremes. The second blank, then, calls for a word that is the opposite of "can be ignored," pointing to "essential" as the correct choice. Similarly, the third blank must be filled with a verb that conveys the opposite of "to be faithful to"; "alter" is the only choice that fits that meaning.

Thus the correct answer is **admit of** (Choice C), **essential** (Choice F), and **alter** (Choice H).

For each of Questions 6 to 11, select <u>one</u> answer choice unless otherwise instructed.

Questions 6 and 7 are based on the following reading passage.

Although exotic, or introduced, plant species are often considered destructive agents, their impact may depend on the degree and type of habitat modification these invaders produce. Indeed, it has been shown that habitat modification by exotics can benefit resident fauna. A case in point is the introduced sea grass *Zostera japonica*. In a 1988 experiment, Posey observed that sedimentary and faunal changes caused by introducing *Z. japonica* into unvegetated areas were similar to those associated with the introduction of native sea grass. Moreover, local faunal richness and abundance within both naturally invaded and transplanted *Z. japonica* patches were higher than in adjacent unvegetated control areas, and no negative effects of *Z. japonica* on resident species were observed.

Description

Questioning the assumption that exotic plant species are harmful to ecosystems where they are introduced, the passage uses the example of *Zostera japonica* to argue that introduced species can in fact have a positive impact on the habitats they modify.

6. According to the passage, which of the following was true of *Zostera japonica* in Posey's experiment?

    Ⓐ Areas where *Z. japonica* was introduced had wider varieties of animals living in them than did those with no vegetation.

    Ⓑ Introducing *Z. japonica* created vegetated patches that were more durable than those composed of native sea grass.

    Ⓒ Some animal species that were present in unvegetated control areas were absent from areas where *Z. japonica* grew.

    Ⓓ Patches where *Z. japonica* had invaded naturally were observed to have more animal life than did those where *Z. japonica* had been introduced.

    Ⓔ *Z. japonica* created habitats that were significantly more beneficial for native animal species than were those created by native sea grass.

Explanation

The question asks about what Posey's experiment revealed about *Zostera japonica*. According to the passage, Posey's experiment found that "local faunal richness" was "higher" in *Z. japonica* patches than in adjacent unvegetated control areas. This points to **Choice A**, which mentions "wider varieties of animals" in areas where *Z. japonica* was introduced, as the correct answer. The passage does not discuss the durability of *Z. japonica* patches (Choice B) or the differences between naturally invaded and transplanted *Z. japonica* patches (Choice D). Nor does it address the relative concentration of specific species in *Z. japonica* patches and in unvegetated control areas (Choice C). Although Posey's experiment indicated that *Z. japonica* modified habitats in ways that were "similar to those associated with the introduction of native sea grass," the passage does not go so far as to claim that *Z. japonica* created habitats that were "significantly more beneficial" for native animal species compared to those created by native sea grass (Choice E).

For the following question, consider each of the choices separately and select all that apply.

7. The author of the passage would be likely to agree with which of the following statements about exotic plant species?

      A They can produce important modifications to the structure of habitats into which they are introduced.

      B They sometimes produce effects that are detrimental to native organisms.

      C They rarely thrive when introduced into areas that previously had no vegetation.

Explanation

Choices A and B are correct. This question asks about the author's views regarding exotic plant species.

Choice A is correct: the author asserts that exotic plant species can have significant impacts on the structure of habitats, depending on the "degree and type of habitat modification" that the introduced species produce.

Choice B is correct: while the overall focus of the passage is on the potential benefits of exotic plant species, the author acknowledges that the "destructive" effects of exotics are well known. Since the nature of their impact depends on the "degree and type" of the modifications they produce, the author admits the possibility that certain modifications might be harmful to native organisms.

Choice C is incorrect: the author describes how *Zostera japonica*—an exotic plant species—was successfully introduced into areas that previously had no vegetation. There is no suggestion in the passage that this is a rare or unusual occurrence for an exotic plant species.

Recognizing that the issue of alcohol reform led many women in the United States to become politically active, historians have generally depicted women as a united force behind Prohibition (legislation banning alcoholic beverages, adopted in 1919 and repealed in 1933). In fact, however, women were divided over Prohibition. The Women's Christian Temperance Union (WCTU), claiming to speak for all women's interests, argued that Prohibition protected family life, but the Women's Organization for National Prohibition Reform (WONPR), while advocating temperance, objected to government regulation of private behavior and argued that the widespread disregard for law fostered by Prohibition undermined social order. By opposing the WCTU's position, WONPR members demonstrated that women were independent in their political thinking, yet even those historians who have discussed the WONPR have failed to recognize this fact. Early studies represented WONPR members as puppets of male brewers, while more recent studies have concluded that the WONPR was a satellite of the similarly minded all-male Association Against the Prohibition Amendment (AAPA), with which the WONPR did work closely, but by no means in a subordinate role.

line 5

10

15

Description

The passage argues that historians have wrongly concluded that women in the United States universally supported Prohibition laws. It discusses two Prohibition-era women's groups that differed in their advocacy of temperance.

8.   The passage is primarily concerned with

    Ⓐ   clarifying the reasons for a divergence of scholarly views

    Ⓑ   questioning the accuracy of evidence on which a conclusion was based

    Ⓒ   correcting a view that the author regards as inaccurate

    Ⓓ   explaining why recent studies of a subject have departed from earlier ones

    Ⓔ   discussing the forces that have shaped a particular historical view

Explanation

The passage begins by explaining that "historians have generally depicted" women as uniformly in favor of Prohibition, before using the phrase "in fact, however" to introduce the author's opposing view. The passage then provides details about the differing approaches of two women's groups in order to correct the impression that women were "a united force behind Prohibition." Thus, **Choice C** is the correct answer. While the passage does mention diverging and evolving scholarly views (Choice A, Choice D, and Choice E) and does challenge how scholars have interpreted certain pieces of evidence about the WONPR (Choice B), it does so only to support its larger claim that historians have overstated the unity of women's sentiments about Prohibition.

9. The author of the passage indicates which of the following about the "historians" mentioned in line 2 ?

     (A) They hold a view of women's reasons for becoming politically active that has been challenged by recent studies.

     (B) They exaggerate the extent to which the issue of alcohol reform mobilized women politically.

     (C) They fail to recognize the extent to which women in the Prohibition era were independent in their political thinking.

     (D) They misrepresent the members of the WCTU as having claimed to speak for the interests of all women.

     (E) They assume that women who held the views espoused by the WONPR were not independent political agents.

Explanation

The first two sentences of the passage argue that on the issue of Prohibition, women were more politically diverse than historians have recognized. **Choice C** is therefore the correct answer. The passage disagrees with the historians about women's attitudes toward alcohol reform but emphasizes that the historians' view is widely held and does not cite any studies that challenge it (Choice A). The author does not disagree with the historians about the extent to which women were motivated politically by the issue of alcohol reform (Choice B). The author also agrees with the historians that the WCTU *claimed* to speak for all women (Choice D), even if they in fact did not. Although the passage mentions that some historians have seen the WONPR as "puppets" (Choice E), this remark only applies to the subset of historians who have studied the WONPR, not the broader group of "historians" referred to in line 2.

10. The author mentions "male brewers" (line 12) primarily in order to

     (A) point out an unexpected finding

     (B) illustrate a point made in the previous sentence

     (C) cast doubt on a point made at the beginning of the passage

     (D) refute a widely held view

     (E) suggest that a certain piece of evidence is ambiguous

Explanation

The passage mentions "male brewers" when describing early studies that depicted the WONPR as controlled by men who were against Prohibition laws. Such studies serve to illustrate the author's claim in the previous sentence that historians have not recognized the politically independent thought of WONPR members, pointing to **Choice B** as the correct answer. These early studies support rather than "refute" (Choice D) the view of women as politically united; they therefore do not "cast doubt on" the author's initial point that such a view is generally held (Choice C). Nothing in the passage suggests that these studies' findings are unexpected (Choice A). Finally, while the passage claims that historians have misunderstood the WONPR, it does not suggest that evidence about the group is ambiguous (Choice E).

11. It can be inferred from the passage that members of the WONPR differed with members of the WCTU over which of the following?

    Ⓐ Whether women's interests lay primarily in the protection of family life

    Ⓑ Whether temperance was beneficial to families

    Ⓒ The extent to which the government's interests were compatible with those of families

    Ⓓ The way in which temperance could best be promoted

    Ⓔ The kinds of issues on which women should be politically active

Explanation

The passage states that while the WONPR was "advocating temperance," it also opposed Prohibition laws. This indicates that the WCTU and WONPR agreed that temperance was beneficial (Choice B) but disagreed over whether Prohibition laws should be used to promote it. Thus, **Choice D** is the correct answer. The passage does not provide enough information to distinguish the two groups' views on family life or the interests of families (Choices A and C). The two groups did not disagree about what issues to address politically (Choice E): both women's groups were politically active around the issue of Prohibition, albeit on opposing sides.

For Questions 12 to 14, select the <u>two</u> answer choices that, when used to complete the sentence, fit the meaning of the sentence as a whole <u>and</u> produce completed sentences that are alike in meaning.

---

12. The company may soon have some legal issues to address, given that some of its new policies appear to _____ recently passed legislation.

    A demarcate

    B contravene

    C buttress

    D infringe

    E demand

    F underlie

Explanation

The sentence makes a prediction about a company's likelihood of facing legal issues as a result of some of the company's new policies, indicating that the policies run contrary to "recently passed legislation." The words that fit in the blank are therefore "contravene" and "infringe," both of which express the idea of going against the legislation.

Thus the correct answer is **contravene** (Choice B) and **infringe** (Choice D).

13. In this instance, aesthetics _____ structure, and the unconventional design of the long, slender-decked bridge allowed its deck to move sideways excessively.

   A prevailed over
   B harmonized with
   C bowed to
   D dominated
   E invigorated
   F complemented

Explanation

This sentence describes a situation in which a bridge with an unusual appearance is not structurally sound: its movement is described as excessive. The blank, then, should be completed with a word indicating that the bridge designers prioritized appearance over function. Both "prevailed over" and "dominated" convey this idea, so they are the correct pair. "Harmonized with" and "complemented," on the other hand, would indicate that the bridge's unconventional design did not negatively affect its structure, so they cannot be correct. "Bowed to" and "invigorated" would likewise suggest that the bridge's aesthetics did not compromise its structure and function.

   Thus the correct answer is **prevailed over** (Choice A) and **dominated** (Choice D).

14. During the opera's most famous aria, the tempo chosen by the orchestra's conductor seemed _____, without necessary relation to what had gone before.

   A arbitrary
   B capricious
   C cautious
   D compelling
   E exacting
   F meticulous

Explanation

Any of the offered words could possibly describe a conductor's choice of tempo. However, the phrase "without necessary relation to what had gone before" is presented as an elaboration on the word in the blank. Among the answer choices, only "arbitrary" and "capricious" could be elaborated that way; none of the other choices would be explained by the final phrase.

   Thus, the correct answer is **arbitrary** (Choice A) and **capricious** (Choice B).

For Question 15, select <u>one</u> answer choice.

Question 15 is based on the following reading passage.

Numerous fragments of Greek household pottery have been unearthed at Gela, the site of an ancient city on the island of Sicily. Those fragments cannot be directly dated. However, the Greeks conquered and then colonized Gela in 689 B.C., and the colonists surely brought their everyday household pottery with them. Since household pottery typically does not last long, the earliest of the Greek household pottery present at Gela is unlikely to have been manufactured much before 689 B.C.

Description

The passage makes an argument about the probable dating of ancient Greek household pottery whose fragments were found at the site of Gela (on the island of Sicily).

15. Which of the following, if true, most seriously weakens the argument?

   (A) There is no record of Gela's having been attacked by the Greeks prior to 689 B.C.
   (B) Greek household pottery that has been securely dated to 300 B.C. is strikingly different from the Greek household pottery unearthed at Gela.
   (C) The Greek colony at Gela survived for almost 300 years.
   (D) Gela is not the only city on the island of Sicily colonized by the Greeks for which a precise date of colonization is known.
   (E) The Greeks engaged in commerce with the inhabitants of Sicily prior to the Greek colonization of the island.

Explanation

The passage argues that the oldest Greek household pottery found at Gela is unlikely to have been manufactured much earlier than 689 B.C. This argument assumes that the arrival of the "earliest of the Greek household pottery present at Gela" coincided with the Greeks' colonization of the site in 689 B.C.; the author of the passage reasons that the colonizers "surely brought their everyday household pottery with them." But **Choice E** describes a way in which the pottery could have arrived before the colonization: earlier commerce between the inhabitants of Gela and the Greeks might have included the exchange of such pottery, meaning that Greek household pottery could have arrived in Gela before Greek colonization. If it were true that commercial ties between Sicily and Greece predated colonization, this could weaken the argument of the passage by offering an alternative explanation for how and when Greek pottery first reached the city. None of the other choices provides additional information that weakens the passage's key assumption regarding the provenance of Greek household pottery at Gela. The difference between Greek pottery found at Gela and newer Greek pottery (Choice B) and the longevity of the Greek colony at Gela (Choice C) have little bearing on the age of the oldest Greek pottery. While evidence of a Greek attack before 689 B.C. (Choice A) could be relevant to the argument, the lack of such evidence neither strengthens nor weakens the argument. Finally, the earlier colonization of another Sicilian city could potentially weaken the argument if it were confirmed that the city had been colonized by the Greeks before 689 B.C. However, on its own, the statement that Greek colonization of other Sicilian cities can be dated precisely (Choice D) does not provide evidence against the passage's argument.

Verbal Practice Set 2
15 Questions

> **For Questions 1 to 5, select one entry for each blank from the corresponding column of choices. Fill all blanks in the way that best completes the text.**

1. The piecrust had not been punctured, so steam built up in it, causing it to _____ and then burst like a balloon, creating a nasty oven-cleaning project where hopes of dinner had once been.

Ⓐ split
Ⓑ warp
Ⓒ distend
Ⓓ shrink
Ⓔ cave in

2. Scholars could not build on each other's work if they could not trust the published work of their colleagues; thus progress depends on the _____ of practicing scholars.

Ⓐ acquisitiveness
Ⓑ mendacity
Ⓒ ambitions
Ⓓ veracity
Ⓔ optimism

3. The brief survey, published under the title *The Work of Nature: How the Diversity of Life Sustains Us*, is surprisingly (i)_____ . Indeed it makes several longer treatments of the effects of lost biodiversity seem (ii) _____ .

Blank (i)	Blank (ii)
Ⓐ distorted	Ⓓ redundant
Ⓑ objective	Ⓔ pithy
Ⓒ comprehensive	Ⓕ premature

4. Although in her personal life Charlotte Brontë did not appear to be impassioned about gender issues, in her art she was anything but (i)_____ about such issues. In *Jane Eyre*, Brontë depicts the female mind as a place of rebellion. Yet, in her own social interactions, she was keen to present a (ii)_____ demeanor with respect to questions of women's place in society.

Blank (i)	Blank (ii)
Ⓐ original	Ⓓ moderate
Ⓑ apathetic	Ⓔ dolorous
Ⓒ zealous	Ⓕ bemused

5. The challenge faced by the ministry's new scheme to help rural farmers is huge: to repair the damage (i)_____ by farm policies motivated by (ii)_____ rather than farmers' needs. Nearly 30,000 rural collectives were born of the postrevolutionary land reform project. Over 385,000 square miles of land were expropriated from big landowners and shared out among the peasantry. (iii)_____ , the reform succeeded, creating wide support for the governing party. Agriculturally, it was a disaster.

Blank (i)	Blank (ii)	Blank (iii)
Ⓐ forestalled	Ⓓ expedience	Ⓖ Politically
Ⓑ mitigated	Ⓔ arrogance	Ⓗ Scientifically
Ⓒ wreaked	Ⓕ productivity	Ⓘ Societally

For each of Questions 6 to 9, select <u>one</u> answer choice unless otherwise instructed.

Questions 6 and 7 are based on the following reading passage.

The United States Congress uses a decision-making model derived from the adversarial traditions of the law. Members listen to testimony by interested parties on all sides of an issue, and from the resulting synthesis and balancing of interests, they collectively discern
line
5   the national interest and act upon it. However, for highly complex problems, especially those involving science and technology, this traditional model may need to be augmented with systematic analysis by experts. Reformers have argued that if Congress is to make wise, well-informed decisions, its committees need more than bare facts and brief inter-actions with technical experts: they need a standing organization of nonpartisan experts inside the legislative branch to help sort, integrate, and analyze technical information.

6. Which of the following best describes the function of the last sentence of the passage?
    Ⓐ To evaluate the last of a series of alternatives
    Ⓑ To synthesize arguments discussed earlier in the passage
    Ⓒ To elaborate on the viewpoint expressed in the preceding sentence
    Ⓓ To summarize objections to a controversial decision
    Ⓔ To cite anecdotal evidence supporting an observation mentioned earlier in the passage

7. In the context in which it appears, "standing" (line 8) most nearly means
    Ⓐ upright
    Ⓑ stagnant
    Ⓒ immovable
    Ⓓ permanent
    Ⓔ reputable

The problem of "old wood" is one of several confronting archaeologists seeking to establish the age of rock paintings in caves by using carbon-dating techniques on the charcoal contained in the paintings' pigments: the time of the paintings' production is not necessarily the same as that of the death of the organism, typically a tree, from which the charcoal comes. While archaeologists usually assume that a charcoal pigment date and the date of the painting are the same, the problem of old wood essentially renders a radiocarbon date as merely a maximum-age estimate. The old-wood effect may, of course, be negligible in many applications, for example, in the humid tropics, where wood deteriorates rapidly. Within the cave environment, however, preservation of wood is often extraordinary.

line
5

8. It can be inferred that what archaeologists "usually assume" (line 5) is flawed because this assumption

   Ⓐ tends to underestimate the age of charcoal pigments
   Ⓑ may rely on flawed carbon-dating techniques
   Ⓒ fails to consider the role played by high humidity in the deterioration of wood
   Ⓓ may result in an overestimation of the maximum age of "old wood"
   Ⓔ can lead to an overestimation of a rock painting's age

9. Which of the following most accurately characterizes the "problem" (line 1) discussed in the passage?

   Ⓐ The charcoal in the pigment of a rock painting within a cave environment may be considerably older than the charcoal in the pigment of a rock painting in a humid environment.
   Ⓑ The pigments within any given rock painting may contain charcoal that varies considerably in age.
   Ⓒ The charcoal in the pigment of a rock painting may yield an earlier date than the date of the painting itself.
   Ⓓ Carbon dating of carbon derived from wood can only approximate the age of the carbon.
   Ⓔ Charcoal pigments tend to deteriorate rapidly in humid environments.

For Questions 10 to 13, select the <u>two</u> answer choices that, when used to complete the sentence, fit the meaning of the sentence as a whole <u>and</u> produce completed sentences that are alike in meaning.

---

10. With regard to foreign policy involvements, the public official exhibited enough _____ human rights to be morally suspect on a number of counts.

   A̅ ignorance of
   B̅ support for
   C̅ disdain for
   D̅ disregard for
   E̅ compliance with
   F̅ observance of

11. The efficiency with which the canals and channels built at the ancient Inca site of Machu Picchu convey water to the site's buildings is not _____ but testifies to the Incas' careful planning and engineering.

    A incidental
    B invariable
    C replicable
    D unexceptional
    E fortuitous
    F repeatable

12. Although information about the particulars of a company's operation is often _____ , some managers are willing to talk in general terms about their companies' strategies.

    A incorrect
    B manifest
    C disclosed
    D proprietary
    E comprehensive
    F private

13. It seems obvious that Miles Davis' _____ the Juilliard School, which resulted in his decision to drop out, was based on the school's training of musicians for a kind of music that he did not want to play.

    A disaffection with
    B dislocation of
    C disentanglement from
    D subversion of
    E displacement of
    F estrangement from

For each of Questions 14 and 15, select <u>one</u> answer choice unless otherwise instructed.

Question 14 is based on the following reading passage.

Much of the archaeological evidence pertaining to the middle Stone Age cultures of Europe consists of stone artifacts, including hand tools and weapons. More sophisticated tools made from leather and wood have been uncovered at middle Stone Age sites in northern Europe, but none have been found at such sites in southern Europe. However, this does not mean that in the middle Stone Age toolmaking was more advanced in northern than in southern Europe, since _____.

14. Which of the following most logically completes the passage?

   Ⓐ at that time southern Europe could sustain a population density greater than northern Europe could

   Ⓑ at that time it was necessary to use stone tools to create tools from leather and wood

   Ⓒ more stone tools have been found at middle Stone Age sites in southern than in northern Europe

   Ⓓ at that time the inhabitants of southern Europe lived in areas with sandy soils in which organic materials degrade quite readily

   Ⓔ archaeological sites in southern Europe from the late Stone Age have yielded numerous sophisticated tools

Question 15 is based on the following reading passage.

More than a third of the bones excavated from middens (refuse piles) at the site of the earliest human settlement on Easter Island belong to dolphins, the largest animal available to the islanders. Nowhere else in Polynesia do dolphins account for even one percent of such bones. Dolphins generally live out to sea, so they could not have been hunted from shore but must have been harpooned from large, seaworthy canoes built from the tall trees that are now extinct on Easter Island. Fish bones and shellfish occur in the middens in only modest quantities compared with other Polynesian islands because Easter's rugged coastline and steep drop-off to the ocean bottom provide few places to fish in shallow water.

For the following question, consider each of the choices separately and select all that apply.

15. The passage suggests that conditions for early human inhabitants of Easter Island differed from conditions for early human inhabitants of other Polynesian islands in which of the following ways?

   ☐A☐ Tall trees were more readily available to Easter Islanders than to other Polynesian islanders.

   ☐B☐ Dolphins were more readily available to Easter Islanders than to other Polynesian islanders.

   ☐C☐ Fish and shellfish were less readily available to Easter Islanders than to other Polynesian islanders.

Answer Key

Practice Set 2. Verbal Reasoning

Question Number	P+	Correct Answer
1	66	**Choice C:** distend
2	60	**Choice D:** veracity
3	41	**Choice C:** comprehensive; **Choice D:** redundant
4	61	**Choice B:** apathetic; **Choice D:** moderate
5	22	**Choice C:** wreaked; **Choice D:** expedience; **Choice G:** Politically
6	77	**Choice C:** To elaborate on the viewpoint expressed in the preceding sentence
7	68	**Choice D:** permanent
8	54	**Choice E:** can lead to an overestimation of a rock painting's age
9	51	**Choice C:** The charcoal in the pigment of a rock painting may yield an earlier date than the date of the painting itself.
10	48	**Choice C:** disdain for AND **Choice D:** disregard for
11	46	**Choice A:** incidental AND **Choice E:** fortuitous
12	62	**Choice D:** proprietary AND **Choice F:** private
13	56	**Choice A:** disaffection with AND **Choice F:** estrangement from
14	62	**Choice D:** at that time the inhabitants of southern Europe lived in areas with sandy soils in which organic materials degrade quite readily
15	37	**Choice C:** Fish and shellfish were less readily available to Easter Islanders than to other Polynesian islanders.

Verbal Practice Set 2
15 Questions with Explanations

> **For Questions 1 to 5, select one entry for each blank from the corresponding column of choices. Fill all blanks in the way that best completes the text.**

1. The piecrust had not been punctured, so steam built up in it, causing it to _____ and then burst like a balloon, creating a nasty oven-cleaning project where hopes of dinner had once been.

Ⓐ	split
Ⓑ	warp
Ⓒ	distend
Ⓓ	shrink
Ⓔ	cave in

Explanation

The sentence presents the unfortunate consequences of a baking project gone awry. The conjunction "so" indicates that what follows in the sentence is a series of effects that result from failing to puncture the piecrust. The clauses after "so" describe a logical sequence of events: the triggering event is the buildup of steam in the crust, and the culminating event is the crust bursting "like a balloon." The blank, therefore, must be filled with a word that characterizes an intermediate stage in the process. In this context, "distend," in the sense of "expand" or "swell," makes most sense. "Shrink" and "cave in" are the opposite of what we would expect a buildup of steam to cause, while "warp" suggests distortion, which does not necessarily result from pressure buildup or end in explosion. Splitting is a possible effect of steam buildup but does not logically fit into a sequence of events that culminates in bursting.

    Thus the correct answer is **distend** (Choice C).

2. Scholars could not build on each other's work if they could not trust the published work of their colleagues; thus progress depends on the _____ of practicing scholars.

Ⓐ	acquisitiveness
Ⓑ	mendacity
Ⓒ	ambitions
Ⓓ	veracity
Ⓔ	optimism

Explanation

The sentence describes a condition that is necessary for scholars to be able to build on each other's work and make progress in their chosen fields: mutual trust among colleagues. The word that fills in the blank must identify a quality that would enable scholars to rely on each other's published work. The only word that justifies such collegial trust is "veracity" (truthfulness). "Acquisitiveness," "mendacity," and having "ambitions" are all characteristics that might call one's trustworthiness into question. While "optimism" is often perceived as a positive quality, a scholar's optimism is no guarantee of the reliability of their work—in fact, in this context, someone's inclination to anticipate the best possible outcome might lead others to doubt the accuracy of their claims.

Thus the correct answer is **veracity** (Choice D).

3. The brief survey, published under the title *The Work of Nature: How the Diversity of Life Sustains Us*, is surprisingly (i)_____. Indeed it makes several longer treatments of the effects of lost biodiversity seem (ii) _____.

Blank (i)	Blank (ii)
Ⓐ distorted	Ⓓ redundant
Ⓑ objective	Ⓔ pithy
Ⓒ comprehensive	Ⓕ premature

Explanation

In this question, it is hard to select an answer for either blank in isolation. The "brief survey," like any survey, could in fact be surprisingly "distorted," "objective," or "comprehensive." The contrast in the following sentence with "longer treatments" suggests that the brevity of the survey is important. Of the three choices, only "comprehensive" is particularly unexpected of a *brief* survey.

Provisionally accepting "comprehensive" makes it easier to analyze the second blank. If the short survey is surprisingly comprehensive, then longer treatments may not convey any useful additional information, making them "redundant." Longer works are unlikely to seem "pithy" in comparison to shorter ones, and "premature" makes little sense in this context.

Reading the sentence again with "comprehensive" and "redundant" filling the blanks confirms that these two choices result in a coherent whole.

Thus, the correct answer is **comprehensive** (Choice C) and **redundant** (Choice D).

4. Although in her personal life Charlotte Brontë did not appear to be impassioned about gender issues, in her art she was anything but (i)_____ about such issues. In *Jane Eyre*, Brontë depicts the female mind as a place of rebellion. Yet, in her own social interactions, she was keen to present a (ii)_____ demeanor with respect to questions of women's place in society.

Blank (i)	Blank (ii)
Ⓐ original	Ⓓ moderate
Ⓑ apathetic	Ⓔ dolorous
Ⓒ zealous	Ⓕ bemused

Explanation

The word "although" suggests a contradiction between Brontë's attitude toward gender issues in her personal life and the handling of such issues in her art. Since in her personal life she "did not appear to be impassioned" about these issues, we can conclude that in her art she *was* impassioned by them or, to put it another way, anything but apathetic (indifferent) about them, making "apathetic" the best answer for Blank (i). The next two sentences give an example to illustrate the contradiction mentioned above: in *Jane Eyre*,

Brontë was impassioned about certain gender issues, shown by her portrayal of "the female mind as a place of rebellion," but in her private life she presented a contrary demeanor with respect to them. The word that fills Blank (ii) should describe such a demeanor. Of the answer choices, "moderate" is best: a moderate demeanor contradicts an impassioned one. Neither "dolorous" nor "bemused" is in opposition to "impassioned."

Thus the correct answer is **apathetic** (Choice B) and **moderate** (Choice D).

5.   The challenge faced by the ministry's new scheme to help rural farmers is huge: to repair the damage (i)_____ by farm policies motivated by (ii)_____ rather than farmers' needs. Nearly 30,000 rural collectives were born of the postrevolutionary land reform project. Over 385,000 square miles of land were expropriated from big landowners and shared out among the peasantry. (iii)_____ , the reform succeeded, creating wide support for the governing party. Agriculturally, it was a disaster.

Blank (i)	Blank (ii)	Blank (iii)
(A) forestalled	(D) expedience	(G) Politically
(B) mitigated	(E) arrogance	(H) Scientifically
(C) wreaked	(F) productivity	(I) Societally

Explanation

The paragraph focuses on the nature of a problem arising in the wake of misguided agricultural policies. The final sentence ("Agriculturally, it was a disaster") confirms that the damage was indeed caused by the policies, so "wreaked" is the best choice for the first blank. Because of the implied contrast between the effects described in the last two sentences, the third blank is best completed by "politically," which is in opposition to "agriculturally" but consistent with "creating wide support for the governing party." At the end of the first sentence, the phrase "rather than" indicates that the word filling the second blank must contrast with "farmers' needs." Of the three choices for Blank (ii), both "expedience" and "arrogance" form such a contrast, but only "expedience" makes sense in the context of the final sentence, which suggests that the postrevolutionary government undertook the ill-advised land reform not out of hubris, but deliberately: to achieve a specific political goal ("wide support for the governing party").

Thus the correct answer is **wreaked** (Choice C), **expedience** (Choice D), and **Politically** (Choice G).

For each of Questions 6 to 9, select one answer choice unless otherwise instructed.

Questions 6 and 7 are based on the following reading passage.

The United States Congress uses a decision-making model derived from the adversarial traditions of the law. Members listen to testimony by interested parties on all sides of an issue, and from the resulting synthesis and balancing of interests, they collectively discern the national interest and act upon it. However, for highly complex problems, especially those involving science and technology, this traditional model may need to be augmented with systematic analysis by experts. Reformers have argued that if Congress is to make wise, well-informed decisions, its committees need more than bare facts and brief interactions with technical experts: they need a standing organization of nonpartisan experts inside the legislative branch to help sort, integrate, and analyze technical information.

Description

The passage explains that legislators currently seek advice from people with diverse opinions on an issue before making decisions. It suggests that this information-gathering process may be inadequate for some types of issues, then describes a proposal to solve this problem by establishing a panel of expert advisors.

6. Which of the following best describes the function of the last sentence of the passage?

   Ⓐ To evaluate the last of a series of alternatives

   Ⓑ To synthesize arguments discussed earlier in the passage

   Ⓒ To elaborate on the viewpoint expressed in the preceding sentence

   Ⓓ To summarize objections to a controversial decision

   Ⓔ To cite anecdotal evidence supporting an observation mentioned earlier in the passage

Explanation

The last sentence of the passage describes certain reformers' reasoning and suggests the need for establishing a more permanent board of experts to advise legislators on complex subjects. It therefore expands on the previous sentence's proposition that the "traditional model may need to be augmented," pointing to **Choice C** as the correct answer. The passage mentions only one alternative, not many (Choice A), and does not present multiple, conflicting arguments (Choice B). Although the sentence describes a proposal that could be controversial, it does not reference any controversial decisions that have been made (Choice D). The last sentence describes a proposal and a justification; it does not provide anecdotal evidence (Choice E).

7. In the context in which it appears, "standing" (line 8) most nearly means

   Ⓐ upright

   Ⓑ stagnant

   Ⓒ immovable

   Ⓓ permanent

   Ⓔ reputable

Explanation

The passage suggests that a "standing organization" of experts could meet the need for systematic analysis by providing "more than . . . brief interactions." An organization dedicated to advising lawmakers that was relatively "permanent" would have more time than one that only provided "brief interactions," so **Choice D** is the correct answer. Although "standing" may suggest the idea of being "upright" and "reputable" (Choice A and Choice E)—and these might be desirable qualities for experts—these qualities would not address the need for more systematic analysis. "Stagnant" (Choice B) and "immovable" (Choice C) suggest unpleasant or inflexible qualities that would be at odds with the passage's recommendation for a standing committee.

Questions 8 and 9 are based on the following reading passage.

The problem of "old wood" is one of several confronting archaeologists seeking to establish the age of rock paintings in caves by using carbon-dating techniques on the charcoal contained in the paintings' pigments: the time of the paintings' production is not necessarily the *line* same as that of the death of the organism, typically a tree, from which the charcoal comes.
5 While archaeologists usually assume that a charcoal pigment date and the date of the painting are the same, the problem of old wood essentially renders a radiocarbon date as merely a maximum-age estimate. The old-wood effect may, of course, be negligible in many applications, for example, in the humid tropics, where wood deteriorates rapidly. Within the cave environment, however, preservation of wood is often extraordinary.

Description

The passage discusses the "old-wood effect," a phenomenon that complicates the use of carbon-dating techniques to determine the age of cave paintings.

8. It can be inferred that what archaeologists "usually assume" (line 5) is flawed because this assumption
    (A) tends to underestimate the age of charcoal pigments
    (B) may rely on flawed carbon-dating techniques
    (C) fails to consider the role played by high humidity in the deterioration of wood
    (D) may result in an overestimation of the maximum age of "old wood"
    (E) can lead to an overestimation of a rock painting's age

Explanation

The passage states that archaeologists "usually assume that a charcoal pigment date and the date of the painting are the same." However, it explains that the charcoal pigment date is determined by the death of the tree from which the charcoal was produced and that there could be a significant gap between the death of the tree and the production and use of the charcoal paint. The charcoal pigment date could therefore be much older than the cave painting, pointing to **Choice E** as the correct answer. The passage suggests that the interpretation of carbon dating needs to be adjusted to account for the old-wood effect, not that the techniques of carbon dating themselves are flawed (Choice B). Indeed, the passage assumes that radiocarbon dating of the pigments and the wood that makes up those pigments is accurate (Choices A and D). Finally, archaeologists' assumptions are flawed not because they overlook certain causes of the deterioration of wood (Option C); rather, they fail to consider that low humidity, such as that found in caves, could result in the "extraordinary" preservation of wood.

9. Which of the following most accurately characterizes the "problem" (line 1) discussed in the passage?

    Ⓐ The charcoal in the pigment of a rock painting within a cave environment may be considerably older than the charcoal in the pigment of a rock painting in a humid environment.

    Ⓑ The pigments within any given rock painting may contain charcoal that varies considerably in age.

    Ⓒ The charcoal in the pigment of a rock painting may yield an earlier date than the date of the painting itself.

    Ⓓ Carbon dating of carbon derived from wood can only approximate the age of the carbon.

    Ⓔ Charcoal pigments tend to deteriorate rapidly in humid environments.

Explanation

The passage specifies that the "problem" occurs when "seeking to establish the age of rock paintings" and that it results from the fact that radiocarbon dating can only determine the charcoal pigment date, which may be much older than the date of the painting itself. Thus, **Choice C** is correct. A difference in the ages of charcoal used in cave paintings in different environments (Choice A) would not, by itself, affect the accuracy of dating those paintings. While pigments with different ages within the same painting (Choice B) or deteriorating pigments (Choice E) could indeed make dating a rock painting more difficult, neither is the problem discussed by the passage. The imprecision of carbon dating (Choice D) is also not discussed.

> **For Questions 10 to 13, select the <u>two</u> answer choices that, when used to complete the sentence, fit the meaning of the sentence as a whole <u>and</u> produce completed sentences that are alike in meaning.**

10. With regard to foreign policy involvements, the public official exhibited enough _____ human rights to be morally suspect on a number of counts.

    A ignorance of
    B support for
    C disdain for
    D disregard for
    E compliance with
    F observance of

Explanation

The sentence describes a public official whose attitude toward human rights makes the official "morally suspect" with regard to foreign policy involvements. "Disdain for" and "disregard for" best fit the blank, since exhibiting such attitudes would justify this suspicion. While "ignorance of" human rights (Choice A) would also be cause for condemnation of the official, this choice lacks the sense of willful defiance that both "disdain for" and "disregard for" convey, and no other choice forms a pair with it.

Thus the correct answer is **disdain for** (Choice C) and **disregard for** (Choice D).

11. The efficiency with which the canals and channels built at the ancient Inca site of Machu Picchu convey water to the site's buildings is not _____ but testifies to the Incas' careful planning and engineering.

   A incidental
   B invariable
   C replicable
   D unexceptional
   E fortuitous
   F repeatable

Explanation

This sentence explains that the Incas intentionally designed Machu Picchu's water system to be efficient. The words "not" and "but" surrounding the blank indicate that the missing word must be inconsistent with "careful planning and engineering." Among the choices, "incidental" and "fortuitous," both of which describe outcomes that happen by chance, meet this requirement and result in sentences alike in meaning. Although "replicable" and "repeatable" would yield sentences with the same meaning, neither they nor the other remaining choices convey the required inconsistency with "careful planning."

Thus the correct answer is **incidental** (Choice A) and **fortuitous** (Choice E).

12. Although information about the particulars of a company's operation is often _____ , some managers are willing to talk in general terms about their companies' strategies.

   A incorrect
   B manifest
   C disclosed
   D proprietary
   E comprehensive
   F private

Explanation

The sentence deals with a constraint on managers' willingness to discuss their business strategies. The word "although" sets up an opposition between managers' attitude regarding the "particulars" of their company's operations and their willingness to describe their companies' strategies "in general terms." The opposition between the two clauses indicates that the blank must be filled with a word that justifies the need for reticence concerning the details of a company's strategies. Both "proprietary" and "private" suggest reasons that managers would refrain from discussing such particulars. Though "manifest" and "disclosed" are somewhat alike, they do not suggest reasons for avoiding particulars: if the particulars were already manifest or disclosed, there would be no reason for managers not to talk about them. The words "incorrect" and "comprehensive" do not suggest plausible reasons for managers' reticence, and neither choice can be paired with another choice to produce sentences that are alike in meaning.

Thus the correct answer is **proprietary** (Choice D) and **private** (Choice F).

13. It seems obvious that Miles Davis's _____ the Juilliard School, which resulted in his decision to drop out, was based on the school's training of musicians for a kind of music that he did not want to play.

    [A] disaffection with
    [B] dislocation of
    [C] disentanglement from
    [D] subversion of
    [E] displacement of
    [F] estrangement from

Explanation

The sentence asserts a logical relationship between Davis's attitude toward the school (as indicated in the blank) and his "decision to drop out." Only "disaffection with" and "estrangement from" are consistent with a decision to drop out and result in sentences nearly alike in meaning.

Thus, the correct answer is **"disaffection with"** (Choice A) and **estrangement from** (Choice F).

For each of Questions 14 and 15, select <u>one</u> answer choice unless otherwise instructed.

Question 14 is based on the following reading passage.

Much of the archaeological evidence pertaining to the middle Stone Age cultures of Europe consists of stone artifacts, including hand tools and weapons. More sophisticated tools made from leather and wood have been uncovered at middle Stone Age sites in northern Europe, but none have been found at such sites in southern Europe. However, this does not mean that in the middle Stone Age toolmaking was more advanced in northern than in southern Europe, since _____.

14. Which of the following most logically completes the passage?

    Ⓐ at that time southern Europe could sustain a population density greater than northern Europe could
    Ⓑ at that time it was necessary to use stone tools to create tools from leather and wood
    Ⓒ more stone tools have been found at middle Stone Age sites in southern than in northern Europe
    Ⓓ at that time the inhabitants of southern Europe lived in areas with sandy soils in which organic materials degrade quite readily
    Ⓔ archaeological sites in southern Europe from the late Stone Age have yielded numerous sophisticated tools

Explanation

The passage must be completed with a reason that would justify its claim that a difference in the types of tools found at sites in northern and southern Europe does not indicate differences in toolmaking practices. If some other factor caused the difference in the types of tools preserved in the two regions, then there would be no reason to assume that practices at the two sites were different. "Sandy soils in which organic materials degrade quite readily" is just such a factor, since any advanced tools made out of leather and wood would likely have disintegrated before archaeologists could discover them in these areas. This points to **Choice D** as the correct answer. A more densely populated area (Choice A) would tend to increase the number of tools produced in the south but not account for the discrepancy between the two regions. The passage does not suggest that Stone Age people in southern Europe had less access to stone tools than people in northern Europe did (Choice B) or that the prevalence of stone tools could account for the absence of leather and wooden ones (Choice C). Similarly, the discovery of sophisticated tools from the *late* Stone Age (Choice E) would not explain why certain tools have not been found at earlier *middle* Stone Age sites.

Question 15 is based on the following reading passage.

More than a third of the bones excavated from middens (refuse piles) at the site of the earliest human settlement on Easter Island belong to dolphins, the largest animal available to the islanders. Nowhere else in Polynesia do dolphins account for even one percent of such bones. Dolphins generally live out to sea, so they could not have been hunted from shore but must have been harpooned from large, seaworthy canoes built from the tall trees that are now extinct on Easter Island. Fish bones and shellfish occur in the middens in only modest quantities compared with other Polynesian islands because Easter's rugged coastline and steep drop-off to the ocean bottom provide few places to fish in shallow water.

Description

The passage offers an explanation for the relatively large proportion of dolphin bones found in Easter Island middens.

For the following question, consider each of the choices separately and select all that apply.

15. The passage suggests that conditions for early human inhabitants of Easter Island differed from conditions for early human inhabitants of other Polynesian islands in which of the following ways?

  A Tall trees were more readily available to Easter Islanders than to other Polynesian islanders.

  B Dolphins were more readily available to Easter Islanders than to other Polynesian islanders.

  C Fish and shellfish were less readily available to Easter Islanders than to other Polynesian islanders.

Explanation

Choice C is correct.

Choice A is incorrect: while the passage does note that dolphins would have been hunted from canoes made of "tall trees," this does not suggest anything about the relative availability of tall trees in different locations.

Choice B is incorrect: the passage does not necessarily imply that Easter Islanders had better access to dolphins, since inhabitants of other Polynesian islands could have had the same access but could have elected not to exploit dolphins.

Choice C is correct: the passage attributes the relative scarcity of fish and shellfish in Easter Island middens to the fact that Easter Island's coasts "provide few places to fish in shallow water," which suggests that Easter Islanders had less access to these foods than did other Polynesian groups.

Verbal Practice Set 3
15 Questions

> **For Questions 1 to 5, select one entry for each blank from the corresponding column of choices. Fill all blanks in the way that best completes the text.**

1. The professor, who enjoys a growing reputation as the first significant philosopher of cyberspace, is among the first to succeed in _____ the worlds of metaphysics and computer technology.

Ⓐ	discrediting
Ⓑ	obviating
Ⓒ	straddling
Ⓓ	protecting
Ⓔ	obfuscating

2. Compared with physics and chemistry, in which superstition was banished long ago, beliefs that seem laughably _____ today were held until quite recently in both meteorology and solar physics.

Ⓐ	abstruse
Ⓑ	controversial
Ⓒ	exotic
Ⓓ	perplexing
Ⓔ	primitive

3. In her reviews of exhibitions surveying contemporary art, the critic often (i)_____ the merits of relatively (ii)_____ artworks, a fact that earned her a reputation as someone oblivious to the possibilities of art that the public had not yet discovered.

Blank (i)		Blank (ii)	
Ⓐ	ignored	Ⓓ	unknown
Ⓑ	reiterated	Ⓔ	accessible
Ⓒ	extolled	Ⓕ	complex

4. In a sharp blow to his reputation as (i)_____ leader, the evidence that the mayor has recently been involved in malfeasance seems to be (ii)_____.

Blank (i)		Blank (ii)	
Ⓐ	a partisan	Ⓓ	fabricated
Ⓑ	an unsuccessful	Ⓔ	sound
Ⓒ	an exemplary	Ⓕ	dubious

5. Singers of the tropicalist movement in Brazil goaded the government by purposefully invoking stereotypical images of Brazil as a tropical paradise only to (i)_____ them with pointed references to political and social problems. But (ii)_____ in giving offense, the tropicalist singers also managed to annoy the Brazilian left, which shared their social concerns. They embraced an irreverent politics and (iii)_____, epitomized by the coexistence of bossa nova and rock in the same song, which ignored certain leftist calls for folkloric authenticity.

Blank (i)	Blank (ii)	Blank (iii)
(A) illustrate	(D) ecumenical	(G) a devotion to tradition
(B) legitimize	(E) parsimonious	(H) a pastiche of styles
(C) subvert	(F) transitory	(I) an exuberant virtuosity

For each of Questions 6 to 11, select <u>one</u> answer choice unless otherwise instructed.

Questions 6 and 7 are based on the following reading passage.

Much of ecological theory consists of models that are so highly idealized that they are of little real-world predictive value. In addition, many of the parameters used in models—such as birth and death rates—are exceedingly difficult to estimate accurately in the field.

line 5   Consequently, ecological theory is rarely directly relevant to the practice of conservation biology. One notable exception is MacArthur's theory of island biogeography, which predicts the species richness of an island on the basis of its size and degree of isolation. This theory could provide important insights into nature preserves, which can be analogous to islands, often consisting of relatively undisturbed ecosystems surrounded by biologically distinct areas.

6. Which of the following best describes the function of the sentence in lines 4–5 ("Consequently . . . biology") ?

    (A) It suggests a direction for future research regarding a theory presented earlier in the passage.

    (B) It presents evidence that will support a theory that is introduced in the following sentence.

    (C) It questions the usefulness of a particular version of a theory.

    (D) It clarifies an ambiguous statement made earlier in the passage.

    (E) It presents a general rule to which the passage will identify an exception.

For the following question, consider each of the choices separately and select all that apply.

7. It can be inferred from the passage that the author would probably agree with which of the following statements?

    [A] The practice of conservation biology may be directly affected by MacArthur's theory of island biogeography.

    [B] Undisturbed systems surrounded by biologically distinct areas may be helpful in estimating birth and death rate parameters more accurately.

    [C] The similarity between nature preserves and the islands studied in MacArthur's biogeography theory may help predict species richness in nature preserves.

Question 8 is based on the following reading passage.

The traditional color of fire trucks is red, but **in cities that have introduced yellow trucks into their fleets, the rate of traffic accidents involving these trucks has been far lower, per mile driven, than the rate involving red trucks**. Some critics of the innovation have questioned whether **this difference should be attributed to color**, given that the yellow trucks were generally newer than the red trucks with which they were compared. But this criticism can readily be dismissed. Admittedly, the mere difference in accident rates is not decisive evidence. The decisive fact is that the rates differed significantly only in the hours around dawn and dusk. At these hours, the visibility of yellow is known to be better than that of red.

8. In the argument given, the two portions in **boldface** play which of the following roles?

    Ⓐ The first is a fact, the explanation of which is at issue in the argument; the second is an explanation that the argument rejects.

    Ⓑ The first is a fact, the explanation of which is at issue in the argument; the second is the position defended in the argument.

    Ⓒ The first provides evidence to support the position defended in the argument; the second is an assumption explicitly made in defending that position.

    Ⓓ The first provides evidence to support the position defended in the argument; the second criticizes the source of that evidence.

    Ⓔ Each provides evidence to support the position defended in the argument.

The transition in European art from the medieval to the early modern period is marked by an increased focus on observing and accurately representing nature. Medieval images tend to be diagrammatic, lacking details typical of images of the early modern period. But the movement toward naturalistic representation is evident in some later medieval images, some of which are accompanied by the artists' claims of firsthand observation. Among these are Villard de Honnecourt's thirteenth-century lion drawings, which the artist indicates were "made from life." Scholars have frequently noted, however, that the sketches paired with this claim are too diagrammatic to support de Honnecourt's comment fully and draw more on earlier lions in art than on any actual animal the artist might have seen. Thus it is generally believed that he simply did not know what it meant to work "from life" as we now understand the phrase. It is possible, however, that de Honnecourt was simply lying; art records abound with examples of misrepresentation. More important than whether de Honnecourt drew the lions "from life" is that he added the inscription saying he did, indicating that he understood the growing importance in art of claiming the authority of eyewitness.

line
5

10

15

9. The primary purpose of the passage is to
   Ⓐ provide an example to substantiate a particular trend
   Ⓑ describe an exception to a generally accepted theory
   Ⓒ introduce two potential explanations for a historical anomaly
   Ⓓ point out certain flaws in a particular interpretation
   Ⓔ propose a revision to a generally accepted theory

10. According to the passage, de Honnecourt's inscription is important primarily because it indicates that
    Ⓐ most European artists did not begin to understand what it meant to work from life until well into the early modern period
    Ⓑ the shift in European art toward drawing from life occurred before the thirteenth century
    Ⓒ the phrase "from life" can be defined in various ways in connection with medieval European art
    Ⓓ de Honnecourt understood the aesthetic challenges involved in accurately representing nature
    Ⓔ de Honnecourt was conscious of an emergent trend in art

11. Which of the following, if true, would most seriously undermine both of the beliefs about de Honnecourt's inscription as they are described in lines 10–12 ("Thus . . . misrepresentation") ?

Ⓐ In his notebooks, de Honnecourt often criticized other artists for being untruthful about their methods.

Ⓑ Various notes and journals discovered to be de Honnecourt's define drawing from life simply as rendering subjects found in the natural world.

Ⓒ Few late-medieval artists other than de Honnecourt kept records about their methods and the inspirations for their art.

Ⓓ De Honnecourt's drawings accurately represent anatomical details of lions that were absent from the earlier images of lions to which de Honnecourt had access.

Ⓔ The lion drawings attributed to de Honnecourt more closely resemble medieval images than images from the early modern period.

For Questions 12 to 14, select the two answer choices that, when used to complete the sentence, fit the meaning of the sentence as a whole and produce completed sentences that are alike in meaning.

---

12. While critics of law enforcement efforts laud the results of ambitious investigations and prosecutions like the Johnson case, they argue that such investigations are _____.

A experimental
B unproductive
C fruitless
D uncommon
E uneconomical
F rare

13. In establishing that the dust she had observed constitutes two percent of the mass in the quadrant, the astronomer showed that the dust's extreme visual prominence _____ its relatively minor contribution to the total mass of the region.

A belies
B masks
C highlights
D nullifies
E disproves
F accentuates

14. Given the wild and fantastical nature of the witness's story, it is not surprising that many believe it to be _____.

- [A] fascinating
- [B] fabricated
- [C] disturbing
- [D] abstruse
- [E] recondite
- [F] spurious

For Question 15, select <u>one</u> answer choice.

Question 15 is based on the following reading passage.

Leslie: Archaeologists in Borneo have recently discovered traces of rice husks embedded in pottery fragments that date from 4,000 years ago. This discovery supports my hypothesis that people in Borneo were cultivating rice at that time.

Sal: But rice was used in China as early as 6,000 years ago as a binding material in pottery making to keep pots from breaking, and it is possible that people in Borneo 4,000 years ago imported pots from China.

15. Sal's reply to Leslie does which of the following?

- (A) It advances an additional hypothesis that can be derived from Leslie's hypothesis.
- (B) It provides evidence that undermines the basis of Leslie's hypothesis.
- (C) It brings new evidence that shows that Leslie's hypothesis cannot be true.
- (D) It provides additional evidence in support of Leslie's hypothesis.
- (E) It shows that the evidence used to support Leslie's hypothesis could well be true without the hypothesis being true.

Answer Key

Practice Set 3. Verbal Reasoning

Question Number	P+	Correct Answer
1	64	**Choice C:** straddling
2	65	**Choice E:** primitive
3	73	**Choice A:** ignored; **Choice D:** unknown
4	50	**Choice C:** an exemplary; **Choice E:** sound
5	25	**Choice C:** subvert; **Choice D:** ecumenical; **Choice H:** a pastiche of styles
6	67	**Choice E:** It presents a general rule to which the passage will identify an exception.
7	49	**Choice A:** The practice of conservation biology may be directly affected by MacArthur's theory of island biogeography. AND **Choice C:** The similarity between nature preserves and the islands studied in MacArthur's biogeography theory may help predict species richness in nature preserves.
8	36	**Choice B:** The first is a fact, the explanation of which is at issue in the argument; the second is the position defended in the argument.
9	39	**Choice A:** provide an example to substantiate a particular trend
10	70	**Choice E:** de Honnecourt was conscious of an emergent trend in art
11	57	**Choice D:** De Honnecourt's drawings accurately represent anatomical details of lions that were absent from the earlier images of lions to which de Honnecourt had access.
12	72	**Choice D:** uncommon AND **Choice F:** rare
13	52	**Choice A:** belies AND **Choice B:** masks
14	42	**Choice B:** fabricated AND **Choice F:** spurious
15	49	**Choice E:** It shows that the evidence used to support Leslie's hypothesis could well be true without the hypothesis being true.

Verbal Practice Set 3
15 Questions with Explanations

> **For Questions 1 to 5, select one entry for each blank from the corresponding column of choices. Fill all blanks in the way that best completes the text.**

1. The professor, who enjoys a growing reputation as the first significant philosopher of cyberspace, is among the first to succeed in _____ the worlds of metaphysics and computer technology.

Ⓐ	discrediting
Ⓑ	obviating
Ⓒ	straddling
Ⓓ	protecting
Ⓔ	obfuscating

Explanation

The phrase "the first significant philosopher of cyberspace" suggests that the professor analyzes issues involving computer networks (cyberspace) using a philosophical approach. Such an approach would require significant involvement in the disciplines of computer technology and of metaphysics (a branch of philosophy); metaphorically, this situation could be described as having a foot in each of these worlds, or "straddling" them.

    Thus the correct answer is **straddling** (Choice C).

2. Compared with physics and chemistry, in which superstition was banished long ago, beliefs that seem laughably _____ today were held until quite recently in both meteorology and solar physics.

Ⓐ	abstruse
Ⓑ	controversial
Ⓒ	exotic
Ⓓ	perplexing
Ⓔ	primitive

Explanation

The sentence is comparing physics and chemistry with meteorology and solar physics, saying that certain beliefs were "banished long ago" in the first group and that the same kinds of beliefs were "held until quite recently" in the second group. Since the beliefs are identified as superstition, the word that fills the blank should, together with "laughably," describe superstitious beliefs. Of the answer choices, "primitive" is best: from a perspective of advanced scientific development, superstitious beliefs might be characterized as primitive in the sense of belonging to an early stage of development.

    Thus the correct answer is **primitive** (Choice E).

3. In her reviews of exhibitions surveying contemporary art, the critic often (i)_____ the merits of relatively (ii)_____ artworks, a fact that earned her a reputation as someone oblivious to the possibilities of art that the public had not yet discovered.

Blank (i)	Blank (ii)
Ⓐ ignored	Ⓓ unknown
Ⓑ reiterated	Ⓔ accessible
Ⓒ extolled	Ⓕ complex

Explanation

This sentence describes a frequent practice of an art critic and the reputation she has earned in consequence of this practice. The critic is characterized as "someone oblivious to the possibilities of art that the public had not yet discovered"; this suggests that she is perceived as someone who fails to pay attention to art whose value has not already been acknowledged by the art-viewing public. Given that the critic's reputation hinges on her treatment of art whose value has not been established, the second blank must be filled with a word that relates to the extent to which an artwork has received public recognition. The only choice that speaks to this attribute is "unknown." An artwork may receive more or less public recognition regardless of whether it is "complex" or "accessible." The behavior toward "relatively unknown artworks" that is consistent with the critic's reputation would be to ignore such work. Reiterating or extolling the merits of unrecognized art would contradict her stated reputation.

Thus the correct answer is **ignored** (Choice A) and **unknown** (Choice D).

4. In a sharp blow to his reputation as (i)_____ leader, the evidence that the mayor has recently been involved in malfeasance seems to be (ii)_____.

Blank (i)	Blank (ii)
Ⓐ a partisan	Ⓓ fabricated
Ⓑ an unsuccessful	Ⓔ sound
Ⓒ an exemplary	Ⓕ dubious

Explanation

By using the expression "in a sharp blow to his reputation," the sentence indicates that the evidence concerning the mayor's involvement in wrongdoing has seriously damaged his image as a certain kind of leader. If the evidence is damaging to the mayor's reputation, then the choice that makes the most sense for Blank (ii) is "sound," since the other two choices would complete the sentence so as to vindicate the mayor or cast doubts on the allegations against him. Since the evidence is damning, the leadership quality that it challenges must be positive; of the three choices, only "exemplary" meets this criterion.

Thus the correct answer is **an exemplary** (Choice C) and **sound** (Choice E).

5. Singers of the tropicalist movement in Brazil goaded the government by purposefully invoking stereotypical images of Brazil as a tropical paradise only to (i)_____ them with pointed references to political and social problems. But (ii)_____ in giving offense, the tropicalist singers also managed to annoy the Brazilian left, which shared their social concerns. They embraced an irreverent politics and (iii)_____, epitomized by the coexistence of bossa nova and rock in the same song, which ignored certain leftist calls for folkloric authenticity.

Blank (i)	Blank (ii)	Blank (iii)
(A) illustrate	(D) ecumenical	(G) a devotion to tradition
(B) legitimize	(E) parsimonious	(H) a pastiche of styles
(C) subvert	(F) transitory	(I) an exuberant virtuosity

Explanation

The paragraph is concerned with explaining how the tropicalist singers "goaded" and "managed to annoy" both the Brazilian government and the Brazilian left. In the first sentence, the word that fills Blank (i) should help explain the government's annoyance with the singers. Of the answer choices, "subvert" is best: the singers subverted positive images of Brazil, thus goading the government. Neither "illustrate" nor "legitimize" makes sense in the blank, since the positive images would not be illustrated or legitimized by references to problems in Brazil.

Moving on to the second sentence, "ecumenical" is the best answer for Blank (ii): the singers offended both the government and the Brazilian left, making them ecumenical—in this context meaning "nonexclusive"—in giving offense. Finally, the last sentence explains the Brazilian left's annoyance with the singers. In addition to embracing "an irreverent politics," the singers rejected "folkloric authenticity" by mixing musical genres, allowing, for example, "the coexistence of bossa nova and rock in the same song"; in so doing, they embraced "a pastiche of styles," the best answer for Blank (iii). Neither "a devotion to tradition" nor "an exuberant virtuosity" makes sense in the third blank, since embracing either does not suggest a rejection of "folkloric authenticity."

Thus the correct answer is **subvert** (Choice C), **ecumenical** (Choice D), and **a pastiche of styles** (Choice H).

For each of Questions 6 to 11, select <u>one</u> answer choice unless otherwise instructed.

Questions 6 and 7 are based on the following reading passage.

Much of ecological theory consists of models that are so highly idealized that they are of little real-world predictive value. In addition, many of the parameters used in models—such as birth and death rates—are exceedingly difficult to estimate accurately in the field.

line
5
Consequently, ecological theory is rarely directly relevant to the practice of conservation biology. One notable exception is MacArthur's theory of island biogeography, which predicts the species richness of an island on the basis of its size and degree of isolation. This theory could provide important insights into nature preserves, which can be analogous to islands, often consisting of relatively undisturbed ecosystems surrounded by biologically distinct areas.

Description

The passage describes how a particular ecological theory is notable for its relevance to the practice of conservation biology.

6.   Which of the following best describes the function of the sentence in lines 4–5 ("Consequently . . . biology") ?

   Ⓐ It suggests a direction for future research regarding a theory presented earlier in the passage.
   Ⓑ It presents evidence that will support a theory that is introduced in the following sentence.
   Ⓒ It questions the usefulness of a particular version of a theory.
   Ⓓ It clarifies an ambiguous statement made earlier in the passage.
   Ⓔ It presents a general rule to which the passage will identify an exception.

Explanation

The sentence in question states that for reasons mentioned earlier in the passage, ecological theory is often not immediately applicable to the practice of conservation biology. But the passage goes on to note an exception to this statement in MacArthur's theory of island biogeography, which could provide relevant insights. The sentence, therefore, presents a general rule to which the subsequent sentence introduces an exception, pointing to **Choice E** as the correct answer choice. Far from questioning the usefulness of MacArthur's theory (Choice C), the passage in fact argues for the theory's potential to provide "important insights" but does not present any evidence that specifically supports the theory (Choice B). The statements that precede the sentence do not present any ambiguity that is clarified by the sentence (Choice D), and although future research is alluded to later in the passage, it is not suggested by the sentence in question (Choice A).

For the following question, consider each of the choices separately and select all that apply.

7.   It can be inferred from the passage that the author would probably agree with which of the following statements?

   [A]   The practice of conservation biology may be directly affected by MacArthur's theory of island biogeography.

   [B]   Undisturbed systems surrounded by biologically distinct areas may be helpful in estimating birth and death rate parameters more accurately.

   [C]   The similarity between nature preserves and the islands studied in MacArthur's biogeography theory may help predict species richness in nature preserves.

Explanation

Choices A and **C** are correct.

   Choice A is correct: the author of the passage suggests that in contrast to most ecological theories, MacArthur's theory of island biogeography may be considered "directly relevant to the practice of conservation biology" and "could provide important insights." It follows that the author would most likely agree that MacArthur's theory could directly affect the practice of conservation biology.

   Choice B is incorrect: although the passage mentions birth and death rates, it does not discuss nor suggest ways by which these may be more accurately estimated.

   Choice C is correct: the passage argues that MacArthur's theory may be applied to conservation by treating nature preserves as "analogous to islands." Thus, the author would probably agree that a similarity between nature preserves and islands could enable biologists to expand the application of MacArthur's theory and thereby help predict species richness in such preserves.

Question 8 is based on the following reading passage.

The traditional color of fire trucks is red, but **in cities that have introduced yellow trucks into their fleets, the rate of traffic accidents involving these trucks has been far lower, per mile driven, than the rate involving red trucks**. Some critics of the innovation have questioned whether **this difference should be attributed to color**, given that the yellow trucks were generally newer than the red trucks with which they were compared. But this criticism can readily be dismissed. Admittedly, the mere difference in accident rates is not decisive evidence. The decisive fact is that the rates differed significantly only in the hours around dawn and dusk. At these hours, the visibility of yellow is known to be better than that of red.

Description

The passage describes how the introduction of yellow fire trucks alongside traditional red ones seems to have resulted in fewer traffic accidents involving yellow trucks than accidents involving red trucks. The rest of the passage considers how to interpret this information.

8. In the argument given, the two portions in **boldface** play which of the following roles?

    Ⓐ The first is a fact, the explanation of which is at issue in the argument; the second is an explanation that the argument rejects.

    Ⓑ The first is a fact, the explanation of which is at issue in the argument; the second is the position defended in the argument.

    Ⓒ The first provides evidence to support the position defended in the argument; the second is an assumption explicitly made in defending that position.

    Ⓓ The first provides evidence to support the position defended in the argument; the second criticizes the source of that evidence.

    Ⓔ Each provides evidence to support the position defended in the argument.

Explanation

The correct answer is **Choice B**: the first portion in **boldface** states a fact about differences in accident rates between yellow fire trucks and red ones, while the second attributes those differences to truck color, thus defending the argument's position that color is the decisive cause of the disparity. Because the second portion does not make an argument that the passage rejects, Choice A is incorrect. The first portion does not present "evidence" in support of any position (Choices C, D, and E) but rather states a fact, so these choices are all incorrect.

Questions 9 to 11 are based on the following reading passage.

The transition in European art from the medieval to the early modern period is marked by an increased focus on observing and accurately representing nature. Medieval images tend to be diagrammatic, lacking details typical of images of the early modern period. But
line
5 the movement toward naturalistic representation is evident in some later medieval images, some of which are accompanied by the artists' claims of firsthand observation. Among these are Villard de Honnecourt's thirteenth-century lion drawings, which the artist indicates were "made from life." Scholars have frequently noted, however, that the sketches paired with this claim are too diagrammatic to support de Honnecourt's comment fully and draw more on earlier lions in art than on any actual animal the artist might have seen.
10 Thus it is generally believed that he simply did not know what it meant to work "from life" as we now understand the phrase. It is possible, however, that de Honnecourt was simply lying; art records abound with examples of misrepresentation. More important than whether de Honnecourt drew the lions "from life" is that he added the inscription saying he did, indicating that he understood the growing importance in art of claiming the authority
15 of eyewitness.

Description

The passage discusses the transition from diagrammatic approaches to art in the medieval period to more naturalistic, observation-based representations in the subsequent early modern period, and in light of that transition, considers how to understand Villard de Honnecourt's claim that his drawings of lions were "made from life."

9. The primary purpose of the passage is to
    (A) provide an example to substantiate a particular trend
    (B) describe an exception to a generally accepted theory
    (C) introduce two potential explanations for a historical anomaly
    (D) point out certain flaws in a particular interpretation
    (E) propose a revision to a generally accepted theory

Explanation

The passage uses the example of de Honnecourt's lion drawings to illustrate a larger point about the trend of art away from the diagrammatic mode of the medieval period, making **Choice A** the correct answer. The view that there was a transition in artistic styles over a certain timespan could arguably represent a "generally accepted theory," but the passage ultimately endorses this view without identifying an exception to it (Choice B) or proposing a revision to it (Choice E). While the passage does introduce two potential explanations for something (Choice C), the explanations pertain to de Honnecourt's claim, which is not presented as a historical anomaly, so Choice C is incorrect.

10. According to the passage, de Honnecourt's inscription is important primarily because it indicates that
    (A) most European artists did not begin to understand what it meant to work from life until well into the early modern period
    (B) the shift in European art toward drawing from life occurred before the thirteenth century
    (C) the phrase "from life" can be defined in various ways in connection with medieval European art
    (D) de Honnecourt understood the aesthetic challenges involved in accurately representing nature
    (E) de Honnecourt was conscious of an emergent trend in art

Explanation

The last sentence of the passage specifies that the significance of de Honnecourt's inscription lies in its indication of his awareness of the trend in art toward naturalism, making **Choice E** the correct answer. Evidence of naturalism in "some later medieval images" would weaken rather than support the idea that "most European artists" did not understand working "from life" at the time (Choice A). However, de Honnecourt's thirteenth-century inscription would not indicate that the shift toward naturalism in European art occurred before the thirteenth century (Choice B). The phrase "from life" mentioned in Choice C was not particularly relevant to medieval art, which was not based on direct observation. Finally, although the passage indicates that de Honnecourt relied on other drawings more than, or along with, direct observation, it does not suggest this was because he "understood the aesthetic challenges" involved in accurate representation (Choice D).

11. Which of the following, if true, would most seriously undermine <u>both</u> of the beliefs about de Honnecourt's inscription as they are described in lines 10–12 ("Thus . . . misrepresentation")?

- Ⓐ In his notebooks, de Honnecourt often criticized other artists for being untruthful about their methods.
- Ⓑ Various notes and journals discovered to be de Honnecourt's define drawing from life simply as rendering subjects found in the natural world.
- Ⓒ Few late-medieval artists other than de Honnecourt kept records about their methods and the inspirations for their art.
- Ⓓ De Honnecourt's drawings accurately represent anatomical details of lions that were absent from the earlier images of lions to which de Honnecourt had access.
- Ⓔ The lion drawings attributed to de Honnecourt more closely resemble medieval images than images from the early modern period.

Explanation

Lines 10–12 present two explanations of de Honnecourt's inscription: first, that de Honnecourt did not understand what it meant to work "from life," and second, that de Honnecourt was lying about having done so. Of the hypothetical claims listed in the answer choices, **Choice D** would most strongly undermine both explanations. If de Honnecourt's drawings accurately represented anatomical details of lions that could not be found in earlier images, then de Honnecourt must have been able to observe real lions, showing that he did understand what working "from life" meant and that he was not lying. Considering Choice B, if de Honnecourt's writings defined drawing from life not as observation but rather as drawing subjects that were simply found in nature (whether directly observed or not), this would undermine the idea that de Honnecourt was lying but not that he had an understanding of what it means to work "from life" as the phrase is understood today—as referring to firsthand observation. Thus, Choice B is incorrect. None of the other answer choices bear directly on the beliefs expressed in lines 10–12, so they cannot be correct.

> **For Questions 12 to 14, select the <u>two</u> answer choices that, when used to complete the sentence, fit the meaning of the sentence as a whole <u>and</u> produce completed sentences that are alike in meaning.**

12. While critics of law enforcement efforts laud the results of ambitious investigations and prosecutions like the Johnson case, they argue that such investigations are _____.

    A experimental
    B unproductive
    C fruitless
    D uncommon
    E uneconomical
    F rare

Explanation

This sentence concerns critics of law enforcement efforts who "laud," or praise, a subset of those efforts ("ambitious investigations and prosecutions"). The blank, then, calls for a word that will reconcile this praise with a generally critical attitude. "Rare" and "uncommon" do exactly this, indicating that the critics believe that only a small proportion of law enforcement efforts produce praiseworthy results. While "unproductive" and "fruitless" do have similar meanings, investigations that are unproductive would be unlikely to be lauded. Ambitious efforts could indeed be "uneconomical" or even "experimental," but neither of these choices can be paired with another word to produce a sentence with the same meaning.

   Thus the correct answer is **uncommon** (Choice D) and **rare** (Choice F).

13. In establishing that the dust she had observed constitutes two percent of the mass in the quadrant, the astronomer showed that the dust's extreme visual prominence _____ its relatively minor contribution to the total mass of the region.

    A belies
    B masks
    C highlights
    D nullifies
    E disproves
    F accentuates

Explanation

The sentence concerns a scientist's observation of dust and the relationship between that dust's "extreme visual prominence" and its "relatively minor" mass. The contrast between those two terms suggests a mismatch between the dust's appearance and its mass; the blank, then, should be completed with a word conveying that the dust's high visibility presents a misleading picture of its mass. "Belies" and "masks," both of which convey a sense of deceptiveness, are the only choices that meet this requirement. "Highlights" and "accentuates" would suggest that the high visibility reveals, rather than conceals, the small contribution of the dust to the region's mass, while "nullifies" and "disproves" would suggest that the mass was not actually small at all.

   Thus the correct answer is **belies** (Choice A) and **masks** (Choice B).

14. Given the wild and fantastical nature of the witness's story, it is not surprising that many believe it to be _____.

     A   fascinating

     B   fabricated

     C   disturbing

     D   abstruse

     E   recondite

     F   spurious

Explanation

The sentence provides a plausible reason for a story to be considered in a certain way by its audience. The blank must be filled with a word that describes the story's reception as a consequence of its "wild and fantastical" nature; by describing the nature of the story as "fantastical" specifically, the sentence suggests that the story might be considered by some to be made-up or not based in reality, thus well described by both "fabricated" and "spurious." Although "abstruse" and "recondite" both mean "obscure or difficult to comprehend," the description of the story as "wild and fantastical" does not sufficiently imply these descriptions: a story can be "fantastical" and still be simple or clear. Although it is conceivable that people might regard a story of this nature as "fascinating" or "disturbing," neither choice can be paired with another choice to produce sentences that are alike in meaning.

Thus the correct answer is **fabricated** (Choice B) and **spurious** (Choice F).

Question 15 is based on the following reading passage.

Leslie: Archaeologists in Borneo have recently discovered traces of rice husks embedded in pottery fragments that date from 4,000 years ago. This discovery supports my hypothesis that people in Borneo were cultivating rice at that time.

Sal: But rice was used in China as early as 6,000 years ago as a binding material in pottery making to keep pots from breaking, and it is possible that people in Borneo 4,000 years ago imported pots from China.

15. Sal's reply to Leslie does which of the following?

    Ⓐ It advances an additional hypothesis that can be derived from Leslie's hypothesis.

    Ⓑ It provides evidence that undermines the basis of Leslie's hypothesis.

    Ⓒ It brings new evidence that shows that Leslie's hypothesis cannot be true.

    Ⓓ It provides additional evidence in support of Leslie's hypothesis.

    Ⓔ It shows that the evidence used to support Leslie's hypothesis could well be true without the hypothesis being true.

Explanation

Sal points out that Chinese pottery containing rice husks may have been imported to Borneo. This possibility shows that Leslie cannot assume that the rice husks discovered by archeologists were grown in Borneo just because they were found there. Thus, **Choice E** is the correct answer. Because Sal's reply casts doubt on whether certain archaeological evidence confirms Leslie's hypothesis, it cannot be said to either build on Leslie's hypothesis (Choice A) or to provide support for it (Choice D). However, questioning one specific piece of evidence does not undermine other evidence that the hypothesis is based on (Choice B), nor does it definitively prove that rice could not have been cultivated in Borneo (Choice C).

Verbal Practice Set 4
15 Questions

> **For Questions 1 to 5, select one entry for each blank from the corresponding column of choices. Fill all blanks in the way that best completes the text.**

1. Unenlightened authoritarian managers rarely recognize a crucial reason for the low levels of serious conflict among members of democratically run work groups: a modicum of tolerance for dissent often prevents _____.

Ⓐ demur
Ⓑ schism
Ⓒ cooperation
Ⓓ compliance
Ⓔ shortsightedness

2. The belief that politicians might become _____ after their election to office led to the appointment of ethics officers at various levels of government.

Ⓐ scrupulous
Ⓑ entrenched
Ⓒ venal
Ⓓ puzzled
Ⓔ artificial

3. There is nothing quite like this movie, and indeed I am not altogether sure there is much more to it than its lovely (i) _____. At a moment when so many films strive to be as (ii)_____ as possible, it is gratifying to find one that is so subtle and puzzling.

Blank (i)	Blank (ii)
Ⓐ peculiarity	Ⓓ indirect
Ⓑ pellucidity	Ⓔ assertive
Ⓒ conventionality	Ⓕ enigmatic

4. The episodes encountered in dreams tend to be quite (i)_____. Yet in this respect dreams' content differs from their causes, for dreams are as likely to have been molded by (ii)_____ events as by extreme and life-changing ones.

Blank (i)	Blank (ii)
Ⓐ trivial	Ⓓ memorable
Ⓑ revealing	Ⓔ traumatic
Ⓒ bizarre	Ⓕ mundane

5.   Elmore Leonard may have had (i)_____ than any other writer in America.
     He was beloved by millions of readers, who reliably propelled each of his books
     onto the best-seller lists; by the Hollywood types, whose (ii)_____ Leonard's
     novels seemingly burned in inverse proportion to their ability to make anything but
     (iii)_____ out of them; and even by the literary establishment, who have in effect
     awarded Leonard, a crime novelist, an honorary membership in the Serious Authors'
     Club.

Blank (i)	Blank (ii)	Blank (iii)
Ⓐ more kinds of fans	Ⓓ indifference towards	Ⓖ mysteries
Ⓑ more interest in popular culture	Ⓔ condescension for	Ⓗ fiascoes
Ⓒ a greater variety of projects	Ⓕ zeal for	Ⓘ hits

For each of Questions 6 to 9, select <u>one</u> answer choice unless otherwise instructed.

Questions 6 and 7 are based on the following reading passage.

Early in the twentieth century, leaders of African American churches in the industrial
North consciously encouraged their congregations—mostly recent migrants from the rural
South—to leave their past, including their music, behind. Church music directors were
line instructed to emphasize European classical works: Bach, Beethoven, and Brahms. Spiri-
5   tuals, in their traditional improvisational forms, were out of the question. Though some
       music directors attempted to address churchgoers' hunger for traditional music by arrang-
       ing spirituals for performance by choirs, they did so presuming that the spirituals should be
       "developed," brought into the classical art-song genre. Harris argues that the inadequacy
       of this response is what prompted the emergence of gospel music—a new blues-influenced
10   genre that provided an identifiably African American church music.

6.   The primary purpose of the passage is to explain
     Ⓐ how the traditional improvisational forms of spirituals were developed into
         an art-song genre
     Ⓑ why African American church music changed in the early twentieth century
     Ⓒ why European classical music had such a strong influence on music in
         African American churches
     Ⓓ why church leaders in the industrial North thought it would be beneficial for
         congregations to distance themselves from their southern, rural pasts
     Ⓔ why music directors of African American churches chose to create new
         arrangements of traditional spirituals

7. The author implies that the reason spirituals were "out of the question" (line 5) was that

    (A) their performance in traditional form would have conflicted with church leaders' aims

    (B) music directors of churches in the industrial North had an inadequate knowledge of the form

    (C) the social context in which churchgoers would have wanted to hear them no longer existed

    (D) they had been displaced by the newer genre of gospel music

    (E) they were not viewed favorably by churchgoers who preferred music influenced by European classical works

Questions 8 and 9 are based on the following reading passage.

One of the most dramatic changes in astronomers' perception of the solar system came when the two Voyager probes reached Jupiter in 1979. The Voyagers astounded everyone by showing that instead of the expected indistinguishable dead ice balls, Jupiter's four large moons had distinct personalities. Callisto had an old, cratered surface, as expected. Ganymede also had old, cratered regions, but they were broken by swaths of bright, fractured ice. Europa turned out to have a very young crust of fractured ice, apparently overlying an ocean of liquid water that could conceivably support life. Io was the biggest surprise, with nearly a dozen actively erupting volcanoes and a colorful surface of sulfur compounds.

8. According to the passage, the Voyager probes suggested which of the following about Europa?

    (A) It is the only one of Jupiter's four large moons to show evidence of life.

    (B) Its surface indicates the presence of liquid water.

    (C) Its crust is not as young as Io's.

    (D) It is the most geologically active of the four moons.

    (E) It is the youngest of the four moons.

For the following question, consider each of the choices separately and select all that apply.

9. According to the passage, the two Voyager probes of Jupiter's four large moons led astronomers to think which of the following?

    A That their assumptions regarding Callisto's surface had been correct

    B That there was greater diversity among the moons than they had expected

    C That at least one of the moons might be capable of supporting life forms

> **For Questions 10 to 13, select the <u>two</u> answer choices that, when used to complete the sentence, fit the meaning of the sentence as a whole <u>and</u> produce completed sentences that are alike in meaning.**

10. The easy success of the theatrical version of her novel unfortunately encouraged what became her subsequent _____ the theater—a form essentially alien to her talents as a writer.
    - [A] facility for
    - [B] infatuation with
    - [C] ambivalence about
    - [D] curiosity about
    - [E] uncertainty about
    - [F] attachment to

11. Because the political situation _____ international communication, French scientific research was at that time uncharacteristically parochial.
    - [A] inhibited
    - [B] stimulated
    - [C] constrained
    - [D] required
    - [E] demanded
    - [F] encouraged

12. Because they lack a strong opposing political party on which to focus their rancor, the ruling party's leaders seem to have concentrated their malevolence on _____ each other.
    - [A] mollifying
    - [B] appeasing
    - [C] lambasting
    - [D] beguiling
    - [E] obliterating
    - [F] excoriating

13. Surprisingly, stories about celebrities, which can at first seem so of the moment and so _____, often have similarities to humanity's oldest and most profound tales.
    - [A] random
    - [B] trivial
    - [C] consequential
    - [D] grave
    - [E] superficial
    - [F] repetitive

For each of Questions 14 and 15, select <u>one</u> answer choice unless otherwise instructed.

Question 14 is based on the following reading passage.

Trying to identify working conditions that promote high worker productivity, a factory's management dimmed the factory's previously uniform lighting in some areas while brightening it in some others in order to see if lighting levels affected productivity. Surprisingly, in every area with changed lighting levels, though not elsewhere, productivity increased, by comparable margins. It can be concluded that what affects productivity are changes in lighting, but not specific levels of lighting.

14. Which of the following, if true, calls the conclusion most seriously into question?

   Ⓐ In the areas where lighting levels were changed, management observed workers particularly carefully and interviewed them about their work and working conditions.

   Ⓑ Workplace safety rules define limits on lighting levels, and the changes in lighting levels did not take lighting levels in any of the factory's work areas beyond these limits.

   Ⓒ At the time of the lighting changes, management made no efforts to boost productivity in the areas where lighting was not changed and made no such efforts other than the lighting changes elsewhere.

   Ⓓ Both in the areas where lighting levels were increased and where they were diminished, management received complaints about the new lighting levels from some workers.

   Ⓔ A year after the lighting changes were made, productivity throughout the factory had returned to its prechange levels even though the lighting levels in the factory had not been changed again.

Question 15 is based on the following reading passage.

Governments often negate their own efforts to nurture public transit by spending large sums to make it easier for people to use cars. When a city's automobile traffic becomes congested, the standard response has long been to provide additional capacity by building new roads or widening existing ones. This approach eventually makes the original problem worse by generating what planners call "induced traffic": every mile of new highway lures passengers from public transit and other more efficient modes of travel and makes it possible for residential and commercial development to spread even farther from urban centers. A better strategy would be to eliminate existing traffic lanes and parking spaces gradually, thereby forcing more drivers to use less environmentally damaging alternatives.

15. According to the passage, the spread of residential and commercial development

   Ⓐ is encouraged by the provision of additional capacity on roads

   Ⓑ is significantly slowed by increasing the capacity of public transit systems

   Ⓒ leads to the improvement of public transit

   Ⓓ is unrelated to increasing traffic congestion

   Ⓔ is largely ignored by governments as a factor in planning for roads and transit systems

Answer Key

Practice Set 4. Verbal Reasoning

Question Number	P+	Correct Answer
1	46	**Choice B:** schism
2	50	**Choice C:** venal
3	54	**Choice A:** peculiarity; **Choice E:** assertive
4	47	**Choice C:** bizarre; **Choice F:** mundane
5	30	**Choice A:** more kinds of fans; **Choice F:** zeal for; **Choice H:** fiascoes
6	43	**Choice B:** why African American church music changed in the early twentieth century
7	70	**Choice A:** their performance in traditional form would have conflicted with church leaders' aims
8	80	**Choice B:** Its surface indicates the presence of liquid water.
9	58	**Choice A:** That their assumptions regarding Callisto's surface had been correct AND **Choice B:** That there was greater diversity among the moons than they had expected AND **Choice C:** That at least one of the moons might be capable of supporting life forms
10	62	**Choice B:** infatuation with AND **Choice F:** attachment to
11	75	**Choice A:** inhibited AND **Choice C:** constrained
12	21	**Choice C:** lambasting AND **Choice F:** excoriating
13	61	**Choice B:** trivial AND **Choice E:** superficial
14	47	**Choice A:** In the areas where lighting levels were changed, management observed workers particularly carefully and interviewed them about their work and working conditions.
15	80	**Choice A:** is encouraged by the provision of additional capacity on roads

Verbal Practice Set 4
15 Questions with Explanations

> **For Questions 1 to 5, select one entry for each blank from the corresponding column of choices. Fill all blanks in the way that best completes the text.**

1. Unenlightened authoritarian managers rarely recognize a crucial reason for the low levels of serious conflict among members of democratically run work groups: a modicum of tolerance for dissent often prevents _____.

Ⓐ	demur
Ⓑ	schism
Ⓒ	cooperation
Ⓓ	compliance
Ⓔ	shortsightedness

Explanation

The blank must be filled with a word that describes a problem that a work group can suffer, a problem that can be a cause of (or associated with) serious conflict. Of the answer choices, only "schism" fits this description.

Thus, the correct answer is **schism** (Choice B).

2. The belief that politicians might become _____ after their election to office led to the appointment of ethics officers at various levels of government.

Ⓐ	scrupulous
Ⓑ	entrenched
Ⓒ	venal
Ⓓ	puzzled
Ⓔ	artificial

Explanation

If a certain belief led to the appointment of ethics officers, that belief must concern some ethical issue. Of the choices provided, only "venal" fits that context. Although several of the other choices are not necessarily positive characteristics, none involves ethics.

Thus, the correct answer is **venal** (Choice C).

3. There is nothing quite like this movie, and indeed I am not altogether sure there is much more to it than its lovely (i) _____. At a moment when so many films strive to be as (ii)_____ as possible, it is gratifying to find one that is so subtle and puzzling.

Blank (i)	Blank (ii)
Ⓐ peculiarity	Ⓓ indirect
Ⓑ pellucidity	Ⓔ assertive
Ⓒ conventionality	Ⓕ enigmatic

Explanation

The two sentences provide the reader with quite a bit of information about the movie. There is "nothing quite like it" and it is "subtle and puzzling." "Peculiarity" is clearly a solid fit for the first blank, while "conventionality" clearly does not work, given the fact that there is "nothing quite like it." That leaves "pellucidity," which, while it could fit logically in the first sentence in isolation, does not fit the later claim that the movie is "subtle and puzzling." The second blank needs simply to provide a contrast with "subtle and puzzling." Of the choices offered, only "assertive" clearly does that.

Thus, the correct answer is **peculiarity** (Choice A) and **assertive** (Choice E).

4. The episodes encountered in dreams tend to be quite (i)_____. Yet in this respect dreams' content differs from their causes, for dreams are as likely to have been molded by (ii)_____ events as by extreme and life-changing ones.

Blank (i)	Blank (ii)
Ⓐ trivial	Ⓓ memorable
Ⓑ revealing	Ⓔ traumatic
Ⓒ bizarre	Ⓕ mundane

Explanation

The passage deals with a contrast between the content of dreams and the real-life events that inspire them. In the second sentence, the first clause asserts that "in this respect dreams' content differs from their causes." This, together with the "yet" occurring at the beginning of that sentence, signals an antithetical relationship between the words that fill Blank (i) and Blank (ii). The nature of the events described at the end of the passage indicates that the second blank also requires a word that contrasts in meaning with "extreme and life-changing." Only "mundane" satisfies this requirement; it follows that "bizarre," which is most clearly in opposition to "mundane," is the best choice for the first blank.

Thus the correct answer is **bizarre** (Choice C) and **mundane** (Choice F).

5. Elmore Leonard may have had (i)_____ than any other writer in America. He was beloved by millions of readers, who reliably propelled each of his books onto the best-seller lists; by the Hollywood types, whose (ii)_____ Leonard's novels seemingly burned in inverse proportion to their ability to make anything but (iii)_____ out of them; and even by the literary establishment, who have in effect awarded Leonard, a crime novelist, an honorary membership in the Serious Authors' Club.

Blank (i)	Blank (ii)	Blank (iii)
Ⓐ more kinds of fans	Ⓓ indifference towards	Ⓖ mysteries
Ⓑ more interest in popular culture	Ⓔ condescension for	Ⓗ fiascoes
Ⓒ a greater variety of projects	Ⓕ zeal for	Ⓘ hits

Explanation

The paragraph focuses on the reception of American writer Elmore Leonard (1925–2013), who was "beloved" by "millions of readers," "by the Hollywood types" and "even by the literary establishment." Since the long second sentence essentially lists the different groups who appreciated Leonard's writing, the attribute described by the phrase in Blank (i) must be "more kinds of fans," which is the only choice that relates to the writer's reception. The words that fill the second and third blanks help elaborate on the relationship between Hollywood filmmakers and Leonard's novels. Based on the understanding that Leonard was "beloved" by Hollywood types, "zeal for" is the best choice for Blank (ii); it is also the phrase that best fits with the verb "burned." Finally, the phrase "in inverse proportion to" indicates a contrast between the filmmakers' positive response to Leonard's work and their capacity to do justice to his novels in film. The only choice that offers a negative value judgment of their film adaptations is "fiascoes" (complete failures).

Thus the correct answer is **more kinds of fans** (Choice A), **zeal for** (Choice F), and **fiascoes** (Choice H).

> **For each of Questions 6 to 9, select _one_ answer choice unless otherwise instructed.**

Questions 6 and 7 are based on the following reading passage.

Early in the twentieth century, leaders of African American churches in the industrial North consciously encouraged their congregations—mostly recent migrants from the rural South—to leave their past, including their music, behind. Church music directors were instructed to emphasize European classical works: Bach, Beethoven, and Brahms. Spirituals, in their traditional improvisational forms, were out of the question. Though some music directors attempted to address churchgoers' hunger for traditional music by arranging spirituals for performance by choirs, they did so presuming that the spirituals should be "developed," brought into the classical art-song genre. Harris argues that the inadequacy of this response is what prompted the emergence of gospel music—a new blues-influenced genre that provided an identifiably African American church music.

line
5

10

Description

The passage describes how music performed within northern African American churches was shaped by churches' policies and churchgoers' musical preferences.

6. The primary purpose of the passage is to explain

    (A) how the traditional improvisational forms of spirituals were developed into an art-song genre

    (B) why African American church music changed in the early twentieth century

    (C) why European classical music had such a strong influence on music in African American churches

    (D) why church leaders in the industrial North thought it would be beneficial for congregations to distance themselves from their southern, rural pasts

    (E) why music directors of African American churches chose to create new arrangements of traditional spirituals

Explanation

This question requires distinguishing the main purpose of the passage from areas of concern that are secondary to that main purpose. Since the passage focuses on the forces that brought about changes in African American church music during the early twentieth century, **Choice B** is the correct answer. While the passage does mention that some music directors attempted to develop spirituals in ways that would bring them closer to art songs (Choice A), this point is ancillary to the main argument. Similarly, Choices D and E touch on important topics, but these topics are not the primary focus of the passage. The passage also mentions that music directors were "instructed" to emphasize European classical music, but it does not say that this music had a "strong influence" on African American church music, ruling out Choice C.

7. The author implies that the reason spirituals were "out of the question" (line 5) was that

   Ⓐ their performance in traditional form would have conflicted with church leaders' aims

   Ⓑ music directors of churches in the industrial North had an inadequate knowledge of the form

   Ⓒ the social context in which churchgoers would have wanted to hear them no longer existed

   Ⓓ they had been displaced by the newer genre of gospel music

   Ⓔ they were not viewed favorably by churchgoers who preferred music influenced by European classical works

Explanation

The passage states that church leaders encouraged churchgoers "to leave their past, including their music, behind." The "traditional improvisational forms" of this music were part of that past; therefore, their performance would have run counter to church leaders' aims, pointing to **Choice A** as the correct answer. The passage does not mention the extent of northern music directors' knowledge of traditional spirituals, thus ruling out Choice B. Choices C and E can be eliminated because the passage specifically points to congregations' "hunger for traditional music," including spirituals. The passage indicates that the development of gospel music came *after* it was deemed that spirituals were "out of the question," thus ruling out Choice D.

Questions 8 and 9 are based on the following reading passage.

One of the most dramatic changes in astronomers' perception of the solar system came when the two Voyager probes reached Jupiter in 1979. The Voyagers astounded everyone by showing that instead of the expected indistinguishable dead ice balls, Jupiter's four large moons had distinct personalities. Callisto had an old, cratered surface, as expected. Ganymede also had old, cratered regions, but they were broken by swaths of bright, fractured ice. Europa turned out to have a very young crust of fractured ice, apparently overlying an ocean of liquid water that could conceivably support life. Io was the biggest surprise, with nearly a dozen actively erupting volcanoes and a colorful surface of sulfur compounds.

Description

The passage describes how in 1979 the Voyager probes changed astronomers' understanding of Jupiter's four large moons by revealing the moons' distinguishing features.

8. According to the passage, the Voyager probes suggested which of the following about Europa?

   Ⓐ It is the only one of Jupiter's four large moons to show evidence of life.

   Ⓑ Its surface indicates the presence of liquid water.

   Ⓒ Its crust is not as young as Io's.

   Ⓓ It is the most geologically active of the four moons.

   Ⓔ It is the youngest of the four moons.

Explanation

In describing the distinguishing features of each of Jupiter's four large moons, the passage states that Europa's crust seemed to overlie an ocean of liquid water, pointing to **Choice B** as the correct answer choice. The passage suggests that this liquid water might be able to support life but does not mention anything to suggest actual evidence of life (Choice A). Although the passage mentions the ages of some of the moons' features, it does not discuss the relative age of the moons themselves (Choice E). No comparison is specifically made between Europa and Io (Choice C), and it is Io, not Europa, in relation to which the passage mentions geological activity (Choice D).

For the following question, consider each of the choices separately and select all that apply.

9. According to the passage, the two Voyager probes of Jupiter's four large moons led astronomers to think which of the following?

    A That their assumptions regarding Callisto's surface had been correct

    B That there was greater diversity among the moons than they had expected

    C That at least one of the moons might be capable of supporting life forms

Explanation

Choices A, B, and **C** are correct.

    Choice A is correct: the passage states that the Voyager probes showed that Callisto had a "cratered surface, as expected," meaning that the astronomers' assumptions about that moon's surface had been correct.

    Choice B is correct: according to the passage, astronomers were "astounded" by the "distinct personalities" of the moons, which displayed far greater diversity than the astronomers had expected.

    Choice C is correct: the passage states that one of the moons, Io, "could conceivably support life."

For Questions 10 to 13, select the _two_ answer choices that, when used to complete the sentence, fit the meaning of the sentence as a whole _and_ produce completed sentences that are alike in meaning.

10. The easy success of the theatrical version of her novel unfortunately encouraged what became her subsequent _____ the theater—a form essentially alien to her talents as a writer.

    A facility for

    B infatuation with

    C ambivalence about

    D curiosity about

    E uncertainty about

    F attachment to

Explanation

The sentence concerns a writer who produced a successful theatrical version of her novel, an experience that shaped her subsequent feelings about theater. The word pair that fills the blank must correspond with that feeling. Since the writer's first theatrical attempt was an "easy success," we can infer that she developed a strong enthusiasm for theater, even though it was a form "alien to her talents."

Thus the correct answer is **infatuation with** (Choice B) and **attachment to** (Choice F).

11. Because the political situation _____ international communication, French scientific research was at that time uncharacteristically parochial.

   - A inhibited
   - B stimulated
   - C constrained
   - D required
   - E demanded
   - F encouraged

Explanation

The sentence describes how at a certain time French politics caused that country's scientific research to become insular (or parochial) by affecting its communication with other countries. The word that fills the blank describes what happened to international communication that would have resulted in this insularity. Although "stimulated" and "encouraged" are alike in meaning, they suggest heightened communication that would reduce rather than contribute to insularity; and although "required" and "demanded" are also alike in meaning, they too suggest a change in communication that would cause scientific research to be less insular. Only "inhibited" and "constrained" suggest what could have happened to international communication that would cause French scientific research to become more parochial—that is, cut off from scientific developments in other countries.

Thus the correct answer is **inhibited** (Choice A) and **constrained** (Choice C).

12. Because they lack a strong opposing political party on which to focus their rancor, the ruling party's leaders seem to have concentrated their malevolence on _____ each other.

   - A mollifying
   - B appeasing
   - C lambasting
   - D beguiling
   - E obliterating
   - F excoriating

Explanation

The sentence describes a reason (lack of opposition) for a certain condition (intraparty rancor) among a political party's leaders. Since there is no opposing party for the ruling party's leaders to attack, we are told that they appear to have turned their rancor against each other, and the word that fills the blank must describe this state of affairs. Both "lambasting" and "excoriating" evoke the scathing verbal attacks exchanged within the party. Although alike in meaning, "mollifying" and "appeasing" suggest moderating actions that do not produce acrimony. "Beguiling" does not suggest a feeling of bitterness or ill will, and while the sense and connotations of "obliterating" would be consistent with the politicians' malevolence, it cannot be paired with another choice to produce sentences alike in meaning.

Thus the correct answer is **lambasting** (Choice C) and **excoriating** (Choice F).

13. Surprisingly, stories about celebrities, which can at first seem so of the moment and so _____, often have similarities to humanity's oldest and most profound tales.

    A random
    B trivial
    C consequential
    D grave
    E superficial
    F repetitive

Explanation

The words "surprisingly" and "at first seem" indicate a mismatch between perception and reality: despite appearances, celebrity stories are actually like our "oldest and most profound tales." The blank calls for a word that describes celebrity stories' appearance rather than their reality; it should therefore convey the opposite of having deep meaning or lasting value. "Trivial" and "superficial" convey this sense and produce sentences alike in meaning. "Grave" and "consequential," on the other hand, suggest that celebrity stories appear to have a weighty significance, the opposite of what the blank requires. Although "random" might suggest that the stories lack significance or value, it cannot be paired with another word to form a sentence with the same meaning. And while such stories might indeed seem "repetitive," that is a quality that could hold true of profound stories as well.

Thus the correct answer is **trivial** (Choice B) and **superficial** (Choice E).

For each of Questions 14 and 15, select <u>one</u> answer choice unless otherwise instructed.

Trying to identify working conditions that promote high worker productivity, a factory's management dimmed the factory's previously uniform lighting in some areas while brightening it in some others in order to see if lighting levels affected productivity. Surprisingly, in every area with changed lighting levels, though not elsewhere, productivity increased, by comparable margins. It can be concluded that what affects productivity are changes in lighting, but not specific levels of lighting.

Description

The passage describes an experiment designed to test the effects of lighting on worker productivity.

14. Which of the following, if true, calls the conclusion most seriously into question?

   Ⓐ In the areas where lighting levels were changed, management observed workers particularly carefully and interviewed them about their work and working conditions.

   Ⓑ Workplace safety rules define limits on lighting levels, and the changes in lighting levels did not take lighting levels in any of the factory's work areas beyond these limits.

   Ⓒ At the time of the lighting changes, management made no efforts to boost productivity in the areas where lighting was not changed and made no such efforts other than the lighting changes elsewhere.

   Ⓓ Both in the areas where lighting levels were increased and where they were diminished, management received complaints about the new lighting levels from some workers.

   Ⓔ A year after the lighting changes were made, productivity throughout the factory had returned to its prechange levels even though the lighting levels in the factory had not been changed again.

Explanation

Since areas with increased worker productivity shared a common factor (altered lighting) that was not present in places with no productivity changes, the passage concludes that altered lighting conditions were responsible for these productivity increases. This reasoning rests on the assumption that there was only one factor common to the areas with increased productivity: if there were others, any of them might have caused the increase, so a conclusion about the effects of a single one would be called into question. If it were indeed true that workers were closely observed in areas where lighting was altered (Choice A), such practices would suggest just such an additional common factor. Since the close observation, rather than the effects of altered lighting, could have led to increased worker productivity, **Choice A** is the correct answer. The factors mentioned in Choice B (limits on lighting levels in all areas) and Choice C (the lack of any conscious efforts by management to boost productivity) were constant throughout the entire factory, so they do not affect the reasoning behind the conclusion. Without additional information, the fact that some workers complained about the new lighting levels (Choice D) is not obviously relevant to the conclusion

(How many complaining workers were there? How productive were these workers?). The fact that productivity increases abated once lighting levels remained stable for some time (Choice E) could be seen as supporting the conclusion rather than calling it into question.

Question 15 is based on the following reading passage.

Governments often negate their own efforts to nurture public transit by spending large sums to make it easier for people to use cars. When a city's automobile traffic becomes congested, the standard response has long been to provide additional capacity by building new roads or widening existing ones. This approach eventually makes the original problem worse by generating what planners call "induced traffic": every mile of new highway lures passengers from public transit and other more efficient modes of travel and makes it possible for residential and commercial development to spread even farther from urban centers. A better strategy would be to eliminate existing traffic lanes and parking spaces gradually, thereby forcing more drivers to use less environmentally damaging alternatives.

Description

The passage explains how governments sabotage their own efforts to encourage the use of public transit by catering to those who drive automobiles.

15. According to the passage, the spread of residential and commercial development

   (A) is encouraged by the provision of additional capacity on roads
   (B) is significantly slowed by increasing the capacity of public transit systems
   (C) leads to the improvement of public transit
   (D) is unrelated to increasing traffic congestion
   (E) is largely ignored by governments as a factor in planning for roads and transit systems

Explanation

The passage notes that sprawling residential and commercial development follows from the expansion of roadways because roadway expansion enables more drivers to live and shop farther away from urban centers. Thus **Choice A** is the correct answer. While the author's overall argument might suggest that residential and commercial development *could* ultimately be slowed by increasing the capacity of public transit systems (Choice B), the passage does not make that point, and whether such slowing would be "significant" is debatable. Rather than suggesting that residential and commercial development "leads to" the improvement of public transit (Choice C), the passage associates such development with policies that weaken public transit. Since the author correlates increasing congestion with increasing development, Choice D is incorrect. The passage does not comment on whether governments consider residential and commercial development when planning for roadways and transit systems, so Choice E is also incorrect.

Verbal Practice Set 5
15 Questions

For Questions 1 to 5, select one entry for each blank from the corresponding column of choices. Fill all blanks in the way that best completes the text.

1. Her problem with postmodernist architecture is not that it is hedonistic but that it is _____: she reproaches postmodernists for making ironic references in their designs that only other architects can fathom.

Ⓐ austere
Ⓑ bland
Ⓒ limpid
Ⓓ esoteric
Ⓔ parsimonious

2. The author would like to see his colleagues in the sciences jettison some of their overweening certainty that they are on the right track and replace it with a countervailing _____ that the difficulty of their enterprise should inspire.

Ⓐ clarity
Ⓑ didacticism
Ⓒ modesty
Ⓓ avidity
Ⓔ staunchness

3. While the company's CEO professes to be (i)_____ and urges the deal forward, its investors are unlikely to be so (ii)_____ about its prospects. Many were uncomfortable with the way the corporation was forced to spend much of its capital in last year's expansion, and this new venture is potentially even more risky.

Blank (i)	Blank (ii)
Ⓐ apprehensive	Ⓓ indifferent
Ⓑ apathetic	Ⓔ sanguine
Ⓒ confident	Ⓕ anxious

4. Any book that sets out to analyze power in Hollywood has constantly to (i)_____ the reality that there are two kinds of power: ownership (or executive) power and star power. A recent work on the subject provides (ii)_____ description of ownership power, but star power, by contrast, is considerably more nebulous.

Blank (i)	Blank (ii)
Ⓐ pay lip service to	Ⓓ an unconvincing
Ⓑ reckon with	Ⓔ a crisp
Ⓒ be skeptical of	Ⓕ a rambling

5. Repression of painful memories is sometimes called "willed forgetting." Yet true forgetting is (i)_____ than the phenomenon of repressed memory. In spite of the effort that it (ii)_____, repressing unwanted memories is less (iii)_____ than truly forgetting them, for repressed memories are prone to come back.

Blank (i)	Blank (ii)	Blank (iii)
Ⓐ less controlled	Ⓓ eases	Ⓖ permanent
Ⓑ different in its effect	Ⓔ conveys	Ⓗ arduous
Ⓒ far more common	Ⓕ entails	Ⓘ immediate

For each of Questions 6 to 11, select <u>one</u> answer choice unless otherwise instructed.

Questions 6 and 7 are based on the following reading passage.

Matisse's art, with its spectacular immediacy and its mysterious depths, poses confounding problems for analysis. When Hilary Spurling writes of *The Piano Lesson* that "the picture cannot be confined to any single source or meaning," she might be writing of any of Matisse's works. Picasso's themes, with their collage of traditional signs and symbols, are far more susceptible to conventional iconographic analysis than anything in Matisse. Similarly, the cubism of Picasso and Braque, while rejecting traditional perspective, can nevertheless be studied as an inversion of traditional norms, using the same tools that one uses to study those norms. But the solutions that Matisse arrives at are always idiosyncratic and tend to be unrelated to any system of ideas. Intuition is his only system.

line
5

For the following question, consider each of the choices separately and select all that apply.

6. It can be inferred that the author of the passage would agree with which of the following comparisons between Picasso's and Matisse's art?

   Ⓐ Picasso's art uses traditional symbolism in a way that Matisse's art does not.
   Ⓑ Picasso's art does not evoke as deep an emotional response as Matisse's art does.
   Ⓒ Picasso's art is guided less completely by intuition than Matisse's art is.

7. In the context in which it appears, "susceptible to" (line 5) most nearly means
   Ⓐ vulnerable to
   Ⓑ amenable to
   Ⓒ influenced by
   Ⓓ prone to
   Ⓔ exploitable by

Questions 8 to 11 are based on the following reading passage.

As part of a larger inquiry into what food resources a group typically shares and which are regarded as private property, anthropologists have attempted to determine whether seeds and piñon nuts fell into the latter category among populations indigenous to the Great Basin (present-day California) around A.D. 1400. Researchers note that seeds and piñon nuts could be harvested and processed by a single individual, unlike other resources that required cooperation for harvesting. For example, although a hunting net could be made by an individual, large numbers of people were required to drive small mammals into the nets. Consequently, any animals trapped were typically shared by all involved. Additionally, people cooperated to cook tubers, which were optimally prepared by steaming in pit hearths. Although a pit hearth could be excavated and used by an individual, in fuel-scarce areas large pits were used to conserve firewood. The large size of such pits required them to be constructed in open areas where everyone could see them. Both of these factors make hoarding foods cooked in pit hearths difficult. Seeds, however, could be cooked in private rather than in a pit hearth. Since seeds and piñon nuts were more amenable than other resources to individual harvesting and processing, sharing them might not have been required.

8. The primary purpose of the passage is to
   Ⓐ present information that sheds light on a particular question
   Ⓑ offer a refutation of a particular argument
   Ⓒ reconcile two conflicting theories
   Ⓓ outline some problems with a type of inquiry
   Ⓔ provide an explanation for an unexpected observation

9. Which of the following best describes the function of the sentence in lines 11–12 ("The large . . . see them")?
   Ⓐ It challenges a claim made earlier in the passage.
   Ⓑ It supplies an example of an activity mentioned earlier in the passage.
   Ⓒ It elaborates on a research finding mentioned earlier in the passage.
   Ⓓ It provides support for a claim made later in the passage.
   Ⓔ It introduces a hypothesis that is further developed later in the passage.

10. The passage suggests which of the following about pit hearths?
   Ⓐ Pit hearths could have been used by single individuals in areas where fuel was abundant.
   Ⓑ Pit hearths probably played an important role in the preparation of seeds and piñon nuts.
   Ⓒ People of the Great Basin were unlikely to have cooperated to build pit hearths.
   Ⓓ When firewood was abundant, pit hearths in the Great Basin tended to be larger.
   Ⓔ Even individually built pit hearths were generally shared with others.

11. The author mentions "tubers" (line 9) primarily in order to

    Ⓐ illustrate conditions under which foods were likely to be shared

    Ⓑ cite evidence suggesting that large pit hearths were used by people of the Great Basin

    Ⓒ contrast two different food preparation methods used by people of the Great Basin

    Ⓓ suggest that food hoarding was rare among the people of the Great Basin

    Ⓔ consider the possibility that some foods that were harvested by individuals were nonetheless treated as shared resources

---

For Questions 12 to 14, select the <u>two</u> answer choices that, when used to complete the sentence, fit the meaning of the sentence as a whole <u>and</u> produce completed sentences that are alike in meaning.

---

12. Edith Wharton described herself as "an omnivorous reader," a fact easily _____ by the impressive range of allusion in her fiction.

    A eclipsed

    B qualified

    C unsettled

    D confirmed

    E overshadowed

    F corroborated

13. The plan, which the engineers said would save the aquifer by reducing pumping to _____ levels, has passed a governmental environmental review but faces opposition from outdoor and environmental groups.

    A innocuous

    B feasible

    C practicable

    D minimal

    E remedial

    F benign

14. The point we might still take from the First World War is the old one that wars are always, as one historian aptly put it, _____: they produce unforeseeable results.

    A unsurprising

    B astounding

    C conventional

    D ruinous

    E stunning

    F devastating

For Question 15, select <u>one</u> answer choice.

Question 15 is based on the following reading passage.

Sensations of nausea in people are accompanied by higher-than-normal blood levels of a particular hormone, vasopressin. Therefore, either nausea triggers the production of vasopressin or abnormally high levels of vasopressin cause nausea.

15. Which of the following is an assumption on which the argument relies?
   - (A) Sensations of nausea are never present when vasopressin is at low levels.
   - (B) High levels of vasopressin have no effect on the body other than to cause sensations of nausea.
   - (C) Sensations of nausea and high levels of vasopressin do not have a common cause that makes them occur together.
   - (D) Mild nausea causes the release of small quantities of vasopressin, and high levels of vasopressin cause intense nausea.
   - (E) People differ in the blood level of vasopressin that is normal for them.

Answer Key

Practice Set 5. Verbal Reasoning

Question Number	P+	Correct Answer
1	67	**Choice D:** esoteric
2	63	**Choice C:** modesty
3	64	**Choice C:** confident; **Choice E:** sanguine
4	67	**Choice B:** reckon with; **Choice E:** a crisp
5	41	**Choice B:** different in its effect; **Choice F:** entails; **Choice G:** permanent
6	66	**Choice A:** Picasso's art uses traditional symbolism in a way that Matisse's art does not. AND **Choice C:** Picasso's art is guided less completely by intuition than Matisse's art is.
7	21	**Choice B:** amenable to
8	72	**Choice A:** present information that sheds light on a particular question
9	57	**Choice D:** It provides support for a claim made later in the passage.
10	51	**Choice A:** Pit hearths could have been used by single individuals in areas where fuel was abundant.
11	42	**Choice A:** illustrate conditions under which foods were likely to be shared
12	67	**Choice D:** confirmed AND **Choice F:** corroborated
13	24	**Choice A:** innocuous AND **Choice F:** benign
14	53	**Choice B:** astounding AND **Choice E:** stunning
15	34	**Choice C:** Sensations of nausea and high levels of vasopressin do not have a common cause that makes them occur together.

Verbal Practice Set 5
15 Questions with Explanations

> For Questions 1 to 5, select one entry for each blank from the corresponding column of choices. Fill all blanks in the way that best completes the text.

1. Her problem with postmodernist architecture is not that it is hedonistic but that it is _____: she reproaches postmodernists for making ironic references in their designs that only other architects can fathom.

Ⓐ	austere
Ⓑ	bland
Ⓒ	limpid
Ⓓ	esoteric
Ⓔ	parsimonious

Explanation

The sentence is concerned with a woman's criticism of postmodernist architecture. The word "but" suggests that the correct answer for Blank (i) should be distinct from "hedonistic"; at the same time, the correct answer must describe postmodernist architecture in a way that corresponds to the woman's criticism of it: that it contains "ironic references" that "only other architects can fathom." Of the answer choices, only "esoteric"—requiring knowledge limited to a small, select group—satisfies both criteria.

   Thus the correct answer is **esoteric** (Choice D).

2. The author would like to see his colleagues in the sciences jettison some of their overweening certainty that they are on the right track and replace it with a countervailing _____ that the difficulty of their enterprise should inspire.

Ⓐ	clarity
Ⓑ	didacticism
Ⓒ	modesty
Ⓓ	avidity
Ⓔ	staunchness

Explanation

The sentence indicates that the author would like an existing attitude toward scientific work to be replaced by a different one. The word "countervailing" suggests that the desired attitude could offset the effects of scientists' current "overweening certainty" in the correctness of their approach. The word that fills the blank, then, must indicate a willingness to question one's methods and allow for the possibility of one's own errors. "Modesty" suggests such willingness, whereas "clarity," "didacticism," "avidity," and "staunchness" all are qualities that might only add to scientists' confidence that their approach is the correct one.

   Thus the correct answer is **modesty** (Choice C).

3.   While the company's CEO professes to be (i)_____ and urges the deal forward, its investors arc unlikely to be so (ii)_____ about its prospects. Many were uncomfortable at the way the corporation was forced to spend much of its capital in last year's expansion, and this new venture is potentially even more risky.

Blank (i)	Blank (ii)
Ⓐ apprehensive	Ⓓ indifferent
Ⓑ apathetic	Ⓔ sanguine
Ⓒ confident	Ⓕ anxious

Explanation

The second sentence of the passage explains the reasoning behind investors' likely attitude toward a business deal. Because the investors were "uncomfortable" about the company's previous spending on an expansion, and because this "new venture" might be "even more risky," it is reasonable to assume that the investors feel anxious about the deal. While "anxious" is among the choices for the second blank, it is important to note that this blank does *not* describe the investors' attitude; rather, it describes an attitude that they are "unlikely" to have. Anxious people are unlikely to be "sanguine" (optimistic), so that is the correct choice for the second blank. In the first sentence, the word "while" suggests that the CEO's attitude toward a deal contrasts with the investors' outlook; the blank, then, should contain a synonym for "sanguine." "Confident" fits that description, and its correctness is confirmed by the information that the CEO "urges the deal forward"—something that an "apprehensive" or "apathetic" CEO would be unlikely to do.

Thus the correct answer is **confident** (Choice C) and **sanguine** (Choice E).

4.   Any book that sets out to analyze power in Hollywood has constantly to (i)_____ the reality that there are two kinds of power: ownership (or executive) power and star power. A recent work on the subject provides (ii)_____ description of ownership power, but star power, by contrast, is considerably more nebulous.

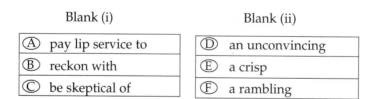

Blank (i)	Blank (ii)
Ⓐ pay lip service to	Ⓓ an unconvincing
Ⓑ reckon with	Ⓔ a crisp
Ⓒ be skeptical of	Ⓕ a rambling

Explanation

The paragraph is concerned with two kinds of power and how they are treated in books that aim to "analyze power in Hollywood." It is hard to select the correct answer for Blank (i) in the first sentence without first considering the second sentence. In the second sentence, "by contrast" suggests that the word that fills Blank (ii) to describe the recent book's description of ownership power should mean the opposite of "nebulous." Of the answer choices, only "crisp" satisfies that criterion: a crisp description is the opposite of a nebulous one. Returning to Blank (i), "reckon with" makes the most sense in the blank: the assessment of the "recent work" in the second sentence confirms that any book about power in Hollywood must consider—rather than pay lip service to or be skeptical of—the two kinds of power in Hollywood.

Thus the correct answer is **reckon with** (Choice B) and **a crisp** (Choice E).

5. Repression of painful memories is sometimes called "willed forgetting." Yet true forgetting is (i)_____ than the phenomenon of repressed memory. In spite of the effort that it (ii)_____ , repressing unwanted memories is less (iii)_____ than truly forgetting them, for repressed memories are prone to come back.

Blank (i)	Blank (ii)	Blank (iii)
Ⓐ less controlled	Ⓓ eases	Ⓖ permanent
Ⓑ different in its effect	Ⓔ conveys	Ⓗ arduous
Ⓒ far more common	Ⓕ entails	Ⓘ immediate

Explanation

This question is best answered by first completing the third blank. The third sentence sets up a comparison between repressing memories and forgetting them. The word "for" indicates that the last part of the sentence—"repressed memories are prone to come back"—presents the basis of that comparison. Choice G, "permanent," is the only choice that is related to the tendency to come back. Working backward, the sentence begins with "In spite of," suggesting that the correct choice for the second blank is contrary to what one might expect. One would ordinarily expect that something entailing effort would be more rather than less permanent. Neither "eases" nor "conveys" sets up such an expectation. Filling the second and third blanks makes it possible to fill the first blank. Nothing in the completed text suggests that true forgetting is "more common" or "less controlled" than the repression of painful memories, but it does suggest that true forgetting is different in its effect—it is more permanent. Thus, Choice B, "different in its effect," is correct.

Thus, the correct answer is **different in its effect** (Choice B), **entails** (Choice F), and **permanent** (Choice G).

For each of Questions 6 to 11, select <u>one</u> answer choice unless otherwise instructed.

Questions 6 and 7 are based on the following reading passage.

Matisse's art, with its spectacular immediacy and its mysterious depths, poses confounding problems for analysis. When Hilary Spurling writes of *The Piano Lesson* that "the picture cannot be confined to any single source or meaning," she might be writing of any of Matisse's works. Picasso's themes, with their collage of traditional signs and symbols,
line 5 are far more susceptible to conventional iconographic analysis than anything in Matisse. Similarly, the cubism of Picasso and Braque, while rejecting traditional perspective, can nevertheless be studied as an inversion of traditional norms, using the same tools that one uses to study those norms. But the solutions that Matisse arrives at are always idiosyncratic and tend to be unrelated to any system of ideas. Intuition is his only system.

Description

The passage argues that Matisse's art is particularly challenging to analyze and justifies this claim by comparing his work to the art of Picasso.

For the following question, consider each of the choices separately and select all that apply.

6.   It can be inferred that the author of the passage would agree with which of the following comparisons between Picasso's and Matisse's art?

   [A] Picasso's art uses traditional symbolism in a way that Matisse's art does not.

   [B] Picasso's art does not evoke as deep an emotional response as Matisse's art does.

   [C] Picasso's art is guided less completely by intuition than Matisse's art is.

Explanation

Choices A and C are correct. The question asks the reader to identify differences between Picasso's and Matisse's art with which the author would agree.

   Choice A is correct: the author argues that Picasso's themes incorporate "traditional signs and symbols" in ways that are "far more susceptible to conventional iconographic analysis" than Matisse's themes; in so doing, the author implies that Picasso's art uses traditional symbolism in a way that Matisse's art does not.

   Choice B is incorrect: the author does not consider the emotional response produced by Picasso's or Matisse's art.

   Choice C is correct: the author argues that Matisse's art is more challenging to analyze than Picasso's art and concludes the passage by suggesting why this is the case: unlike Picasso's art, which relates to "traditional perspective" in that it represents "an inversion of traditional norms," Matisse's art tends to be "unrelated to any system of ideas," with "intuition [being] his only system." In making this claim, the author implies that Picasso's art is guided less completely by intuition than Matisse's art.

7.   In the context in which it appears, "susceptible to" (line 5) most nearly means

   (A) vulnerable to

   (B) amenable to

   (C) influenced by

   (D) prone to

   (E) exploitable by

Explanation

The author uses "susceptible to" when comparing Picasso's art to Matisse's. In the surrounding context, the author argues that Matisse's art is more challenging to analyze than Picasso's art. Given this and the fact that Picasso's themes incorporate "traditional signs and symbols," it is reasonable to infer that the author thinks Picasso's art is more open or receptive to "conventional iconographic analysis" than Matisse's art. This points to **Choice B**: of the answer choices, "amenable to" is closest in meaning to "open to." Though "vulnerable to" (Choice A) and "prone to" (Choice D) may be tempting—since both could be synonyms of "susceptible to" in certain contexts—the former suggests a sense of weakness and the latter a sense of being naturally inclined to something, neither of which the author attributes to Picasso's art.

Questions 8 to 11 are based on the following reading passage.

As part of a larger inquiry into what food resources a group typically shares and which are regarded as private property, anthropologists have attempted to determine whether seeds and piñon nuts fell into the latter category among populations indigenous to the Great Basin (present-day California) around A.D. 1400. Researchers note that seeds and piñon nuts could be harvested and processed by a single individual, unlike other resources that required cooperation for harvesting. For example, although a hunting net could be made by an individual, large numbers of people were required to drive small mammals into the nets. Consequently, any animals trapped were typically shared by all involved. Additionally, people cooperated to cook tubers, which were optimally prepared by steaming in pit hearths. Although a pit hearth could be excavated and used by an individual, in fuel-scarce areas large pits were used to conserve firewood. The large size of such pits required them to be constructed in open areas where everyone could see them. Both of these factors make hoarding foods cooked in pit hearths difficult. Seeds, however, could be cooked in private rather than in a pit hearth. Since seeds and piñon nuts were more amenable than other resources to individual harvesting and processing, sharing them might not have been required.

line 5

line 10

line 15

Description

The passage contextualizes a research question—whether seeds and piñon nuts in the Great Basin were considered communal or private food resources—by giving examples of communal foods and discussing some factors that might have influenced how foods were categorized.

8. The primary purpose of the passage is to
   - Ⓐ present information that sheds light on a particular question
   - Ⓑ offer a refutation of a particular argument
   - Ⓒ reconcile two conflicting theories
   - Ⓓ outline some problems with a type of inquiry
   - Ⓔ provide an explanation for an unexpected observation

Explanation

This question requires summarizing the main purpose of the passage. Since the passage is focused on explaining the context of a research question by discussing examples of the categories involved (what food resources are typically shared and which are regarded as private property) and considerations affecting how categorizations were made, the correct answer is **Choice A**, "present information that sheds light on a particular question." The passage does not present a specific argument that could be refuted (Choice B) or two conflicting theories (Choice C), nor does it suggest any problems associated with the line of inquiry it discusses (Choice D). While it makes several observations, there is no indication that any of them are "unexpected" (Choice E).

9. Which of the following best describes the function of the sentence in lines 11-12 ("The large . . . see them")?
   - Ⓐ It challenges a claim made earlier in the passage.
   - Ⓑ It supplies an example of an activity mentioned earlier in the passage.
   - Ⓒ It elaborates on a research finding mentioned earlier in the passage.
   - Ⓓ It provides support for a claim made later in the passage.
   - Ⓔ It introduces a hypothesis that is further developed later in the passage.

Explanation

The sentence this question asks about points out that the large size and the exposed location of pit hearths made them conspicuous; the following sentence cites these qualities when claiming that "hoarding foods cooked in pit hearths" was "difficult." This points to **Choice D**, which mentions providing "support for a claim made later in the passage," as the correct answer.

10. The passage suggests which of the following about pit hearths?

    Ⓐ Pit hearths could have been used by single individuals in areas where fuel was abundant.

    Ⓑ Pit hearths probably played an important role in the preparation of seeds and piñon nuts.

    Ⓒ People of the Great Basin were unlikely to have cooperated to build pit hearths.

    Ⓓ When firewood was abundant, pit hearths in the Great Basin tended to be larger.

    Ⓔ Even individually built pit hearths were generally shared with others.

Explanation

The passage states that while pit hearths "could be excavated and used by an individual, in fuel-scarce areas large pits were used to conserve firewood." By portraying fuel scarcity as the constraint preventing individual pit hearth use, the passage suggests that individual use might have been possible where fuel was abundant, pointing to **Choice A** as the correct answer. The passage directly contradicts the idea that pit hearths were important for preparing seeds and piñon nuts (Choice B). Although the passage allows that pit hearths could have been individually excavated, it does not imply that cooperative building was unlikely (Choice C), nor does it suggest how individually built pits might have been used (Choice E). The passage also does not suggest that conditions of greater fuel abundance led to larger pit hearths (Choice D).

11. The author mentions "tubers" (line 9) primarily in order to

    Ⓐ illustrate conditions under which foods were likely to be shared

    Ⓑ cite evidence suggesting that large pit hearths were used by people of the Great Basin

    Ⓒ contrast two different food preparation methods used by people of the Great Basin

    Ⓓ suggest that food hoarding was rare among the people of the Great Basin

    Ⓔ consider the possibility that some foods that were harvested by individuals were nonetheless treated as shared resources

Explanation

In discussing the question of whether seeds and piñon nuts were communal or private food resources, the passage introduces two examples of communal foods. The first is animals trapped by netting, a cooperative hunting strategy; the second is tubers, root vegetables requiring a preparation method that was likely cooperative, or at least difficult to hide from others. The passage uses both examples to discuss some conditions under which food was likely seen as a communal (shared) resource, pointing to **Choice A** as the correct answer. While the passage does mention that tubers were cooked in large pit hearths, the existence of such hearths is presented as a given: tubers are not mentioned as evidence for their use (Choice B). The preparation of tubers does contrast with that of seeds, which could be "cooked in private," but developing that contrast is not the primary reason that tubers are mentioned (Choice C); rather, the contrast serves to further the passage's distinction between communal and private foods. Finally, the passage mentions nothing about the prevalence of food hoarding (Choice D) or whether tubers were harvested by individuals (Choice E), so those choices cannot be correct.

For Questions 12 to 14, select the <u>two</u> answer choices that, when used to complete the sentence, fit the meaning of the sentence as a whole <u>and</u> produce completed sentences that are alike in meaning.

---

12. Edith Wharton described herself as "an omnivorous reader," a fact easily _____ by the impressive range of allusion in her fiction.

    A eclipsed
    B qualified
    C unsettled
    D confirmed
    E overshadowed
    F corroborated

Explanation

The sentence suggests that an aspect of Wharton's fiction (its "impressive range of allusion") illustrates something pertinent about Wharton's description of herself as "an omnivorous reader." Since this description emphasizes the wide range of reading material that Wharton consumed, the word that fills the blank should indicate that her description matches her ability to refer to a wide variety of other texts in her own writing. Only "confirmed" and "corroborated" suggest such an agreement between her self-description and her densely allusive prose. Although "eclipsed" and "overshadowed" are alike in meaning, they suggest that Wharton's self-description is *not* in accord with, and in fact falls short of, the allusive quality of her fiction. Likewise, "qualified" and "unsettled" do not suggest agreement between her claim and her writing, and neither choice can be paired with another choice to produce sentences that are alike in meaning.

Thus the correct answer is **confirmed** (Choice D) and **corroborated** (Choice F).

13. The plan, which the engineers said would save the aquifer by reducing pumping to _____ levels, has passed a governmental environmental review but faces opposition from outdoor and environmental groups.

    A innocuous
    B feasible
    C practicable
    D minimal
    E remedial
    F benign

Explanation

If the engineers think that the reduced levels will save the aquifer, they may describe the reduced levels as innocuous, minimal, remedial, or benign. Of these words, only "innocuous" and "benign" produce sentences with the same meaning. The two words "feasible" and "practicable" are similar in meaning, but do not fit the context well, because they imply that the current levels are not feasible or practicable, conflicting with the implication that the current levels, though perhaps undesirable, are nevertheless entirely feasible.

Thus, the correct answer is **innocuous** (Choice A) and **benign** (Choice F).

14. The point we might still take from the First World War is the old one that wars are always, as one historian aptly put it, _____: they produce unforeseeable results.

  [A] unsurprising
  [B] astounding
  [C] conventional
  [D] ruinous
  [E] stunning
  [F] devastating

Explanation

The colon after the blank indicates a definitional relationship between the blanked word and the phrase that follows the colon. The two answer choices for which "they produce unforeseeable results" would most clearly serve as a definition are "astounding" and "stunning." While "ruinous" and "devastating" might be adjectives describing the effects of war, they clearly do not fit the logical structure of this sentence, since they are not by definition "unforeseeable."

Thus, the correct answer is **astounding** (Choice B) and **stunning** (Choice E).

For Question 15, select <u>one</u> answer choice.

Question 15 is based on the following reading passage.

Sensations of nausea in people are accompanied by higher-than-normal blood levels of a particular hormone, vasopressin. Therefore, either nausea triggers the production of vasopressin or abnormally high levels of vasopressin cause nausea.

15. Which of the following is an assumption on which the argument relies?

  (A) Sensations of nausea are never present when vasopressin is at low levels.
  (B) High levels of vasopressin have no effect on the body other than to cause sensations of nausea.
  (C) Sensations of nausea and high levels of vasopressin do not have a common cause that makes them occur together.
  (D) Mild nausea causes the release of small quantities of vasopressin, and high levels of vasopressin cause intense nausea.
  (E) People differ in the blood level of vasopressin that is normal for them.

Explanation

In stating its conclusion, the passage assumes that there are only two possible lines of causation for the observed correlation between nausea and vasopressin levels: either nausea triggers elevated vasopressin or abnormal levels of vasopressin cause nausea. It is conceivable, however, that another underlying factor, a "common cause," could simultaneously produce both elevated vasopressin levels and nausea, making **Choice C** the correct answer. The passage neither states nor implies that nausea and high levels of vasopressin *always* occur together; its conclusions could be true even if the correlation between nausea and elevated vasopressin applies to only a subset of all cases of nausea. Therefore, its argument does not depend on an assumption that nausea never occurs when vasopressin levels are low (Choice A). The passage does not touch on the question of whether high levels of vasopressin have effects other than causing nausea, ruling out Choice B. It also does not correlate the intensity of nausea with levels of vasopressin, ruling out Choice D. And the assumption presented in Choice E is not implicit in the logic of the passage: the argument concerns "higher-than-normal" or "elevated" levels of vasopressin without assuming that people have varying baseline levels of the hormone.

6 GRE Quantitative Reasoning: Overview

Your goals for this chapter

◣ Learn the four types of GRE Quantitative Reasoning questions
◣ Learn general problem-solving steps and strategies
◣ Get tips for answering each question type
◣ Study sample Quantitative Reasoning questions with explanations
◣ Learn how to use the on-screen calculator

Overview of the Quantitative Reasoning Measure

The Quantitative Reasoning measure of the GRE General Test assesses your:

- basic mathematical skills
- understanding of elementary mathematical concepts
- ability to reason quantitatively and to model and solve problems with quantitative methods

Some of the Quantitative Reasoning questions are posed in real-life settings, while others are posed in purely mathematical settings. Many of the questions are word problems, which must be translated and modeled mathematically. The skills, concepts, and abilities are assessed in the following four content areas:

Arithmetic topics include properties and types of integers, such as divisibility, factorization, prime numbers, remainders, and odd and even integers; arithmetic operations, exponents, and roots; and concepts such as estimation, percent, ratio, rate, absolute value, the number line, decimal representation, and sequences of numbers.

Algebra topics include operations with exponents; factoring and simplifying algebraic expressions; relations, functions, equations, and inequalities; solving linear and quadratic equations and inequalities; solving simultaneous equations and inequalities; setting up equations to solve word problems; and coordinate geometry, including graphs of functions, equations, and inequalities, intercepts, and slopes of lines.

Geometry topics include parallel and perpendicular lines, circles, triangles— including isosceles, equilateral, and 30°-60°-90° triangles—quadrilaterals, other polygons, congruent and similar figures, three-dimensional figures, area, perimeter, volume, the Pythagorean theorem, and angle measurement in degrees. The ability to construct proofs is not tested.

Data analysis topics include basic descriptive statistics, such as mean, median, mode, range, standard deviation, interquartile range, quartiles, and percentiles; interpretation of data in tables and graphs, such as line graphs, bar graphs, circle graphs, boxplots, scatterplots, and frequency distributions; elementary probability, such as probabilities of compound events and independent events; conditional probability; random variables and probability distributions, including normal distributions; and counting methods, such as combinations, permutations, and Venn diagrams. These topics are typically taught in high school algebra courses or introductory statistics courses. Inferential statistics is not tested.

The content in these areas includes high school mathematics and statistics at a level that is generally no higher than a second course in algebra; it does not include trigonometry, calculus, or other higher-level mathematics. The publication *Math Review for the GRE General Test*, which is available at **www.ets.org/gre/prepare**, provides detailed information about the content of the Quantitative Reasoning measure. The *Math Review* is Chapter 9 in this book.

The mathematical symbols, terminology, and conventions used in the Quantitative Reasoning measure are those that are standard at the high school level. For example, the positive direction of a number line is to the right, distances are nonnegative, and prime numbers are greater than 1. Whenever nonstandard notation is used in a question, it is explicitly introduced in the question.

In addition to conventions, there are some important assumptions about numbers and figures that are listed in the Quantitative Reasoning section directions:

- All numbers used are real numbers.
- All figures are assumed to lie in a plane unless otherwise indicated.
- Geometric figures, such as lines, circles, triangles, and quadrilaterals, **are not necessarily** drawn to scale. That is, you should **not** assume that quantities such as lengths and angle measures are as they appear in a figure. You should assume, however, that lines shown as straight are actually straight, points on a line are in the order shown, and more generally, all geometric objects are in the relative positions shown. For questions with geometric figures, you should base your answers on geometric reasoning, not on estimating or comparing quantities by sight or by measurement.
- Coordinate systems, such as xy-planes and number lines, **are** drawn to scale; therefore, you can read, estimate, or compare quantities in such figures by sight or by measurement.
- Graphical data presentations, such as bar graphs, circle graphs, and line graphs, **are** drawn to scale; therefore, you can read, estimate, or compare data values by sight or by measurement.

More about conventions and assumptions appears in the publication *Mathematical Conventions for the GRE General Test*, which is available at **www.ets.org/gre/prepare** and at the end of this chapter.

General Problem-Solving Steps

Questions in the Quantitative Reasoning measure ask you to model and solve problems using quantitative, or mathematical, methods. Generally, there are three basic steps in solving a mathematics problem:

Step 1: Understand the problem
Step 2: Carry out a strategy for solving the problem
Step 3: Check your answer

Here is a description of the three steps, followed by a list of useful strategies for solving mathematics problems.

Step 1: Understand the Problem

The first step is to read the statement of the problem carefully to make sure you understand the information given and the problem you are being asked to solve.

Some information may describe certain quantities. Quantitative information may be given in words or mathematical expressions, or a combination of both. Also, in some problems you may need to read and understand quantitative information in data presentations, geometric figures, or coordinate systems. Other information may take the form of formulas, definitions, or conditions that must be satisfied by the quantities. For example, the conditions may be equations or inequalities, or may be words that can be translated into equations or inequalities.

In addition to understanding the information you are given, it is important to understand what you need to accomplish in order to solve the problem. For example, what unknown quantities must be found? In what form must they be expressed?

Step 2: Carry Out a Strategy for Solving the Problem

Solving a mathematics problem requires more than understanding a description of the problem, that is, more than understanding the quantities, the data, the conditions, the unknowns, and all other mathematical facts related to the problem. It requires determining *what* mathematical facts to use and *when* and *how* to use those facts to develop a solution to the problem. It requires a strategy.

Mathematics problems are solved by using a wide variety of strategies. Also, there may be different ways to solve a given problem. Therefore, you should develop a repertoire of problem-solving strategies, as well as a sense of which strategies are likely to work best in solving particular problems. Attempting to solve a problem without a strategy may lead to a lot of work without producing a correct solution.

After you determine a strategy, you must carry it out. If you get stuck, check your work to see if you made an error in your solution. It is important to have a flexible, open mindset. If you check your solution and cannot find an error or if your solution strategy is simply not working, look for a different strategy.

Step 3: Check Your Answer

When you arrive at an answer, you should check that it is reasonable and computationally correct.

- Have you answered the question that was asked?
- Is your answer reasonable in the context of the question? Checking that an answer is reasonable can be as simple as recalling a basic mathematical fact and checking whether your answer is consistent with that fact. For example, the probability of an event must be between 0 and 1, inclusive, and the area of a geometric figure must be positive. In other cases, you can use estimation to check that your answer is reasonable. For example, if your solution involves adding three numbers, each of which is between 100 and 200, estimating the sum tells you that the sum must be between 300 and 600.
- Did you make a computational mistake in arriving at your answer? A key-entry error using the calculator? You can check for errors in each step in your solution. Or you may be able to check directly that your solution is correct. For example, if you solved the equation $7(3x - 2) + 4 = 95$ for x and got the answer $x = 5$, you can check your answer by substituting $x = 5$ into the equation to see that $7(3(5) - 2) + 4 = 95$.

Strategies

There are no set rules—applicable to all mathematics problems—to determine the best strategy. The ability to determine a strategy that will work grows as you solve more and more problems. What follows are brief descriptions of useful strategies, along with references to questions in this chapter that you can answer with the help of particular strategies. These strategies do not form a complete list, and, aside from grouping the first four strategies together, they are not presented in any particular order.

The first four strategies are translation strategies, where one representation of a mathematics problem is translated into another.

Strategy 1: Translate from Words to an Arithmetic or Algebraic Representation

Word problems are often solved by translating textual information into an arithmetic or algebraic representation. For example, an "odd integer" can be represented by the expression $2n + 1$, where n is an integer; and the statement "the cost of a taxi trip is $3.00, plus $1.25 for each mile" can be represented by the equation $c = 3 + 1.25m$. More generally, translation occurs when you understand a word problem in mathematical terms in order to model the problem mathematically.

• See question 4 on page 192 and question 5 on page 199.

Strategy 2: Translate from Words to a Figure or Diagram

To solve a problem in which a figure is described but not shown, draw your own figure. Draw the figure as accurately as possible, labeling as many parts as possible, including any unknowns.

Drawing figures can help in geometry problems as well as in other types of problems. For example, in probability and counting problems, drawing a diagram can sometimes make it easier to analyze the relevant data and to notice relationships and dependencies.

• See question 2 on page 190.

Strategy 3: Translate from an Algebraic to a Graphical Representation

Many algebra problems can be represented graphically in a coordinate system, whether the system is a number line if the problem involves one variable, or a coordinate plane if the problem involves two variables. Such graphs can clarify relationships that may be less obvious in algebraic representations.

• See question 3 on page 191.

Strategy 4: Translate from a Figure to an Arithmetic or Algebraic Representation

When a figure is given in a problem, it may be effective to express relationships among the various parts of the figure using arithmetic or algebra.

• See question 4 on page 184 and question 3 on page 198.

Strategy 5: Simplify an Arithmetic or Algebraic Representation

Arithmetic and algebraic representations include both expressions and equations. Your facility in simplifying a representation can often lead to a quick solution. Examples include converting from a percent to a decimal, converting from one measurement unit to another, combining like terms in an algebraic expression, and simplifying an equation until its solutions are evident.

- See question 6 on page 176 and question 4 on page 199.

Strategy 6: Add to a Geometric Figure

Sometimes you can add useful lines, points, or circles to a geometric figure to facilitate solving a problem. You can also add any given information—as well as any new information as you derive it—to the figure to help you see relationships within the figure more easily, for example, the length of a line segment or the measure of an angle.

- See question 3 on page 191.

Strategy 7: Find a Pattern

Patterns are found throughout mathematics. Identifying a pattern is often the first step in understanding a complex mathematical situation. Pattern recognition yields insight that may point in the direction of a complete solution to the problem or simply help you generate a hypothesis, which requires further exploration using another strategy. In a problem where you suspect there is a pattern but don't recognize it yet, working with particular instances can help you identify the pattern. Once a pattern is identified, it can be used to answer questions.

- See question 4 on page 196.

Strategy 8: Search for a Mathematical Relationship

More general than patterns, mathematical relationships exist throughout mathematics. Problems may involve quantities that are related algebraically, sets that are related logically, or figures that are related geometrically. Also, there may be relationships between information given textually, algebraically, graphically, etc. To express relationships between quantities, it is often helpful to introduce one or more variables to represent the quantities. Once a relationship is understood and expressed, it is often the key to solving a problem.

- See question 8 on page 187 and question 3 on page 195.

Strategy 9: Estimate

Sometimes it is not necessary to perform extensive calculations to solve a problem—it is sufficient to estimate the answer. The degree of accuracy needed depends on the particular question being asked. Care should be taken to determine how far off your estimate could possibly be from the actual answer to the question. Estimation can also be used to check whether the answer to a question is reasonable.

- See question 3 on page 184 and question 4 on page 192.

Strategy 10: Trial and Error

Version 1: Make a Reasonable Guess and Then Refine It
For some problems, the fastest way to a solution is to make a reasonable guess at the answer, check it, and then improve on your guess. This is especially useful if the number of possible answers is limited. In other problems, this approach may help you at least to understand better what is going on in the problem.

- See question 1 on page 194.

Version 2: Try More Than One Value of a Variable

To explore problems containing variables, it is useful to substitute values for the variables. It often helps to substitute more than one value for each variable. How many values to choose and what values are good choices depends on the problem. Also dependent on the problem is whether this approach, by itself, will yield a solution or whether the approach will simply help you generate a hypothesis that requires further exploration using another strategy.

- See question 2 on page 183 and question 5 on page 185.

Strategy 11: Divide into Cases

Some problems are quite complex. To solve such problems you may need to divide them into smaller, less complex problems, which are restricted cases of the original problem. When you divide a problem into cases, you should consider whether or not to include all possibilities. For example, if you want to prove that a certain statement is true for all integers, it may be best to show that it is true for all positive integers, then show it is true for all negative integers, and then show it is true for zero. In doing that, you will have shown that the statement is true for all integers, because each integer is either positive, negative, or zero.

- See question 1 on page 183 and question 2 on page 194.

Strategy 12: Adapt Solutions to Related Problems

When solving a new problem that seems similar to a problem that you know how to solve, you can try to solve the new problem by adapting the solution—both the strategies and the results—of the problem you know how to solve.

If the differences between the new problem and the problem you know how to solve are only surface features—for example, different numbers, different labels, or different categories—that is, features that are not fundamental to the structure of the problem, then solve the new problem using the same strategy as you used before.

If the differences between the new problem and the problem you know how to solve are more than just surface features, try to modify the solution to the problem you know how to solve to fit the conditions given in the new problem.

- See question 3 on page 195 and question 4 on page 196.

Strategy 13: Determine Whether a Conclusion Follows from the Information Given

In some problems, you are given information and a statement describing a possible conclusion, which may or may not follow from the information. You need to determine whether or not the conclusion is a logical consequence of the information given.

If you think that the conclusion follows from the information, try to show it. Using the information and any relevant mathematical relationships, try to reason step-by-step from the information to the conclusion. Another way to show that the conclusion follows from the information is to show that in *all* cases in which the information is true, the conclusion is also true.

If you think that the conclusion does *not* follow from the information, try to show that instead. One way to show that a conclusion does not follow from the information is to produce a counterexample. A counterexample is a case where the given information is true but the conclusion is false. If you are unsuccessful in producing a counterexample, it does not necessarily mean that the conclusion does not follow from the information—it may mean that although a counterexample exists, you were not successful in finding it.

- See question 9 on page 188 and question 3 on page 201.

Strategy 14: Determine What Additional Information Is Sufficient to Solve a Problem

Some problems cannot be solved directly from the information given, and you need to determine what other information will help you answer the question. In that case, it is useful to list all the information given in the problem, along with the information that would be contained in a complete solution, and then evaluate what is missing. Sometimes the missing information can be derived from the information given, and sometimes it cannot.

- See question 3 on page 201.

Quantitative Reasoning Question Types

The Quantitative Reasoning measure has four types of questions:

- Quantitative Comparison questions
- Multiple-choice questions—Select One Answer Choice
- Multiple-choice questions—Select One or More Answer Choices
- Numeric Entry questions

Each question appears either independently as a discrete question or as part of a set of questions called a Data Interpretation set. All of the questions in a Data Interpretation set are based on the same data presented in tables, graphs, or other displays of data.

In the computer-delivered test, you are allowed to use a basic calculator—provided on-screen—on the Quantitative Reasoning measure. Information about using the calculator appears later in this chapter.

Quantitative Comparison Questions

Description

Questions of this type ask you to compare two quantities—Quantity A and Quantity B—and then determine which of the following statements describes the comparison.

- Quantity A is greater.
- Quantity B is greater.
- The two quantities are equal.
- The relationship cannot be determined from the information given.

Tips for Answering

- **Become familiar with the answer choices.** Quantitative Comparison questions always have the same answer choices, so get to know them, especially the last choice, "The relationship cannot be determined from the information given." Never select this last choice if it is clear that the values of the two quantities can be determined by computation. Also, if you determine that one quantity is greater than the other, make sure you carefully select the corresponding choice so as not to reverse the first two choices.

- **Avoid unnecessary computations.** Don't waste time performing needless computations in order to compare the two quantities. Simplify, transform, or estimate one or both of the given quantities only as much as is necessary to compare them.

- **Remember that geometric figures are not necessarily drawn to scale.** If any aspect of a given geometric figure is not fully determined, try to redraw the figure, keeping those aspects that are completely determined by the given information fixed but changing the aspects of the figure that are not determined. Examine the results. What variations are possible in the relative lengths of line segments or measures of angles?

- **Plug in numbers.** If one or both of the quantities are algebraic expressions, you can substitute easy numbers for the variables and compare the resulting quantities in your analysis. Consider all kinds of appropriate numbers before you give an answer: e.g., zero, positive and negative numbers, small and large numbers, fractions and decimals. If you see that Quantity A is greater than Quantity B in one case and Quantity B is greater than Quantity A in another case, choose "The relationship cannot be determined from the information given."

- **Simplify the comparison.** If both quantities are algebraic or arithmetic expressions and you cannot easily see a relationship between them, you can try to simplify the comparison. Try a step-by-step simplification that is similar to the steps involved when you solve the equation $5 = 4x + 3$ for x, or similar to the steps involved when you determine that the inequality $\frac{3y + 2}{5} < y$ is equivalent to the simpler inequality $1 < y$. Begin by setting up a comparison involving the two quantities, as follows:

$$\text{Quantity A} \boxed{?} \text{Quantity B}$$

where $\boxed{?}$ is a "placeholder" that could represent the relationship *greater than* (>), *less than* (<), or *equal to* (=) or could represent the fact that the relationship cannot be determined from the information given. Then try to simplify the comparison, step by step, until you can determine a relationship between simplified quantities. For example, you may conclude after the last step that $\boxed{?}$ represents equal to (=). Based on this conclusion, you may be able to compare Quantities A and B. To understand this strategy more fully, see sample questions 6 to 9.

Sample Questions

Compare Quantity A and Quantity B, using additional information centered above the two quantities if such information is given, and select one of the following four answer choices:

(A) Quantity A is greater.

(B) Quantity B is greater.

(C) The two quantities are equal.

(D) The relationship cannot be determined from the information given.

A symbol that appears more than once in a question has the same meaning throughout the question.

Quantity A	Quantity B
1. The least prime number greater than 24	The greatest prime number less than 28

(A) Quantity A is greater.

(B) Quantity B is greater.

(C) The two quantities are equal.

(D) The relationship cannot be determined from the information given.

Explanation

For the integers greater than 24, note that 25, 26, 27, and 28 are not prime numbers, but 29 is a prime number, as are 31 and many other greater integers. Thus, 29 is the least prime number greater than 24, and Quantity A is 29. For the integers less than 28, note that 27, 26, 25, and 24 are not prime numbers, but 23 is a prime number, as are 19 and several other lesser integers. Thus, 23 is the greatest prime number less than 28, and Quantity B is 23.

The correct answer is Choice A, Quantity A is greater.

This explanation uses the following strategy.

Strategy 11: Divide into Cases

Lionel is younger than Maria.

Quantity A	Quantity B
2. Twice Lionel's age	Maria's age

(A) Quantity A is greater.

(B) Quantity B is greater.

(C) The two quantities are equal.

(D) The relationship cannot be determined from the information given.

Explanation

If Lionel's age is 6 years and Maria's age is 10 years, then Quantity A is greater, but if Lionel's age is 4 years and Maria's age is 10 years, then Quantity B is greater. Thus, the relationship cannot be determined.

The correct answer is Choice D, the relationship cannot be determined from the information given.

This explanation uses the following strategies.

Strategy 10: Trial and Error

Strategy 13: Determine Whether a Conclusion Follows from the Information Given

---

Quantity A	Quantity B
3. 54% of 360	150

     (A) Quantity A is greater.

     (B) Quantity B is greater.

     (C) The two quantities are equal.

     (D) The relationship cannot be determined from the information given.

Explanation

Without doing the exact computation, you can see that 54 percent of 360 is greater than $\frac{1}{2}$ of 360, which is 180, and 180 is greater than Quantity B, 150.

Thus, the correct answer is Choice A, Quantity A is greater.

This explanation uses the following strategy.

Strategy 9: Estimate

Figure 1

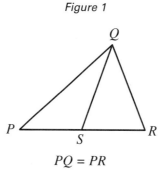

$PQ = PR$

Quantity A	Quantity B
4. PS	SR

     (A) Quantity A is greater.

     (B) Quantity B is greater.

     (C) The two quantities are equal.

     (D) The relationship cannot be determined from the information given.

Explanation

From Figure 1, you know that PQR is a triangle and that point S is between points P and R, so $PS < PR$ and $SR < PR$. You are also given that $PQ = PR$. However, this information is not sufficient to compare PS and SR. Furthermore, because the figure is not necessarily drawn to scale, you cannot determine the relative sizes of PS and SR visually from the figure, though they may appear to be equal. The position of S can vary alongside PR anywhere between P and R. Following are two possible variations of Figure 1, each of which is drawn to be consistent with the information $PQ = PR$.

Figure 2   Figure 3

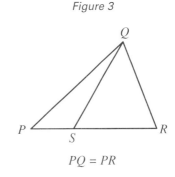

$$PQ = PR \qquad\qquad\qquad PQ = PR$$

Note that Quantity A is greater in Figure 2 and Quantity B is greater in Figure 3.

Thus, the correct answer is Choice D, the relationship cannot be determined from the information given.

This explanation uses the following strategies.

Strategy 4: Translate from a Figure to an Arithmetic or Algebraic Representation

Strategy 13: Determine Whether a Conclusion Follows from the Information Given

---

$$y = 2x^2 + 7x - 3$$

Quantity A	Quantity B

5. x y

    (A) Quantity A is greater.

    (B) Quantity B is greater.

    (C) The two quantities are equal.

    (D) The relationship cannot be determined from the information given.

Explanation

If $x = 0$, then $y = 2(0^2) + 7(0) - 3 = -3$, so in this case, $x > y$; but if $x = 1$, then $y = 2(1^2) + 7(1) - 3 = 6$, so in that case, $y > x$.

Thus, the correct answer is Choice D, the relationship cannot be determined from the information given.

This explanation uses the following strategies.

Strategy 10: Trial and Error

Strategy 13: Determine Whether a Conclusion Follows from the Information Given

Note that plugging numbers into expressions *may not* be conclusive. It *is* conclusive, however, if you get different results after plugging in different numbers: the conclusion is that the relationship cannot be determined from the information given. It is also conclusive if there are only a small number of possible numbers to plug in and all of them yield the same result, say, that Quantity B is greater.

Now suppose that there are an infinite number of possible numbers to plug in. If you plug many of them in and each time the result is, for example, that Quantity A is greater, you still cannot conclude that Quantity A is greater for every possible number that could be plugged in. Further analysis would be necessary and should focus on whether Quantity A is greater for all possible numbers or whether there are numbers for which Quantity A is not greater.

The following sample questions focus on simplifying the comparison.

$$y > 4$$

Quantity A	Quantity B
6. $\dfrac{3y+2}{5}$	y

   Ⓐ Quantity A is greater.
   Ⓑ Quantity B is greater.
   Ⓒ The two quantities are equal.
   Ⓓ The relationship cannot be determined from the information given.

Explanation

Set up the initial comparison:

$$\frac{3y+2}{5} \;\boxed{?}\; y$$

Then simplify:

Step 1: Multiply both sides by 5 to get

$$3y + 2 \;\boxed{?}\; 5y$$

Step 2: Subtract 3y from both sides to get

$$2 \;\boxed{?}\; 2y$$

Step 3: Divide both sides by 2 to get

$$1 \;\boxed{?}\; y$$

The comparison is now simplified as much as possible. In order to compare 1 and y, note that you are given the information $y > 4$ (above Quantities A and B). It follows from $y > 4$ that $y > 1$, or $1 < y$, so that in the comparison $1 \;\boxed{?}\; y$, the placeholder $\boxed{?}$ represents *less than* (<): $1 < y$.

    However, the problem asks for a comparison between Quantity A and Quantity B, not a comparison between 1 and y. To go from the comparison between 1 and y to a comparison between Quantities A and B, start with the last comparison, $1 < y$, and carefully consider each simplification step in reverse order to determine what each comparison implies about the preceding comparison, all the way back to the comparison between Quantities A and B if possible. Since step 3 was "*divide* both sides by 2," *multiplying* both sides of the comparison $1 < y$ by 2 implies the preceding comparison $2 < 2y$, thus reversing step 3. Each simplification step can be reversed as follows:

- Reverse step 3: *multiply* both sides by 2.
- Reverse step 2: *add 3y* to both sides.
- Reverse step 1: *divide* both sides by 5.

    When each step is reversed, the relationship remains *less than* (<), so Quantity A is less than Quantity B.
    Thus, the correct answer is Choice B, Quantity B is greater.

This explanation uses the following strategy.

Strategy 5: Simplify an Arithmetic or Algebraic Representation

While some simplification steps like subtracting 3 from both sides or dividing both sides by 10 are always reversible, it is important to note that some steps, like squaring both sides, may not be reversible.

Also, note that when you simplify an *inequality*, the steps of multiplying or dividing both sides by a negative number change the direction of the inequality; for example, if $x < y$, then $-x > -y$. So the relationship in the final, simplified inequality may be the *opposite* of the relationship between Quantities A and B. This is another reason to consider the impact of each step carefully.

	Quantity A	Quantity B

7. $\dfrac{2^{30} - 2^{29}}{2}$ 2^{28}

   Ⓐ Quantity A is greater.
   Ⓑ Quantity B is greater.
   Ⓒ The two quantities are equal.
   Ⓓ The relationship cannot be determined from the information given.

Explanation

Set up the initial comparison:

$$\frac{2^{30} - 2^{29}}{2} \boxed{?} \; 2^{28}$$

Then simplify:

Step 1: Multiply both sides by 2 to get

$$2^{30} - 2^{29} \boxed{?} \; 2^{29}$$

Step 2: Add 2^{29} to both sides to get

$$2^{30} \boxed{?} \; 2^{29} + 2^{29}$$

Step 3: Simplify the right-hand side using the fact that $(2)(2^{29}) = 2^{30}$ to get

$$2^{30} \boxed{?} \; 2^{30}$$

The resulting relationship is *equal to* (=). In reverse order, each simplification step implies *equal to* in the preceding comparison. So Quantities A and B are also equal.

Thus, the correct answer is Choice C, the two quantities are equal.

This explanation uses the following strategy.

Strategy 5: Simplify an Arithmetic or Algebraic Representation

	Quantity A	Quantity B

8. $x^2 + 1$ $2x - 1$

   Ⓐ Quantity A is greater.
   Ⓑ Quantity B is greater.
   Ⓒ The two quantities are equal.
   Ⓓ The relationship cannot be determined from the information given.

Explanation

Set up the initial comparison:

$$x^2 + 1 \;\boxed{?}\; 2x - 1$$

Then simplify by noting that the quadratic polynomial $x^2 - 2x + 1$ can be factored:

Step 1: Subtract $2x$ from both sides to get

$$x^2 - 2x + 1 \;\boxed{?}\; -1$$

Step 2: Factor the left-hand side to get

$$(x - 1)^2 \;\boxed{?}\; -1$$

The left-hand side of the comparison is the square of a number. Since the square of a number is always greater than or equal to 0, and 0 is greater than -1, the simplified comparison is the inequality $(x - 1)^2 > -1$ and the resulting relationship is *greater than* (>). In reverse order, each simplification step implies the inequality *greater than* (>) in the preceding comparison. Therefore, Quantity A is greater than Quantity B.

The correct answer is Choice A, Quantity A is greater.

This explanation uses the following strategies.
Strategy 5: Simplify an Arithmetic or Algebraic Representation
Strategy 8: Search for a Mathematical Relationship

$$w > 1$$

Quantity A	Quantity B
$7w - 4$	$2w + 5$

9.

Ⓐ Quantity A is greater.
Ⓑ Quantity B is greater.
Ⓒ The two quantities are equal.
Ⓓ The relationship cannot be determined from the information given.

Explanation

Set up the initial comparison:

$$7w - 4 \;\boxed{?}\; 2w + 5$$

Then simplify:

Step 1: Subtract $2w$ from both sides and add 4 to both sides to get

$$5w \;\boxed{?}\; 9$$

Step 2: Divide both sides by 5 to get

$$w \boxed{?} \frac{9}{5}$$

The comparison cannot be simplified any further. Although you are given that $w > 1$, you still don't know how w compares to $\frac{9}{5}$, or 1.8. For example, if $w = 1.5$, then $w < 1.8$, but if $w = 2$, then $w > 1.8$. In other words, the relationship between w and $\frac{9}{5}$ cannot be determined. Note that each of these simplification steps is reversible, so in reverse order, each simplification step implies that the *relationship cannot be determined* in the preceding comparison. Thus, the relationship between Quantities A and B cannot be determined.

The correct answer is Choice D, the relationship cannot be determined from the information given.

This explanation uses the following strategies.
Strategy 5: Simplify an Arithmetic or Algebraic Representation
Strategy 13: Determine Whether a Conclusion Follows from the Information Given

The strategy of simplifying the comparison works most efficiently when you note that a simplification step is reversible while actually taking the step. Here are some common steps that are always reversible:

- Adding any number or expression to both sides of a comparison
- Subtracting any number or expression from both sides
- Multiplying both sides by any nonzero number or expression
- Dividing both sides by any nonzero number or expression

Remember that if the relationship is an inequality, multiplying or dividing both sides by any *negative* number or expression will yield the opposite inequality. Be aware that some common operations like squaring both sides are generally not reversible and may require further analysis using other information given in the question in order to justify reversing such steps.

Multiple-choice Questions—Select One Answer Choice

Description

These questions are multiple-choice questions that ask you to select only one answer choice from a list of five choices.

> **Tips for Answering**
> - **Use the fact that the answer is there.** If your answer is not one of the five answer choices given, you should assume that your answer is incorrect and do the following:
>   - Reread the question carefully—you may have missed an important detail or misinterpreted some information.
>   - Check your computations—you may have made a mistake, such as mis-keying a number on the calculator.
>   - Reevaluate your solution method—you may have a flaw in your reasoning.

● **Examine the answer choices.** In some questions you are asked explicitly which of the choices has a certain property. You may have to consider each choice separately, or you may be able to see a relationship between the choices that will help you find the answer more quickly. In other questions, it may be helpful to work backward from the choices, say, by substituting the choices in an equation or inequality to see which one works. However, be careful, as that method may take more time than using reasoning.

● **For questions that require approximations, scan the answer choices to see how close an approximation is needed.** In other questions, too, it may be helpful to scan the choices briefly before solving the problem to get a better sense of what the question is asking. If computations are involved in the solution, it may be necessary to carry out all computations exactly and round only your final answer in order to get the required degree of accuracy. In other questions, you may find that estimation is sufficient and will help you avoid spending time on long computations.

Sample Questions

Select a single answer choice.

1. If $5x + 32 = 4 - 2x$, what is the value of x?

    (A) −4

    (B) −3

    (C) 4

    (D) 7

    (E) 12

Explanation
Solving the equation for x, you get $7x = -28$, and so $x = -4$.
    The correct answer is Choice A, −4.

This explanation uses the following strategy.
Strategy 5: Simplify an Arithmetic or Algebraic Representation

2. Which of the following numbers is farthest from the number 1 on the number line?

    (A) −10

    (B) −5

    (C) 0

    (D) 5

    (E) 10

Explanation

Circling each of the answer choices in a sketch of the number line (Figure 4) shows that of the given numbers, −10 is the greatest distance from 1.

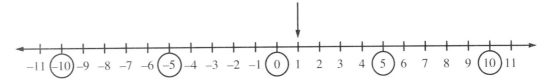

Figure 4

Another way to answer the question is to remember that the distance between two numbers on the number line is equal to the absolute value of the difference of the two numbers. For example, the distance between −10 and 1 is $|-10 - 1| = 11$, and the distance between 10 and 1 is $|10 - 1| = |9| = 9$.

The correct answer is Choice A, −10.

This explanation uses the following strategy.

Strategy 2: Translate from Words to a Figure or Diagram

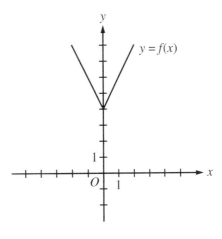

Figure 5

3. The figure above shows the graph of the function f defined by $f(x) = |2x| + 4$ for all numbers x. For which of the following functions g, defined for all numbers x, does the graph of g intersect the graph of f?

    Ⓐ $g(x) = x - 2$

    Ⓑ $g(x) = x + 3$

    Ⓒ $g(x) = 2x - 2$

    Ⓓ $g(x) = 2x + 3$

    Ⓔ $g(x) = 3x - 2$

Explanation

You can see that all five choices are linear functions whose graphs are lines with various slopes and *y*-intercepts. The graph of Choice A is a line with slope 1 and *y*-intercept –2, shown in Figure 6.

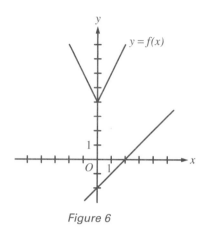

Figure 6

It is clear that this line will not intersect the graph of *f* to the left of the *y*-axis. To the right of the *y*-axis, the graph of *f* is a line with slope 2, which is greater than slope 1. Consequently, as the value of *x* increases, the value of *y* increases faster for *f* than for *g*, and therefore the graphs do not intersect to the right of the *y*-axis. Choice B is similarly ruled out. Note that if the *y*-intercept of either of the lines in Choices A and B were greater than or equal to 4 instead of less than 4, they would intersect the graph of *f*.

Choices C and D are lines with slope 2 and *y*-intercepts less than 4. Hence, they are parallel to the graph of *f* (to the right of the *y*-axis) and therefore will not intersect it. Any line with a slope greater than 2 and a *y*-intercept less than 4, like the line in Choice E, will intersect the graph of *f* (to the right of the *y*-axis).
The correct answer is Choice E, $g(x) = 3x - 2$.

This explanation uses the following strategies.
Strategy 3: Translate from an Algebraic to a Graphical Representation
Strategy 6: Add to a Geometric Figure
Strategy 8: Search for a Mathematical Relationship

4. A car got 33 miles per gallon using gasoline that cost $2.95 per gallon. Approximately what was the cost, in dollars, of the gasoline used in driving the car 350 miles?

     (A) $10   (B) $20   (C) $30   (D) $40   (E) $50

Explanation

Scanning the answer choices indicates that you can do at least some estimation and still answer confidently. The car used $\dfrac{350}{33}$ gallons of gasoline, so the cost was $\left(\dfrac{350}{33}\right)(2.95)$ dollars. You can estimate the product $\left(\dfrac{350}{33}\right)(2.95)$ by estimating $\dfrac{350}{33}$ a little low, 10, and estimating 2.95 a little high, 3, to get approximately $(10)(3) = 30$ dollars. You can also use the calculator to compute a more exact answer and then round the answer to the nearest 10 dollars, as suggested by the answer choices. The calculator yields the decimal 31.287... , which rounds to 30 dollars.

Thus, the correct answer is Choice C, $30.

This explanation uses the following strategies.

Strategy 1: Translate from Words to an Arithmetic or Algebraic Representation
Strategy 9: Estimate

---

5.   A certain jar contains 60 jelly beans—22 white, 18 green, 11 yellow, 5 red, and 4 purple. If a jelly bean is to be chosen at random, what is the probability that the jelly bean will be neither red nor purple?

   (A)   0.09
   (B)   0.15
   (C)   0.54
   (D)   0.85
   (E)   0.91

Explanation

Since there are 5 red and 4 purple jelly beans in the jar, there are 51 that are neither red nor purple, and the probability of selecting one of these is $\frac{51}{60}$.

Since all of the answer choices are decimals, you must convert the fraction to its decimal equivalent, 0.85.

Thus, the correct answer is Choice D, 0.85.

This explanation uses the following strategies.

Strategy 1: Translate from Words to an Arithmetic or Algebraic Representation
Strategy 5: Simplify an Arithmetic or Algebraic Representation

Multiple-Choice Questions—Select One or More Answer Choices

Description

These questions are multiple-choice questions that ask you to select one or more answer choices from a list of choices. A question may or may not specify the number of choices to select. These questions are marked with square boxes beside the answer choices, not circles or ovals.

Tips for Answering
- Note whether you are asked to indicate a specific number of answer choices or all choices that apply. In the latter case, be sure to consider all of the choices, determine which ones are correct, and select all of those and only those choices. Note that there may be only one correct choice.
- In some questions that involve conditions that limit the possible values of numerical answer choices, it may be efficient to determine the least and/or the greatest possible value. Knowing the least and/or greatest possible value may enable you to quickly determine all of the choices that are correct.
- Avoid lengthy calculations by recognizing and continuing numerical patterns.

Sample Questions

> **Select one or more answer choices according to the specific question directions.**
>
> **If the question does not specify how many answer choices to select, select all that apply.**
>
> - **The correct answer may be just one of the choices or as many as all of the choices, depending on the question.**
> - **No credit is given unless you select all of the correct choices and no others.**
>
> **If the question specifies how many answer choices to select, select exactly that number of choices.**

1. Which two of the following numbers have a product that is between −1 and 0?

    Indicate <u>both</u> of the numbers.

    A   −20   C 2^{-4}

    B   −10   D 3^{-2}

Explanation

For this question, you must select a pair of answer choices. The product of the pair must be negative, so the possible products are $(-20)(2^{-4})$, $(-20)(3^{-2})$, $(-10)(2^{-4})$, and $(-10)(3^{-2})$. The product must also be greater than −1. The first product is $\dfrac{-20}{2^4} = -\dfrac{20}{16} < -1$, the second product is $\dfrac{-20}{3^2} = -\dfrac{20}{9} < -1$, and the third product is $\dfrac{-10}{2^4} = -\dfrac{10}{16} > -1$, so you can stop there.

The correct answer consists of Choices B (−10) and C (2^{-4}).

This explanation uses the following strategies.
Strategy 1: Translate from Words to an Arithmetic or Algebraic Representation
Strategy 10: Trial and Error

---

2. Which of the following integers are multiples of both 2 and 3?

    Indicate <u>all</u> such integers.

    A   8   D   18
    B   9   E   21
    C   12   F   36

Explanation

You can first identify the multiples of 2, which are 8, 12, 18, and 36, and then among the multiples of 2 identify the multiples of 3, which are 12, 18, and 36. Alternatively, if you realize that every number that is a multiple of 2 and 3 is also a multiple of 6, you can identify the choices that are multiples of 6.

The correct answer consists of Choices C (12), D (18), and F (36).

This explanation uses the following strategies.
Strategy 1: Translate from Words to an Arithmetic or Algebraic Representation
Strategy 11: Divide into Cases

3. Each employee of a certain company is in either Department X or Department Y, and there are more than twice as many employees in Department X as in Department Y. The average (arithmetic mean) salary is $25,000 for the employees in Department X and $35,000 for the employees in Department Y. Which of the following amounts could be the average salary for all of the employees of the company?

    Indicate <u>all</u> such amounts.

    A $26,000

    B $28,000

    C $29,000

    D $30,000

    E $31,000

    F $32,000

    G $34,000

Explanation

One strategy for answering this kind of question is to find the least and/or greatest possible value. Clearly the average salary is between $25,000 and $35,000, and all of the answer choices are in this interval. Since you are told that there are more employees with the lower average salary, the average salary of all employees must be less than the average of $25,000 and $35,000, which is $30,000. If there were exactly twice as many employees in Department X as in Department Y, then the average salary for all employees would be, to the nearest dollar, the following weighted mean,

$$\frac{(2)(25,000)+(1)(35,000)}{2+1} \approx 28,333 \text{ dollars}$$

where the weight for $25,000 is 2 and the weight for $35,000 is 1. Since there are *more* than twice as many employees in Department X as in Department Y, the actual average salary must be even closer to $25,000 because the weight for $25,000 is greater than 2. This means that $28,333 is the greatest possible average. Among the choices given, the possible values of the average are therefore $26,000 and $28,000.

   Thus, the correct answer consists of Choices A ($26,000) and B ($28,000).

   Intuitively, you might expect that any amount between $25,000 and $28,333 is a possible value of the average salary. To see that $26,000 is possible, in the weighted mean above, use the respective weights 9 and 1 instead of 2 and 1. To see that $28,000 is possible, use the respective weights 7 and 3.

This explanation uses the following strategies.

Strategy 1: Translate from Words to an Arithmetic or Algebraic Representation
Strategy 8: Search for a Mathematical Relationship
Strategy 12: Adapt Solutions to Related Problems

4. Which of the following could be the units digit of 57^n, where n is a positive integer?

    Indicate all such digits.

A	0		F	5
B	1		G	6
C	2		H	7
D	3		I	8
E	4		J	9

    ### Explanation

    The units digit of 57^n is the same as the units digit of 7^n for all positive integers n. To see why this is true for $n = 2$, compute 57^2 by hand and observe how its units digit results from the units digit of 7^2. Because this is true for every positive integer n, you need to consider only powers of 7. Beginning with $n = 1$ and proceeding consecutively, the units digits of 7, 7^2, 7^3, 7^4, and 7^5 are 7, 9, 3, 1, and 7, respectively. In this sequence, the first digit, 7, appears again, and the pattern of four digits, 7, 9, 3, 1, repeats without end. Hence, these four digits are the only possible units digits of 7^n and therefore of 57^n.

    The correct answer consists of Choices B (1), D (3), H (7), and J (9).

    This explanation uses the following strategies.
    Strategy 7: Find a Pattern
    Strategy 12: Adapt Solutions to Related Problems

Numeric Entry Questions

Description

Questions of this type ask you either to enter your answer as an integer or a decimal in a single answer box or to enter it as a fraction in two separate boxes—one for the numerator and one for the denominator. In the computer-delivered test, use the computer mouse and keyboard to enter your answer.

Tips for Answering

- **Make sure you answer the question that is asked.** Since there are no answer choices to guide you, read the question carefully and make sure you provide the type of answer required. Sometimes there will be labels before or after the answer box to indicate the appropriate type of answer. Pay special attention to units such as feet or miles, to orders of magnitude such as millions or billions, and to percents as compared with decimals.

- **If you are asked to round your answer, make sure you round to the required degree of accuracy.** For example, if an answer of 46.7 is to be rounded to the nearest integer, you need to enter the number 47. If your solution strategy involves intermediate computations, you should carry out all computations exactly and round only your final answer in order to get the required degree of accuracy. If no rounding instructions are given, enter the exact answer.

- **Examine your answer to see if it is reasonable with respect to the information given.** You may want to use estimation or another solution path to double-check your answer.

Sample Questions

Enter your answer as an integer or a decimal if there is a single answer box OR as a fraction if there are two separate answer boxes—one for the numerator and one for the denominator.

To enter an integer or a decimal, either type the number in the answer box using the keyboard or use the Transfer Display button on the calculator.

- First, select the answer box—a cursor will appear in the box—and then type the number.
- For a negative sign, type a hyphen. For a decimal point, type a period.
- The Transfer Display button on the calculator will transfer the calculator display to the answer box.
- Equivalent forms of the correct answer, such as 2.5 and 2.50, are all correct.
- Enter the exact answer unless the question asks you to round your answer.

To enter a fraction, type the numerator and the denominator in their respective answer boxes using the keyboard.

- Select each answer box—a cursor will appear in the box—and then type an integer. A decimal point cannot be used in either box.
- For a negative sign, type a hyphen in either box.
- The Transfer Display button on the calculator cannot be used for a fraction.
- Fractions do not need to be reduced to lowest terms, though you may need to reduce your fraction to fit in the boxes

1. One pen costs $0.25 and one marker costs $0.35. At those prices, what is the total cost of 18 pens and 100 markers?

$ [＿＿＿＿＿]

Explanation

Multiplying $0.25 by 18 yields $4.50, which is the cost of the 18 pens; and multiplying $0.35 by 100 yields $35.00, which is the cost of the 100 markers. The total cost is therefore $4.50 + $35.00 = $39.50. Equivalent decimals, such as $39.5 or $39.500, are considered correct.

Thus, the correct answer is $39.50 (or equivalent).

Note that the dollar symbol is in front of the answer box, so the symbol $ does not need to be entered in the box. In fact, only numbers, a decimal point, and a negative sign can be entered in the answer box.

This explanation uses the following strategy.

Strategy 1: Translate from Words to an Arithmetic or Algebraic Representation

2. Rectangle *R* has length 30 and width 10, and square *S* has length 5. The perimeter of *S* is what fraction of the perimeter of *R*?

Explanation

The perimeter of *R* is $30 + 10 + 30 + 10 = 80$, and the perimeter of *S* is $(4)(5) = 20$. Therefore, the perimeter of *S* is $\frac{20}{80}$ of the perimeter of *R*. To enter the answer $\frac{20}{80}$, you should enter the numerator 20 in the top box and the denominator 80 in the bottom box. Because the fraction does not need to be reduced to lowest terms, any fraction that is equivalent to $\frac{20}{80}$ is also considered correct, as long as it fits in the boxes. For example, both of the fractions $\frac{2}{8}$ and $\frac{1}{4}$ are considered correct.

Thus, the correct answer is $\frac{20}{80}$ (or any equivalent fraction).

This explanation uses the following strategy.

Strategy 1: Translate from Words to an Arithmetic or Algebraic Representation

---

RESULTS OF A USED-CAR AUCTION

	Small Cars	Large Cars
Number of cars offered	32	23
Number of cars sold	16	20
Projected sales total for cars offered (in thousands)	$70	$150
Actual sales total (in thousands)	$41	$120

Figure 7

3. For the large cars sold at an auction that is summarized in the table above, what was the average sale price per car?

$

Explanation

From Figure 7, you see that the number of large cars sold was 20 and the sales total for large cars was $120,000 (not $120). Thus the average sale price per car was

$$\frac{\$120{,}000}{20} = \$6{,}000 .$$

The correct answer is $6,000 (or equivalent).

(In numbers that are 1,000 or greater, you do not need to enter commas in the answer box.)

This explanation uses the following strategy.

Strategy 4: Translate from a Figure to an Arithmetic or Algebraic Representation

4. A merchant made a profit of $5 on the sale of a sweater that cost the merchant $15. What is the profit expressed as a percent of the merchant's cost?

Give your answer to the <u>nearest whole percent</u>.

 %

Explanation

The percent profit is $\left(\dfrac{5}{15}\right)(100) = 33.333... = 33.\overline{3}$ percent, which is 33%, to the nearest whole percent.

Thus, the correct answer is 33% (or equivalent).

If you use the calculator and the Transfer Display button, the number that will be transferred to the answer box is 33.333333, which is incorrect since it is not given to the nearest whole percent. You will need to adjust the number in the answer box by deleting all of the digits to the right of the decimal point.

Also, since you are asked to give the answer as a percent, the decimal equivalent of 33 percent, which is 0.33, is incorrect. The percent symbol next to the answer box indicates that the form of the answer must be a percent. Entering 0.33 in the box would give the erroneous answer 0.33%.

This explanation uses the following strategies.

Strategy 1: Translate from Words to an Arithmetic or Algebraic Representation
Strategy 5: Simplify an Arithmetic or Algebraic Representation

---

5. Working alone at its constant rate, machine A produces k liters of a chemical in 10 minutes. Working alone at its constant rate, machine B produces k liters of the chemical in 15 minutes. How many minutes does it take machines A and B, working simultaneously at their respective constant rates, to produce k liters of the chemical?

 minutes

Explanation

Machine A produces $\dfrac{k}{10}$ liters per minute, and machine B produces $\dfrac{k}{15}$ liters per minute. So when the machines work simultaneously, the rate at which the chemical is produced is the sum of these two rates, which is $\dfrac{k}{10} + \dfrac{k}{15} = k\left(\dfrac{1}{10} + \dfrac{1}{15}\right) = k\left(\dfrac{25}{150}\right) = \dfrac{k}{6}$ liters per minute. To compute the time required to produce k liters at this rate, divide the amount k by the rate $\dfrac{k}{6}$ to get $\dfrac{k}{\frac{k}{6}} = 6.$

Therefore, the correct answer is 6 minutes (or equivalent).

One way to check that the answer of 6 minutes is reasonable is to observe that if the slower rate of machine B were the same as machine A's faster rate of k liters in 10 minutes, then the two machines, working simultaneously, would take half the time, or 5 minutes, to produce the k liters. So the answer has to be *greater than 5 minutes.* Similarly, if the faster rate of machine A were the same as machine B's slower rate of k liters in 15 minutes, then the two machines would take half the time, or 7.5 minutes, to produce the k liters. So the answer has to be *less than 7.5 minutes*. Thus, the answer of 6 minutes is reasonable compared to the lower estimate of 5 minutes and the upper estimate of 7.5 minutes.

This explanation uses the following strategies.

Strategy 1: Translate from Words to an Arithmetic or Algebraic Representation
Strategy 5: Simplify an Arithmetic or Algebraic Representation
Strategy 8: Search for a Mathematical Relationship

Data Interpretation Sets

Description

Data Interpretation questions are grouped together and refer to the same table, graph, or other data presentation. These questions ask you to interpret or analyze the given data. The types of questions may be Multiple-choice (both types) or Numeric Entry.

> ### Tips for Answering
>
> ● Scan the data presentation briefly to see what it is about, but do not spend time studying all of the information in detail. Focus on those aspects of the data that are necessary to answer the questions. Pay attention to the axes and scales of graphs; to the units of measurement or orders of magnitude (such as *billions*) that are given in the titles, labels, and legends; and to any notes that clarify the data.
> ● When graphical data presentations, such as bar graphs and line graphs, are shown with scales, you should read, estimate, or compare quantities by sight or by measurement, according to the corresponding scales. For example, you can use the relative sizes of bars or sectors to compare the quantities that they represent, but be aware of broken scales and of bars that do not start at 0.
> ● The questions are to be answered only on the basis of the data presented, everyday facts (such as the number of days in a year), and your knowledge of mathematics. Do not make use of specialized information you may recall from other sources about the particular context on which the questions are based unless the information can be derived from the data presented.

Sample Questions

Questions 1 to 3 are based on the following data.

ANNUAL PERCENT CHANGE IN DOLLAR AMOUNT OF SALES AT FIVE RETAIL STORES FROM 2006 TO 2008

Store	Percent Change from 2006 to 2007	Percent Change from 2007 to 2008
P	10	−10
Q	−20	9
R	5	12
S	−7	−15
T	17	−8

Figure 8

1. If the dollar amount of sales at Store P was $800,000 for 2006, what was the dollar amount of sales at that store for 2008?

         (A) $727,200   (D) $880,000

         (B) $792,000   (E) $968,000

         (C) $800,000

Explanation

According to Figure 8, if the dollar amount of sales at Store P was $800,000 for 2006, then it was 10 percent greater for 2007, which is 110 percent of that amount, or $880,000. For 2008 the amount was 90 percent of $880,000, which is $792,000.

The correct answer is Choice B, $792,000.

    Note that an increase of 10 percent for one year and a decrease of 10 percent for the following year does not result in the same dollar amount as the original dollar amount, because the base that is used in computing the percents is $800,000 for the first change but $880,000 for the second change.

This explanation uses the following strategies.

Strategy 4: Translate from a Figure to an Arithmetic or Algebraic Representation
Strategy 5: Simplify an Arithmetic or Algebraic Representation

---

2. At Store T, the dollar amount of sales for 2007 was what percent of the dollar amount of sales for 2008?

    Give your answer to the <u>nearest 0.1 percent</u>.

                  [   ] %

Explanation

If A is the dollar amount of sales at Store T for 2007, then 8 percent of A, or $0.08A$, is the amount of decrease from 2007 to 2008. Thus $A - 0.08A = 0.92A$ is the dollar amount for 2008. Therefore, the desired percent can be obtained by dividing A by $0.92A$, which equals $\dfrac{A}{0.92\,A} = \dfrac{1}{0.92} = 1.0869565$. Expressed as a percent and rounded to the nearest 0.1 percent, this number is 108.7%.

Thus, the correct answer is 108.7% (or equivalent).

This explanation uses the following strategies.

Strategy 4: Translate from a Figure to an Arithmetic or Algebraic Representation
Strategy 5: Simplify an Arithmetic or Algebraic Representation

---

3. Based on the information given, which of the following statements must be true?

    Indicate <u>all</u> such statements.

    [A]   For 2008 the dollar amount of sales at Store R was greater than that at each of the other four stores.

    [B]   The dollar amount of sales at Store S for 2008 was 22 percent less than that for 2006.

    [C]   The dollar amount of sales at Store R for 2008 was more than 17 percent greater than that for 2006.

Explanation

For Choice A, since the only data given in Figure 8 are percent changes from year to year, there is no way to compare the actual dollar amount of sales at the stores for 2008 or for any other year. Even though Store R had the greatest percent increase from 2006 to 2008, its actual dollar amount of sales for 2008 may have been much smaller than that for any of the other four stores, and therefore Choice A is not necessarily true.

For Choice B, even though the sum of the two percent decreases would suggest a 22 percent decrease, the bases of the percents are different. If B is the dollar amount of sales at Store S for 2006, then the dollar amount for 2007 is 93 percent of B, or $0.93B$, and the dollar amount for 2008 is given by $(0.85)(0.93)B$, which is $0.7905B$. Note that this represents a percent decrease of $100 - 79.05$, or 20.95 percent, which is not equal to 22 percent, and so Choice B is not true.

For Choice C, if C is the dollar amount of sales at Store R for 2006, then the dollar amount for 2007 is given by $1.05C$ and the dollar amount for 2008 is given by $(1.12)(1.05)C$, which is $1.176C$. Note that this represents a 17.6 percent increase, which is greater than 17 percent, so Choice C must be true.

Therefore, the correct answer consists of only Choice C (The dollar amount of sales at Store R for 2008 was more than 17 percent greater than that for 2006).

This explanation uses the following strategies.

Strategy 1: Translate from Words to an Arithmetic or Algebraic Representation
Strategy 4: Translate from a Figure to an Arithmetic or Algebraic Representation
Strategy 5: Simplify an Arithmetic or Algebraic Representation
Strategy 13: Determine Whether a Conclusion Follows from the Information Given
Strategy 14: Determine What Additional Information Is Sufficient to Solve a Problem

Using the Calculator

Sometimes the computations you need to do in order to answer a question in the Quantitative Reasoning measure are somewhat time-consuming, like long division, or involve square roots. For such computations, you can use the on-screen calculator provided in the computer-delivered test. The on-screen calculator is shown in Figure 9.

Figure 9

Although the calculator can shorten the time it takes to perform computations, keep in mind that the calculator provides results that supplement, but do not replace, your knowledge of mathematics. You must use your mathematical knowledge to determine whether the calculator's results are reasonable and how the results can be used to answer a question.

Here are some general guidelines for calculator use in the Quantitative Reasoning measure:

- Most of the questions don't require difficult computations, so don't use the calculator just because it's available.
- Use it for calculations that you know are tedious, such as long division, square roots, and addition, subtraction, or multiplication of numbers that have several digits.
- Avoid using it for simple computations that are quicker to do mentally, such as $10 - 490$, $(4)(70)$, $\frac{4,300}{10}$, $\sqrt{25}$, and 30^2.
- Avoid using it to introduce decimals if you are asked to give an answer as a fraction.
- Some questions can be answered more quickly by reasoning and estimating than by using the calculator.
- If you use the calculator, estimate the answer beforehand so that you can determine whether the calculator's answer is reasonable. This may help you avoid key-entry errors.

The following guidelines are specific to the on-screen calculator in the computer-delivered test:

- When you use the computer mouse or the keyboard to operate the calculator, take care not to mis-key a number or operation.
- Note all of the calculator's buttons, including Transfer Display.
- The Transfer Display button can be used on Numeric Entry questions with a single answer box. This button will transfer the calculator display to the answer box. You should check that the transferred number has the correct form to answer the question. For example, if a question requires you to round your answer or convert your answer to a percent, make sure that you adjust the transferred number accordingly.
- Take note that the calculator respects *order of operations*, which is a mathematical convention that establishes which operations are performed before others in a mathematical expression that has more than one operation. The order is as follows: parentheses, exponentiation (including square roots), multiplications and divisions (from left to right), additions and subtractions (from left to right). With respect to order of operations, the value of the expression $1 + 2 \times 4$ is 9 because the expression is evaluated by first multiplying 2 and 4 and then by adding 1 to the result. This is how the on-screen calculator in the Quantitative Reasoning measure performs the operations. (Note that many basic calculators follow a different convention, whereby they perform multiple operations in the order that they are entered into the calculator. For such calculators,

the result of entering $1+2\times4$ is 12. To get this result, the calculator adds 1 and 2, displays a result of 3, then multiplies 3 and 4, and displays a result of 12.)

- In addition to parentheses, the on-screen calculator has one memory location and three memory buttons that govern it: memory recall $\boxed{MR}$, memory clear $\boxed{MC}$, and memory sum $\boxed{M+}$. These buttons function as they normally do on most basic calculators.

- Some computations are not defined for real numbers: for example, division by zero or taking the square root of a negative number. If you enter $6\boxed{\div}0\boxed{=}$, the word **ERROR** will be displayed. Similarly, if you enter $1\boxed{\pm}\boxed{\sqrt{}}$, then **ERROR** will be displayed. To clear the display, you must press the clear button $\boxed{C}$.

- The calculator displays up to eight digits. If a computation results in a number greater than 99,999,999, then **ERROR** will be displayed. For example, the calculation $10,000,000\boxed{\times}10\boxed{=}$ results in **ERROR**. The clear button $\boxed{C}$ must be used to clear the display. If a computation results in a positive number less than 0.0000001, or 10^{-7}, then 0 will be displayed.

Below are some examples of computations using the calculator.

1. Compute $4+\dfrac{6.73}{2}$.

Explanation

Enter $4\boxed{+}6.73\boxed{\div}2\boxed{=}$ to get 7.365. Alternatively, enter $6.73\boxed{\div}2\boxed{=}$ to get 3.365, and then enter $\boxed{+}4\boxed{=}$ to get **7.365**.

---

2. Compute $-\dfrac{8.4+9.3}{70}$.

Explanation

Since division takes precedence over addition in the order of operations, you need to override that precedence in order to compute this fraction. Here are two ways to do that. You can use the parentheses for the addition in the numerator, entering $\boxed{(}8.4\boxed{+}9.3\boxed{)}\boxed{\div}70\boxed{=}\boxed{\pm}$ to get –0.2528571. Or you can use the equals sign after 9.3, entering $8.4\boxed{+}9.3\boxed{=}\boxed{\div}70\boxed{=}\boxed{\pm}$ to get the same result. In the second way, note that pressing the first $\boxed{=}$ is essential, because without it, $8.4\boxed{+}9.3\boxed{\div}70\boxed{=}\boxed{\pm}$ would erroneously compute $-\left(8.4+\dfrac{9.3}{70}\right)$ instead.

Incidentally, the exact value of the expression $-\dfrac{8.4+9.3}{70}$ is the repeating decimal $-0.25\overline{285714}$, where the digits 285714 repeat without end, but the calculator rounds the decimal to **–0.2528571**.

---

3. Find the length, to the nearest 0.01, of the hypotenuse of a right triangle with legs of length 21 and 54; that is, use the Pythagorean theorem and calculate $\sqrt{21^2+54^2}$.

Explanation

Enter 21 $\times$ 21 $+$ 54 $\times$ 54 $=$ $\sqrt{}$ to get 57.939624. Again, pressing the $=$ before the $\sqrt{}$ is essential because 21 $\times$ 21 $+$ 54 $\times$ 54 $\sqrt{}$ $=$ would erroneously compute $21^2 + 54\sqrt{54}$. This is because the square root would take precedence over the multiplication in the order of operations. Note that parentheses could be used, as in $($ 21 $\times$ 21 $)$ $+$ $($ 54 $\times$ 54 $)$ $=$ $\sqrt{}$, but they are not necessary because the multiplications already take precedence over the addition.

Incidentally, the exact answer is a nonterminating, nonrepeating decimal, or an irrational number, but the calculator rounds the decimal to 57.939624. Finally, note that the problem asks for the answer to the nearest 0.01, so the correct answer is **57.94**.

---

4. Compute $(-15)^3$.

Explanation

Enter 15 $\pm$ $\times$ 15 $\pm$ $\times$ 15 $\pm$ $=$ to get **–3,375.**

---

5. Convert 6 miles per hour to feet per second.

Explanation

The solution to this problem uses the conversion factors 1 mile = 5,280 feet and 1 hour = 3,600 seconds as follows:

$$\left(\frac{6\ \text{miles}}{1\ \text{hour}}\right)\left(\frac{5{,}280\ \text{feet}}{1\ \text{mile}}\right)\left(\frac{1\ \text{hour}}{3{,}600\ \text{seconds}}\right) = ?\ \frac{\text{feet}}{\text{second}}$$

Enter 6 $\times$ 5280 $\div$ 3600 $=$ to get 8.8. Alternatively, enter 6 $\times$ 5280 $=$ to get the result 31,680, and then enter $\div$ 3600 $=$ to get **8.8 feet per second.**

---

6. At a fund-raising event, 43 participants donated $60 each, 21 participants donated $80 each, and 16 participants donated $100 each. What was the average (arithmetic mean) donation per participant, in dollars?

Explanation

The solution to this problem is to compute the weighted mean $\dfrac{(43)(60) + (21)(80) + (16)(100)}{43 + 21 + 16}$. You can use the memory buttons and parentheses for this computation as follows:

Enter 43 $\times$ 60 $=$ $M+$ 21 $\times$ 80 $=$ $M+$ 16 $\times$ 100 $=$ $M+$ MR $\div$ $($ 43 $+$ 21 $+$ 16 $)$ $=$ to get 73.25, or **$73.25 per participant**.

When the $M+$ button is first used, the number in the calculator display is stored in memory and an **M** appears to the left of the display to show that the memory function is in use. Each subsequent use of the $M+$ button adds the number in the current display to the number stored in memory and replaces the number stored in memory by the sum. When the MR button is pressed in the computation, the current value in memory, 5,860, is displayed. To clear the memory, use the MC button, and the **M** next to the display disappears.

Mathematical Conventions for the Quantitative Reasoning Measure of the GRE General Test

The mathematical symbols and terminology used in the Quantitative Reasoning measure of the test are conventional at the high school level, and most of these appear in the *Math Review*. Whenever nonstandard or special notation or terminology is used in a test question, it is explicitly introduced in the question. However, there are some particular assumptions about numbers and geometric figures that are made throughout the test. These assumptions appear in the test at the beginning of the Quantitative Reasoning sections, and they are elaborated below.

Also, some notation and terminology, while standard at the high school level in many countries, may be different from those used in other countries or from those used at higher or lower levels of mathematics. Such notation and terminology are clarified below. Because it is impossible to ascertain which notation and terminology should be clarified for an individual test taker, more material than necessary may be included.

Finally, there are some guidelines for how certain information given in test questions should be interpreted and used in the context of answering the questions—information such as certain words, phrases, quantities, mathematical expressions, and displays of data. These guidelines appear at the end.

Numbers and Quantities

1. All numbers used in the test questions are real numbers. In particular, integers and both rational and irrational numbers are to be considered, but imaginary numbers are not. This is the main assumption regarding numbers. Also, all quantities are real numbers, although quantities may involve units of measurement.

2. Numbers are expressed in base 10 unless otherwise noted, using the 10 digits 0 through 9 and a period to the right of the ones digit, or units digit, for the decimal point. When commas appear in a number, they are used to separate groups of three digits to the left of the decimal point.

3. When a positive integer is described by the number of its digits, for example, a two-digit integer, the digits that are counted include the ones digit and all the digits farther to the left, where the leftmost digit is not 0. For example, 5,000 is a four-digit integer, whereas 031 is not considered to be a three-digit integer.

4. Some other conventions involving numbers:

   one billion means 1,000,000,000, or 10^9 (not 10^{12}, as in some countries);

   one dozen means 12;

   the Greek letter π represents the ratio of the circumference of a circle to its diameter and is approximately 3.14.

5. When a positive number is to be rounded to a certain decimal place and the number is halfway between the two nearest possibilities, the number should be rounded to the greater possibility.

Example A: 23.5 rounded to the nearest integer is 24.

Example B: 123.985 rounded to the nearest 0.01 is 123.99.

When the number to be rounded is negative, the number should be rounded to the lesser possibility.

Example C: −36.5 rounded to the nearest integer is −37.

6. Repeating decimals are sometimes written with a bar over the digits that repeat, as in $\frac{25}{12} = 2.08\overline{3}$ and $\frac{1}{7} = 0.\overline{142857}$.

7. If r, s, and t are integers and $rs = t$, then r and s are **factors**, or **divisors**, of t; also, t is a **multiple** of r (and of s) and t is **divisible** by r (and by s). The factors of an integer include positive and negative integers.

Example A: −7 is a factor of 35.

Example B: 8 is a factor of −40.

Example C: The integer 4 has six factors: −4, −2, −1, 1, 2, and 4.

The terms **factor**, **divisor**, and **divisible** are used only when r, s, and t are integers. However, the term **multiple** can be used with any real numbers s and t provided that r is an integer.

Example A: 1.2 is a multiple of 0.4.

Example B: -2π is a multiple of π.

8. The **least common multiple** of two nonzero integers a and b is the least positive integer that is a multiple of both a and b. The **greatest common divisor** (or **greatest common factor**) of a and b is the greatest positive integer that is a divisor of both a and b.

9. If an integer n is divided by a nonzero integer d resulting in a quotient q with remainder r, then $n = qd + r$, where $0 \leq r < d$. Furthermore, $r = 0$ if and only if n is a multiple of d.

Example A: When 20 is divided by 7, the quotient is 2 and the remainder is 6.

Example B: When 21 is divided by 7, the quotient is 3 and the remainder is 0.

Example C: When −17 is divided by 7, the quotient is −3 and the remainder is 4.

10. A **prime number** is an integer greater than 1 that has only two positive divisors: 1 and itself. The first five prime numbers are 2, 3, 5, 7, and 11. A **composite number** is an integer greater than 1 that is not a prime number. The first five composite numbers are 4, 6, 8, 9, and 10.

11. Odd and even integers are not necessarily positive.

Example A: −7 is odd.

Example B: −18 and 0 are even.

12. The integer 0 is neither positive nor negative.

Mathematical Expressions, Symbols, and Variables

1. As is common in algebra, italic letters like x are used to denote numbers, constants, and variables. Letters are also used to label various objects, such as line $\pounds$, point P, function f, set S, list T, event E, random variable X, Brand X, City Y, and Company Z. The meaning of a letter is determined by the context.

2. When numbers, constants, or variables are given, their possible values are all real numbers unless otherwise restricted. It is common to restrict the possible values in various ways. Here are three examples.

    Example A: n is a nonzero integer.

    Example B: $1 \le x < \pi$

    Example C: T is the tens digits of a two-digit positive integer, so T is an integer from 1 to 9.

3. Standard mathematical symbols at the high school level are used. These include the standard symbols for the arithmetic operations of addition, subtraction, multiplication, and division ($+$, $-$, $\times$, and $\div$), though multiplication is usually denoted by juxtaposition, often with parentheses, for example, $2y$ and $(3)(4.5)$, and division is usually denoted with a horizontal fraction bar, for example, $\frac{w}{3}$. Sometimes mixed numbers, or mixed fractions, are used, like $4\frac{3}{8}$ and $-10\frac{1}{2}$. (The mixed number $4\frac{3}{8}$ is equal to the fraction $\frac{35}{8}$, and the mixed number $-10\frac{1}{2}$ is equal to the fraction $-\frac{21}{2}$.) Exponents are also used, for example, $2^{10} = 1{,}024$, $10^{-2} = \frac{1}{100}$, and $x^0 = 1$ for all nonzero numbers x.

4. Mathematical expressions are to be interpreted with respect to **order of operations**, which establishes which operations are performed before others in an expression. The order is as follows: parentheses, exponentiation, negation, multiplication and division (from left to right), addition and subtraction (from left to right).

    Example A: The value of the expression $1 + 2 \times 4$ is 9, because the expression is evaluated by first multiplying 2 and 4 and then adding 1 to the result.

    Example B: -3^2 means "the negative of 3 squared" because exponentiation takes precedence over negation. Therefore, $-3^2 = -9$, but $(-3)^2 = 9$ because parentheses take precedence over exponentiation.

5. Here are examples of ten other standard symbols with their meanings.

Symbol	**Meaning**
$x \leq y$	x is less than or equal to y
$x \neq y$	x is not equal to y
$x \approx y$	x is approximately equal to y
$|x|$	the absolute value of x
$\sqrt{x}$	the nonnegative square root of x, where $x \geq 0$
$-\sqrt{x}$	the negative square root of x, where $x > 0$
$n!$	n factorial, which is the product of all positive integers less than or equal to n, where n is any positive integer and, as a special definition, $0! = 1$.
$k \parallel m$	lines k and m are parallel
$k \perp m$	lines k and m are perpendicular
$\angle B$	angle B

6. Because all numbers are assumed to be real, some expressions are not defined. Here are three examples.

   Example A: For every number x, the expression $\dfrac{x}{0}$ is not defined.

   Example B: If $x < 0$, then $\sqrt{x}$ is not defined.

   Example C: 0^0 is not defined.

7. Sometimes special symbols or notation are introduced in a question. Here are two examples.

   Example A: The operation $\lozenge$ is defined for all integers r and s by $r \lozenge s = \dfrac{rs}{1 + r^2}$.

   Example B: The operation $\sim$ is defined for all nonzero numbers x by $\sim x = -\dfrac{1}{x}$.

8. Sometimes juxtaposition of letters does *not* denote multiplication, as in "consider a three-digit positive integer denoted by BCD, where B, C, and D are digits." Whether or not juxtaposition of letters denotes multiplication depends on the context in which the juxtaposition occurs.

9. Standard function notation is used in the test, as shown in the following three examples.

   Example A: The function g is defined for all $x \neq 2$ by $g(x) = \dfrac{1}{2 - x}$.

   Example B: If the domain of a function f is not given explicitly, it is assumed to be the set of all real numbers x for which $f(x)$ is a real number.

   Example C: If f and g are two functions, then the **composition** of g with f is denoted by $g(f(x))$.

Geometry

1. In questions involving geometry, the conventions of plane (or Euclidean) geometry are followed, including the assumption that the sum of the measures of the interior angles of a triangle is 180 degrees.

2. Lines are assumed to be "straight" lines that extend in both directions without end.

3. Angle measures are in degrees and are assumed to be positive and less than or equal to 360 degrees.

4. When a square, circle, polygon, or other closed geometric figure is described in words but not shown, the figure is assumed to enclose a convex region. It is also assumed that such a closed geometric figure is not just a single point or a line segment. For example, a description of a quadrilateral *cannot* refer to any of the following geometric figures.

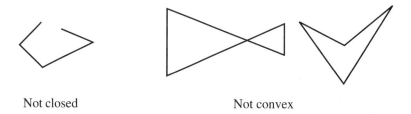

Not closed   Not convex

Mathematical Conventions Figure 1

5. The phrase **area of a rectangle** means the area of the region enclosed by the rectangle. The same terminology applies to circles, triangles, and other closed figures.

6. The **distance between a point and a line** is the length of the perpendicular line segment from the point to the line, which is the shortest distance between the point and the line. Similarly, the **distance between two parallel lines** is the distance between a point on one line and the other line.

7. In a geometric context, the phrase **similar triangles** (or other figures) means that the figures have the same shape. See the Geometry part of the *Math Review* for further explanation of the terms **similar** and **congruent**.

Geometric Figures

1. Geometric figures consist of points, lines, line segments, curves (such as circles), angles, and regions; also included are labels, markings, or shadings that identify these objects or their sizes. A point is indicated by a dot, a label, or the intersection of two or more lines or curves. Points, lines, angles, etc., that are shown as distinct are indeed distinct. All figures are assumed to lie in a plane unless otherwise indicated.

2. If points A, B, and C do not lie on the same line, then line segments AB and BC form two angles with vertex B: one angle with measure less than $180°$ and the other with measure greater than $180°$, as shown in the following figure. Unless otherwise indicated, angle ABC, also called angle B, refers to the *smaller* of the two angles.

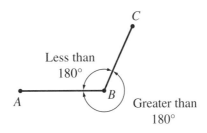

Mathematical Conventions Figure 2

3. The notation *AB* may mean the line segment with endpoints *A* and *B*, or it may mean the length of the line segment. It may also mean the line containing points *A* and *B*. The meaning can be determined from the context.

4. Geometric figures *are not necessarily* drawn to scale. That is, you should *not* assume that quantities such as lengths and angle measures are as they appear in a figure. However, you should assume that lines shown as straight are actually straight, and when curves are shown, you should assume they are not straight. Also, assume that points on a line or a curve are in the order shown, points shown to be on opposite sides of a line or curve are so oriented, and more generally, assume all geometric objects are in the relative positions shown. For questions with geometric figures, you should base your answers on geometric reasoning, not on estimating or comparing quantities by sight or by measurement.

    To illustrate some of the conventions regarding geometric figures, consider the following figure.

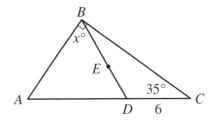

Mathematical Conventions Figure 3

The following seven statements about the preceding figure are consistent with the way the figure is drawn, and you should assume that they are in fact true.

Statement 1:   Points *A*, *D*, and *C* are distinct. Point *D* lies between points *A* and *C*, and the line containing them is straight.

Statement 2:   The length of line segment *AD* is less than the length of line segment *AC*.

Statement 3:   *ABC*, *ABD*, and *DBC* are triangles.

Statement 4:   Point *E* lies on line segment *BD*.

Statement 5:   Angle *ABC* is a right angle, as indicated by the small square symbol at point *B*.

Statement 6:   The length of line segment *DC* is 6, and the measure of angle *C* is 35 degrees.

Statement 7:   The measure of angle *ABD* is *x* degrees, and $x < 90$.

The following four statements about the preceding figure are consistent with the way the figure is drawn; however, you should *not* assume that they are in fact true.

Statement 1: The length of line segment *AD* is greater than the length of line segment *DC*.

Statement 2: The measures of angles *BAD* and *BDA* are equal.

Statement 3: The measure of angle *DBC* is less than *x* degrees.

Statement 4: The area of triangle *ABD* is greater than the area of triangle *DBC*.

For another illustration, consider the following figure.

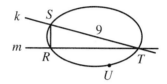

Mathematical Conventions Figure 4

The following five statements about the preceding figure are consistent with the way the figure is drawn, and according to the preceding conventions, you should assume that they are in fact true.

Statement 1: Points *R*, *S*, *T*, and *U* lie on a closed curve.

Statement 2: Line *k* intersects the closed curve at points *S* and *T*.

Statement 3: Points *S* and *U* are on opposite sides of line *m*.

Statement 4: The length of side *ST* is 9.

Statement 5: The area of the region enclosed by the curve is greater than the area of triangle *RST*.

The statement "angle *SRT* is a right angle" is consistent with the way the figure is drawn, but you should *not* assume that angle *SRT* is a right angle.

Coordinate Systems

1. Coordinate systems, such as *xy*-planes and number lines, are drawn to scale. Therefore, you can read, estimate, or compare quantities in such figures by sight or by measurement, including geometric figures that appear in coordinate systems.

2. When a number line is drawn horizontally, the positive direction is to the right unless otherwise noted. When a number line is drawn vertically, the positive direction is upward unless otherwise noted.

3. As in geometry, distances in a coordinate system are nonnegative.

4. The *xy*-plane may also be referred to as the rectangular coordinate plane or the rectangular coordinate system.

5. In the *xy*-plane, the *x*-axis is horizontal and the positive direction of the *x*-axis is to the right. The *y*-axis is vertical, and the positive direction is upward. The *x*-axis and

the *y*-axis may have different scales. The *x*-axis and the *y*-axis intersect at the origin *O*, and they partition the plane into four quadrants, as shown in the following figure.

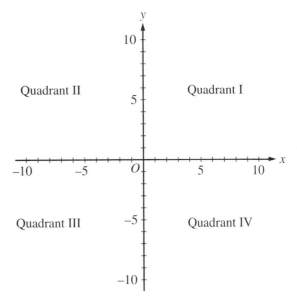

Mathematical Conventions Figure 5

6. Each point in the *xy*-plane has coordinates (*x*, *y*) that give its location with respect to the axes; for example, the point *P*(2, −8) is located 2 units to the right of the *y*-axis and 8 units below the *x*-axis, as shown in the following figure.

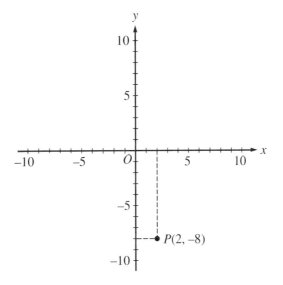

Mathematical Conventions Figure 6

7. Intermediate grid lines or tick marks in a coordinate system are evenly spaced unless otherwise noted.

8. The term **x-intercept** refers to the *x*-coordinate of the point at which a graph in the *xy*-plane intersects the *x*-axis. The term **y-intercept** is used analogously. Sometimes the terms **x-intercept** and **y-intercept** refer to the actual intersection points.

Sets, Lists, and Sequences

1. Sets of numbers or other elements appear in some questions. Some sets are infinite, such as the set of integers; other sets are finite and may have all of their elements listed within curly brackets, such as the set {2, 4, 6, 8}. When the elements of a set are given, repetitions are *not* counted as additional elements and the order of the elements is *not* relevant. Elements are also called **members**. A set with one or more members is called **nonempty**; there is a set with no members, called the **empty set** and denoted by $\varnothing$. If A and B are sets, then the **intersection** of A and B, denoted by $A \cap B$, is the set of elements that are in both A and B, and the **union** of A and B, denoted by $A \cup B$, is the set of elements that are in A or B, or both. If all of the elements in A are also in B, then A is a **subset** of B. By convention, the empty set is a subset of every set. If A and B have no elements in common, they are called **disjoint** sets or **mutually exclusive** sets.

2. Lists of numbers or other elements are also used in the test. When the elements of a list are given, repetitions *are* counted as additional elements and the order of the elements *is* relevant.

    Example: The list 3, 1, 2, 3, 3 contains five numbers, and the first, fourth, and fifth numbers in the list are each 3.

3. The terms **data set** and **set of data** are not sets in the mathematical sense given above. Rather they refer to a list of data because there may be repetitions in the data, and if there are repetitions, they would be relevant.

4. Sequences are lists that may have a finite or infinite number of elements, or terms. The terms of a sequence can be represented by a fixed letter along with a subscript that indicates the order of a term in the sequence. Ellipsis dots are used to indicate the presence of terms that are not explicitly listed. Ellipsis dots at the end of a list of terms indicate that there is no last term; that is, the sequence is infinite.

    Example: $a_1, a_2, a_3, \ldots, a_n, \ldots$ represents an infinite sequence in which the first term is a_1, the second term is a_2, and more generally, the nth term is a_n for every positive integer n.

    Sometimes the nth term of a sequence is given by a formula, such as $b_n = 2^n + 1$. Sometimes the first few terms of a sequence are given explicitly, as in the following sequence of consecutive even negative integers: $-2, -4, -6, -8, -10, \ldots$.

5. Sets of consecutive integers are sometimes described by indicating the first and last integer, as in "the integers from 0 to 9, inclusive." This phrase refers to 10 integers, with or without "inclusive" at the end. Thus, the phrase "during the years from 1985 to 2005" refers to 21 years.

Data and Statistics

1. Numerical data are sometimes given in lists and sometimes displayed in other ways, such as in tables, bar graphs, or circle graphs. Various statistics, or measures of data, appear in questions: measures of central tendency—mean, median, and mode; measures of position—quartiles and percentiles; and measures of dispersion—standard deviation, range, and interquartile range.

2. The term **average** is used in two ways, with and without the qualification "(arithmetic mean)." For a list of data, the **average (arithmetic mean)** of the data is the sum of the data divided by the number of data. The term **average** does not refer to either **median** or **mode** in the test. Without the qualification of "arithmetic mean," **average** can refer to a rate or the ratio of one quantity to another, as in "average number of miles per hour" or "average weight per truckload."

3. For a finite set or list of numbers, the **mean** of the numbers refers to the *arithmetic mean* unless otherwise noted.

4. The **median** of an odd number of data is the middle number when the data are listed in increasing order; the **median** of an even number of data is the arithmetic mean of the two middle numbers when the data are listed in increasing order.

5. For a list of data, the **mode** of the data is the most frequently occurring number in the list. Thus, there may be more than one mode for a list of data.

6. For data listed in increasing order, the **first quartile**, **second quartile**, and **third quartile** of the data are three numbers that divide the data into four groups that are roughly equal in size. The first group of numbers is from the least number up to the first quartile. The second group is from the first quartile up to the second quartile, which is also the median of the data. The third group is from the second quartile up to the third quartile, and the fourth group is from the third quartile up to the greatest number. Note that the four groups themselves are sometimes referred to as quartiles—**first quartile**, **second quartile**, **third quartile**, and **fourth quartile**. The latter usage is clarified by the word "in," as in the phrase "the cow's weight is *in* the third quartile of the weights of the herd."

7. For data listed in increasing order, the **percentiles** of the data are 99 numbers that divide the data into 100 groups that are roughly equal in size. The 25th percentile equals the first quartile; the 50th percentile equals the second quartile, or median; and the 75th percentile equals the third quartile.

8. For a list of data, where the arithmetic mean is denoted by m, the **standard deviation** of the data refers to the nonnegative square root of the mean of the squared differences between m and each of the data. The standard deviation is a measure of the spread of the data about the mean. The greater the standard deviation, the greater the spread of the data about the mean. This statistic is also known as the **population standard deviation** (not to be confused with the "sample standard deviation," a closely related statistic).

9. For a list of data, the **range** of the data is the greatest number in the list minus the least number. The **interquartile range** of the data is the third quartile minus the first quartile.

Data Distributions and Probability Distributions

1. Some questions display data in **frequency distributions**, where discrete data values are repeated with various frequencies or where preestablished intervals of possible values have frequencies corresponding to the numbers of values in the intervals.

   Example: The lifetimes, rounded to the nearest hour, of 300 lightbulbs are in the following 10 intervals: 501 to 550 hours, 551 to 600 hours, 601 to 650 hours, and so on, up to 951 to 1,000 hours. Consequently, each of the intervals has a number, or frequency, of lifetimes, and the sum of the 10 frequencies is 300.

2. Questions may involve **relative frequency distributions**, where each frequency of a frequency distribution is divided by the total number of data in the distribution, resulting in a relative frequency. In the example above, the 10 frequencies of the 10 intervals would each be divided by 300, yielding 10 relative frequencies.

3. When a question refers to a random selection or a random sample, all possible samples of equal size have the same probability of being selected unless there is information to the contrary.

4. Some questions describe **probability experiments**, or **random experiments**, that have a finite number of possible **outcomes**. In a random experiment, any particular set of outcomes is called an **event**, and every event E has a **probability**, denoted by $P(E)$, where $0 \le P(E) \le 1$. If each outcome of an experiment is equally likely, then the probability of an event E is defined as the following ratio.

$$P(E) = \frac{\text{the number of outcomes in the event } E}{\text{the number of possible outcomes in the experiment}}$$

5. If E and F are two events in an experiment, then "E and F" is an event, which is the set of outcomes that are in the intersection of events E and F. Another event is "E or F," which is the set of outcomes that are in the union of events E and F.

6. If E and F are two events and E and F are mutually exclusive, then $P(E \text{ and } F) = 0$.

7. If E and F are two events such that the occurrence of either event does not affect the occurrence of the other, then E and F are said to be **independent** events. Events E and F are independent if and only if $P(E \text{ and } F) = P(E)P(F)$.

8. A **random variable** is a variable that represents values resulting from a random experiment. The values of the random variable may be the actual outcomes of the experiment if the outcomes are numerical, or the random variable may be related to the outcomes more indirectly. In either case, random variables can be used to describe events in terms of numbers.

9. A random variable from an experiment with only a finite number of possible outcomes also has only a finite number of values and is called a **discrete random variable**. When the values of a random variable form a continuous interval of real numbers, such as all of the numbers between 0 and 2, the random variable is called a **continuous random variable**.

10. Every value of a discrete random variable X, say $X = a$, has a probability denoted by $P(X = a)$, or by just $P(a)$. A histogram (or a table) showing all of the values of X and their probabilities $P(X)$ is called the **probability distribution** of X. The **mean of the random variable** X is the sum of the products $XP(X)$ for all values of X.

11. The mean of a random variable X is also called the **expected value** of X or the **mean of the probability distribution** of X.

12. For a continuous random variable X, every interval of values, say $a \leq X \leq b$, has a probability, which is denoted by $P(a \leq X \leq b)$. The **probability distribution** of X can be represented by a curve in the xy-plane. The curve is the graph of a function f whose values are nonnegative. The curve $y = f(x)$ is related to the probability of each interval $a \leq X \leq b$ in the following way: $P(a \leq X \leq b)$ is equal to the area of the region that is below the curve, above the x-axis, and between the vertical lines $x = a$ and $x = b$. The area of the entire region under the curve is 1, where the x-axis and the y-axis may have different scales.

13. The **mean of a continuous random variable** X is the point m on the x-axis at which the region under the distribution curve would perfectly balance if a fulcrum were placed at $x = m$. The **median** of X is the point M on the x-axis at which the line $x = M$ divides the region under the distribution curve into two regions of equal area.

14. The **standard deviation of a random variable** X is a measure of dispersion, which indicates how spread out the probability distribution of X is from its mean. The greater the standard deviation of a random variable, the greater the spread of its distribution about its mean. This statistic is also known as the **standard deviation of the probability distribution** of X.

15. One of the most important probability distributions is the **normal distribution**, whose distribution curve is shaped like a bell. A random variable X with this distribution is called **normally distributed**. The curve is symmetric about the line $x = m$, where m is the mean as well as the median. The right and left tails of the distribution approach the x-axis but never touch it.

16. The **standard normal distribution** has mean 0 and standard deviation 1. The following figure shows the standard normal distribution, including approximate probabilities corresponding to the six intervals shown.

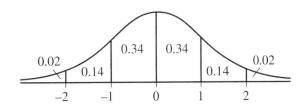

Mathematical Conventions Figure 7

Graphical Representations of Data

1. When graphical data presentations, such as bar graphs and line graphs, are shown with scales, you should read, estimate, or compare quantities by sight or by measurement, according to the corresponding scales.

2. Scales, grid lines, dots, bars, shadings, solid and dashed lines, legends, etc., are used on graphs to indicate the data. Sometimes scales that do not begin at 0 are used, and sometimes broken scales are used.

3. Standard conventions apply to graphs of data unless otherwise indicated. For example, a circle graph represents 100 percent of the data indicated in the graph's title, and the areas of the individual sectors are proportional to the percents they represent.

4. In Venn diagrams, various sets of objects are represented by circular regions and by regions formed by intersections of the circles. In some Venn diagrams, all of the circles are inside a rectangular region that represents a universal set. A number placed in a region is the number of elements in the subset represented by the smallest region containing the number, unless otherwise noted. Sometimes a number is placed above a circular region to indicate the number of elements in the set represented by the circular region.

Miscellaneous Guidelines for Interpreting and Using Information in Test Questions

1. Numbers given in a question are to be used as exact numbers, even though in some real-life settings they are likely to have been rounded.

    Example: If a question states that "30 percent of the company's profit was from health products," then 30 is to be used as an exact number; it is not to be treated as though it were a nearby number, say, 29 or 30.1, that has been rounded up or down.

2. An integer that is given as the number of certain objects, whether in a real-life or pure-math setting, is to be taken as the total number of such objects.

    Example: If a question states that "a bag contains 50 marbles, and 23 of the marbles are red," then 50 is to be taken as the total number of marbles in the bag and 23 is to be taken as the total number of red marbles in the bag, so that the other 27 marbles are not red. Fractions and percents are understood in a similar way, so "one-fifth, or 20 percent, of the 50 marbles in the bag are green" means that 10 marbles in the bag are green and 40 marbles are not green.

3. When a multiple-choice question asks for an approximate quantity without stipulating a degree of approximation, the correct answer is the choice that is closest in value to the quantity that can be computed from the information given.

4. Unless otherwise indicated, the phrase "difference between two quantities" is assumed to mean "positive difference," that is, the greater quantity minus the lesser quantity.

    Example: "For which two consecutive years was the difference in annual rainfall least?" means "for which two consecutive years was the *absolute value of the difference in annual rainfall least?*"

5. When the term **profit** is used in a question, it refers to **gross profit**, which is the sales revenue minus the cost of production or acquisition. The profit does not involve any other amounts unless they are explicitly given.

6. The common meaning of terms such as **months** and **years** and other everyday terms are assumed in questions where the terms appear.

7. In questions involving real-life scenarios in which a variable is given to represent a number of existing objects or a monetary amount, the context implies that the variable is greater than 0 unless otherwise noted.

    Example: "Jane sold x rugs and deposited her profit of y dollars into her savings account" implies that x and y are greater than 0.

8. Some quantities may involve units, such as inches, pounds, and Celsius degrees, while other quantities are pure numbers. Any units of measurement, such as English units or metric units, may be used. However, if an answer to a question requires converting one unit of measurement to another, then the relationship between the units is given in the question, unless the relationship is a common one, such as the relationships between minutes and hours, dollars and cents, and metric units like centimeters and meters.

9. In any question, there may be some information that is not needed for obtaining the correct answer.

10. When reading questions, do not introduce unwarranted assumptions.

    Example A: If a question describes a trip that begins and ends at certain times, the intended answer will assume that the times are unaffected by crossing time zones or by changes to the local time for daylight savings, unless those matters are explicitly mentioned.

    Example B: Do not consider sales taxes on purchases unless explicitly mentioned.

11. The display of data in a Data Interpretation set of questions is the same for each question in the set. Also, the display may contain more than one graph or table. Each question will refer to the data presentation, but it may happen that some part of the data will have no question that refers to it.

12. In a Data Interpretation set of questions, each question should be considered separately from the others. No information except what is given in the display of data should be carried over from one question to another.

13. In many questions, mathematical expressions and words appear together in a phrase. In such a phrase, each mathematical expression should be interpreted *separately* from the words before it is interpreted *along with* the words. For example, if n is an integer, then the phrase "the sum of the first two consecutive integers greater than $n + 6$" means $(n + 7) + (n + 8)$; it does not mean "the sum of the first two consecutive integers greater than n" plus 6, or $(n + 1) + (n + 2) + 6$. That is, the expression $n + 6$ should be interpreted first, separately from the words. However, in a phrase like "the function g is defined for all $x \geq 0$," the phrase "for all $x \geq 0$," is mathematical shorthand for "for all numbers x such that $x \geq 0$."

7 GRE Quantitative Reasoning: Practice Questions

Your goals for this chapter

▸ Practice answering GRE Quantitative Reasoning questions on your own
▸ Review answers and explanations, particularly for questions you answered incorrectly

This chapter contains four sets of GRE Quantitative Reasoning practice questions. Each of the first three practice sets consists of Quantitative Comparison questions, both types of Multiple-choice questions, and Numeric Entry questions. These three sets are arranged in order of increasing difficulty. The first is easy, the second is medium, and the third is hard. The fourth practice set consists of Data Interpretation questions of varying levels of difficulty.

Following the last set is an answer key for quick reference. Then, at the end of the chapter, you will find complete explanations for every question. Each explanation is presented with the corresponding question for easy reference.

Sharpen your GRE Quantitative Reasoning skills by working your way through these question sets. For the Discrete question sets, begin with the easy sets and then move on to the medium and hard sets. Review the answers and explanations carefully, paying particular attention to explanations for questions that you answered incorrectly.

For the practice questions in this chapter, use the section directions that begin on the following page.

Section Directions

For each question, indicate the best answer, using the directions given.

Notes: All numbers used are real numbers.

All figures are assumed to lie in a plane unless otherwise indicated.

Geometric figures, such as lines, circles, triangles, and quadrilaterals, **are not necessarily** drawn to scale. That is, you should **not** assume that quantities such as lengths and angle measures are as they appear in a figure. You should assume, however, that lines shown as straight are actually straight, points on a line are in the order shown, and more generally, all geometric objects are in the relative positions shown. For questions with geometric figures, you should base your answers on geometric reasoning, not on estimating or comparing quantities by sight or by measurement.

Coordinate systems, such as xy-planes and number lines, **are** drawn to scale; therefore, you can read, estimate, or compare quantities in such figures by sight or by measurement.

Graphical data presentations, such as bar graphs, circle graphs, and line graphs, **are** drawn to scale; therefore, you can read, estimate, or compare data values by sight or by measurement.

Directions for Quantitative Comparison questions

Compare Quantity A and Quantity B, using additional information centered above the two quantities if such information is given. Select one of the following four answer choices and fill in the corresponding oval to the right of the question.

(A) **Quantity A is greater.**

(B) **Quantity B is greater.**

(C) **The two quantities are equal.**

(D) **The relationship cannot be determined from the information given.**

A symbol that appears more than once in a question has the same meaning throughout the question.

	Quantity A	Quantity B	Correct Answer
Example 1:	(2)(6)	2 + 6	(A) (B) (C) (D)

	Quantity A	Quantity B	Correct Answer
Example 2:	PS	SR	(A) (B) (C) (D)

(since equal lengths cannot be assumed, even though PS and SR appear equal)

Directions for Numeric Entry questions

Enter your answer in the answer box(es) below the question.

- Your answer may be an integer, a decimal, or a fraction, and it may be negative.
- If a question asks for a fraction, there will be two boxes—one for the numerator and one for the denominator.
- Equivalent forms of the correct answer, such as 2.5 and 2.50, are all correct. Fractions do not need to be reduced to lowest terms.
- Enter the exact answer unless the question asks you to round your answer.

SET 1. Practice Questions: Easy

Quantitative Comparison

For Questions 1 to 6, compare Quantity A and Quantity B, using additional information centered above the two quantities if such information is given. Select one of the following four answer choices and fill in the corresponding oval to the right of the question.

(A) Quantity A is greater.

(B) Quantity B is greater.

(C) The two quantities are equal.

(D) The relationship cannot be determined from the information given.

A symbol that appears more than once in a question has the same meaning throughout the question.

Emma spent $75 buying a used bicycle and $27 repairing it. Then she sold the bicycle for 40 percent more than the total amount she spent buying and repairing it.

	Quantity A	Quantity B	
1.	The price at which Emma sold the bicycle	$140	(A) (B) (C) (D)

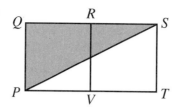

In the figure above, squares *PQRV* and *VRST* have sides of length 6.

Quantity A	Quantity B	
2. The area of the shaded region	36	Ⓐ Ⓑ Ⓒ Ⓓ

In 2009 the property tax on each home in Town *X* was *p* percent of the assessed value of the home, where *p* is a constant. The property tax in 2009 on a home in Town *X* that had an assessed value of $125,000 was $2,500.

Quantity A	Quantity B	
3. The property tax in 2009 on a home in Town *X* that had an assessed value of $160,000	$3,000	Ⓐ Ⓑ Ⓒ Ⓓ

$$x + y = -1$$

Quantity A	Quantity B	
4. x	y	Ⓐ Ⓑ Ⓒ Ⓓ

---

r, *s*, and *t* are three consecutive odd integers such that $r < s < t$.

Quantity A	Quantity B	
5. $r + s + 1$	$s + t - 1$	Ⓐ Ⓑ Ⓒ Ⓓ

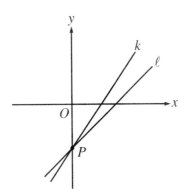

Quantity A	Quantity B
6. The slope of line k	The slope of line ℓ

Ⓐ Ⓑ Ⓒ Ⓓ

Multiple-choice Questions—Select One Answer Choice

For Questions 7 to 11, select a single answer choice.

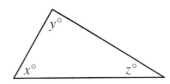

7. In the figure above, what is the value of $\dfrac{x+y+z}{45}$?

    Ⓐ 2

    Ⓑ 3

    Ⓒ 4

    Ⓓ 5

    Ⓔ 6

8. A certain store sells two types of pens: one type for $2 per pen and the other type for $3 per pen. If a customer can spend up to $25 to buy pens at the store and there is no sales tax, what is the greatest number of pens the customer can buy?

    Ⓐ 9

    Ⓑ 10

    Ⓒ 11

    Ⓓ 12

    Ⓔ 20

9. If $y = 3x$ and $z = 2y$, what is $x + y + z$ in terms of x?

  (A) $10x$

  (B) $9x$

  (C) $8x$

  (D) $6x$

  (E) $5x$

10. A certain shipping service charges an insurance fee of $0.75 when shipping any package with contents worth $25.00 or less and an insurance fee of $1.00 when shipping any package with contents worth over $25.00. If Dan uses the shipping company to ship three packages with contents worth $18.25, $25.00, and $127.50, respectively, what is the total insurance fee that the company charges Dan to ship the three packages?

  (A) $1.75

  (B) $2.25

  (C) $2.50

  (D) $2.75

  (E) $3.00

11. Last year, all purchases of a certain product were made either online or in a store. If 55 percent of the purchases were made online, what was the ratio of the number of purchases made online to the number of purchases made in a store?

  (A) 11 to 9

  (B) 11 to 5

  (C) 10 to 9

  (D) 9 to 11

  (E) 9 to 10

Numeric Entry

For Questions 12 and 13, enter your answer in the answer box(es) below the question.

- Your answer may be an integer, a decimal, or a fraction, and it may be negative.
- If a question asks for a fraction, there will be two boxes—one for the numerator and one for the denominator.
- Equivalent forms of the correct answer, such as 2.5 and 2.50, are all correct. Fractions do not need to be reduced to lowest terms.
- Enter the exact answer unless the question asks you to round your answer.

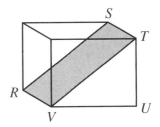

12. In the rectangular solid above, $TU = 3$, $UV = 4$, and $VR = 2$. What is the area of the shaded rectangular region?

13. A list of numbers has a mean of 8 and a standard deviation of 2.5. If x is a number in the list that is 2 standard deviations above the mean, what is the value of x?

$x = $ _____

Multiple-choice Questions—Select One or More Answer Choices

For Question 14, select all the answer choices that apply.

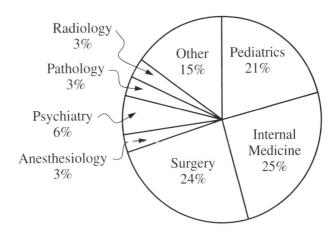

14. The circle graph above shows the distribution of 200,000 physicians by specialty. Which of the following sectors of the circle graph represent more than 40,000 physicians?

Indicate <u>all</u> such sectors.

A   Pediatrics

B   Internal Medicine

C   Surgery

D   Anesthesiology

E   Psychiatry

SET 2. Practice Questions: Medium

Quantitative Comparison

For Questions 1 to 5, compare Quantity A and Quantity B, using additional information centered above the two quantities if such information is given. Select one of the following four answer choices and fill in the corresponding oval to the right of the question.

Ⓐ Quantity A is greater.

Ⓑ Quantity B is greater.

Ⓒ The two quantities are equal.

Ⓓ The relationship cannot be determined from the information given.

A symbol that appears more than once in a question has the same meaning throughout the question.

Machine R, working alone at a constant rate, produces x units of a product in 30 minutes, and machine S, working alone at a constant rate, produces x units of the product in 48 minutes, where x is a positive integer.

Quantity A	Quantity B

1. The number of units of the product that machine R, working alone at its constant rate, produces in 3 hours

   The number of units of the product that machine S, working alone at its constant rate, produces in 4 hours

Frequency Distribution for List X

Number	1	2	3	5
Frequency	10	20	18	12

Frequency Distribution for List Y

Number	6	7	8	9
Frequency	24	17	10	9

List X and list Y each contain 60 numbers. Frequency distributions for each list are given. The average (arithmetic mean) of the numbers in list X is 2.7, and the average of the numbers in list Y is 7.1. List Z contains 120 numbers: the 60 numbers in list X and the 60 numbers in list Y.

Quantity A	Quantity B

2. The average of the 120 numbers in list Z

   The median of the 120 numbers in list Z

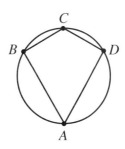

In the figure above, the diameter of the circle is 10.

Quantity A	Quantity B	
3. The area of quadrilateral *ABCD*	40	Ⓐ Ⓑ Ⓒ Ⓓ

$$x^2y > 0$$
$$xy^2 < 0$$

Quantity A	Quantity B	
4. x	y	Ⓐ Ⓑ Ⓒ Ⓓ

Among the 9,000 people attending a football game at College *C*, there were *x* students from College *C* and *y* students who were <u>not</u> from College *C*.

Quantity A	Quantity B	
5. The number of people attending the game who were <u>not</u> students	$9{,}000 - x - y$	Ⓐ Ⓑ Ⓒ Ⓓ

Multiple-choice Questions—Select One Answer Choice

For Questions 6 to 10, select a single answer choice.

6. If $x \neq 0$, which of the following is equivalent to $\dfrac{x(x^2)^3}{x^2}$?

 Ⓐ x^2

 Ⓑ x^3

 Ⓒ x^4

 Ⓓ x^5

 Ⓔ x^6

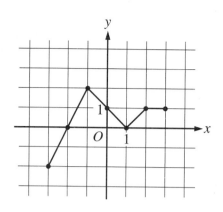

7. The figure above shows the graph of the function *f* in the *xy*-plane. What is the value of $f(f(-1))$?
    - (A) −2
    - (B) −1
    - (C) 0
    - (D) 1
    - (E) 2

8. If $\dfrac{d-3n}{7n-d}=1$, which of the following statements describes *d* in terms of *n*?

    - (A) *d* is 4 less than *n*.
    - (B) *d* is 4 more than *n*.
    - (C) *d* is $\dfrac{3}{7}$ of *n*.
    - (D) *d* is 2 times *n*.
    - (E) *d* is 5 times *n*.

9. By weight, liquid *A* makes up 8 percent of solution *R* and 18 percent of solution *S*. If 3 grams of solution *R* are mixed with 7 grams of solution *S*, then liquid *A* accounts for what percent of the weight of the resulting solution?
    - (A) 10%
    - (B) 13%
    - (C) 15%
    - (D) 19%
    - (E) 26%

10. Of the 700 members of a certain organization, 120 are lawyers. Two members of the organization will be selected at random. Which of the following is closest to the probability that <u>neither</u> of the members selected will be a lawyer?
    - (A) 0.5
    - (B) 0.6
    - (C) 0.7
    - (D) 0.8
    - (E) 0.9

Numeric Entry

For Questions 11 and 12, enter your answer in the answer box(es) below the question.

- Your answer may be an integer, a decimal, or a fraction, and it may be negative.
- If a question asks for a fraction, there will be two boxes—one for the numerator and one for the denominator.
- Equivalent forms of the correct answer, such as 2.5 and 2.50, are all correct. Fractions do not need to be reduced to lowest terms.
- Enter the exact answer unless the question asks you to round your answer.

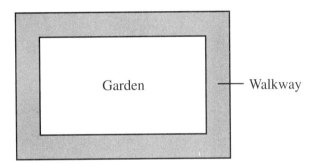

11. The figure above represents a rectangular garden with a walkway around it. The garden is 18 feet long and 12 feet wide. The walkway is uniformly 3 feet wide, and its edges meet at right angles. What is the area of the walkway?

      [_____] square feet

12. Line *k* lies in the *xy*-plane. The *x*-intercept of line *k* is −4, and line *k* passes through the midpoint of the line segment whose endpoints are (2, 9) and (2, 0). What is the slope of line *k*?

   Give your answer as a fraction.

   $$\frac{[\quad]}{[\quad]}$$

Multiple-Choice Questions—Select One or More Answer Choices

For Questions 13 and 14, select all the answer choices that apply.

13. If the lengths of two sides of a triangle are 5 and 9, respectively, which of the following could be the length of the third side of the triangle?

Indicate <u>all</u> such lengths.

   A   3

   B   5

   C   8

   D   15

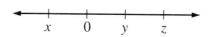

14. On the number line shown above, the tick marks are equally spaced. Which of the following statements about the numbers x, y, and z must be true?

Indicate <u>all</u> such statements.

   A $xyz < 0$

   B $x + z = y$

   C $z(y - x) > 0$

SET 3. Practice Questions: Hard

Quantitative Comparison

For Questions 1 to 6, compare Quantity A and Quantity B, using additional information centered above the two quantities if such information is given. Select one of the following four answer choices and fill in the corresponding oval to the right of the question.

Ⓐ   Quantity A is greater.

Ⓑ   Quantity B is greater.

Ⓒ   The two quantities are equal.

Ⓓ   The relationship cannot be determined from the information given.

A symbol that appears more than once in a question has the same meaning throughout the question.

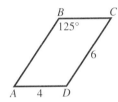

In the figure above, *ABCD* is a parallelogram.

	Quantity A	Quantity B	
1.	The area of the *ABCD*	24	Ⓐ Ⓑ Ⓒ Ⓓ

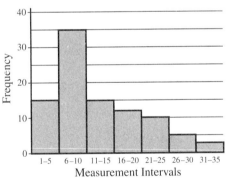

In the course of an experiment, 95 measurements were recorded, and all of the measurements were integers. The 95 measurements were then grouped into 7 measurement intervals. The graph above shows the frequency distribution of the 95 measurements by measurement interval.

	Quantity A	Quantity B	
2.	The average (arithmetic mean) of the 95 measurements	The median of the 95 measurements	Ⓐ Ⓑ Ⓒ Ⓓ

x is an integer greater than 1.

	Quantity A	Quantity B	
3.	3^{x+1}	4^x	Ⓐ Ⓑ Ⓒ Ⓓ

A, B, and C are three rectangles. The length and width of rectangle A are 10 percent greater and 10 percent less, respectively, than the length and width of rectangle C. The length and width of rectangle B are 20 percent greater and 20 percent less, respectively, than the length and width of rectangle C.

	Quantity A	Quantity B	
4.	The area of rectangle A	The area of rectangle B	Ⓐ Ⓑ Ⓒ Ⓓ

The random variable X is normally distributed. The values 650 and 850 are at the 60th and 90th percentiles of the distribution of X, respectively.

	Quantity A	Quantity B	
5.	The value at the 75th percentile of the distribution of X	750	Ⓐ Ⓑ Ⓒ Ⓓ

Set S consists of all positive integers less than 81 that are <u>not</u> equal to the square of an integer.

	Quantity A	Quantity B	
6.	The number of integers in set S	72	Ⓐ Ⓑ Ⓒ Ⓓ

Multiple-choice Questions—Select One Answer Choice

For Questions 7 to 12, select a single answer choice.

7. A manager is forming a 6-person team to work on a certain project. From the 11 candidates available for the team, the manager has already chosen 3 to be on the team. In selecting the other 3 team members, how many different combinations of 3 of the remaining candidates does the manager have to choose from?

    (A) 6
    (B) 24
    (C) 56
    (D) 120
    (E) 462

8. Which of the following could be the graph of all values of x that satisfy the inequality $2 - 5x \leq -\dfrac{6x-5}{3}$?

    (A)

    (B)

    (C)

    (D)

    (E)

9. If $1 + x + x^2 + x^3 = 60$, then the average (arithmetic mean) of x, x^2, x^3, and x^4 is equal to which of the following?

    (A) $12x$
    (B) $15x$
    (C) $20x$
    (D) $30x$
    (E) $60x$

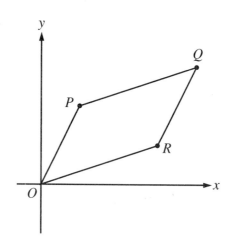

10. Parallelogram *OPQR* lies in the *xy*-plane, as shown in the figure above. The coordinates of point *P* are (2, 4) and the coordinates of point *Q* are (8, 6). What are the coordinates of point *R*?

    (A) (3, 2)

    (B) (3, 3)

    (C) (4, 4)

    (D) (5, 2)

    (E) (6, 2)

11. The relationship between the area *A* of a circle and its circumference *C* is given by the formula $A = kC^2$, where *k* is a constant. What is the value of *k*?

    (A) $\dfrac{1}{4\pi}$

    (B) $\dfrac{1}{2\pi}$

    (C) $\dfrac{1}{4}$

    (D) 2π

    (E) $4\pi^2$

12. The sequence of numbers $a_1, a_2, a_3, \ldots, a_n, \ldots$ is defined by $a_n = \dfrac{1}{n} - \dfrac{1}{n+2}$ for each integer $n \geq 1$. What is the sum of the first 20 terms of the sequence?

    (A) $\left(1 + \dfrac{1}{2}\right) - \dfrac{1}{20}$

    (B) $\left(1 + \dfrac{1}{2}\right) - \left(\dfrac{1}{21} + \dfrac{1}{22}\right)$

    (C) $1 - \left(\dfrac{1}{20} + \dfrac{1}{22}\right)$

    (D) $1 - \dfrac{1}{22}$

    (E) $\dfrac{1}{20} - \dfrac{1}{22}$

Numeric Entry

> **For Question 13, enter your answer in the answer box(es) below the question.**
>
> - Your answer may be an integer, a decimal, or a fraction, and it may be negative.
> - If a question asks for a fraction, there will be two boxes—one for the numerator and one for the denominator.
> - Equivalent forms of the correct answer, such as 2.5 and 2.50, are all correct. Fractions do not need to be reduced to lowest terms.
> - Enter the exact answer unless the question asks you to round your answer.

Y	Frequency
$\dfrac{1}{2}$	2
$\dfrac{3}{4}$	7
$\dfrac{5}{4}$	8
$\dfrac{3}{2}$	8
$\dfrac{7}{4}$	9

13. The table above shows the frequency distribution of the values of a variable Y. What is the mean of the distribution?

   Give your answer to the <u>nearest 0.01</u>.

   [   ]

Multiple-choice Questions—Select One or More Answer Choices

> **For Questions 14 and 15, select all the answer choices that apply.**

14. Let S be the set of all positive integers n such that n^2 is a multiple of both 24 and 108. Which of the following integers are divisors of every integer n in S?

   Indicate <u>all</u> such integers.

   A 12

   B 24

   C 36

   D 72

15. The penguins currently living on an island are of two types, Chinstrap penguins and Gentoo penguins. The range of the heights of the Chinstrap penguins on the island is 13.2 centimeters, and the range of the heights of the Gentoo penguins on the island is 15.4 centimeters.

Which of the following statements individually provide(s) sufficient additional information to determine the range of the heights of all the penguins on the island?

Indicate all such statements.

A The tallest Gentoo penguin on the island is 5.8 centimeters taller than the tallest Chinstrap penguin on the island.

B The median height of the Gentoo penguins on the island is 1.1 centimeters greater than the median height of the Chinstrap penguins on the island.

C The average (arithmetic mean) height of the Gentoo penguins on the island is 4.6 centimeters greater than the average height of the Chinstrap penguins on the island.

SET 4. Data Interpretation Sets

For Questions 1 to 7, select a single answer choice unless otherwise directed.

Questions 1 to 3 are based on the following data.

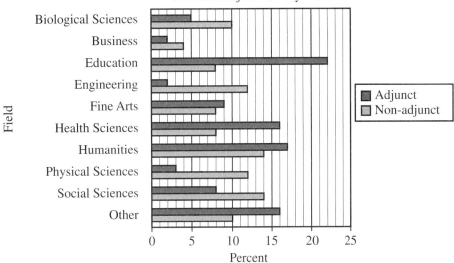

PERCENT OF ADJUNCT FACULTY AND PERCENT OF NON-ADJUNCT
FACULTY AT COLLEGE *X*, BY FIELD
Total adjunct faculty: 200
Total non-adjunct faculty: 250

Medium Question

1. There are 275 students in the field of engineering at College *X*.
    Approximately what is the ratio of the number of students in engineering to
    the number of faculty in engineering?

    Ⓐ 8 to 1
    Ⓑ 10 to 1
    Ⓒ 12 to 1
    Ⓓ 14 to 1
    Ⓔ 20 to 1

Medium Question

2. Approximately what percent of the faculty in humanities are non-adjunct
    faculty?

    Ⓐ 35%
    Ⓑ 38%
    Ⓒ 41%
    Ⓓ 45%
    Ⓔ 51%

For Question 3, use the directions for Numeric Entry questions.

Hard Question

3. For the biological sciences and health sciences faculty combined, $\frac{1}{3}$ of the adjunct faculty and $\frac{2}{9}$ of the non-adjunct faculty are medical doctors. What fraction of all the faculty in those two fields combined are medical doctors?

Questions 4 to 7 are based on the following data.

VALUE OF IMPORTS TO AND EXPORTS FROM COUNTRY T, 2000–2009
(in United States dollars)

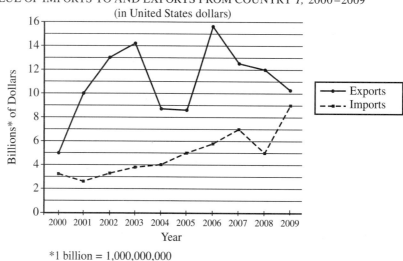

*1 billion = 1,000,000,000

For Question 4, select all the answer choices that apply.

Easy Question

4. For which of the eight years from 2001 to 2008 did exports exceed imports by more than $5 billion?

Indicate <u>all</u> such years.

- [A] 2001
- [B] 2002
- [C] 2003
- [D] 2004
- [E] 2005
- [F] 2006
- [G] 2007
- [H] 2008

Medium Question

5. Which of the following is closest to the average (arithmetic mean) of the 9 changes in the value of imports between consecutive years from 2000 to 2009?

    (A) $260 million

    (B) $320 million

    (C) $400 million

    (D) $480 million

    (E) $640 million

Medium Question

6. In 2008 the value of exports was approximately what percent greater than the value of imports?

    (A) 40%

    (B) 60%

    (C) 70%

    (D) 120%

    (E) 140%

Hard Question

7. If it were discovered that the value of imports shown for 2007 was incorrect and should have been $5 billion instead, then the average (arithmetic mean) value of imports per year for the 10 years shown would have been approximately how much less?

    (A) $200 million

    (B) $50 million

    (C) $20 million

    (D) $7 million

    (E) $5 million

<u>ANSWER KEY</u>

SET 1. Practice Questions: Easy

1. **Choice A**: Quantity A is greater.
2. **Choice C**: The two quantities are equal.
3. **Choice A**: Quantity A is greater.
4. **Choice D**: The relationship cannot be determined from the information given.
5. **Choice B**: Quantity B is greater.
6. **Choice A**: Quantity A is greater.
7. **Choice C**: 4
8. **Choice D**: 12
9. **Choice A**: $10x$
10. **Choice C**: $2.50
11. **Choice A**: 11 to 9
12. **10**
13. **13**
14. **Choice A**: Pediatrics
    AND
    Choice B: Internal Medicine
    AND
    Choice C: Surgery

SET 2. Practice Questions: Medium

1. **Choice A**: Quantity A is greater.
2. **Choice B**: Quantity B is greater.
3. **Choice D**: The relationship cannot be determined from the information given.
4. **Choice B**: Quantity B is greater.
5. **Choice C**: The two quantities are equal.
6. **Choice D**: x^5
7. **Choice D**: 1
8. **Choice E**: d is 5 times n.
9. **Choice C**: 15%
10. **Choice C**: 0.7
11. **216**
12. $\frac{3}{4}$ (or any equivalent fraction)
13. **Choice B**: 5
    AND
    Choice C: 8
14. **Choice A**: $xyz < 0$
    AND
    Choice B: $x + z = y$
    AND
    Choice C: $z(y - x) > 0$

SET 3. Practice Questions: Hard

1. **Choice B**: Quantity B is greater.
2. **Choice A**: Quantity A is greater.
3. **Choice D**: The relationship cannot be determined from the information given.
4. **Choice A**: Quantity A is greater.
5. **Choice B**: Quantity B is greater.
6. **Choice C**: The two quantities are equal.
7. **Choice C**: 56
8. **Choice C**:
9. **Choice B**: $15x$ 0
10. **Choice E**: (6, 2)
11. **Choice A**: $\dfrac{1}{4\pi}$
12. **Choice B**: $\left(1+\dfrac{1}{2}\right)-\left(\dfrac{1}{21}+\dfrac{1}{22}\right)$
13. **1.29**
14. **Choice A**: 12
    AND
    Choice C: 36
15. **Choice A**: The tallest Gentoo penguin on the island is 5.8 centimeters taller than the tallest Chinstrap penguin on the island.

SET 4. Data Interpretation Sets

1. **Choice A**: 8 to 1
2. **Choice E**: 51%
3. $\dfrac{24}{87}$ (or any equivalent fraction)
4. **Choice A**: 2001
   AND
   Choice B: 2002
   AND
   Choice C: 2003
   AND
   Choice F: 2006
   AND
   Choice G: 2007
   AND
   Choice H: 2008
5. **Choice E**: $640 million
6. **Choice E**: 140%
7. **Choice A**: $200 million

Answers and Explanations

For the practice questions in this chapter, use the following directions.

Section Directions

For each question, indicate the best answer, using the directions given.

Notes: All numbers used are real numbers.

All figures are assumed to lie in a plane unless otherwise indicated.

Geometric figures, such as lines, circles, triangles, and quadrilaterals, **are not necessarily** drawn to scale. That is, you should **not** assume that quantities such as lengths and angle measures are as they appear in a figure. You should assume, however, that lines shown as straight are actually straight, points on a line are in the order shown, and more generally, all geometric objects are in the relative positions shown. For questions with geometric figures, you should base your answers on geometric reasoning, not on estimating or comparing quantities by sight or by measurement.

Coordinate systems, such as xy-planes and number lines, **are** drawn to scale; therefore, you can read, estimate, or compare quantities in such figures by sight or by measurement.

Graphical data presentations, such as bar graphs, circle graphs, and line graphs, **are** drawn to scale; therefore, you can read, estimate, or compare data values by sight or by measurement.

Directions for Quantitative Comparison questions

Compare Quantity A and Quantity B, using additional information centered above the two quantities if such information is given. Select one of the following four answer choices and fill in the corresponding oval to the right of the question.

Ⓐ Quantity A is greater.

Ⓑ Quantity B is greater.

Ⓒ The two quantities are equal.

Ⓓ The relationship cannot be determined from the information given.

A symbol that appears more than once in a question has the same meaning throughout the question.

Directions for Numeric Entry questions

Enter your answer in the answer box(es) below the question.

- Your answer may be an integer, a decimal, or a fraction, and it may be negative.
- If a question asks for a fraction, there will be two boxes—one for the numerator and one for the denominator.
- Equivalent forms of the correct answer, such as 2.5 and 2.50, are all correct. Fractions do not need to be reduced to lowest terms.
- Enter the exact answer unless the question asks you to round your answer.

SET 1. Practice Questions: Easy

Quantitative Comparison

For Questions 1 to 6, use the directions for Quantitative Comparison questions.

Emma spent $75 buying a used bicycle and $27 repairing it. Then she sold the bicycle for 40 percent more than the total amount she spent buying and repairing it.

	Quantity A	Quantity B	
1.	The price at which Emma sold the bicycle	$140	Ⓐ Ⓑ Ⓒ Ⓓ

Explanation

In this question you are asked to compare the price at which Emma sold the bicycle with $140. From the information given, you can conclude that Emma spent a total of $75 + 27 = 102$ dollars buying and repairing the bicycle and that she sold it for 40 percent more than the $102 she spent buying and repairing it. If you notice that 140 is 40 percent more than 100, you can conclude that 40 percent more than 102 is greater than 40 percent more than 100, and therefore, Quantity A is greater than Quantity B. The correct answer is **Choice A**. (If you solve the problem in this way, you do not have to calculate the value of Quantity A.)

Another way to solve the problem is by explicitly calculating the value of Quantity A and comparing the result with $140 directly. Since 40 percent of 102 is $(0.4)(102) = 40.8$, it follows that Quantity A, the price at which Emma sold the bicycle, is $102.00 + 40.80 = 142.80$ dollars. Thus Quantity A, $142.80, is greater than Quantity B, $140, and the correct answer is **Choice A**.

This explanation uses the following strategy.

Strategy 1: Translate from Words to an Arithmetic or Algebraic Representation

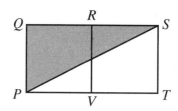

In the figure above, squares *PQRV* and *VRST* have sides of length 6.

Quantity A	Quantity B	
2. The area of the shaded region	36	Ⓐ Ⓑ Ⓒ Ⓓ

Explanation

In this question you are asked to compare the area of the shaded region with 36. You are given that both *PQRV* and *VRST* are squares with sides of length 6. Therefore, you can conclude that the length of *QS* is 12, and the area of the shaded right triangle *PQS* is $\frac{1}{2}(12)(6)$, or 36. Thus Quantity A is equal to Quantity B, and the correct answer is **Choice C**.

This explanation uses the following strategy.

Strategy 4: Translate from a Figure to an Arithmetic or Algebraic Representation

---

In 2009 the property tax on each home in Town *X* was *p* percent of the assessed value of the home, where *p* is a constant. The property tax in 2009 on a home in Town *X* that had an assessed value of $125,000 was $2,500.

Quantity A	Quantity B	
3. The property tax in 2009 on a home in Town *X* that had an assessed value of $160,000	$3,000	Ⓐ Ⓑ Ⓒ Ⓓ

Explanation

Before making the comparison in this problem, you need to analyze the information given to see what it tells you about the value of Quantity A, the property tax in 2009 on a home in Town *X* that had an assessed value of $160,000. One way of doing this is to determine the value of the constant *p* and then use that value to calculate the tax on the home that had an assessed value of $160,000.

Since it is given that a home that had an assessed value of $125,000 had a property tax of $2,500, you can conclude that *p* is equal to $\frac{2,500}{125,000}$, or 2%. Once you know that the property tax is 2% of the assessed value, you can determine that tax on the home that had an assessed value of $160,000 was 2% of 160,000, or 3,200. The correct answer is **Choice A**.

Another way to calculate the property tax on a home with an assessed value of $160,000 is by setting up a proportion. Because the tax rate is the same for each home in Town X, you can let the variable x represent the tax for the home assessed at \$160,000 and solve for x as follows.

$$\frac{x}{160,000} = \frac{2,500}{125,000}$$

$$125,000\,x = (160,000)(2,500)$$

$$x = \frac{(160,000)(2,500)}{125,000}$$

$$x = 3,200$$

The correct answer is **Choice A**.

This explanation uses the following strategies.

Strategy 1: Translate from Words to an Arithmetic or Algebraic Representation
Strategy 8: Search for a Mathematical Relationship

$$x + y = -1$$

	Quantity A	Quantity B	
4.	x	y	Ⓐ Ⓑ Ⓒ Ⓓ

Explanation

One way to approach this question is to plug in values for one of the variables and determine the corresponding value for the other variable.

One way to plug in: Plug in easy values. For example, you can plug in $x = 0$ and find that the corresponding value of y is -1; then you can plug in $y = 0$ and find that the corresponding value of x is -1. Since in the first case x is greater than y and in the second case y is greater than x, the correct answer is **Choice D**, the relationship cannot be determined from the information given.

A second way to plug in: If you prefer to always plug in values of x to determine corresponding values of y, you can begin by writing the equation $x + y = -1$ as $y = -x - 1$. Writing it in this form makes it easier to find the corresponding values of y.

You can start by plugging in the value $x = 0$. For this value of x, the corresponding value of y is $y = -1$, and therefore, x is greater than y. If you continue plugging in a variety of values of x, some negative and some positive, you will see that sometimes x is greater than y and sometimes y is greater than x.

If you inspect the equation $y = -x - 1$, you can conclude that since there is a negative sign in front of the x but not in front of the y, for each value of x that is greater than 0, the corresponding value of y is less than 0; therefore, for each $x > 0$, x is greater than y.

What about negative values of x? A quick inspection of the equation $y = -x - 1$ allows you to conclude that if $x < -1$, then $y > 0$, so y is greater than x.

So for some values of x and y that satisfy the equation, x is greater than y; and for other values, y is greater than x. Therefore, the relationship between the two quantities x and y cannot be determined from the information given, and the correct answer is **Choice D**.

This explanation uses the following strategies.

Strategy 10: Trial and Error
Strategy 13: Determine Whether a Conclusion Follows from the Information Given

---

r, s, and t are three consecutive odd integers such that $r < s < t$.

	Quantity A	Quantity B	
5.	$r + s + 1$	$s + t - 1$	Ⓐ Ⓑ Ⓒ Ⓓ

Explanation

You are given that three numbers, r, s, and t, are consecutive odd integers and that $r < s < t$. This means that if you express the three consecutive odd integers in terms of r, they are r, $r + 2$, and $r + 4$.

One way to approach this problem is to set up a placeholder relationship between the two quantities and simplify it to see what conclusions you can draw.

Simplification 1: Begin simplifying by expressing s and t in terms of r. The steps in this simplification can be done as follows.

$$r + s + 1 \boxed{?} s + t - 1$$
$$r + (r + 2) + 1 \boxed{?} (r + 2) + (r + 4) - 1$$
$$2r + 3 \boxed{?} 2r + 5$$
$$3 \boxed{?} 5$$

In the last step of the simplification, you can easily see that $3 < 5$. If you follow the simplification steps in reverse, you can see that the placeholder in each step remains unchanged, so you can conclude that Quantity B is greater than Quantity A, and the correct answer is **Choice B**.

Simplification 2: Since the number s appears in both quantities, you can begin the simplification by subtracting s from both sides of the relationship and then express t in terms of r. The steps in this simplification can be done as follows.

$$r + s + 1 \boxed{?} s + t - 1$$
$$r + 1 \boxed{?} t - 1$$
$$r + 1 \boxed{?} (r + 4) - 1$$
$$r + 1 \boxed{?} r + 3$$
$$1 \boxed{?} 3$$

In the last step of the simplification, you can easily see that $1 < 3$. If you follow the simplification steps in reverse, you can see that the placeholder in each step remains unchanged, so you can conclude that Quantity B is greater than Quantity A, and the correct answer is **Choice B**.

Note that in this solution, the fact that r is odd is not used; what is used is the fact that the consecutive odd integers differ by 2.

This explanation uses the following strategies.

Strategy 5: Simplify an Arithmetic or Algebraic Representation
Strategy 8: Search for a Mathematical Relationship

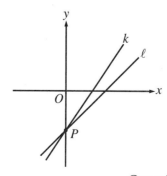

Quantity A	Quantity B	
6. The slope of line k	The slope of line ℓ	

Explanation

Note that the slope of each of the lines is positive, since each line rises as it goes to the right. Since the slopes of both lines are positive and line k rises faster (or is steeper) than line ℓ, line k has the greater slope, and the correct answer is **Choice A**.

You can also use the definition of the slope to arrive at the correct answer. Slope can be defined as the ratio of "rise" to "run" between any two points on a line, where the rise is the vertical distance between the points and the run is the horizontal distance, and the slope is respectively positive or negative depending on whether the line rises or falls when viewed from left to right. Because both lines pass through point P on the y-axis, they have the same rise from P to the x-axis. However, line ℓ intersects the x-axis at a greater value than line k. Thus, the run of line ℓ from the y-axis to the x-intercept is greater than the run of line k. When the slope is expressed as a ratio, both lines have the same numerator (rise), but line ℓ has a greater denominator (run). The greater denominator results in a lesser fraction and a lesser slope for line ℓ. Therefore, the correct answer is **Choice A**.

This explanation uses the following strategy.

Strategy 4: Translate from a Figure to an Arithmetic or Algebraic Representation

Multiple-choice Questions—Select One Answer Choice

For Questions 7 to 11, select a single answer choice.

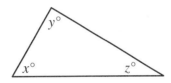

7. In the figure above, what is the value of $\dfrac{x+y+z}{45}$?

  (A) 2

  (B) 3

  (C) 4

  (D) 5

  (E) 6

Explanation

The sum of the measures, in degrees, of the three interior angles of any triangle is 180°. As shown in the figure, the three angles of the triangle have measures of $x°$, $y°$, and $z°$, so $x + y + z = 180$. Therefore, $\dfrac{x+y+z}{45} = \dfrac{180}{45} = 4$, and the correct answer is **Choice C**.

This explanation uses the following strategy.

Strategy 4: Translate from a Figure to an Arithmetic or Algebraic Representation

8.   A certain store sells two types of pens: one type for $2 per pen and the other type for $3 per pen. If a customer can spend up to $25 to buy pens at the store and there is no sales tax, what is the greatest number of pens the customer can buy?

(A) 9   (D) 12

(B) 10   (E) 20

(C) 11

Explanation

It is fairly clear that the greatest number of pens that can be bought for $25 will consist mostly, if not entirely, of $2 pens. In fact, it is reasonable to begin by looking at how many of the $2 pens the customer can buy if the customer does not buy any $3 pens. It is easy to see that the customer could buy 12 of the $2 pens, with $1 left over.

If the customer bought 11 of the $2 pens, there would be $3 left over with which to buy a $3 pen. In this case, the customer could still buy 12 pens.

If the customer bought 10 of the $2 pens, there would be $5 left over. Only 1 of the $3 pens could be bought with the $5, so in this case, the customer could buy only 11 pens.

As the number of $2 pens decreases, the total number of pens that the customer can buy with $25 decreases as well. Thus the greatest number of pens the customer can buy with $25 is 12. The correct answer is **Choice D**.

This explanation uses the following strategies.

Strategy 1: Translate from Words to an Arithmetic or Algebraic Representation

Strategy 10: Trial and Error

---

9.   If $y = 3x$ and $z = 2y$, what is $x + y + z$ in terms of x?

(A) $10x$ (D) $6x$

(B) $9x$ (E) $5x$

(C) $8x$

Explanation

It is not necessary to find the individual values of x, y, and z to answer the question. You are asked to rewrite the expression $x + y + z$ as an equivalent expression in terms of x. This means that you need to use the information provided about y and z to express them in terms of the variable x. The variable y is already given in terms of x; that is, $y = 3x$; and because $z = 2y$, it follows that $z = (2)(3x) = 6x$. Using substitution, you can rewrite the expression as follows.

$$x + y + z = x + (3x) + (6x)$$

$$= (1 + 3 + 6)x$$

$$= 10x$$

The correct answer is **Choice A**.

This explanation uses the following strategy.

Strategy 5: Simplify an Arithmetic or Algebraic Representation

10. A certain shipping service charges an insurance fee of $0.75 when shipping any package with contents worth $25.00 or less and an insurance fee of $1.00 when shipping any package with contents worth over $25.00. If Dan uses the shipping company to ship three packages with contents worth $18.25, $25.00, and $127.50, respectively, what is the total insurance fee that the company charges Dan to ship the three packages?

   (A) $1.75
   (B) $2.25
   (C) $2.50
   (D) $2.75
   (E) $3.00

Explanation

Note that two of the packages being shipped have contents that are worth $25.00 or less. Therefore, each of them has an insurance fee of $0.75, for a total of $1.50. The third package has contents worth over $25.00, and it has an insurance fee of $1.00. Therefore, the total insurance fee for the three packages is $1.50 + $1.00 = $2.50, and the correct answer is **Choice C**.

This explanation uses the following strategy.

Strategy 1: Translate from Words to an Arithmetic or Algebraic Representation

11. Last year, all purchases of a certain product were made either online or in a store. If 55 percent of the purchases were made online, what was the ratio of the number of purchases made online to the number of purchases made in a store?

   (A)   11 to 9
   (B)   11 to 5
   (C)   10 to 9
   (D)   9 to 11
   (E)   9 to 10

Explanation

Note that because 55 percent of the purchases were made online, it follows that 45 percent of the purchases were made in a store. Therefore, the ratio of the number of purchases made online to the number of purchases made in a store is 55 to 45, or 11 to 9, and the correct answer is **Choice A**.

This explanation uses the following strategy.

Strategy 1: Translate from Words to an Arithmetic or Algebraic Representation

Numeric Entry

For Questions 12 and 13, use the directions for Numeric Entry questions.

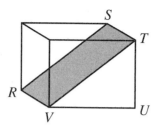

12.   In the rectangular solid above, $TU = 3$, $UV = 4$, and $VR = 2$. What is the area of the shaded rectangular region?

Explanation

To find the area of the shaded rectangular region, you need to multiply the length of the rectangular region by its width. In this question you are given the lengths of three edges: $TU = 3$, $UV = 4$, and $VR = 2$. Note that VR is the length of the shaded rectangle. To find the width of the shaded rectangle, you need to find either RS or VT. Note that VT lies on the front face of the rectangular solid. It is the hypotenuse of right triangle VUT. You know that $UV = 4$ and $TU = 3$, so by the Pythagorean theorem you can conclude that $VT = \sqrt{3^2 + 4^2} = \sqrt{9 + 16} = \sqrt{25} = 5$. Therefore, the area of the shaded rectangular region is $(5)(2) = 10$. The correct answer is **10**.

This explanation uses the following strategies.

Strategy 4: Translate from a Figure to an Arithmetic or Algebraic Representation
Strategy 8: Search for a Mathematical Relationship

---

13.   A list of numbers has a mean of 8 and a standard deviation of 2.5. If x is a number in the list that is 2 standard deviations above the mean, what is the value of x?

$$x = \boxed{}$$

Explanation

You are given that x is 2 standard deviations above the mean, 8. Because the standard deviation of the numbers in the list is 2.5, it follows that x is $(2)(2.5)$, or 5 units above the mean 8. Therefore, $x = 8 + 5 = 13$, and the correct answer is **13**.

This explanation uses the following strategy.

Strategy 8: Search for a Mathematical Relationship

Multiple-choice Questions—Select One or More Answer Choices

> **For Question 14, select all the answer choices that apply.**

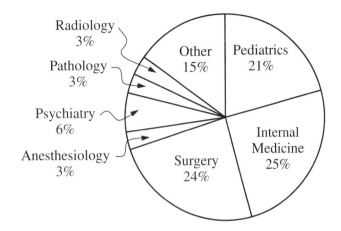

14. The circle graph above shows the distribution of 200,000 physicians by specialty. Which of the following sectors of the circle graph represent more than 40,000 physicians?

Indicate <u>all</u> such sectors.

- [A] Pediatrics
- [B] Internal Medicine
- [C] Surgery
- [D] Anesthesiology
- [E] Psychiatry

Explanation

One approach to solve this problem is to find out what percent of 200,000 is 40,000 and then compare this percent with the percents given in the circle graph. Because $\frac{40,000}{200,000} = 0.2$, it follows that 40,000 is 20% of 200,000, and any specialty that has more than 20% of the distribution has more than 40,000 physicians. This is true for the specialties of pediatrics, internal medicine, and surgery. The correct answer consists of **Choices A, B, and C**.

This explanation uses the following strategy.

Strategy 4: Translate from a Figure to an Arithmetic or Algebraic Representation

SET 2. Practice Questions: Medium

Quantitative Comparison

For Questions 1 to 5, use the directions for Quantitative Comparison questions.

Machine R, working alone at a constant rate, produces x units of a product in 30 minutes, and machine S, working alone at a constant rate, produces x units of the product in 48 minutes, where x is a positive integer.

Quantity A	Quantity B

1. The number of units of the product that machine R, working alone at its constant rate, produces in 3 hours   The number of units of the product that machine S, working alone at its constant rate, produces in 4 hours

Explanation

In this question you are given that machine R, working alone at its constant rate, produces x units of a product in 30 minutes. Since it is easy to see that 3 hours is 6 times 30 minutes, you can conclude that Quantity A is $6x$.

You can compare $6x$ with Quantity B in two ways.

One: In the additional information centered above the quantities, you are given that machine S, working alone at its constant rate, produces x units of the product in 48 minutes, so you can conclude that machine S can produce $6x$ units of the product in $(6)(48)$ minutes, or 4.8 hours. So in 4 hours, machine S produces less than $6x$ units, and Quantity B is less than $6x$.

Two: First, convert 48 minutes to $\frac{4}{5}$ hour, then find the number of 48-minute periods there are in 4 hours by computing $\dfrac{4}{\frac{4}{5}} = (4)\left(\frac{5}{4}\right) = 5$. Thus, Quantity B is $5x$.

Either way, Quantity A is greater than Quantity B, and the correct answer is **Choice A**.

This explanation uses the following strategies.

Strategy 1: Translate from Words to an Arithmetic or Algebraic Representation
Strategy 8: Search for a Mathematical Relationship

Frequency Distribution for List X

Number	1	2	3	5
Frequency	10	20	18	12

Frequency Distribution for List Y

Number	6	7	8	9
Frequency	24	17	10	9

List X and list Y each contain 60 numbers. Frequency distributions for each list are given above. The average (arithmetic mean) of the numbers in list X is 2.7, and the average of the numbers in list Y is 7.1. List Z contains 120 numbers: the 60 numbers in list X and the 60 numbers in list Y.

Quantity A	Quantity B	
2. The average of the 120 numbers in list Z	The median of the 120 numbers in list Z	

Explanation

In this problem you are asked to compare the average with the median of the 120 numbers in list Z. Since list Z consists of the numbers in lists X and Y combined, it is reasonable to try to use the information about lists X and Y to calculate the average and the median of the numbers in list Z.

To determine the average of the 120 numbers in list Z, you can use the information given about the individual averages of the numbers in lists X and Y. Because lists X and Y each contain 60 numbers, the average of the numbers in list Z is the average of the individual averages of the numbers in lists X and Y. Thus, the average of the numbers in list Z is $\frac{2.7+7.1}{2}$, or 4.9.

To determine the median of the 120 numbers in list Z, first note that list Z contains an even number of numbers, so the median of the numbers in list Z is the average of the middle two numbers when the numbers are listed in increasing order. If you look at the numbers in the two lists, you will see that the 60 numbers in list X are all less than or equal to 5, and the 60 numbers in list Y are all greater than or equal to 6. Thus, the two middle numbers in list Z are 5 and 6, and the average of these numbers is $\frac{5+6}{2}$ or 5.5. Therefore, the median of the numbers in list Z is 5.5, and this is greater than the average of 4.9. The correct answer is **Choice B**.

This explanation uses the following strategies.

Strategy 4: Translate from a Figure to an Arithmetic or Algebraic Representation
Strategy 8: Search for a Mathematical Relationship

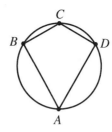

In the figure above, the diameter of the circle is 10.

Quantity A   Quantity B

3.   The area of quadrilateral   40   Ⓐ Ⓑ Ⓒ Ⓓ
      ABCD

Explanation

You are given that the circle has a diameter of 10, and from the figure you can assume that points *A*, *B*, *C*, and *D* lie on the circle in the order shown. However, because figures are not necessarily drawn to scale, you cannot assume anything else about the positions of points *A*, *B*, *C*, and *D* on the circle. Therefore, to get an idea of how various possible positions of these four points could affect the area of quadrilateral *ABCD*, it is a good idea to see how the figure can vary but still have points *A*, *B*, *C*, and *D* in the same order as in the figure above.

One way that you might vary the figure is to evenly space the four points along the circle, as shown below.

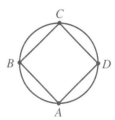

Another way is to draw points *A* and *C* opposite each other, with points *B* and *D* close to point *C*, as shown below.

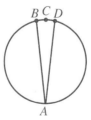

From these figures you can draw some basic conclusions about the area of *ABCD*.

If points *A* and *C* are opposite each other, with points *B* and *D* very close to point *C*, the area of quadrilateral *ABCD* is very close to 0. Clearly, the area can be less than 40 (Quantity B).

If points *A*, *B*, *C*, and *D* are evenly spaced, the area is not close to 0. How does the area compare with 40? To calculate the area of *ABCD*, draw the diameters *AC* and *BD* in the figure. The two diameters are perpendicular bisectors of each other, so they divide *ABCD* into four right triangles, as shown.

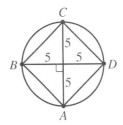

The area of each of the right triangles is $\left(\dfrac{1}{2}\right)(5)(5)$, or 12.5. Thus, the area of $ABCD$ is $(4)(12.5)$, or 50.

Since the area of the quadrilateral in the first figure is less than 40 and the area of the quadrilateral in the second figure is greater than 40, the relationship cannot be determined from the information given. The correct answer is **Choice D**.

This explanation uses the following strategies.

Strategy 4: Translate from a Figure to an Arithmetic or Algebraic Representation
Strategy 6: Add to a Geometric Figure
Strategy 13: Determine Whether a Conclusion Follows from the Information Given

---

$$x^2 y > 0$$
$$xy^2 < 0$$

	Quantity A	Quantity B	
4.	x	y	Ⓐ Ⓑ Ⓒ Ⓓ

Explanation

You are given that $x^2 y > 0$, which means that the product of the two numbers x^2 and y is positive. Recall that the product of two numbers is positive only if both numbers are positive or both numbers are negative. The square of a number is always greater than or equal to 0. In this case, x^2 cannot equal 0 because the product $x^2 y$ is not 0. Thus, x^2 is positive and it follows that y is also positive.

You are also given that $xy^2 < 0$, which means that the product of the two numbers x and y^2 is negative. The product of two numbers is negative only if one of the numbers is negative and the other number is positive. In this case, y^2 cannot be negative because it is the square of a number, and it cannot be 0 because the product $x^2 y$ is not 0. Thus, y^2 is positive and so x must be negative.

Because x is negative and y is positive, y must be greater than x, and the correct answer is **Choice B**.

This explanation uses the following strategy.

Strategy 8: Search for a Mathematical Relationship

Among the 9,000 people attending a football game at College C, there were x students from College C and y students who were <u>not</u> from College C.

	Quantity A	Quantity B	
5.	The number of people attending the game who were <u>not</u> students	$9{,}000 - x - y$	Ⓐ Ⓑ Ⓒ Ⓓ

Explanation

In this question you are not told whether all of the 9,000 people attending the game were students. Let z be the number of people attending the game who were not students. The people attending the game can be broken down into three groups: students from College C, students not from College C, and people who were not students. This can be expressed algebraically as $9{,}000 = x + y + z$, where x represents the number of students from College C attending the game and y represents the number of students attending the game who were not from College C. Therefore, $9{,}000 - x - y = z$ is the number of people attending the game who were not students. The correct answer is **Choice C**.

This explanation uses the following strategy.
Strategy 1: Translate from Words to an Arithmetic or Algebraic Representation

Multiple-Choice Questions—Select One Answer Choice

> **For Questions 6 to 10, select a single answer choice.**

6. If $x \neq 0$, which of the following is equivalent to $\dfrac{x(x^2)^3}{x^2}$?

   Ⓐ x^2

   Ⓑ x^3

   Ⓒ x^4

   Ⓓ x^5

   Ⓔ x^6

Explanation

To simplify $\dfrac{x(x^2)^3}{x^2}$, it can be helpful to write $(x^2)^3$ as $(x^2)(x^2)(x^2)$ in the given expression; that is, $\dfrac{x(x^2)^3}{x^2} = \dfrac{x(x^2)(x^2)(x^2)}{x^2}$. Because $x \neq 0$, both numerator and denominator can be divided by x^2, and the expression simplifies to $x(x^2)(x^2)$, which, by the rules of exponents, is equal to x^5.

Another way to simplify the expression using the rules of exponents directly is as follows.

$$\frac{x(x^2)^3}{x^2} = \frac{x(x^6)}{x^2} = \frac{x^7}{x^2} = x^5$$

The correct answer is **Choice D**.

This explanation uses the following strategy.
Strategy 5: Simplify an Arithmetic or Algebraic Representation

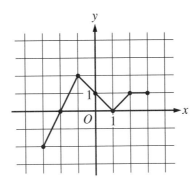

7. The figure above shows the graph of the function f in the xy-plane. What is the value of $f(f(-1))$?

(A) -2 (D) 1

(B) -1 (E) 2

(C) 0

Explanation

Note that to find $f(f(-1))$, you must apply the function f twice, first to find the value of $f(-1)$ and then to find the value of $f(f(-1))$. To find the value of $f(-1)$, find the point on the graph of the function f whose x-coordinate is $x = -1$. This point has y-coordinate $y = 2$. Therefore, the value of $f(-1)$ is 2, and $f(f(-1)) = f(2)$. Next you need to find the value of $f(2)$. To find the value of $f(2)$, find the point on the graph whose x-coordinate is $x = 2$. This point has y-coordinate $y = 1$. Therefore, $f(2) = 1$, and because $f(f(-1)) = f(2)$, you can conclude that $f(f(-1)) = 1$. The correct answer is **Choice D**.

This explanation uses the following strategies.

Strategy 4: Translate from a Figure to an Arithmetic or Algebraic Representation
Strategy 12: Adapt Solutions to Related Problems

---

8. If $\dfrac{d-3n}{7n-d} = 1$, which of the following statements describes d in terms of n?

(A) d is 4 less than n.   (D) d is 2 times n.

(B) d is 4 more than n.   (E) d is 5 times n.

(C) d is $\dfrac{3}{7}$ of n.

Explanation

To describe d in terms of n, you need to solve the equation $\dfrac{d-3n}{7n-d} = 1$ for d. To simplify the equation, you can begin by multiplying both sides by $7n - d$ and then proceed as follows.

$$(7n-d)\left(\frac{d-3n}{7n-d}\right) = (7n-d)(1)$$
$$d - 3n = 7n - d$$
$$d = 10n - d$$
$$2d = 10n$$
$$d = 5n$$

The correct answer is **Choice E**.

This explanation uses the following strategy.

Strategy 5: Simplify an Arithmetic or Algebraic Representation

9. By weight, liquid A makes up 8 percent of solution R and 18 percent of solution S. If 3 grams of solution R are mixed with 7 grams of solution S, then liquid A accounts for what percent of the weight of the resulting solution?

(A) 10%
(B) 13%
(C) 15%
(D) 19%
(E) 26%

Explanation

Liquid A makes up 8 percent of the weight of solution R and 18 percent of the weight of solution S. Therefore, 3 grams of solution R contain (0.08)(3), or 0.24 gram of liquid A, and 7 grams of solution S contain (0.18)(7), or 1.26 grams of liquid A. When the two solutions are mixed, the resulting solution weighs 3 + 7, or 10 grams, and contains 0.24 + 1.26, or 1.5 grams of liquid A. This means that liquid A makes up $\frac{1.5}{10}$, or $\frac{15}{100}$, or 15 percent of the weight of the resulting solution. The correct answer is **Choice C**.

This explanation uses the following strategy.

Strategy 1: Translate from Words to an Arithmetic or Algebraic Representation

---

10. Of the 700 members of a certain organization, 120 are lawyers. Two members of the organization will be selected at random. Which of the following is closest to the probability that <u>neither</u> of the members selected will be a lawyer?

(A) 0.5
(B) 0.6
(C) 0.7
(D) 0.8
(E) 0.9

Explanation

The probability that neither of the members selected will be a lawyer is equal to the fraction

$$\frac{\text{the number of ways 2 members who are not lawyers can be selected}}{\text{the number of ways 2 members can be selected}}$$

where the order of selection does not matter.

Since there are 120 members who are lawyers, there must be 700 − 120, or 580, members who are not lawyers. There are 580 ways of selecting a first member who is not a lawyer and 579 ways of selecting a second member who is not a lawyer. Multiplying these two numbers gives the number of ways to select 2 members who are not lawyers. However, in the (580)(579) ways, each group of 2 members who are not lawyers is counted twice. You can see this by considering 2 members, A and B. The 2 members can be chosen in 2 ways: A first, followed by B, and B first, followed by A. To adjust for double counting, you need to divide (580)(579) by 2.

Similarly, the number of ways 2 members can be selected from among the 700 members is (700)(699) divided by 2. Thus, the desired probability is

$$\frac{\dfrac{(580)(579)}{2}}{\dfrac{(700)(699)}{2}} = \frac{(580)(579)}{(700)(699)}$$

Since the answer choices are all tenths, you need to approximate the value of this fraction to the nearest tenth. There are several ways to do this approximation. One way is to use your calculator to convert the fraction to a decimal and round the decimal to the nearest tenth.

Another way is to approximate the value of the fraction as follows.

$$\frac{(580)(579)}{(700)(699)} \approx \frac{(600)(600)}{(700)(700)} = \left(\frac{6}{7}\right)^2 = \frac{36}{49} \approx \frac{36}{50} = 0.72$$

Either way, the answer choice that is closest to the value of the fraction is 0.7. The correct answer is **Choice C**.

Another approach to this problem is to consider the random selections as two separate but successive events. The probability of selecting a first member who is not a lawyer is $\frac{580}{700}$, because there are 580 members out of the 700 members who are not lawyers. For the second selection, there are only 699 members left to select from, because one member has already been selected. If the first member selected is not a lawyer, then there are only 579 members left who are not lawyers. So the probability of selecting a second member who is not a lawyer, given the condition that the first member selected was not a lawyer, is $\frac{579}{699}$. The probability that both members selected will not be lawyers is the product of the two probabilities, or $\left(\frac{580}{700}\right)\left(\frac{579}{699}\right)$, which is approximated above as 0.72. The correct answer is **Choice C**.

This explanation uses the following strategies.
Strategy 8: Search for a Mathematical Relationship
Strategy 9: Estimate

Numeric Entry

For Questions 11 and 12, use the directions for Numeric Entry questions.

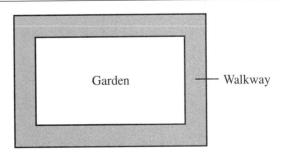

Garden — Walkway

11.   The figure above represents a rectangular garden with a walkway around it. The garden is 18 feet long and 12 feet wide. The walkway is uniformly 3 feet wide, and its edges meet at right angles. What is the area of the walkway?

[   ] square feet

Explanation

You can see from the figure that the shaded region is the region between the two rectangles. Looking at the shaded region in this way suggests that the area of the walkway can be calculated as the difference between the area of the larger rectangle and the area of the smaller rectangle.

The region represented by the smaller rectangle is the garden. Since the garden is 18 feet long and 12 feet wide, its area is (18)(12), or 216 square feet.

The region represented by the larger rectangle is the garden and the walkway combined. The length of the region is the length of the garden plus twice the width of the walkway, or 18 + (2)(3) = 24 feet. The width of the region is the width of the garden plus twice the width of the walkway, or 12 + (2)(3) = 18 feet. Therefore, the area of the region represented by the larger rectangle is (24)(18), or 432 square feet, and the area of the walkway is 432 – 216, or 216 square feet.

Another way to approach this problem is to think of the walkway as being composed of four rectangles and four squares, as shown in the figure below.

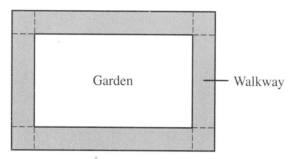

Each of the four squares is 3 feet long and 3 feet wide. The two rectangles running along the length of the garden are 18 feet long and 3 feet wide, and the two rectangles running along the width of the garden are 12 feet long and 3 feet wide. Thus, the area of the walkway is

$$4(3)(3) + 2(18)(3) + 2(12)(3) = 36 + 108 + 72 = 216 \text{ square feet}$$

The correct answer is **216**.

This explanation uses the following strategies.

Strategy 4: Translate from a Figure to an Arithmetic or Algebraic Representation
Strategy 8: Search for a Mathematical Relationship

---

12.   Line k lies in the xy-plane. The x-intercept of line k is –4, and line k passes through the midpoint of the line segment whose endpoints are (2, 9) and (2, 0). What is the slope of line k?

Give your answer as a fraction.

Explanation

You can calculate the slope of a line if you know the coordinates of two points on the line. In this question you are given information about two points on line k, namely,

- the point at which line k crosses the x-axis has x-coordinate –4;
- the midpoint of the line segment with endpoints at (2, 9) and (2, 0) is on line k.

The coordinates of the first point are (–4, 0), since the x-coordinate is –4 and the y-coordinate of every point on the x-axis is 0. For the second point, the midpoint of the line segment is halfway between the endpoints (2, 9) and (2, 0). Thus, the midpoint has x-coordinate 2 and y-coordinate $\frac{9}{2}$, the number halfway between 9 and 0. Based on the coordinates (–4, 0) and $\left(2, \frac{9}{2}\right)$, the slope of line k is

$$\frac{\frac{9}{2} - 0}{2 - (-4)} = \frac{\frac{9}{2}}{6} = \frac{3}{4}$$

The correct answer is $\frac{3}{4}$ (or any equivalent fraction).

This explanation uses the following strategies.

Strategy 1: Translate from Words into an Arithmetic or Algebraic Representation
Strategy 8: Search for a Mathematical Relationship

Multiple-Choice Questions—Select One or More Answer Choices

For Questions 13 and 14, select all the answer choices that apply.

13. If the lengths of two sides of a triangle are 5 and 9, respectively, which of the following could be the length of the third side of the triangle?

Indicate <u>all</u> such lengths.

- [A] 3
- [B] 5
- [C] 8
- [D] 15

Explanation

A good way to approach this problem is to think about how much the length of the third side of a triangle with two fixed side lengths can vary. If you think about it a bit, you will see that the smaller the interior angle between the two sides of the triangle is, the smaller the length of the third side is; and the larger the interior angle between the two sides of the triangle is, the larger the length of the third side is. This suggests drawing two triangles, one in which the angle between the two sides is close to 0 degrees and one in which the angle between the two sides is close to 180 degrees, like the triangles below.

In the triangle in which the angle between the sides of length 5 and 9 is small, you can see that the length of the third side is a bit greater than 9 – 5, or 4. If it were equal to 4, the triangle would degenerate into a line segment.

In the triangle in which the angle between the sides of length 5 and 9 is large, you can see that the length of the third side is a bit less than 9 + 5, or 14. If it were equal to 14, the triangle would degenerate into a line segment.

Therefore, the length of the third side of the triangle must be greater than 4 and less than 14. Furthermore, it is intuitive that any length between these two numbers can be achieved by some triangle. The correct answer consists of **Choices B and C**.

This explanation uses the following strategies.
Strategy 2: Translate from Words to a Figure or Diagram
Strategy 11: Divide into Cases

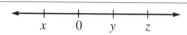

14.   On the number line shown above, the tick marks are equally spaced. Which of the following statements about the numbers x, y, and z must be true?

Indicate <u>all</u> such statements.

|A| $xyz < 0$ |B| $x + z = y$ |C| $z(y - x) > 0$

Explanation
You can see from their positions on the number line that x is less than 0 and both y and z are greater than 0. Because the tick marks are equally spaced, you can also see that $x = -y$ and $z = 2y$. You need to evaluate each answer choice separately to determine whether it must be true.

Choice A says that the product of the three numbers x, y, and z is less than 0. Recall that the product of three numbers is negative under either of the following two conditions.

- All three numbers are negative.
- One of the numbers is negative and the other two numbers are positive.

Choice A must be true, since x is negative and y and z are positive.

Choice B is the equation $x + z = y$. To see whether the equation must be true, it is a good idea to express two of the variables in terms of the third (that is, to "get rid of" two of the variables). The equations $x = -y$ and $z = 2y$ give x and z in terms of y, so the equation $x + z = y$ can be rewritten, substituting $-y$ for x and $2y$ for z, as $-y + 2y = y$. In this form you can quickly conclude that the equation must be true.

Choice C says that the product of the two numbers z and $y - x$ is greater than 0. Recall that the product of two numbers is positive under either of the following two conditions.

- Both numbers are positive.
- Both numbers are negative.

Since you already know that z is positive, you can conclude that the product $z(y - x)$ will be positive if $y - x$ is positive. By adding x to both sides of the inequality $y - x > 0$, you can see that it is equivalent to the inequality $y > x$, which is clearly true from the number line. Since $y - x$ is positive, the product $z(y - x)$ must be positive.

Therefore, the correct answer consists of **Choices A, B, and C**.

This explanation uses the following strategies.
Strategy 4: Translate from a Figure to an Arithmetic or Algebraic Representation
Strategy 8: Search for a Mathematical Relationship
Strategy 13: Determine Whether a Conclusion Follows from the Information Given

SET 3. Practice Questions: Hard

Quantitative Comparison

For Questions 1 to 6, use the directions for Quantitative Comparison questions.

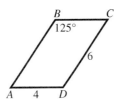

In the figure above, *ABCD* is a parallelogram.

Quantity A	Quantity B	
1. The area of the *ABCD*	24	

Explanation

In this question you are asked to compare the area of a parallelogram with an area of 24, given two side lengths and the measure of one interior angle of the parallelogram. Since the measure of the interior angle given is 125°, you can conclude that the parallelogram is not a rectangle.

Recall that the area of a parallelogram is found by multiplying the length of a base by the height corresponding to the base. It is helpful to draw the vertical height from vertex *C* to base *AD* of the parallelogram, as shown in the figure below.

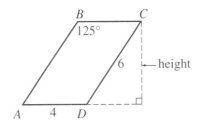

Note that the newly drawn height is a leg in a newly formed right triangle. The hypotenuse of the triangle is a side of the parallelogram and has length 6. Thus, the leg of the triangle, which is the height of the parallelogram, must be less than the hypotenuse 6. The area of the parallelogram is equal to the length of base *AD*, which is 4, times the height, which is less than 6. Since the product of 4 and a number less than 6 must be less than 24, the area of the parallelogram must be less than 24. Quantity B is greater than Quantity A, and the correct answer is **Choice B**.

This explanation uses the following strategies.
Strategy 6: Add to a Geometric Figure
Strategy 8: Search for a Mathematical Relationship

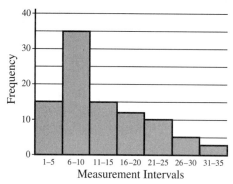

In the course of an experiment, 95 measurements were recorded, and all of the measurements were integers. The 95 measurements were then grouped into 7 measurement intervals. The graph above shows the frequency distribution of the 95 measurements by measurement interval.

Quantity A	Quantity B	
2. The average (arithmetic mean) of the 95 measurements	The median of the 95 measurements	

Explanation

From the histogram, you can observe that

- all of the measurement intervals are the same size,
- the distribution has a peak at the measurement interval 6–10, and
- more of the measurement intervals are to the right of the peak than are to the left of the peak.

Since in the histogram the 95 measurements have been grouped into intervals, you cannot calculate the exact value of either the average or the median; you must compare them without being able to determine the exact value of either one.

The median of the 95 measurements is the middle measurement when the measurements are listed in increasing order. The middle measurement is the 48th measurement. From the histogram, you can see that the measurement interval 1–5 contains the first 15 measurements, and the measurement interval 6–10 contains the next 35 measurements (that is, measurements 16 through 50). Therefore, the median is in the measurement interval 6–10 and could be 6, 7, 8, 9, or 10.

Estimating the average of the 95 measurements is more complicated.

Since you are asked to compare the average and the median, not necessarily to calculate them, you may ask yourself if you can tell whether the average is greater than or less than the median. Note that visually the measurements in the first three measurement intervals are symmetric around the measurement interval 6–10, so you would expect the average of the measurements in just these three measurement intervals to lie in the 6–10 measurement interval. The 30 measurements in the remaining four measurement intervals are all greater than 10, some significantly greater than 10. Therefore, the average of the 95 measurements is greater than the average of the measurements in the first three measurement intervals, probably greater than 10. At this point it seems likely that the average of the 95 measurements is greater than the median of the 95 measurements. It turns out that this is true.

To actually show that the average must be greater than 10, you can make the average as small as possible and see if the smallest possible average is greater than 10. To make the average as small as possible, assume that all of the measurements in each interval are as small as possible. That is to say, all 15 measurements in the measurement interval 1–5 are equal to 1, all 35 measurements in the measurement interval 6–10 are equal to 6, etc. Under this assumption, the average of the 95 measurements is

$$\frac{(1)(15)+(6)(35)+(11)(15)+(16)(12)+(21)(10)+(26)(5)+(31)(3)}{95}=\frac{1,015}{95}$$

The value of the smallest possible average, $\frac{1,015}{95}$, is greater than 10.

Therefore, since the average of the 95 measurements is greater than 10 and the median is in the measurement interval 6–10, it follows that the average is greater than the median, and the correct answer is **Choice A**.

This explanation uses the following strategies.

Strategy 4: Translate from a Figure to an Arithmetic or Algebraic Representation
Strategy 8: Search for a Mathematical Relationship
Strategy 9: Estimate
Strategy 11: Divide into Cases

x is an integer greater than 1.

Quantity A	Quantity B	
3. $\quad 3^{x+1}$	4^x	Ⓐ Ⓑ Ⓒ Ⓓ

Explanation

One way to approach this question is to plug in numbers for the variables and see what the relationship between the two quantities is for each of the numbers you plug in.

If you plug in $x = 2$, you see that Quantity A is $3^{x+1} = 3^3$, or 27, and Quantity B is $4^x = 4^2$, or 16. In this case, Quantity A is greater than Quantity B.

If you plug in $x = 3$, you see that Quantity A is $3^{x+1} = 3^4$, or 81, and Quantity B is $4^x = 4^3$, or 64. In this case, Quantity A is greater than Quantity B.

If you plug in $x = 4$, you see that Quantity A is $3^{x+1} = 3^5$, or 243, and Quantity B is $4^x = 4^4$, or 256. In this case, Quantity B is greater than Quantity A. Since for $x = 2$ and for $x = 3$, Quantity A is greater than Quantity B, and for $x = 4$, Quantity B is greater than Quantity A, it follows that the relationship between the two quantities cannot be determined. The correct answer is **Choice D**.

Since both quantities are algebraic expressions, another way to approach this problem is to set up a placeholder relationship between the two quantities and simplify it to see what conclusions you can draw.

$$3^{x+1} \boxed{?} 4^x$$

$$3(3^x) \boxed{?} 4^x$$

$$\frac{3(3^x)}{3^x} \boxed{?} \frac{4^x}{3^x}$$

$$3 \boxed{?} \left(\frac{4}{3}\right)^x$$

For any value of x, the value of 3^x is positive, so dividing by 3^x does not change any inequality that could be put in the placeholder. Since each step in this simplification is reversible, this reduces the problem to comparing 3 with $\left(\frac{4}{3}\right)^x$.

You can see that because $\frac{4}{3}$ is greater than 1, the value of $\left(\frac{4}{3}\right)^x$ becomes greater as x becomes larger. In particular, it is greater than 3 for large-enough values of x. For the smallest value of x, $x = 2$, the relationship is $\left(\frac{4}{3}\right)^2 = \frac{16}{9} < 3$.

Since for $x = 2$, Quantity A is greater than Quantity B and for large values of x, Quantity B is greater than Quantity A, it follows that the relationship between the two quantities cannot be determined. The correct answer is **Choice D**.

This explanation uses the following strategies.

Strategy 10: Trial and Error

Strategy 13: Determine Whether a Conclusion Follows from the Information Given

---

A, B, and C are three rectangles. The length and width of rectangle A are 10 percent greater and 10 percent less, respectively, than the length and width of rectangle C. The length and width of rectangle B are 20 percent greater and 20 percent less, respectively, than the length and width of rectangle C.

Quantity A	Quantity B	
4. The area of rectangle A	The area of rectangle B	

Explanation

In this question you are asked to compare the area of rectangle A and the area of rectangle B. Since the information given relates the dimensions of both rectangle A and rectangle B to the corresponding dimensions of rectangle C, you can try to use the relationships to make the desired comparison.

If ℓ represents the length of rectangle C and w represents its width, then the length and width of rectangles A and B can be translated into algebraic expressions as follows.

- The length of rectangle A is 10 percent greater than the length of rectangle C, or 1.1ℓ.
- The width of rectangle A is 10 percent less than the width of rectangle C, or $0.9w$.
- The length of rectangle B is 20 percent greater than the length of rectangle C, or 1.2ℓ.
- The width of rectangle B is 20 percent less than the width of rectangle C, or $0.8w$.

In terms of ℓ and w, the area of rectangle A is $(1.1\ell)(0.9w)$, or $0.99\ell w$.
In terms of ℓ and w, the area of rectangle B is $(1.2\ell)(0.8w)$, or $0.96\ell w$.
Since $0.99\ell w$ is greater than $0.96\ell w$, Quantity A is greater than Quantity B, and the correct answer is **Choice A**.

This explanation uses the following strategy.

Strategy 1: Translate from Words into an Arithmetic or Algebraic Representation

---

The random variable X is normally distributed. The values 650 and 850 are at the 60th and 90th percentiles of the distribution of X, respectively.

Quantity A	Quantity B	
5. The value at the 75th percentile of the distribution of X	750	

Explanation

You are given that the distribution of random variable X is normal and that the values 650 and 850 are at the 60th and 90th percentiles of the distribution, respectively.

Both of the values 650 and 850 are greater than the mean of the distribution. If you draw a rough sketch of the graph of the normal distribution, the sketch could look something like the one below. Note that it is not necessary to know the exact location of 650 and 850, just that both values are above the mean.

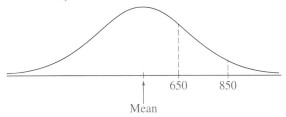

To say that the value 650 is at the 60th percentile of the distribution means, graphically, that 60 percent of the area between the normal curve and the horizontal axis lies to the left of the vertical line segment at 650. To say that 850 is at the 90th percentile of the distribution means that 90 percent of the area between the normal curve and the horizontal axis lies to the left of the vertical line segment at 850.

The value 750 is halfway between 650 and 850. However, because the curve is decreasing in that interval, the area between 650 and 750 is greater than the area between 750 and 850. Since the value at the 75th percentile should divide in half the <u>area</u> between the value at the 60th percentile (650) and the value at the 90th percentile (850), this value is closer to 650 than to 850. Thus you can conclude that Quantity A, the value at the 75th percentile of the distribution of X, is less than Quantity B. The correct answer is **Choice B**.

This explanation uses the following strategies.

Strategy 2: Translate from Words to a Figure or Diagram
Strategy 8: Search for a Mathematical Relationship
Strategy 9: Estimate

Set S consists of all positive integers less than 81 that are <u>not</u> equal to the square of an integer.

Quantity A	Quantity B	
6. The number of integers in set S	72	Ⓐ Ⓑ Ⓒ Ⓓ

Explanation

Set S consists of all integers from 1 to 80, except those that are equal to the square of an integer. So, Quantity A, the number of integers in set S, is equal to the number of positive integers that are less than 81 minus the number of positive integers less than 81 that <u>are</u> equal to the square of an integer.

Clearly, there are 80 positive integers that are less than 81.

One way to determine the number of positive integers less than 81 that are squares of integers is by noticing that 81 is equal to 9^2 and concluding that the squares of the integers from 1 to 8 are all positive integers that are less than 81.

You can also draw this conclusion by squaring each of the positive integers, beginning with 1, until you get to an integer n such that n^2 is greater than or equal to 81. Either way, there are 8 positive integers less than 81 that are squares of integers.

Therefore, the number of integers in set S is $80 - 8$, or 72, which is equal to Quantity B. So Quantity A is equal to Quantity B, and the correct answer is **Choice C**.

This explanation uses the following strategy.

Strategy 1: Translate from Words to an Arithmetic or Algebraic Representation

Multiple-Choice Questions—Select One Answer Choice

For Questions 7 to 12, select a single answer choice.

7. A manager is forming a 6-person team to work on a certain project. From the 11 candidates available for the team, the manager has already chosen 3 to be on the team. In selecting the other 3 team members, how many different combinations of 3 of the remaining candidates does the manager have to choose from?

(A) 6   (D) 120
(B) 24   (E) 462
(C) 56

Explanation

To determine the number of different combinations of 3 of the remaining candidates that the manager has to choose from, you first have to know the number of remaining candidates. Since you know that the manager has already chosen 3 of the 11 candidates to be on the team, it is easy to see that there are 8 remaining candidates. Now you need to count how many different combinations of 3 objects can be chosen from a group of 8 objects.

If you remember the combinations formula, you know that the number of combinations is $\frac{8!}{3!(8-3)!}$ (which is denoted symbolically as $\binom{8}{3}$ or $_8C_3$). You can then calculate the number of different combinations of 3 of the remaining candidates as follows.

$$\frac{8!}{3!(8-3)!} = \frac{(8)(7)(6)(5!)}{(3!)(5!)} = \frac{(8)(7)(6)}{6} = 56$$

The correct answer is **Choice C**.

This explanation uses the following strategy.

Strategy 8: Search for a Mathematical Relationship

8. Which of the following could be the graph of all values of x that satisfy the inequality $2 - 5x \le -\frac{6x-5}{3}$?

(A)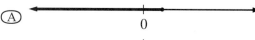
0

(B)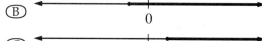
0

(C)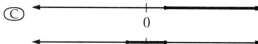
0

(D)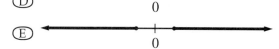
0

(E)
0

Explanation

To determine which of the graphs is the correct answer, you first need to determine all values of x that satisfy the inequality. To do that you need to simplify the inequality until you isolate x.

You can begin by multiplying both sides of the inequality by 3 to obtain $(3)(2 - 5x) \leq -(6x - 5)$. Note that when you multiply by 3, the right-hand side of the inequality becomes $-(6x - 5)$, <u>not</u> $-6x - 5$.

The rest of the simplification is as follows.

$$(3)(2 - 5x) \leq -6x + 5$$

$$6 - 15x \leq -6x + 5$$

$$-15x \leq -6x - 1$$

$$-9x \leq -1$$

$$x \geq \frac{1}{9}$$

Note that when an inequality is multiplied (or divided) by a negative number, the direction of the inequality reverses.

The graphs in the answer choices are number lines on which only the number 0 is indicated. Therefore, you do not need to locate $\frac{1}{9}$ on the number line; it is enough to know that $\frac{1}{9}$ is a positive number. Choice C is the only choice in which the shaded part of the line is equal to or greater than a positive number. Therefore, the correct answer is **Choice C**.

This explanation uses the following strategy.

Strategy 3: Translate from an Algebraic to a Graphical Representation

---

9.   If $1 + x + x^2 + x^3 = 60$, then the average (arithmetic mean) of x, x^2, x^3, and x^4 is equal to which of the following?

     (A) $12x$
     (B) $15x$
     (C) $20x$
     (D) $30x$
     (E) $60x$

Explanation

A quick inspection of the answer choices shows that it is not necessary to solve the equation $1 + x + x^2 + x^3 = 60$ for x to answer this question. You are being asked to express the average of the four quantities x, x^2, x^3, and x^4 in terms of x. To express this average in terms of x, you need to add the 4 quantities and divide the result by 4; that is, $\dfrac{x + x^2 + x^3 + x^4}{4}$.

The only information given in the question is that the sum of the 4 quantities, $1 + x + x^2 + x^3$, is 60, so you need to think of a way to use this information to simplify the expression $\dfrac{x + x^2 + x^3 + x^4}{4}$.

Note that the numerator of the fraction is a sum of 4 quantities, each of which has an x term raised to a power. Thus, the expression in the numerator can be factored as $x + x^2 + x^3 + x^4 = x(1 + x + x^2 + x^3)$. By using the information in the question, you can make the following simplification.

$$\frac{x + x^2 + x^3 + x^4}{4} = \frac{x(1 + x + x^2 + x^3)}{4} = \frac{x(60)}{4} = 15x$$

Therefore, the correct answer is **Choice B**.

This explanation uses the following strategy.

Strategy 5: Simplify an Arithmetic or Algebraic Representation

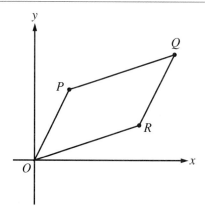

10. Parallelogram *OPQR* lies in the *xy*-plane, as shown in the figure above. The coordinates of point *P* are (2, 4) and the coordinates of point *Q* are (8, 6). What are the coordinates of point *R*?

Ⓐ (3, 2)
Ⓑ (3, 3)
Ⓒ (4, 4)
Ⓓ (5, 2)
Ⓔ (6, 2)

Explanation

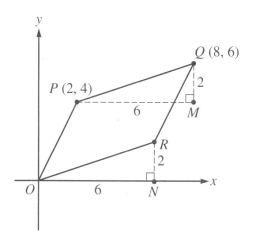

Since *OPQR* is a parallelogram, line segments *PQ* and *OR* have the same length and the same slope. Therefore, in the figure above, *PQM* and *ORN* are congruent right triangles. From the coordinates of P and Q, the lengths of the legs of triangle PQM are $PM = 8 - 2 = 6$ and $QM = 6 - 4 = 2$. Thus, the lengths of the legs ON and RN of triangle ORN are also 6 and 2, respectively. So the coordinates of point R are $(6, 2)$. The correct answer is **Choice E**.

This explanation uses the following strategies.

Strategy 6: Add to a Geometric Figure
Strategy 8: Search for a Mathematical Relationship

---

11.   The relationship between the area A of a circle and its circumference C is given by the formula $A = kC^2$, where k is a constant. What is the value of k?

(A) $\dfrac{1}{4\pi}$

(B) $\dfrac{1}{2\pi}$

(C) $\dfrac{1}{4}$

(D) 2π

(E) $4\pi^2$

Explanation

One way to approach this problem is to realize that the value of the constant k is the same for all circles. Therefore, you can pick a specific circle and substitute the circumference and the area of that particular circle into the formula and calculate the value of k.

Say, for example, that you pick a circle with radius 1. The area of the circle is π and the circumference of the circle is 2π. Inserting these values into the formula gives $\pi = k(2\pi)^2$. Solving this equation for k gives $k = \dfrac{1}{4\pi}$, and the correct answer is **Choice A**.

Another way to approach the problem is to express A and C in terms of a common variable and then solve the resulting equation for k. Recall the commonly used formulas for the area and the circumference of a circle: $A = \pi r^2$ and $C = 2\pi r$. Note that in these formulas, both A and C are expressed in terms of the radius r. So, in the formula $A = kC^2$, you can substitute expressions for A and C in terms of r.

Substituting πr^2 for A and $2\pi r$ for C gives $\pi r^2 = k(2\pi r)^2$.

Now you can determine the value of k by solving the equation for k as follows.

$$\pi r^2 = k(2\pi r)^2$$
$$\pi r^2 = k(4\pi^2 r^2)$$
$$\pi = k(4\pi^2)$$
$$\frac{1}{4\pi} = k$$

The correct answer is **Choice A**.

This explanation uses the following strategies.

Strategy 5: Simplify an Arithmetic or Algebraic Representation
Strategy 8: Search for a Mathematical Relationship

12. The sequence of numbers $a_1, a_2, a_3, \ldots, a_n, \ldots$ is defined by $a_n = \dfrac{1}{n} - \dfrac{1}{n+2}$ for each integer $n \geq 1$. What is the sum of the first 20 terms of the sequence?

Ⓐ $\left(1 + \dfrac{1}{2}\right) - \dfrac{1}{20}$

Ⓑ $\left(1 + \dfrac{1}{2}\right) - \left(\dfrac{1}{21} + \dfrac{1}{22}\right)$

Ⓒ $1 - \left(\dfrac{1}{20} + \dfrac{1}{22}\right)$

Ⓓ $1 - \dfrac{1}{22}$

Ⓔ $\dfrac{1}{20} - \dfrac{1}{22}$

Explanation

This question asks for the sum of the first 20 terms of the sequence. Obviously, it would be very time-consuming to write out the first 20 terms of the sequence and add them together, so it is reasonable to try to find a more efficient way to calculate the sum. Questions involving sequences can often be answered by looking for a pattern. Scanning the answer choices and noting that they contain fractions with denominators 2, 20, 21, and 22, and nothing in between, seems to confirm that looking for a pattern is a good approach to try.

To look for a pattern, begin by adding the first two terms of the sequence.

$$\left(\frac{1}{1} - \frac{1}{3}\right) + \left(\frac{1}{2} - \frac{1}{4}\right) = \left(\frac{1}{1} + \frac{1}{2}\right) - \left(\frac{1}{3} + \frac{1}{4}\right)$$

Now, if you add the first three terms of the sequence, you get

$$\left(\frac{1}{1} - \frac{1}{3}\right) + \left(\frac{1}{2} - \frac{1}{4}\right) + \left(\frac{1}{3} - \frac{1}{5}\right)$$

Note that you can simplify the sum by canceling the fraction $\frac{1}{3}$; that is, the sum of positive $\frac{1}{3}$ and negative $\frac{1}{3}$ is 0.

$$\left(\frac{1}{1} - \frac{\cancel{1}}{\cancel{3}}\right) + \left(\frac{1}{2} - \frac{1}{4}\right) + \left(\frac{\cancel{1}}{\cancel{3}} - \frac{1}{5}\right) = \left(\frac{1}{1} + \frac{1}{2}\right) - \left(\frac{1}{4} + \frac{1}{5}\right)$$

If you add the first four terms, you get

$$\left(\frac{1}{1} - \frac{1}{3}\right) + \left(\frac{1}{2} - \frac{1}{4}\right) + \left(\frac{1}{3} - \frac{1}{5}\right) + \left(\frac{1}{4} - \frac{1}{6}\right)$$

Again, you can simplify the sum by canceling. This time, you can cancel the fractions $\frac{1}{3}$ and $\frac{1}{4}$.

$$\left(\frac{1}{1} - \frac{\cancel{1}}{\cancel{3}}\right) + \left(\frac{1}{2} - \frac{\cancel{1}}{\cancel{4}}\right) + \left(\frac{\cancel{1}}{\cancel{3}} - \frac{1}{5}\right) + \left(\frac{\cancel{1}}{\cancel{4}} - \frac{1}{6}\right) = \left(\frac{1}{1} + \frac{1}{2}\right) - \left(\frac{1}{5} + \frac{1}{6}\right)$$

If you write out the next two sums and simplify them, you will see that they are

$$\left(\frac{1}{1}+\frac{1}{2}\right)-\left(\frac{1}{6}+\frac{1}{7}\right) \text{ and } \left(\frac{1}{1}+\frac{1}{2}\right)-\left(\frac{1}{7}+\frac{1}{8}\right)$$

Working with the sums makes it clear that this pattern continues to hold as you add more and more terms of the sequence together and that a formula for the sum of the first k terms of the sequence is

$$\left(\frac{1}{1}+\frac{1}{2}\right)-\left(\frac{1}{k+1}+\frac{1}{k+2}\right)$$

Therefore, the sum of the first 20 terms of the sequence is equal to

$$\left(\frac{1}{1}+\frac{1}{2}\right)-\left(\frac{1}{20+1}+\frac{1}{20+2}\right)=\left(1+\frac{1}{2}\right)-\left(\frac{1}{21}+\frac{1}{22}\right)$$

The correct answer is **Choice B**.

This explanation uses the following strategies.
Strategy 5: Simplify an Arithmetic or Algebraic Representation
Strategy 7: Find a Pattern

Numeric Entry

For Question 13, use the directions for Numeric Entry questions.

Y	Frequency
$\frac{1}{2}$	2
$\frac{3}{4}$	7
$\frac{5}{4}$	8
$\frac{3}{2}$	8
$\frac{7}{4}$	9

13. The table above shows the frequency distribution of the values of a variable Y. What is the mean of the distribution?
    Give your answer to the <u>nearest 0.01</u>.

    [   ]

Explanation

The mean of the distribution of the variable Y is the sum of all the values of Y divided by the number of values of Y. However, before you begin the summing process, you need to understand how the information is presented in the question. Information about the variable is given in a table, where any repetitions of values have been summarized in the column labeled "Frequency." Reading from the table, you can see that the value $\frac{1}{2}$ occurs twice, the value $\frac{3}{4}$ occurs seven times, and so on. To sum all the values of Y, you could add the value $\frac{1}{2}$ twice, add the value $\frac{3}{4}$ seven times, and continue the addition process in this manner. It is easier, however, to multiply the values by their corresponding frequencies and then sum the individual products, as shown below.

$$(2)\left(\frac{1}{2}\right)+(7)\left(\frac{3}{4}\right)+(8)\left(\frac{5}{4}\right)+(8)\left(\frac{3}{2}\right)+(9)\left(\frac{7}{4}\right)=\frac{4}{4}+\frac{21}{4}+\frac{40}{4}+\frac{48}{4}+\frac{63}{4}$$

$$=\frac{176}{4}$$

$$=44$$

To find the average, you need to divide the sum, 44, by the number of values of Y. The number of values can be found by looking at the column of frequencies in the table. The sum of the numbers in this column, $2 + 7 + 8 + 8 + 9$, or 34, is the number of values of Y. Thus, the mean of the distribution is $\frac{44}{34}$, which, as a decimal, equals 1.2941.... Rounded to the nearest 0.01, the correct answer is **1.29**.

This explanation uses the following strategies.
Strategy 4: Translate from a Figure to an Arithmetic or Algebraic Representation
Strategy 8: Search for a Mathematical Relationship

Multiple-Choice Questions—Select One or More Answer Choices

> For Questions 14 and 15, select all the answer choices that apply.

14. Let S be the set of all positive integers n such that n^2 is a multiple of both 24 and 108. Which of the following integers are divisors of every integer n in S?
Indicate <u>all</u> such integers.

   A 12

   B 24

   C 36

   D 72

Explanation
To determine which of the integers in the answer choices is a divisor of every positive integer n in S, you must first understand the integers that are in S. Note that in this question you are given information about n^2, not about n itself. Therefore, you must use the information about n^2 to derive information about n.

The fact that n^2 is a multiple of both 24 and 108 implies that n^2 is a multiple of the least common multiple of 24 and 108. To determine the least common multiple of 24 and 108, factor 24 and 108 into prime factors as $(2^3)(3)$ and $(2^2)(3^3)$, respectively. Because these are prime factorizations, you can conclude that the least common multiple of 24 and 108 is $(2^3)(3^3)$.

Knowing that n^2 must be a multiple of $(2^3)(3^3)$ does not mean that every multiple of $(2^3)(3^3)$ is a possible value of n^2, because n^2 must be the square of an integer. The prime factorization of a square number must contain only even exponents. Thus, the least multiple of $(2^3)(3^3)$ that is a square is $(2^4)(3^4)$. This is the least possible value of n^2, and so the least possible value of n is $(2^2)(3^2)$, or 36. Furthermore, since every value of n^2 is a multiple of $(2^4)(3^4)$, the values of n are the positive multiples of 36; that is, $S = \{36, 72, 108, 144, 180, \ldots\}$.

The question asks for integers that are divisors of every integer n in S, that is, divisors of every positive multiple of 36. Since Choice A, 12, is a divisor of 36, it is also a divisor of every multiple of 36. The same is true for Choice C, 36. Choices B and D, 24 and 72, are not divisors of 36, so they are not divisors of every integer in S. The correct answer consists of **Choices A and C**.

This explanation uses the following strategies.

Strategy 8: Search for a Mathematical Relationship
Strategy 12: Adapt Solutions to Related Problems

---

15. The penguins currently living on an island are of two types, Chinstrap penguins and Gentoo penguins. The range of the heights of the Chinstrap penguins on the island is 13.2 centimeters, and the range of the heights of the Gentoo penguins on the island is 15.4 centimeters.

    Which of the following statements <u>individually</u> provide(s) sufficient additional information to determine the range of the heights of all the penguins on the island?

    Indicate <u>all</u> such statements.

    A   The tallest Gentoo penguin on the island is 5.8 centimeters taller than the tallest Chinstrap penguin on the island.

    B   The median height of the Gentoo penguins on the island is 1.1 centimeters greater than the median height of the Chinstrap penguins on the island.

    C   The average (arithmetic mean) height of the Gentoo penguins on the island is 4.6 centimeters greater than the average height of the Chinstrap penguins on the island.

Explanation

Choice A tells you that the tallest Gentoo penguin is 5.8 centimeters taller than the tallest Chinstrap penguin. You can combine this information with the given information about the Gentoo and Chinstrap height ranges to place four penguins—the shortest Gentoo, the shortest Chinstrap, the tallest Gentoo, and the tallest Chinstrap—in relative order according to height, as shown in the figure below.

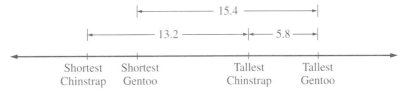

You can see from the figure that the tallest penguin must be a Gentoo and the shortest penguin must be a Chinstrap. You can also see the difference in height between those two penguins, which is the range of the heights of all the penguins. Therefore, Choice A provides sufficient additional information to determine the range.

Choice B provides information about one of the centers of the data—the median; it does not say anything about how spread out the data are around that center. You are given that the median height of the Gentoos is 1.1 centimeters greater than that of the Chinstraps. First note that it is possible for two different sets of data to have the same median but have very different ranges. Choice B gives the difference between the medians of the Gentoo heights and the Chinstrap heights, without giving the actual medians. However, even if you knew the medians, the fact that the ranges can vary widely indicates that the range of the heights of all the penguins can also vary widely.

It is possible to construct examples of heights of penguins that satisfy all of the information in the question and in Choice B but have different ranges for the heights of all the penguins. Here are two such examples, each of which has only three Chinstraps and three Gentoos. Although the examples are small, they illustrate the fact that the range of the heights of all the penguins can vary. In both examples, the range of Chinstrap heights is 13.2 centimeters, the range of Gentoo heights is 15.4 centimeters, and the difference between the median heights is 1.1 centimeters.

Example 1
Chinstrap heights: 50.0   56.6   63.2   which have a median of 56.6
Gentoo heights: 50.0   57.7   65.4   which have a median of 57.7
Range of heights of all the penguins: 15.4

Example 2
Chinstrap heights: 50.0   56.6   63.2   which have a median of 56.6
Gentoo heights: 51.0   57.7   66.4   which have a median of 57.7
Range of heights of all the penguins: 16.4

Therefore, Choice B does not provide sufficient additional information to determine the range of the heights of all the penguins.

Choice C provides information about another center of the data—the average. You are given that the average height of the Gentoos is 4.6 centimeters greater than that of the Chinstraps. However, like Choice B, the statement gives no information about how spread out the data are around that center. Again, it is possible for two different sets of data to have the same average but have very different ranges. Examples similar to the two examples above can be constructed that satisfy all of the information in the question and in Choice C but have different ranges for the heights of all the penguins. Therefore, Choice C does not provide sufficient additional information to determine the range of the heights of all the penguins.

The correct answer consists of **Choice A**.

This explanation uses the following strategies.
Strategy 2: Translate from Words to a Figure or Diagram
Strategy 11: Divide into Cases
Strategy 14: Determine What Additional Information Is Sufficient to Solve a Problem

SET 4. Data Interpretation Sets

For Questions 1 to 7, select a single answer choice unless otherwise directed.

Questions 1 to 3 are based on the following data.

PERCENT OF ADJUNCT FACULTY AND PERCENT OF NON-ADJUNCT
FACULTY AT COLLEGE *X*, BY FIELD
Total adjunct faculty: 200
Total non-adjunct faculty: 250

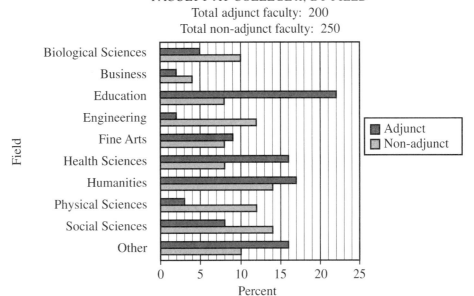

Medium Question

1. There are 275 students in the field of engineering at College *X*. Approximately what is the ratio of the number of students in engineering to the number of faculty in engineering?

    (A) 8 to 1
    (B) 10 to 1
    (C) 12 to 1
    (D) 14 to 1
    (E) 20 to 1

Explanation

According to the graph, 2 percent of the adjunct faculty and 12 percent of the non-adjunct faculty are in the engineering field. To determine the total number of faculty in engineering, you need to add 2 percent of 200, which is 4, to 12 percent of 250, which is 30, to get 34. Thus, the ratio of the numbers of students to faculty in engineering is 275 to 34, which is approximately equal to 280 to 35, or 8 to 1. The correct answer is **Choice A**.

This explanation uses the following strategies.

Strategy 4: Translate from a Figure to an Arithmetic or Algebraic Representation
Strategy 5: Simplify an Arithmetic or Algebraic Representation
Strategy 9: Estimate

Medium Question

2. Approximately what percent of the faculty in humanities are non-adjunct faculty?

   (A) 35%   (D) 45%

   (B) 38%   (E) 51%

   (C) 41%

Explanation

You need to determine the numbers of adjunct and non-adjunct faculty in the humanities field. According to the graph, 17 percent of the 200 adjunct faculty, or 34, and 14 percent of the 250 non-adjunct faculty, or 35, are in humanities. Thus, the fraction of humanities faculty who are non-adjunct faculty is $\dfrac{35}{34+35} = \dfrac{35}{69}$, or approximately 0.507. As a percent, the answer choice that is closest to 0.507 is 51 percent. The correct answer is **Choice E**.

This explanation uses the following strategies.

Strategy 4: Translate from a Figure to an Arithmetic or Algebraic Representation
Strategy 5: Simplify an Arithmetic or Algebraic Representation
Strategy 9: Estimate

For Question 3, use the directions for Numeric Entry questions.

Hard Question

3. For the biological sciences and health sciences faculty combined, $\dfrac{1}{3}$ of the adjunct faculty and $\dfrac{2}{9}$ of the non-adjunct faculty are medical doctors. What fraction of all the faculty in those two fields combined are medical doctors?

Explanation

You need to determine the number of adjunct faculty and the number of non-adjunct faculty in the combined group. According to the graph, 5 percent of the adjunct faculty, or 10, and 10 percent of the non-adjunct faculty, or 25, are in the biological sciences. Similarly, 16 percent of the adjunct faculty, or 32, and 8 percent of the non-adjunct faculty, or 20, are in the health sciences. When you combine the groups, you get a total of 42 adjunct faculty (10 + 32) and 45 non-adjunct faculty (25 + 20), which is a total of 87 faculty. Medical doctors are $\dfrac{1}{3}$ of the 42 adjunct faculty, or 14 adjuncts, and $\dfrac{2}{9}$ of the 45 non-adjunct faculty, or 10 non-adjuncts. Thus, there are 24 medical doctors, and the fraction that are medical doctors is $\dfrac{24}{87}$. The correct answer is $\dfrac{24}{87}$ (or any equivalent fraction).

This explanation uses the following strategies.

Strategy 4: Translate from a Figure to an Arithmetic or Algebraic Representation
Strategy 5: Simplify an Arithmetic or Algebraic Representation

VALUE OF IMPORTS TO AND EXPORTS FROM COUNTRY *T*, 2000–2009
(in United States dollars)

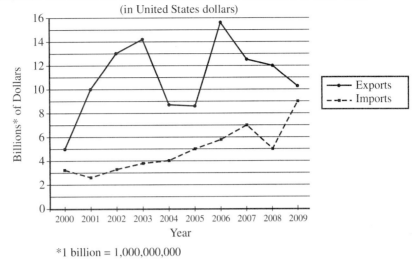

*1 billion = 1,000,000,000

For Question 4, select all the answer choices that apply.

Easy Question

4. For which of the eight years from 2001 to 2008 did exports exceed imports by more than $5 billion?

    Indicate <u>all</u> such years.

    - [A] 2001
    - [B] 2002
    - [C] 2003
    - [D] 2004
    - [E] 2005
    - [F] 2006
    - [G] 2007
    - [H] 2008

    Explanation

    Note that for all years shown, the dollar value of exports is greater than the dollar value of imports. For each year, the difference between the dollar value of exports and the dollar value of imports can be read directly from the graph. The difference was more than $5 billion for each of the years 2001, 2002, 2003, 2006, 2007, and 2008. The correct answer consists of **Choices A, B, C, F, G, and H**.

    This explanation uses the following strategy.
    Strategy 4: Translate from a Figure to an Arithmetic or Algebraic Representation

Medium Question

5. Which of the following is closest to the average (arithmetic mean) of the 9 changes in the value of imports between consecutive years from 2000 to 2009?

    (A) $260 million

    (B) $320 million

    (C) $400 million

    (D) $480 million

    (E) $640 million

Explanation

The average of the 9 changes in the value of imports between consecutive years can be represented as follows, where the function v(year) represents the value of imports for the indicated year.

$$\frac{(v(2001) - v(2000)) + (v(2002) - v(2001)) + (v(2003) - v(2002)) + \cdots + (v(2009) - v(2008))}{9}$$

Note that in the numerator of the fraction, each term, with the exception of $v(2000)$ and $v(2009)$, appears first as positive and then again as negative. The positive and negative pairs sum to 0, and the fraction simplifies to

$$\frac{v(2009) - v(2000)}{9}$$

Reading the values from the graph, you can approximate the value of the simplified fraction as $\frac{9.0 - 3.2}{9} = \frac{5.8}{9} \approx 0.644$ billion dollars. The answer choice that is closest to $0.644 billion is $640 million. The correct answer is **Choice E**.

This explanation uses the following strategies.

Strategy 4: Translate from a Figure to an Arithmetic or Algebraic Representation
Strategy 5: Simplify an Arithmetic or Algebraic Representation
Strategy 9: Estimate

Medium Question

6. In 2008 the value of exports was approximately what percent greater than the value of imports?

    (A) 40%

    (B) 60%

    (C) 70%

    (D) 120%

    (E) 140%

Explanation

The difference between the value of exports and the value of imports expressed as a percent of the value of imports is

$$\left(\frac{(\text{value of exports}) - (\text{value of imports})}{\text{value of imports}}\right)(100\%)$$

In 2008 the value of imports was approximately $5 billion and the value of exports was approximately $12 billion, so the value of the fraction is approximately $\dfrac{12-5}{5}$, or $\dfrac{7}{5}$.

Since the fraction is greater than 1, expressing it as a percent will give a percent greater than 100. The fraction is equal to 1.4, or 140 percent. The correct answer is **Choice E**.

This explanation uses the following strategies.

Strategy 4: Translate from a Figure to an Arithmetic or Algebraic Representation
Strategy 5: Simplify an Arithmetic or Algebraic Representation

Hard Question

7.   If it were discovered that the value of imports shown for 2007 was incorrect and should have been $5 billion instead, then the average (arithmetic mean) value of imports per year for the 10 years shown would have been approximately how much less?

    Ⓐ $200 million

    Ⓑ $50 million

    Ⓒ $20 million

    Ⓓ $7 million

    Ⓔ $5 million

Explanation

To answer this question, you do not need to compute either of the two 10-year averages referred to in the question; you just need to calculate the difference between the two averages.

The average value of imports for the 10 years shown in the graph is found by adding the 10 values and then dividing the sum by 10. The value of imports in 2007 is $7 billion. If that amount were $5 billion instead, then the sum of the values would be $2 billion less. If the sum were $2 billion less than what it was, then the average would decrease by 2 billion divided by 10, or $\dfrac{2,000,000,000}{10} = 200,000,000$. The average would therefore be $200 million less, and the correct answer is **Choice A**.

A more algebraic approach to the problem is to let S represent the sum, in billions, of the 10 values of imports in the graph. The average of the 10 values is $\dfrac{S}{10}$. Note that $S - 2$ represents the sum, in billions, of the 10 values adjusted for the $2 billion correction for 2007. The average of the adjusted sum is $\dfrac{S-2}{10}$. The difference between the two averages is

$$\frac{S}{10} - \frac{S-2}{10} = \frac{S-(S-2)}{10}$$

$$= \frac{S-S+2}{10}$$

$$= \frac{2}{10}$$

The difference is 0.2 billion dollars, or $200 million. The correct answer is **Choice A**.

This explanation uses the following strategies.

Strategy 4: Translate from a Figure to an Arithmetic or Algebraic Representation
Strategy 5: Simplify an Arithmetic or Algebraic Representation

8 GRE Quantitative Reasoning: Mixed Practice Sets

Your goals for this chapter	◤ Practice answering GRE Quantitative Reasoning questions on your own
	◤ Review answers and explanations, particularly for questions you answered incorrectly

This chapter contains five GRE Quantitative Reasoning practice sets. Each practice set contains a mixture of Quantitative Reasoning question types and difficulty levels, similar to a mixture of questions on the actual GRE Quantitative Reasoning measure.

Each practice set is followed by an answer key and explanations for the questions in the set. As in Chapter 7, each explanation is presented with the corresponding question so that you can easily see what is being asked and what the various answer choices are.

Review the answer explanations carefully, paying particular attention to the explanations for questions that you answered incorrectly. Begin the first Quantitative Reasoning practice set on the next page.

Quantitative Reasoning Practice Set 1
15 Questions

For each of Questions 1 to 6, select one of the following answer choices.

(A)   **Quantity A is greater.**

(B)   **Quantity B is greater.**

(C)   **The two quantities are equal.**

(D)   **The relationship cannot be determined from the information given.**

$$x \neq 0$$

	Quantity A	Quantity B	
1.	$\dfrac{5 + x^2}{10 + x^2}$	$\dfrac{1}{2}$	Ⓐ Ⓑ Ⓒ Ⓓ

In the rectangular coordinate system, the "D-length" between points (x_1, y_1) and (x_2, y_2) is defined as the greater of the two quantities $|x_1 - x_2|$ and $|y_1 - y_2|$. Points R, S, and T have coordinates $(-3,1), (3,5)$, and $(4,1)$, respectively.

	Quantity A	Quantity B	
2.	The D-length between points R and S	The D-length between points R and T	Ⓐ Ⓑ Ⓒ Ⓓ

x and y are integers, and $x + y < 0$.

	Quantity A	Quantity B	
3.	xy	0	Ⓐ Ⓑ Ⓒ Ⓓ

$$x < y < z$$

	Quantity A	Quantity B	
4.	$\dfrac{x + y + z}{3}$	y	Ⓐ Ⓑ Ⓒ Ⓓ

	Quantity A	Quantity B	

5. The area enclosed by a square with a side of length 2   Twice the area enclosed by an equilateral triangle with a side of length 2   

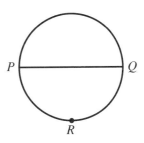

PQ is a diameter of the circle above. Point R divides the lower semicircle into two arcs of equal lengths. Point S (not shown) lies on the upper semicircle and is distinct from points P and Q.

	Quantity A	Quantity B	

6. The measure of angle RPS   150°

For each of questions 7 to 15, select <u>one</u> answer choice unless otherwise instructed.

---

7. What is the value of 2.673285, rounded to the nearest tenth?

   (A) 2.6
   (B) 2.7
   (C) 2.67
   (D) 2.68
   (E) 2.673

8. A pencil holder holds 30 pencils. When a pencil is chosen at random from the pencil holder, the probability of choosing a pencil that is yellow is 0.4 and the probability of choosing a yellow pencil that has an eraser is 0.3. How many yellow pencils that have <u>no</u> erasers are in the pencil holder?

   (A) 1
   (B) 3
   (C) 4
   (D) 9
   (E) 12

For the following question, select all the answer choices that apply.

9. Two water pumps, *P* and *Q*, working at their respective constant rates, will fill an empty water tank. Pump *P*, working alone at its constant rate, can fill the tank in 30 minutes.

    Which of the following statements individually provide(s) sufficient additional information to determine how long it will take to fill the tank if both pumps work simultaneously at their respective constant rates?

    Indicate all such statements.

    | A | The capacity of the tank is 600 gallons.

    | B | Pump *Q*, working alone at its constant rate, can fill $\frac{1}{20}$ of the tank in 1 minute.

    | C | If pump *P* works alone for 5 minutes at its constant rate and then both pumps work simultaneously at their respective constant rates, the tank can be filled in a total of 15 minutes.

Questions 10 to 13 are based on the following data.

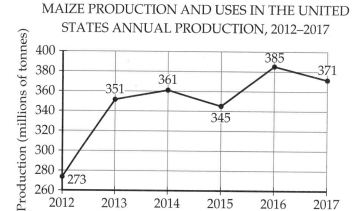

MAIZE PRODUCTION AND USES IN THE UNITED STATES ANNUAL PRODUCTION, 2012–2017

Note: 1 tonne = 1,000 kilograms.

Uses, 2017

Use	Percent of Production
Feed	39%
Ethanol and fuel	27%
Exports	16%
Food and industrial use	9%
Residual	9%

10. Approximately how much greater was the average (arithmetic mean) annual maize production for the years 2013 through 2017 than the maize production, in tonnes, for 2012?

    (A) 70 million
    (B) 75 million
    (C) 85 million
    (D) 90 million
    (E) 95 million

For the following question, enter your answer in the box.

11. In 2017 the maize production that was used for ethanol and fuel was what percent of the maize production that was <u>not</u> used for exports?

    Give your answer to the <u>nearest whole percent</u>.

    [   ] %

12. Which of the following is closest to the average rate of change, in tonnes per year, for maize production from 2012 to 2017?

    (A) 20 million
    (B) 19 million
    (C) 18 million
    (D) 17 million
    (E) 16 million

13. If the mass of 1 bushel of maize is 0.0254 tonne of maize, approximately how many bushels of the maize produced in 2017 were used for exports?

    (A) 2 million
    (B) 9 million
    (C) 59 million
    (D) 2,337 million
    (E) 3,944 million

14. Which of the following integers has only two different prime factors?

    (A) 4
    (B) 5
    (C) 12
    (D) 27
    (E) 30

For the following question, enter your answer in the boxes.

15. Lists R and S consist of numbers, and R has twice as many numbers as S. The average (arithmetic mean) of the numbers in R is 8, and the average of the numbers in S is 7. What is the average of the numbers in lists R and S combined?

Give your answer as a fraction.

$$\frac{\boxed{}}{\boxed{}}$$

Quantitative Reasoning Practice Set 2
15 Questions

For each of Questions 1 to 6, select one of the following answer choices.

(A)   **Quantity A is greater.**

(B)   **Quantity B is greater.**

(C)   **The two quantities are equal.**

(D)   **The relationship cannot be determined from the information given.**

$$x < 0 \text{ and } y < 0$$

	Quantity A	Quantity B	
1.	$4xy$	$\dfrac{2xy}{0.5}$	(A) (B) (C) (D)

In a certain sequence, each term after the first term is obtained by subtracting 1 from the preceding term and then dividing that difference by 3. The fourth term of the sequence is $\frac{4}{3}$.

	Quantity A	Quantity B	
2.	The first term of the sequence	46	(A) (B) (C) (D)

Number of gallons of milk	Less than 0.5	0.5	1.0	1.5	2.0	2.5	3.0 or more
Number of consumers	10	13	15	16	10	6	5

Each of the 75 consumers in a survey reported the number of gallons of milk that the consumer purchased last week. The preceding table shows the frequency distribution of the numbers of gallons reported.

	Quantity A	Quantity B	
3.	The median number of gallons of milk reported by the 75 consumers surveyed	1.5	(A) (B) (C) (D)

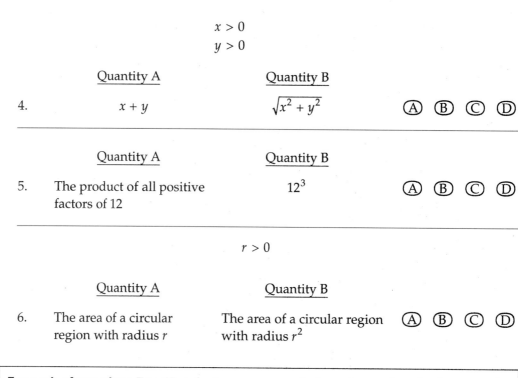

$$x > 0$$
$$y > 0$$

Quantity A	Quantity B	
4. $x + y$	$\sqrt{x^2 + y^2}$	Ⓐ Ⓑ Ⓒ Ⓓ

Quantity A	Quantity B	
5. The product of all positive factors of 12	12^3	Ⓐ Ⓑ Ⓒ Ⓓ

$$r > 0$$

Quantity A	Quantity B	
6. The area of a circular region with radius r	The area of a circular region with radius r^2	Ⓐ Ⓑ Ⓒ Ⓓ

For each of questions 7 to 15, select <u>one</u> answer choice unless otherwise instructed.

7. There are 10 different books available to a librarian for purchase, each for the same price, but the librarian has only enough money to purchase 9 of them. How many different collections of 9 books are there that can be selected from the 10 books?

Ⓐ   9
Ⓑ   10
Ⓒ   45
Ⓓ   90
Ⓔ   100

Questions 8 to 11 are based on the following data.

Selected Sales Data for Store X, 2014–2016
Total Sales by Year

Year	Total Sales (billions of dollars)
2014	$80.0
2015	$84.8
2016	$90.7

Percent of Total Sales by Department and Year

Department	2014	2015	2016
Gardening	16.0%	16.0%	17.0%
Paint	9.0%	8.5%	8.0%
Appliances	7.0%	7.5%	8.0%
Kitchen and Bath	8.0%	8.0%	7.5%
Plumbing	6.5%	7.0%	7.0%
Other	53.5%	53.0%	52.5%
Total	100%	100%	100%

8. For the years 2014 to 2016, which of the following is closest to the average (arithmetic mean) annual sales of the Appliances department?

   (A) $6.4 billion
   (B) $6.6 billion
   (C) $6.8 billion
   (D) $7.0 billion
   (E) $7.2 billion

9. For the years 2014 to 2016, which of the following is closest to the median annual sales of the Kitchen and Bath department?

   (A) $6.23 billion
   (B) $6.40 billion
   (C) $6.66 billion
   (D) $6.78 billion
   (E) $7.05 billion

For the following question, select all the answer choices that apply.

10. For which of the following departments were the combined departmental sales for the three years from 2014 to 2016 greater than $18 billion?

    Indicate <u>all</u> such departments.

    A Gardening
    B Paint
    C Appliances
    D Kitchen and Bath
    E Plumbing

11. Which of the following is closest to the percent change in annual sales of the Paint department from 2014 to 2016?

    (A) 11.1% decrease
    (B) 1.0% decrease
    (C) 0.8% increase
    (D) 8.0% increase
    (E) 12.5% increase

For the following question, enter your answer in the box.

12. The five points $P, Q, R, S,$ and T lie on the number line in that order, where $PQ = QR, PR = RS,$ and $PS = ST.$ If $PT = 16,$ what is the value of QS?

    [   ]

13. The operation Δ is defined by $a\Delta b = a^2 - 4b^2$ for all numbers a and b. For which of the following values of x is $(2x)\Delta 3 = (x-1)\Delta 2$?

    (A) $\dfrac{7}{3}$
    (B) 3
    (C) $\sqrt{7}$
    (D) $-1 + \sqrt{6}$
    (E) $-1 + \sqrt{22}$

For the following question, select all the answer choices that apply.

14. Gerald has a collection consisting of coins valued at $0.25 each and coins valued at $0.10 each. The total value of all the coins in the collection is less than $10.00, and there are 3 times as many coins valued at $0.25 as coins valued at $0.10. Which of the following statements about the coins in the collection must be true?

    Indicate all such statements.

    [A] The total value of the coins is a multiple of $0.85.

    [B] The total number of coins is less than or equal to 44.

    [C] The number of coins valued at $0.25 is a multiple of 5.

15. Each postal code for a certain area is a sequence of 5 digits, where each digit is selected from the digits 0 through 9. How many such postal codes have the property that the first digit is 9, the second digit is selected from the digits 0 through 6, and the third digit is 7 if the second digit is less than 6, and the third digit is 7 or 8 if the second digit is 6?

    (A) 567
    (B) 648
    (C) 700
    (D) 729
    (E) 800

Quantitative Reasoning Practice Set 3
15 Questions

For each of Questions 1 to 5, select one of the following answer choices.

(A) Quantity A is greater.

(B) Quantity B is greater.

(C) The two quantities are equal.

(D) The relationship cannot be determined from the information given.

On a certain day, Danielle invested $150 in shares of stock M and Ricardo invested $170 in shares of stock P. After one month, the value of Danielle's investment had increased by 5 percent, the value of Ricardo's investment had decreased by x percent, and the value of Danielle's investment was equal to the value of Ricardo's investment.

	Quantity A	Quantity B	
1.	x	10	(A) (B) (C) (D)

In pentagon $ABCDE$, points M, N, P, Q, and R are the midpoints of sides AB, BC, CD, DE, and EA, respectively.

	Quantity A	Quantity B	
2.	The perimeter of pentagon $ABCDE$	The perimeter of pentagon $MNPQR$	(A) (B) (C) (D)

$$5, 5, 5, x, x$$

m is the mean and q is the median of the five numbers in the list shown, and $m = q + 2$.

	Quantity A	Quantity B	
3.	x	8	(A) (B) (C) (D)

$$r^3 - r = r - r^3$$

Quantity A	Quantity B	
4. r	0	Ⓐ Ⓑ Ⓒ Ⓓ

Let X be the set of integers that are greater than or equal to 1 and less than or equal to 100.

Quantity A	Quantity B	
5. The number of integers in X that are multiples of 3 but <u>not</u> multiples of 4	The number of integers in X that are multiples of 4	Ⓐ Ⓑ Ⓒ Ⓓ

For each of questions 6 to 15, select <u>one</u> answer choice unless otherwise instructed.

---

6.   If n is an odd integer, which of the following must be an even integer?

Ⓐ $3n$
Ⓑ n^2
Ⓒ $(n + 1)^2$
Ⓓ $(n + 2)^2$
Ⓔ $(2n - 1)^2$

For the following question, select all the answer choices that apply.

7.   A group of students equally divided 60 bottles of water so that each student received the same whole number of bottles of water, and nothing was left over. Similarly, the students equally divided 84 packs of gum and equally divided 72 energy bars, and nothing was left over in either case. Which of the following could be the number of students in the group?

Indicate <u>all</u> such numbers.

A   4
B   5
C   6
D   8
E   9
F   10
G   12

For the following question, select all the answer choices that apply.

8. The lengths of the sides of a triangle are 7.5, 11, and x, where x is an integer. Which of the following could be the integer x?

    Indicate <u>all</u> such integers.

    A   1
    B   6
    C   11
    D   16
    E   21

Questions 9 to 12 are based on the following data.

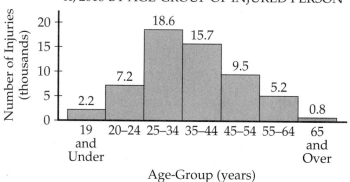

NUMBER OF OCCUPATIONAL INJURIES IN STATE X, 2018 BY AGE-GROUP OF INJURED PERSON

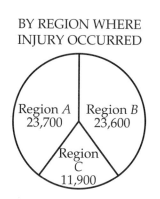

BY REGION WHERE INJURY OCCURRED

9. Of the total number of occupational injuries in State X in 2018, the fraction of the occupational injuries of people in the age-group 35–44 is closest to which of the following?

    Ⓐ $\frac{1}{3}$

    Ⓑ $\frac{1}{4}$

    Ⓒ $\frac{1}{5}$

    Ⓓ $\frac{1}{6}$

    Ⓔ $\frac{1}{7}$

10. For the age-group 55–64, the average (arithmetic mean) number of work hours lost per occupational injury in 2018 was 48.5. If a workweek consists of 40 work hours, which of the following is closest to the total number of workweeks lost due to occupational injuries in the age-group 55–64 in 2018?

    Ⓐ 4,500
    Ⓑ 5,200
    Ⓒ 5,500
    Ⓓ 5,900
    Ⓔ 6,300

11. For the two age-groups 19 and Under and 20 – 24 combined, 25 percent of all occupational injuries were bone fractures and 35 percent of all occupational injuries occurred in Region B. For the two age-groups combined, which of the following could be the number of occupational injuries that were bone fractures occurring in Region B?

    Ⓐ 2,300
    Ⓑ 2,400
    Ⓒ 2,500
    Ⓓ 2,600
    Ⓔ 2,700

For the following question, enter your answer in the box.

12. In 2018, if one-fourth of the occupational injuries in the age-groups 35 – 44 and 45 – 54 combined occurred in Region C, what percent of the occupational injuries that occurred in Region C were in the age-groups 35 – 44 and 45 – 54 combined?

    Give your answer to the <u>nearest whole percent</u>.

    ☐ %

13. In responding to a poll, 500 people answered either yes or no to each of 2 questions. Of the 500 respondents, 410 answered yes to the first question and 220 answered yes to the second question. If n is the number of respondents who answered yes to both questions, what is the least possible value of n?

(A) 90

(B) 110

(C) 130

(D) 190

(E) 220

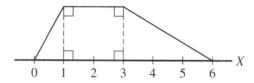

14. The figure above shows the probability distribution of a continuous random variable X. What is the probability that $4 < X < 5$?

(A) $\frac{1}{12}$

(B) $\frac{1}{8}$

(C) $\frac{1}{6}$

(D) $\frac{1}{5}$

(E) $\frac{1}{4}$

For the following question, enter your answer in the boxes.

15. In the xy-plane, ℓ and m are two perpendicular lines that intersect at the point $(2,3)$. Line ℓ passes through the origin. What is the y-intercept of line m?

Give your answer as a fraction.

$$\frac{\boxed{}}{\boxed{}}$$

Quantitative Reasoning Practice Set 4
15 Questions

For each of Questions 1 to 5, select one of the following answer choices.

(A)   **Quantity A is greater.**

(B)   **Quantity B is greater.**

(C)   **The two quantities are equal.**

(D)   **The relationship cannot be determined from the information given.**

A group of children is divided into r teams of 7 players each and 1 team of 10 players. The group has more than 30 but less than 50 children, and each child belongs to only one team.

	Quantity A	Quantity B	
1.	The number of children in the group	38	(A) (B) (C) (D)

$$0 < s < t$$

	Quantity A	Quantity B	
2.	$0.60s$	$0.58t$	(A) (B) (C) (D)

$$r < s < t < x < y < z$$

The average (arithmetic mean) of r, s, t, x, y, and z is 0.

	Quantity A	Quantity B	
3.	$r + s + t$	$-(x + y + z)$	(A) (B) (C) (D)

$$x < 0$$

	Quantity A	Quantity B	
4.	x^{-2}	$\dfrac{1}{-\left(x^2\right)}$	(A) (B) (C) (D)

In parallelogram QRST (not shown), the measure of angle R is (y + 15) degrees, and the measure of angle S is (225 − 2y) degrees.

	Quantity A	Quantity B	
5.	The measure of angle S	90 degrees	

6. Charley bought 200 small items for $0.75 each in order to resell as many of them as possible at an open market. He rented a table at the market for $20.00 and sold a number of the items for $1.25 each. He gave the remaining items to a neighboring vendor. If his profit from the sale of the items at the market was $67.50, how many of the items did he sell?

   Ⓐ 142
   Ⓑ 158
   Ⓒ 174
   Ⓓ 182
   Ⓔ 190

For each of questions 7 to 15, select <u>one</u> answer choice unless otherwise instructed.

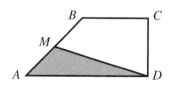

7. In the figure above, angle BCD and angle ADC are right angles, AD = 2(BC), and M is the midpoint of side AB. If the area of the shaded region is 10, what is the area of ABCD?

   Ⓐ 20
   Ⓑ 25
   Ⓒ 30
   Ⓓ 35
   Ⓔ 40

8. If d is the standard deviation of the three numbers w, p, and u, what is the standard deviation of the three numbers $w + 6$, $p + 6$, and $u + 6$?

   Ⓐ d
   Ⓑ $d + 6$
   Ⓒ $d + 18$
   Ⓓ $6d$
   Ⓔ $18d$

9.   For how many different values of x is $(2x + 4)(x - 3)(x + 2)^2 = 0$?

    (A) One
    (B) Two
    (C) Three
    (D) Four
    (E) An infinite number

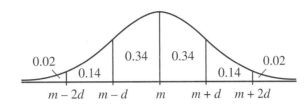

The figure above shows a normal distribution with mean m and standard deviation d, including approximate probabilities corresponding to the six intervals shown.

10.   The distribution of heights of a large group of students is approximately normal with mean 140 centimeters and standard deviation 2 centimeters. One student will be selected at random from the group. Of the following, which is the best estimate of the probability that the student selected will have a height greater than 141 centimeters?

    (A) 0.14
    (B) 0.16
    (C) 0.31
    (D) 0.48
    (E) 0.50

For the following question, enter your answer in the box.

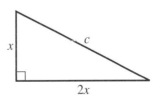

11.   If $c = \sqrt{31.25}$ in the triangle shown, what is the value of x?

$$x = \boxed{}$$

12.   If x and y are positive and x is $\frac{27}{36}$ of y, then x is what percent of y?

    (A) 9%
    (B) 33%
    (C) 75%
    (D) 133%
    (E) 175%

13. In a group of 200 college students, each student is a member of the orchestra or the tennis club or both. Of the 200 students, 150 students are members of the orchestra only and 10 students are members of both the orchestra and the tennis club. If a student is to be selected at random from the 200 students, what is the probability that the student selected will be a student who is a member of the tennis club only?

   (A) $\frac{1}{40}$

   (B) $\frac{1}{20}$

   (C) $\frac{1}{5}$

   (D) $\frac{1}{4}$

   (E) $\frac{3}{4}$

14. If $-1 < 2x - 1 < 3$ and $1 < y + 2 < 5$, which of the following could be true?

   (A) $x = 0$ and $y = 0$
   (B) $x = 1$ and $y = -2$
   (C) $x = 1.2$ and $y = -1.2$
   (D) $x = 1.5$ and $y = 0.5$
   (E) $x = 2$ and $y = 2.5$

For the following question, select all the answer choices that apply.

15. George's total monthly earnings consist of a base monthly salary of $2,000 plus up to three commissions. The first commission is equal to 10 percent of his monthly sales up to $10,000, the second commission is equal to 20 percent of his monthly sales in excess of $10,000 and up to $30,000, and the third commission is equal to 50 percent of his monthly sales in excess of $30,000.

   Which of the following statements <u>individually</u> provide(s) sufficient additional information to determine George's total earnings last month?

   Indicate <u>all</u> such statements.

   A Last month, George's second commission was $3,000 greater than his first commission.

   B Last month, George's third commission was $5,000 greater than his first commission.

   C Last month, George's third commission was $2,000 greater than his second commission.

Quantitative Reasoning Practice Set 5
15 Questions

> **For each of Questions 1 to 5, select one of the following answer choices.**
>
> **(A)** Quantity A is greater.
> **(B)** Quantity B is greater.
> **(C)** The two quantities are equal.
> **(D)** The relationship cannot be determined from the information given.

n and p are positive.

	Quantity A	Quantity B	
1.	$(n - p)(n^2 + np + p^2)$	$n^3 - p^3$	Ⓐ Ⓑ Ⓒ Ⓓ

The sequence $a_1, a_2, a_3, \ldots$ is defined by $a_n = \dfrac{1}{2}n - 7$ for all integers $n \geq 1$.

	Quantity A	Quantity B	
2.	$a_3 + a_5$	8	Ⓐ Ⓑ Ⓒ Ⓓ

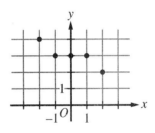

	Quantity A	Quantity B	
3.	The standard deviation of the x-coordinates of the 5 points shown in the xy-plane above	The standard deviation of the y-coordinates of the 5 points shown in the xy-plane above	Ⓐ Ⓑ Ⓒ Ⓓ

For a certain triangular region, each side has length 1 and the area is t.

Quantity A	Quantity B	
4. $\quad t\sqrt{3}$	1	Ⓐ Ⓑ Ⓒ Ⓓ

x and y are integers and $0 < x < y$.

Quantity A	Quantity B	
5. $\quad x^y$	y^x	Ⓐ Ⓑ Ⓒ Ⓓ

For each of questions 6 to 15, select one answer choice unless otherwise instructed.

For the following question, enter your answer in the boxes.

6. A lighthouse, a bell tower, and a clock tower are represented by three points on a map. On the map, the lighthouse is 6 inches due north of the bell tower and the clock tower is 1.75 inches due east of the bell tower. The distance on the map between the lighthouse and the clock tower is how many inches greater than the distance on the map between the lighthouse and the bell tower?

   Give your answer as a fraction.

 inch

7. In the sophomore class of a certain university, 85 percent of the students were taking English composition, 70 percent were taking biology, and 60 percent were taking both English composition and biology. What percent of the students in the class were taking neither English composition nor biology?

   Ⓐ 0%
   Ⓑ 5%
   Ⓒ 10%
   Ⓓ 15%
   Ⓔ 25%

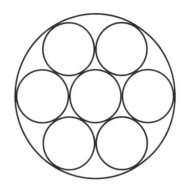

8. A paperweight in the shape of a right circular cylinder consists of 7 parallel right circular cylinders that are made of solid glass, where the space between the 7 cylinders is filled with resin. The figure shows a horizontal cross section of the paperweight, where each circle is tangent to any adjacent circles. The height of the paperweight is 10 centimeters and is equal to the height of each glass cylinder. The radius of each glass cylinder is 1 centimeter. Approximately what is the volume, in cubic centimeters, of the resin in the paperweight?

    (A) 16
    (B) 20
    (C) 42
    (D) 63
    (E) 80

For the following question, select all the answer choices that apply.

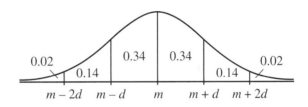

The figure shows a normal distribution with mean m and standard deviation d, including approximate probabilities corresponding to the six intervals shown.

9. The random variable G is normally distributed with mean 32.5 and standard deviation 4.2. The random variable H is normally distributed with mean 200 and standard deviation 100. Which of the following statements are true?

    Indicate <u>all</u> such statements.

    A $P(G \geq 36.7) = P(H \leq 100)$
    B $P(G \geq 38.8) = P(H \geq 350)$
    C $2(P(28.3 \leq G \leq 36.7)) = P(200 \leq H \leq 300)$

10. A music store owner bought a violin at a cost of $500 and then sold the violin for a price of $625. The owner's profit from the sale of the violin was what percent of the cost of the violin? (Profit equals price minus cost.)

    (A) 20%
    (B) 25%
    (C) 30%
    (D) 35%
    (E) 80%

11. If $0 < x < 1$, which of the following has the greatest value?

    (A) $\dfrac{1}{x}$

    (B) $\dfrac{1}{x^2}$

    (C) 1

    (D) x

    (E) x^2

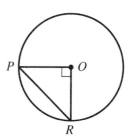

12. The figure above shows a circle with center O and circumference 10π. What is the perimeter of $\triangle POR$?

    (A) $12\sqrt{2}$
    (B) $10 + 5\sqrt{2}$
    (C) $12 + 5\sqrt{2}$
    (D) $20 + 5\sqrt{2}$
    (E) $20 + 10\sqrt{2}$

$$S = \{2, 3, 7, 9, 12, 13, 15\}$$

13. How many subsets of set S consist of 3 integers such that the product of the 3 integers is even?

    (A) 14
    (B) 21
    (C) 25
    (D) 30
    (E) 35

For the following question, enter your answer in the box.

14. For each of its cars, a rental-car company measured the fuel consumption in gallons of fuel consumed per 1,000 miles traveled. In the distribution of measurements, 41.25 is 1.3 standard deviations below the mean and 47.50 is 1.2 standard deviations above the mean. What is the mean of the distribution?

   [   ]

15. How many integers x are there such that $|x + 2| < 4$ and $|2x - 1| < 7$?

   (A) None
   (B) One
   (C) Two
   (D) Three
   (E) Four

Answer Key

Quantitative Reasoning: Practice Section 1

Question Number	P+	Correct Answer
1	67	**Choice A:** Quantity A is greater.
2	58	**Choice B:** Quantity B is greater.
3	53	**Choice D:** The relationship cannot be determined from the information given.
4	48	**Choice D:** The relationship cannot be determined from the information given.
5	43	**Choice A:** Quantity A is greater.
6	35	**Choice B:** Quantity B is greater.
7	91	**Choice B:** 2.7
8	52	**Choice B:** 3
9	50	**Choice B:** Pump Q, working alone at its constant rate, can fill $\frac{1}{20}$ of the tank in 1 minute. **AND** **Choice C:** If pump P works alone for 5 minutes at its constant rate and then both pumps work simultaneously at their respective constant rates, the tank can be filled in a total of 15 minutes.
10	88	**Choice D:** 90 million
11	42	**32%**
12	54	**Choice A:** 20 million
13	55	**Choice D:** 2,337 million
14	28	**Choice C:** 12
15	25	$\frac{23}{3}$

Practice Set 2: Quantitative Reasoning

Question Number	P+	Correct Answer
1	70	**Choice C:** The two quantities are equal.
2	61	**Choice A:** Quantity A is greater.
3	55	**Choice B:** Quantity B is greater.
4	58	**Choice A:** Quantity A is greater.
5	54	**Choice C:** The two quantities are equal.
6	38	**Choice D:** The relationship cannot be determined from the information given.
7	38	**Choice B:** 10
8	81	**Choice A:** $6.4 billion
9	61	**Choice D:** $6.78 billion
10	48	**Choice A:** Gardening **AND** **Choice B:** Paint **AND** **Choice C:** Appliances **AND** **Choice D:** Kitchen and Bath

Question Number	P+	Correct Answer
11	42	**Choice C:** 0.8% increase
12	24	**6**
13	19	**Choice A:** $\dfrac{7}{3}$
14	22	**Choice A:** The total value of the coins is an integer multiple of $0.85. **AND** **Choice B:** The total number of coins is less than or equal to 44.
15	05	**Choice E:** 800

Practice Set 3: Quantitative Reasoning

Question Number	P+	Correct Answer
1	77	**Choice B:** Quantity B is greater.
2	54	**Choice A:** Quantity A is greater.
3	51	**Choice A:** Quantity A is greater.
4	49	**Choice D:** The relationship cannot be determined from the information given.
5	28	**Choice C:** The two quantities are equal.
6	89	**Choice C:** $(n + 1)^2$
7	86	**Choice A:** 4 **AND** **Choice C:** 6 **AND** **Choice G:** 12
8	30	**Choice B:** 6 **AND** **Choice C:** 11 **AND** **Choice D:** 16
9	73	**Choice B:** $\dfrac{1}{4}$
10	40	**Choice E:** 6,300
11	39	**Choice A:** 2,300
12	25	**53%**
13	35	**Choice C:** 130
14	31	**Choice B:** $\dfrac{1}{8}$
15	11	$\dfrac{13}{3}$

Quantitative Reasoning: Practice Section 4

Question Number	P+	Correct Answer
1	62	**Choice D:** The relationship cannot be determined from the information given.
2	44	**Choice D:** The relationship cannot be determined from the information given.

Question Number	P+	Correct Answer
3	51	**Choice C:** The two quantities are equal.
4	66	**Choice A:** Quantity A is greater.
5	55	**Choice A:** Quantity A is greater.
6	60	**Choice E:** 190
7	38	**Choice C:** 30
8	44	**Choice A:** d
9	33	**Choice B:** Two
10	35	**Choice C:** 0.31
11	30	**2.5**
12	90	**Choice C:** 75%
13	76	**Choice C:** $\frac{1}{5}$
14	82	**Choice D:** $x = 1.5$ and $y = 0.5$
15	18	**Choice B:** Last month, George's third commission was $5,000 greater than his first commission. **AND** **Choice C:** Last month, George's third commission was $2,000 greater than his second commission.

Practice Set 5: Quantitative Reasoning

Question Number	P+	Correct Answer
1	61	**Choice C:** The two quantities are equal.
2	72	**Choice B:** Quantity B is greater.
3	61	**Choice A:** Quantity A is greater.
4	47	**Choice B:** Quantity B is greater.
5	51	**Choice D:** The relationship cannot be determined from the information given.
6	56	$\frac{1}{4}$ (or any equivalent fraction)
7	37	**Choice B:** 5%
8	39	**Choice D:** 63
9	23	**Choice A:** $P(G \geq 36.7) = P(H \leq 100)$ **AND** **Choice B:** $P(G \geq 38.8) = P(H \geq 350)$
10	94	**Choice B:** 25%
11	72	**Choice B:** $\frac{1}{x^2}$
12	75	**Choice B:** $10 + 5\sqrt{2}$
13	18	**Choice C:** 25
14	14	**44.5**
15	28	**Choice E:** Four

Answers and Explanations

Quantitative Reasoning Practice Set 1
15 Questions with Explanations

For each of Questions 1 to 6, select one of the following answer choices.

(A)   **Quantity A is greater.**

(B)   **Quantity B is greater.**

(C)   **The two quantities are equal.**

(D)   **The relationship cannot be determined from the information given.**

$$x \neq 0$$

<table>
<tr><td>Quantity A</td><td>Quantity B</td></tr>
</table>

1. $\dfrac{5 + x^2}{10 + x^2}$ $\dfrac{1}{2}$ (A)   (B)   (C)   (D)

Explanation

When divided by $\dfrac{1}{2}$ Quantity A becomes

$$\frac{\frac{5+x^2}{10+x^2}}{\frac{1}{2}} = \frac{2(5+x^2)}{10+x^2} = \frac{10+2x^2}{10+x^2} = \frac{(10+x^2)+x^2}{(10+x^2)} = 1 + \frac{x^2}{10+x^2} \text{ and Quantity B becomes 1.}$$

Since $\dfrac{x^2}{10+x^2}$ is greater than 0, $1 + \dfrac{x^2}{10+x^2}$ is greater than 1. But the problem asks

for a comparison between Quantity A and Quantity B, not between $1 + \dfrac{x^2}{10+x^2}$ and 1.

To go from a comparison between $1 + \dfrac{x^2}{10+x^2}$ and 1, start with this comparison and work backward until you get to the comparison between Quantity A and Quantity B.

Step 1: $1 + \dfrac{x^2}{10+x^2} > 1$.

Step 2: Substituting $\dfrac{10+x^2}{10+x^2}$ for 1, $\dfrac{10+x^2}{10+x^2} + \dfrac{x^2}{10+x^2} > 1$.

Step 3: Adding the fractions, $\dfrac{10+x^2+x^2}{10+x^2} > 1$.

Step 4: Combining terms, $\dfrac{10+2x^2}{10+x^2} > 1$.

Step 5: Factoring out 2, $\dfrac{2(5 + x^2)}{10 + x^2} > 1$.

Step 6: Dividing both sides by 2, $\dfrac{5 + x^2}{10 + x^2} > \dfrac{1}{2}$.

This implies that Quantity A is greater than Quantity B. So, the correct answer is **Choice A**.

Alternative Explanation

Quantity A: $\dfrac{5 + x^2}{10 + x^2} = \dfrac{1}{2}\left(\dfrac{10 + 2x^2}{10 + x^2}\right) = \dfrac{1}{2}\left(\dfrac{10 + x^2}{10 + x^2} + \dfrac{x^2}{10 + x^2}\right) = \dfrac{1}{2} + \dfrac{x^2}{2(10 + x^2)} > \dfrac{1}{2}$

because x^2 is positive. The correct answer is **Choice A**.

These explanations use the following strategies.
Strategy 5: Simplify an Arithmetic or Algebraic Representation
Strategy 8: Search for a Mathematical Relationship

In the rectangular coordinate system, the "D-length" between points (x_1, y_1) and (x_2, y_2) is defined as the greater of the two quantities $|x_1 - x_2|$ and $|y_1 - y_2|$. Points R, S, and T have coordinates $(-3,1)$, $(3,5)$, and $(4,1)$, respectively.

Quantity A	Quantity B	
2. The D-length between points R and S	The D-length between points R and T	

Explanation

From the given definition of the "D-Length," Quantity A is the greater of the two quantities $(-3) - 3| = |-6| = 6$ and $|1 - 5| = |-4| = 4$, which is 6.

Quantity B is the greater of the two quantities $(-3) - 4| = |-7| = 7$ and $|1 - 1| = |0| = 0$, which is 7. Therefore, Quantity B is greater than Quantity A. So, the correct answer is **Choice B**.

This explanation uses the following strategy.
Strategy 5: Simplify an Arithmetic or Algebraic Representation

---

x and y are integers, and $x + y < 0$.

Quantity A	Quantity B	
3. xy	0	

Explanation

Since $x + y < 0$, both integers can be less than 0 or one can be less than 0 and the other integer can be greater than 0 such that $x < -y$.

If both integers are less than 0, then their product is greater than 0.

If one of the integers is less than 0 and one of the integers is greater than 0, such that $x < -y$, then their product is less than 0. For example, suppose $x = -3$ and $y = -1$. Then $x + y < 0$ and $xy > 0$, making Quantity A greater than Quantity B.

On the other hand, suppose $x = -3$ and $y = 1$. Then $x + y < 0$ and $xy < 0$, making Quantity B greater than Quantity A. Therefore, the relationship between the two quantities cannot be determined from the given information. So, the correct answer is **Choice D**.

This explanation uses the following strategies.
Strategy 8: Search for a Mathematical Relationship
Strategy 10: Trial and Error, *Version 2: Try More Than One Value of a Variable*
Strategy 11: Divide into Cases

$$x < y < z$$

Quantity A	Quantity B

4. $\dfrac{x + y + z}{3}$ $\qquad\qquad\qquad$ y $\qquad$ Ⓐ Ⓑ Ⓒ Ⓓ

Explanation

One approach to this problem is use trial-and-error and then divide into several cases.

First, suppose that $x = 1$, $y = 3$, and $z = 4$. Then, $\dfrac{x + y + z}{3} = \dfrac{8}{3}$, which is less than $y = 3$, making Quantity B greater than Quantity A.

Next, suppose that $x = 1$, $y = 3$, and $z = 5$. Then, $\dfrac{x + y + z}{3} = \dfrac{9}{3}$, which is equal to $y = 3$, making the two quantities equal.

Finally, suppose $x = 1$, $y = 3$, and $z = 6$. Then, $\dfrac{x + y + z}{3} = \dfrac{10}{3}$, which is greater than $y = 3$, making Quantity A greater than Quantity B. Therefore, the relationship between the two quantities cannot be determined from the given information. So, the correct answer is **Choice D**.

Alternative Explanation

Quantity A represents the average (arithmetic mean) of three numbers, and Quantity B represents the median of the three numbers. The average can be less than, equal to, or greater than the median. The correct answer is **Choice D**.

These explanations use the following strategies.
Strategy 8: Search for a Mathematical Relationship
Strategy 10: Trial and Error, *Version 2: Try More Than One Value of a Variable*
Strategy 11: Divide into Cases

Quantity A	Quantity B	
5. The area enclosed by a square with a side of length 2	Twice the area enclosed by an equilateral triangle with a side of length 2	

Explanation

Quantity A is the area of a square; the area is (2)(2) = 4.

In an equilateral triangle, all side lengths are equal, and all angles have the same measure. The height of an equilateral triangle with sides of length 2 is perpendicular to the base and therefore forms two right triangles, each with a hypotenuse of length 2. In each right triangle, the height is across from an angle that measures 60 degrees. So, height is equal to $\frac{\sqrt{3}}{2}(2) = \sqrt{3}$. Therefore, Quantity B = $2\left(\frac{bh}{2}\right) = bh = 2\sqrt{3}$. Since $\sqrt{3}$ is less than 2, Quantity B is less than 4. Therefore, Quantity A is greater than Quantity B. Thus, the correct answer is **Choice A**.

This explanation uses the following strategies.

Strategy 1: Translate from Words to an Arithmetic or Algebraic Representation
Strategy 5: Simplify an Arithmetic or Algebraic Representation
Strategy 8: Search for a Mathematical Relationship
Strategy 9: Estimate

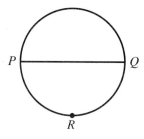

PQ is a diameter of the circle above. Point *R* divides the lower semicircle into two arcs of equal lengths. Point *S* (not shown) lies on the upper semicircle and is distinct from points *P* and *Q*.

Quantity A	Quantity B	
6. The measure of angle *RPS*	150°	

Explanation

S is a point on the upper semicircle. Let *T* be a point above *P* on the line tangent to the circle at *P*, as shown in the figure below. The measure of ∠*RPS* is less than the measure of ∠*RPT*.

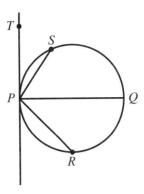

Since PQ is a diameter of the circle and R divides the lower semicircle into two arcs of equal length, the measure of each arc is 90°, which is equal to the measure of the central angle formed by P and R and by R and Q. Let point C be the center of the circle. Then in triangle RPC, $\angle RCP$ is a right angle and sides CP and CR are radii of the circle and therefore equal in length. Therefore, the degree measure of $\angle RPC$ and the degree measure of $\angle PRC$ are both 45°, as shown in the figure.

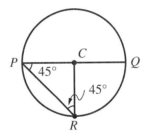

Since T is on the line tangent to the circle at P, the degree measure of $\angle CPT$ is 90° and the degree measure of $\angle RPT$ is 45° + 90° = 135°.

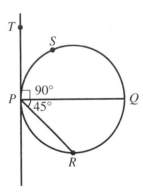

Since the measure of $\angle RPS$ is less than the measure of $\angle RPT$, in the figure we see that the degree measure of $\angle RPS$ is less than 135°, which is less than 150°. This implies that Quantity B is greater than Quantity A. Thus, the correct answer is **Choice B**.

This explanation uses the following strategies.

Strategy 2: Translate from Words to a Figure or Diagram
Strategy 6: Add to a Geometric Figure
Strategy 8: Search for a Mathematical Relationship

For each of questions 7 to 15, select <u>one</u> answer choice unless otherwise instructed.

7. What is the value of 2.673285, rounded to the nearest tenth?

   (A) 2.6
   (B) 2.7
   (C) 2.67
   (D) 2.68
   (E) 2.673

Explanation

Since the hundredths digit of 2.673285 is greater than 5, when the number is rounded to the nearest tenth, the tenths digit is increased by 1 and the remaining digits are truncated. Therefore, the value of 2.673285 rounded to the nearest tenth is 2.7. So, the correct answer is **Choice B**.

This explanation uses the following strategies.

Strategy 1: Translate from Words to an Arithmetic or Algebraic Representation
Strategy 12: Adapt Solutions to Related Problems

---

8. A pencil holder holds 30 pencils. When a pencil is chosen at random from the pencil holder, the probability of choosing a pencil that is yellow is 0.4 and the probability of choosing a yellow pencil that has an eraser is 0.3. How many yellow pencils that have <u>no</u> erasers are in the pencil holder?

   (A) 1
   (B) 3
   (C) 4
   (D) 9
   (E) 12

Explanation

In this question it is given that the probability of selecting a yellow pencil at random from the holder is 0.4. It is also given that there are 30 pencils in the holder, so the number of yellow pencils must be $(0.4)(30) = 12$. Of those 12 yellow pencils, some have erasers and the rest have no erasers. The probability of choosing a yellow pencil with an eraser from all the pencils is 0.3, so the number of yellow pencils with erasers must be $(0.3)(30) = 9$. Therefore, the number of yellow pencils that have no erasers is $12 - 9 = 3$. The correct answer is **Choice B**.

Alternative Explanation

Another way to approach the problem is to draw a two-way table to represent the situation. The 30 pencils are either yellow or not yellow, and the pencils either have erasers or do not have erasers, as shown in the following table.

	Yellow	Not Yellow	Total
Eraser			
No eraser			
Total			30

Since it is given that the probability of selecting a yellow pencil at random is 0.4, the total for the Yellow column is (0.4)(30) = 12. The number of yellow pencils that have erasers is represented in the table by the value in the cell in the Yellow column and the Eraser row. It is given that the probability of selecting a yellow pencil with an eraser is 0.3, so (0.3)(30) = 9 is the value for that cell, as shown.

	Yellow	Not Yellow	Total
Eraser	9		
No eraser			
Total			

The total of the values in the two cells in the Yellow column must be 12. One of the cells contains the value of 9, so the number of yellow pencils with no erasers must be 3. The correct answer is **Choice B**.

These explanations use the following strategies.
Strategy 1: Translate from Words to an Arithmetic or Algebraic Representation
Strategy 2: Translate from Words to a Figure or Diagram

For the following question, select all the answer choices that apply.

9.   Two water pumps, P and Q, working at their respective constant rates, will fill an empty water tank. Pump P, working alone at its constant rate, can fill the tank in 30 minutes.

Which of the following statements <u>individually</u> provide(s) sufficient additional information to determine how long it will take to fill the tank if both pumps work simultaneously at their respective constant rates?

Indicate <u>all</u> such statements.

- [A] The capacity of the tank is 600 gallons.
- [B] Pump Q, working alone at its constant rate, can fill $\frac{1}{20}$ of the tank in 1 minute.
- [C] If pump P works alone for 5 minutes at its constant rate and then both pumps work simultaneously at their respective constant rates, the tank can be filled in a total of 15 minutes.

Explanation
One way to solve problems involving two machines working at constant rates is to recognize that the product of rate and time for the first machine plus the product of rate and time for the second machine is equal to the entire job. Represent the rates of pumps P and Q by r_1 and r_2, respectively, and the amount of time the pumps work together is given by t. Therefore, to determine how long it will take both pumps working simultaneously to fill the tank, you can use an equation of the form $r_1 t + r_2 t = 1$.
        Pump P can fill the empty tank in 30 minutes when working alone, which indicates that P fills the tank at a rate of $\frac{1}{30}$ of the tank per minute. Therefore, any

additional information that would allow you to determine the rate at which pump Q works would be sufficient to determine how long it will take both pumps working simultaneously to fill the tank. Consider each of the three statements individually, as follows:

Choice A: The capacity of the tank is 600 gallons. This statement does not provide any information on the rate of pump Q, so Choice A does not provide sufficient additional information to determine how long it will take both pumps working simultaneously to fill the tank.

Choice B: Pump Q, working alone at its constant rate, can fill $\frac{1}{20}$ of the tank in 1 minute. This statement provides the rate of pump Q, which allows you to set up the equation $\frac{t}{30} + \frac{t}{20} = 1$ and solve it for t, so Choice B provides sufficient additional information to determine how long it will take both pumps working simultaneously to fill the tank.

Choice C: If pump P works alone for 5 minutes at its constant rate and then both pumps work simultaneously at their respective constant rates, the tank can be filled in a total of 15 minutes. This statement implies that if pump P works for 15 minutes and pump Q works for 10 minutes, then the tank will be filled. The times are different, but they allow you to set up the equation $\frac{15}{30} + 10r_2 = 1$. You can solve this equation to find r_2, which is the rate of pump Q. So, Choice C provides sufficient information to determine how long it will take both pumps working simultaneously to fill the tank.

Choices B and C individually provide sufficient additional information to determine how long it will take both pumps working simultaneously to fill the tank. Therefore, the correct answer consists of **Choices B and C**.

This explanation uses the following strategies.
Strategy 8: Search for a Mathematical Relationship
Strategy 1: Translate from Words to an Arithmetic or Algebraic Representation
Strategy 5: Simplify an Arithmetic or Algebraic Representation
Strategy 14: Determine What Additional Information is Sufficient to Solve a Problem

Questions 10 to 13 are based on the following data.

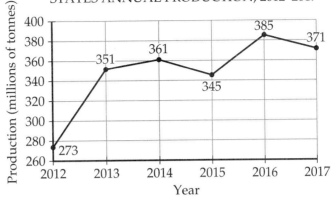

MAIZE PRODUCTION AND USES IN THE UNITED
STATES ANNUAL PRODUCTION, 2012–2017

Note: 1 tonne = 1,000 kilograms.

Uses, 2017

Use	Percent of Production
Feed	39%
Ethanol and fuel	27%
Exports	16%
Food and industrial use	9%
Residual	9%

10. Approximately how much greater was the average (arithmetic mean) annual maize production for the years 2013 through 2017 than the maize production, in tonnes, for 2012?

   (A) 70 million
   (B) 75 million
   (C) 85 million
   (D) 90 million
   (E) 95 million

Explanation

The data accompanying questions 10 to 13 consists of two displays, a line graph and a table. It is a good idea to look at the displays before trying to answer the questions and become familiar with the information contained in the displays. Then, as you read each question, you should think about which of the displays contains the information you need to solve the problem. It could be that all the information you need to solve the problem is contained in one of the displays, or it could be that you need to get information from both of the displays.

To solve this problem, find the average (arithmetic mean) annual maize production for the years 2013 through 2017, subtract the maize production for 2012 from the average, and then find the choice that is closest to the result. Therefore, all the information can be found using the line graph alone. You also need to remember that the values on the line graph represent the annual maize production in millions of tonnes. Keeping this in mind, find the average by calculating the sum of the values for the annual production given for each year and then dividing by 5, as follows.

$$\frac{351 + 361 + 345 + 385 + 371}{5} = \frac{1813}{5} = 362.6, \text{ in millions of tonnes}$$

The maize production for 2012 is given as 273 million tonnes. To find how much greater the average was, subtract, $362.6 - 273 = 89.6$, which represents 89.6 million tonnes. Of the choices given, 90 million tonnes is closest to 89.6 million tonnes. The correct answer is **Choice D**.

This explanation uses the following strategies.

Strategy 4: Translate from a Figure to an Arithmetic or Algebraic Relationship
Strategy 1: Translate from Words to an Arithmetic or Algebraic Representation
Strategy 8: Search for a Mathematical Relationship

For the following question, enter your answer in the box.

11. In 2017 the maize production that was used for ethanol and fuel was what percent of the maize production that was NOT used for exports?

Give your answer to the <u>nearest whole percent</u>.

[   ] %

Explanation

One way to solve the problem is by only using information in the table, which gives the percents that correspond to the uses of the maize produced in 2017. The percent the problem asks for can be found by dividing the percent of maize used for ethanol and fuel by the percent of maize that was not used for exports and then rewriting the resulting decimal as a percent. The table shows that 27 percent of the maize was used for ethanol and fuel. Since 16 percent of the maize was used for exports, $100 - 16 = 84$ percent of the maize was not used for exports. Since 27 percent = 0.27 and 84 percent = 0.84, you can divide 0.27 by 0.84, and  $\frac{0.27}{0.84} \approx 0.3214$, which is about 32.14 percent. You are asked to give the answer to the nearest whole percent, so the correct answer is **32**.

Alternative Explanation

Another way to solve the problem is to compare the actual amounts of maize production by using information from both displays. The line graph shows that the total maize production in 2017 was 371 million tonnes. The amount of maize used for ethanol and fuel was 27 percent of 371 million tonnes, or $(0.27)(371) = 100.17$ million tonnes. The amount of maize that was not used for exports was 84 percent of

371 million tonnes, or $(0.84)(371) = 311.64$ million tonnes. To find the percent the problem asks for, divide 101.17 by 311.64, and $\frac{100.17}{311.64} \approx 0.3214$, or about 32.14 percent. When rounded to the nearest whole percent, the correct answer is **32**.

These explanations use the following strategies.
Strategy 4: Translate from a Figure to an Arithmetic or Algebraic Relationship
Strategy 1: Translate from Words to an Arithmetic or Algebraic Representation
Strategy 8: Search for a Mathematical Relationship

12. Which of the following is closest to the average rate of change, in tonnes per year, for maize production from 2012 to 2017?

Ⓐ 20 million
Ⓑ 19 million
Ⓒ 18 million
Ⓓ 17 million
Ⓔ 16 million

Explanation
Since the average rate of change between two points is defined by the slope of the line between the points, only information from the line graph is needed to answer this question. Draw a line from the production in 2012 to the production in 2017. In 2012, 273 million tonnes of maize were produced, so one point on the line has the coordinates $(2012, 273)$. In 2017, 371 million tonnes of maize were produced, so another point on the line has the coordinates $(2017, 371)$. The formula for the slope m of a line is $m = \frac{y_2 - y_1}{x_2 - x_1}$, where (x_1, y_1) and (x_2, y_2) are the coordinates of two points on the line. Let $(x_1, y_1) = (2012, 273)$ and $(x_2, y_2) = (2017, 371)$, then the slope of the line through the points is $\frac{371 - 273}{2017 - 2012} = \frac{98}{5} = 19.6$. Using the units on the axes of the line graph, this means that the average rate of change is 19.6 million tonnes per year. Of the choices given, 20 million tonnes is closest to 19.6 million tonnes. The correct answer is **Choice A**.

These explanations use the following strategies.
Strategy 1: Translate from Words to an Arithmetic or Algebraic Representation
Strategy 4: Translate from a Figure to an Arithmetic or Algebraic Representation
Strategy 8: Search for a Mathematical Relationship

13. If the mass of 1 bushel of maize is 0.0254 tonne of maize, approximately how many bushels of the maize produced in 2017 were used for exports?

(A) 2 million
(B) 9 million
(C) 59 million
(D) 2,337 million
(E) 3,944 million

Explanation

To solve this problem, find how many million tonnes of the maize produced in 2017 were used for exports, convert from million tonnes to bushels and then find the choice that is closest to the result. Therefore, information from both displays will be used to answer the problem.

The line graph shows that 371 million tonnes of maize were produced in 2017. The table shows that 16 percent of this maize was used for exports, and 16 percent of 371 million tonnes is $(0.16)(371) = 59.36$ million tonnes.

It is given that 1 bushel is equivalent to 0.0254 tonnes, so set up a proportion to convert 59.36 million tonnes to bushels. One way to set up the proportion is $\frac{1 \text{ bushel}}{0.0254 \text{ tonne}} = \frac{x \text{ bushels}}{59.36 \text{ tonnes}}$, which yields $59.36 = 0.0254x$. Then, $x = \frac{59.36}{0.0254} \approx 2337.008$. This means that approximately 2,337 million bushels of the maize produced in 2017 were used for exports. The correct answer is **Choice D**.

This explanation uses the following strategies.

Strategy 1: Translate from Words to an Arithmetic or Algebraic Representation
Strategy 4: Translate from a Figure to an Arithmetic or Algebraic Representation
Strategy 8: Search for a Mathematical Relationship

14. Which of the following integers has only two different prime factors?

(A) 4
(B) 5
(C) 12
(D) 27
(E) 30

Explanation

For Choice A, $4 = (2)(2)$, so 4 has only one prime factor, namely 2. For Choice B, 5 is a prime number, so 5 has only one prime factor. For Choice C, $12 = (2)(2)(3)$, so 12 does have only two different prime factors, 2 and 3. For Choice D, $27 = (3)(3)(3)$, so 27 has only one prime factor, namely 3. For Choice E, $30 = (2)(3)(5)$, so 30 has three different prime factors, 2, 3, and 5. Of the five choices given, only 12 has two different prime factors. Thus, the correct answer is **Choice C**.

This explanation uses the following strategy.

Strategy 5: Simplify an Arithmetic or Algebraic Representation

For the following question, enter your answer in the boxes.

15. Lists R and S consist of numbers, and R has twice as many numbers as S. The average (arithmetic mean) of the numbers in R is 8, and the average of the numbers in S is 7. What is the average of the numbers in lists R and S combined?

Give your answer as a fraction.

Explanation

Let list S contain n numbers and let list R contain $2n$ numbers. Since the average of the numbers in S is 7, the sum of the numbers in S is $7n$. Since the average of the numbers in R is 8, the sum of the numbers in R is $(8)(2n) = 16n$. The sum of the numbers in lists R and S combined is $16n + 7n = 23n$. Since there are n numbers in list S and $2n$ numbers in list R, there are $3n$ numbers in lists R and S combined. Thus, the average of the numbers in lists R and S combined is

$$\frac{23n}{3n} = \frac{23}{3}.$$

The correct answer is $\frac{23}{3}$.

This explanation uses the following strategies.

Strategy 1: Translate from Words to an Arithmetic or Algebraic Representation
Strategy 8: Search for a Mathematical Relationship

Quantitative Reasoning Practice Set 2
15 Questions with Explanations

For each of Questions 1 to 6, select one of the following answer choices.

(A)   **Quantity A is greater.**

(B)   **Quantity B is greater.**

(C)   **The two quantities are equal.**

(D)   **The relationship cannot be determined from the information given.**

$$x < 0 \text{ and } y < 0$$

Quantity A	Quantity B

1. $4xy$ $\dfrac{2xy}{0.5}$ Ⓐ Ⓑ Ⓒ Ⓓ

Explanation

In this question, it is given that $x < 0$ and $y < 0$, and you are asked to compare $4xy$ with $\dfrac{2xy}{0.5}$.

Note that

$$\frac{2xy}{0.5} = \frac{2xy}{\frac{1}{2}} = 4xy$$

Consequently, the correct answer is **Choice C**.

This explanation uses the following strategy.

Strategy 5: Simplify an Arithmetic or Algebraic Representation

---

In a certain sequence, each term after the first term is obtained by subtracting 1 from the preceding term and then dividing that difference by 3. The fourth term of the sequence is $\dfrac{4}{3}$.

Quantity A	Quantity B

2.   The first term of the sequence   46   Ⓐ Ⓑ Ⓒ Ⓓ

Explanation

It is given that each term in the sequence after the first term is derived from the previous term by subtracting 1 and then dividing by 3. If these steps are reversed (that is, if a term after the first term is multiplied by 3 and then 1 is added to the result), the previous term will be obtained. Thus, if the fourth term is $\dfrac{4}{3}$, then the third term is $3\left(\dfrac{4}{3}\right) + 1 = 5$, the second term is $3(5) + 1 = 16$, and the first term is $3(16) + 1 = 49$,

which is greater than 46. The correct answer is **Choice A**.

This explanation uses the following strategies.
Strategy 1: Translate from Words to an Arithmetic or Algebraic Representation
Strategy 8: Search for a Mathematical Relationship

Number of gallons of milk	Less than 0.5	0.5	1.0	1.5	2.0	2.5	3.0 or more
Number of consumers	10	13	15	16	10	6	5

Each of the 75 consumers in a survey reported the number of gallons of milk that the consumer purchased last week. The preceding table shows the frequency distribution of the numbers of gallons reported.

Quantity A	Quantity B	
3. The median number of gallons of milk reported by the 75 consumers surveyed	1.5	Ⓐ Ⓑ Ⓒ Ⓓ

Explanation

There are 75 responses to the survey, so the median position is in the middle of the ordered list, the 38th position, since $\dfrac{75 + 1}{2} = 38$. The response categories are ordered from least to greatest in the table, so the median of the responses is found by counting from the left ($10 + 13 + 15 = 38$), and therefore the 38th response is in the 1.0-gallon category. The median for this data set is 1.0 gallon. Therefore, Quantity B is greater than Quantity A, and the correct answer is **Choice B**.

This explanation uses the following strategies.
Strategy 4: Translate from a Figure to an Arithmetic or Algebraic Representation
Strategy 8: Search for a Mathematical Relationship

$$x > 0$$
$$y > 0$$

Quantity A	Quantity B	
4. $x + y$	$\sqrt{x^2 + y^2}$	Ⓐ Ⓑ Ⓒ Ⓓ

Explanation

Since both x and y are positive both Quantity A and Quantity B are positive so that the comparison is the same if both sides are squared. Quantity A becomes $(x + y)^2 = x^2 + 2xy + y^2$. Quantity B becomes $x^2 + y^2$. The comparison is the same if

$x^2 + y^2$ is subtracted from both quantities. Quantity A becomes $2xy$ and Quantity B becomes 0. Since x and y are positive, Quantity A is greater than Quantity B. The correct answer is **Choice A**.

This explanation uses the following strategies.
Strategy 5: Simplify an Arithmetic or Algebraic Representation
Strategy 8: Search for a Mathematical Relationship

Quantity A	Quantity B	
5. The product of all positive factors of 12	12^3	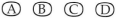

Explanation
The positive factors of 12 are 1, 2, 3, 4, 6, and 12. The product of the factors is
$(1)(2)(3)(4)(6)(12) = ((2)(6))((3)(4))(12) = 12^3$.
  Thus, the correct answer is **Choice C**.

This explanation uses the following strategies.
Strategy 1: Translate from Words to an Arithmetic or Algebraic Representation
Strategy 8: Search for a Mathematical Relationship

$$r > 0$$

Quantity A	Quantity B	
6. The area of a circular region with radius r	The area of a circular region with radius r^2	

Explanation
The area of a circular region with radius r is πr^2. The area of a circular region with radius r^2 is $\pi(r^2)^2 = \pi r^4$. Therefore, the comparison is between πr^2 and πr^4. Since r is positive, the comparison is the same after dividing both quantities by πr^2. Therefore, the comparison is between 1 and r^2. If $r < 1$, Quantity A is greater. If $r = 1$, Quantity A is equal to Quantity B. If $r > 1$. Quantity B is greater. The correct answer is **Choice D**.

This explanation uses the following strategies.
Strategy 1: Translate from Words to an Arithmetic or Algebraic Representation
Strategy 8: Search for a Mathematical Relationship
Strategy 11: Divide into Cases

For each of questions 7 to 15, select <u>one</u> answer choice unless otherwise instructed.

7. There are 10 different books available to a librarian for purchase, each for the same price, but the librarian has only enough money to purchase 9 of them. How many different collections of 9 books are there that can be selected from the 10 books?

 Ⓐ 9
 Ⓑ 10
 Ⓒ 45
 Ⓓ 90
 Ⓔ 100

Explanation

The librarian must choose 9 books from the 10 books. The number of ways to choose 9 objects from 10 is defined to be "10 choose 9," or the number of combinations of 10 objects taken 9 at a time. The combinations formula states that the number of combinations of n objects taken r at a time is $\begin{pmatrix} n \\ r \end{pmatrix} = \dfrac{n!}{r!(n-r)!}$. Thus, the number of combinations of 10 objects taken 9 at a time is $\dfrac{10!}{9!(10-9)!}$. The value of $\dfrac{10!}{9!(10-9)!}$ is $\dfrac{(10)(9!)}{(9!)(1!)} = 10$.

The correct answer is **Choice B**.

Alternative Explanation

If the librarian is choosing 9 books from 10, then 1 book is left out. Since any 1 of the 10 books can be left out, creating a combination, there are 10 ways to leave out 1 book, and thus there are 10 combinations consisting of the remaining 9 books. The correct answer is **Choice B**.

These explanations use the following strategies.

Strategy 1: Translate from Words to an Arithmetic or Algebraic Representation
Strategy 5: Simplify an Arithmetic or Algebraic Representation

Questions 8 to 11 are based on the following data.

SELECTED SALES DATA FOR STORE X, 2014–2016

TOTAL SALES BY YEAR

Year	Total Sales (billions of dollars)
2014	$80.0
2015	$84.8
2016	$90.7

PERCENT OF TOTAL SALES BY DEPARTMENT AND YEAR

Department	2014	2015	2016
Gardening	16.0%	16.0%	17.0%
Paint	9.0%	8.5%	8.0%
Appliances	7.0%	7.5%	8.0%
Kitchen and Bath	8.0%	8.0%	7.5%
Plumbing	6.5%	7.0%	7.0%
Other	53.5%	53.0%	52.5%
Total	100%	100%	100%

8. For the years 2014 to 2016, which of the following is closest to the average (arithmetic mean) annual sales of the Appliances department?

(A) $6.4 billion
(B) $6.6 billion
(C) $6.8 billion
(D) $7.0 billion
(E) $7.2 billion

Explanation

This question asks for the average of several numbers that are not directly given. The values for the annual sales in Appliances are found by converting the percent of each year's total sales for Appliances to a decimal and multiplying by that year's total sales.

- For 2014, 7.0% of $80.0 billion is 0.07($80.0) billion, which is $5.6 billion.

- For 2015, 7.5% of $84.8 billion is 0.075($84.8) billion, which is $6.36 billion.

- For 2016, 8.0% of $90.7 billion is 0.08($90.7) billion, which is $7.256 billion.

Thus, the total sales for all three years combined is $19.216 billion, and the desired answer is $19.216 billion divided by 3, which is approximately $6.405 billion. The closest answer choice is $6.4 billion, so the correct answer is **Choice A**.

This explanation uses the following strategies.

Strategy 4: Translate from a Figure to an Arithmetic or Algebraic Representation
Strategy 5: Simplify an Arithmetic or Algebraic Representation

9. For the years 2014 to 2016, which of the following is closest to the median annual sales of the Kitchen and Bath department?

    Ⓐ $6.23 billion
    Ⓑ $6.40 billion
    Ⓒ $6.66 billion
    Ⓓ $6.78 billion
    Ⓔ $7.05 billion

Explanation

This question asks for the median of a set of values that are not directly given. First, the values for the annual sales of the Kitchen and Bath department are found.

- For 2014, 0.08($80.0) billion is $6.4 billion.

- For 2015, 0.08($84.8) billion is $6.784 billion.

- For 2016, 0.075($90.7) billion is $6.8025 billion.

The median of three values is the second value when placed in order from least to greatest. In this case, the values are already in order, so the median is $6.784 billion. The closest answer choice is $6.78 billion, so the correct answer is **Choice D**.

This explanation uses the following strategies.

Strategy 4: Translate from a Figure to an Arithmetic or Algebraic Representation
Strategy 5: Simplify an Arithmetic or Algebraic Representation

---

For the following question, select all the answer choices that apply.

10. For which of the following departments were the combined departmental sales for the three years from 2014 to 2016 greater than $18 billion?

    Indicate <u>all</u> such departments.

    A Gardening
    B Paint
    C Appliances
    D Kitchen and Bath
    E Plumbing

Explanation

This question asks for a comparison of several values that are not directly given to a specific number. To find these values, determine the sum of the annual sales of each department for the three years.
    The calculations needed are summarized:

- For Gardening, the total sales are
    0.16($80 billion) + 0.16($84.8 billion) + 0.17($90.7 billion) = $41.787 billion

- For Paint, the total sales are
    0.09($80 billion) + 0.085($84.8 billion) + 0.08($90.7 billion) = $21.664 billion

- For Appliances, the total sales are
    0.07($80 billion) + 0.075($84.8 billion) + 0.08($90.7 billion) = $19.216 billion

- For Kitchen and Bath, the total sales are
  0.08($80 billion) + 0.08($84.8 billion) + 0.075($90.7 billion) = $19.9865 billion

- For Plumbing, the total sales are
  0.065($80 billion) + 0.07($84.8 billion) + 0.07($90.7 billion) = $17.485 billion

The departments with total annual sales greater than $18 billion from 2014 to 2016 are Gardening, Paint, Appliances, and Kitchen and Bath. The correct answer consists of **Choices A, B, C, and D**.

Alternative Explanation

The problem could also be solved using estimation. The percent of total sales for the three years needed to obtain $18 billion is

$$\frac{18 \text{ billion}}{(80 + 84.8 + 90.7) \text{ billion}} \approx 7.05\%.$$

Based on the data given, the departments for Gardening, Paint, and Kitchen and Bath satisfy that the percent of total sales for all three years is at least 7.05%, and the Plumbing department is less than 7.05% for all three years. For Appliances, the percents for 2015 and 2016 are significantly above 7.05% and that for 2014 is only slightly below 7.05%. The amount for total sales by year was the least for 2014, so the percent of total sales for the three years combined will clearly be above 7.05%.

Thus, the correct answer consists of **Choices A, B, C, and D**.

These explanations use the following strategies.

Strategy 4: Translate from a Figure to an Arithmetic or Algebraic Representation
Strategy 5: Simplify an Arithmetic or Algebraic Representation
Strategy 9: Estimate

---

11. Which of the following is closest to the percent change in annual sales of the Paint department from 2014 to 2016?

    Ⓐ 11.1% decrease
    Ⓑ 1.0% decrease
    Ⓒ 0.8% increase
    Ⓓ 8.0% increase
    Ⓔ 12.5% increase

Explanation

This question asks for the percent change in a value that is not directly given. To find the percent change, the total sales for the Paint department in each of 2014 and 2016 must be found.

- For 2014, 0.09($80.0) billion is $7.2 billion.

- For 2016, 0.08($90.7) billion is $7.256 billion.

The percent change can be found by dividing the change in the total sales from 2014 to 2016 by the 2014 value:

$\dfrac{2016 \text{ value} - 2014 \text{ value}}{2014 \text{ value}} = \dfrac{7.256 - 7.2}{7.2} \approx 0.00778$, which is closest to a 0.8 percent

increase. Note that a negative result would indicate a percent decrease. The correct answer is **Choice C**.

This explanation uses the following strategies.
Strategy 4: Translate from a Figure to an Arithmetic or Algebraic Representation
Strategy 5: Simplify an Arithmetic or Algebraic Representation

For the following question, enter your answer in the box.

12.   The five points $P, Q, R, S,$ and T lie on the number line in that order, where $PQ = QR, PR = RS,$ and $PS = ST.$ If $PT = 16,$ what is the value of QS?

Explanation

This question asks for the length of a line segment given the relative positions of a set of points on a number line. It is helpful to sketch the number line using the given information to locate the points. Even though the exact locations are not known, the relative positions can be determined. For example, since PR is given as equal to RS and there are two equally spaced tick marks from P to R, there must be two equally spaced tick marks from R to S. This allows the number line to be drawn as shown.

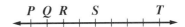

The length of segment QS is needed, which can be viewed as the combined lengths of QR and RS. It is given that PT is 16. Since PS and ST are equal, $PS = ST = \dfrac{PT}{2} = 8.$ Since PR and RS are equal, $PR = RS = \dfrac{PS}{2} = 4.$ Since PQ and QR are equal, $PQ = QR = \dfrac{PR}{2} = 2.$ Thus, $QS = QR + RS = 2 + 4 = 6.$ The correct answer is **6**.

Alternative Explanation

Since PT is 16 and there are 8 intervals of equal length between P and T, it is clear that each tick mark denotes a length of 2. Thus, since there are 3 tick marks from Q to S, the length of QS is 3 times 2, or **6**.

These explanations use the following strategies.
Strategy 2: Translate from Words to a Figure or Diagram
Strategy 5: Simplify an Arithmetic or Algebraic Representation

13.   The operation Δ is defined by $a \Delta b = a^2 - 4b^2$ for all numbers a and b. For which of the following values of x is $(2x) \Delta 3 = (x - 1) \Delta 2$?

Ⓐ $\dfrac{7}{3}$

Ⓑ 3

Ⓒ $\sqrt{7}$

Ⓓ $-1 + \sqrt{6}$

Ⓔ $-1 + \sqrt{22}$

Explanation

This question asks for values that satisfy an equation in terms of a newly defined function. These values are found by first expanding the new function and then solving the resulting equation. Expanding the left and right sides of the given equation and then collecting all terms on one side of the equation gives

$$(2x) \,\Delta\, 3 = (x-1)\Delta 2$$
$$(2x)^2 - 4\left(3^2\right) = (x-1)^2 - 4\left(2^2\right)$$
$$4x^2 - 36 = x^2 - 2x + 1 - 16$$
$$3x^2 + 2x - 21 = 0$$

The left-hand side factors as $(3x-7)(x+3)$, and one of those two factors must be equal to 0 since their product is 0. Thus, $x = \dfrac{7}{3}$ or $x = -3$. Only the first possibility is among the given choices, so the correct answer is **Choice A**.

This explanation uses the following strategy.

Strategy 5: Simplify an Arithmetic or Algebraic Representation

---

For the following question, select all the answer choices that apply.

14. Gerald has a collection consisting of coins valued at $0.25 each and coins valued at $0.10 each. The total value of all the coins in the collection is less than $10.00, and there are 3 times as many coins valued at $0.25 as coins valued at $0.10. Which of the following statements about the coins in the collection must be true?

Indicate <u>all</u> such statements.

> A The total value of the coins is an integer multiple of $0.85.
> B The total number of coins is less than or equal to 44.
> C The number of coins valued at $0.25 is a multiple of 5.

Explanation

One way to determine if the statements are true is to set up an equation and an inequality using the number of $0.25 and $0.10 coins as variables. Note that the question asks which statement <u>must</u> be true, so finding an example that works for each statement is not enough to answer the question.

Define q as the number of coins worth $0.25 and d as the number of coins worth $0.10. This generates the following two statements.

- $0.25q + 0.10d < 10.00$, since the total value is less than $10.00

- $q = 3d$, since there are three times as many coins worth $0.25 as those worth $0.10

Substitute $3d$ for q into the inequality to obtain $0.25(3d) + 0.10d = 0.85d < 10.00$. Divide both sides by 0.85 to obtain the inequality $d < \dfrac{1000}{85} = 11 + \dfrac{13}{17}$. Since d must be an integer, it is 11 or less, and so q is a multiple of 3 that is 33 or less.

- *Choice A*: For every $0.10 coin, there are three $0.25 coins, so the coins can be split into groups of one $0.10 coin and three $0.25 coins, which have a total value of $0.85. So this statement must be true.

- *Choice B*: There are at most 11 coins worth $0.10, which would mean there are at most 33 coins worth $0.25, for a total of at most 44 coins. So this statement must be true.

- *Choice C*: The number of $0.25 coins is a multiple of 3 that is at most 33, and there are no other constraints. Thus, since 5 is not a multiple of 3, it cannot be determined whether the number of $0.25 coins is also a multiple of 5; it could be 15 or 30, but it could also be any other multiple of 3 between 3 and 33. Thus, this statement does not have to be true.

The correct answer consists of **Choices A and B**.

This explanation uses the following strategies.

Strategy 1: Translate from Words to an Arithmetic or Algebraic Representation
Strategy 5: Simplify an Arithmetic or Algebraic Representation
Strategy 8: Search for a Mathematical Relationship
Strategy 13: Determine Whether a Conclusion Follows from the Information Given

---

15. Each postal code for a certain area is a sequence of 5 digits, where each digit is selected from the digits 0 through 9. How many such postal codes have the property that the first digit is 9, the second digit is selected from the digits 0 through 6, and the third digit is 7 if the second digit is less than 6, and the third digit is 7 or 8 if the second digit is 6?

(A) 567
(B) 648
(C) 700
(D) 729
(E) 800

Explanation

This question asks for the number of digit permutations that satisfy a set of conditions. This is found by summing the number of possibilities for each of a limited number of mutually exclusive cases. In this question, it is easiest to look at two cases:

1) The second digit is less than 6

2) The second digit equals 6

If the second digit is less than 6, there is 1 option for the first digit (it must equal 9), 6 options for the second digit (0 through 5), 1 option for the third digit (it must equal 7), and 10 options each for the fourth and fifth digits (0 through 9). So the number of postal codes possible for this case is the product of the possibilities for each digit, or $(1)(6)(1)(10)(10) = 600$.

If the second digit equals 6, there is 1 option for the first digit (it must be 9), 1 option for the second digit (it must equal 6), 2 options for the third digit (it must equal 7 or 8), and 10 options each for the fourth and fifth digits. So the number of postal codes possible for this case is $(1)(1)(2)(10)(10) = 200$.

Thus, there are $600 + 200 = 800$ postal codes possible with the given conditions. The correct answer is **Choice E**.

This explanation uses the following strategies.

Strategy 1: Translate from Words to an Arithmetic or Algebraic Representation
Strategy 11: Divide into Cases

Quantitative Reasoning Practice Set 3
15 Questions with Explanations

For each of Questions 1 to 5, select one of the following answer choices.

(A)   Quantity A is greater.

(B)   Quantity B is greater.

(C)   The two quantities are equal.

(D)   The relationship cannot be determined from the information given.

On a certain day, Danielle invested $150 in shares of stock M and Ricardo invested $170 in shares of stock P. After one month, the value of Danielle's investment had increased by 5 percent, the value of Ricardo's investment had decreased by x percent, and the value of Danielle's investment was equal to the value of Ricardo's investment.

	Quantity A	Quantity B	
1.	x	10	(A) (B) (C) (D)

Explanation

Since the value of Danielle's stock increased by 5 percent after one month, the value was $(1.05)(\$150) = \$157.50$. Since the value of Ricardo's stock decreased by x percent, the value was $\left(1 - \dfrac{x}{100}\right)(170) = 170 - 1.7x$. Since the values are equal, solve for x as follows.

$$170 - 1.7x = 157.50$$
$$1.7x = 12.5$$
$$x \approx 7.35$$

Thus, $x < 10$ and the correct answer is **Choice B**.

This explanation uses the following strategies.

Strategy 1: Translate from Words to an Arithmetic or Algebraic Representation
Strategy 8: Search for a Mathematical Relationship

In pentagon $ABCDE$, points M, N, P, Q, and R are the midpoints of sides AB, BC, CD, DE, and EA, respectively.

Quantity A	Quantity B	
2.	The perimeter of pentagon $ABCDE$	The perimeter of pentagon $MNPQR$	Ⓐ Ⓑ Ⓒ Ⓓ

Explanation

A strategy that is often helpful in working with geometry problems is drawing a figure that represents the given information.

For this question, sketch a pentagon $ABCDE$ and then mark the midpoints of each side and connect the midpoints to form pentagon $MNPQR$, as shown in the following figure.[1]

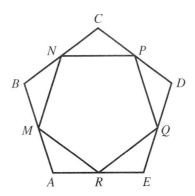

Thus, the perimeter of $ABCDE$ is:

$$AB + BC + CD + DE + EA = AM + MB + BN + NC + CP + PD + DQ + QE + ER + RA.$$

Consider one of the triangles formed, for example, triangle RAM.
By the Triangle Inequality, $RM < RA + AM$, as shown in the following figure.

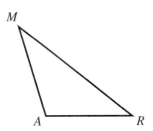

The perimeter of pentagon $MNPQR$ is $RM + MN + NP + PQ + QR$, and by multiple applications of the Triangle Inequality, one can determine that

$$RM + MN + NP + PQ + QR < (RA + AM) + (MB + BN) + (NC + CP) + (PD + DQ) + (QE + ER).$$

---

[1] The figure shows a regular pentagon. However, to answer the question the pentagon does not have to be regular.

The right-hand side of the inequality is equal to $AB + BC + CD + DE + EA$, which is the perimeter of $ABCDE$. Thus, the perimeter of $ABCDE$ is greater than the perimeter of $MNPQR$, and the correct answer is **Choice A**.

This explanation uses the following strategies.

Strategy 2: Translate from Words to a Figure or Diagram
Strategy 4: Translate from a Figure to an Arithmetic or Algebraic Representation
Strategy 8: Search for a Mathematical Relationship

$$5, 5, 5, x, x$$

m is the mean and q is the median of the five numbers in the list shown, and $m = q + 2$.

Quantity A	Quantity B	
3. x	8	Ⓐ Ⓑ Ⓒ Ⓓ

Explanation

The median of a set of n numbers, where n is odd, can be obtained by ordering the numbers from least to greatest and then identifying the middle number. If $x \le 5$, then the list ordered from least to greatest is $x, x, 5, 5, 5$, so the median would be 5. If $x > 5$, then the list ordered from least to greatest is $5, 5, 5, x, x$, so the median would still be 5. Therefore, q must equal 5, which means the mean m must equal $5 + 2 = 7$.

The mean of a set of n numbers can be found by calculating the sum of the numbers and then dividing the sum by n. This results in the equation $\dfrac{5 + 5 + 5 + x + x}{5} = 7$, which simplifies to $\dfrac{15 + 2x}{5} = 7$. Solve this equation for x as follows.

$$\frac{15 + 2x}{5} = 7$$
$$15 + 2x = 35$$
$$2x = 20$$
$$x = 10$$

Since $x = 10$ and $10 > 8$, the correct answer is **Choice A**.

This explanation uses the following strategies.

Strategy 1: Translate from Words to an Arithmetic or Algebraic Representation
Strategy 5: Simplify an Arithmetic or Algebraic Representation
Strategy 8: Search for a Mathematical Relationship

$$r^3 - r = r - r^3$$

Quantity A	Quantity B	
4. $\quad r$	0	Ⓐ Ⓑ Ⓒ Ⓓ

Explanation

A strategy that is often helpful in working with problems involving polynomial equations or expressions is rewriting the polynomials so they can be factored. In this question, solve the equation $r^3 - r = r - r^3$ for r as follows.

$$r^3 - r = r - r^3$$
$$2r^3 - 2r = 0$$
$$r^3 - r = 0$$
$$r(r^2 - 1) = 0$$
$$r(r - 1)(r + 1) = 0$$

Note that the equation is now written as a product that is equal to 0. Recall that for a product to equal 0, at least one of its factors must equal 0.

Thus, $r = 0$, or $r - 1 = 0$, or $r + 1 = 0$, which means that $r = 0$, or $r = 1$, or $r = -1$.

If $r = 0$, then Quantity A is equal to Quantity B. If $r = 1$, then Quantity A is greater than Quantity B. If $r = -1$, then Quantity B is greater than Quantity A.

Thus, the relationship cannot be determined from the information given, so the correct answer is **Choice D**.

This explanation uses the following strategies.

Strategy 5: Simplify an Arithmetic or Algebraic Representation
Strategy 8: Search for a Mathematical Relationship
Strategy 13: Determine Whether a Conclusion Follows from the Information Given

---

Let X be the set of integers that are greater than or equal to 1 and less than or equal to 100.

Quantity A	Quantity B	
5. The number of integers in X that are multiples of 3 but <u>not</u> multiples of 4	The number of integers in X that are multiples of 4	Ⓐ Ⓑ Ⓒ Ⓓ

Explanation

The integers in the set X that are multiples of 3 but not multiples of 4 are the same as the integers that are multiples of 3 that are not multiples of 12, since the multiples of 12 in X are multiples of both 3 and 4, and 3 and 4 have no factors in common other than 1.

Since X consists of the integers from 1 to 100, one way to determine the number of multiples of an integer in X is to divide 100 by the integer because the whole number part of the result will be the number of multiples of the integer in X.

Since $\frac{100}{3} = 33\frac{1}{3}$, there are 33 multiples of 3 in X. Since $\frac{100}{12} = 8\frac{1}{3}$, there are 8 multiples of 12 in X. The multiples of 12 are multiples of 3 and 4, and the number of integers in X that are multiples of 3 but not multiples of 4 is $33 - 8 = 25$. Then, since

$\frac{100}{4} = 25$, there are 25 multiples of 4 in X. Both quantities are equal to 25, and thus the correct answer is **Choice C**.

Alternative Explanation

Another way to solve the problem is to list the multiples in Quantity A. The multiples of 3 in X that are not multiples of 4 are 3, 6, 9, 15, 18, 21, 27, 30, 33, 39, 42, 45, 51, 54, 57, 63, 66, 69, 75, 78, 81, 87, 90, 93, and 99. There are 25 numbers in this list. Since $4(25) = 100$, there are 25 multiples of 4 in X. Thus, the correct answer is **Choice C**.

These explanations use the following strategies.

Strategy 1: Translate from Words to an Arithmetic or Algebraic Representation
Strategy 7: Find a Pattern
Strategy 8: Search for a Mathematical Relationship

For each of questions 6 to 15, select <u>one</u> answer choice unless otherwise instructed.

6.   If n is an odd integer, which of the following must be an even integer?

     Ⓐ $3n$
     Ⓑ n^2
     Ⓒ $(n+1)^2$
     Ⓓ $(n+2)^2$
     Ⓔ $(2n-1)^2$

Explanation

One way to solve the problem is to start by recalling the following facts about the sums and products of odd and even integers.

- The sum of two odd integers is even.
- The sum of two even integers is even.
- The sum of an odd integer and an even integer is odd.
- The product of two odd integers is odd.
- The product of two even integers is even.
- The product of an odd integer and an even integer is even.

Then examine each choice, using the given information that n is odd.

Choice A: Since 3 is odd and the product of two odd integers is odd, $3n$ is odd.

Choice B: Since $n^2 = (n)(n)$ and the product of two odd integers is odd, n^2 is odd.

Choice C: Since 1 is odd and the sum of two odd integers is even, $n + 1$ is even. Then $(n + 1)^2$ is a product of two even integers, so $(n + 1)^2$ is even.

Choice D: Since 2 is even and the sum of an odd integer and an even integer is odd, $n + 2$ is odd. Then $(n + 2)^2$ is a product of two odd integers, so $(n + 2)^2$ is odd.

Choice E: Since 2 is even and the product of an odd integer and an even integer is even, $2n$ is even. Since $2n - 1 = 2n + (-1)$ and -1 is an odd integer, then $2n - 1$ is the sum of an odd integer and an even integer, so $2n - 1$ is odd. Then $(2n - 1)^2$ is a product of two odd integers, so $(2n - 1)^2$ is odd.

The only choice that must be even is $(n + 1)^2$, so the correct answer is **Choice C**.

Alternative Explanation

Another way to solve the problem is to recall that for any integer k, $2k$ is an even integer and $2k + 1$ is an odd integer. Since n is an odd integer, let $n = 2j + 1$ for some integer j. Then examine each choice by substituting for n and determining whether the result can be written in the form $2k$, which means the expression is even, or in the form $2k + 1$, which means the expression is odd:

Choice A:

$$3n = (3)(2j + 1) = 6j + 3 = 2(3j + 1) + 1, \text{ so } 3n \text{ is odd.}$$

Choice B:

$$n^2 = (2j + 1)(2j + 1) = 4j^2 + 4j + 1 = 2(2j^2 + 2j) + 1, \text{ so } n^2 \text{ is odd.}$$

Choice C:

$$(n + 1)^2 = (2j + 1 + 1)^2 = (2j + 2)^2 = 4j^2 + 8j + 4$$
$$= 2(2j^2 + 4j + 2), \text{ so } (n + 1)^2 \text{ is even.}$$

Choice D:

$$(n + 2)^2 = (2j + 1 + 2)^2 = (2j + 3)^2 = 4j^2 + 12j + 9 = 4j^2 + 12j + 8 + 1$$
$$= 2(2j^2 + 6j + 4) + 1, \text{ so } (n + 2)^2 \text{ is odd.}$$

Choice E:

$$(2n - 1)^2 = (2[2j + 1] - 1)^2 = (4j + 2 - 1)^2 = (4j + 1)^2$$
$$= 16j^2 + 8j + 1 = 2(8j^2 + 4j) + 1, \text{ so } (2n - 1)^2 \text{ is odd.}$$

Thus, the correct answer is **Choice C**.

These explanations use the following strategies.

Strategy 1: Translate from Words to an Arithmetic or Algebraic Representation
Strategy 5: Simplify an Arithmetic or Algebraic Representation
Strategy 8: Search for a Mathematical Relationship

For the following question, select all the answer choices that apply.

7. A group of students equally divided 60 bottles of water so that each student received the same whole number of bottles of water, and nothing was left over. Similarly, the students equally divided 84 packs of gum and equally divided 72 energy bars, and nothing was left over in either case. Which of the following could be the number of students in the group?

    Indicate <u>all</u> such numbers.

    |A| 4
    |B| 5
    |C| 6
    |D| 8
    |E| 9
    |F| 10
    |G| 12

Explanation

In all three cases of sharing, there were no items left over after the sharing. This means that the number of students in the group divides 60, 84, and 72 with no remainder. In other words, the number of students in the group is a factor of 60, 84, and 72. The prime factorization of each number is as follows.

$$60 = \left(2^2\right)(3)(5)$$

$$84 = \left(2^2\right)(3)(7)$$

$$72 = \left(2^3\right)\left(3^2\right)$$

The greatest common factor of 60, 84, and 72 is $\left(2^2\right)(3) = 12$. Therefore, the number of students in the group could be 12 or any factor of 12. The correct answer consists of **Choices A, C, and G**.

This explanation uses the following strategies.
Strategy 1: Translate from Words to an Arithmetic or Algebraic Representation
Strategy 8: Search for a Mathematical Relationship

For the following question, select all the answer choices that apply.

8. The lengths of the sides of a triangle are 7.5, 11, and x, where x is an integer. Which of the following could be the integer x?

    Indicate <u>all</u> such integers.

    A   1
    B   6
    C   11
    D   16
    E   21

Explanation

By the Triangle Inequality, the sum of the lengths of any two sides of a triangle must be greater than or equal to the length of the third side. Therefore, the following statements or inequalities must be true: $7.5 + 11 > x$ and $7.5 + x > 11$. So, $x < 18.5$ and $x > 3.5$. Therefore, $3.5 < x < 18.5$.

Among the choices given the integer x can be 6, 11, or 16. The correct answer consists of **Choices B, C, and D**.

This explanation uses the following strategies.
Strategy 1: Translate from Words to an Arithmetic or Algebraic Representation
Strategy 5: Simplify an Arithmetic or Algebraic Representation
Strategy 8: Search for a Mathematical Relationship

Questions 9 to 12 are based on the following data.

NUMBER OF OCCUPATIONAL INJURIES IN STATE
X, 2018 BY AGE-GROUP OF INJURED PERSON

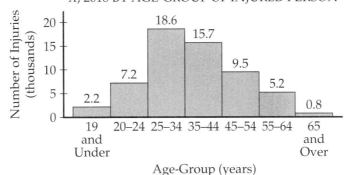

BY REGION WHERE
INJURY OCCURRED

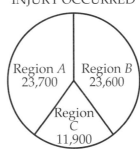

9.   Of the total number of occupational injuries in State X in 2018, the fraction of the occupational injuries of people in the age-group 35 – 44 is closest to which of the following?

(A) $\frac{1}{3}$

(B) $\frac{1}{4}$

(C) $\frac{1}{5}$

(D) $\frac{1}{6}$

(E) $\frac{1}{7}$

Explanation

According to the histogram, the number of occupational injuries of people who were in the age-group 35 to 44 is 15.7 thousand. The total number of injuries across all the age-groups in the histogram is the sum $(2.2 + 7.2 + 18.6 + 15.7 + 9.5 + 5.2 + 0.8)$ thousand or 59.2 thousand.

The fraction of the injured persons who were in the 35 to 44 age-group is $\frac{15.7}{59.2} \approx 0.265$.

Among the choices given, 0.265 is closest to $\frac{1}{4}$. The correct answer is **Choice B**.

This explanation uses the following strategies.

Strategy 1: Translate from Words to an Arithmetic or Algebraic Representation
Strategy 4: Translate from a Figure to an Arithmetic or Algebraic Representation
Strategy 9: Estimate

10. For the age-group 55–64, the average (arithmetic mean) number of work hours lost per occupational injury in 2018 was 48.5. If a workweek consists of 40 work hours, which of the following is closest to the total number of workweeks lost due to occupational injuries in the age-group 55–64 in 2018?

    (A) 4,500
    (B) 5,200
    (C) 5,500
    (D) 5,900
    (E) 6,300

Explanation

According to the histogram, the total number of injuries for the age-group 55 to 64 is 5.2 thousand, or 5,200. To obtain the total number of work hours lost due to occupational injury, multiply the average number of work hours lost per injury by the number of injuries.

$$(48.5)(5,200) = 252,200$$

To convert hours to workweeks, divide the total number of hours by the number of hours per workweek.

$$\frac{252,000}{40} = 6,305$$

or about 6,300 workweeks.

Therefore, the total number of workweeks lost is closest to 6,300. The correct answer is **Choice E**.

This explanation uses the following strategies.

Strategy 1: Translate from Words to an Arithmetic or Algebraic Representation
Strategy 4: Translate from a Figure to an Arithmetic or Algebraic Representation
Strategy 9: Estimate

---

11. For the two age-groups 19 and under and 20–24 combined, 25 percent of all occupational injuries were bone fractures and 35 percent of all occupational injuries occurred in Region B. For the two age-groups combined, which of the following could be the number of occupational injuries that were bone fractures occurring in Region B?

    (A) 2,300
    (B) 2,400
    (C) 2,500
    (D) 2,600
    (E) 2,700

Explanation

Based on the histogram, the total number of injuries for the age-groups 19 and under and 20 to 24 combined is (2.2 + 7.2) thousand or 9,400. Since 25 percent of injuries in this age range were bone fractures, there were $(9,400)(0.25) = 2,350$ injuries that were bone fractures. Since 35 percent of injuries in this age range occurred in region B, there were $(9,400)(0.35) = 3,290$ injuries in Region B. From this information, there were 2,350 or less bone fractures that could have occurred in Region B. Only Choice A is less than 2,350. The correct answer is **Choice A**.

This explanation uses the following strategies.
Strategy 1: Translate from Words to an Arithmetic or Algebraic Representation
Strategy 4: Translate from a Figure to an Arithmetic or Algebraic Representation
Strategy 9: Estimate
Strategy 13: Determine Whether a Conclusion Follows from the Information Given

For the following question, enter your answer in the box.

12. In 2018, if one-fourth of the occupational injuries in the age-groups 35–44 and 45–54 combined occurred in Region C, what percent of the occupational injuries that occurred in Region C were in the age-groups 35–44 and 45–54 combined?

Give your answer to the <u>nearest whole percent</u>.

 %

Explanation
According to the histogram, the total number of injuries for the combined age-groups of 35 to 44 and 45 to 54 is $(15.7 + 9.5)$ thousand, or 25,200. One-fourth (25%) of those injuries would be $(25,200)(0.25) = 6,300$. To find the percent of injuries in Region C that came from these two age-groups combined, we divide the number of injuries of the age-groups in Region C by the total number of injuries in Region C, $\frac{6,300}{11,900} \approx 0.529$ or 53% to the nearest whole percent. The correct answer is **53**.

This explanation uses the following strategies.
Strategy 1: Translate from Words to an Arithmetic or Algebraic Representation
Strategy 4: Translate from a Figure to an Arithmetic or Algebraic Representation
Strategy 9: Estimate

13. In responding to a poll, 500 people answered either yes or no to each of 2 questions. Of the 500 respondents, 410 answered yes to the first question and 220 answered yes to the second question. If n is the number of respondents who answered yes to both questions, what is the least possible value of n?

Ⓐ 90
Ⓑ 110
Ⓒ 130
Ⓓ 190
Ⓔ 220

Explanation

Consider the incomplete table below, where n is the number of respondents who answered yes to both questions.

		Second Question	
		Yes	No
First Question	Yes	n	
	No		

Since 410 answered yes to the first question and 220 answered yes to the second question, two more cells in the table can be filled in as shown below.

		Second Question	
		Yes	No
First Question	Yes	n	$410 - n$
	No	$220 - n$	

Since 500 people answered either yes or no to each of 2 questions, the bottom right cell is $500 - (n + (410 - n) + (220 - n)) = n - 130$.

		Second Question	
		Yes	No
First Question	Yes	n	$410 - n$
	No	$220 - n$	$n - 130$

Since all the numbers in the table are nonnegative numbers, we have the inequalities:

$$n \geq 0$$

$$410 - n \geq 0, \text{ which is equivalent to } n \leq 410$$

$$220 - n \geq 0, \text{ which is equivalent to } n \leq 220$$

$$n - 130 \geq 0, \text{ which is equivalent to } n \geq 130.$$

Combining the 4 inequalities above gives $130 \leq n \leq 220$. The least possible value of n is 130, and the greatest possible value of n is 220. The correct answer is **Choice C**.

This explanation uses the following strategies.

Strategy 2: Translate from Words to a Figure or Diagram
Strategy 8: Search for a Mathematical Relationship
Strategy 13: Determine Whether a Conclusion Follows from the Information Given

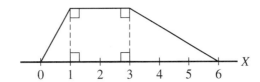

14. The figure above shows the probability distribution of a continuous random variable X. What is the probability that 4 < X < 5?

(A) $\frac{1}{12}$

(B) $\frac{1}{8}$

(C) $\frac{1}{6}$

(D) $\frac{1}{5}$

(E) $\frac{1}{4}$

Explanation

In the probability distribution, the probability that 4 < X < 5 is the ratio of the area of the region under the line from 4 to 5 to the total area of the figure

$$P(4 < X < 5) = \frac{\text{Area of the Region from 4 to 5}}{\text{Total Area of the Figure}}.$$

Let h represent the height of the figure. The total area of the figure is the area of right triangle A plus the area of rectangle B plus the area of right triangle C, as shown in the figure below.

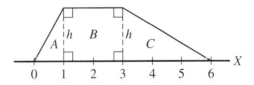

The area of right triangle A is $\frac{1}{2}(1)(h) = \frac{h}{2}$. The area of rectangle B is $(3-1)(h) = 2h$.

The area of right triangle C is $\frac{1}{2}(6-3)(h) = \frac{3h}{2}$. Thus, the total area of the figure is

$$\frac{h}{2} + 2h + \frac{3h}{2} = \frac{h + 4h + 3h}{2} = \frac{8h}{2} = 4h.$$

The region under the line between 4 and 5 is a trapezoid, the shaded region in the figure below. The height of the trapezoid is 5 − 4 = 1, and to find the lengths of the bases of the trapezoid we can use similar triangles.

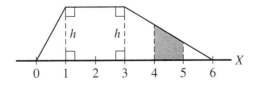

The triangle with vertices 3, Y, and 6 is similar to the triangle with vertices 4, Z, and 6, as shown in the following figure, where the length of the segment from 4 to Z is k.

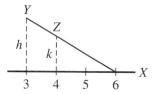

Then since the triangles are similar, we get the following equations.

$$\frac{k}{6-4} = \frac{h}{6-3}$$

$$\frac{k}{2} = \frac{h}{3}$$

$$k = \frac{2}{3}h$$

Also, the triangle with vertices 3, Y, and 6 is similar to the triangle with vertices 5, W, and 6, as shown in the following figure, where the length of the segment from 5 to W is ℓ.

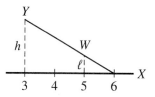

Then since the triangles are similar, we get the following equations.

$$\frac{\ell}{6-5} = \frac{h}{6-3}$$

$$\ell = \frac{1}{3}h$$

The area of the part of the figure where $4 < X < 5$ is the area of the trapezoid shown.

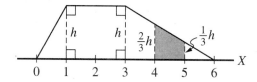

The area of the trapezoid is

$$\frac{1}{2}(k + \ell)(5 - 4) = \frac{k + \ell}{2} = \frac{\frac{2}{3}h + \frac{1}{3}h}{2} = \frac{h}{2}.$$

Therefore, the probability that $4 < X < 5$ is equal to

$$\frac{\text{Area of the Trapezoid}}{\text{Total Area of Figure}} = \frac{\left(\frac{h}{2}\right)}{4h} = \frac{1}{8}.$$

The correct answer is **Choice B**.

This explanation uses the following strategies.

Strategy 4: Translate from a Figure to an Arithmetic or Algebraic Representation
Strategy 6: Add to a Geometric Figure
Strategy 8: Search for a Mathematical Relationship
Strategy 12: Adapt Solutions to Related Problems

For the following question, enter your answer in the boxes.

15. In the xy-plane, ℓ and m are two perpendicular lines that intersect at the point $(2,3)$. Line ℓ passes through the origin. What is the y-intercept of line m?

Give your answer as a fraction.

Explanation

The slope of a line is the ratio of the change in y-coordinates of two points on the line to the change in x-coordinates of the two points. Line ℓ passes through the origin $(0, 0)$ and $(2, 3)$, thus the slope of line ℓ is $\frac{3-0}{2-0} = \frac{3}{2}$.

If two lines in the xy-plane are perpendicular, the slopes of the lines are negative reciprocals of each other. The slope of line m is then the negative reciprocal of the slope of line ℓ. Therefore the slope of line m is $-\frac{2}{3}$.

To obtain the y-intercept of line m, use the slope-intercept form of the line, $y = -\frac{2}{3}x + b$, where b is the y-intercept. Since it is given that line m passes through the point $(2, 3)$, it follows that $3 = -\frac{2}{3}(2) + b$, and solving for b, we obtain $b = 3 + \frac{2}{3}(2) = 3 + \frac{4}{3} = \frac{13}{3}$.

The correct answer is $\frac{13}{3}$.

This explanation uses the following strategies.

Strategy 1: Translate from Words to an Arithmetic or Algebraic Representation
Strategy 5: Simplify an Arithmetic or Algebraic Representation
Strategy 8: Search for a Mathematical Relationship

Quantitative Reasoning Practice Set 4
15 Questions with Explanations

For each of Questions 1 to 5, select one of the following answer choices.

- (A) **Quantity A is greater.**
- (B) **Quantity B is greater.**
- (C) **The two quantities are equal.**
- (D) **The relationship cannot be determined from the information given.**

A group of children is divided into r teams of 7 players each and 1 team of 10 players. The group has more than 30 but less than 50 children, and each child belongs to only one team.

Quantity A	Quantity B	
1. The number of children in the group	38	(A) (B) (C) (D)

Explanation

There are r teams with 7 players each, so there are $7r$ players on these teams. Then there is 1 team of 10 players. Therefore, altogether, there are $7r + 10$ children in the group. This number is strictly between 30 and 50, which yields the inequality $30 < 7r + 10 < 50$; subtract 10 from all parts of the inequality to yield $20 < 7r < 40$; dividing by 7 then yields $2\frac{6}{7} < r < 5\frac{5}{7}$.

Since r is an integer, r could be 3, 4, or 5. This means that the number of children in the group could be 31, 38, or 45. Therefore, Quantity A could be less than, equal to, or greater than Quantity B and the relationship between the two quantities cannot be determined from the given information. So, the correct answer is **Choice D**.

This explanation uses the following strategies.
Strategy 1: Translate from Words to an Arithmetic or Algebraic Representation
Strategy 5: Simplify an Arithmetic or Algebraic Representation
Strategy 8: Search for a Mathematical Relationship

$$0 < s < t$$

Quantity A	Quantity B	
2. $0.60s$	$0.58t$	(A) (B) (C) (D)

Explanation

One way to compare the two quantities is to substitute a few values for s and t. Let $s = 0.58$ and $t = 0.60$, and see that $0.60s = (0.60)(0.58) = 0.348$ and $0.58t = (0.58)(0.60) = 0.348$, so Quantity A is equal to Quantity B. If $s = 1$ and $t = 10$, then $0.60s = (0.60)(1) = 0.60$ and $0.58t = (0.58)(10) = 5.8$, so Quantity B is greater than Quantity A. Additionally, if $s = 100$ and $t = 101$, then $0.60s = (0.60)(100) = 60$ and $0.58t = (0.58)(101) = 58.58$, so Quantity A is greater than Quantity B. Therefore, the correct answer is **Choice D**.

Alternative Explanation

Another way to compare the two quantities is to perform algebraic manipulations. Since $s < t$, you can multiply both sides of the inequality by 0.60 to obtain $0.60s < 0.60t$. Since s and t are positive, you also know that $0.58t < 0.60t$. Although you know that $0.60s$ and $0.58t$ are both less than $0.60t$, the comparison between $0.60s$ and $0.58t$ cannot be determined.

Similarly, you could start by assuming that $0.60s = 0.58t$ and solve for t, which results in $t \approx 1.03s$. However, this leads to the conclusion that if $t = 1.02s$, then $s < t$ and $0.6s > 0.58t$, and if $t = 1.04s$, then $s < t$ and $0.6s < 0.58t$. Therefore, the comparison between $0.60s$ and $0.58t$ cannot be determined, and the correct answer is **Choice D**.

These explanations use the following strategies.

Strategy 8: Search for a Mathematical Relationship
Strategy 9: Estimate
Strategy 10: Trial and Error (both versions)
Strategy 11: Divide into Cases
Strategy 13: Determine Whether a Conclusion Follows from the Information Given

---

$$r < s < t < x < y < z$$

The average (arithmetic mean) of $r, s, t, x, y,$ and z is 0.

	Quantity A	Quantity B	
3.	$r + s + t$	$-(x + y + z)$	Ⓐ Ⓑ Ⓒ Ⓓ

Explanation

The average of $r, s, t, x, y,$ and z is $\dfrac{r + s + t + x + y + z}{6}$. The average is 0, so it follows that $\dfrac{r + s + t + x + y + z}{6} = 0$.

Multiplying both sides of the equation by 6, we have $r + s + t + x + y + z = 0$, and subtracting $x + y + z$ from both sides of the equation, we have $r + s + t = -(x + y + z)$. Therefore, the two quantities are equal. Thus, the correct answer is **Choice C**.

This explanation uses the following strategies.

Strategy 1: Translate from Words to an Arithmetic or Algebraic Representation
Strategy 5: Simplify an Arithmetic or Algebraic Representation
Strategy 8: Search for a Mathematical Relationship

$$x < 0$$

	Quantity A	Quantity B	
4.	x^{-2}	$\dfrac{1}{-\left(x^2\right)}$	Ⓐ Ⓑ Ⓒ Ⓓ

Explanation

On one hand, the expression x^{-2} is equal to $\dfrac{1}{x^2}$ so that if $x < 0$ then $\dfrac{1}{x^2}$ is positive. On the other hand, $\dfrac{1}{-\left(x^2\right)}$ is equal to $-\dfrac{1}{x^2}$ so that if $x < 0$ then $-\dfrac{1}{x^2}$ is negative.

Consequently, $x^{-2} > \dfrac{1}{-\left(x^2\right)}$ and the correct answer is **Choice A**.

This explanation uses the following strategies.

Strategy 5: Simplify an Arithmetic or Algebraic Representation
Strategy 8: Search for a Mathematical Relationship

In parallelogram $QRST$ (not shown), the measure of angle R is $(y + 15)$ degrees, and the measure of angle S is $(225 - 2y)$ degrees.

	Quantity A	Quantity B	
5.	The measure of angle S	90 degrees	Ⓐ Ⓑ Ⓒ Ⓓ

Explanation

In parallelogram $QRST$, angle R and angle S are consecutive angles and the sum of their measures must therefore be 180 degrees. One way of reaching this conclusion is to observe that opposite angles of a parallelogram have the same measure, so angle Q has the same measure as angle S, and angle T has the same measure as angle R. The sum for R and S is the same as the sum for Q and T, so the sum for R and S must be half the total sum of the measures of the four angles, which is 360 degrees. Therefore, the sum of the measures of angle R and angle S must be $\dfrac{360}{2} = 180$ degrees.

In this situation, it is given that angle R has measure $(y + 15)$ degrees and angle S has measure $(225 - 2y)$ degrees, so the total of the measures of angle R and angle S is $(240 - y)$ degrees, which is 180 degrees. Solving for y gives $y = 60$. Substituting 60 for y in the expressions for the measures of angle R and angle S, the measure of angle R is 75 degrees and the measure of angle S is 105 degrees.

Since $105 > 90$, the correct answer is **Choice A**.

This explanation uses the following strategies.

Strategy 1: Translate from Words to an Arithmetic or Algebraic Representation
Strategy 8: Search for a Mathematical Relationship
Strategy 12: Adapt Solutions to Related Problems

6.   Charley bought 200 small items for $0.75 each in order to resell as many of them as possible at an open market. He rented a table at the market for $20.00 and sold a number of the items for $1.25 each. He gave the remaining items to a neighboring vendor. If his profit from the sale of the items at the market was $67.50, how many of the items did he sell?

(A) 142

(B) 158

(C) 174

(D) 182

(E) 190

Explanation

For this problem translate the given information into an algebraic equation. The solution to the problem uses the relationship between cost and profit; that is, Profit is equal to Revenue minus Cost.

The total cost to Charley is the cost of the items plus the cost of the table rental. The cost of the items is $(200)($0.75) = 150.00, and the cost of the table rental is $20.00, so the total cost is $150.00 + $20.00 = 170.00.

Let x be the number of items sold at the market. Because the items were sold for $1.25 each, the revenue from the sale of the items can be expressed as $1.25x$. It is given that the profit was $67.50. Substitute the expressions for profit, revenue, and cost into the equation and solve for x as follows:

$$\text{Profit} = \text{Revenue} - \text{Cost}$$

$$67.50 = 1.25x - 170.00$$

$$237.50 = 1.25x$$

$$190 = x$$

Therefore, the number of items that Charley sold at the market was 190. The correct answer is **Choice E**.

This explanation uses the following strategies.

Strategy 8: Search for a Mathematical Relationship
Strategy 1: Translate from Words to an Arithmetic or Algebraic Representation
Strategy 5: Simplify an Arithmetic or Algebraic Representation

For each of questions 7 to 15, select <u>one</u> answer choice unless otherwise instructed.

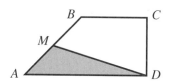

7.   In the figure above, angle BCD and angle ADC are right angles, $AD = 2(BC)$, and M is the midpoint of side AB. If the area of the shaded region is 10, what is the area of $ABCD$?

Ⓐ 20
Ⓑ 25
Ⓒ 30
Ⓓ 35
Ⓔ 40

Explanation

In this question, it is given that angles BCD and ADC are right angles, so $ABCD$ is a trapezoid with height CD and bases AD and BC. Let k be the length of CD and let x represent the length of BC. Since it is given that $AD = 2(BC)$, the length of AD is $2x$.

The area of a trapezoid is given by $\frac{1}{2}(b_1 + b_2)h$, where b_1 and b_2 are the lengths of the bases and h is the height. Therefore, the area of $ABCD$ can be expressed as $\frac{1}{2}(x + 2x)(k) = \frac{1}{2}(3x)(k) = \frac{3kx}{2}$.

The shaded region is triangle AMD with base AD. The height of the triangle is the distance from M to AD. Because M is the midpoint of AB, the height of the triangle must be equal to $\frac{k}{2}$, as shown in the following figure.

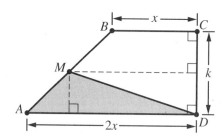

The area of a triangle is given by $\frac{1}{2}bh$, where b is the length of the base and h is the height. Therefore, the area of triangle AMD can be expressed as $\frac{1}{2}(2x)\left(\frac{k}{2}\right) = \frac{kx}{2}$. Since it is given that the area of AMD is 10, you can conclude that $\frac{kx}{2} = 10$, so $kx = 20$. Finally, substitute 20 for the kx in the expression for the area of $ABCD$, which yields $\frac{3kx}{2} = \frac{3(20)}{2} = 30$. The correct answer is **Choice C**.

Alternative Explanation

Another approach to solving this problem is to add point E on AD such that E is the midpoint of AD and then draw triangles ABE, BCE, and CDE in $ABCD$. The following figure shows these additions with triangle AMD removed for clarity.

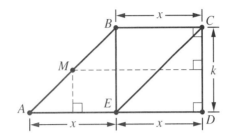

Note that the height of triangle AMD (base AD) is half the height of triangle ABE (base AE) and the base of ABE is half the base of AMD, which means the area of AMD is equal to the area of ABE, since $\frac{1}{2}(2x)\left(\frac{k}{2}\right) = \frac{1}{2}(x)(k)$. Also, the areas of ABE, BCE, and CDE are all equal, since the three triangles are congruent. Finally, since it is given that the area of AMD is 10, you can conclude that ABE, BCE, and CDE each have an area of 10. The area of trapezoid $ABCD$ is the sum of the areas of triangles ABE, BCE, and CDE, which means the area of trapezoid $ABCD$ is $10 + 10 + 10 = 30$. The correct answer is **Choice C**.

These explanations use the following strategies.

Strategy 4: Translate from a Figure to an Arithmetic or Algebraic Representation
Strategy 6: Add to a Geometric Figure
Strategy 8: Search for a Mathematical Relationship

---

8.   If d is the standard deviation of the three numbers w, p, and u, what is the standard deviation of the three numbers $w + 6$, $p + 6$, and $u + 6$?

Ⓐ d
Ⓑ $d + 6$
Ⓒ $d + 18$
Ⓓ $6d$
Ⓔ $18d$

Explanation

It is given that d is the standard deviation of numbers w, p, and u. The standard deviation of a set of numerical data measures the spread of the data around their mean. The numbers $w + 6$, $p + 6$, and $u + 6$ are each 6 greater than the numbers w, p, and u, respectively. So, while the numbers w, p, and u have each increased by 6 to become the numbers $w + 6$, $p + 6$, and $u + 6$, they are still spread out in exactly the same way around their mean. Therefore, the standard deviation d remains unchanged, and the correct answer is **Choice A**.

This explanation uses the following strategies.

Strategy 8: Search for a Mathematical Relationship
Strategy 12: Adapt Solutions to Related Problems

9.   For how many different values of x is $(2x + 4)(x - 3)(x + 2)^2 = 0$?

   (A) One
   (B) Two
   (C) Three
   (D) Four
   (E) An infinite number

Explanation

Note that the equation is written as a product that is equal to 0. Recall that for a product to equal 0, at least one of its factors must equal 0. One way to solve the problem is to set each factor equal to 0 and solve for x.

$$2x + 4 = 0 \qquad\qquad x - 3 = 0 \qquad\qquad (x + 2)^2 = 0$$
$$2x = -4 \qquad\qquad x = 3 \qquad\qquad x + 2 = 0$$
$$x = -2 \qquad\qquad\qquad\qquad\qquad\qquad x = -2$$

There are only two different values for x; namely, 3 and –2. The correct answer is **Choice B**.

Alternative Explanation

Another way to solve the problem is to notice that the factor $2x + 4$ can be written as $2(x + 2)$, so the equation is equivalent to $2(x - 3)(x + 2)^3 = 0$. When written in this form, it is seen that the two values of x are 3 and –2. The correct answer is **Choice B**.

These explanations use the following strategies.
Strategy 8: Search for a Mathematical Relationship
Strategy 5: Simplify an Arithmetic or Algebraic Representation

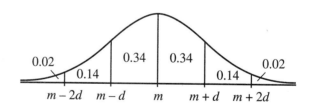

The figure above shows a normal distribution with mean m and standard deviation d, including approximate probabilities corresponding to the six intervals shown.

10.   The distribution of heights of a large group of students is approximately normal with mean 140 centimeters and standard deviation 2 centimeters. One student will be selected at random from the group. Of the following, which is the best estimate of the probability that the student selected will have a height greater than 141 centimeters?

   (A) 0.14
   (B) 0.16
   (C) 0.31
   (D) 0.48
   (E) 0.50

Explanation

From the information given, $m = 140$ and $d = 2$. If a vertical line is drawn at a height of 141 centimeters (cm) (halfway between m and $m + d$), the probability that the student selected will have a height greater than 141 cm would be the sum of the probabilities of the three intervals to the right of 141 centimeters. The probability that the height will be between 141 cm and 142 cm is less than half of 0.34, and consequently, the probability that the student selected will have a height greater than 141 cm is less than $\left(\dfrac{0.34}{2}\right) + 0.14 + 0.02 = 0.33$. The probability is also greater than the sum of the two rightmost intervals $(0.14 + 0.02) = 0.16$. Therefore, the probability must be greater than 0.16 and less than 0.33. Among the choices, only Choice C meets these requirements, so the correct answer is **Choice C**.

This explanation uses the following strategies.

Strategy 4: Translate from a Figure to an Arithmetic or Algebraic Representation
Strategy 8: Search for a Mathematical Relationship
Strategy 9: Estimate

For the following question, enter your answer in the box.

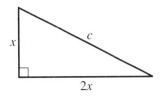

11.   If $c = \sqrt{31.25}$ in the triangle shown, what is the value of x?

$$x = \boxed{}$$

Explanation

Since the given triangle is a right triangle, use the Pythagorean theorem to get

$$x^2 + (2x)^2 = c^2$$
$$5x^2 = \left(\sqrt{31.25}\right)^2$$
$$5x^2 = 31.25$$
$$x^2 = 6.25$$
$$x = \sqrt{6.25}$$
$$x = 2.5$$

The correct answer is **2.5**.

This explanation uses the following strategy.

Strategy 4: Translate from a Figure to an Arithmetic or Algebraic Representation

12. If x and y are positive and x is $\frac{27}{36}$ of y, then x is what percent of y?

  (A) 9%

  (B) 33%

  (C) 75%

  (D) 133%

  (E) 175%

Explanation

The fraction $\frac{27}{36}$ is equivalent to the fraction $\frac{3}{4}$, which is equal to the decimal 0.75. As a percent, 0.75 equals 75 percent. Thus, "x is $\frac{27}{36}$ of y" can be restated as "x is 75 percent of y."

  The correct answer is **Choice C**.

This explanation uses the following strategies.

Strategy 5: Simplify an Arithmetic or Algebraic Representation
Strategy 8: Search for a Mathematical Relationship

---

13. In a group of 200 college students, each student is a member of the orchestra or the tennis club or both. Of the 200 students, 150 students are members of the orchestra only and 10 students are members of both the orchestra and the tennis club. If a student is to be selected at random from the 200 students, what is the probability that the student selected will be a student who is a member of the tennis club only?

  (A) $\frac{1}{40}$

  (B) $\frac{1}{20}$

  (C) $\frac{1}{5}$

  (D) $\frac{1}{4}$

  (E) $\frac{3}{4}$

Explanation

The desired probability is given by the fraction

$$\frac{\text{the number of students that are members of the tennis club only}}{\text{the total number of students}}.$$

  Since the group consists of 200 students, the value of the denominator in the fraction is 200.

To calculate the value of the numerator, the following Venn diagram is used to represent the given situation.

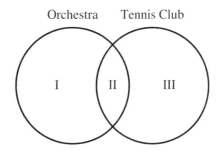

Orchestra   Tennis Club

I   II   III

Region I represents the number of students that are members of the orchestra only, region II represents the number of students that are members of both the orchestra and the tennis club, and region III represents the number of students that are members of the tennis club only.

It is given that I = 150, II = 10, and I + II + III = 200. Thus, the number of students that are members of the tennis club only is III = 200 − 150 − 10 = 40.

Therefore, if a student is selected at random from the 200 students, the probability that the student will be a member of the tennis club only is $\frac{40}{200} = \frac{1}{5}$.

The correct answer is **Choice C**.

This explanation uses the following strategies.

Strategy 2: Translate from Words to a Figure or Diagram
Strategy 8: Search for a Mathematical Relationship

---

14. If $-1 < 2x - 1 < 3$ and $1 < y + 2 < 5$, which of the following could be true?

    (A) $x = 0$ and $y = 0$
    (B) $x = 1$ and $y = -2$
    (C) $x = 1.2$ and $y = -1.2$
    (D) $x = 1.5$ and $y = 0.5$
    (E) $x = 2$ and $y = 2.5$

Explanation

To determine which pair of x and y values satisfies the inequalities, it is best to simplify the inequalities. To simplify the first inequality, first add 1 to all parts of the inequality. This results in the inequality $0 < 2x < 4$. Then divide all parts of this inequality by 2. This results in the inequality $0 < x < 2$.

To simplify the second inequality, subtract 2 from all parts of the inequality. This results in $-1 < y < 3$.

Only the values in Choice D satisfy both inequalities. The correct answer is **Choice D**.

This explanation uses the following strategies.

Strategy 5: Simplify an Arithmetic or Algebraic Representation
Strategy 10: Trial and Error

For the following question, select all the answer choices that apply.

15. George's total monthly earnings consist of a base monthly salary of $2,000 plus up to three commissions. The first commission is equal to 10 percent of his monthly sales up to $10,000, the second commission is equal to 20 percent of his monthly sales in excess of $10,000 and up to $30,000, and the third commission is equal to 50 percent of his monthly sales in excess of $30,000.

Which of the following statements <u>individually</u> provide(s) sufficient additional information to determine George's total earnings last month?

Indicate <u>all</u> such statements.

- A   Last month, George's second commission was $3,000 greater than his first commission.
- B   Last month, George's third commission was $5,000 greater than his first commission.
- C   Last month, George's third commission was $2,000 greater than his second commission.

Explanation

If George gets a second commission, then his monthly sales must be greater than $10,000 and he must receive a first commission of 10 percent of $10,000, or $1,000. If George gets a third commission, then his monthly sales must be greater than $30,000 and he must receive the first commission of $1,000 plus a second commission of 20 percent of $20,000 ($30,000 minus $10,000), or $4,000.

- For *Choice A*, if George's second commission was $3,000 greater than his first commission, then his second commission was $4,000, the maximum possible second commission; therefore, George may have also received a third commission, but there is not enough information to know what it was. Hence, in Choice A there is not enough information to determine George's total earnings last month.

- For *Choice B*, since George received a third commission, he received a first commission of $1,000 and a second commission of $4,000. Since his third commission was $5,000 greater than his first commission, his third commission was $6,000. Consequently, George's total earnings last month were the sum of his base salary and the three commissions he received, or

$$2,000 + \$1,000 + \$4,000 + \$6,000 = \$13,000.$$

- For *Choice C*, since George received a third commission, he received a first commission of $1,000 and a second commission of $4,000. Since his third commission was $2,000 greater than his second commission, his third commission was $6,000. Consequently, George's total earnings last month were the sum of his base salary and the three commissions he received, or

$$2,000 + \$1,000 + \$4,000 + \$6,000 = \$13,000.$$

The correct answer consists of **Choices B and C**.

This explanation uses the following strategies.
Strategy 1: Translate from Words to an Arithmetic or Algebraic Representation
Strategy 14: Determine What Additional Information Is Sufficient to Solve a Problem

Quantitative Reasoning Practice Set 5
15 Questions with Explanations

For each of Questions 1 to 5, select one of the following answer choices.

(A)   **Quantity A is greater.**

(B)   **Quantity B is greater.**

(C)   **The two quantities are equal.**

(D)   **The relationship cannot be determined from the information given.**

---

n and p are positive.

Quantity A	Quantity B

1. $(n-p)\left(n^2 + np + p^2\right)$ $n^3 - p^3$ (A)   (B)   (C)   (D)

Explanation

Observe that

$$(n-p)\left(n^2 + np + p^2\right) = n\left(n^2 + np + p^2\right) - p\left(n^2 + np + p^2\right)$$
$$= n^3 + n^2 p + np^2 - n^2 p - np^2 - p^3$$
$$= n^3 - p^3$$

The correct answer is **Choice C**.

This explanation uses the following strategy.

Strategy 5: Simplify an Arithmetic or Algebraic Representation

---

The sequence $a_1, a_2, a_3, \ldots$ is defined by $a_n = \dfrac{1}{2}n - 7$ for all integers $n \geq 1$.

Quantity A	Quantity B

2. $a_3 + a_5$ 8   (A)   (B)   (C)   (D)

Explanation

One way to solve this problem is to use the given definition of the sequence to calculate $a_3 + a_5$ and then compare the result to 8.

$$a_3 + a_5 = \left[\left(\frac{1}{2}\right)(3) - 7\right] + \left[\left(\frac{1}{2}\right)(5) - 7\right]$$

$$= \left[\frac{3}{2} - 7\right] + \left[\frac{5}{2} - 7\right] = \frac{8}{2} - 14 = 4 - 14 = -10$$

Since $-10 < 8$, the correct answer is **Choice B**.

Alternative Explanation

You could also observe that $a_n < 0$ for $n < 14$. Therefore, $a_3 < 0$ and $a_5 < 0$, which means that $a_3 + a_5 < 0$. Since $0 < 8$, the correct answer is **Choice B**.

These explanations use the following strategies.

Strategy 5: Simplify an Arithmetic or Algebraic Representation
Strategy 9: Estimate

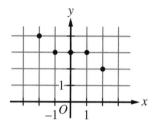

Quantity A	Quantity B	
3. The standard deviation of the x-coordinates of the 5 points shown in the xy-plane above	The standard deviation of the y-coordinates of the 5 points shown in the xy-plane above	Ⓐ Ⓑ Ⓒ Ⓓ

Explanation

In this problem you are asked to compare two standard deviations. Standard deviation is a measure of the spread of the numbers in a data set. Using the mean as the center of the data set, the standard deviation examines how much each value in the list differs from the mean and then takes a type of average of these differences.

One way to solve this problem is to reason about the spread of the x-coordinates and the spread of the y-coordinates of the 5 points, or how far the coordinates are from the mean. For the x-coordinates in the graph, the mean is 0 since $\frac{-2 + (-1) + 0 + 1 + 2}{5} = \frac{0}{5} = 0$. Only 1 x-coordinate is equal to the mean, 2 are 1 unit away from the mean, and 2 are 2 units away from the mean. For the y-coordinates in the graph, the mean is 3 since $\frac{4 + 3 + 3 + 3 + 2}{5} = 3$. In this case, 3 y-coordinates are equal to the mean, and the other 2 are only 1 unit away from the mean. Thus, the spread of the x-coordinates is greater than the spread of the y-coordinates, so Quantity A is greater, and the correct answer is **Choice A**.

Alternative Explanation

Another way to solve this problem is to calculate the two standard deviations. The standard deviation of n values $x_1, x_2, x_3, \dots, x_n$ with mean $\overline{x}$ is equal to $\sqrt{\frac{S}{n}}$, where S is the sum of the squared differences $\left(x_i - \overline{x}\right)^2$ for $1 \le i \le n$.

The mean of the x-coordinates is 0, so the standard deviation of the x-coordinates is equal to

$$\sqrt{\frac{(-2-0)^2 + (-1-0)^2 + (0-0)^2 + (1-0)^2 + (2-0)^2}{5}}$$

$$= \sqrt{\frac{4+1+0+1+4}{5}} = \sqrt{\frac{10}{5}} = \sqrt{2} \approx 1.414.$$

The mean of the y-coordinates is 3, so the standard deviation of the y-coordinates is equal to

$$\sqrt{\frac{(4-3)^2 + (3-3)^2 + (3-3)^2 + (3-3)^2 + (2-3)^2}{5}}$$

$$= \sqrt{\frac{1+0+0+0+1}{5}} = \sqrt{\frac{2}{5}} \approx 0.632.$$

Since 1.414 > 0.632, Quantity A is greater, and the correct answer is **Choice A**.

These explanations use the following strategies.
Strategy 4: Translate from a Figure to an Arithmetic or Algebraic Representation
Strategy 5: Simplify an Arithmetic or Algebraic Representation
Strategy 9: Estimate

For a certain triangular region, each side has length 1 and the area is t.

	Quantity A	Quantity B	
4.	$t\sqrt{3}$	1	Ⓐ Ⓑ Ⓒ Ⓓ

Explanation

A strategy that is often helpful in working with geometry problems is drawing a figure that represents the given information.

For this question sketch a triangle ABC such that each side has length 1. Since each side has length 1, the triangle is equilateral, which means that the angle at each vertex measures 60 degrees. Since $AB = BC$, add an altitude BD to the sketch, which will be the perpendicular bisector of AC. This means that $AD = \frac{1}{2}$ and triangle BAD is a 30-60-90 triangle, as shown in the following figure.

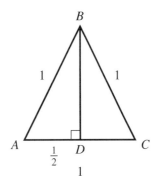

Since $AD = \frac{1}{2}$ and $AB = 1$, the length of BD can be determined using the Pythagorean theorem, as follows.

$$AD^2 + BD^2 = AB^2$$

$$\left(\frac{1}{2}\right)^2 + BD^2 = 1^2$$

$$\frac{1}{4} + BD^2 = 1$$

$$BD^2 = \frac{3}{4}$$

$$BD = \sqrt{\frac{3}{4}} = \frac{\sqrt{3}}{\sqrt{4}} = \frac{\sqrt{3}}{2}$$

In general, the area of a triangle is given by $\frac{1}{2}bh$, where b is the length of the base and h is the height. Therefore, the area of the triangle is $t = \left(\frac{1}{2}\right)(1)\left(\frac{\sqrt{3}}{2}\right) = \frac{\sqrt{3}}{4}$. This implies that $t\sqrt{3} = \left(\frac{\sqrt{3}}{4}\right)(\sqrt{3}) = \frac{3}{4}$, which is less than 1, so Quantity B is greater. Thus, the correct answer is **Choice B**.

Alternative Explanation

Another way to solve the problem is to use estimation. Since AB is the hypotenuse of a right triangle and the hypotenuse is the longest side of a right triangle, the height of triangle ABC, which corresponds to BD, must be less than 1. Therefore, the area of triangle ABC must be less than $\frac{1}{2}(1)(1) = \frac{1}{2}$. That means t must be less than $\frac{1}{2}$, so $t\sqrt{3}$ must be less than $\frac{\sqrt{3}}{2}$. Since $\frac{\sqrt{3}}{2} < \frac{\sqrt{4}}{2} = 1$, $t\sqrt{3}$ must be less than 1, so Quantity B is greater, and the correct answer is **Choice B**.

These explanations use the following strategies.

Strategy 2: Translate from Words to a Figure or Diagram
Strategy 4: Translate from a Figure to an Arithmetic or Algebraic Representation
Strategy 5: Simplify an Arithmetic or Algebraic Representation
Strategy 6: Add to a Geometric Figure
Strategy 8: Search for a Mathematical Relationship
Strategy 9: Estimate

---

x and y are integers and $0 < x < y$.

Quantity A	Quantity B	
5. x^y	y^x	Ⓐ Ⓑ Ⓒ Ⓓ

Explanation

One approach to this problem is to divide the analysis into several cases.

First, suppose that $x = 2$ and $y = 3$. Then, Quantity A is $2^3 = 8$ and Quantity B is $3^2 = 9$, making Quantity B greater than Quantity A.

Next, suppose that $x = 2$ and $y = 4$. Then, Quantity A is $2^4 = 16$ and Quantity B is $4^2 = 16$, making the two quantities equal.

Finally, suppose that $x = 2$ and $y = 5$. Then, Quantity A is $2^5 = 32$ and Quantity B is $5^2 = 25$, making Quantity A greater than Quantity B.

Therefore, the relationship between the two quantities cannot be determined from the given information. So, the correct answer is **Choice D**.

This explanation uses the following strategies.

Strategy 8: Search for a Mathematical Relationship
Strategy 10: Trial and Error, *Version 2: Try More Than One Value of a Variable*
Strategy 11: Divide into Cases

For each of questions 6 to 15, select <u>one</u> answer choice unless otherwise instructed.

For the following question, enter your answer in the boxes.

6. A lighthouse, a bell tower, and a clock tower are represented by three points on a map. On the map, the lighthouse is 6 inches due north of the bell tower and the clock tower is 1.75 inches due east of the bell tower. The distance on the map between the lighthouse and the clock tower is how many inches greater than the distance on the map between the lighthouse and the bell tower?

Give your answer as a fraction.

 inch

Explanation

Using the information given, the following diagram of a right triangle represents the geometric relationship of the three landmarks, where point *L* represents the lighthouse, point *B* represents the bell tower, point *C* represents the clock tower, and the measurements are in inches.

The goal is to find the length of line segment *CL*, which represents the distance between the lighthouse and the clock tower, and compare it to the length of line segment *BL*, which represents the distance between the lighthouse and the bell tower.

Line segments BL and BC are perpendicular because the directions due north and due east are perpendicular. Thus, angle LBC is a right angle and CL is the hypotenuse of right triangle LBC; the Pythagorean theorem can be used to determine the length of CL as follows.

$$CL^2 = BL^2 + BC^2$$

$$CL = \sqrt{BL^2 + BC^2}$$

$$CL = \sqrt{6^2 + 1.75^2} = \sqrt{6^2 + \left(\frac{7}{4}\right)^2} = \sqrt{36 + \frac{49}{16}} = \sqrt{\frac{576 + 49}{16}} = \sqrt{\frac{625}{16}} = \frac{25}{4} = 6\frac{1}{4}$$

Thus, $CL - BL = 6\frac{1}{4} - 6 = \frac{1}{4}$. The distance on the map between the lighthouse and the clock tower is $\frac{1}{4}$ inch greater than the distance between the lighthouse and the bell tower.

The correct answer is $\frac{1}{4}$.

This explanation uses the following strategies.

Strategy 2: Translate from Words to a Figure or Diagram
Strategy 5: Simplify an Arithmetic or Algebraic Representation
Strategy 8: Search for a Mathematical Relationship

---

7. In the sophomore class of a certain university, 85 percent of the students were taking English composition, 70 percent were taking biology, and 60 percent were taking both English composition and biology. What percent of the students in the class were taking neither English composition nor biology?

    (A) 0%
    (B) 5%
    (C) 10%
    (D) 15%
    (E) 25%

Explanation

Drawing a Venn diagram is often helpful in solving problems of this type that involve overlapping sets. In this problem, there are two sets of students—one set consisting of students taking English composition and one set consisting of students taking biology. The sets overlap for students taking both courses. The following Venn diagram can be drawn to represent the information given in the question, where region I represents students taking only English composition, region III represents students taking only biology, and region II represents students taking both courses.

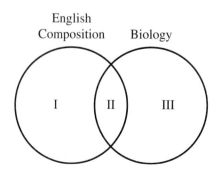

Note that the group of students taking English composition consists of regions I and II and that the group taking biology consists of regions II and III. It is given that 60 percent of the students were taking both courses. So, region II contains 60 percent of the students. Since 85 percent of the students were taking English composition, then region I contains 85 − 60 = 25 percent of the students. Similarly, since 70 percent of the students were taking biology, then region III contains 70 − 60 = 10 percent of the students.

Adding the percent of students in each of the three regions together gives a total of 25 + 60 + 10 = 95 percent of the students in the sophomore class who were taking at least one of the two courses. Thus, 5 percent of the students in the class were taking neither course, since 100 − 95 = 5. The correct answer is **Choice B**.

This explanation uses the following strategies.
Strategy 2: Translate from Words to a Figure or Diagram
Strategy 8: Search for a Mathematical Relationship

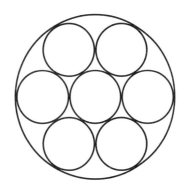

8. A paperweight in the shape of a right circular cylinder consists of 7 parallel right circular cylinders that are made of solid glass, where the space between the 7 cylinders is filled with resin. The figure shows a horizontal cross section of the paperweight, where each circle is tangent to any adjacent circles. The height of the paperweight is 10 centimeters and is equal to the height of each glass cylinder. The radius of each glass cylinder is 1 centimeter. Approximately what is the volume, in cubic centimeters, of the resin in the paperweight?

   (A) 16
   (B) 20
   (C) 42
   (D) 63
   (E) 80

Explanation

This question asks for the difference between two volumes: that of the main cylinder and the total volume of the 7 glass cylinders. The volume of the resin in the paperweight is equal to this difference, which is
the volume of the resin = the total volume of the paperweight − the volume of the 7 glass cylinders.

For any cylinder, the volume V is given by $V = \pi r^2 h$, where r is the radius of the circular base and h is the height of the cylinder. The radius of each glass cylinder is 1 centimeter, which means the diameter of each glass cylinder is 2 centimeters. The diameter of the paperweight is the same as 3 glass cylinders across, so the diameter of the paperweight is 6 centimeters. This means that the radius of the paperweight is 3 centimeters.

The total volume of the paperweight is $\pi(3^2)(10) = 90\pi$ cubic centimeters. The volume of the 7 glass cylinders is $7(\pi(1^2)(10)) = 70\pi$ cubic centimeters. Thus, the volume of the resin in the paperweight is $90\pi - 70\pi = 20\pi$ cubic centimeters.

The question asks for an approximate volume in cubic centimeters. The number π is an irrational number, and to find an answer use an approximation of $\pi \approx 3.14159$. Then $20\pi \approx 62.8318$ and among the choices given, 63 is the closest value to 20π. The correct answer is **Choice D**.

This explanation uses the following strategies.

Strategy 4: Translate from a Figure to an Arithmetic or Algebraic Representation
Strategy 5: Simplify an Arithmetic or Algebraic Representation

---

For the following question, select all the answer choices that apply.

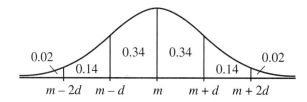

0.02   0.34   0.34   0.02
   0.14   0.14
$m - 2d$ $m - d$ m $m + d$ $m + 2d$

The figure shows a normal distribution with mean m and standard deviation d, including approximate probabilities corresponding to the six intervals shown.

9.   The random variable G is normally distributed with mean 32.5 and standard deviation 4.2. The random variable H is normally distributed with mean 200 and standard deviation 100. Which of the following statements are true?

Indicate <u>all</u> such statements.

A $P(G \geq 36.7) = P(H \leq 100)$
B $P(G \geq 38.8) = P(H \geq 350)$
C $2(P(28.3 \leq G \leq 36.7)) = P(200 \leq H \leq 300)$

Explanation

This question asks for several comparisons of two normal distributions. As the provided graphic indicates, the normal distribution is symmetric and probabilities are determined by the number of standard deviations above or below the mean.

For each statement, identifying the number of standard deviations from the mean at which each value lies allows the comparison to be made.

- *Choice A*, the value 36.7 is 4.2 above the mean of G, so the left-hand side is the probability that a value is at least 1 deviation above the mean, or 0.16. The value 100 is 100 below the mean of H, so the right-hand side is the probability that a value is at least 1 deviation below the mean, or 0.16. Thus, they are equal. Note that the symmetry of the normal distribution would allow this determination to be made even without knowing the probabilities.

- *Choice B*, the value 38.8 is 6.3 above the mean of G, so the left-hand side is the probability that a value is at least 1.5 deviations above the mean. The value

350 is 150 above the mean of H, so the right-hand side is also the probability that a value is at least 1.5 deviations above the mean. Thus, they are equal.

- *Choice C*, the values 28.3 and 36.7 are 4.2 away from the mean of G, so the left-hand side is twice the probability that a value is within 1 deviation of the mean, or $2(0.68) = 1.36$. The right-hand side is just that probability, and so it is at most 1. Thus, they are not equal.

The correct answer consists of **Choices A and B**.

This explanation uses the following strategies.
Strategy 4: Translate from a Figure to an Arithmetic or Algebraic Representation
Strategy 8: Search for a Mathematical Relationship
Strategy 12: Adapt Solutions to Related Problems

10.   A music store owner bought a violin at a cost of $500 and then sold the violin for a price of $625. The owner's profit from the sale of the violin was what percent of the cost of the violin? (Profit equals price minus cost.)

(A) 20%
(B) 25%
(C) 30%
(D) 35%
(E) 80%

Explanation

The profit from the sale of the violin is the purchase price subtracted from the selling price or $625 - $500 = 125. The percent profit of the sale is the ratio of the profit to the purchase price or $\frac{125}{500} = \frac{1}{4} = 25\%$. The correct answer is **Choice B**.

This explanation uses the following strategies.
Strategy 1: Translate from Words to an Arithmetic or Algebraic Representation
Strategy 5: Simplify an Arithmetic or Algebraic Representation

11.   If $0 < x < 1$, which of the following has the greatest value?

(A) $\frac{1}{x}$
(B) $\frac{1}{x^2}$
(C) 1
(D) x
(E) x^2

Explanation

This question asks about the relationship between several expressions given that $0 < x < 1$. The given inequality states that x is a positive number less than 1. Therefore, each time an expression is multiplied by x, the value of the expression is decreased.

This means that $0 < x^4 < x^3 < x^2 < x < 1$. Dividing all the expressions by x^2 yields $0 < x^2 < x < 1 < \frac{1}{x} < \frac{1}{x^2}$. Therefore, among the choices given the greatest value is $\frac{1}{x^2}$. The correct answer is **Choice B**.

Alternative Explanation

Another way to approach this problem is to make a numeric substitution for x. For example, let $x = \frac{1}{2} < 1$. Then $\frac{1}{x} = 2$, $\frac{1}{x^2} = 4$, $x = \frac{1}{2}$, and $x^2 = \frac{1}{4}$. So the greatest value among the choices is $\frac{1}{x^2} = 4$. The correct answer is **Choice B**.

These explanations use the following strategies.
Strategy 5: Simplify an Arithmetic or Algebraic Representation
Strategy 8: Search for a Mathematical Relationship
Strategy 10: Trial and Error

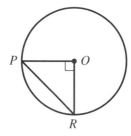

12. The figure above shows a circle with center O and circumference 10π. What is the perimeter of $\triangle POR$?

   (A) $12\sqrt{2}$
   (B) $10 + 5\sqrt{2}$
   (C) $12 + 5\sqrt{2}$
   (D) $20 + 5\sqrt{2}$
   (E) $20 + 10\sqrt{2}$

Explanation

The formula for the circumference C of a circle is $C = 2\pi r$, where r is the radius. Since the circumference of the circle is given as 10π, then $10\pi = 2\pi r$; and therefore, $r = 5$.

Since PO and OR are radii of the circle, triangle POR is an isosceles right triangle, with hypotenuse PR. In an isosceles right triangle, each of the other two angles has a measure of 45 degrees and the hypotenuse is $\sqrt{2}$ times one of the legs. Therefore, $PR = 5\sqrt{2}$.

Alternatively, the Pythagorean theorem could be applied to find PR:

$(OP)^2 + (OR)^2 = (PR)^2$. So, $(PR)^2 = 5^2 + 5^2 = 50$ and therefore $PR = \sqrt{50} = \sqrt{(25)(2)} = 5\sqrt{2}$.

Thus, the perimeter of triangle POR is $OP + OR + PR = 5 + 5 + 5\sqrt{2} = 10 + 5\sqrt{2}$. The correct answer is **Choice B**.

This explanation uses the following strategies.
Strategy 4: Translate from a Figure to an Arithmetic or Algebraic Representation
Strategy 5: Simplify an Arithmetic or Algebraic Representation
Strategy 8: Search for a Mathematical Relationship

$$S = \{2, 3, 7, 9, 12, 13, 15\}$$

13. How many subsets of set S consist of 3 integers such that the product of the 3 integers is even?

  (A) 14
  (B) 21
  (C) 25
  (D) 30
  (E) 35

Explanation

Set S consists of 5 odd integers and 2 even integers. In a subset, each number can only appear once, so there are two ways in which the product of the three numbers from set S can be even, one even number and two odd numbers, or two even numbers and one odd number.

The number of combinations of one even number and two odd numbers is $\binom{2}{1}\binom{5}{2}$, that is, choose 1 of the 2 even numbers and 2 of the 5 odd numbers, where $\binom{n}{k} = \frac{n!}{k!(n-k)!}$.

The number of combinations of 2 even numbers and 1 odd number is $\binom{2}{2}\binom{5}{1}$, that is, choose 2 of the 2 even numbers and 1 of the 5 odd numbers.

The total number of combinations is then equal to

$$\binom{2}{1}\binom{5}{2} + \binom{2}{2}\binom{5}{1} = \left(\frac{2}{1}\right)\left(\frac{(5)(4)}{(2)(1)}\right) + \left(\frac{2}{(2)(1)}\right)\left(\frac{5}{1}\right) = 20 + 5 = 25.$$

Thus, the correct answer is **Choice C**.

This explanation uses the following strategies.
Strategy 1: Translate from Words to an Arithmetic or Algebraic Representation
Strategy 5: Simplify an Arithmetic or Algebraic Representation
Strategy 11: Divide into Cases

For the following question, enter your answer in the box.

14. For each of its cars, a rental-car company measured the fuel consumption in gallons of fuel consumed per 1,000 miles traveled. In the distribution of measurements, 41.25 is 1.3 standard deviations below the mean and 47.50 is 1.2 standard deviations above the mean. What is the mean of the distribution?

$$\boxed{}$$

Explanation

Let s be the standard deviation and m be the mean of the distribution. From the question, it is given that $m - 1.3s = 41.25$ and $m + 1.2s = 47.50$. Subtracting the first equation from the second yields $2.5s = 6.25$ or $s = 2.5$. Substituting s into the first equation and solving for m yields

$$m = 41.25 + 1.3(2.5) = 41.25 + 3.25 = 44.50.$$

The correct answer is **44.5**.

Alternative Explanation

The mean is $\dfrac{1.3}{1.3 + 1.2} = \dfrac{13}{25}$ of the way from 41.25 to 47.50. So,

$$m = 41.25 + \frac{13}{25}(47.50 - 41.25) = 41.25 + \frac{13}{25}(6.25) = 41.25 + 3.25 = 44.50.$$

The correct answer is **44.5**.

These explanations use the following strategies.
Strategy 1: Translate from Words to an Arithmetic or Algebraic Representation
Strategy 8: Search for a Mathematical Relationship

---

15. How many integers x are there such that $|x + 2| < 4$ and $|2x - 1| < 7$?

   (A) None
   (B) One
   (C) Two
   (D) Three
   (E) Four

Explanation

Since it is given that $x + 2| < 4$, it follows that $-4 < x + 2 < 4$, and therefore $-6 < x < 2$.
   Since it is also given that $2x - 1| < 7$, it follows that $-7 < 2x - 1 < 7$, so $-6 < 2x < 8$, and therefore $-3 < x < 4$.
   The inequalities $-6 < x < 2$ and $-3 < x < 4$ together imply that $-3 < x < 2$. Therefore, since x is an integer, x can be $-2, -1, 0$, or 1. There are 4 integer solutions.
   The correct answer is **Choice E**.

This explanation uses the following strategy.
Strategy 5: Simplify an Arithmetic or Algebraic Representation

9 GRE Math Review

This Math Review will familiarize you with the mathematical skills and concepts that are important for solving problems and reasoning quantitatively on the Quantitative Reasoning measure of the GRE General Test. The skills and concepts are in the areas of Arithmetic, Algebra, Geometry, and Data Analysis. The material covered includes many definitions, properties, and examples, as well as a set of exercises (with answers) at the end of each part. Note, however, that this review is not intended to be all-inclusive—the test may include some concepts that are not explicitly presented in this review.

If any material in this review seems especially unfamiliar or is covered too briefly, you may also wish to consult appropriate mathematics texts for more information. Another resource is the Khan Academy® page on the GRE website at **www.ets.org/gre/khan**, where you will find links to free instructional videos about concepts in this review.

PART 1. ARITHMETIC

The review of arithmetic begins with integers, fractions, and decimals and progresses to the set of real numbers. The basic arithmetic operations of addition, subtraction, multiplication, and division are discussed, along with exponents and roots. The review of arithmetic ends with the concepts of ratio and percent.

1.1 Integers

The **integers** are the numbers 1, 2, 3, ..., together with their negatives, −1, −2, −3, ..., and 0. Thus, the set of integers is {..., −3, −2, −1, 0, 1, 2, 3, ...}.

The positive integers are greater than 0, the negative integers are less than 0, and 0 is neither positive nor negative. When integers are added, subtracted, or multiplied, the result is always an integer; division of integers is addressed below. The many elementary number facts for these operations, such as $7 + 8 = 15$, $78 − 87 = −9$, $7 − (−18) = 25$, and $(7)(8) = 56$, should be familiar to you; they are not reviewed here. Here are three general facts regarding multiplication of integers.

Fact 1: The product of two positive integers is a positive integer.
Fact 2: The product of two negative integers is a positive integer.
Fact 3: The product of a positive integer and a negative integer is a negative integer.

When integers are multiplied, each of the multiplied integers is called a **factor** or **divisor** of the resulting product. For example, $(2)(3)(10) = 60$, so 2, 3, and 10 are factors of 60. The integers 4, 15, 5, and 12 are also factors of 60, since $(4)(15) = 60$ and $(5)(12) = 60$. The positive factors of 60 are 1, 2, 3, 4, 5, 6, 10, 12, 15, 20, 30, and 60. The negatives of these integers are also factors of 60, since, for example, $(−2)(−30) = 60$. There are no other factors of 60. We say that 60 is a **multiple** of each of its factors and that 60 is **divisible** by each of its divisors. Here are five more examples of factors and multiples.

Example 1.1.1: The positive factors of 100 are 1, 2, 4, 5, 10, 20, 25, 50, and 100.

Example 1.1.2: 25 is a multiple of only six integers: 1, 5, 25, and their negatives.

Example 1.1.3: The list of positive multiples of 25 has no end: 25, 50, 75, 100, ... ; likewise, every nonzero integer has infinitely many multiples.

Example 1.1.4: 1 is a factor of every integer; 1 is not a multiple of any integer except 1 and −1.

Example 1.1.5: 0 is a multiple of every integer; 0 is not a factor of any integer except 0.

The **least common multiple** of two nonzero integers c and d is the least positive integer that is a multiple of both c and d. For example, the least common multiple of 30 and 75 is 150. This is because the positive multiples of 30 are 30, 60, 90, 120, 150, 180, 210, 240, 270, 300, 330, 390, 420, 450, ... , and the positive multiples of 75 are 75, 150, 225, 300, 375, 450, ... Thus, the *common* positive multiples of 30 and 75 are 150, 300, 450, ... , and the least of these is 150.

The **greatest common divisor** (or **greatest common factor**) of two nonzero integers c and d is the greatest positive integer that is a divisor of both c and d. For example, the greatest common divisor of 30 and 75 is 15. This is because the positive divisors of 30 are 1, 2, 3, 5, 6, 10, 15, and 30, and the positive divisors of 75 are 1, 3, 5, 15, 25, and 75. Thus, the *common* positive divisors of 30 and 75 are 1, 3, 5, and 15, and the greatest of these is 15.

When an integer c is divided by an integer d, where d is a divisor of c, the result is always a divisor of c. For example, when 60 is divided by 6 (one of its divisors), the result is 10, which is another divisor of 60. If d is *not* a divisor of c, then the result can be viewed in three different ways. The result can be viewed as a fraction or as a decimal, both of which are discussed later, or the result can be viewed as a **quotient** with a **remainder**, where both are integers. Each view is useful, depending on the context. Fractions and decimals are useful when the result must be viewed as a single number, while quotients with remainders are useful for describing the result in terms of integers only.

Regarding quotients with remainders, consider the integer c and the positive integer d, where d is *not* a divisor of c; for example, the integers 19 and 7. When 19 is divided by 7, the result is greater than 2, since $(2)(7) < 19$, but less than 3, since $19 < (3)(7)$. Because 19 is 5 more than $(2)(7)$, we say that the result of 19 divided by 7 is the quotient 2 with remainder 5, or simply 2 remainder 5. In general, when an integer c is divided by a positive integer d, you first find the greatest multiple of d that is less than or equal to c. That multiple of d can be expressed as the product qd, where q is the quotient. Then the remainder is equal to c minus that multiple of d, or $r = c - qd$, where r is the remainder. The remainder is always greater than or equal to 0 and less than d.

Here are four examples that illustrate a few different cases of division resulting in a quotient and remainder.

Example 1.1.6: 100 divided by 45 is 2 remainder 10, since the greatest multiple of 45 that is less than or equal to 100 is $(2)(45)$, or 90, which is 10 less than 100.

Example 1.1.7: 24 divided by 4 is 6 remainder 0, since the greatest multiple of 4 that is less than or equal to 24 is 24 itself, which is 0 less than 24. In general, the remainder is 0 if and only if c is divisible by d.

Example 1.1.8: 6 divided by 24 is 0 remainder 6, since the greatest multiple of 24 that is less than or equal to 6 is $(0)(24)$, or 0, which is 6 less than 6.

Example 1.1.9: −32 divided by 3 is −11 remainder 1, since the greatest multiple of 3 that is less than or equal to −32 is $(-11)(3)$, or −33, which is 1 less than −32.

Here are five more examples.

Example 1.1.10: 100 divided by 3 is 33 remainder 1, since $100 = (33)(3) + 1$.

Example 1.1.11: 100 divided by 25 is 4 remainder 0, since $100 = (4)(25) + 0$.

Example 1.1.12: 80 divided by 100 is 0 remainder 80, since $80 = (0)(100) + 80$.

Example 1.1.13: −13 divided by 5 is −3 remainder 2, since $-13 = (-3)(5) + 2$.

Example 1.1.14: −73 divided by 10 is −8 remainder 7, since $-73 = (-8)(10) + 7$.

If an integer is divisible by 2, it is called an **even integer**; otherwise, it is an **odd integer**. Note that when an odd integer is divided by 2, the remainder is always 1. The set of even integers is $\{\ldots, -6, -4, -2, 0, 2, 4, 6, \ldots\}$, and the set of odd integers is $\{\ldots, -5, -3, -1, 1, 3, 5, \ldots\}$. Here are six useful facts regarding the sum and product of even and odd integers.

Fact 1: The sum of two even integers is an even integer.
Fact 2: The sum of two odd integers is an even integer.
Fact 3: The sum of an even integer and an odd integer is an odd integer.
Fact 4: The product of two even integers is an even integer.
Fact 5: The product of two odd integers is an odd integer.
Fact 6: The product of an even integer and an odd integer is an even integer.

A **prime number** is an integer greater than 1 that has only two positive divisors: 1 and itself. The first ten prime numbers are 2, 3, 5, 7, 11, 13, 17, 19, 23, and 29. The integer 14 is not a prime number, since it has four positive divisors: 1, 2, 7, and 14. The integer 1 is not a prime number, and the integer 2 is the only prime number that is even.

Every integer greater than 1 either is a prime number or can be uniquely expressed as a product of factors that are prime numbers, or **prime divisors**. Such an expression is called a **prime factorization**. Here are six examples of prime factorizations.

Example 1.1.15: $12 = (2)(2)(3) = (2^2)(3)$
Example 1.1.16: $14 = (2)(7)$
Example 1.1.17: $81 = (3)(3)(3)(3) = 3^4$
Example 1.1.18: $338 = (2)(13)(13) = (2)(13^2)$
Example 1.1.19: $800 = (2)(2)(2)(2)(2)(5)(5) = (2^5)(5^2)$
Example 1.1.20: $1{,}155 = (3)(5)(7)(11)$

An integer greater than 1 that is not a prime number is called a **composite number**. The first ten composite numbers are 4, 6, 8, 9, 10, 12, 14, 15, 16, and 18.

1.2 Fractions

A **fraction** is a number of the form $\frac{c}{d}$, where c and d are integers and $d \neq 0$. The integer c is called the **numerator** of the fraction, and d is called the **denominator**. For example, $\frac{-7}{5}$ is a fraction in which -7 is the numerator and 5 is the denominator. Such numbers are also called **rational numbers**. Note that every integer n is a rational number, because n is equal to the fraction $\frac{n}{1}$.

If both the numerator c and the denominator d, where $d \neq 0$, are multiplied by the same nonzero integer, the resulting fraction will be equivalent to $\frac{c}{d}$.

Example 1.2.1: Multiplying the numerator and denominator of the fraction $\frac{-7}{5}$ by 4 gives

$$\frac{-7}{5} = \frac{(-7)(4)}{(5)(4)} = \frac{-28}{20}$$

Multiplying the numerator and denominator of the fraction $\frac{-7}{5}$ by -1 gives

$$\frac{-7}{5} = \frac{(-7)(-1)}{(5)(-1)} = \frac{7}{-5}$$

For all integers c and d, the fractions $\frac{-c}{d}$, $\frac{c}{-d}$, and $-\frac{c}{d}$ are equivalent.

Example 1.2.2: $\frac{-7}{5} = \frac{7}{-5} = -\frac{7}{5}$

If both the numerator and denominator of a fraction have a common factor, then the numerator and denominator can be factored and the fraction can be reduced to an equivalent fraction.

Example 1.2.3: $\frac{40}{72} = \frac{(8)(5)}{(8)(9)} = \frac{5}{9}$

Adding and Subtracting Fractions

To add two fractions with the same denominator, you add the numerators and keep the same denominator.

Example 1.2.4: $-\dfrac{8}{11} + \dfrac{5}{11} = \dfrac{-8+5}{11} = \dfrac{-3}{11} = -\dfrac{3}{11}$

To add two fractions with different denominators, first find a **common denominator**, which is a common multiple of the two denominators. Then convert both fractions to equivalent fractions with the same denominator. Finally, add the numerators and keep the common denominator.

Example 1.2.5: To add the two fractions $\dfrac{1}{3}$ and $-\dfrac{2}{5}$, first note that 15 is a common denominator of the fractions.

Then convert the fractions to equivalent fractions with denominator 15 as follows.

$$\frac{1}{3} = \frac{1(5)}{3(5)} = \frac{5}{15} \quad \text{and} \quad -\frac{2}{5} = -\frac{2(3)}{5(3)} = -\frac{6}{15}$$

Therefore, the two fractions can be added as follows.

$$\frac{1}{3} + \frac{-2}{5} = \frac{5}{15} + \frac{-6}{15} = \frac{5+(-6)}{15} = -\frac{1}{15}$$

The same method applies to subtraction of fractions.

Multiplying and Dividing Fractions

To multiply two fractions, multiply the two numerators and multiply the two denominators. Here are two examples.

Example 1.2.6: $\left(\dfrac{10}{7}\right)\left(\dfrac{-1}{3}\right) = \dfrac{(10)(-1)}{(7)(3)} = \dfrac{-10}{21} = -\dfrac{10}{21}$

Example 1.2.7: $\left(\dfrac{8}{3}\right)\left(\dfrac{7}{3}\right) = \dfrac{56}{9}$

To divide one fraction by another, first **invert** the second fraction (that is, find its **reciprocal),** then multiply the first fraction by the inverted fraction. Here are two examples.

Example 1.2.8: $\dfrac{17}{8} \div \dfrac{3}{5} = \left(\dfrac{17}{8}\right)\left(\dfrac{5}{3}\right) = \dfrac{85}{24}$

Example 1.2.9: $\dfrac{\frac{3}{10}}{\frac{7}{13}} = \left(\dfrac{3}{10}\right)\left(\dfrac{13}{7}\right) = \dfrac{39}{70}$

Mixed Numbers

An expression such as $4\dfrac{3}{8}$ is called a **mixed number**. It consists of an integer part and a fraction part, where the fraction part has a value between 0 and 1; the mixed number $4\dfrac{3}{8}$ means $4 + \dfrac{3}{8}$.

To convert a mixed number to a fraction, convert the integer part to an equivalent fraction with the same denominator as the fraction, and then add it to the fraction part.

Example 1.2.10: To convert the mixed number $4\frac{3}{8}$ to a fraction, first convert the integer 4 to a fraction with denominator 8, as follows.

$$4 = \frac{4}{1} = \frac{4(8)}{1(8)} = \frac{32}{8}$$

Then add $\frac{3}{8}$ to it to get

$$4\frac{3}{8} = \frac{32}{8} + \frac{3}{8} = \frac{35}{8}$$

Fractional Expressions

Numbers of the form $\frac{c}{d}$, where either c or d is not an integer and $d \neq 0$, are called fractional expressions. Fractional expressions can be manipulated just like fractions. Here are two examples.

Example 1.2.11: Add the numbers $\frac{\pi}{2}$ and $\frac{\pi}{3}$.

Solution: Note that 6 is a common denominator of both numbers.

The number $\frac{\pi}{2}$ is equivalent to the number $\frac{3\pi}{6}$, and the number $\frac{\pi}{3}$ is equivalent to the number $\frac{2\pi}{6}$.

Therefore

$$\frac{\pi}{2} + \frac{\pi}{3} = \frac{3\pi}{6} + \frac{2\pi}{6} = \frac{5\pi}{6}$$

Example 1.2.12: Simplify the number $\dfrac{\frac{1}{\sqrt{2}}}{\frac{3}{\sqrt{5}}}$.

Solution: Note that the numerator of the number is $\frac{1}{\sqrt{2}}$ and the denominator of the number is $\frac{3}{\sqrt{5}}$. Note also that the reciprocal of the denominator is $\frac{\sqrt{5}}{3}$.

Therefore,

$$\dfrac{\frac{1}{\sqrt{2}}}{\frac{3}{\sqrt{5}}} = \left(\frac{1}{\sqrt{2}}\right)\left(\frac{\sqrt{5}}{3}\right)$$

which can be simplified to $\dfrac{\sqrt{5}}{3\sqrt{2}}$.

Thus, the number $\dfrac{\frac{1}{\sqrt{2}}}{\frac{3}{\sqrt{5}}}$ simplifies to the number $\dfrac{\sqrt{5}}{3\sqrt{2}}$.

1.3 Exponents and Roots

Exponents

Exponents are used to denote the repeated multiplication of a number by itself; for example, $3^4 = (3)(3)(3)(3) = 81$ and $5^3 = (5)(5)(5) = 125$. In the expression 3^4, 3 is called the **base**, 4 is called the **exponent**, and we read the expression as "3 to the fourth power." Similarly, 5 to the third power is 125.

When the exponent is 2, we call the process **squaring**. Thus, 6 squared is 36; that is, $6^2 = (6)(6) = 36$. Similarly, 7 squared is 49; that is, $7^2 = (7)(7) = 49$.

When negative numbers are raised to powers, the result may be positive or negative; for example, $(-3)^2 = (-3)(-3) = 9$ and $(-3)^5 = (-3)(-3)(-3)(-3)(-3) = -243$. A negative number raised to an even power is always positive, and a negative number raised to an odd power is always negative. Note that $(-3)^2 = (-3)(-3) = 9$, but $-3^2 = -((3)(3)) = -9$. Exponents can also be negative or zero; such exponents are defined as follows.

The exponent zero: For all nonzero numbers a, $a^0 = 1$. The expression 0^0 is undefined.

Negative exponents: For all nonzero numbers a, $a^{-1} = \dfrac{1}{a}$, $a^{-2} = \dfrac{1}{a^2}$, $a^{-3} = \dfrac{1}{a^3}$, and so on.

Note that $(a)(a^{-1}) = (a)\left(\dfrac{1}{a}\right) = 1$.

Roots

A **square root** of a nonnegative number n is a number r such that $r^2 = n$. For example, 4 is a square root of 16 because $4^2 = 16$. Another square root of 16 is -4, since $(-4)^2 = 16$. All positive numbers have two square roots, one positive and one negative. The only square root of 0 is 0. The expression consisting of the square root symbol $\sqrt{}$ placed over a nonnegative number denotes the *nonnegative* square root (or the positive square root if the number is greater than 0) of that nonnegative number. Therefore, $\sqrt{100} = 10$, $-\sqrt{100} = -10$, and $\sqrt{0} = 0$. Square roots of negative numbers are not defined in the real number system.

Here are four important rules regarding operations with square roots, where $a > 0$ and $b > 0$.

Rule 1: $(\sqrt{a})^2 = a$

Example A: $(\sqrt{3})^2 = 3$

Example B: $(\sqrt{\pi})^2 = \pi$

Rule 2: $\sqrt{a^2} = a$

Example A: $\sqrt{4} = \sqrt{2^2} = 2$

Example B: $\sqrt{\pi^2} = \pi$

Rule 3: $\sqrt{a}\sqrt{b} = \sqrt{ab}$

Example A: $\sqrt{3}\sqrt{10} = \sqrt{30}$

Example B: $\sqrt{24} = \sqrt{4}\sqrt{6} = 2\sqrt{6}$

Rule 4: $\dfrac{\sqrt{a}}{\sqrt{b}} = \sqrt{\dfrac{a}{b}}$

Example A: $\dfrac{\sqrt{5}}{\sqrt{15}} = \sqrt{\dfrac{5}{15}} = \sqrt{\dfrac{1}{3}}$

Example B: $\dfrac{\sqrt{18}}{\sqrt{2}} = \sqrt{\dfrac{18}{2}} = \sqrt{9} = 3$

A square root is a root of order 2. Higher order roots of a positive number n are defined similarly. For orders 3 and 4, the **cube root** of n, written as $\sqrt[3]{n}$, and **fourth root** of n, written as $\sqrt[4]{n}$, represent numbers such that when they are raised to the powers 3 and 4, respectively, the result is n. These roots obey rules similar to those above but with the exponent 2 replaced by 3 or 4 in the first two rules.

There are some notable differences between odd order roots and even order roots (in the real number system):

For odd order roots, there is *exactly one* root for *every* number n, even when n is negative.

For even order roots, there are *exactly two* roots for every *positive* number n and *no* roots for any *negative* number n.

For example, 8 has exactly one cube root, $\sqrt[3]{8} = 2$, but 8 has two fourth roots, $\sqrt[4]{8}$ and $-\sqrt[4]{8}$, whereas -8 has exactly one cube root, $\sqrt[3]{-8} = -2$, but -8 has no fourth root, since it is negative.

1.4 Decimals

The decimal number system is based on representing numbers using powers of 10. The place value of each digit corresponds to a power of 10. For example, the digits of the number 7,532.418 have the following place values.

Arithmetic Figure 1

That is, the number 7,532.418 can be written as

$$7(1,000) + 5(100) + 3(10) + 2(1) + 4\left(\frac{1}{10}\right) + 1\left(\frac{1}{100}\right) + 8\left(\frac{1}{1,000}\right)$$

Alternatively, it can be written as

$$7\left(10^3\right) + 5\left(10^2\right) + 3\left(10^1\right) + 2\left(10^0\right) + 4\left(10^{-1}\right) + 1\left(10^{-2}\right) + 8\left(10^{-3}\right)$$

If there are a finite number of digits to the right of the decimal point, converting a decimal to an equivalent fraction with integers in the numerator and denominator is a straightforward process. Since each place value is a power of 10, every decimal can be converted to an integer divided by a power of 10. Here are three examples.

Example 1.4.1: $2.3 = 2 + \dfrac{3}{10} = \dfrac{20}{10} + \dfrac{3}{10} = \dfrac{23}{10}$

Example 1.4.2: $90.17 = 90 + \dfrac{17}{100} = \dfrac{9,000 + 17}{100} = \dfrac{9,017}{100}$

Example 1.4.3: $0.612 = \dfrac{612}{1,000}$

Conversely, every fraction with integers in the numerator and denominator can be converted to an equivalent decimal by dividing the numerator by the denominator using long division (which is not in this review). The decimal that results from the long division will either **terminate**, as in $\frac{1}{4} = 0.25$ and $\frac{52}{25} = 2.08$, or **repeat** without end, as in

$\frac{1}{9} = 0.111\ldots$, $\frac{1}{22} = 0.0454545\ldots$, and $\frac{25}{12} = 2.08333\ldots$. One way to indicate the repeating part of a decimal that repeats without end is to use a bar over the digits that repeat. Here are four examples of fractions converted to decimals.

Example 1.4.4: $\frac{3}{8} = 0.375$

Example 1.4.5: $\frac{259}{40} = 6.475$

Example 1.4.6: $-\frac{1}{3} = -0.\overline{3}$

Example 1.4.7: $\frac{15}{14} = 1.0\overline{714285}$

Every fraction with integers in the numerator and denominator is equivalent to a decimal that either terminates or repeats. That is, every rational number can be expressed as a terminating or repeating decimal. The converse is also true; that is, every terminating or repeating decimal represents a rational number.

Not all decimals are terminating or repeating; for instance, the decimal that is equivalent to $\sqrt{2}$ is $1.41421356237\ldots$, and it can be shown that this decimal does not terminate or repeat. Another example is $0.020220222022220222220\ldots$, which has groups of consecutive 2s separated by a 0, where the number of 2s in each successive group increases by one. Since these two decimals do not terminate or repeat, they are not rational numbers. Such numbers are called **irrational numbers**.

1.5 Real Numbers

The set of **real numbers** consists of all rational numbers and all irrational numbers. The real numbers include all integers, fractions, and decimals. The set of real numbers can be represented by a number line called the **real number line**. Arithmetic Figure 2 below is a number line.

Arithmetic Figure 2

Every real number corresponds to a point on the number line, and every point on the number line corresponds to a real number. On the number line, all numbers to the left of 0 are negative and all numbers to the right of 0 are positive. As shown in Arithmetic Figure 2, the negative numbers $-0.4, -1, -\frac{3}{2}, -2, -\sqrt{5}$, and -3 are to the left of 0, and the positive numbers $\frac{1}{2}, 1, \sqrt{2}, 2, 2.6$, and 3 are to the right of 0. Only the number 0 is neither negative nor positive.

A real number x is **less than** a real number y if x is to the left of y on the number line, which is written as $x < y$. A real number y is **greater than** a real number x if y is to the right of x on the number line, which is written as $y > x$. For example, the number line in Arithmetic Figure 2 shows the following three relationships.

Relationship 1: $-\sqrt{5} < -2$

Relationship 2: $\dfrac{1}{2} > 0$

Relationship 3: $1 < \sqrt{2} < 2$

A real number x is **less than or equal to** a real number y if x is to the left of, *or corresponds to the same point as*, y on the number line, which is written as $x \le y$. A real number y is **greater than or equal to** a real number x if y is to the right of, *or corresponds to the same point as*, x on the number line, which is written as $y \ge x$.

To say that a real number x is between 2 and 3 on the number line means that $x > 2$ and $x < 3$, which can also be written as $2 < x < 3$. The set of all real numbers that are between 2 and 3 is called an **interval**, and $2 < x < 3$ is often used to represent that interval. Note that the endpoints of the interval, 2 and 3, are not included in the interval. Sometimes one or both of the endpoints are to be included in an interval. The following inequalities represent four types of intervals, depending on whether or not the endpoints are included.

Interval type 1: $2 < x < 3$
Interval type 2: $2 \le x < 3$
Interval type 3: $2 < x \le 3$
Interval type 4: $2 \le x \le 3$

There are also four types of intervals with only one endpoint, each of which consists of all real numbers to the right or to the left of the endpoint and include or do not include the endpoint. The following inequalities represent these types of intervals.

Interval type 1: $x < 4$
Interval type 2: $x \le 4$
Interval type 3: $x > 4$
Interval type 4: $x \ge 4$

The entire real number line is also considered to be an interval.

Absolute Value

The distance between a number x and 0 on the number line is called the **absolute value** of x, written as $|x|$. Therefore, $|3| = 3$ and $|-3| = 3$ because each of the numbers 3 and -3 is a distance of 3 from 0. Note that if x is positive, then $|x| = x$; if x is negative, then $|x| = -x$; and lastly, $|0| = 0$. It follows that the absolute value of any nonzero number is positive. Here are three examples.

Example 1.5.1: $\left|\sqrt{5}\right| = \sqrt{5}$

Example 1.5.2: $|-23| = -(-23) = 23$

Example 1.5.3: $\left|-10.2\right| = 10.2$

Properties of Real Numbers

Here are twelve general properties of real numbers that are used frequently. In each property, r, s, and t are real numbers.

Property 1: $r + s = s + r$ and $rs = sr$.

　　Example A: $8 + 2 = 2 + 8 = 10$

　　Example B: $(-3)(17) = (17)(-3) = -51$

Property 2: $(r + s) + t = r + (s + t)$ and $(rs)t = r(st)$.

　　Example A: $(7 + 3) + 8 = 7 + (3 + 8) = 18$

　　Example B: $\left(7\sqrt{2}\right)\sqrt{2} = 7\left(\sqrt{2}\,\sqrt{2}\right) = (7)(2) = 14$

Property 3: $r(s + t) = rs + rt$

　　Example: $5(3 + 16) = (5)(3) + (5)(16) = 95$

Property 4: $r + 0 = r$, $(r)(0) = 0$, and $(r)(1) = r$.

Property 5: If $rs = 0$, then either $r = 0$ or $s = 0$ or both.

　　Example: If $-2s = 0$, then $s = 0$.

Property 6: Division by 0 is undefined.

　　Example A: $5 \div 0$ is undefined.

　　Example B: $\dfrac{-7}{0}$ is undefined.

　　Example C: $\dfrac{0}{0}$ is undefined.

Property 7: If both r and s are positive, then both $r + s$ and rs are positive.

Property 8: If both r and s are negative, then $r + s$ is negative and rs is positive.

Property 9: If r is positive and s is negative, then rs is negative.

Property 10: $|r + s| \le |r| + |s|$. This is known as the **triangle inequality**.

　　Example: If $r = 5$ and $s = -2$, then $|5 + (-2)| = |5 - 2| = |3| = 3$ and

　　$|5| + |-2| = 5 + 2 = 7$. Therefore, $|5 + (-2)| \le |5| + |-2|$.

Property 11: $|r||s| = |rs|$

　　Example: $|5||-2| = |(5)(-2)| = |-10| = 10$

Property 12: If $r > 1$, then $r^2 > r$. If $0 < s < 1$, then $s^2 < s$.

　　Example: $5^2 = 25 > 5$, but $\left(\dfrac{1}{5}\right)^2 = \dfrac{1}{25} < \dfrac{1}{5}$.

1.6 Ratio

The **ratio** of one quantity to another is a way to express their relative sizes, often in the form of a fraction, where the first quantity is the numerator and the second quantity is the denominator. Thus, if s and t are positive quantities, then the ratio of s to t can be written as the fraction $\dfrac{s}{t}$. The notation "s to t" and the notation "$s : t$" are also used to express this ratio. For example, if there are 2 apples and 3 oranges in a basket, we can say that the ratio of the number of apples to the number of oranges is $\dfrac{2}{3}$, or that it is 2 to 3, or that it is 2 : 3. Like fractions, ratios can be reduced to lowest terms. For example, if there are 8 apples and 12 oranges in a basket, then the ratio of the number of apples to the number of oranges is still 2 to 3. Similarly, the ratio 9 to 12 is equivalent to the ratio 3 to 4.

　　If three or more positive quantities are being considered, say r, s, and t, then their relative sizes can also be expressed as a ratio with the notation "r to s to t". For example, if there are 5 apples, 30 pears, and 20 oranges in a basket, then the ratio of the number of apples to the number of pears to the number of oranges is 5 to 30 to 20. This ratio can be reduced to 1 to 6 to 4 by dividing each number by the greatest common divisor of 5, 30, and 20, which is 5.

A **proportion** is an equation relating two ratios; for example, $\dfrac{9}{12} = \dfrac{3}{4}$. To solve a problem involving ratios, you can often write a proportion and solve it by **cross multiplication**.

Example 1.6.1: To find a number x so that the ratio of x to 49 is the same as the ratio of 3 to 21, you can first write the following equation.

$$\frac{x}{49} = \frac{3}{21}$$

You can then cross multiply to get $21x = (3)(49)$, and finally you can solve for x to get $x = \dfrac{(3)(49)}{21} = 7.$

1.7 Percent

The term **percent** means *per hundred*, or *hundredths*. Percents are ratios that are often used to represent *parts of a whole*, where the whole is considered as having 100 parts. Percents can be converted to fraction or decimal equivalents. Here are three examples of percents.

Example 1.7.1: 1 percent means 1 part out of 100 parts. The fraction equivalent of 1 percent is $\dfrac{1}{100}$, and the decimal equivalent is 0.01.

Example 1.7.2: 32 percent means 32 parts out of 100 parts. The fraction equivalent of 32 percent is $\dfrac{32}{100}$, and the decimal equivalent is 0.32.

Example 1.7.3: 50 percent means 50 parts out of 100 parts. The fraction equivalent of 50 percent is $\dfrac{50}{100}$, and the decimal equivalent is 0.50.

Note that in the fraction equivalent, the *part* is the numerator of the fraction and the *whole* is the denominator. Percents are often written using the percent symbol, %, instead of the word "percent." Here are five examples of percents written using the % symbol, along with their fraction and decimal equivalents.

Example 1.7.4: $100\% = \dfrac{100}{100} = 1$

Example 1.7.5: $12\% = \dfrac{12}{100} = 0.12$

Example 1.7.6: $8\% = \dfrac{8}{100} = 0.08$

Example 1.7.7: $10\% = \dfrac{10}{100} = 0.1$

Example 1.7.8: $0.3\% = \dfrac{0.3}{100} = 0.003$

Be careful not to confuse 0.01 with 0.01%. The percent symbol matters. For example, $0.01 = 1\%$, but $0.01\% = \dfrac{0.01}{100} = 0.0001$.

To compute a *percent*, given the *part* and the *whole*, first divide the part by the whole to get the decimal equivalent, then multiply the result by 100. The percent is that number followed by the word "percent" or the % symbol.

Example 1.7.9: If the whole is 20 and the part is 13, you can find the percent as follows.

$$\frac{part}{whole} = \frac{13}{20} = 0.65 = 65\%$$

Example 1.7.10: What percent of 150 is 12.9 ?

Solution: Here, the whole is 150 and the part is 12.9, so

$$\frac{part}{whole} = \frac{12.9}{150} = 0.086 = 8.6\%$$

To find the *part* that is a certain *percent* of a *whole*, you can either multiply the *whole* by the decimal equivalent of the percent or set up a proportion to find the part.

Example 1.7.11: To find 30% of 350, you can multiply 350 by the decimal equivalent of 30%, or 0.3, as follows.

$$(350)(0.3) = 105$$

Alternatively, to use a proportion to find 30% of 350, you need to find the number of parts of 350 that yields the same ratio as 30 parts out of 100 parts. You want a number x that satisfies the proportion

$$\frac{part}{whole} = \frac{30}{100} \text{ or}$$
$$\frac{x}{350} = \frac{30}{100}$$

Solving for x yields $x = \dfrac{(30)(350)}{100} = 105$, so 30% of 350 is 105.

Given the *percent* and the *part*, you can calculate the *whole*. To do this, either you can use the decimal equivalent of the percent or you can set up a proportion and solve it.

Example 1.7.12: 15 is 60% of what number?

Solution: Use the decimal equivalent of 60%. Because 60% of some number z is 15, multiply z by the decimal equivalent of 60%, or 0.6.

$$0.6z = 15$$

Now solve for z by dividing both sides of the equation by 0.6 as follows.

$$z = \frac{15}{0.6} = 25$$

Using a proportion, look for a number z such that

$$\frac{part}{whole} = \frac{60}{100} \text{ or}$$
$$\frac{15}{z} = \frac{60}{100}$$

Hence, $60z = (15)(100)$, and therefore, $z = \dfrac{(15)(100)}{60} = \dfrac{1,500}{60} = 25$. That is, 15 is 60% of 25.

Percents Greater than 100%

Although the discussion about percent so far assumes a context of a *part* and a *whole*, it is not necessary that the part be less than the whole. In general, the whole is called the **base** of the percent. When the numerator of a percent is greater than the base, the percent is greater than 100%.

Example 1.7.13: 15 is 300% of 5, since

$$\frac{15}{5} = \frac{300}{100}$$

Example 1.7.14: 250% of 16 is 40, since

$$\left(\frac{250}{100}\right)(16) = (2.5)(16) = 40$$

Note that the decimal equivalent of 300% is 3.0 and the decimal equivalent of 250% is 2.5.

Percent Increase, Percent Decrease, and Percent Change

When a quantity changes from an initial positive amount to another positive amount (for example, an employee's salary that is raised), you can compute the amount of change as a percent of the initial amount. This is called **percent change**. If a quantity increases from 600 to 750, then the base of the increase is the initial amount, 600, and the amount of the increase is $750 - 600$, or 150. The **percent increase** is found by dividing the amount of increase by the base, as follows.

$$\frac{amount\ of\ increase}{base} = \frac{750 - 600}{600} = \frac{150}{600} = \frac{25}{100} = 25\%$$

We say the percent increase is 25%. Sometimes this computation is written as follows.

$$\left(\frac{750 - 600}{600}\right)(100\%) = \left(\frac{150}{600}\right)(100\%) = 25\%$$

If a quantity doubles in size, then the percent increase is 100%. For example, if a quantity increases from 150 to 300, then the percent increase is calculated as follows.

$$\frac{amount\ of\ increase}{base} = \frac{300 - 150}{150} = \frac{150}{150} = 100\%$$

If a quantity decreases from 500 to 400, calculate the **percent decrease** as follows.

$$\frac{amount\ of\ decrease}{base} = \frac{500 - 400}{500} = \frac{100}{500} = \frac{20}{100} = 20\%$$

The quantity decreased by 20%.

When computing a percent *increase*, the base is the *smaller* number. When computing a percent *decrease*, the base is the *larger* number. In either case, the base is the initial number, before the change.

Example 1.7.15: An investment in a mutual fund increased by 12% in a single day. If the value of the investment before the increase was $1,300, what was the value after the increase?

Solution: The percent increase is 12%. Therefore, the value of the increase is 12% of $1,300, or, using the decimal equivalent, the increase is (0.12)($1,300) = $156. Thus, the value of the investment after the change is

$$\$1,300 + \$156 = 1,456$$

Because the final result is the sum of the initial investment (100% of $1,300) and the increase (12% of $1,300), the final result is 100% + 12% = 112% of $1,300. Thus, another way to get the final result is to multiply the value of the investment by the decimal equivalent of 112%, which is 1.12:

$$(\$1,300)(1.12) = \$1,456$$

A quantity may have several successive percent changes, where the base of each successive change is the result of the preceding percent change, as is the case in the following example.

Example 1.7.16: On September 1, 2013, the number of children enrolled in a certain preschool was 8% less than the number of children enrolled at the preschool on September 1, 2012. On September 1, 2014, the number of children enrolled in the preschool was 6% greater than the number of children enrolled in the preschool on September 1, 2013. By what percent did the number of students enrolled change from September 1, 2012, to September 1, 2014?

Solution: The *initial* base is the enrollment on September 1, 2012. The first percent change was the 8% decrease in the enrollment from September 1, 2012, to September 1, 2013. As a result of this decrease, the enrollment on September 1, 2013, was (100 − 8)%, or 92%, of the enrollment on September 1, 2012. The decimal equivalent of 92% is 0.92.

So, if n represents the number of children enrolled on September 1, 2012, then the number of children enrolled on September 1, 2013, is equal to $0.92n$.

The *new* base is the enrollment on September 1, 2013, which is $0.92n$. The second percent change was the 6% increase in enrollment from September 1, 2013, to September 1, 2014. As a result of this increase, the enrollment on September 1, 2014, was (100 + 6)%, or 106%, of the enrollment on September 1, 2013. The decimal equivalent of 106% is 1.06.

Thus, the number of children enrolled on September 1, 2014, was $(1.06)(0.92n)$, which is equal to $0.9752n$.

The percent equivalent of 0.9752 is 97.52%, which is 2.48% less than 100%. Thus, the percent change in the enrollment from September 1, 2012, to September 1, 2014, is a 2.48% decrease.

ARITHMETIC EXERCISES

Exercise 1. Evaluate the following.

(a) $15 - (6 - 4)(-2)$

(b) $(2 - 17) \div 5$

(c) $(60 \div 12) - (-7 + 4)$

(d) $3^4 - (-2)^3$

(e) $(-5)(-3) - 15$

(f) $(-2)^4(15 - 18)^4$

(g) $(20 \div 5)^2(-2 + 6)^3$

(h) $(-85)(0) - (-17)(3)$

Exercise 2. Evaluate the following.

(a) $\dfrac{1}{2} - \dfrac{1}{3} + \dfrac{1}{12}$

(b) $\left(\dfrac{3}{4} + \dfrac{1}{7}\right)\left(\dfrac{-2}{5}\right)$

(c) $\left(\dfrac{7}{8} - \dfrac{4}{5}\right)^2$

(d) $\left(\dfrac{3}{-8}\right) \div \left(\dfrac{27}{32}\right)$

Exercise 3. Which of the integers 312, 98, 112, and 144 are divisible by 8 ?

Exercise 4. (a) What is the prime factorization of 372 ?

(b) What are the positive divisors of 372 ?

Exercise 5. (a) What are the prime divisors of 100 ?

(b) What are the prime divisors of 144 ?

Exercise 6. Which of the integers 2, 9, 19, 29, 30, 37, 45, 49, 51, 83, 90, and 91 are prime numbers?

Exercise 7. What is the prime factorization of 585 ?

Exercise 8. Which of the following statements are true?

(a) $-5 < 3.1$

(b) $\sqrt{16} = 4$

(c) $7 \div 0 = 0$

(d) $0 < \left|-\dfrac{1}{7}\right|$

(e) $0.3 < \dfrac{1}{3}$

(f) $(-1)^{87} = -1$

(g) $\sqrt{(-3)^2} < 0$

(h) $\dfrac{21}{28} = \dfrac{3}{4}$

(i) $-|-23| = 23$

(j) $\dfrac{1}{2} > \dfrac{1}{17}$

(k) $(59^3)(59^2) = 59^6$

(l) $-\sqrt{25} < -4$

Exercise 9. Find the following.

(a) 40% of 15

(b) 150% of 48

(c) 0.6% of 800

(d) 15 is 30% of which number?

(e) 11 is what percent of 55?

Exercise 10. If a person's salary increases from $200 per week to $234 per week, what is the percent increase in the person's salary?

Exercise 11. If an athlete's weight decreases from 160 pounds to 152 pounds, what is the percent decrease in the athlete's weight?

Exercise 12. A particular stock is valued at $40 per share. If the value increases by 20 percent and then decreases by 25 percent, what will be the value of the stock per share after the decrease?

Exercise 13. There are a total of 20 dogs and cats at a kennel. If the ratio of the number of dogs to the number of cats at the kennel is 3 to 2, how many cats are at the kennel?

Exercise 14. The integer c is even, and the integer d is odd. For each of the following integers, indicate whether the integer is even or odd.

(a) $c + 2d$ (d) c^d

(b) $2c + d$ (e) $(c + d)^2$

(c) cd (f) $c^2 - d^2$

Exercise 15. When the positive integer n is divided by 3, the remainder is 2, and when n is divided by 5, the remainder is 1. What is the least possible value of n ?

ANSWERS TO ARITHMETIC EXERCISES

Exercise 1. (a) 19   (e) 0
             (b) −3   (f) 1,296
             (c) 8   (g) 1,024
             (d) 89   (h) 51

Exercise 2. (a) $\dfrac{1}{4}$ (c) $\dfrac{9}{1,600}$

             (b) $-\dfrac{5}{14}$ (d) $-\dfrac{4}{9}$

Exercise 3. 312, 112, and 144

Exercise 4. (a) $372 = (2^2)(3)(31)$

             (b) The positive divisors of 372 are 1, 2, 3, 4, 6, 12, 31, 62, 93, 124, 186, and 372.

Exercise 5. (a) $100 = (2^2)(5^2)$, so the prime divisors are 2 and 5.

             (b) $144 = (2^4)(3^2)$, so the prime divisors are 2 and 3.

Exercise 6. 2, 19, 29, 37, and 83

Exercise 7. $585 = (3^2)(5)(13)$

Exercise 8. (a) True   (g) False; $\sqrt{(-3)^2} = \sqrt{9} = 3 > 0$
             (b) True   (h) True
             (c) False; division by 0 is undefined.   (i) False; $-|-23| = -23$
             (d) True   (j) True
             (e) True   (k) False; $(59^3)(59^2) = 59^{3+2} = 59^5$
             (f) True   (l) True

Exercise 9.   (a)   6   (d) 50
               (b)   72   (e) 20%
               (c)   4.8

Exercise 10.   17%

Exercise 11.   5%

Exercise 12. $36 per share

Exercise 13.   8 cats

Exercise 14.   (a) $c + 2d$ is even.   (d) c^d is even.

               (b) $2c + d$ is odd.   (e) $(c + d)^2$ is odd.

               (c) cd is even.   (f) $c^2 - d^2$ is odd.

Exercise 15.   11

PART 2. ALGEBRA

The review of algebra begins with algebraic expressions, equations, inequalities, and functions and then progresses to several examples of applying them to solve real-life word problems. The review of algebra ends with coordinate geometry and graphs of functions as other important algebraic tools for solving problems.

2.1 Algebraic Expressions

A **variable** is a letter that represents a quantity whose value is unknown. The letters x and y are often used as variables, although any symbol can be used. An **algebraic expression** has one or more variables and can be written as a single **term** or as a sum of terms. Here are four examples of algebraic expressions.

Example 2.1.1: $2x$

Example 2.1.2: $y - \dfrac{1}{4}$

Example 2.1.3: $w^3z + 5z^2 - z^2 + 6$

Example 2.1.4: $\dfrac{8}{n + p}$

In the examples above, $2x$ is a single term, $y - \dfrac{1}{4}$ has two terms, $w^3z + 5z^2 - z^2 + 6$ has four terms, and $\dfrac{8}{n + p}$ has one term.

In the expression $w^3z + 5z^2 - z^2 + 6$, the terms $5z^2$ and $-z^2$ are called **like terms** because they have the same variables, and the corresponding variables have the same exponents. A term that has no variable is called a **constant** term. A number that is multiplied by variables is called the **coefficient** of a term.

A **polynomial** is the sum of a finite number of terms in which each term is either a constant term or a product of a coefficient and one or more variables with positive integer exponents. The **degree** of each term is the sum of the exponents of the variables in the term. A variable that is written without an exponent has degree 1. The degree of a constant term is 0. The **degree of a polynomial** is the greatest degree of its terms.

Polynomials of degrees 2 and 3 are known as quadratic and cubic polynomials, respectively.

Example 2.1.5: The expression $4x^6 + 7x^5 - 3x + 2$ is a polynomial in one variable, x. The polynomial has four terms.

The first term is $4x^6$. The coefficient of this term is 4, and its degree is 6.
The second term is $7x^5$. The coefficient of this term is 7, and its degree is 5.
The third term is $-3x$. The coefficient of this term is -3, and its degree is 1.
The fourth term is 2. This term is a constant, and its degree is 0.

Example 2.1.6: The expression $2x^2 - 7xy^3 - 5$ is a polynomial in two variables, x and y. The polynomial has three terms.

The first term is $2x^2$. The coefficient of this term is 2, and its degree is 2.

The second term is $-7xy^3$. The coefficient of this term is -7; and, since the degree of x is 1 and the degree of y^3 is 3, the degree of the term $-7xy^3$ is 4.

The third term is -5, which is a constant term. The degree of this term is 0.

In this example, the degrees of the three terms are 2, 4, and 0, so the degree of the polynomial is 4.

Example 2.1.7: The expression $4x^3 - 12x^2 - x + 36$ is a cubic polynomial in one variable.

Operations with Algebraic Expressions

The same rules that govern operations with numbers apply to operations with algebraic expressions.

In an algebraic expression, like terms can be combined by simply adding their coefficients, as the following three examples show.

Example 2.1.8: $2x + 5x = 7x$

Example 2.1.9: $w^3z + 5z^2 - z^2 + 6 = w^3z + 4z^2 + 6$

Example 2.1.10: $3xy + 2x - xy - 3x = 2xy - x$

A number or variable that is a factor of each term in an algebraic expression can be factored out, as the following three examples show.

Example 2.1.11: $4x + 12 = 4(x + 3)$

Example 2.1.12: $15y^2 - 9y = 3y\,(5y - 3)$

Example 2.1.13: For values of x where it is defined, the algebraic expression $\dfrac{7x^2 + 14x}{2x + 4}$

can be simplified as follows.

First factor the numerator and the denominator to get $\dfrac{7x(x + 2)}{2(x + 2)}$.

Since $x + 2$ occurs as a factor in both the numerator and the denominator of the expression, canceling it out will give an equivalent fraction for all values of x for which the expression is defined. Thus, for all values of x for which the expression is defined, the expression is equivalent to $\dfrac{7x}{2}$.

(A fraction is not defined when the denominator is equal to 0. The denominator of the original expression was $2(x + 2)$, which is equal to 0 when $x = -2$, so the original expression is defined for all $x \neq -2$.)

To multiply two algebraic expressions, each term of the first expression is multiplied by each term of the second expression and the results are added, as the following example shows.

Example 2.1.14: Multiply $(x + 2)(3x - 7)$ as follows.

First multiply each term of the expression $x + 2$ by each term of the expression $3x - 7$ to get the expression $x(3x) + x(-7) + 2(3x) + 2(-7)$.

Then simplify each term to get $3x^2 - 7x + 6x - 14$.

Finally, combine like terms to get $3x^2 - x - 14$.

So you can conclude that $(x + 2)(3x - 7) = 3x^2 - x - 14$.

A statement of equality between two algebraic expressions that is true for all possible values of the variables involved is called an **identity**. Here are seven examples of identities.

Identity 1: $ca + cb = c(a + b)$

Identity 2: $ca - cb = c(a - b)$

Identity 3: $(a + b)^2 = a^2 + 2ab + b^2$

Identity 4: $(a - b)^2 = a^2 - 2ab + b^2$

Identity 5: $a^2 - b^2 = (a + b)(a - b)$

Identity 6: $(a + b)^3 = a^3 + 3a^2b + 3ab^2 + b^3$

Identity 7: $(a - b)^3 = a^3 - 3a^2b + 3ab^2 - b^3$

Identities can be used to modify and simplify algebraic expressions, as in the following example.

Example 2.1.15: Simplify the algebraic expression $\dfrac{x^2 - 9}{4x - 12}$.

Solution: Use the identity $a^2 - b^2 = (a + b)(a - b)$ to factor the numerator of the expression, and use the identity $ca - cb = c(a - b)$ to factor the denominator of the expression to get

$$\frac{x^2 - 9}{4x - 12} = \frac{(x + 3)(x - 3)}{4(x - 3)}$$

Now, since $x - 3$ occurs as a factor in both the numerator and the denominator, it can be canceled out when $x - 3 \neq 0$, that is, when $x \neq 3$ (since the fraction is not defined when the denominator is 0). Therefore, for all $x \neq 3$, the expression is equivalent to $\dfrac{x + 3}{4}$.

2.2 Rules of Exponents

In the algebraic expression x^a, where x is raised to the power a, x is called the **base** and a is called the **exponent**. For all integers a and b and all positive numbers x, except $x = 1$, the following property holds: If $x^a = x^b$, then $a = b$.

Example: If $2^{3c+1} = 2^{10}$, then $3c + 1 = 10$, and therefore, $c = 3$.

Here are seven basic rules of exponents. In each rule, the bases x and y are nonzero real numbers and the exponents a and b are integers, unless stated otherwise.

Rule 1: $x^{-a} = \dfrac{1}{x^a}$

Example A: $4^{-3} = \dfrac{1}{4^3} = \dfrac{1}{64}$

Example B: $x^{-10} = \dfrac{1}{x^{10}}$

Example C: $\dfrac{1}{2^{-a}} = 2^{a}$

Rule 2: $\left(x^{a}\right)\left(x^{b}\right) = x^{a+b}$

Example A: $\left(3^{2}\right)\left(3^{4}\right) = 3^{2+4} = 3^{6} = 729$

Example B: $\left(y^{3}\right)\left(y^{-1}\right) = y^{2}$

Rule 3: $\dfrac{x^{a}}{x^{b}} = x^{a-b} = \dfrac{1}{x^{b-a}}$

Example A: $\dfrac{5^{7}}{5^{4}} = 5^{7-4} = 5^{3} = 125$

Example B: $\dfrac{t^{3}}{t^{8}} = t^{-5} = \dfrac{1}{t^{5}}$

Rule 4: $x^{0} = 1$

Example A: $7^{0} = 1$

Example B: $(-3)^{0} = 1$

Note that 0^{0} is not defined.

Rule 5: $\left(x^{a}\right)\left(y^{a}\right) = (xy)^{a}$

Example A: $\left(2^{3}\right)\left(3^{3}\right) = 6^{3} = 216$

Example B: $(10z)^{3} = 10^{3}z^{3} = 1{,}000z^{3}$

Rule 6: $\left(\dfrac{x}{y}\right)^{a} = \dfrac{x^{a}}{y^{a}}$

Example A: $\left(\dfrac{3}{4}\right)^{2} = \dfrac{3^{2}}{4^{2}} = \dfrac{9}{16}$

Example B: $\left(\dfrac{r}{4t}\right)^{3} = \dfrac{r^{3}}{64t^{3}}$

Rule 7: $\left(x^{a}\right)^{b} = x^{ab}$

Example A: $\left(2^{5}\right)^{2} = 2^{10} = 1{,}024$

Example B: $\left(3y^{6}\right)^{2} = \left(3^{2}\right)\left(y^{6}\right)^{2} = 9y^{12}$

The rules above are identities that are used to simplify expressions. Sometimes algebraic expressions look like they can be simplified in similar ways, but in fact they cannot. In order to avoid mistakes commonly made when dealing with exponents, keep the following six cases in mind.

Case 1: $(x^{a})(y^{b}) \neq (xy)^{a+b}$

For example, $(2^{4})(3^{2}) \neq (2 \times 3)^{4+2}$, since $(2^{4})(3^{2}) = 144$ and $6^{4+2} = 6^{6} = 46{,}656$.

Case 2: $(x^{a})^{b} \neq x^{a}x^{b}$

Instead, $(x^{a})^{b} = x^{ab}$ and $x^{a}x^{b} = x^{a+b}$; for example, $(4^{2})^{3} = 4^{6}$ and $4^{2}4^{3} = 4^{5}$.

Case 3: $(x + y)^a \neq x^a + y^a$.

In particular, note that $(x + y)^2 = x^2 + 2xy + y^2$; that is, the correct expansion contains the additional term $2xy$.

Case 4: $(-x)^2 \neq -x^2$

Instead, $(-x)^2 = x^2$. Note carefully where each negative sign appears.

Case 5: $\sqrt{x^2 + y^2} \neq x + y$

Case 6: $\dfrac{a}{x + y} \neq \dfrac{a}{x} + \dfrac{a}{y}$

But it *is* true that $\dfrac{x + y}{a} = \dfrac{x}{a} + \dfrac{y}{a}$.

2.3 Solving Linear Equations

An **equation** is a statement of equality between two mathematical expressions. If an equation involves one or more variables, the values of the variables that make the equation true are called the **solutions** of the equation. To **solve an equation** means to find the values of the variables that make the equation true, that is, the values that **satisfy the equation**. Two equations that have the same solutions are called **equivalent equations**. For example, $x + 1 = 2$ and $2x + 2 = 4$ are equivalent equations; both are true when $x = 1$ and are false otherwise. The general method for solving an equation is to find successively simpler equivalent equations so that the simplest equivalent equation makes the solutions obvious.

The following three rules are important for producing equivalent equations.

Rule 1: When the same constant is added to or subtracted from both sides of an equation, the equality is preserved and the new equation is equivalent to the original equation.

Rule 2: When both sides of an equation are multiplied or divided by the same nonzero constant, the equality is preserved and the new equation is equivalent to the original equation.

Rule 3: When an expression that occurs in an equation is replaced by an equivalent expression, the equality is preserved and the new equation is equivalent to the original equation.

Example: Since the expression $2(x + 1)$ is equivalent to the expression $2x + 2$, when the expression $2(x + 1)$ occurs in an equation, it can be replaced by the expression $2x + 2$, and the new equation will be equivalent to the original equation.

A **linear equation** is an equation involving one or more variables in which each term in the equation is either a constant term or a variable multiplied by a coefficient. None of the variables are multiplied together or raised to a power greater than 1. For example, $2x + 1 = 7x$ and $10x - 9y - z = 3$ are linear equations, but $x + y^2 = 0$ and $xz = 3$ are not.

Linear Equations in One Variable

To solve a linear equation in one variable, find successively simpler equivalent equations by combining like terms and applying the rules for producing simpler equivalent equations until the solution is obvious.

Example 2.3.1: Solve the equation $11x - 4 - 8x = 2(x + 4) - 2x$ as follows.

Combine like terms on the left side to get $3x - 4 = 2(x + 4) - 2x$.

Replace $2(x + 4)$ by $2x + 8$ on the right side to get $3x - 4 = 2x + 8 - 2x$.

Combine like terms on the right side to get $3x - 4 = 8$.

Add 4 to both sides to get $3x = 12$.

Divide both sides by 3 to get $\dfrac{3x}{3} = \dfrac{12}{3}$.

Simplify to get $x = 4$.

You can always check your solution by substituting it into the original equation. If the resulting value of the right-hand side of the equation is equal to the resulting value of the left-hand side of the equation, your solution is correct.

Substituting the solution $x = 4$ into the left-hand side of the equation $11x - 4 - 8x = 2(x + 4) - 2x$ gives

$$11x - 4 - 8x = 11(4) - 4 - 8(4) = 44 - 4 - 32 = 8$$

Substituting the solution $x = 4$ into the right-hand side of the equation gives

$$2(x + 4) - 2x = 2(4 + 4) - 2(4) = 2(8) - 8 = 8$$

Since both substitutions give the same result, 8, the solution $x = 4$ is correct.

Note that it is possible for a linear equation to have no solutions. For example, the equation $2x + 3 = 2(7 + x)$ has no solution, since it is equivalent to the equation $3 = 14$, which is false. Also, it is possible that what looks to be a linear equation could turn out to be an identity when you try to solve it. For example, $3x - 6 = -3(2 - x)$ is true for all values of x, so it is an identity.

Linear Equations in Two Variables

A linear equation in two variables, x and y, can be written in the form

$$ax + by = c$$

where a, b, and c are real numbers and neither a nor b is equal to 0. For example, $3x + 2y = 8$ is a linear equation in two variables.

A solution of such an equation is an **ordered pair** of numbers (x, y) that makes the equation true when the values of x and y are substituted into the equation. For example, both the ordered pair $(2, 1)$ and the ordered pair $\left(-\dfrac{2}{3}, 5\right)$ are solutions of the equation $3x + 2y = 8$, but the ordered pair $(1, 2)$ is not a solution. Every linear equation in two variables has infinitely many solutions.

A set of equations in two or more variables is called a **system of equations**, and the equations in the system are called **simultaneous equations**. To solve a system of equations in two variables, x and y, means to find ordered pairs of numbers (x, y) that satisfy all of the equations in the system. Similarly, to solve a system of equations in three variables, x, y, and z, means to find ordered triples of numbers (x, y, z) that satisfy all of the equations in the system. Solutions of systems with more than three variables are defined in a similar way.

Generally, systems of linear equations in two variables consist of two linear equations, each of which contains one or both of the variables. Often, such systems have a unique solution; that is, there is only one ordered pair of numbers that satisfies both equations in the system. However, it is possible that the system will not have any solutions, or that it will have infinitely many solutions.

There are two basic methods for solving systems of linear equations, by **substitution** or by **elimination**. In the substitution method, one equation is manipulated to express one variable in terms of the other. Then the expression is substituted in the other equation.

Example 2.3.2: Use substitution to solve the following system of two equations.

$$4x + 3y = 13$$
$$x + 2y = 2$$

Solution:

Part 1: You can solve for y as follows.

Express x in the second equation in terms of y as $x = 2 - 2y$.

Substitute $2 - 2y$ for x in the first equation to get $4(2 - 2y) + 3y = 13$.

Replace $4(2 - 2y)$ by $8 - 8y$ on the left side to get $8 - 8y + 3y = 13$.

Combine like terms to get $8 - 5y = 13$.

Solving for y gives $y = -1$.

Part 2: Now, you can use the fact that $y = -1$ to solve for x as follows.

Substitute -1 for y in the second equation to get $x + 2(-1) = 2$.

Solving for x gives $x = 4$.

Thus, the solution of the system is $x = 4$ and $y = -1$, or $(x, y) = (4, -1)$.

In the elimination method, the object is to make the coefficients of one variable the same in both equations so that one variable can be eliminated either by adding the equations together or by subtracting one from the other.

Example 2.3.3: Use elimination to solve the following system of two equations.

$$4x + 3y = 13$$
$$x + 2y = 2$$

(Note that this is the same system of equations that was solved by substitution in Example 2.3.2.)

Solution: Multiplying both sides of the second equation by 4 yields $4(x + 2y) = 4(2)$, or $4x + 8y = 8$.

Now you have two equations with the same coefficient of x.

$$4x + 3y = 13$$
$$4x + 8y = 8$$

If you subtract the equation $4x + 8y = 8$ from the equation $4x + 3y = 13$, the result is $-5y = 5$. Thus, $y = -1$, and substituting -1 for y in either of the original equations yields $x = 4$.

Again, the solution of the system is $x = 4$ and $y = -1$, or $(x, y) = (4, -1)$.

2.4 Solving Quadratic Equations

A **quadratic equation** in the variable x is an equation that can be written in the form

$$ax^2 + bx + c = 0$$

where a, b, and c are real numbers and $a \neq 0$. Quadratic equations have zero, one, or two real solutions.

The Quadratic Formula

One way to find solutions of a quadratic equation is to use the **quadratic formula**:

$$x = \frac{-b \pm \sqrt{b^2 - 4ac}}{2a}$$

where the notation $\pm$ is shorthand for indicating two solutions—one that uses the plus sign and the other that uses the minus sign.

Example 2.4.1: In the quadratic equation $2x^2 - x - 6 = 0$, we have $a = 2$, $b = -1$, and $c = -6$. Therefore, the quadratic formula yields

$$x = \frac{-(-1) \pm \sqrt{(-1)^2 - 4(2)(-6)}}{2(2)}$$

When the expression under the square root sign is simplified, we get

$$x = \frac{-(-1) \pm \sqrt{49}}{2(2)}$$

which can be further simplified to

$$x = \frac{1 \pm \sqrt{49}}{4}$$

Finally, since $\sqrt{49} = 7$, we get that

$$x = \frac{1 \pm 7}{4}$$

Hence this quadratic equation has two real solutions: $x = \frac{1+7}{4} = 2$ and $x = \frac{1-7}{4} = -\frac{3}{2}$.

Example 2.4.2: In the quadratic equation $x^2 + 4x + 4 = 0$, we have $a = 1$, $b = 4$, and $c = 4$. Therefore, the quadratic formula yields

$$x = \frac{-4 \pm \sqrt{4^2 - 4(1)(4)}}{2(1)}$$

When the expression under the square root sign is simplified, we get

$$x = \frac{-4 \pm \sqrt{0}}{2(1)}$$

The expression under the square root sign is equal to 0 and $\sqrt{0} = 0$. Therefore, the expression can be simplified to

$$x = \frac{-4}{2(1)} = -2$$

Thus this quadratic equation has only one solution, $x = -2$.

Example 2.4.3: In the quadratic equation $x^2 + x + 5 = 0$, we have $a = 1$, $b = 1$, and $c = 5$. Therefore, the quadratic formula yields

$$x = \frac{-1 \pm \sqrt{(1)^2 - 4(1)(5)}}{2(1)}$$

The expression under the square root sign is equal to -19. Since square roots of negative numbers are not real numbers, x is not a real number, and there is no real solution to this quadratic equation.

Solving Quadratic Equations by Factoring

Some quadratic equations can be solved more quickly by factoring.

Example 2.4.4: The quadratic equation $2x^2 - x - 6 = 0$ in Example 2.4.1 can be factored as $(2x + 3)(x - 2) = 0$. When a product is equal to 0, at least one of the factors must be equal to 0, so either $2x + 3 = 0$ or $x - 2 = 0$.

If $2x + 3 = 0$, then $2x = -3$ and $x = -\frac{3}{2}$.

If $x - 2 = 0$, then $x = 2$.

Thus the solutions are $-\frac{3}{2}$ and 2.

Example 2.4.5: The quadratic equation $5x^2 + 3x - 2 = 0$ can be factored as $(5x - 2)(x + 1) = 0$.

Therefore, either $5x - 2 = 0$ or $x + 1 = 0$.

If $5x - 2 = 0$, then $x = \frac{2}{5}$.

If $x + 1 = 0$, then $x = -1$.

Thus the solutions are $\frac{2}{5}$ and -1.

2.5 Solving Linear Inequalities

A mathematical statement that uses one of the following four inequality signs is called an **inequality**.

$<$ less than
$>$ greater than
$\leq$ less than or equal to
$\geq$ greater than or equal to

Inequalities can involve variables and are similar to equations, except that the two sides are related by one of the inequality signs instead of the equality sign used in equations. For example, the inequality $4x + 1 \leq 7$ is a linear inequality in one variable, which states that $4x + 1$ is less than or equal to 7. To **solve an inequality** means to find the set of all values of the variable that make the inequality true. This set of values is also known as the **solution set** of an inequality. Two inequalities that have the same solution set are called **equivalent inequalities**.

The procedure used to solve a linear inequality is similar to that used to solve a linear equation, which is to simplify the inequality by isolating the variable on one side of the inequality, using the following two rules.

Rule 1: When the same constant is added to or subtracted from both sides of an inequality, the direction of the inequality is preserved and the new inequality is equivalent to the original.

Rule 2: When both sides of the inequality are multiplied or divided by the same nonzero constant, the direction of the inequality is *preserved if the constant is positive* but the direction is *reversed if the constant is negative*. In either case, the new inequality is equivalent to the original.

Example 2.5.1: The inequality $-3x + 5 \leq 17$ can be solved as follows.

Subtract 5 from both sides to get $-3x \leq 12$.

Divide both sides by -3 and reverse the direction of the inequality to get $\dfrac{-3x}{-3} \geq \dfrac{12}{-3}$.
That is, $x \geq -4$.

Therefore, the solution set of $-3x + 5 \leq 17$ consists of all numbers greater than or equal to -4.

Example 2.5.2: The inequality $\dfrac{4x + 9}{11} < 5$ can be solved as follows.

Multiply both sides by 11 to get $4x + 9 < 55$.

Subtract 9 from both sides to get $4x < 46$.

Divide both sides by 4 to get $x < \dfrac{46}{4}$.
That is, $x < 11.5$.

Therefore, the solution set of the inequality $\dfrac{4x + 9}{11} < 5$ consists of all numbers less than 11.5.

2.6 Functions

An algebraic expression in one variable can be used to define a **function** of that variable. Functions are usually denoted by letters such as f, g, and h. For example, the algebraic expression $3x + 5$ can be used to define a function f by

$$f(x) = 3x + 5$$

where $f(x)$ is called the value of f at x and is obtained by substituting the value of x in the expression above. For example, if $x = 1$ is substituted in the expression above, the result is $f(1) = 3(1) + 5 = 8$.

It might be helpful to think of a function f as a machine that takes an input, which is a value of the variable x, and produces the corresponding output, $f(x)$. For any function, each input x gives exactly one output $f(x)$. However, more than one value of x can give the same output $f(x)$. For example, if g is the function defined by $g(x) = x^2 - 2x + 3$, then $g(0) = 3$ and $g(2) = 3$.

The **domain** of a function is the set of all permissible inputs, that is, all permissible values of the variable x. For the functions f and g defined above, the domain is the set of all real numbers. Sometimes the domain of the function is given explicitly and is restricted to a specific set of values of x. For example, we can define the function h by $h(x) = x^2 - 4$ for $-2 \leq x \leq 2$. Without an explicit restriction, the domain is assumed to be the set of all values of x for which $f(x)$ is a real number.

Example 2.6.1: Let f be the function defined by $f(x) = \dfrac{2x}{x-6}$. In this case, f is not defined at $x = 6$, because $\dfrac{12}{0}$ is not defined. Hence, the domain of f consists of all real numbers except for 6.

Example 2.6.2: Let g be the function defined by $g(x) = x^3 + \sqrt{x+2} - 10$. In this case, $g(x)$ is not a real number if $x < -2$. Hence, the domain of g consists of all real numbers x such that $x \geq -2$.

Example 2.6.3: Let h be the function defined by $h(x) = |x|$, which is the distance between x and 0 on the number line (see Arithmetic, Section 1.5). The domain of h is the set of all real numbers. Also, $h(x) = h(-x)$ for all real numbers x, which reflects the property that on the number line the distance between x and 0 is the same as the distance between $-x$ and 0.

2.7 Applications

Translating verbal descriptions into algebraic expressions is an essential initial step in solving word problems. Three examples of verbal descriptions and their translations are given below.

Example 2.7.1: If the square of the number x is multiplied by 3 and then 10 is added to that product, the result can be represented algebraically by $3x^2 + 10$.

Example 2.7.2: If John's present salary s is increased by 14 percent, then his new salary can be represented algebraically by $1.14s$.

Example 2.7.3: If y gallons of syrup are to be distributed among 5 people so that one particular person gets 1 gallon and the rest of the syrup is divided equally among the remaining 4, then the number of gallons of syrup that each of the 4 people will get can be represented algebraically by $\dfrac{y-1}{4}$.

The remainder of this section gives examples of various applications.

Average, Mixture, Rate, and Work Problems

Example 2.7.4: Ellen has received the following scores on 3 exams: 82, 74, and 90. What score will Ellen need to receive on the next exam so that the average (arithmetic mean) score for the 4 exams will be 85?

Solution: Let x represent the score on Ellen's next exam. This initial step of assigning a variable to the quantity that is sought is an important beginning to solving the problem. Then in terms of x, the average of the 4 exam scores is

$$\frac{82 + 74 + 90 + x}{4}$$

which is supposed to equal 85. Now simplify the expression and set it equal to 85:

$$\frac{82 + 74 + 90 + x}{4} = \frac{246 + x}{4} = 85$$

Solving the resulting linear equation for x, you get $246 + x = 340$, and so $x = 94$.

Therefore, Ellen will need to attain a score of 94 on the next exam.

Example 2.7.5: A mixture of 12 grams of vinegar and oil is 40 percent vinegar, where all of the measurements are by weight. How many grams of oil must be added to the mixture to produce a new mixture that is only 25 percent vinegar?

Solution: Let x represent the number of grams of oil to be added. Then the total number of grams of the new mixture will be $12 + x$, and the total number of grams of vinegar in the new mixture will be $(0.40)(12)$. Since the new mixture must be 25 percent vinegar,

$$\frac{(0.40)(12)}{12 + x} = 0.25$$

Therefore, $(0.40)(12) = (12 + x)(0.25)$.

Simplifying further gives $4.8 = 3 + 0.25x$, so $1.8 = 0.25x$, and $7.2 = x$.

Thus, 7.2 grams of oil must be added to produce a new mixture that is 25 percent vinegar.

Example 2.7.6: In a driving competition, Jeff and Dennis drove the same course at average speeds of 51 miles per hour and 54 miles per hour, respectively. If it took Jeff 40 minutes to drive the course, how long did it take Dennis?

Solution: Let x be the time, in minutes, that it took Dennis to drive the course. The distance d, in miles, is equal to the product of the rate r, in miles per hour, and the time t, in hours; that is,

$$d = rt$$

Note that since the rates are given in miles per *hour*, it is necessary to express the times in hours; for example, 40 minutes equals $\frac{40}{60}$ of an hour. Thus, the distance traveled by Jeff is the product of his speed and his time, $(51)\left(\frac{40}{60}\right)$ miles, and the distance traveled by Dennis is similarly represented by $(54)\left(\frac{x}{60}\right)$ miles.

Since the distances are equal, it follows that $(51)\left(\frac{40}{60}\right) = (54)\left(\frac{x}{60}\right)$.

From this equation it follows that $(51)(40) = 54x$ and $x = \frac{(51)(40)}{54} \approx 37.8$.

Thus, it took Dennis approximately 37.8 minutes to drive the course.

Example 2.7.7: A batch of computer parts consists of n identical parts, where n is a multiple of 60. Working alone at its constant rate, machine A takes 3 hours to produce a batch of computer parts. Working alone at its constant rate, machine B takes 2 hours to produce a batch of computer parts. How long will it take the two machines, working simultaneously at their respective constant rates, to produce a batch of computer parts?

Solution: Since machine A takes 3 hours to produce a batch, machine A can produce $\frac{1}{3}$ of the batch in 1 hour. Similarly, machine B can produce $\frac{1}{2}$ of the batch in 1 hour. If we let x represent the number of hours it takes both machines, working simultaneously, to produce the batch, then the two machines will produce $\frac{1}{x}$ of the batch in 1 hour. When the two machines work together, adding their individual production rates, $\frac{1}{3}$ and $\frac{1}{2}$, gives their combined production rate $\frac{1}{x}$.

Therefore, it follows that $\frac{1}{3}+\frac{1}{2}=\frac{1}{x}$.

This equation is equivalent to $\frac{2}{6}+\frac{3}{6}=\frac{1}{x}$. So $\frac{5}{6}=\frac{1}{x}$ and $\frac{6}{5}=x$.

Thus, working together, the machines will take $\frac{6}{5}$ hours or 1 hour 12 minutes, to produce a batch of computer parts.

Example 2.7.8: At a fruit stand, apples can be purchased for $0.15 each and pears for $0.20 each. At these rates, a bag of apples and pears was purchased for $3.80. If the bag contained 21 pieces of fruit, how many of the pieces were pears?

Solution: If a represents the number of apples purchased and p represents the number of pears purchased, then the total cost of the fruit can be represented by the equation $0.15a + 0.20p = 3.80$, and the total number of pieces of fruit can be represented by the equation $a + p = 21$. Thus to answer the question, you need to solve the following system of equations.

$$0.15a + 0.20p = 3.80$$
$$a + p = 21$$

From the equation for the total number of fruit, $a = 21 - p$.

Substituting $21 - p$ for a in the equation for the total cost gives the equation

$$0.15(21 - p) + 0.20p = 3.80$$

So, $(0.15)(21) - 0.15p + 0.20p = 3.80$, which is equivalent to

$$3.15 - 0.15p + 0.20p = 3.80$$

Therefore $0.05p = 0.65$, and $p = 13$.

Thus, of the 21 pieces of fruit, 13 were pears.

Example 2.7.9: To produce a particular radio model, it costs a manufacturer $30 per radio, and it is assumed that if 500 radios are produced, all of them will be sold. What must be the selling price per radio to ensure that the profit (revenue from the sales minus the total production cost) on the 500 radios is greater than $8,200 ?

Solution: If the selling price per radio is y dollars, then the profit is $500(y - 30)$ dollars.

Therefore, $500(y - 30) > 8{,}200$.

Simplifying further gives $500y - 15{,}000 > 8{,}200$, which simplifies to $500y > 23{,}200$ and then to $y > 46.4$.

Thus, the selling price must be greater than $46.40 to ensure that the profit is greater than $8,200.

Interest

Some applications involve computing **interest** earned on an investment during a specified time period. The interest can be computed as simple interest or compound interest.

Simple interest is based only on the initial deposit, which serves as the amount on which interest is computed, called the **principal**, for the entire time period. If the amount P is invested at a *simple annual interest rate of r percent*, then the value V of the investment at the end of t years is given by the formula

$$V = P\left(1 + \frac{rt}{100}\right)$$

In the case of **compound interest**, interest is added to the principal at regular time intervals, such as annually, quarterly, and monthly. Each time interest is added to the principal, the interest is said to be compounded. After each compounding, interest is earned on the new principal, which is the sum of the preceding principal and the interest just added. If the amount P is invested at an *annual interest rate of r percent, compounded annually*, then the value V of the investment at the end of t years is given by the formula

$$V = P\left(1 + \frac{r}{100}\right)^t$$

If the amount P is invested at an *annual interest rate of r percent, compounded n times per year*, then the value V of the investment at the end of t years is given by the formula

$$V = P\left(1 + \frac{r}{100n}\right)^{nt}$$

Example 2.7.10: If $10,000 is invested at a simple annual interest rate of 6 percent, what is the value of the investment after half a year?

Solution: According to the formula for simple interest, the value of the investment after $\frac{1}{2}$ year is

$$\$10,000\left(1 + 0.06\left(\frac{1}{2}\right)\right) = \$10,000(1.03) = \$10,300$$

Example 2.7.11: If an amount P is to be invested at an annual interest rate of 3.5 percent, compounded annually, what should be the value of P so that the value of the investment is $1,000 at the end of 3 years? (Give your answer to the nearest dollar.)

Solution: According to the formula for 3.5 percent annual interest, compounded annually, the value of the investment after 3 years is

$$P(1 + 0.035)^3$$

and we set it to be equal to $1,000 as follows.

$$P(1 + 0.035)^3 = \$1,000$$

To find the value of P, we divide both sides of the equation by $(1 + 0.035)^3$.

$$P = \frac{\$1,000}{(1 + 0.035)^3} \approx \$902$$

Thus, to the nearest dollar, $902 should be invested.

Example 2.7.12: A college student expects to earn at least $1,000 in interest on an initial investment of $20,000. If the money is invested for one year at an annual interest rate of r percent, compounded quarterly, what is the least annual interest rate that would achieve the goal? (Give your answer to the nearest 0.1 percent.)

Solution: According to the formula for r percent annual interest, compounded quarterly, the value of the investment after 1 year is

$$\$20,000\left(1+\frac{r}{400}\right)^4$$

By setting this value greater than or equal to $21,000 and solving for r, we get

$$\$20,000\left(1+\frac{r}{400}\right)^4 \geq \$21,000$$

which simplifies to

$$\left(1+\frac{r}{400}\right)^4 \geq 1.05$$

We can use the fact that taking the positive fourth root of each side of an inequality preserves the direction of the inequality. It is also true that taking the positive square root or any other positive root of each side of an inequality preserves the direction of the inequality. Using this fact, take the positive fourth root of both sides of

$$\left(1+\frac{r}{400}\right)^4 \geq 1.05$$

to get

$$1+\frac{r}{400} \geq \sqrt[4]{1.05}$$

which simplifies to

$$r \geq 400(\sqrt[4]{1.05}-1)$$

To compute the positive fourth root of 1.05, we can use the fact that for any number $x \geq 0$, $\sqrt[4]{x} = \sqrt{\sqrt{x}}$.

This allows us to compute the positive fourth root of 1.05 by taking the positive square root of 1.05 and then taking the positive square root of the result.

Therefore we can conclude that

$$400(\sqrt[4]{1.05}-1) = 400\left(\sqrt{\sqrt{1.05}}-1\right) \approx 4.9$$

Since $r \geq 400(\sqrt[4]{1.05}-1)$ and $400(\sqrt[4]{1.05}-1)$, rounded to the nearest 0.1, is 4.9, the least interest rate is approximately 4.9 percent per year, compounded quarterly.

2.8 Coordinate Geometry

Two real number lines that are perpendicular to each other and that intersect at their respective zero points define a **rectangular coordinate system**, often called the **xy-coordinate system** or **xy-plane**. The horizontal number line is called the **x-axis** and the vertical number line is called the **y-axis**. The point where the two axes intersect is called the **origin**, denoted by O. The positive half of the x-axis is to the right of the origin, and the positive half of the y-axis is above the origin. The two axes divide the plane into four regions called **quadrants**. The four quadrants are labeled I, II, III, and IV, as shown in Algebra Figure 1 below.

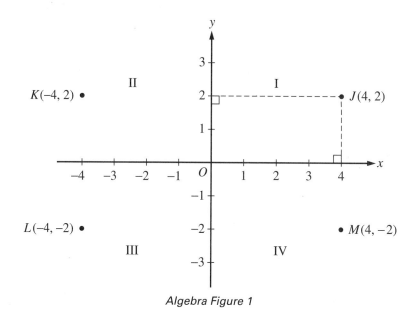

Algebra Figure 1

Each point J in the xy-plane can be identified with an ordered pair (x, y) of real numbers and is denoted by J(x, y). The first number in the ordered pair is called the **x-coordinate**, and the second number is called the **y-coordinate**. A point with coordinates (x, y) is located $|x|$ units to the right of the y-axis if x is positive, or it is located $|x|$ units to the left of the y-axis if x is negative. Also, the point is located $|y|$ units above the x-axis if y is positive, or it is located $|y|$ units below the x-axis if y is negative. If x = 0, the point lies on the y-axis, and if y = 0, the point lies on the x-axis. The origin has coordinates (0, 0). Unless otherwise noted, the units used on the x-axis and the y-axis are the same.

In Algebra Figure 1 above, the point J(4, 2) is 4 units to the right of the y-axis and 2 units above the x-axis, the point K(−4, 2) is 4 units to the left of the y-axis and 2 units above the x-axis, the point L(−4, −2) is 4 units to the left of the y-axis and 2 units below the x-axis, and the point M(4, −2) is 4 units to the right of the y-axis and 2 units below the x-axis.

Note that the three points K(−4, 2), L(−4, −2), and M(4, −2) have the same coordinates as J except for the signs. These points are geometrically related to J as follows.

- *M* is the **reflection of J about the x-axis**, or M and J are **symmetric about the x-axis**.

- *K* is the **reflection of J about the y-axis**, or K and J are **symmetric about the y-axis**.

- *L* is the **reflection of J about the origin**, or L and J are **symmetric about the origin**.

Calculating the Distance Between Two Points

The distance between two points in the xy-plane can be found by using the Pythagorean theorem. For example, the distance between the two points Q(−2, −3) and R(4, 1.5) in Algebra Figure 2 below is the length of line segment QR. To find this length, construct a right triangle with hypotenuse QR by drawing a vertical line segment downward from R and a horizontal line segment rightward from Q until these two line segments intersect at the point $S(4, -3)$ forming a right angle, as shown in Algebra Figure 2. Then note that the horizontal side of the triangle has length $4 - (-2) = 6$ and the vertical side of the triangle has length $1.5 - (-3) = 4.5$.

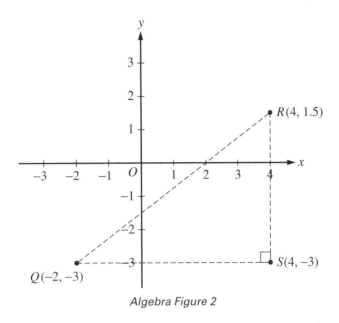

Algebra Figure 2

Since line segment QR is the hypotenuse of the triangle, you can apply the Pythagorean theorem:

$$QR = \sqrt{6^2 + 4.5^2} = \sqrt{56.25} = 7.5$$

(For a discussion of right triangles and the Pythagorean theorem, see Geometry, Section 3.3.)

Graphing Linear Equations and Inequalities

Equations in two variables can be represented as graphs in the coordinate plane. In the xy-plane, the **graph of an equation** in the variables x and y is the set of all points whose ordered pairs (x, y) satisfy the equation.

The graph of a linear equation of the form $y = mx + b$ is a straight line in the xy-plane, where m is called the **slope** of the line and b is called the **y-intercept**.

The **x-intercepts** of a graph are the x-coordinates of the points at which the graph intersects the x-axis. Similarly, the **y-intercepts** of a graph are the y-coordinates of the points at which the graph intersects the y-axis. Sometimes the terms **x-intercept** and **y-intercept** refer to the actual intersection points.

The slope of a line passing through two points $Q(x_1, y_1)$ and $R(x_2, y_2)$, where $x_1 \neq x_2$, is defined as

$$\frac{y_2 - y_1}{x_2 - x_1}$$

This ratio is often called "rise over run," where *rise* is the change in y when moving from Q to R and *run* is the change in x when moving from Q to R. A horizontal line has a slope of 0, since the rise is 0 for any two points on the line. Therefore, the equation of every horizontal line has the form $y = b$, where b is the y-intercept. The slope of a vertical line is not defined, since the run is 0. The equation of every vertical line has the form $x = a$, where a is the x-intercept.

Two lines are **parallel** if their slopes are equal. Two lines are **perpendicular** if their slopes are negative reciprocals of each other. For example, the line with equation $y = 2x + 5$ is perpendicular to the line with equation $y = -\dfrac{1}{2}x + 9$.

Example 2.8.1: Algebra Figure 3 below shows the graph of the line through the points $Q(-2, -3)$ and $R(4, 1.5)$.

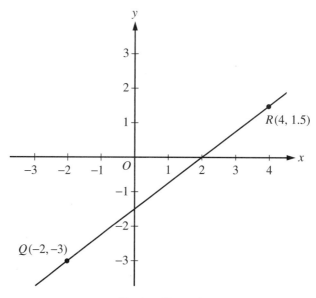

Algebra Figure 3

In Algebra Figure 3 above, the slope of the line passing through the points

$Q(-2, -3)$ and $R(4, 1.5)$ is

$$\frac{1.5 - (-3)}{4 - (-2)} = \frac{4.5}{6} = 0.75$$

Line QR appears to intersect the y-axis close to the point $(0, -1.5)$ so the y-intercept of the line must be close to -1.5. To get the exact value of the y-intercept, substitute the coordinates of any point on the line into the equation $y = 0.75x + b$, and solve it for b.

For example, if you pick the point $Q(-2, -3)$ and substitute its coordinates into the equation, you get $-3 = (0.75)(-2) + b$.

Then adding $(0.75)(2)$ to both sides of the equation yields $b = -3 + (0.75)(2)$, or $b = -1.5$.

Therefore, the equation of line QR is $y = 0.75x - 1.5$.

You can see from the graph in Algebra Figure 3 that the x-intercept of line QR is 2, since QR passes through the point $(2, 0)$. More generally, you can find the x-intercept of a line by setting $y = 0$ in an equation of the line and solving it for x. So you can find the x-intercept of line QR by setting $y = 0$ in the equation $y = 0.75x - 1.5$ and solving it for x as follows.

Setting $y = 0$ in the equation $y = 0.75x - 1.5$ gives the equation $0 = 0.75x - 1.5$. Then adding 1.5 to both sides yields $1.5 = 0.75x$. Finally, dividing both sides by 0.75 yields $x = \dfrac{1.5}{0.75} = 2$.

Graphs of linear equations can be used to illustrate solutions of systems of linear equations and inequalities, as can be seen in Examples 2.8.2 and 2.8.3.

Example 2.8.2: Consider the following system of two linear equations in two variables.

$$4x + 3y = 13$$
$$x + 2y = 2$$

(Note that this system was solved by substitution and by elimination in Section 2.3.) Solving each equation for y in terms of x yields the following equivalent system of equations.

$$y = -\frac{4}{3}x + \frac{13}{3}$$
$$y = -\frac{1}{2}x + 1$$

Algebra Figure 4 below shows the graphs of the two equations in the xy-plane. The solution of the system of equations is the point at which the two graphs intersect, which is $(4, -1)$.

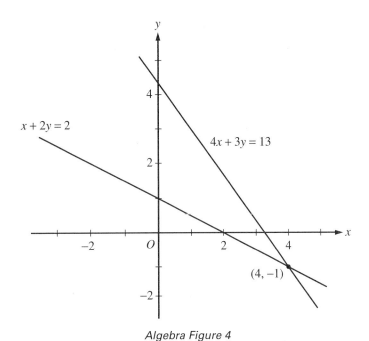

Algebra Figure 4

Example 2.8.3: Consider the following system of two linear inequalities.

$$x - 3y \geq -6$$
$$2x + y \geq -1$$

Solving each inequality for y in terms of x yields the following equivalent system of inequalities.

$$y \le \frac{1}{3}x + 2$$
$$y \ge -2x - 1$$

Each point (x, y) that satisfies the first inequality, $y \le \frac{1}{3}x + 2$, is either on the line $y = \frac{1}{3}x + 2$ or *below* the line because the y-coordinate is either equal to or *less than* $\frac{1}{3}x + 2$. Therefore, the graph of $y \le \frac{1}{3}x + 2$ consists of the line $y = \frac{1}{3}x + 2$ and the entire region below it. Similarly, the graph of $y \ge -2x - 1$ consists of the line $y = -2x - 1$ and the entire region *above* it. Thus, the solution set of the system of inequalities consists of all of the points that lie in the intersection of the two graphs described, which is represented by the shaded region shown in Algebra Figure 5 below, including the two half-lines that form the boundary of the shaded region.

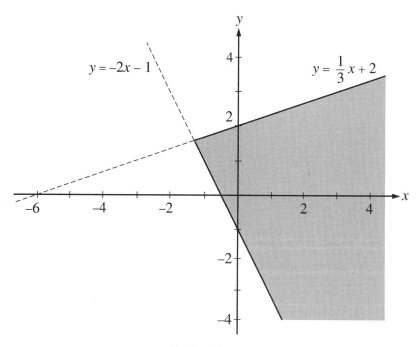

Algebra Figure 5

Symmetry with respect to the x-axis, the y-axis, and the origin is mentioned earlier in this section. Another important symmetry is symmetry with respect to the line with equation $y = x$. The line $y = x$ passes through the origin, has a slope of 1, and makes a 45-degree angle with each axis. For any point with coordinates (a, b), the point with interchanged coordinates (b, a) is the reflection of (a, b) about the line $y = x$; that is, (a, b) and (b, a) are symmetric about the line $y = x$. It follows that interchanging x and y in the equation of any graph yields another graph that is the reflection of the original graph about the line $y = x$.

Example 2.8.4: Consider the line whose equation is $y = 2x + 5$. Interchanging x and y in the equation yields $x = 2y + 5$. Solving this equation for y yields $y = \frac{1}{2}x - \frac{5}{2}$. The line $y = 2x + 5$ and its reflection $y = \frac{1}{2}x - \frac{5}{2}$ are graphed in Algebra Figure 6 that follows.

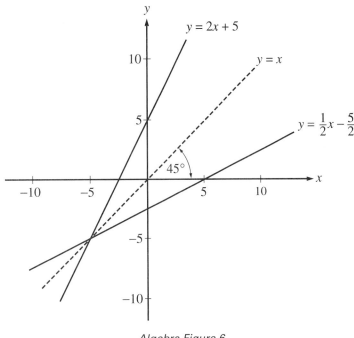

Algebra Figure 6

The line $y = x$ is a **line of symmetry** for the graphs of $y = 2x + 5$ and $y = \dfrac{1}{2}x - \dfrac{5}{2}$.

Graphing Quadratic Equations

The graph of a quadratic equation of the form $y = ax^2 + bx + c$, where a, b, and c are constants and $a \neq 0$, is a **parabola**. The x-intercepts of the parabola are the solutions of the equation $ax^2 + bx + c = 0$. If a is positive, the parabola opens upward and the **vertex** is its lowest point. If a is negative, the parabola opens downward and the vertex is its highest point. Every parabola that is the graph of a quadratic equation of the form $y = ax^2 + bx + c$ is symmetric with itself about the vertical line that passes through its vertex. In particular, the two x-intercepts are equidistant from this line of symmetry.

Example 2.8.5: The quadratic equation $y = x^2 - 2x - 3$ has the graph shown in Algebra Figure 7 below.

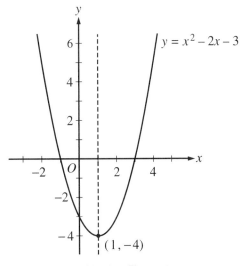

Algebra Figure 7

The graph indicates that the x-intercepts of the parabola are -1 and 3. The values of the x-intercepts can be confirmed by solving the quadratic equation $x^2 - 2x - 3 = 0$ to get $x = -1$ and $x = 3$. The point $(1, -4)$ is the vertex of the parabola, and the line $x = 1$ is its line of symmetry. The y-intercept is the y-coordinate of the point on the parabola at which $x = 0$, which is $y = 0^2 - 2(0) - 3 = -3$.

Graphing Circles

The graph of an equation of the form $(x - a)^2 + (y - b)^2 = r^2$ is a **circle** with its center at the point (a, b) and with radius $r > 0$.

Example 2.8.6: Algebra Figure 8 below shows the graph of two circles in the xy-plane. The larger of the two circles is centered at the origin and has radius 10, so its equation is $x^2 + y^2 = 100$. The smaller of the two circles has center $(6, -5)$ and radius 3, so its equation is $(x - 6)^2 + (y + 5)^2 = 9$.

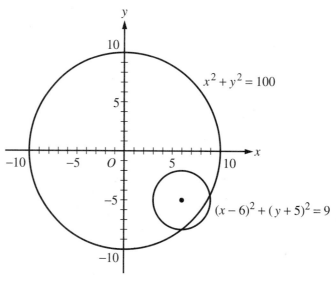

Algebra Figure 8

2.9 Graphs of Functions

The coordinate plane can be used for graphing functions. To graph a function in the xy-plane, you represent each input x and its corresponding output $f(x)$ as a point (x, y), where $y = f(x)$. In other words, you use the x-axis for the input and the y-axis for the output.

Below are several examples of graphs of elementary functions.

Example 2.9.1: Consider the linear function defined by $f(x) = -\dfrac{1}{2}x + 1$. Its graph in the xy-plane is the line with the linear equation $y = -\dfrac{1}{2}x + 1$.

Example 2.9.2: Consider the quadratic function defined by $g(x) = x^2$. The graph of g is the parabola with the quadratic equation $y = x^2$.

The graph of both the linear equation $y = -\frac{1}{2}x + 1$ and the quadratic equation $y = x^2$ are shown in Algebra Figure 9 below.

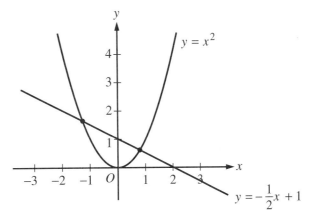

Algebra Figure 9

Note that the graphs of f and g in Algebra Figure 9 above intersect at two points. These are the points at which $g(x) = f(x)$. We can find these points algebraically as follows.

Set $g(x) = f(x)$ and get $x^2 = -\frac{1}{2}x + 1$, which is equivalent to $x^2 + \frac{1}{2}x - 1 = 0$, or $2x^2 + x - 2 = 0$.

Then solve the equation $2x^2 + x - 2 = 0$ for x using the quadratic formula and get

$$x = \frac{-1 \pm \sqrt{1 + 16}}{4}$$

which represents the x-coordinates of the two solutions

$$x = \frac{-1 + \sqrt{17}}{4} \approx 0.78 \quad \text{and} \quad x = \frac{-1 - \sqrt{17}}{4} \approx -1.28.$$

With these input values, the corresponding y-coordinates can be found using either f or g:

$$g\left(\frac{-1 + \sqrt{17}}{4}\right) = \left(\frac{-1 + \sqrt{17}}{4}\right)^2 \approx 0.61 \quad \text{and} \quad g\left(\frac{-1 - \sqrt{17}}{4}\right) = \left(\frac{-1 - \sqrt{17}}{4}\right)^2 \approx 1.64.$$

Thus, the two intersection points can be approximated by $(0.78, 0.61)$ and $(-1.28, 1.64)$.

Example 2.9.3: Consider the absolute value function defined by $h(x) = |x|$. By using the definition of absolute value (see Arithmetic, Section 1.5), h can be expressed as a **piecewise-defined** function:

$$h(x) = \begin{cases} x, & x \geq 0 \\ -x, & x < 0 \end{cases}$$

The graph of this function is V-shaped and consists of two linear pieces, $y = x$ and $y = -x$, joined at the origin, as shown in Algebra Figure 10 that follows.

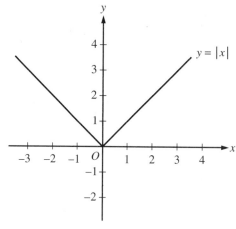

Algebra Figure 10

Example 2.9.4: Consider the positive square root function defined by $j(x) = \sqrt{x}$ for $x \geq 0$. The graph of this function is the upper half of a parabola lying on its side.

Also consider the negative square root function defined by $k(x) = -\sqrt{x}$ for $x \geq 0$. The graph of this function is the lower half of the parabola lying on its side.

The graphs of both of these functions, along with the graph of the parabola $y = x^2$, are shown in Algebra Figure 11 below.

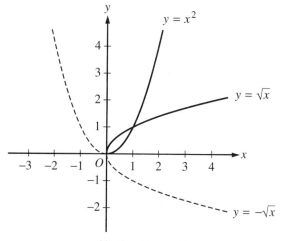

Algebra Figure 11

The graphs of $y = \sqrt{x}$ and $y = -\sqrt{x}$ are halves of a parabola because they are reflections of the right and left halves, respectively, of the parabola $y = x^2$ about the line $y = x$. This follows from squaring both sides of the two square root equations to get $y^2 = x$ and then interchanging x and y to get $y = x^2$.

Also note that $y = -\sqrt{x}$ is the reflection of $y = \sqrt{x}$ about the x-axis. In general, for any function h, the graph of $y = -h(x)$ is the **reflection** of the graph of $y = h(x)$ about the x-axis.

Example 2.9.5: Consider the function defined by $f(x) = |x| + 2$.

The graph of $f(x) = |x| + 2$ is the graph of $y = |x|$ shifted upward by 2 units, as shown in Algebra Figure 12 that follows.

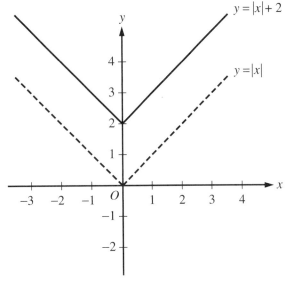

Algebra Figure 12

Similarly, the graph of the function $k(x) = |x| - 5$ is the graph of $y = |x|$ shifted downward by 5 units. (The graph of this function is not shown.)

Example 2.9.6: Consider the function defined by $g(x) = (x + 1)^2$.

The graph of $g(x) = (x + 1)^2$ is the graph of $y = x^2$ shifted to the left by 1 unit, as shown in Algebra Figure 13 below.

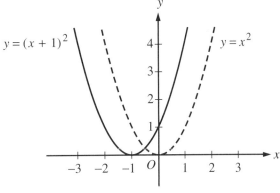

Algebra Figure 13

Similarly, the graph of the function $j(x) = (x - 4)^2$ is the graph of $y = x^2$ shifted to the right by 4 units. (The graph of this function is not shown.)

Note that in Example 2.9.5, the graph of the function $y = |x|$ was shifted upward and downward, and in Example 2.9.6, the graph of the function $y = x^2$ was shifted to the left and to the right. To double-check the direction of a shift, you can plot some corresponding values of the original function and the shifted function.

In general, for any function $h(x)$ and any positive number c, the following are true.

The graph of $h(x) + c$ is the graph of $h(x)$ **shifted upward** by c units.

The graph of $h(x) - c$ is the graph of $h(x)$ **shifted downward** by c units.

The graph of $h(x + c)$ is the graph of $h(x)$ **shifted to the left** by c units.

The graph of $h(x - c)$ is the graph of $h(x)$ **shifted to the right** by c units.

Example 2.9.7: Consider the functions defined by $f(x) = 2|x-1|$ and $g(x) = -\dfrac{x^2}{4}$.

These functions are related to the absolute value function $|x|$ and the quadratic function x^2, respectively, in more complicated ways than in the preceding two examples.

The graph of $f(x) = 2|x-1|$ is the graph of $y = |x|$ shifted to the right by 1 unit and then stretched, or dilated, vertically away from the x-axis by a factor of 2, as shown in Algebra Figure 14 below.

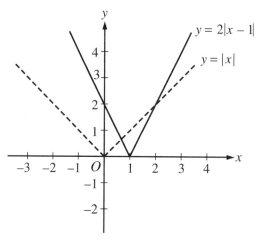

Algebra Figure 14

Similarly, the graph of the function $h(x) = \dfrac{1}{2}|x-1|$ is the graph of $y = |x|$ shifted to the right by 1 unit and then shrunk, or contracted, vertically toward the x-axis by a factor of $\dfrac{1}{2}$. (The graph of this function is not shown.)

The graph of $g(x) = -\dfrac{x^2}{4}$ is the graph of $y = x^2$ contracted vertically toward the x-axis by a factor of $\dfrac{1}{4}$ and then reflected in the x-axis, as shown in Algebra Figure 15 below.

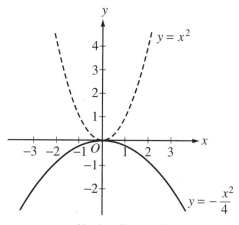

Algebra Figure 15

In general, for any function $h(x)$ and any positive number c, the following are true.
The graph of $ch(x)$ is the graph of $h(x)$ **stretched vertically** by a factor of c if $c > 1$.
The graph of $ch(x)$ is the graph of $h(x)$ **shrunk vertically** by a factor of c if $0 < c < 1$.

ALGEBRA EXERCISES

Exercise 1. Find an algebraic expression to represent each of the following.

(a) The square of y is subtracted from 5, and the result is multiplied by 37.

(b) Three times x is squared, and the result is divided by 7.

(c) The product of $x + 4$ and y is added to 18.

Exercise 2. Simplify each of the following algebraic expressions.

(a) $3x^2 - 6 + x + 11 - x^2 + 5x$

(b) $3(5x - 1) - x + 4$

(c) $\dfrac{x^2 - 16}{x - 4}$, where $x \neq 4$

(d) $(2x + 5)(3x - 1)$

Exercise 3. (a) What is the value of $f(x) = 3x^2 - 7x + 23$, when $x = -2$?

(b) What is the value of $h(x) = x^3 - 2x^2 + x - 2$, when $x = 2$?

(c) What is the value of $k(x) = \dfrac{5}{3}x - 7$ when $x = 0$?

Exercise 4. If the function g is defined for all nonzero numbers y by $g(y) = \dfrac{y}{|y|}$, find the value of each of the following.

(a) $g(2)$

(b) $g(-2)$

(c) $g(2) - g(-2)$

Exercise 5. Use the rules of exponents to simplify the following.

(a) $(n^5)(n^{-3})$

(b) $(s^7)(t^7)$

(c) $\dfrac{r^{12}}{r^4}$

(d) $\left(\dfrac{2a}{b}\right)^5$

(e) $\left(w^5\right)^{-3}$

(f) $(5^0)(d^3)$

(g) $\dfrac{\left(x^{10}\right)\left(y^{-1}\right)}{\left(x^{-5}\right)\left(y^5\right)}$

(h) $\left(\dfrac{3x}{y}\right)^2 \div \left(\dfrac{1}{y}\right)^5$

Exercise 6. Solve each of the following equations for x.

(a) $5x - 7 = 28$

(b) $12 - 5x = x + 30$

(c) $5(x + 2) = 1 - 3x$

(d) $(x + 6)(2x - 1) = 0$

(e) $x^2 + 5x - 14 = 0$

(f) $x^2 - x - 1 = 0$

Exercise 7. Solve each of the following systems of equations for x and y.

(a) $x + y = 24$
$\ \ \ \ x - y = 18$

(b) $3x - y = -5$
$\ \ \ \ x + 2y = 3$

(c) $15x - 18 - 2y = -3x + y$
$\ \ \ \ 10x + 7y + 20 = 4x + 2$

Exercise 8.   Solve each of the following inequalities for x.

(a) $-3x > 7 + x$
(b) $25x + 16 \geq 10 - x$
(c) $16 + x > 8x - 12$

Exercise 9.   For a given two-digit positive integer, the tens digit is 5 more than the units digit. The sum of the digits is 11. Find the integer.

Exercise 10.   If the ratio of $2x$ to $5y$ is 3 to 4, what is the ratio of x to y ?

Exercise 11.   Kathleen's weekly salary was increased by 8 percent to $712.80. What was her weekly salary before the increase?

Exercise 12.   A theater sells children's tickets for half the adult ticket price. If 5 adult tickets and 8 children's tickets cost a total of $81, what is the cost of an adult ticket?

Exercise 13.   Pat invested a total of $3,000. Part of the money was invested in a money market account that paid 10 percent simple annual interest, and the remainder of the money was invested in a fund that paid 8 percent simple annual interest. If the total interest earned at the end of the first year from these investments was $256, how much did Pat invest at 10 percent and how much at 8 percent?

Exercise 14.   Two cars started from the same point and traveled on a straight course in opposite directions for 2 hours, at which time they were 208 miles apart. If one car traveled, on average, 8 miles per hour faster than the other car, what was the average speed of each car for the 2-hour trip?

Exercise 15.   A group can charter a particular aircraft at a fixed total cost. If 36 people charter the aircraft rather than 40 people, then the cost per person is greater by $12.

(a) What is the fixed total cost to charter the aircraft?

(b) What is the cost per person if 40 people charter the aircraft?

Exercise 16.   An antiques dealer bought c antique chairs for a total of x dollars. The dealer sold each chair for y dollars.

(a) Write an algebraic expression for the profit, P, earned from buying and selling the chairs.

(b) Write an algebraic expression for the profit per chair.

Exercise 17.   Algebra Figure 16 that follows shows right triangle PQR in the xy-plane. Find the following.

(a) The coordinates of point Q

(b) The lengths of line segment PQ, line segment QR, and line segment PR

(c) The perimeter of triangle PQR

(d) The area of triangle PQR

(e) The slope, y-intercept, and equation of the line passing through points P and R

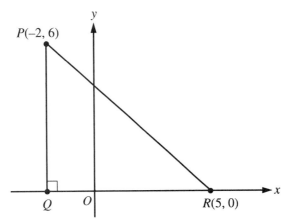

Algebra Figure 16

Exercise 18.   In the xy-plane, find the following.

(a) The slope and y-intercept of the line with equation $2y + x = 6$

(b) The equation of the line passing through the point $(3, 2)$ with y-intercept 1

(c) The y-intercept of a line with slope 3 that passes through the point $(-2, 1)$

(d) The x-intercepts of the graphs in parts (a), (b), and (c)

Exercise 19.   For the parabola $y = x^2 - 4x - 12$ in the xy-plane, find the following.

(a) The x-intercepts

(b) The y-intercept

(c) The coordinates of the vertex

Exercise 20.   For the circle $(x - 1)^2 + (y + 1)^2 = 20$ in the xy-plane, find the following.

(a) The coordinates of the center

(b) The radius

(c) The area

Exercise 21.   For each of the following functions, give the domain and a description of the graph $y = f(x)$ in the xy-plane, including its shape, and the x- and y- intercepts.

(a) $f(x) = -4$

(b) $f(x) = 100 - 900x$

(c) $f(x) = 5 - (x + 20)^2$

(d) $f(x) = \sqrt{x + 2}$

(e) $f(x) = x + |x|$

ANSWERS TO ALGEBRA EXERCISES

Exercise 1.   (a) $37(5 - y^2)$, or $185 - 37y^2$

(b) $\dfrac{(3x)^2}{7}$, or $\dfrac{9x^2}{7}$

(c) $18 + (x + 4)(y)$, or $18 + xy + 4y$

Exercise 2.   (a) $2x^2 + 6x + 5$ (c) $x + 4$

(b) $14x + 1$ (d) $6x^2 + 13x - 5$

Exercise 3.   (a) 49

(b) 0

(c) -7

Exercise 4.   (a) 1

(b) -1

(c) 2

Exercise 5.   (a) n^2 (e) $\dfrac{1}{w^{15}}$

(b) $(st)^7$ (f) d^3

(c) r^8 (g) $\dfrac{x^{15}}{y^6}$

(d) $\dfrac{32a^5}{b^5}$ (h) $9x^2 y^3$

Exercise 6.   (a) 7

(b) -3

(c) $-\dfrac{9}{8}$

(d) The two solutions are -6 and $\dfrac{1}{2}$.

(e) The two solutions are -7 and 2.

(f) The two solutions are $\dfrac{1+\sqrt{5}}{2}$ and $\dfrac{1-\sqrt{5}}{2}$.

Exercise 7.   (a) $x = 21$ and $y = 3$

(b) $x = -1$ and $y = 2$

(c) $x = \dfrac{1}{2}$ and $y = -3$

Exercise 8.   (a) $x < -\dfrac{7}{4}$

(b) $x \geq -\dfrac{3}{13}$

(c) $x < 4$

Exercise 9.   83

Exercise 10.   15 to 8

Exercise 11. $660

Exercise 12. $9

Exercise 13. $800 at 10% and $2,200 at 8%

Exercise 14.   48 miles per hour and 56 miles per hour

Exercise 15. (a) $4,320

(b) $108

Exercise 16. (a) $P = cy - x$

(b) Profit per chair: $\dfrac{P}{c} = \dfrac{cy - x}{c} = y - \dfrac{x}{c}$

Exercise 17. (a) The coordinates of point Q are $(-2, 0)$.

(b) The length of PQ is 6, the length of QR is 7, and the length of PR is $\sqrt{85}$.

(c) $13 + \sqrt{85}$

(d) 21

(e) Slope: $-\dfrac{6}{7}$; y-intercept: $\dfrac{30}{7}$

equation of line: $y = -\dfrac{6}{7}x + \dfrac{30}{7}$, or $7y + 6x = 30$

Exercise 18. (a) Slope: $-\dfrac{1}{2}$; y-intercept: 3

(b) $y = \dfrac{x}{3} + 1$

(c) 7

(d) $6, -3,$ and $-\dfrac{7}{3}$

Exercise 19. (a) $x = -2$ and $x = 6$

(b) $y = -12$

(c) $(2, -16)$

Exercise 20. (a) $(1, -1)$

(b) $\sqrt{20}$

(c) 20π

Exercise 21. (a) Domain: the set of all real numbers. The graph is a horizontal line with y-intercept 4 and no x intercept.

(b) Domain: the set of all real numbers. The graph is a line with slope -900, y intercept 100, and x-intercept $\dfrac{1}{9}$.

(c) Domain: the set of all real numbers. The graph is a parabola opening downward with vertex at $(-20, 5)$, line of symmetry $x = -20$, y-intercept -395, and x-intercepts $-20 \pm \sqrt{5}$.

(d) Domain: the set of numbers greater than or equal to -2. The graph is the upper half of a parabola opening to the right with vertex at $(-2, 0)$, x-intercept -2, and y-intercept $\sqrt{2}$.

(e) Domain: the set of all real numbers. The graph is two half-lines joined at the origin: one half-line is the negative x-axis and the other is a line starting at the origin with slope 2. Every nonpositive number is an x-intercept, and the y-intercept is 0. The function is equal to the following piecewise-defined function

$$f(x) = \begin{cases} 2x, & x \geq 0 \\ 0, & x < 0 \end{cases}$$

PART 3. GEOMETRY

The review of geometry begins with lines and angles and progresses to other plane figures, such as polygons, triangles, quadrilaterals, and circles. The review of geometry ends with some basic three-dimensional figures. Coordinate geometry is covered in the Algebra part.

3.1 Lines and Angles

A **line** is understood to be a straight line that extends in both directions without ending. Given any two points on a line, a **line segment** is the part of the line that contains the two points and all the points between them. The two points are called **endpoints**. Line segments that have equal lengths are called **congruent line segments**. The point that divides a line segment into two congruent line segments is called the **midpoint** of the line segment.

In Geometry Figure 1 below, A, B, C, and D are points on line m.

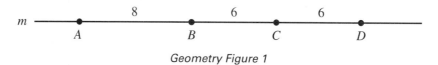

Geometry Figure 1

Line segment AB is the part of line m that consists of points A and B and all the points between A and B. According to Geometry Figure 1 above, the lengths of line segments AB, BC, and CD are 8, 6, and 6, respectively. Hence, line segments BC and CD are congruent. Since C is halfway between B and D, point C is the midpoint of line segment BD.

Sometimes the notation AB denotes line segment AB, and sometimes it denotes the **length** of line segment AB. The meaning of the notation can be determined from the context.

When two lines intersect at a point, they form four **angles**. Each angle has a **vertex** at the point of intersection of the two lines. For example, in Geometry Figure 2 below, lines k and m intersect at point P, forming the four angles APC, CPB, BPD, and DPA.

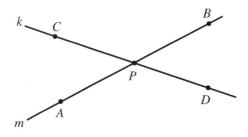

Geometry Figure 2

The first and third of the angles, that is, angles APC and BPD, are called **opposite angles**, also known as **vertical angles**. The second and fourth of the angles, that is, angles CPB and DPA, are also opposite angles. Opposite angles have equal measure, and angles that have equal measure are called **congruent angles**. Hence, opposite angles are congruent. The sum of the measures of the four angles is **360°**.

Sometimes the angle symbol $\angle$ is used instead of the word "angle." For example, angle APC can be written as $\angle APC$.

Two lines that intersect to form four congruent angles are called **perpendicular lines**. Each of the four angles has a measure of **90°**. An angle with a measure of **90°** is called a **right angle**. Geometry Figure 3 below shows two lines, k and m, that are perpendicular, denoted by $k \perp m$.

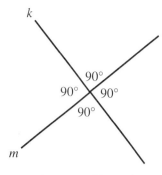

Geometry Figure 3

A common way to indicate that an angle is a right angle is to draw a small square at the vertex of the angle, as shown in Geometry Figure 4 below, where *PON* is a right angle.

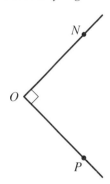

Geometry Figure 4

An angle with measure less than 90° is called an **acute angle**, and an angle with measure between 90° and 180° is called an **obtuse angle**.

Two lines in the same plane that do not intersect are called **parallel lines**. Geometry Figure 5 below shows two lines, k and m, that are parallel, denoted by $k \mid\mid m$. The two lines are intersected by a third line, p, forming eight angles.

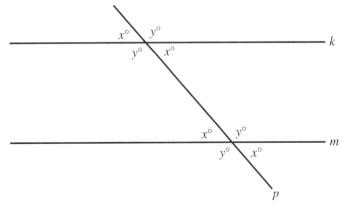

Geometry Figure 5

Note that four of the eight angles in Geometry Figure 5 have the measure $x°$, and the remaining four angles have the measure $y°$, where $x + y = 180$.

3.2 Polygons

A **polygon** is a closed figure formed by three or more line segments, all of which are in the same plane. The line segments are called the **sides** of the polygon. Each side is joined to two other sides at its endpoints, and the endpoints are called **vertices**. In this discussion, the term "polygon" means "convex polygon," that is, a polygon in which the measure of each interior angle is less than 180°. Geometry Figure 6 below contains examples of a triangle, a quadrilateral, and a pentagon, all of which are convex.

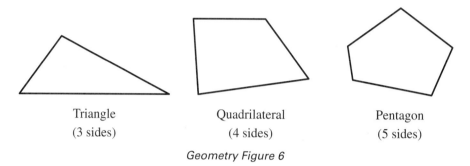

Triangle   Quadrilateral   Pentagon
(3 sides)   (4 sides)   (5 sides)

Geometry Figure 6

The simplest polygon is a **triangle**. Note that a **quadrilateral** can be divided into 2 triangles by drawing a diagonal; and a **pentagon** can be divided into 3 triangles by selecting one of the vertices and drawing 2 line segments connecting the selected vertex to the two nonadjacent vertices, as shown in Geometry Figure 7 below.

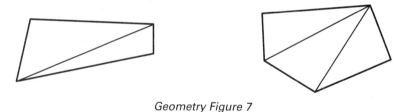

Geometry Figure 7

If a polygon has n sides, it can be divided into $n - 2$ triangles. Since the sum of the measures of the interior angles of a triangle is 180°, it follows that the sum of the measures of the interior angles of an n-sided polygon is $(n - 2)(180°)$. For example, since a quadrilateral has 4 sides, the sum of the measures of the interior angles of a quadrilateral is $(4 - 2)(180°) = 360°$, and since a **hexagon** has 6 sides, the sum of the measures of the interior angles of a hexagon is $(6 - 2)(180°) = 720°$.

A polygon in which all sides are congruent and all interior angles are congruent is called a **regular polygon**. For example, since an **octagon** has 8 sides, the sum of the measures of the interior angles of an octagon is $(8 - 2)(180°) = 1,080°$. Therefore, in a **regular octagon** the measure of each angle is $\dfrac{1,080°}{8} = 135°$.

The **perimeter** of a polygon is the sum of the lengths of its sides. The **area** of a polygon refers to the area of the region enclosed by the polygon.

In the next two sections, we will look at some basic properties of triangles and quadrilaterals.

3.3 Triangles

Every triangle has three sides and three interior angles. The measures of the interior angles add up to 180°. The length of each side must be less than the sum of the lengths of the other two sides. For example, the sides of a triangle could not have the lengths 4, 7, and 12 because 12 is greater than 4 + 7.

The following are 3 types of special triangles.

Type 1: A triangle with three congruent sides is called an **equilateral triangle**. The measures of the three interior angles of such a triangle are equal, and each measure is 60°.

Type 2: A triangle with at least two congruent sides is called an **isosceles triangle**. If a triangle has two congruent sides, then the angles opposite the two congruent sides are congruent. The converse is also true. For example, in triangle ABC in Geometry Figure 8 below, the measure of angle A is 50°, the measure of angle C is 50°, and the measure of angle B is $x°$. Since both angle A and angle C measure 50°, it follows that the length of AB is equal to the length of BC. Also, since the sum of the three angles of a triangle is 180°, it follows that $50 + 50 + x = 180$, and the measure of angle B is 80°.

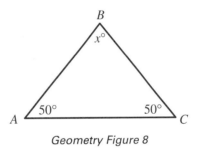

Geometry Figure 8

Type 3: A triangle with an interior right angle is called a **right triangle**. The side opposite the right angle is called the **hypotenuse**; the other two sides are called **legs**. For example, in right triangle DEF in Geometry Figure 9 below, side EF is the side opposite right angle D; therefore EF is the hypotenuse and DE and DF are legs.

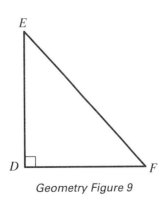

Geometry Figure 9

The Pythagorean Theorem

The **Pythagorean theorem** states that in a right triangle, the square of the length of the hypotenuse is equal to the sum of the squares of the lengths of the legs. Thus, for triangle *DEF* in Geometry Figure 9,

$$(EF)^2 = (DE)^2 + (DF)^2$$

This relationship can be used to find the length of one side of a right triangle if the lengths of the other two sides are known. For example, consider a right triangle with hypotenuse of length 8, a leg of length 5, and another leg of unknown length x, as shown in Geometry Figure 10 below.

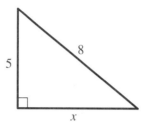

Geometry Figure 10

By the Pythagorean theorem, $8^2 = 5^2 + x^2$. Therefore, $64 = 25 + x^2$ and $39 = x^2$. Since $x^2 = 39$ and x must be positive, it follows that $x = \sqrt{39}$, or approximately 6.2.

The Pythagorean theorem can be used to determine the ratios of the lengths of the sides of two special right triangles. One special right triangle is an isosceles right triangle, as shown in Geometry Figure 11 below.

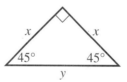

Geometry Figure 11

In Geometry Figure 11, the hypotenuse of the right triangle is of length y, both legs are of length x, and the angles opposite the legs are both 45-degree angles.

Applying the Pythagorean theorem to the isosceles right triangle in Geometry Figure 11 above shows that the lengths of its sides are in the ratio 1 to 1 to $\sqrt{2}$, as follows.

By the Pythagorean theorem, $y^2 = x^2 + x^2$. Therefore $y^2 = 2x^2$ and $y = \sqrt{2}x$. So the lengths of the sides are in the ratio x to x to $\sqrt{2}x$, which is the same as the ratio 1 to 1 to $\sqrt{2}$.

The other special right triangle is a 30°-60°-90° right triangle, which is half of an equilateral triangle, as shown in Geometry Figure 12 below.

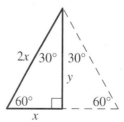

Geometry Figure 12

Note that the length of the horizontal side, x, is one-half the length of the hypotenuse, $2x$. Applying the Pythagorean theorem to the 30°-60°-90° right triangle shows that the lengths of its sides are in the ratio 1 to $\sqrt{3}$ to 2, as follows.

By the Pythagorean theorem, $x^2 + y^2 = (2x)^2$, which simplifies to $x^2 + y^2 = 4x^2$. Subtracting x^2 from both sides gives $y^2 = 4x^2 - x^2$ or $y^2 = 3x^2$. Therefore, $y = \sqrt{3}x$. Hence, the ratio of the lengths of the three sides of a 30°-60°-90° right triangle is x to $\sqrt{3}x$ to $2x$, which is the same as the ratio 1 to $\sqrt{3}$ to 2.

The Area of a Triangle

The **area** A of a triangle is given by the formula

$$A = \frac{bh}{2}$$

where b is the length of a base, and h is the length of the corresponding height. Geometry Figure 13 below shows a triangle: the length of the horizontal base of the triangle is denoted by b and the length of the corresponding vertical height is denoted by h.

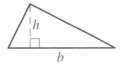

Geometry Figure 13

Any side of a triangle can be used as a base; the height that corresponds to the base is the perpendicular line segment from the opposite vertex to the base (or an extension of the base). Depending on the context, the term "base" can also refer to the *length* of a side of the triangle, and the term "height" can refer to the *length* of the perpendicular line segment from the opposite vertex to that side. The examples in Geometry Figure 14 below show three different configurations of a base and the corresponding height.

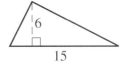  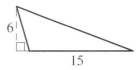

Geometry Figure 14

In all three triangles in Geometry Figure 14 above, the area is $\frac{(15)(6)}{2}$, or 45.

Congruent Triangles and Similar Triangles

Two triangles that have the same shape and size are called **congruent triangles**. More precisely, two triangles are congruent if their vertices can be matched up so that the corresponding angles and the corresponding sides are congruent.

By convention, the statement "triangles PQR and STU are congruent" does not just tell you that the two triangles are congruent, it also tells you what the corresponding parts of the two triangles are. In particular, because the letters in the name of the first triangle are given in the order PQR, and the letters in the name of the second triangle are given in the order STU, the statement tells you that angle P is congruent to angle S, angle Q is congruent to angle T, and angle R is congruent to angle U. It also tells you that sides PQ, QR, and PR in triangle PQR are congruent to sides ST, TU, and SU in triangle STU, respectively.

The following three propositions can be used to determine whether two triangles are congruent by comparing only some of their sides and angles.

Proposition 1: If the three sides of one triangle are congruent to the three sides of another triangle, then the triangles are congruent. This proposition is called Side-Side-Side, or SSS, congruence.

Proposition 2: If two sides and the included angle of one triangle are congruent to two sides and the included angle of another triangle, then the triangles are congruent. This proposition is called Side-Angle-Side, or SAS, congruence.

Proposition 3: If two angles and the included side of one triangle are congruent to two angles and the included side of another triangle, then the triangles are congruent. This proposition is called Angle-Side-Angle, or ASA, congruence. Note that if two angles of one triangle are congruent to two angles of another triangle, then the remaining angles are also congruent to each other, since the sum of the angle measures in any triangle is 180 degrees. Therefore, a similar proposition, called Angle-Angle-Side, or AAS, congruence, follows from ASA congruence.

Two triangles that have the same shape but not necessarily the same size are called **similar triangles**. More precisely, two triangles are similar if their vertices can be matched up so that the corresponding angles are congruent or, equivalently, the lengths of the corresponding sides have the same ratio, called the **scale factor of similarity**. For example, all 30°-60°-90° right triangles are similar triangles, though they may differ in size.

Geometry Figure 15 below shows two similar triangles, triangle ABC and triangle DEF.

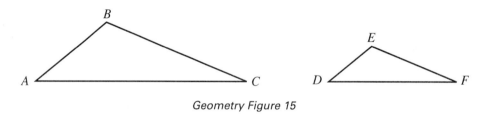

Geometry Figure 15

As with the convention for congruent triangles, the letters in similar triangles ABC and DEF indicate their corresponding parts.

Since triangles ABC and DEF are similar, we have $\dfrac{AB}{DE} = \dfrac{BC}{EF} = \dfrac{AC}{DF}$. By cross multiplication, we can obtain other proportions, such as $\dfrac{AB}{BC} = \dfrac{DE}{EF}$.

3.4 Quadrilaterals

Every quadrilateral has four sides and four interior angles. The measures of the interior angles add up to 360°.

Special Types of Quadrilaterals

The following are four special types of quadrilaterals.

Type 1: A quadrilateral with four right angles is called a **rectangle**. Opposite sides of a rectangle are parallel and congruent, and the two diagonals are also congruent.

Geometry Figure 16 below shows rectangle *ABCD*. In rectangle *ABCD*, opposite sides *AD* and *BC* are parallel and congruent, opposite sides *AB* and *DC* are parallel and congruent, and diagonal *AC* is congruent to diagonal *BD*.

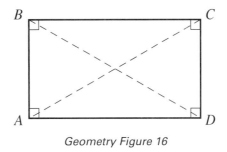

Geometry Figure 16

Type 2: A rectangle with four congruent sides is called a **square**.

Type 3: A quadrilateral in which both pairs of opposite sides are parallel is called a **parallelogram**. In a parallelogram, opposite sides are congruent and opposite angles are congruent.

Note that all rectangles are parallelograms.

Geometry Figure 17 below shows parallelogram *PQRS*. In parallelogram *PQRS*:

Opposite sides *PQ* and *SR* are parallel and congruent.
Opposite sides *QR* and *PS* are parallel and congruent.
Opposite angles *Q* and *S* are congruent.
Opposite angles *P* and *R* are congruent.

In the figure, angles *Q* and *S* are both labeled $x°$, and angles *P* and *R* are both labeled $y°$.

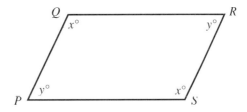

Geometry Figure 17

Type 4: A quadrilateral in which at least one pair of opposite sides is parallel is called a **trapezoid**. Two opposite, parallel sides of the trapezoid are called **bases** of the trapezoid.

Geometry Figure 18 below shows trapezoid *KLMN*. In trapezoid *KLMN*, horizontal side *KN* is parallel to horizontal side *LM*. Sides *KN* and *LM* are the bases of the trapezoid.

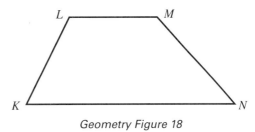

Geometry Figure 18

The Areas of the Special Types of Quadrilaterals

For all parallelograms, including rectangles and squares, the **area** A is given by the formula

$$A = bh$$

where b is the length of a base and h is the length of the corresponding height.

    Any side of a parallelogram can be used as a base. The height corresponding to the base is the perpendicular line segment from any point on the side opposite the base to the base (or an extension of that base). Depending on the context, the term "base" can also refer to the *length* of a side of the parallelogram, and the term "height" can refer to the *length* of the perpendicular line segment from that side to the opposite side. Examples of finding the areas of a rectangle and a parallelogram are shown in Geometry Figure 19 below.

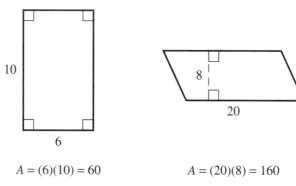

$$A = (6)(10) = 60 \qquad\qquad A = (20)(8) = 160$$

Geometry Figure 19

The **area** A of a trapezoid is given by the formula

$$A = \frac{1}{2}(b_1 + b_2)(h)$$

where b_1 and b_2 are the lengths of the bases of the trapezoid, and h is the corresponding height. For example, for the trapezoid in Geometry Figure 20 below with bases of length 10 and 18 and a height of 7.5, the area is

$$\frac{1}{2}(10 + 18)(7.5) = 105$$

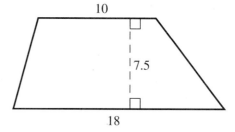

Geometry Figure 20

3.5 Circles

Given a point O in a plane and a positive number r, the set of points in the plane that are a distance of r units from O is called a **circle**. The point O is called the **center** of the circle and the distance r is called the **radius** of the circle. The **diameter** of the circle is twice the radius. Two circles with equal radii are called **congruent circles**.

Any line segment joining two points on the circle is called a **chord**. The terms "radius" and "diameter" can also refer to line segments: A **radius** is any line segment joining a point on the circle and the center of the circle, and a **diameter** is a chord that passes through the center of the circle. In Geometry Figure 21 below, O is the center of the circle, r is length of a radius, PQ is a chord, and ST is a diameter, as well as a chord.

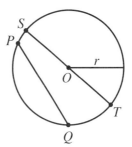

Geometry Figure 21

The distance around a circle is called the **circumference** of the circle, which is analogous to the perimeter of a polygon. The ratio of the circumference C to the diameter d is the same for all circles and is denoted by the Greek letter π; that is,

$$\frac{C}{d} = \pi$$

The value of π is approximately 3.14 and can also be approximated by the fraction $\frac{22}{7}$.

If r is the radius of a circle, then $\frac{C}{d} = \frac{C}{2r} = \pi$, and so the circumference is related to the radius by the equation

$$C = 2\pi r$$

For example, if a circle has a radius of 5.2, then its circumference is
$$(2)(\pi)(5.2) = (10.4)(\pi) \approx (10.4)(3.14)$$

which is approximately 32.7.

Given any two points on a circle, an **arc** is the part of the circle containing the two points and all the points between them. Two points on a circle are always the endpoints of two arcs. An arc is frequently identified by three points to avoid ambiguity. In Geometry Figure 22 below, there are four points on a circle. Going clockwise around the circle, the four points are A, B, C, and D. There are two different arcs between points A and C: arc ABC is the shorter arc between A and C, and arc ADC is the longer arc between A and C.

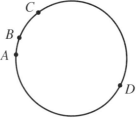

Geometry Figure 22

A **central angle** of a circle is an angle with its vertex at the center of the circle. The **measure of an arc** is the measure of its central angle, which is the angle formed by two radii that connect the center of the circle to the two endpoints of the arc. An entire circle is considered to be an arc with measure 360°.

In Geometry Figure 23 below, there are four points on a circle: points A, B, C, and D. It is given that the radius of the circle is 5.

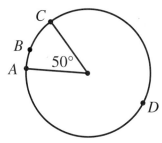

Geometry Figure 23

In Geometry Figure 23, the measure of the shorter arc between points A and C, that is arc ABC, is 50°; and the measure of the longer arc, between points A and C, that is arc ADC, is 310°.

To find the **length of an arc** of a circle, note that the ratio of the length of an arc to the circumference is equal to the ratio of the degree measure of the arc to 360°. For example, since the radius of the circle in Geometry Figure 23 is 5, the circumference of the circle is 10π. Therefore,

$$\frac{\text{length of arc } ABC}{10\pi} = \frac{50}{360}$$

Multiplying both sides by 10π gives

$$\text{length of arc } ABC = \frac{50}{360}(10\pi)$$

Then, since

$$\frac{50}{360}(10\pi) = \frac{25\pi}{18} \approx \frac{(25)(3.14)}{18} \approx 4.4$$

it follows that the length of arc ABC is approximately 4.4.

The **area** of a circle with radius r is equal to πr^2. For example, since the radius of the circle in Geometry Figure 23 above is 5, the area of the circle is $\pi(5^2) = 25\pi$.

A **sector** of a circle is a region bounded by an arc of the circle and two radii. To find the **area of a sector**, note that the ratio of the area of a sector of a circle to the area of the entire circle is equal to the ratio of the degree measure of its arc to 360°. For example, in the circle in Geometry Figure 23 the region bounded by arc ABC and the two radii is a sector with central angle 50°, and the radius of the circle is 5. Therefore, if S represents the area of the sector with central angle 50°, then

$$\frac{S}{25\pi} = \frac{50}{360}$$

Multiplying both sides by 25π gives

$$S = \left(\frac{50}{360}\right)(25\pi)$$

Then, since

$$\left(\frac{50}{360}\right)(25\pi) = \frac{125\pi}{36} \approx \frac{(125)(3.14)}{36} \approx 10.9$$

it follows that the area of the sector with central angle 50° is approximately 10.9.

A **tangent** to a circle is a line that lies in the same plane as the circle and intersects the circle at exactly one point, called the **point of tangency**. If a line is tangent to a circle, then a radius drawn to the point of tangency is perpendicular to the tangent line. The converse is also true; that is, if a radius and a line intersect at a point on the circle and the line is perpendicular to the radius, then the line is a tangent to the circle at the point of intersection. Geometry Figure 24 below shows a circle, a line tangent to the circle at point P, and a radius drawn to point P.

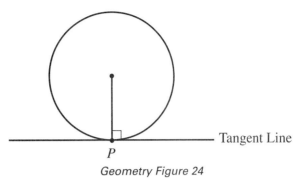

Geometry Figure 24

A polygon is **inscribed** in a circle if all its vertices lie on the circle, or equivalently, the circle is **circumscribed** about the polygon.

Geometry Figure 25 below shows triangle RST inscribed in a circle with center O. The center of the circle is inside the triangle.

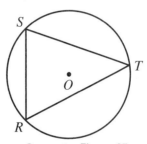

Geometry Figure 25

It is not always the case that if a triangle is inscribed in a circle, the center of the circle is inside the inscribed triangle. It is also possible for the center of the circle to be outside the inscribed triangle, or on one of the sides of the inscribed triangle. Note that if the center of the circle is on one of the sides of the inscribed triangle, that side is a diameter of the circle.

If one side of an inscribed triangle is a diameter of the circle, then the triangle is a right triangle. Conversely, if an inscribed triangle is a right triangle, then one of its sides is a diameter of the circle. Geometry Figure 26 below shows right triangle XYZ inscribed in a circle with center W. In triangle XYZ, side XZ is a diameter of the circle and angle Y is a right angle.

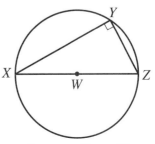

Geometry Figure 26

A polygon is circumscribed about a circle if each side of the polygon is tangent to the circle, or equivalently, the circle is inscribed in the polygon. Geometry Figure 27 below shows quadrilateral *ABCD* circumscribed about a circle with center *O*.

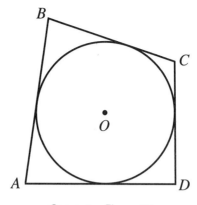

Geometry Figure 27

Two or more circles with the same center are called **concentric circles**, as shown in Geometry Figure 28 below.

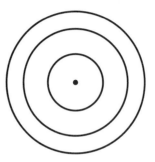

Geometry Figure 28

3.6 Three-Dimensional Figures

Basic three-dimensional figures include rectangular solids, cubes, cylinders, spheres, pyramids, and cones. In this section, we look at some properties of rectangular solids and right circular cylinders.

A **rectangular solid**, or **right rectangular prism**, has 6 rectangular surfaces called **faces**, as shown in Geometry Figure 29 below. Adjacent faces are perpendicular to each other. Each line segment that is the intersection of two faces is called an **edge**, and each point at which the edges intersect is called a **vertex**. There are 12 edges and 8 vertices. The dimensions of a rectangular solid are the length *l*, the width *w*, and the height *h*.

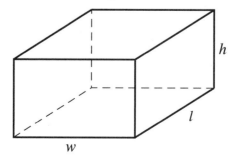

Geometry Figure 29

A rectangular solid with six square faces is called a **cube**, in which case $l = w = h$. The **volume** V of a rectangular solid is the product of its three dimensions, or

$$V = lwh$$

The **surface area** A of a rectangular solid is the sum of the areas of the six faces, or

$$A = 2(lw + lh + wh)$$

For example, if a rectangular solid has length 8.5, width 5, and height 10, then its volume is

$$V = (8.5)(5)(10) = 425$$

and its surface area is

$$A = 2((8.5)(5) + (8.5)(10) + (5)(10)) = 355$$

A **circular cylinder** consists of two bases that are congruent circles lying in parallel planes and a **lateral surface** made of all line segments that join points on the two circles and that are parallel to the line segment joining the centers of the two circles. The latter line segment is called the **axis** of the cylinder.

A **right circular cylinder** is a circular cylinder whose axis is perpendicular to its bases. The **height** of a right circular cylinder is the perpendicular distance between the two bases. Because the axis of a right circular cylinder is perpendicular to both bases, the height of a right circular cylinder is equal to the length of the axis.

The right circular cylinder shown in Geometry Figure 30 below has circular bases with centers P and Q. Line segment PQ is the axis of the cylinder and is perpendicular to both bases. The height of the cylinder is equal to the length of PQ.

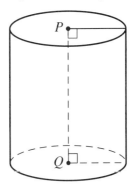

Geometry Figure 30

The **volume** V of a right circular cylinder that has height h and a base with radius r is the product of the height and the area of the base, or

$$V = \pi r^2 h$$

The **surface area** A of a right circular cylinder is the sum of the areas of the two bases and the area of its lateral surface, or

$$A = 2(\pi r^2) + 2\pi rh$$

For example, if a right circular cylinder has height 6.5 and a base with radius 3, then its volume is

$$V = \pi (3^2)(6.5) = 58.5\pi$$

and its surface area is

$$A = 2\pi (3^2) + 2\pi (3)(6.5) = 57\pi$$

GEOMETRY EXERCISES

Exercise 1. In Geometry Figure 31 below, the two horizontal lines are parallel. Find the values of x and y.

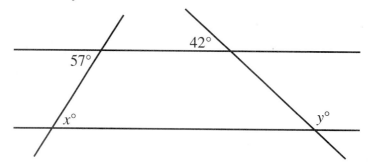

Geometry Figure 31

Exercise 2. In Geometry Figure 32 below, $AC = BC$. Find the values of x and y.

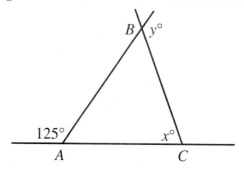

Geometry Figure 32

Exercise 3. In Geometry Figure 33 below, what is the relationship between x, y, and z?

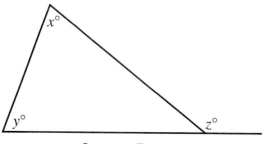

Geometry Figure 33

Exercise 4. What is the sum of the measures of the interior angles of a decagon (10-sided polygon)?

Exercise 5. If the polygon in exercise 4 is regular, what is the measure of each interior angle?

Exercise 6. The lengths of two sides of an isosceles triangle are 15 and 22. What are the possible values of the perimeter?

Exercise 7. Triangles PQR and XYZ are similar. If $PQ = 6$, $PR = 4$, and $XY = 9$, what is the length of side XZ?

Exercise 8. What are the lengths of sides NO and OP of triangle NOP in Geometry Figure 34 below?

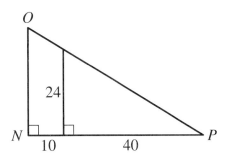

Geometry Figure 34

Exercise 9.   In Geometry Figure 35 below, $AB = BC = CD$. If the area of triangle CDE is 42, what is the area of triangle ADG?

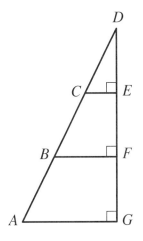

Geometry Figure 35

Exercise 10.   In Geometry Figure 36 below, $ABCD$ is a rectangle, $AB = 5$, $AF = 7$, and $FD = 3$. Find the following.

(a) The area of rectangle $ABCD$

(b) The area of triangle AEF

(c) The length of diagonal BD

(d) The perimeter of rectangle $ABCD$

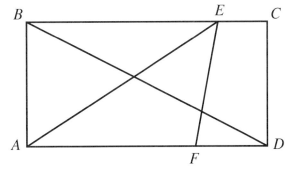

Geometry Figure 36

Exercise 11.   In Geometry Figure 37 below, *ABCD* is a parallelogram. Find the following.

(a) The area of *ABCD*

(b) The perimeter of *ABCD*

(c) The length of diagonal *BD*

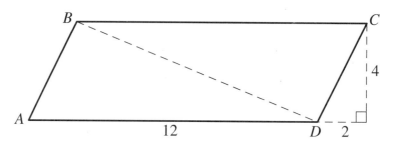

Geometry Figure 37

Exercise 12.   In Geometry Figure 38 below, the circle with center *O* has radius 4. Find the following.

(a) The circumference of the circle

(b) The length of arc *ABC*

(c) The area of the shaded region

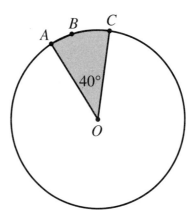

Geometry Figure 38

Exercise 13. Geometry Figure 39 below shows two concentric circles, each with center O. Given that the larger circle has radius 12 and the smaller circle has radius 7, find the following.

(a) The circumference of the larger circle

(b) The area of the smaller circle

(c) The area of the shaded region

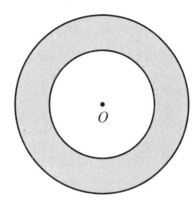

Geometry Figure 39

Exercise 14. For the rectangular solid in Geometry Figure 40 below, find the following.

(a) The surface area of the solid

(b) The length of diagonal AB

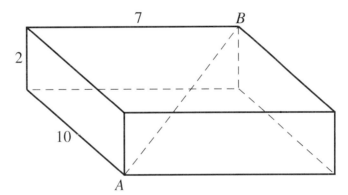

Geometry Figure 40

ANSWERS TO GEOMETRY EXERCISES

Exercise 1. $x = 57$ and $y = 138$

Exercise 2. $x = 70$ and $y = 125$

Exercise 3. $z = x + y$

Exercise 4. $1,440°$

Exercise 5. $144°$

Exercise 6.   52 and 59

Exercise 7.   6

Exercise 8.   The length of side NO is 30 and the length of side OP is $10\sqrt{34}$.

Exercise 9.   378

Exercise 10.   (a) 50

             (b) 17.5

             (c) $5\sqrt{5}$

             (d) 30

Exercise 11.   (a) 48

             (b) $24 + 4\sqrt{5}$

             (c) $2\sqrt{29}$

Exercise 12.   (a) 8π

             (b) $\dfrac{8\pi}{9}$

             (c) $\dfrac{16\pi}{9}$

Exercise 13.   (a) 24π

             (b) 49π

             (c) 95π

Exercise 14.   (a) 208

             (b) $3\sqrt{17}$

PART 4. DATA ANALYSIS

The review of data analysis begins with methods for presenting data, followed by counting methods and probability, and then progresses to distributions of data, random variables, and probability distributions. The review of data analysis ends with examples of data interpretation.

4.1 Methods for Presenting Data

Data can be organized and presented using a variety of methods. Tables are commonly used, and there are many graphical and numerical methods as well. In this section, we review tables and some common graphical methods for presenting and summarizing data.

In data analysis, a variable is any characteristic that can vary for a population of individuals or objects. Variables can be **quantitative**, or **numerical**, such as the age of individuals. Variables can also be **categorical**, or **nonnumerical**, such as the eye color of individuals.

Data are collected from a population by observing one or more variables. The **distribution of a variable**, or **distribution of data**, indicates how frequently different categorical or numerical data values are observed in the data.

> **Example 4.1.1**: In a population of students in a sixth-grade classroom, a variable that can be observed is the height of each student. Note that the variable in this example is numerical.

> **Example 4.1.2**: In a population of voters in a city's mayoral election, a variable that can be observed is the candidate that each voter voted for. Note that the variable in this example is nonnumerical.

The **frequency**, or **count**, of a particular category or numerical value is the number of times that the category or numerical value appears in the data. A **frequency distribution** is a table or graph that presents the categories or numerical values along with their corresponding frequencies. The **relative frequency** of a category or a numerical value is the corresponding frequency divided by the total number of data. Relative frequencies may be expressed in terms of percents, fractions, or decimals. A **relative frequency distribution** is a table or graph that presents the relative frequencies of the categories or numerical values.

Tables

Tables are used to present a wide variety of data, including frequency distributions and relative frequency distributions. The rows and columns provide clear associations between categories and data. A frequency distribution is often presented as a 2-column table in which the categories or numerical values of the data are listed in the first column and the corresponding frequencies are listed in the second column. A relative frequency distribution table has the same layout but with relative frequencies instead of frequencies. When data include a large number of categories or numerical values, the categories or values are often grouped together in a smaller number of groups and the corresponding frequencies are given.

Example 4.1.3: A survey was taken to find the number of children in each of 25 families. A list of the 25 values collected in the survey follows.

1 2 0 4 1 3 3 1 2 0 4 5 2 3 2 3 2 4 1 2 3 0 2 3 1

Here are tables that present the resulting frequency distribution and relative frequency distribution of the data.

Frequency Distribution

Number of Children	Frequency
0	3
1	5
2	7
3	6
4	3
5	1
Total	25

Relative Frequency Distribution

Number of Children	Relative Frequency
0	12%
1	20%
2	28%
3	24%
4	12%
5	4%
Total	100%

Note that in the relative frequency distribution table the relative frequencies are expressed as percents and that the total for the relative frequencies is 100%. If the relative frequencies were expressed as decimals or fractions instead of percents, the total would be 1.

Example 4.1.4: Thirty students took a history test. Here is a list of the 30 scores on the test, from least to greatest.

62 63 68 70 72 72 72 75 76 76 76 76 78 78 82
82 85 85 85 85 85 86 87 88 91 91 92 95 97 100

The 30 students achieved 18 different scores on the test. Displaying the frequency distribution of this many different scores would make the frequency distribution table very large, so instead we group the scores into four groups: the scores from 61 to 70, the scores from 71 to 80, the scores from 81 to 90, and the scores from 91 to 100. Here is the frequency distribution of the scores with these groups.

Score	Frequency
61 to 70	4
71 to 80	10
81 to 90	10
91 to 100	6

In addition to being used to present frequency and relative frequency distributions, tables are used to display a wide variety of other data. Here are two examples.

Example 4.1.5: The following table shows the annual per capita income in a certain state, from 1930 to 1980.

Year	Annual Per Capita Income
1930	$656
1940	$680
1950	$1,717
1960	$2,437
1970	$4,198
1980	$10,291

Example 4.1.6: The following table shows the closest and farthest distance of the eight planets from the Sun, in millions of kilometers.

Planet	Closest Distance from the Sun (in millions of kilometers)	Farthest Distance from the Sun (in millions of kilometers)
Mercury	46	70
Venus	107	109
Earth	147	152
Mars	205	249
Jupiter	741	817
Saturn	1,350	1,510
Uranus	2,750	3,000
Neptune	4,450	4,550

Bar Graphs

A frequency distribution or relative frequency distribution of data collected from a population by observing one or more variables can be presented using a **bar graph**, or **bar chart**. In a bar graph, each of the data categories or numerical values is represented by a rectangular bar, and the height of each bar is proportional to the corresponding frequency or relative frequency. All of the bars are drawn with the same width, and the bars can be presented either vertically or horizontally. When data include a large number of different categories of numerical values, the categories or values are often grouped together in several groups and the corresponding frequencies or relative frequencies are given. Bar graphs enable comparisons across several categories more easily than tables do. For example, in a bar graph it is easy to identify the category with the greatest frequency by looking for the bar with the greatest height.

Here are two examples of frequency distributions presented as bar graphs.

Example 4.1.7: Data Analysis Figure 1 is a bar graph with vertical bars. It shows the frequency distribution of one variable, fall 2009 enrollment. The variable is observed for five data categories, Colleges *A*, *B*, *C*, *D*, and *E*.

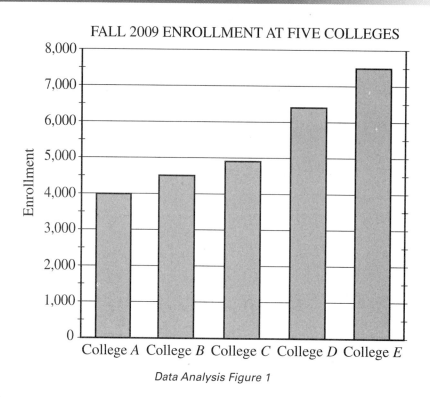

Data Analysis Figure 1

From the graph, we can conclude that the college with the greatest fall 2009 enrollment was College *E* and the college with the least enrollment was College *A*. Also, we can estimate that the enrollment for College *D* was about 6,400.

Example 4.1.8: Data Analysis Figure 2 is a bar graph with vertical bars. It shows the frequency distributions of two variables, fall 2009 enrollment and spring 2010 enrollment. Both variables are observed for three data categories, Colleges *A*, *B*, and *C*.

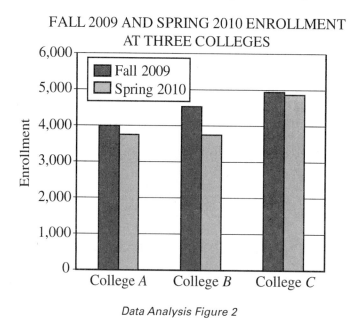

Data Analysis Figure 2

Observe that for all three colleges, the fall 2009 enrollment was greater than the spring 2010 enrollment. Also, the greatest decrease in the enrollment from fall 2009 to spring 2010 occurred at College B.

Segmented Bar Graphs

A **segmented bar graph**, or **stacked bar graph**, is similar to a regular bar graph except that in a segmented bar graph, each rectangular bar is divided, or segmented, into smaller rectangles that show how the variable is "separated" into other related variables. For example, rectangular bars representing enrollment can be divided into two smaller rectangles, one representing full-time enrollment and the other representing part-time enrollment, as shown in the following example.

Example 4.1.9: In Data Analysis Figure 3, the fall 2009 enrollment at the five colleges shown in Data Analysis Figure 1 is presented again, but this time each bar has been divided into two segments: one representing full-time enrollment and one representing part-time enrollment.

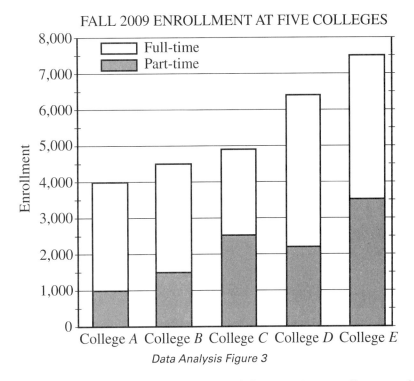

Data Analysis Figure 3

The total enrollment, the full-time enrollment, and the part-time enrollment at the five colleges can be estimated from the segmented bar graph in Data Analysis Figure 3. For example, for College D, the total enrollment was a little below 6,500, or approximately 6,400 students; the part-time enrollment was approximately 2,200; and the full-time enrollment was approximately $6,400 - 2,200$, or 4,200 students.

Although bar graphs are commonly used to compare frequencies, as in the examples above, they are sometimes used to compare numerical data that could be displayed in a table, such as temperatures, dollar amounts, percents, heights, and weights. Also, the categories sometimes are numerical in nature, such as years or other time intervals.

Histograms

When a list of data is large and contains many different values of a numerical variable, it is useful to organize the data by grouping the values into intervals, often called classes. To do this, divide the entire interval of values into smaller intervals of equal length and then count the values that fall into each interval. In this way, each interval has a frequency and a relative frequency. The intervals and their frequencies (or relative frequencies) are often displayed in a **histogram**. Histograms are graphs of frequency distributions that are similar to bar graphs, but they must have a number line for the horizontal axis, which represents the numerical variable. Also, in a histogram, there are no regular spaces between the bars. Any spaces between bars in a histogram indicate that there are no data in the intervals represented by the spaces.

Example 4.5.1 in Section 4.5 illustrates a histogram with 50 bars.

Numerical variables with just a few values can also be displayed using histograms, where the frequency or relative frequency of each value is represented by a bar centered over the value.

Example 4.1.10: In Example 4.1.3, the relative frequency distribution of the number of children of each of 25 families was presented as a 2-column table. For convenience, the table is repeated below.

Relative Frequency Distribution

Number of Children	Relative Frequency
0	12%
1	20%
2	28%
3	24%
4	12%
5	4%
Total	100%

This relative frequency distribution can also be displayed as a histogram, as shown in the following figure.

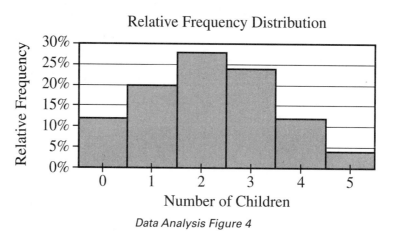

Relative Frequency Distribution

Data Analysis Figure 4

Histograms are useful for identifying the general shape of a distribution of data. Also evident are the "center" and degree of "spread" of the distribution, as well as high-frequency and low-frequency intervals. From the histogram in Data Analysis Figure 4 above, you can see that the distribution is shaped like a mound with one peak; that is, the data are frequent in the middle and sparse at both ends. The central values are 2 and 3, and the distribution is close to being symmetric about those values. Because the bars all have the same width, the area of each bar is proportional to the amount of data that the bar represents. Thus, the areas of the bars indicate where the data are concentrated and where they are not.

Finally, note that because each bar has a width of 1, the sum of the areas of the bars equals the sum of the relative frequencies, which is 100% or 1, depending on whether percents or decimals are used. This fact is central to the discussion of probability distributions in Section 4.5.

Circle Graphs

Circle graphs, often called **pie charts**, are used to represent data that have been separated into a small number of categories. They illustrate how a whole is separated into parts. The data are presented in a circle such that the area of the circle representing each category is proportional to the part of the whole that the category represents.

A circle graph may be used to represent a frequency distribution or a relative frequency distribution. More generally, a circle graph may represent any total amount that is distributed into a small number of categories, as in the following example.

Example 4.1.11:

UNITED STATES PRODUCTION OF PHOTOGRAPHIC
EQUIPMENT AND SUPPLIES IN 1971

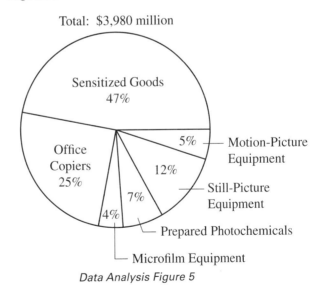

Data Analysis Figure 5

From the graph you can see that Sensitized Goods is the category with the greatest dollar value.

Each part of a circle graph is called a **sector**. Because the area of each sector is proportional to the percent of the whole that the sector represents, the measure of the central angle of a sector is proportional to the percent of 360 degrees that the sector represents.

For example, the measure of the central angle of the sector representing the category Prepared Photochemicals is 7 percent of 360 degrees, or 25.2 degrees.

Scatterplots

A **scatterplot** is a type of graph that is useful for showing the relationship between two numerical variables whose values can be observed in a single population of individuals or objects. In a scatterplot, the values of one variable appear on the horizontal axis of a rectangular coordinate system and the values of the other variable appear on the vertical axis. For each individual or object in the data, an ordered pair of numbers is collected, one number for each variable, and the pair is represented by a point in the coordinate system.

A scatterplot makes it possible to observe an overall pattern, or **trend**, in the relationship between the two variables. Also, the strength of the trend as well as striking deviations from the trend are evident. In many cases, a line or a curve that best represents the trend is also displayed in the graph and is used to make predictions about the population.

Example 4.1.12: A bicycle trainer studied 50 bicyclists to examine how the finishing time for a certain bicycle race was related to the amount of physical training each bicyclist did in the three months before the race. To measure the amount of training, the trainer developed a training index, measured in "units" and based on the intensity of each bicyclist's training. The data and the trend of the data, represented by a line, are displayed in the scatterplot in Data Analysis Figure 6 below.

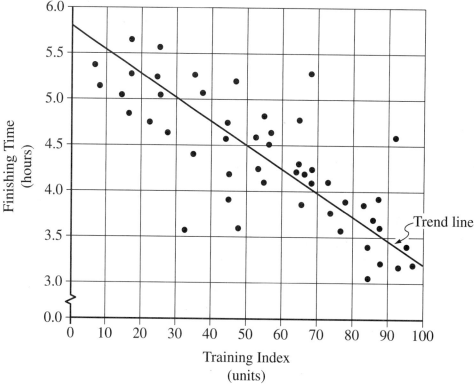

Data Analysis Figure 6

When a trend line is included in the presentation of a scatterplot, you can observe how scattered or close the data are to the trend line, or to put it another way, how well the trend line fits the data. In the scatterplot in Data Analysis Figure 6 above, almost all of the data points are relatively close to the trend line. The scatterplot also shows that the finishing times generally decrease as the training indices increase.

The trend line can be used to make predictions. For example, it can be predicted, based on the trend line, that a bicyclist with a training index of 70 units will finish the race in approximately 4 hours. This value is obtained by noting that the vertical line at the training index of 70 units intersects the trend line very close to 4 hours.

Another prediction that can be made, based on the trend line, is the approximate number of minutes by which a bicyclist will lower their finishing time for each increase of 10 training index units. This prediction is derived from the ratio of the change in finishing time to the change in training index, or the slope of the trend line. Note that the slope is negative. To estimate the slope, estimate the coordinates of any two points on the line, for instance, the points at the extreme left and right ends of the line: (0, 5.8) and (100, 3.2). The slope, which is measured in hours per unit, can be computed as follows:

$$\frac{3.2 - 5.8}{100 - 0} = \frac{-2.6}{100} = -0.026$$

The slope can be interpreted as follows: The finishing time is predicted to decrease 0.026 hour for every unit by which the training index increases. Since we want to know how much the finishing time decreases for an increase of *10 units*, we multiply the rate by 10 to get 0.26 hour per 10 units. To compute the decrease in *minutes* per 10 units, we multiply 0.26 by 60 to get approximately 16 minutes. Based on the trend line, it can be predicted that the bicyclist will decrease their finishing time by approximately 16 minutes for every increase of 10 training index units.

Line Graphs

A **line graph** is another type of graph that is useful for showing the relationship between two numerical variables, especially if one of the variables is time. A line graph uses a coordinate plane, where each data point represents a pair of values observed for the two numerical variables. There is at most one data point for each value on the horizontal axis, similar to a function. The data points are in order from left to right, and consecutive data points are connected by a line segment.

When one of the variables is time, it is associated with the horizontal axis, which is labeled with regular time intervals. The data points may represent an interval of time, such as an entire day or year, or just an instant of time. Such a line graph is often called a **time series**.

Example 4.1.13:

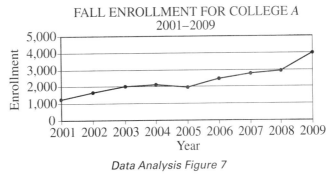

Data Analysis Figure 7

The line graph shows that the greatest increase in fall enrollment between consecutive years was the change from 2008 to 2009. One way to determine this is by noting that the slope of the line segment joining the values for 2008 and 2009 is greater than the slopes of the line segments joining all other consecutive years. Another way to determine this is by noting that the increase in enrollment from 2008 to 2009 was greater than 1,000, but all other increases in enrollment were less than 1,000.

Although line graphs are commonly used to compare frequencies, as in Example 4.1.13 above, they can be used to compare any numerical data as the data change over time, such as temperatures, dollar amounts, percents, heights, and weights.

4.2 Numerical Methods for Describing Data

Data can be described numerically by various **statistics**, or **statistical measures**. These statistical measures are often grouped in three categories: measures of central tendency, measures of position, and measures of dispersion.

Measures of Central Tendency

Measures of **central tendency** indicate the "center" of the data along the number line and are usually reported as values that represent the data. There are three common measures of central tendency:

1. the **arithmetic mean**—usually called the **average** or simply the **mean**
2. the **median**
3. the **mode**

To calculate the **mean** of n numbers, take the sum of the n numbers and divide it by n.

Example 4.2.1: For the five numbers 6, 4, 7, 10, and 4, the mean is

$$\frac{6+4+7+10+4}{5} = \frac{31}{5} = 6.2.$$

When several values are repeated in a list, it is helpful to think of the mean of the numbers as a **weighted mean** of only those values in the list that are *different*.

Example 4.2.2: Consider the following list of 16 numbers.

$$2, 4, 4, 5, 7, 7, 7, 7, 7, 7, 8, 8, 9, 9, 9, 9$$

There are only 6 different values in the list: 2, 4, 5, 7, 8, and 9. The mean of the numbers in the list can be computed as

$$\frac{1(2)+2(4)+1(5)+6(7)+2(8)+4(9)}{1+2+1+6+2+4} = \frac{109}{16} = 6.8125$$

The number of times a value appears in the list, or the frequency, is called the **weight** of that value. So the mean of the 16 numbers is the weighted mean of the values 2, 4, 5, 7, 8, and 9, where the respective weights are 1, 2, 1, 6, 2, and 4. Note that the sum of the weights is the number of numbers in the list, 16.

The mean can be affected by just a few values that lie far above or below the rest of the data, because these values contribute directly to the sum of the data and therefore to the mean. By contrast, the **median** is a measure of central tendency that is fairly unaffected by unusually high or low values relative to the rest of the data.

To calculate the median of n numbers, first order the numbers from least to greatest. If n is odd, then the median is the middle number in the ordered list of numbers. If n is even, then there are *two* middle numbers, and the median is the average of these two numbers.

Example 4.2.3: The five numbers 6, 4, 7, 10, and 4 listed in increasing order are 4, 4, 6, 7, 10, so the median is 6, the middle number. Note that if the number 10 in the list is replaced by the number 24, the mean increases from 6.2 to

$$\frac{4+4+6+7+24}{5} = \frac{45}{5} = 9$$

but the median remains equal to 6. This example shows how the median is relatively unaffected by an unusually large value.

The median, as the "middle value" of an ordered list of numbers, divides the list into roughly two equal parts. However, if the median is equal to one of the data values and it is repeated in the list, then the numbers of data above and below the median may be rather different. For example, the median of the 16 numbers 2, 4, 4, 5, 7, 7, 7, 7, 7, 7, 8, 8, 9, 9, 9, 9 is 7, but four of the data are less than 7 and six of the data are greater than 7.

The **mode** of a list of numbers is the number that occurs most frequently in the list.

Example 4.2.4: The mode of the 6 numbers in the list 1, 3, 6, 4, 3, 5 is 3. A list of numbers may have more than one mode. For example, the list of 11 numbers 1, 2, 3, 3, 3, 5, 7, 10, 10, 10, 20 has two modes, 3 and 10.

Measures of Position

The three most basic **positions**, or locations, in a list of numerical data ordered from least to greatest are the beginning, the end, and the middle. It is useful here to label these as L for the least, G for the greatest, and M for the median. Aside from these, the most common measures of position are **quartiles** and **percentiles**. Like the median M, quartiles and percentiles are numbers that divide the data into roughly equal groups after the data have been ordered from the least value L to the greatest value G. There are three quartile numbers, called the **first quartile**, the **second quartile**, and the **third quartile**, that divide the data into four roughly equal groups; and there are 99 percentile numbers that divide the data into 100 roughly equal groups. As with the mean and median, the quartiles and percentiles may or may not themselves be values in the data.

In the following discussion of quartiles, the symbol Q_1 will be used to denote the first quartile, Q_2 will be used to denote the second quartile, and Q_3 will be used to denote the third quartile.

The numbers Q_1, Q_2, and Q_3 divide the data into 4 roughly equal groups as follows. After the data are listed in increasing order, the first group consists of the data from L to Q_1, the second group is from Q_1 to Q_2, the third group is from Q_2 to Q_3, and the fourth group is from Q_3 to G. Because the number of data may not be divisible by 4, there are various rules to determine the exact values of Q_1 and Q_3, and some statisticians use different rules, but in all cases Q_2 is equal to the median M. We use perhaps the most common rule for determining the values of Q_1 and Q_3. According to this rule, after the data are listed in increasing order, Q_1 is the median of the first half of the data in the ordered list and Q_3 is the median of the second half of the data in the ordered list, as illustrated in the following example.

Example 4.2.5: To find the quartiles for the list of 16 numbers 2, 4, 4, 5, 7, 7, 7, 7, 7, 7, 8, 8, 9, 9, 9, 9 (which are already listed in increasing order), first divide the numbers in the list into two groups of 8 numbers each. The first group of 8 numbers is 2, 4, 4, 5, 7, 7, 7, 7, and the second group of 8 numbers is 7, 7, 8, 8, 9, 9, 9, 9, so that the second quartile, or median, is 7. To find the other quartiles, you can take each of the two smaller groups and find its median: the first quartile, Q_1, is 6 (the average of 5 and 7) and the third quartile, Q_3, is 8.5 (the average of 8 and 9).

In this example, note that the number 4 is in the lowest 25 percent of the distribution of data. There are different ways to describe this. We can say that 4 is below the first quartile, that is, below Q_1. We can also say that 4 is *in* the first quartile. The phrase "in a quartile" refers to being in one of the four groups determined by Q_1, Q_2, and Q_3.

Percentiles are mostly used for very large lists of numerical data ordered from least to greatest. Instead of dividing the data into four groups, the 99 percentiles P_1, P_2, P_3, ..., P_{99} divide the data into 100 groups. Consequently, $Q_1 = P_{25}$, $M = Q_2 = P_{50}$, and $Q_3 = P_{75}$. Because the number of data in a list may not be divisible by 100, statisticians apply various rules to determine values of percentiles.

Measures of Dispersion

Measures of **dispersion** indicate the degree of spread of the data. The most common statistics used as measures of dispersion are the range, the interquartile range, and the standard deviation. These statistics measure the spread of the data in different ways.

The **range** of the numbers in a group of data is the difference between the greatest number G in the data and the least number L in the data; that is, $G - L$. For example, the range of the five numbers 11, 10, 5, 13, 21 is $21 - 5 = 16$.

The simplicity of the range is useful in that it reflects the maximum spread of the data. Sometimes a data value is unusually small or unusually large in comparison with the rest of the data. Such data are called **outliers** because they lie so far out from the rest of the data. The range is directly affected by outliers.

A measure of dispersion that is not usually affected by outliers is the **interquartile range**. It is defined as the difference between the third quartile and the first quartile; that is, $Q_3 - Q_1$. Thus, the interquartile range measures the spread of the middle half of the data.

One way to summarize a group of numerical data and to illustrate its center and spread is to use the five numbers L, Q_1, Q_2, Q_3 and G. These five numbers can be plotted along a number line to show where the four quartile groups lie. Such plots are called **boxplots** or **box-and-whisker plots**, because a box is used to identify each of the two middle quartile groups of data, and "whiskers" extend outward from the boxes to the least and greatest values.

Example 4.2.6: In the list of 16 numbers 2, 4, 4, 5, 7, 7, 7, 7, 7, 7, 8, 8, 9, 9, 9, 9, the range is $9 - 2 = 7$, the first quartile, $Q_1 = 6$, and the third quartile, $Q_3 = 8.5$. So the interquartile range for the numbers in this list is $8.5 - 6 = 2.5$.

A boxplot for this list of 16 numbers is shown in the following figure.

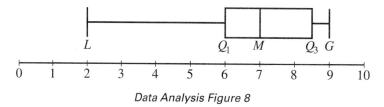

Data Analysis Figure 8

There are a few variations in the way boxplots are drawn—the position of the ends of the boxes can vary slightly, and some boxplots identify outliers with certain symbols—but all boxplots show the center of the data at the median and illustrate the spread of the data in each of the four quartile groups. As such, boxplots are useful for comparing sets of data side by side.

Example 4.2.7: Two large lists of numerical data, list 1 and list 2, are summarized by the boxplots in the following figure.

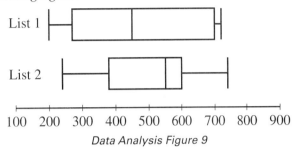

Data Analysis Figure 9

Based on the boxplots, several different comparisons of the two lists can be made. First, the median of list 2, which is approximately 550, is greater than the median of list 1, which is approximately 450. Second, the two measures of spread, range and interquartile range, are greater for list 1 than for list 2. For list 1, these measures are approximately 520 and 430, respectively, and for list 2, they are approximately 500 and 220, respectively.

Unlike the range and the interquartile range, the **standard deviation** is a measure of spread that depends on each number in the list. Using the mean as the center of the data, the standard deviation takes into account how much each value differs from the mean and then takes a type of average of these differences. As a result, the more the data are spread away from the mean, the greater the standard deviation; and the more the data are clustered around the mean, the lesser the standard deviation.

The standard deviation of a group of numerical data is computed by

1. calculating the mean of the values,
2. finding the difference between the mean and each of the values,
3. squaring each of the differences,
4. finding the average of the squared differences, and
5. taking the nonnegative square root of the average of the squared differences.

Example 4.2.8: For the five data 0, 7, 8, 10, and 10, the standard deviation can be computed as follows. First, the mean of the data is 7, and the squared differences from the mean are

$$(7-0)^2, (7-7)^2, (7-8)^2, (7-10)^2, (7-10)^2$$

or 49, 0, 1, 9, 9. The average of the five squared differences is $\frac{68}{5}$, or 13.6, and the positive square root of 13.6 is approximately 3.7.

Note on terminology: The term "standard deviation" defined above is slightly different from another measure of dispersion, the **sample standard deviation**. The latter term is qualified with the word "sample" and is computed by dividing the sum of the squared differences by $n-1$ instead of n. The sample standard deviation is only slightly different from the standard deviation but is preferred for technical reasons for a sample of data that is taken from a larger population of data. Sometimes the standard deviation is called the **population standard deviation** to help distinguish it from the sample standard deviation.

Example 4.2.9: Six hundred applicants for several post office jobs were rated on a scale from 1 to 50 points. The ratings had a mean of 32.5 points and a standard deviation of 7.1 points. How many standard deviations above or below the mean is a rating of 48 points? A rating of 30 points? A rating of 20 points?

Solution: Let d be the standard deviation, so $d = 7.1$ points. Note that 1 standard deviation above the mean is

$$32.5 + d = 32.5 + 7.1 = 39.6$$

and 2 standard deviations above the mean is

$$32.5 + 2d = 32.5 + 2(7.1) = 46.7$$

Using the same reasoning, if 48 is r standard deviations above the mean, then

$$32.5 + rd = 32.5 + r(7.1) = 48$$

Solving the equation $32.5 + r(7.1) = 48$ for r gives

$$r = \frac{48 - 32.5}{7.1} = \frac{15.5}{7.1} \approx 2.2$$

Similarly, any rating of p points is $\dfrac{p - 32.5}{7.1}$ standard deviations from the mean.

The number of standard deviations that a rating of 30 is away from the mean is

$$\frac{30 - 32.5}{7.1} = \frac{-2.5}{7.1} \approx -0.4$$

where the negative sign indicates that the rating is 0.4 standard deviation *below* the mean.

The number of standard deviations that a rating of 20 is away from the mean is

$$\frac{20 - 32.5}{7.1} = \frac{-12.5}{7.1} \approx -1.8$$

where the negative sign indicates that the rating is 1.8 standard deviations *below* the mean.

To summarize:

1. 48 points is 15.5 points above the mean, or approximately 2.2 standard deviations above the mean.
2. 30 points is 2.5 points below the mean, or approximately 0.4 standard deviation below the mean.
3. 20 points is 12.5 points below the mean, or approximately 1.8 standard deviations below the mean.

One more instance, which may seem trivial, is important to note:

32.5 points is 0 points from the mean, or 0 standard deviations from the mean.

Example 4.2.9 above shows that for a group of data, each value can be located with respect to the mean by using the standard deviation as a ruler. The process of subtracting the mean from each value and then dividing the result by the standard deviation is called

standardization. Standardization is a useful tool because for each data value, it provides a measure of position relative to the rest of the data independently of the variable for which the data was collected and the units of the variable.

Note that the standardized values 2.2, –0.4, and –1.8 from the last example are all between –3 and 3; that is, the corresponding ratings 48, 30, and 20 are all within 3 standard deviations of the mean. This is not surprising, based on the following fact about the standard deviation.

Fact: In *any group of data*, most of the data are within 3 standard deviations of the mean.

Thus, when *any group of data* are standardized, most of the data are transformed to an interval on the number line centered about 0 and extending from –3 to 3. The mean is always transformed to 0.

4.3 Counting Methods

When a set contains a small number of objects, it is easy to list the objects and count them one by one. When the set is too large to count that way, and when the objects are related in a patterned or systematic way, there are some useful techniques for counting the objects without actually listing them.

Sets and Lists

The term **set** has been used informally in this review to mean a collection of objects that have some property, whether it is the collection of all positive integers, all points in a circular region, or all students in a school that have studied French. The objects of a set are called **members** or **elements**. Some sets are **finite**, which means that their members can be completely counted. Finite sets can, in principle, have all of their members listed, using curly brackets, such as the set of even digits {0, 2, 4, 6, 8}. Sets that are not finite are called **infinite** sets, such as the set of all integers. A set that has no members is called the **empty set** and is denoted by the symbol $\varnothing$. A set with one or more members is called **nonempty**. If A and B are sets and all of the members of A are also members of B, then A is a **subset** of B. For example, {2, 8} is a subset of {0, 2, 4, 6, 8}. Also, by convention, $\varnothing$ is a subset of every set.

A **list** is like a finite set, having members that can all be listed, but with two differences. In a list, the members are ordered—that is, rearranging the members of a list makes it a different list. Thus, the terms "first element," "second element," and so on, make sense in a list. Also, elements can be repeated in a list and the repetitions matter. For example, the list 1, 2, 3, 2 and the list 1, 2, 2, 3 are different lists, each with four elements, and they are both different from the list 1, 2, 3, which has three elements.

In contrast to a list, when the elements of a set are given, repetitions are not counted as additional elements and the order of the elements does not matter. For example, the set {1, 2, 3, 2} and the set {3, 1, 2} are the same set, which has three elements. For any finite set S, the number of elements of S is denoted by $|S|$. Thus, if S = {6.2, –9, π, 0.01,0}, then $|S|$ = 5. Also, $|\varnothing|$ = 0.

Sets can be formed from other sets. If S and T are sets, then the **intersection** of S and T is the set of all elements that are in both S and T and is denoted by $S \cap T$. The **union** of S and T is the set of all elements that are in either S or T or both and is denoted by $S \cup T$. If sets S and T have no elements in common, they are called **disjoint** or **mutually exclusive**.

A useful way to represent two or three sets and their possible intersections and unions is a **Venn diagram**. In a Venn diagram, sets are represented by circular regions that overlap if they have elements in common but do not overlap if they are disjoint. Sometimes the circular regions are drawn inside a rectangular region, which represents a **universal set**, of which all other sets involved are subsets.

Example 4.3.1: Data Analysis Figure 10 below is a Venn diagram using circular regions to represent the three sets A, B, and C. In the Venn diagram, the three circular regions are drawn in a rectangular region representing a universal set U.

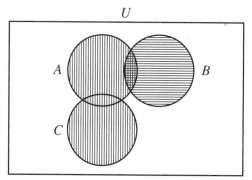

Data Analysis Figure 10

The regions with vertical stripes represent the set $A \cup C$. The regions with horizontal stripes represent the set B. The region with both kinds of stripes represents the set $A \cap B$. The sets B and C are mutually exclusive, often written as $B \cap C = \varnothing$.

The last example can be used to illustrate an elementary counting principle involving intersecting sets, called the **inclusion-exclusion principle**. This principle relates the numbers of elements in the union and intersection of two finite sets. The number of elements in the union of two sets equals the sum of their individual numbers of elements minus the number of elements in their intersection. If the sets in the example are finite, then we have for the union of A and B,

$$|A \cup B| = |A| + |B| - |A \cap B|$$

Because $A \cap B$ is a subset of both A and B, the subtraction is necessary to avoid counting the elements in $A \cap B$ twice. For the union of B and C, we have

$$|B \cup C| = |B| + |C|$$

because $B \cap C = \varnothing$.

Multiplication Principle

Suppose there are two choices to be made sequentially and that the second choice is independent of the first choice. Suppose also that there are k different possibilities for the first choice and m different possibilities for the second choice. The **multiplication principle** states that under those conditions, there are km different possibilities for the pair of choices.

For example, suppose that a meal is to be ordered from a restaurant menu and that the meal consists of one entrée and one dessert. If there are 5 entrées and 3 desserts on the menu, then there are (5)(3) = 15 different meals that can be ordered from the menu.

The multiplication principle applies in more complicated situations as well. If there are more than two independent choices to be made, then the number of different possible outcomes of all of the choices is the product of the numbers of possibilities for each choice.

Example 4.3.2: Suppose that a computer password consists of four characters such that the first character is one of the 10 digits from 0 to 9 and each of the next 3 characters is any one of the uppercase letters from the 26 letters of the English alphabet. How many different passwords are possible?

Solution: The description of the password allows repetitions of letters. Thus, there are 10 possible choices for the first character in the password and 26 possible choices for each of the next 3 characters in the password. Therefore, applying the multiplication principle, the number of possible passwords is (10)(26)(26)(26) = 175,760.

Note that if repetitions of letters are not allowed in the password, then the choices are not all independent, but a modification of the multiplication principle can still be applied. There are 10 possible choices for the first character in the password, 26 possible choices for the second character, 25 for the third character because the first letter cannot be repeated, and 24 for the fourth character because the first two letters cannot be repeated. Therefore, the number of possible passwords is (10)(26)(25)(24) = 156,000.

Example 4.3.3: Each time a coin is tossed, there are 2 possible outcomes—either it lands heads up or it lands tails up. Using this fact and the multiplication principle, you can conclude that if a coin is tossed 8 times, there are $(2)(2)(2)(2)(2)(2)(2)(2) = 2^8 = 256$ possible outcomes.

Permutations and Factorials

Suppose you want to determine the number of different ways the 3 letters A, B, and C can be placed in order from 1st to 3rd. The following is a list of all the possible orders in which the letters can be placed.

ABC ACB BAC BCA CAB CBA

There are 6 possible orders for the 3 letters.

Now suppose you want to determine the number of different ways the 4 letters A, B, C, and D can be placed in order from 1st to 4th. Listing all of the orders for 4 letters is time-consuming, so it would be useful to be able to count the possible orders without listing them.

To order the 4 letters, one of the 4 letters must be placed first, one of the remaining 3 letters must be placed second, one of the remaining 2 letters must be placed third, and the last remaining letter must be placed fourth. Therefore, applying the multiplication principle, there are (4)(3)(2)(1), or 24, ways to order the 4 letters.

More generally, suppose n objects are to be ordered from 1st to nth, and we want to count the number of ways the objects can be ordered. There are n choices for the first object, $n - 1$ choices for the second object, $n - 2$ choices for the third object, and so on, until there is only 1 choice for the nth object. Thus, applying the multiplication principle, the number of ways to order the n objects is equal to the product

$$n(n-1)(n-2)\cdots(3)(2)(1)$$

Each order is called a **permutation**, and the product above is called the number of permutations of n objects.

Because products of the form $n(n-1)(n-2)\cdots(3)(2)(1)$ occur frequently when counting objects, a special symbol $n!$, called **n-factorial**, is used to denote this product.

For example,

$$1! = 1$$
$$2! = (2)(1)$$
$$3! = (3)(2)(1)$$
$$4! = (4)(3)(2)(1)$$

As a special definition, $0! = 1$.

Note that $n! = n(n-1)! = n(n-1)(n-2)! = n(n-1)(n-2)(n-3)!$ and so on.

Example 4.3.4: Suppose that 10 students are going on a bus trip, and each of the students will be assigned to one of the 10 available seats. Then the number of possible different seating arrangements of the students on the bus is

$$10! = (10)(9)(8)(7)(6)(5)(4)(3)(2)(1) = 3{,}628{,}800$$

Now suppose you want to determine the number of ways in which you can select 3 of the 5 letters A, B, C, D, and E and place them in order from 1st to 3rd. Reasoning as in the preceding examples, you find that there are $(5)(4)(3)$, or 60, ways to select and order them.

More generally, suppose that k objects will be selected from a set of n objects, where $k \le n$, and the k objects will be placed in order from 1st to kth. Then there are n choices for the first object, $n-1$ choices for the second object, $n-2$ choices for the third object, and so on, until there are $n-k+1$ choices for the kth object. Thus, applying the multiplication principle, the number of ways to select and order k objects from a set of n objects is $n(n-1)(n-2)\ldots(n-k+1)$. It is useful to note that

$$n(n-1)(n-2)\cdots(n-k+1) = n(n-1)(n-2)\cdots(n-k+1)\frac{(n-k)!}{(n-k)!} = \frac{n!}{(n-k)!}$$

This expression represents the number of **permutations of n objects taken k at a time**—that is, the number of ways to select and order k objects out of n objects. This number is commonly denoted by the notation $_nP_k$.

Example 4.3.5: How many different 5-digit positive integers can be formed using the digits 1, 2, 3, 4, 5, 6, and 7 if none of the digits can occur more than once in the integer?

Solution: This example asks how many ways there are to order 5 integers chosen from a set of 7 integers. According to the counting principle above, there are $(7)(6)(5)(4)(3) = 2{,}520$ ways to do this. Note that this is equal to $\dfrac{7!}{(7-5)!} = \dfrac{(7)(6)(5)(4)(3)(2!)}{2!} = (7)(6)(5)(4)(3)$.

Combinations

Given the 5 letters A, B, C, D, and E, suppose that you want to determine the number of ways in which you can select 3 of the 5 letters, but unlike before, you do not want to count different orders for the 3 letters. The following is a list of all of the ways in which 3 of the 5 letters can be selected without regard to the order of the letters.

$$\text{ABC} \quad \text{ABD} \quad \text{ABE} \quad \text{ACD} \quad \text{ACE}$$
$$\text{ADE} \quad \text{BCD} \quad \text{BCE} \quad \text{BDE} \quad \text{CDE}$$

There are 10 ways of selecting the 3 letters without order. There is a relationship between selecting with order and selecting without order.

The number of ways to select 3 of the 5 letters without order, which is 10, *multiplied by* the number of ways to order the 3 letters, which is 3!, or 6, *is equal to* the number of ways to select 3 of the 5 letters and order them, which is $\dfrac{5!}{2!} = 60$. In short,

(number of ways to select without order) × (number of ways to order)
= (number of ways to select with order)

This relationship can also be rewritten as follows.

$$\text{(number of ways to select without order)} = \frac{\text{(number of ways to select with order)}}{\text{(number of ways to order)}}$$

For the example above, the number of ways to select without order is $\dfrac{\frac{5!}{2!}}{3!} = \dfrac{5!}{3!2!} = 10$.

More generally, suppose that k objects will be chosen from a set of n objects, where $k \le n$, but that the k objects will not be put in order. The number of ways in which this can be done is called the number of **combinations of n objects taken k at a time** and is given by the formula $\dfrac{n!}{k!(n-k)!}$.

Another way to refer to the number of combinations of n objects taken k at a time is **n choose k**, and two notations commonly used to denote this number are $_nC_k$ and $\dbinom{n}{k}$.

Example 4.3.6: Suppose you want to select a 3-person committee from a group of 9 students. How many ways are there to do this?

Solution: Since the 3 students on the committee are not ordered, you can use the formula for the combination of 9 objects taken 3 at a time, or "9 choose 3":

$$\frac{9!}{3!(9-3)!} = \frac{9!}{3!6!} = \frac{(9)(8)(7)}{(3)(2)(1)} = 84$$

Using the terminology of sets, given a set S consisting of n elements, n choose k is simply the number of subsets of S that consist of k elements.

The formula for n choose k, which is $\dfrac{n!}{k!(n-k)!}$ also holds when $k = 0$ and $k = n$. Therefore

1. n choose 0 is $\dfrac{n!}{0!n!} = 1$.

    (This reflects the fact that there is only one subset of S with 0 elements, namely the empty set).

2. n choose n is $\dfrac{n!}{n!0!} = 1$.

    (This reflects the fact that there is only one subset of S with n elements, namely the set S itself).

Finally, note that n choose k is always equal to n choose $n - k$, because

$$\frac{n!}{(n-k)!\,(n-(n-k))!} = \frac{n!}{(n-k)!k!} = \frac{n!}{k!(n-k)!}$$

4.4 Probability

Probability is a way of describing uncertainty in numerical terms. In this section, we review some of the terminology used in elementary probability theory.

A **probability experiment**, also called a **random experiment**, is an experiment for which the result, or **outcome**, is uncertain. We assume that all of the possible outcomes of an experiment are known before the experiment is performed, but which outcome will actually occur is unknown. The set of all possible outcomes of a random experiment is called the **sample space**, and any particular set of outcomes is called an **event**. For example, consider a cube with faces numbered 1 to 6, called a 6-sided die. Rolling the die once is an experiment in which there are 6 possible outcomes: either 1, 2, 3, 4, 5, or 6 will appear on the top face. The sample space for this experiment is {1, 2, 3, 4, 5, 6}. Here are two examples of events for this experiment.

Event 1: Rolling the number 4. This event has only one outcome.

Event 2: Rolling an odd number. This event has three outcomes.

The **probability** of an event is a number from 0 to 1, inclusive, that indicates the likelihood that the event occurs when the experiment is performed. The greater the number, the more likely the event.

Example 4.4.1: Consider the following experiment. A box contains 15 pieces of paper, each of which has the name of one of the 15 students in a high school class consisting of 7 juniors and 8 seniors, all with different names. The instructor will shake the box for a while and then choose a piece of paper at random and read the name. Here the sample space is the set of 15 names. The assumption of **random selection** means that each of the names is **equally likely** to be selected. If this assumption is made, then the probability that any one particular name will be selected is equal to $\frac{1}{15}$.

For any event E, the probability that E occurs is often written as $P(E)$. For the sample space in this example, $P(E)$, that is, the probability that event E occurs, is equal to

$$\frac{\text{the number of names in the event } E}{15}$$

If J is the event that the student selected is a junior, then $P(J) = \frac{7}{15}$.

In general, for a random experiment with a finite number of possible outcomes, if each outcome is equally likely to occur, then the probability that an event E occurs is defined by

$$P(E) = \frac{\text{the number of outcomes in the event } E}{\text{the number of possible outcomes in the experiment}}$$

In the case of rolling a 6-sided die, if the die is "fair," then the 6 outcomes are equally likely. So the probability of rolling a 4 is $\frac{1}{6}$, and the probability of rolling an odd number (that is, rolling a 1, 3, or 5) can be calculated as $\frac{3}{6} = \frac{1}{2}$.

The following are six general facts about probability.

Fact 1: If an event E is certain to occur, then $P(E) = 1$.

Fact 2: If an event E is certain *not* to occur, then $P(E) = 0$.

Fact 3: If an event E is possible but not certain to occur, then $0 < P(E) < 1$.

Fact 4: The probability that an event E will not occur is equal to $1 - P(E)$.

Fact 5: If E is an event, then the probability of E is the sum of the probabilities of the outcomes in E.

Fact 6: The sum of the probabilities of all possible outcomes of an experiment is 1.

If E and F are two events of an experiment, we consider two other events related to E and F.

Event 1: The event that both E and F occur, that is, outcomes in the set $E \cap F$
Event 2: The event that E or F, or both, occur, that is, outcomes in the set $E \cup F$

Events that cannot occur at the same time are said to be **mutually exclusive**. For example, if a 6-sided die is rolled once, the event of rolling an odd number and the event of rolling an even number are mutually exclusive. But rolling a 4 and rolling an even number are not mutually exclusive, since 4 is an outcome that is common to both events.

For events E and F, we have the following three rules.

Rule 1: P(either E or F, or both, occur) $= P(E) + P(F) - P$(both E and F occur), which is the inclusion-exclusion principle applied to probability.

Rule 2: If E and F are mutually exclusive, then P(both E and F occur) $= 0$, and therefore, P(either E or F, or both, occur) $= P(E) + P(F)$.

Rule 3: E and F are said to be **independent** if the occurrence of either event does not affect the occurrence of the other. If two events E and F are independent, then P(both E and F occur) $= P(E)P(F)$. For example, if a fair 6-sided die is rolled twice, the event E of rolling a 3 on the first roll and the event F of rolling a 3 on the second roll are independent, and the probability of rolling a 3 on both rolls is $P(E)P(F) = \left(\frac{1}{6}\right)\left(\frac{1}{6}\right) = \frac{1}{36}$. In this example, the experiment is actually "rolling the die twice," and each outcome is an ordered pair of results like "4 on the first roll and 1 on the second roll." But event E restricts only the first roll—to a 3—having no effect on the second roll; similarly, event F restricts only the second roll—to a 3—having no effect on the first roll.

Note that if $P(E) \neq 0$ and $P(F) \neq 0$, then events E and F cannot be both mutually exclusive and independent. For if E and F are independent, then P(both E and F occur) $= P(E)P(F) \neq 0$, but if E and F are mutually exclusive, then P(both E and F occur) $= 0$.

It is common to use the shorter notation "E and F" instead of "both E and F occur" and use "E or F" instead of "E or F or both occur." With this notation, we can restate the previous three rules as follows.

Rule 1: $P(E \text{ or } F) = P(E) + P(F) - P(E \text{ and } F)$
Rule 2: $P(E \text{ or } F) = P(E) + P(F)$ if E and F are mutually exclusive.
Rule 3: $P(E \text{ and } F) = P(E)P(F)$ if E and F are independent.

Example 4.4.2: If a fair 6-sided die is rolled once, let E be the event of rolling a 3 and let F be the event of rolling an odd number. These events are *not* independent. This is because rolling a 3 makes certain that the event of rolling an odd number occurs. Note that $P(E \text{ and } F) \neq P(E)P(F)$, since

$$P(E \text{ and } F) = P(E) = \frac{1}{6} \quad \text{and} \quad P(E)P(F) = \left(\frac{1}{6}\right)\left(\frac{1}{2}\right) = \frac{1}{12}$$

Example 4.4.3: A 12-sided die, with faces numbered 1 to 12, is to be rolled once, and each of the 12 possible outcomes is equally likely to occur. The probability of rolling a 4 is $\frac{1}{12}$, so the probability of rolling a number that is *not* a 4 is $1 - \frac{1}{12} = \frac{11}{12}$.
The probability of rolling a number that is either a multiple of 5 (that is, rolling a 5 or a 10) or an odd number (that is, rolling a 1, 3, 5, 7, 9, or 11) is equal to

$$P(\text{multiple of } 5) + P(\text{odd}) - P(\text{multiple of } 5 \text{ and odd}) = \frac{2}{12} + \frac{6}{12} - \frac{1}{12} = \frac{7}{12}$$

Another way to calculate this probability is to notice that rolling a number that is either a multiple of 5 or an odd number is the same as rolling one of the seven numbers 1, 3, 5, 7, 9, 10, and 11, which are equally likely outcomes. So by using the ratio formula to calculate the probability, the required probability is $\frac{7}{12}$.

Example 4.4.4: Consider an experiment with events A, B, and C for which $P(A) = 0.23$, $P(B) = 0.40$, and $P(C) = 0.85$.

Suppose that events A and B are mutually exclusive and events B and C are independent. What is $P(A \text{ or } B)$ and $P(B \text{ or } C)$?

Solution: Since A and B are mutually exclusive,

$$P(A \text{ or } B) = P(A) + P(B) = 0.23 + 0.40 = 0.63$$

Since B and C are independent, $P(B \text{ and } C) = P(B)P(C)$. So

$$P(B \text{ or } C) = P(B) + P(C) - P(B \text{ and } C) = P(B) + P(C) - P(B) P(C)$$

Therefore,

$$P(B \text{ or } C) = 0.40 + 0.85 - (0.40)(0.85) = 1.25 - 0.34 = 0.91$$

Example 4.4.5: Suppose that there is a 6-sided die that is weighted in such a way that each time the die is rolled, the probabilities of rolling any of the numbers from 1 to 5 are all equal, but the probability of rolling a 6 is twice the probability of rolling a 1. When you roll the die once, the 6 outcomes are *not equally likely*. What are the probabilities of the 6 outcomes?

Solution: Let p equal the probability of rolling a 1. Then each of the probabilities of rolling a 2, 3, 4, or 5 is equal to p, and the probability of rolling a 6 is equal to $2p$. Therefore, since the sum of the probabilities of all possible outcomes is 1, it follows that

$$1 = P(1) + P(2) + P(3) + P(4) + P(5) + P(6) = p + p + p + p + p + 2p = 7p$$

So the probability of rolling each of the numbers from 1 to 5 is $\frac{1}{7}$, and the probability of rolling a 6 is $\frac{2}{7}$.

Example 4.4.6: Suppose that you roll the weighted 6-sided die from Example 4.4.5 twice. What is the probability that the first roll will be an odd number and the second roll will be an even number?

Solution: To calculate the probability that the first roll will be odd and the second roll will be even, note that these two events are independent. To calculate the probability that both occur, you must multiply the probabilities of the two independent events. First compute the individual probabilities.

$$P(\text{odd}) = P(1) + P(3) + P(5) = \frac{3}{7}$$

$$P(\text{even}) = P(2) + P(4) + P(6) = \frac{4}{7}$$

Then $P(\text{first roll is odd and second roll is even}) = P(\text{odd})\, P(\text{even}) = \left(\frac{3}{7}\right)\left(\frac{4}{7}\right) = \frac{12}{49}$.

Two events that happen sequentially are not always independent. The occurrence of the first event may affect the occurrence of the second event. In this case, the probability that *both* events happen is equal to the probability that the first event happens multiplied by the probability that, *given that the first event has already happened*, the second event will happen as well.

Example 4.4.7: A box contains 5 orange disks, 4 red disks, and 1 blue disk. You are to select two disks at random and without replacement from the box. What is the probability that the first disk you select will be red and the second disk you select will be orange?

Solution: To solve, you need to calculate the following two probabilities and then multiply them.

1. The probability that the first disk selected from the box will be red
2. The probability that the second disk selected from the box will be orange, given that the first disk selected from the box is red

The probability that the first disk you select will be red is $\frac{4}{10} = \frac{2}{5}$. If the first disk you select is red, there will be 5 orange disks, 3 red disks, and 1 blue disk left in the box, for a total of 9 disks. Therefore, the probability that the second disk you select will be orange, given that the first disk you selected is red, is $\frac{5}{9}$. Multiply the two probabilities to get $\left(\frac{2}{5}\right)\left(\frac{5}{9}\right) = \frac{2}{9}$.

4.5 Distributions of Data, Random Variables, and Probability Distributions

In data analysis, variables whose values depend on chance play an important role in linking distributions of data to probability distributions. Such variables are called random variables. We begin with a review of distributions of data.

Distributions of Data

Recall that relative frequency distributions given in a table or histogram are a common way to show how numerical data are distributed. In a histogram, the areas of the bars indicate where the data are concentrated. The histogram of the relative frequency distribution of the number of children in each of 25 families in Data Analysis Figure 4 below illustrates a small group of data, with only 6 distinct data values and 25 data values altogether. (Note: This is the second occurrence of Data Analysis Figure 4, it was first encountered in Example 4.1.10.)

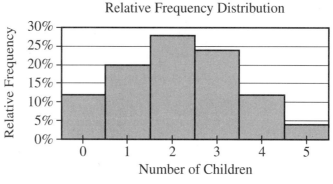

Data Analysis Figure 4 (repeated)

Many groups of data are much larger than 25 and have many more than 6 possible values, which are often measurements of quantities like length, money, or time.

Example 4.5.1: The lifetimes of 800 electric devices were measured. Because the lifetimes had many different values, the measurements were grouped into 50 intervals, or **classes**, of 10 hours each: 601 to 610 hours, 611 to 620 hours, and so on, up to 1,091 to 1,100 hours. The resulting relative frequency distribution, as a histogram, has 50 thin bars and many different bar heights, as shown in Data Analysis Figure 11 below.

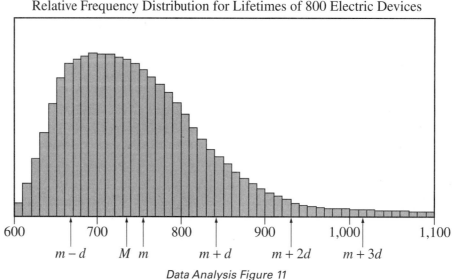

Data Analysis Figure 11

In the histogram, the median is represented by M, the mean is represented by m, and the standard deviation is represented by d.

According to the graph:

- A data value 1 standard deviation below the mean, represented by $m - d$, is between 660 and 670.
- The median, represented by M, is between 730 and 740.
- The mean, represented by m, is between 750 and 760.

- A data value 1 standard deviation above the mean, represented by $m + d$, is between 840 and 850.
- A data value 2 standard deviations above the mean, represented by $m + 2d$, is approximately 930.
- A data value 3 standard deviations above the mean, represented by $m + 3d$, is between 1,010 and 1,020.

The standard deviation marks show how most of the data are within 3 standard deviations of the mean, that is, between the numbers $m - 3d$ and $m + 3d$. Note that $m + 3d$ is shown in the figure, but $m - 3d$ is not.

The tops of the bars of the relative frequency distribution in the histogram in Data Analysis Figure 11 have a relatively smooth appearance and begin to look like a curve. In general, histograms that represent very large data sets grouped into many classes have a relatively smooth appearance. Consequently, the distribution can be modeled by a smooth curve that is close to the tops of the bars. Such a model retains the shape of the distribution but is independent of classes.

Recall from Example 4.1.10 that the sum of the areas of the bars of a relative frequency histogram is 1. Although the units on the horizontal axis of a histogram vary from one data set to another, the vertical scale can be adjusted (stretched or shrunk) so that the sum of the areas of the bars is 1. With this vertical scale adjustment, the area under the curve that models the distribution is also 1. This model curve is called a **distribution curve**, but it has other names as well, including **density curve** and **frequency curve**.

The purpose of the distribution curve is to give a good illustration of a large distribution of numerical data that does not depend on specific classes. To achieve this, the main property of a distribution curve is that the area under the curve in any vertical slice, just like a histogram bar, represents the proportion of the data that lies in the corresponding interval on the horizontal axis, which is at the base of the slice.

Random Variables

When analyzing data, it is common to choose a value of the data at random and consider that choice as a random experiment, as introduced in Section 4.4. Then, the probabilities of events involving the randomly chosen value may be determined. Given a distribution of data, a variable, say X, may be used to represent a randomly chosen value from the distribution. Such a variable X is an example of a **random variable**, which is a variable whose value is a numerical outcome of a random experiment.

Example 4.5.2: In Example 4.1.3, data consisting of numbers of children in each of 25 families was summarized in a frequency distribution table. For convenience, the frequency distribution table is repeated below.

Frequency Distribution

Number of Children	Frequency
0	3
1	5
2	7
3	6
4	3
5	1
Total	25

Let X be the random variable representing the number of children in a randomly chosen family among the 25 families. What is the probability that $X = 3$? That $X > 3$? That X is less than the mean of the distribution?

Solution: To determine the probability that $X = 3$, realize that this is the same as determining the probability that a family with 3 children will be chosen.

Since there are 6 families with 3 children and each of the 25 families is equally likely to be chosen, the probability that a family with 3 children will be chosen is $\frac{6}{25}$. That is, $X = 3$ is an event, and its probability is $P(X = 3) = \frac{6}{25}$, or 0.24. It is common to use the shorter notation $P(3)$ instead of $P(X = 3)$, so you could write $P(3) = 0.24$.

Note that in the histogram shown in Data Analysis Figure 4 below, the area of the bar corresponding to $X = 3$ as a proportion of the combined areas of all of the bars is equal to this probability. This indicates how probability is related to area in a histogram for a relative frequency distribution. (Note: This is the third occurrence of Data Analysis Figure 4, it was previously encountered in Example 4.1.10 and at the beginning of this section.)

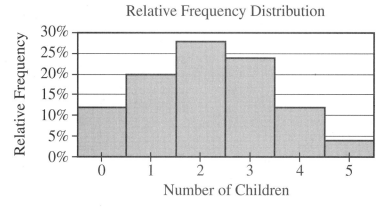

Data Analysis Figure 4 (repeated)

To determine the probability that $X > 3$, notice that the event $X > 3$ is the same as the event "$X = 4$ or $X = 5$". Because $X = 4$ and $X = 5$ are mutually exclusive events, we can use the rules of probability from Section 4.4.

$$P(X > 3) = P(4) + P(5) = \frac{3}{25} + \frac{1}{25} = 0.12 + 0.04 = 0.16$$

To determine the probability that X is less than the mean of the distribution, first compute the mean of the distribution as follows.

$$\frac{0(3) + 1(5) + 2(7) + 3(6) + 4(3) + 5(1)}{25} = \frac{54}{25} = 2.16$$

Then, calculate the probability that X is less than the mean of the distribution (that is, the probability that X is less than 2.16).

$$P(X < 2.16) = P(0) + P(1) + P(2) = \frac{3}{25} + \frac{5}{25} + \frac{7}{25} = \frac{15}{25} = 0.6$$

The following table shows all 6 possible values of X and their probabilities. This table is called the **probability distribution** of the random variable X.

X	$P(X)$
0	0.12
1	0.20
2	0.28
3	0.24
4	0.12
5	0.04

Note that the probabilities are simply the relative frequencies of the 6 possible values expressed as decimals instead of percents. The following statement indicates a fundamental link between data distributions and probability distributions.

Statement: For a random variable that represents a randomly chosen value from a distribution of data, the probability distribution of the random variable is the same as the relative frequency distribution of the data.

Because the probability distribution and the relative frequency distribution are essentially the same, the probability distribution can be represented by a histogram. Also, all of the descriptive statistics—such as mean, median, and standard deviation—that apply to the distribution of data also apply to the probability distribution. For example, we say that the probability distribution above has a mean of 2.16, a median of 2, and a standard deviation of about 1.3, since the 25 data values have these statistics, as you can check.

These statistics are similarly defined for the random variable X above. Thus, we would say that the **mean of the random variable X** is 2.16. Another name for the mean of a random variable is **expected value**. So we would also say that the expected value of X is 2.16.

Note that the mean of X is equal to

$$\frac{0(3) + 1(5) + 2(7) + 3(6) + 4(3) + 5(1)}{25}$$

which can also be expressed as

$$0\left(\frac{3}{25}\right) + 1\left(\frac{5}{25}\right) + 2\left(\frac{7}{25}\right) + 3\left(\frac{6}{25}\right) + 4\left(\frac{3}{25}\right) + 5\left(\frac{1}{25}\right)$$

which is the same as

$$0P(0) + 1P(1) + 2P(2) + 3P(3) + 4P(4) + 5P(5)$$

Therefore, the mean of the random variable X is the sum of the products $XP(X)$ for all values of X, that is, the sum of each value of X multiplied by its corresponding probability $P(X)$.

The preceding example involves a common type of random variable—one that represents a randomly chosen value from a distribution of data. However, the concept of a random variable is more general. A random variable can be any quantity whose value is the result of a random experiment. The possible values of the random variable are the same as the outcomes of the experiment. So any random experiment with numerical outcomes naturally has a random variable associated with it, as in the following example.

Example 4.5.3: Let Y represent the outcome of the experiment of rolling the weighted 6-sided die in Example 4.4.5. (In that example, the probabilities of rolling any of the numbers from 1 to 5 are all equal, but the probability of rolling a 6 is twice the probability of rolling a 1.) Then Y is a random variable with 6 possible values, the numbers 1 through 6. Each of the six values of Y has a probability. The probability distribution of the random variable Y is shown below, first in a table, then as a histogram.

Table Representing the Probability Distribution of Random Variable Y

Y	$P(Y)$
1	$\frac{1}{7}$
2	$\frac{1}{7}$
3	$\frac{1}{7}$
4	$\frac{1}{7}$
5	$\frac{1}{7}$
6	$\frac{2}{7}$

Histogram Representing the Probability Distribution of Random Variable Y

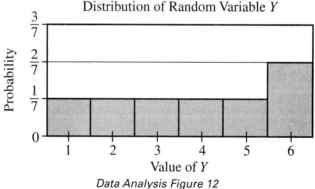

Data Analysis Figure 12

The mean, or expected value, of Y can be computed as

$$P(1) + 2P(2) + 3P(3) + 4P(4) + 5P(5) + 6P(6)$$

which is equal to

$$\left(\frac{1}{7}\right) + 2\left(\frac{1}{7}\right) + 3\left(\frac{1}{7}\right) + 4\left(\frac{1}{7}\right) + 5\left(\frac{1}{7}\right) + 6\left(\frac{2}{7}\right)$$

This sum simplifies to $\frac{1}{7} + \frac{2}{7} + \frac{3}{7} + \frac{4}{7} + \frac{5}{7} + \frac{12}{7}$, or $\frac{27}{7}$, which is approximately 3.86.

Both of the random variables X and Y above are examples of **discrete random variables** because their values consist of discrete points on a number line.

A basic fact about probability from Section 4.4 is that the sum of the probabilities of all possible outcomes of an experiment is 1, which can be confirmed by adding all of the probabilities in each of the probability distributions for the random variables X and Y above. Also, the sum of the areas of the bars in a histogram for the probability distribution of a random variable is 1. This fact is related to the following fundamental link between the areas of the bars of a histogram and the probabilities of a discrete random variable.

Fundamental Link: In a histogram representing the probability distribution of a random variable, the area of each bar is proportional to the probability represented by the bar.

If the die in Example 4.4.5 were a fair die instead of weighted, then the probability of each of the outcomes would be $\frac{1}{6}$, and consequently, each of the bars in the histogram of the probability distribution would have the same height. Such a flat histogram indicates a **uniform distribution**, since the probability is distributed uniformly over all possible outcomes.

The Normal Distribution

Many natural processes yield data that have a relative frequency distribution shaped somewhat like a bell, as in the distribution with mean m and standard deviation d in Data Analysis Figure 13 below.

Approximately Normal Relative Frequency Distribution

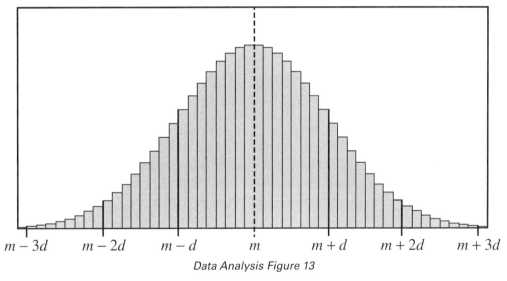

Data Analysis Figure 13

Such data are said to be **approximately normally distributed** and have the following four properties.

Property 1: The mean, median, and mode are all nearly equal.

Property 2: The data are grouped fairly symmetrically about the mean.

Property 3: About two-thirds of the data are within 1 standard deviation of the mean.

Property 4: Almost all of the data are within 2 standard deviations of the mean.

As stated above, you can always associate a random variable X with a distribution of data by letting X be a randomly chosen value from the distribution. If X is such a random variable for the distribution in Data Analysis Figure 13, we say that X is approximately normally distributed.

As described in the example about the lifetimes of 800 electric devices, relative frequency distributions are often approximated using a smooth curve—a distribution curve or density curve—for the tops of the bars in the histogram. The region below such a curve represents a distribution called a **continuous probability distribution**. There are many different continuous probability distributions, but the most important one is the **normal distribution**, which has a bell-shaped curve like the one shown in Data Analysis Figure 14 below.

Normal Distribution

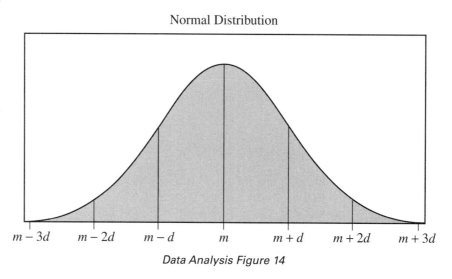

Data Analysis Figure 14

Just as a data distribution has a mean and standard deviation, the normal probability distribution has a mean and standard deviation. Also, the properties listed above for the approximately normal distribution of data hold for the normal distribution, except that the mean, median, and mode are exactly the same and the distribution is perfectly symmetric about the mean.

A normal distribution, though always shaped like a bell, can be centered around any mean and can be spread out to a greater or lesser degree, depending on the standard deviation. The less the standard deviation, the less spread out the curve is; that is to say, at the mean the curve is higher and as you move away from the mean in either direction it drops down toward the horizontal axis faster.

In Data Analysis Figure 15 below, there are two normal distributions that have different centers, −10 and 5, respectively, but the spread of the distributions is the same. The two distributions have the same shape, so one can be shifted horizontally onto the other.

Two Normal Distributions with the Same Spread

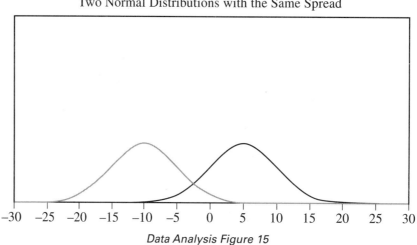

Data Analysis Figure 15

In Data Analysis Figure 16 below, there are two normal distributions that have different spreads, but the same center. The mean of both distributions is 0. One of the distributions is high and spread narrowly about the mean; and the other is low and spread widely about the mean. The standard deviation of the high, narrow distribution is less than the standard deviation of the low, wide distribution.

Two Normal Distributions with the Same Center

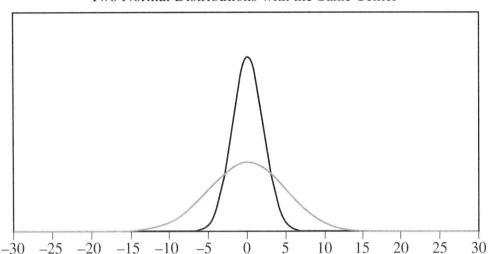

Data Analysis Figure 16

As mentioned earlier, areas of the bars in a histogram for a discrete random variable correspond to probabilities for the values of the random variable; the sum of the areas is 1 and the sum of the probabilities is 1. This is also true for a continuous probability distribution: the area of the region under the curve is 1, and the areas of vertical slices of the region, like the areas of the bars of a histogram, are equal to probabilities of a random variable associated with the distribution. Such a random variable is called a **continuous random variable**, and it plays the same role as a random variable that represents a randomly chosen value from a distribution of data. The main difference is that we seldom consider the event in which a continuous random variable is equal to a single value like $X = 3$; rather, we consider events that are described by intervals of values such as $1 < X < 3$ and $X > 10$. Such events correspond to vertical slices under a continuous probability distribution, and the areas of the vertical slices are the probabilities of the corresponding events. (Consequently, the probability of an event such as $X = 3$ would correspond to the area of a line segment, which is 0.)

Example 4.5.4: If W is a random variable that is normally distributed with a mean of 5 and a standard deviation of 2, what is $P(W > 5)$? Approximately what is $P(3 < W < 7)$? Which of the four numbers 0.5, 0.1, 0.05, or 0.01 is the best estimate of $P(W < -1)$?

Solution: Data Analysis Figure 17 below is a graph of a normal distribution with a mean of 5 and a standard deviation of 2.

The numbers 3 and 7 are 1 standard deviation away from the mean, the numbers 1 and 9 are 2 standard deviations away from the mean, and the numbers -1 and 11 are 3 standard deviations away from the mean.

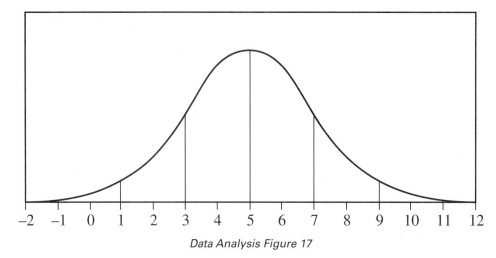

Data Analysis Figure 17

Since the mean of the distribution is 5, and the distribution is symmetric about the mean, the event $W > 5$ corresponds to exactly half of the area under the normal distribution. So $P(W > 5) = \dfrac{1}{2}$.

For the event $3 < W < 7$, note that since the standard deviation of the distribution is 2, the values 3 and 7 are one standard deviation below and above the mean, respectively. Since about two-thirds of the area is within one standard deviation of the mean,

$P(3 < W < 7)$ is approximately $\dfrac{2}{3}$.

For the event $W < -1$, note that -1 is 3 standard deviations below the mean. Since the graph makes it fairly clear that the area of the region under the normal curve to the left of -1 is much less than 5 percent of all of the area, the best of the four estimates given for $P(W < -1)$ is 0.01.

The **standard normal distribution** is a normal distribution with a mean of 0 and standard deviation equal to 1. To transform a normal distribution with a mean of m and a standard deviation of d to a standard normal distribution, you standardize the values; that is, you subtract m from any observed value of the normal distribution and then divide the result by d.

Very precise values for probabilities associated with normal distributions can be computed using calculators, computers, or statistical tables for the standard normal distribution. In the preceding example, more precise values for $P(3 < W < 7)$ and $P(W < -1)$ are 0.683 and 0.0013, respectively. Such calculations are beyond the scope of this review.

4.6 Data Interpretation Examples

Example 4.6.1: This example is based on the following table.

DISTRIBUTION OF CUSTOMER COMPLAINTS RECEIVED BY
AIRLINE *P,* 2003 and 2004

Category	2003	2004
Flight problem	20.0%	22.1%
Baggage	18.3	21.8
Customer service	13.1	11.3
Reservation and ticketing	5.8	5.6
Credit	1.0	0.8
Special passenger accommodation	0.9	0.9
Other	40.9	37.5
Total	100.0%	100.0%
Total number of complaints	22,998	13,278

(a) Approximately how many complaints concerning credit were received by Airline P in 2003 ?

(b) By approximately what percent did the total number of complaints decrease from 2003 to 2004 ?

(c) Based on the information in the table, which of the following three statements are true?

Statement 1: In each of the years 2003 and 2004, complaints about flight problems, baggage, and customer service together accounted for more than 50 percent of all customer complaints received by Airline P.

Statement 2: The number of special passenger accommodation complaints was unchanged from 2003 to 2004.

Statement 3: From 2003 to 2004, the number of flight problem complaints increased by more than 2 percent.

Solutions:

(a) According to the table, in 2003, 1 percent of the total number of complaints concerned credit. Therefore, the number of complaints concerning credit is equal to 1 percent of 22,998. By converting 1 percent to its decimal equivalent, you obtain that the number of complaints in 2003 is equal to (0.01)(22,998), or about 230.

(b) The decrease in the total number of complaints from 2003 to 2004 was 22,998 − 13,278, or 9,720. Therefore, the percent decrease was $\left(\dfrac{9,720}{22,998} \right) (100\%)$, or approximately 42 percent.

(c) Since $20.0 + 18.3 + 13.1$ and $22.1 + 21.8 + 11.3$ are both greater than 50, statement 1 is true. For statement 2, the *percent* of special passenger accommodation complaints *did* remain the same from 2003 to 2004, but the number of such complaints decreased because the total number of complaints decreased. Thus, statement 2 is false. For statement 3, the *percents* shown in the table for flight problems do in fact increase by more than 2 percentage points, but the bases of the percents are different. The total number of complaints in 2004 was much lower than the total number of complaints in 2003, and clearly 20 percent of 22,998 is greater than 22.1 percent of 13,278. So, the number of flight problem complaints actually decreased from 2003 to 2004, and statement 3 is false.

Example 4.6.2: This example is based on the following circle graph.

UNITED STATES PRODUCTION OF PHOTOGRAPHIC
EQUIPMENT AND SUPPLIES IN 1971

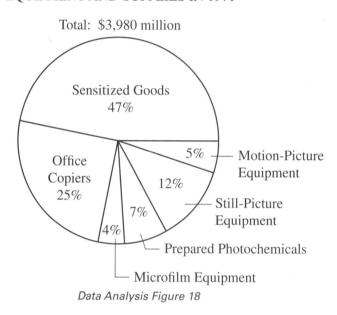

Data Analysis Figure 18

(a) Approximately what was the ratio of the value of sensitized goods to the value of still-picture equipment produced in 1971 in the United States?

(b) If the value of office copiers produced in 1971 was 30 percent greater than the corresponding value in 1970, what was the value of office copiers produced in 1970 ?

Solutions:

(a) The ratio of the value of sensitized goods to the value of still-picture equipment is equal to the ratio of the corresponding percents shown because the percents have the same base, which is the total value. Therefore, the ratio is 47 to 12, or approximately 4 to 1.

(b) The value of office copiers produced in 1971 was 0.25 times $3,980 million, or $995 million. Therefore, if the corresponding value in 1970 was x million dollars, then $1.3x = 995$ million. Solving for x yields $x = \dfrac{995}{1.3} \approx 765$, so the value of office copiers produced in 1970 was approximately $765 million.

Example 4.6.3: In a survey of 250 European travelers, 93 have traveled to Africa, 155 have traveled to Asia, and of these two groups, 70 have traveled to both continents, as illustrated in the Venn diagram below.

TRAVELERS SURVEYED: 250

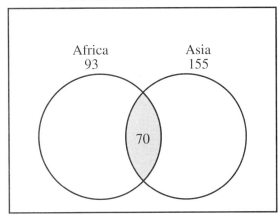

Data Analysis Figure 19

(a) How many of the travelers surveyed have traveled to Africa but *not* to Asia?

(b) How many of the travelers surveyed have traveled to *at least one* of the two continents of Africa and Asia?

(c) How many of the travelers surveyed have traveled *neither* to Africa *nor* to Asia?

Solutions:

In the Venn diagram in Data Analysis Figure 19, the rectangular region represents the set of all travelers surveyed; the two circular regions represent the two sets of travelers to Africa and Asia, respectively; and the shaded region represents the subset of those who have traveled to both continents.

(a) The travelers surveyed who have traveled to Africa but not to Asia are represented in the Venn diagram by *the part of the left circle that is not shaded*. This suggests that the answer can be found by taking the shaded part away from the leftmost circle, in effect, subtracting the 70 from the 93, to get 23 travelers who have traveled to Africa, but not to Asia.

(b) The travelers surveyed who have traveled to at least one of the two continents of Africa and Asia are represented in the Venn diagram by that part of the rectangle that is *in at least one of the two circles*. This suggests adding the two numbers 93 and 155. But the 70 travelers who have traveled to both continents would be counted twice in the sum $93 + 155$. To correct the double counting, subtract 70 from the sum so that these 70 travelers are counted only once:

$$93 + 155 - 70 = 178$$

(c) The travelers surveyed who have traveled neither to Africa nor to Asia are represented in the Venn diagram by the part of the rectangle that is not in either circle. Let N be the number of these travelers. Note that the entire rectangular region has two main nonoverlapping parts: the part outside the circles and the part inside the circles. The first part represents N travelers and the second part represents $93 + 155 - 70 = 178$ travelers (from part b). Therefore, $250 = N + 178$, and solving for N yields $N = 250 - 178 = 72$.

DATA ANALYSIS EXERCISES

Exercise 1. The daily temperatures, in degrees Fahrenheit, for 10 days in May were 61, 62, 65, 65, 65, 68, 74, 74, 75, and 77.

    (a) Find the mean, median, mode, and range of the temperatures.

    (b) If each day had been 7 degrees warmer, what would have been the mean, median, mode, and range of those 10 temperatures?

Exercise 2. The numbers of passengers on 9 airline flights were 22, 33, 21, 28, 22, 31, 44, 50, and 19. The standard deviation of these 9 numbers is approximately equal to 10.22.

    (a) Find the mean, median, mode, range, and interquartile range of the 9 numbers.

    (b) If each flight had had 3 times as many passengers, what would have been the mean, median, mode, range, interquartile range, and standard deviation of the 9 numbers?

    (c) If each flight had had 2 fewer passengers, what would have been the interquartile range and standard deviation of the 9 numbers?

Exercise 3. A group of 20 values has a mean of 85 and a median of 80. A different group of 30 values has a mean of 75 and a median of 72.

    (a) What is the mean of the 50 values?

    (b) What is the median of the 50 values?

Exercise 4. Find the mean and median of the values of the random variable X, whose relative frequency distribution is given in the following table.

X	Relative Frequency
0	0.18
1	0.33
2	0.10
3	0.06
4	0.33

Exercise 5. Eight hundred insects were weighed, and the resulting measurements, in milligrams, are summarized in the following boxplot.

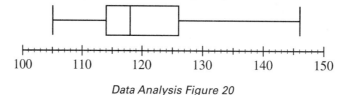

Data Analysis Figure 20

    (a) What are the range, the three quartiles, and the interquartile range of the measurements?

    (b) If the 80th percentile of the measurements is 130 milligrams, about how many measurements are between 126 milligrams and 130 milligrams?

Exercise 6. In how many different ways can the letters in the word STUDY be ordered?

Exercise 7.   Martha invited 4 friends to go with her to the movies. There are 120 different ways in which they can sit together in a row of 5 seats, one person per seat. In how many of those ways is Martha sitting in the middle seat?

Exercise 8.   How many 3-digit positive integers are odd and do not contain the digit 5?

Exercise 9.   From a box of 10 lightbulbs, you are to remove 4. How many different sets of 4 lightbulbs could you remove?

Exercise 10.   A talent contest has 8 contestants. Judges must award prizes for first, second, and third places, with no ties.

    (a)   In how many different ways can the judges award the 3 prizes?

    (b)   How many different groups of 3 people can get prizes?

Exercise 11.   If an integer is randomly selected from all positive 2-digit integers, what is the probability that the integer chosen has

    (a)   a 4 in the tens place?

    (b)   at least one 4 in the tens place or the units place?

    (c)   no 4 in either place?

Exercise 12.   In a box of 10 electrical parts, 2 are defective.

    (a)   If you choose one part at random from the box, what is the probability that it is *not* defective?

    (b)   If you choose two parts at random from the box, without replacement, what is the probability that both are defective?

Exercise 13.   A certain college has 8,978 full-time students, some of whom live on campus and some of whom live off campus.

The following table shows the distribution of the 8,978 full-time students, by class and living arrangement.

	Freshmen	Sophomores	Juniors	Seniors
Live on campus	1,812	1,236	950	542
Live off campus	625	908	1,282	1,623

    (a)   If one full-time student is selected at random, what is the probability that the student who is chosen will not be a freshman?

    (b)   If one full-time student who lives off campus is selected at random, what is the probability that the student will be a senior?

    (c)   If one full-time student who is a freshman or sophomore is selected at random, what is the probability that the student will be a student who lives on campus?

Exercise 14.   Let A, B, C, and D be events for which

$$P(A \text{ or } B) = 0.6, P(A) = 0.2, P(C \text{ or } D) = 0.6, \text{ and } P(C) = 0.5.$$

The events A and B are mutually exclusive, and the events C and D are independent.

    (a)   Find $P(B)$.

    (b)   Find $P(D)$.

Exercise 15.   Lin and Mark each attempt independently to decode a message. If the probability that Lin will decode the message is 0.80 and the probability that Mark will decode the message is 0.70, find the probability that

(a)   both will decode the message

(b)   at least one of them will decode the message

(c)   neither of them will decode the message

Exercise 16.   Data Analysis Figure 21 below shows the graph of a normal distribution with mean *m* and standard deviation *d*, including approximate percents of the distribution corresponding to the six regions shown.

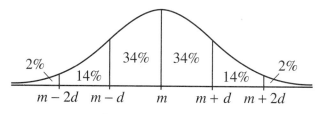

Data Analysis Figure 21

Suppose the heights of a population of 3,000 adult penguins are approximately normally distributed with a mean of 65 centimeters and a standard deviation of 5 centimeters.

(a)   Approximately how many of the adult penguins are between 65 centimeters and 75 centimeters tall?

(b)   If an adult penguin is chosen at random from the population, approximately what is the probability that the penguin's height will be less than 60 centimeters? Give your answer to the nearest 0.05.

Exercise 17.   This exercise is based on the following graph.

PUBLIC AND PRIVATE SCHOOL
EXPENDITURES, 1995–2001
(in billions of dollars)

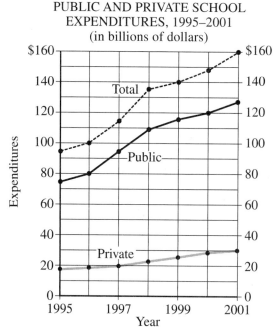

Data Analysis Figure 22

(a) For which year did total expenditures increase the most from the year before?

(b) For 2001, private school expenditures were what percent of total expenditures? Give your answer to the nearest percent.

Exercise 18.   This exercise is based on the following data.

DISTRIBUTION OF WORKFORCE BY OCCUPATIONAL CATEGORY
FOR REGION Y IN 2001 AND PROJECTED FOR 2025

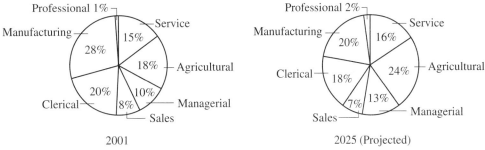

2001

2025 (Projected)

Data Analysis Figure 23

(a) In 2001, how many categories each comprised more than 25 million workers?

(b) What is the ratio of the number of workers in the Agricultural category in 2001 to the projected number of such workers in 2025?

(c) From 2001 to 2025, there is a projected increase in the number of workers in which of the following three categories?

Category 1: Sales

Category 2: Service

Category 3: Clerical

Exercise 19.   This exercise is based on the following data.

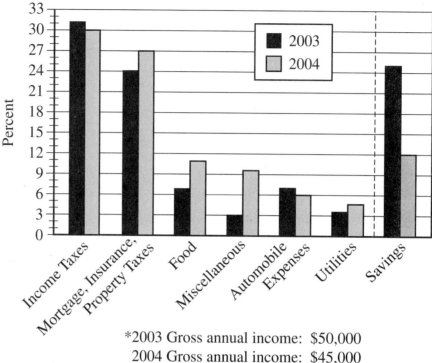

A FAMILY'S EXPENDITURES AND SAVINGS
AS A PERCENT OF ITS GROSS ANNUAL INCOME*

*2003 Gross annual income: $50,000
2004 Gross annual income: $45,000

Data Analysis Figure 24

(a) In 2003 the family used a total of 49 percent of its gross annual income
for two of the categories listed. What was the total amount of the family's
income used for those same categories in 2004?

(b) Of the seven categories listed, which category of expenditure had the
greatest percent increase from 2003 to 2004?

ANSWERS TO DATA ANALYSIS EXERCISES

Exercise 1. In degrees Fahrenheit, the statistics are

(a) mean = 68.6, median = 66.5, mode = 65, range = 16

(b) mean = 75.6, median = 73.5, mode = 72, range = 16

Exercise 2. (a) mean = 30, median = 28, mode = 22,

range = 31, interquartile range = 17

(b) mean = 90, median = 84, mode = 66,

range = 93, interquartile range = 51,

standard deviation ≈ 3(10.22) = 30.66

(c) interquartile range = 17, standard deviation ≈ 10.22

Exercise 3. (a) mean = 79

(b) The median cannot be determined from the information given.

Exercise 4. mean = 2.03, median = 1

Exercise 5. (a) range = 41, $Q_1 = 114$, $Q_2 = 118$, $Q_3 = 126$, interquartile range = 12

(b) 40 measurements

Exercise 6. 5! = 120

Exercise 7. 24

Exercise 8. 288

Exercise 9. 210

Exercise 10. (a) 336   (b) 56

Exercise 11. (a) $\dfrac{1}{9}$ (b) $\dfrac{1}{5}$ (c) $\dfrac{4}{5}$

Exercise 12. (a) $\dfrac{4}{5}$ (b) $\dfrac{1}{45}$

Exercise 13. (a) $\dfrac{6,541}{8,978}$ (b) $\dfrac{1,623}{4,438}$ (c) $\dfrac{3,048}{4,581}$

Exercise 14. (a) 0.4   (b) 0.2

Exercise 15. (a) 0.56   (b) 0.94   (c) 0.06

Exercise 16. (a) 1,440   (b) 0.15

Exercise 17. (a) 1998   (b) 19%

Exercise 18. (a) Three   (b) 9 to 14, or $\dfrac{9}{14}$ (c) Categories 1, 2, and 3

Exercise 19. (a) $17,550   (b) Miscellaneous

10 GRE Practice Test 1

Your goals for this chapter	◥ Take the first full-length authentic GRE General Test under actual test time limits ◥ Check your answers and read explanations for every question ◥ Use your results to identify your strengths and weaknesses

Taking Practice Test 1

Now that you have become familiar with the three measures of the General Test, it is time to take the first practice General Test to see how well you do. Practice Test 1 begins on the following pages. The total time that you should allow for this practice test is 2 hours and 15 minutes. The time allotted for each section appears at the beginning of that section.

Try to take Practice Test 1 under actual test conditions. Find a quiet place to work, and set aside enough time to complete the test without being disturbed. Work on only one section at a time. Use your watch or a timer to keep track of the time limit for each section.

For the Verbal Reasoning and Quantitative Reasoning portions of this practice test, mark your answers directly in this book. However, when you take the real GRE General Test on computer, you will use your mouse or keyboard to select your answer choices. For the Analytical Writing section of this test, you should type your responses.

The number of questions and time allowed per section on this practice test will give you an accurate guide to your readiness to take the test.

Following this practice test you will find an answer key. Check your answers against the key, then follow the instructions for calculating your Verbal Reasoning and Quantitative Reasoning scores and evaluating your Analytical Writing performance. You will also find explanations for each test question. Review the explanations, paying particular attention to the ones for the questions that you answered incorrectly.

Once you have worked your way through Practice Test 1, you will have a better idea of how ready you are to take the actual GRE General Test. You will also have a better sense of whether you are able to work fast enough to finish each section within the time allowed, or whether you need to improve your test-taking speed. After you have evaluated your test-taking performance, you can determine what type of additional preparation you might want to do for the test. For Official GRE prep resources, including practice tests that simulate the real test, visit the GRE website at **www.ets.org/gre/prepare**. Once you feel you have sufficiently prepared, you can take Practice Test 2 (Chapter 11).

SECTION 1
Analytical Writing

30 minutes

You will be given a brief quotation that states or implies an issue of general interest and specific instructions on how to respond to that issue. You will then have 30 minutes to plan and compose a response according to the specific instructions. A response to any other issue will receive a score of zero.

Make sure that you respond according to the specific instructions and support your position on the issue with reasons and examples drawn from such areas as your reading, experience, observations, and/or academic studies.

Trained GRE readers will evaluate your response for its overall quality, based on how well you:

- Respond to the specific task instructions
- Consider the complexities of the issue
- Organize, develop, and express your ideas
- Support your ideas with relevant reasons and/or examples
- Control the elements of standard written English

Before you begin writing, you may want to think for a few minutes about the issue and the specific task instructions and then plan your response. Be sure to develop your position fully and organize it coherently, but leave time to reread what you have written and make any revisions you think are necessary.

Analytical Writing Topic

The best way to teach is to praise positive actions and ignore negative ones.

Write a response in which you discuss the extent to which you agree or disagree with the recommendation and explain your reasoning for the position you take.
In developing and supporting your position, describe specific circumstances in which adopting the recommendation would or would not be advantageous and explain how these examples shape your position.

SECTION 2
Verbal Reasoning
Time—21 Minutes
15 Questions

For each of Questions 1 to 3, select <u>one</u> answer choice unless otherwise instructed.

Questions 1 to 3 are based on the following reading passage.

Whether the languages of the ancient American peoples were used for expressing abstract universal concepts can be clearly answered in the case of Nahuatl. Nahuatl, like Greek and German, is a language that allows the formation of extensive compounds. By the combination of radicals or semantic elements, single compound words can express complex conceptual relations, often of an abstract universal character.

line
5

The *tlamatinime* (those who know) were able to use this rich stock of abstract terms to express the nuances of their thought. They also availed themselves of other forms of expression with metaphorical meaning, some probably original, some derived from Toltec coinages. Of these forms, the most characteristic in Nahuatl is the juxtaposition of two words that, because they are synonyms, associated terms, or even contraries, complement each other to evoke one single idea. Used metaphorically, the juxtaposed terms connote specific or essential traits of the being they refer to, introducing a mode of poetry as an almost habitual form of expression.

10

For the following question, consider each of the choices separately and select all that apply.

1. Which of the following can be inferred from the passage regarding present-day research relating to Nahuatl?

    A Some record or evidence of the thought of the *tlamatinime* is available.
    B For at least some Nahuatl expressions, researchers are able to trace their derivation from another ancient language.
    C Researchers believe that in Nahuatl, abstract universal concepts are always expressed metaphorically.

2. Select the sentence in the passage in which the author introduces a specific Nahuatl mode of expression that is not identified as being shared with certain European languages.

3. In the context in which it appears, "coinages" (line 9) most nearly means

    Ⓐ adaptations
    Ⓑ creations
    Ⓒ idiosyncrasies
    Ⓓ pronunciations
    Ⓔ currencies

> **For Questions 4 and 5, select one entry for each blank from the corresponding column of choices. Fill all blanks in the way that best completes the text.**

4. In her later years, Bertha Pappenheim was an apostle of noble but already (i)_____ notions, always respected for her integrity, her energy, and her resolve but increasingly out of step and ultimately (ii)_____ even her own organization.

Blank (i)	Blank (ii)
(A) anachronistic	(D) emulated by
(B) accepted	(E) appreciated by
(C) exotic	(F) alienated from

5. The reception given to Kimura's radical theory of molecular evolution shows that when _____ fights orthodoxy to a draw, then novelty has seized a good chunk of space from convention.

(A) imitation
(B) reaction
(C) dogmatism
(D) invention
(E) caution

GO ON TO NEXT PAGE

For Question 6, select <u>one</u> answer choice unless otherwise instructed.

Question 6 is based on the following reading passage.

In the past ten years, there have been several improvements in mountain-climbing equipment. These improvements have made the sport both safer and more enjoyable for experienced climbers. Despite these improvements, however, the rate of mountain-climbing injuries has doubled in the past ten years.

6.   Which of the following, if true, best reconciles the apparent discrepancy presented in the passage?

   (A) Many climbers, lulled into a false sense of security, use the new equipment to attempt climbing feats of which they are not capable.

   (B) Some mountain-climbing injuries are caused by unforeseeable weather conditions.

   (C) Mountain climbing, although a dangerous sport, does not normally result in injury to the experienced climber.

   (D) In the past ten years there have been improvements in mountain-climbing techniques as well as in mountain-climbing equipment.

   (E) Although the rate of mountain-climbing injuries has increased, the rate of mountain-climbing deaths has not changed.

For Questions 7 to 9, select one entry for each blank from the corresponding column of choices. Fill all blanks in the way that best completes the text.

7.   The novelist devotes so much time to avid descriptions of his characters' clothes that the reader soon feels that such _____ concerns, although worthy of attention, have superseded any more directly literary aims.

   | (A) didactic |
   | (B) syntactical |
   | (C) irrelevant |
   | (D) sartorial |
   | (E) frivolous |

8.   Belanger dances with an (i)_____ that draws one's attention as if by seeking to (ii)_____ it; through finesse and understatement, he manages to seem at once intensely present and curiously detached.

Blank (i)	Blank (ii)
(A) undemonstrative panache	(D) focus
(B) unrestrained enthusiasm	(E) overwhelm
(C) unattractive gawkiness	(F) deflect

9. The most striking thing about the politician is how often his politics have been (i)_____ rather than ideological, as he adapts his political positions at any particular moment to the political realities that constrain him. He does not, however, piously (ii)_____ political principles only to betray them in practice. Rather, he attempts in subtle ways to balance his political self-interest with a (iii)_____, viewing himself as an instrument of some unchanging higher purpose.

Blank (i)	Blank (ii)	Blank (iii)
(A) quixotic	(D) brandish	(G) profound cynicism
(B) self-righteous	(E) flout	(H) deeply felt moral code
(C) strategic	(F) follow	(I) thoroughgoing pragmatism

GO ON TO NEXT PAGE ↘

For each of Questions 10 to 12, select <u>one</u> answer choice unless otherwise instructed.

Questions 10 to 12 are based on the following reading passage.

The condition of scholarship devoted to the history of women in photography is confounding. Recent years have witnessed the posthumous inflation of the role of the hobbyist Alice Austen into that of a pioneering documentarian while dozens of notable senior
line figures—Marion Palfi, whose photographs of civil-rights activities in the South served as
5 early evidence of the need for protective legislation, to name one—received scant attention from scholars. And, while Naomi Rosenblum's synoptic *History of Women Photographers* covers the subject through 1920 in a generally useful fashion, once she reaches the 1920s, when the venues, forms, applications, and movements of the medium expanded exponentially, she resorts to an increasingly terse listing of unfamiliar names, with approaches and
10 careers summarized in a sentence or two.

10. The author of the passage cites Rosenblum's book most likely in order to
- (A) suggest that the works documented most thoroughly by historians of women in photography often do not warrant that attention
- (B) offer an explanation for the observation that not all aspects of the history of women in photography have received the same level of attention
- (C) provide an example of a way in which scholarship on the history of women in photography has been unsatisfactory
- (D) suggest that employing a strictly chronological approach when studying the history of women in photography may be unproductive
- (E) provide support for the notion that certain personalities in women's photography have attained undue prominence

For the following question, consider each of the choices separately and select all that apply.

11. Which of the following statements about Marion Palfi is supported by the passage?
- [A] Marion Palfi's photographs would have received greater recognition from historians had her work been done in an era when most aspects of photography were static rather than in a state of transition.
- [B] Alice Austen has achieved greater notoriety than has Marion Palfi primarily because the subjects that Austen photographed were more familiar to her contemporaries.
- [C] In addition to providing a record of certain historical events, Marion Palfi's photographs played a role in subsequent events.

12. In the context in which it appears, "inflation" (line 2) most nearly means
- (A) exaggeration
- (B) acquisition
- (C) evaluation
- (D) distortion
- (E) attenuation

> **For Questions 13 to 15, select the <u>two</u> answer choices that, when used to complete the sentence, fit the meaning of the sentence as a whole <u>and</u> produce completed sentences that are alike in meaning.**

13. Though feminist in its implications, Yvonne Rainer's 1974 film _____ the filmmaker's active involvement in feminist politics.
    - A antedated
    - B cloaked
    - C portrayed
    - D preceded
    - E renewed
    - F represented

14. Congress is having great difficulty developing a consensus on energy policy, primarily because the policy objectives of various members of Congress rest on such _____ assumptions.
    - A commonplace
    - B disparate
    - C divergent
    - D fundamental
    - E trite
    - F trivial

15. Because they had expected the spacecraft Voyager 2 to be able to gather data only about the planets Jupiter and Saturn, scientists were _____ the wealth of information it sent back from Neptune twelve years after leaving Earth.
    - A anxious for
    - B confident in
    - C thrilled about
    - D keen on
    - E elated by
    - F eager for

STOP. This is the end of Section 2.

GO ON TO NEXT PAGE ↘

SECTION 3
Verbal Reasoning
Time—28 Minutes
20 Questions

For Questions 1 to 4, select the <u>two</u> answer choices that, when used to complete the sentence, fit the meaning of the sentence as a whole and produce completed sentences that are alike in meaning.

1. Only by ignoring decades of mismanagement and inefficiency could investors conclude that a fresh infusion of cash would provide anything other than a _____ solution to the company's financial woes.

    A complete

    B fleeting

    C momentary

    D premature

    E trivial

    F total

2. Some scientists argue that carbon compounds play such a central role in life on Earth because of the possibility of _____ resulting from the carbon atom's ability to form an unending series of different molecules.

    A diversity

    B deviation

    C variety

    D reproduction

    E stability

    F invigoration

3. Given the flood of information presented by the mass media, the only way for someone to keep abreast of the news is to rely on _____ accounts.

    A synoptic

    B abridged

    C sensational

    D copious

    E lurid

    F understated

4. Always circumspect, she was reluctant to make judgments, but once arriving at a conclusion, she was _____ in its defense.

    A   deferential

    B   intransigent

    C   lax

    D   negligent

    E   obsequious

    F   resolute

For each of Questions 5 to 7, select **one** answer choice unless otherwise instructed.

Questions 5 and 6 are based on the following reading passage.

When marine organisms called phytoplankton photosynthesize, they absorb carbon dioxide dissolved in seawater, potentially causing a reduction in the concentration of atmospheric carbon dioxide, a gas that contributes to global warming. However, phytoplankton flourish only in surface waters where iron levels are sufficiently high. Martin therefore hypothesized that adding iron to iron-poor regions of the ocean could help alleviate global warming. While experiments subsequently confirmed that such a procedure increases phytoplankton growth, field tests have shown that such growth does not significantly lower atmospheric carbon dioxide. When phytoplankton utilize carbon dioxide for photosynthesis, the carbon becomes a building block for organic matter, but the carbon leaks back into the atmosphere when predators consume the phytoplankton and respire carbon dioxide.

For the following question, consider each of the choices separately and select all that apply.

5. It can be inferred from the passage that Martin's hypothesis includes which of the following elements?

  A. A correct understanding of how phytoplankton photosynthesis utilizes carbon dioxide

  B. A correct prediction about how the addition of iron to iron-poor waters would affect phytoplankton growth

  C. An incorrect prediction about how phytoplankton growth would affect the concentration of atmospheric carbon dioxide

6. It can be inferred that the author of the passage mentions predators (line 10) primarily in order to

  (A) help explain why Martin's hypothesis is incorrect

  (B) identify one effect of adding iron to iron-poor waters

  (C) indicate how some carbon dioxide is converted to solid organic matter

  (D) help account for differences in the density of phytoplankton between different regions of the ocean

  (E) point out a factor that was not anticipated by the scientists who conducted the field tests mentioned in the passage

Question 7 is based on the following reading passage.

Sparva, unlike Treland's other provinces, requires automobile insurers to pay for any medical treatment sought by someone who has been involved in an accident; in the other provinces, insurers pay for nonemergency treatment only if they preapprove the treatment. Clearly, Sparva's less restrictive policy must be the explanation for the fact that altogether insurers there pay for far more treatments after accidents than insurers in other provinces, even though Sparva does not have the largest population.

7. Which of the following, if true, most strengthens the argument?

(A) Car insurance costs more in Sparva than in any other province.

(B) The cost of medical care in Sparva is higher than the national average.

(C) Different insurance companies have different standards for determining what constitutes emergency treatment.

(D) Fewer insurance companies operate in Sparva than in any other province.

(E) There are fewer traffic accidents annually in Sparva than in any of the provinces of comparable or greater population.

For Questions 8 to 11, select one entry for each blank from the corresponding column of choices. Fill all blanks in the way that best completes the text.

---

8. Ironically, the writer so wary of (i)_____ was (ii)_____ with ink and paper, his novel running to 2,500 shagreen-bound folio pages—a fortune in stationery at the time.

Blank (i)	Blank (ii)
(A) probity	(D) acquisitive
(B) extravagance	(E) illiberal
(C) disapprobation	(F) profligate

9. What readers most commonly remember about John Stuart Mill's classic exploration of the liberty of thought and discussion concerns the danger of (i)_____: in the absence of challenge, one's opinions, even when they are correct, grow weak and flabby. Yet Mill had another reason for encouraging the liberty of thought and discussion: the danger of partiality and incompleteness. Since one's opinions, even under the best circumstances, tend to (ii)_____, and because opinions opposed to one's own rarely turn out to be completely (iii)_____, it is crucial to supplement one's opinions with alternative points of view.

Blank (i)	Blank (ii)	Blank (iii)
(A) tendentiousness	(D) embrace only a portion of the truth	(G) erroneous
(B) complacency	(E) change over time	(H) antithetical
(C) fractiousness	(F) focus on matters close at hand	(I) immutable

GO ON TO NEXT PAGE ➘

10. Just as the authors' book on eels is often a key text for courses in marine vertebrate zoology, their ideas on animal development and phylogeny _____ teaching in this area.

Ⓐ prevent
Ⓑ defy
Ⓒ replicate
Ⓓ inform
Ⓔ use

11. Mechanisms develop whereby every successful species can _____ its innate capacity for population growth with the constraints that arise through its interactions with the natural environment.

Ⓐ enhance
Ⓑ replace
Ⓒ produce
Ⓓ surpass
Ⓔ reconcile

For each of Questions 12 to 14, select <u>one</u> answer choice unless otherwise instructed.

Questions 12 to 14 are based on the following reading passage.

It would be expected that a novel by a figure as prominent as W. E. B. DuBois would attract the attention of literary critics. Additionally, when the novel subtly engages the issue of race, as DuBois' *The Quest of the Silver Fleece* (1911) does, it would be a surprise not to encounter an abundance of scholarly work about that text. But though valuable scholarship has examined DuBois' political and historical thought, his novels have received scant attention. Perhaps DuBois the novelist must wait his turn behind DuBois the philosopher, historian, and editor. But what if the truth lies elsewhere: what if his novels do not speak to current concerns?

12. Which of the following can be inferred from the passage regarding DuBois' *The Quest of the Silver Fleece*?
    - (A) The lack of attention devoted to *The Quest of the Silver Fleece* can be attributed to the fact that it was DuBois' first novel.
    - (B) Among DuBois' novels, *The Quest of the Silver Fleece* is unusual in that it has received scant attention from scholars.
    - (C) *The Quest of the Silver Fleece* has at least one feature that typically would attract the attention of literary scholars.
    - (D) *The Quest of the Silver Fleece*, given its subtle exploration of race, is probably the best novel written by DuBois.
    - (E) Much of the scholarly work that has focused on *The Quest of the Silver Fleece* has been surprisingly critical of it.

13. In the fourth sentence ("Perhaps DuBois . . . editor."), the author of the passage is most likely suggesting that
    - (A) scholars will find that DuBois' novels are more relevant to current concerns than is his work as philosopher, historian, and editor
    - (B) more scholarly attention will be paid to *The Quest of the Silver Fleece* than to DuBois' other novels
    - (C) DuBois' novels will come to overshadow his work as philosopher, historian, and editor
    - (D) DuBois' novels may eventually attract greater scholarly interest than they have to date
    - (E) it will be shown that DuBois' work as philosopher, historian, and editor had an important influence on his work as novelist

GO ON TO NEXT PAGE

14. Which of the following best describes the central issue with which the passage is concerned?

   Ⓐ The perfunctoriness of much of the critical work devoted to DuBois' novels
   Ⓑ The nature of DuBois' engagement with the issue of race in *The Quest of the Silver Fleece*
   Ⓒ Whether DuBois' novels are of high quality and relevant to current concerns
   Ⓓ The relationship between DuBois the novelist and DuBois the philosopher, historian, and editor
   Ⓔ The degree of consideration that has been given to DuBois' novels, including *The Quest of the Silver Fleece*

> **For Questions 15 and 16, select one entry for each blank from the corresponding column of choices. Fill all blanks in the way that best completes the text.**

15. The activists' energetic work in the service of both woman suffrage and the temperance movement in the late nineteenth century (i)_____ the assertion that the two movements were (ii)_____.

Blank (i)	Blank (ii)
Ⓐ undermines	Ⓓ diffuse
Ⓑ supports	Ⓔ inimical
Ⓒ underscores	Ⓕ predominant

16. Wills argues that certain malarial parasites are especially (i)_____ because they have more recently entered humans than other species and therefore have had (ii)_____ time to evolve toward (iii)_____. Yet there is no reliable evidence that the most harmful *Plasmodium* species has been in humans for a shorter time than less harmful species.

Blank (i)	Blank (ii)	Blank (iii)
Ⓐ populous	Ⓓ ample	Ⓖ virulence
Ⓑ malignant	Ⓔ insufficient	Ⓗ benignity
Ⓒ threatened	Ⓕ adequate	Ⓘ variability

For each of Questions 17 to 20, select <u>one</u> answer choice unless otherwise instructed.

Question 17 is based on the following reading passage.

Observations of the Arctic reveal that the Arctic Ocean is covered by less ice each summer than the previous summer. If this warming trend continues, within 50 years the Arctic Ocean will be ice free during the summer months. This occurrence would in itself have little or no effect on global sea levels, since the melting of ice floating in water does not affect the water level. However, serious consequences to sea levels would eventually result, because _____.

17.   Which of the following most logically completes the passage?

    Ⓐ large masses of floating sea ice would continue to form in the wintertime

    Ⓑ significant changes in Arctic sea temperatures would be accompanied by changes in sea temperatures in more temperate parts of the world

    Ⓒ such a warm Arctic Ocean would trigger the melting of massive land-based glaciers in the Arctic

    Ⓓ an ice-free Arctic Ocean would support a very different ecosystem than it does presently

    Ⓔ in the spring, melting sea ice would cause more icebergs to be created and to drift south into shipping routes

GO ON TO NEXT PAGE ↘

In a recent study, David Cressy examines two central questions concerning English immigration to New England in the 1630s: what kinds of people immigrated and why? Using contemporary literary evidence, shipping lists, and customs records, Cressy finds that most adult immigrants were skilled in farming or crafts, were literate, and were organized in families. Each of these characteristics sharply distinguishes the 21,000 people who left for New England in the 1630s from most of the approximately 377,000 English people who had immigrated to America by 1700.

With respect to their reasons for immigrating, Cressy does not deny the frequently noted fact that some of the immigrants of the 1630s, most notably the organizers and clergy, advanced religious explanations for departure, but he finds that such explanations usually assumed primacy only in retrospect. When he moves beyond the principal actors, he finds that religious explanations were less frequently offered, and he concludes that most people immigrated because they were recruited by promises of material improvement.

For the following question, consider each of the choices separately and select all that apply.

18. The passage indicates that Cressy would agree with which of the following statements about the organizers among the English immigrants to New England in the 1630s?

   [A] Some of them offered a religious explanation for their immigration.

   [B] They did not offer any reasons for their immigration until some time after they had immigrated.

   [C] They were more likely than the average immigrant to be motivated by material considerations.

19. Select the sentence that provides Cressy's opinion about what motivated English immigrants to go to New England in the 1630s.

20. In the passage, the author is primarily concerned with

   (A) summarizing the findings of an investigation
   (B) analyzing a method of argument
   (C) evaluating a point of view
   (D) hypothesizing about a set of circumstances
   (E) establishing categories

STOP. This is the end of Section 3.

SECTION 4
Quantitative Reasoning
Time—24 Minutes
15 Questions

For each question, indicate the best answer, using the directions given.

Notes: All numbers used are real numbers.

All figures are assumed to lie in a plane unless otherwise indicated. Geometric figures, such as lines, circles, triangles, and quadrilaterals, **are not necessarily** drawn to scale. That is, you should **not** assume that quantities such as lengths and angle measures are as they appear in a figure. You should assume, however, that lines shown as straight are actually straight, points on a line are in the order shown, and more generally, all geometric objects are in the relative positions shown. For questions with geometric figures, you should base your answers on geometric reasoning, not on estimating or comparing quantities by sight or by measurement.

Coordinate systems, such as xy-planes and number lines, **are** drawn to scale; therefore, you can read, estimate, or compare quantities in such figures by sight or by measurement.

Graphical data presentations, such as bar graphs, circle graphs, and line graphs, **are** drawn to scale; therefore, you can read, estimate, or compare data values by sight or by measurement.

For each of Questions 1 to 5, compare Quantity A and Quantity B, using additional information centered above the two quantities if such information is given. Select one of the following four answer choices and fill in the corresponding oval to the right of the question.

(A)   Quantity A is greater.

(B)   Quantity B is greater.

(C)   The two quantities are equal.

(D)   The relationship cannot be determined from the information given.

A symbol that appears more than once in a question has the same meaning throughout the question.

	Quantity A	Quantity B	Correct Answer
Example 1:	(2)(6)	2 + 6	(A) (B) (C) (D)

	Quantity A	Quantity B	Correct Answer
Example 2:	PS	SR	(A) (B) (C) (D)

(since equal lengths cannot be assumed, even though *PS* and *SR* appear equal)

Ⓐ **Quantity A is greater.**
Ⓑ **Quantity B is greater.**
Ⓒ **The two quantities are equal.**
Ⓓ **The relationship cannot be determined from the information given.**

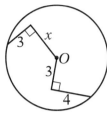

O is the center of the circle above.

	Quantity A	Quantity B	
1.	x	5	Ⓐ Ⓑ Ⓒ Ⓓ

$$x < y < z$$

	Quantity A	Quantity B	
2.	$\dfrac{x+y+z}{3}$	y	Ⓐ Ⓑ Ⓒ Ⓓ

Ⓐ **Quantity A is greater.**
Ⓑ **Quantity B is greater.**
Ⓒ **The two quantities are equal.**
Ⓓ **The relationship cannot be determined from the information given.**

p is the probability that event *E* will occur, and *s* is the probability that event *E* will <u>not</u> occur.

	Quantity A	Quantity B	
3.	$p + s$	ps	Ⓐ Ⓑ Ⓒ Ⓓ

X is the set of all integers n that satisfy the inequality $2 \leq |n| \leq 5$.

Quantity A	Quantity B	
4. The absolute value of the greatest integer in X	The absolute value of the least integer in X	Ⓐ Ⓑ Ⓒ Ⓓ

A random variable Y is normally distributed with a mean of 200 and a standard deviation of 10.

Quantity A	Quantity B	
5. The probability of the event that the value of Y is greater than 220	$\dfrac{1}{6}$	Ⓐ Ⓑ Ⓒ Ⓓ

GO ON TO NEXT PAGE ⬃

Questions 6 to 15 have several different formats. Unless otherwise directed, select a single answer choice. For Numeric Entry questions, follow the instructions below.

Numeric Entry Questions
Enter your answer in the answer box(es) below the question.

- Your answer may be an integer, a decimal, or a fraction, and it may be negative.
- If a question asks for a fraction, there will be two boxes—one for the numerator and one for the denominator.
- Equivalent forms of the correct answer, such as 2.5 and 2.50, are all correct. Fractions do not need to be reduced to lowest terms.
- Enter the exact answer unless the question asks you to round your answer.

6. The ratio of $\frac{1}{3}$ to $\frac{3}{8}$ is equal to the ratio of

   (A) 1 to 8
   (B) 8 to 1
   (C) 8 to 3
   (D) 8 to 9
   (E) 9 to 8

For the following question, enter your answer in the box.

7. In a graduating class of 236 students, 142 took algebra and 121 took chemistry. What is the greatest possible number of students that could have taken both algebra and chemistry?

   [   ] students

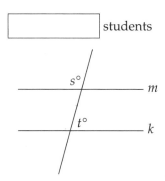

8. In the figure above, if $m \parallel k$ and $s = t + 30$, then $t =$
   (A) 30
   (B) 60
   (C) 75
   (D) 80
   (E) 105

For the following question, select all the answer choices that apply.

9. The total amount that Mary paid for a book was equal to the price of the book plus a sales tax that was 4 percent of the price of the book. Mary paid for the book with a $10 bill and received the correct change, which was less than $3.00. Which of the following statements must be true?

   Indicate _all_ such statements.

   [A] The price of the book was less than $9.50.

   [B] The price of the book was greater than $6.90.

   [C] The sales tax was less than $0.45.

10. If $\dfrac{1}{(2^{11})(5^{17})}$ is expressed as a terminating decimal, how many nonzero digits will the decimal have?

    (A) One
    (B) Two
    (C) Four
    (D) Six
    (E) Eleven

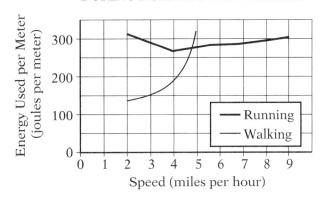

ENERGY USED PER METER VERSUS SPEED
DURING RUNNING AND WALKING

11. If s is a speed, in miles per hour, at which the energy used per meter during running is twice the energy used per meter during walking, then, according to the graph above, s is between

    (A) 2.5 and 3.0
    (B) 3.0 and 3.5
    (C) 3.5 and 4.0
    (D) 4.0 and 4.5
    (E) 4.5 and 5.0

GO ON TO NEXT PAGE ↘

12. If $n = 2^3$, then $n^n =$

    Ⓐ 2^6

    Ⓑ 2^{11}

    Ⓒ 2^{18}

    Ⓓ 2^{24}

    Ⓔ 2^{27}

For the following question, select all the answer choices that apply.

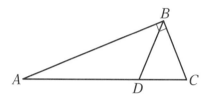

The length of AB is $10\sqrt{3}$.

13. Which of the following statements <u>individually</u> provide(s) sufficient additional information to determine the area of triangle ABC above?

Indicate <u>all</u> such statements.

    A DBC is an equilateral triangle.

    B ABD is an isosceles triangle.

    C   The length of BC is equal to the length of AD.

    D   The length of BC is 10.

    E   The length of AD is 10.

For the following question, enter your answer in the box.

$$a_1, a_2, a_3, \ldots, a_n, \ldots$$

14. In the sequence above, each term after the first term is equal to the preceding term plus the constant c. If $a_1 + a_3 + a_5 = 27$, what is the value of $a_2 + a_4$?

$$a_2 + a_4 = \boxed{}$$

15. A desert outpost has a water supply that is sufficient to last 21 days for 15 people. At the same average rate of water consumption per person, how many days would the water supply last for 9 people?

    Ⓐ 28.0

    Ⓑ 32.5

    Ⓒ 35.0

    Ⓓ 37.5

    Ⓔ 42.0

STOP. This is the end of Section 4.

SECTION 5
Quantitative Reasoning
Time — 32 Minutes
20 Questions

For each question, indicate the best answer, using the directions given.

Notes: All numbers used are real numbers.

All figures are assumed to lie in a plane unless otherwise indicated. Geometric figures, such as lines, circles, triangles, and quadrilaterals, **are not necessarily** drawn to scale. That is, you should **not** assume that quantities such as lengths and angle measures are as they appear in a figure. You should assume, however, that lines shown as straight are actually straight, points on a line are in the order shown, and more generally, all geometric objects are in the relative positions shown. For questions with geometric figures, you should base your answers on geometric reasoning, not on estimating or comparing quantities by sight or by measurement.

Coordinate systems, such as xy-planes and number lines, **are** drawn to scale; therefore, you can read, estimate, or compare quantities in such figures by sight or by measurement.

Graphical data presentations, such as bar graphs, circle graphs, and line graphs, **are** drawn to scale; therefore, you can read, estimate, or compare data values by sight or by measurement.

For each of Questions 1 to 7, compare Quantity A and Quantity B, using additional information centered above the two quantities if such information is given. Select one of the following four answer choices and fill in the corresponding oval to the right of the question.

(A) Quantity A is greater.

(B) Quantity B is greater.

(C) The two quantities are equal.

(D) The relationship cannot be determined from the information given.

A symbol that appears more than once in a question has the same meaning throughout the question.

	Quantity A	Quantity B	Correct Answer
Example 1:	(2)(6)	2 + 6	(A) (B) (C) (D)

	Quantity A	Quantity B	Correct Answer
Example 2:	PS	SR	(A) (B) (C) (D)

(since equal lengths cannot be assumed, even though *PS* and *SR* appear equal)

GO ON TO NEXT PAGE ➘

Ⓐ **Quantity A is greater.**
Ⓑ **Quantity B is greater.**
Ⓒ **The two quantities are equal.**
Ⓓ **The relationship cannot be determined from the information given.**

Country	Value of 1 United States Dollar
Argentina	0.93 peso
Kenya	32.08 shillings

	Quantity A	Quantity B	
1.	The dollar value of 1 Argentine peso according to the table above	The dollar value of 1 Kenyan shilling according to the table above	Ⓐ Ⓑ Ⓒ Ⓓ

k is a digit in the decimal 1.3k5, and 1.3k5 is less than 1.33.

	Quantity A	Quantity B	
2.	k	1	Ⓐ Ⓑ Ⓒ Ⓓ

AB is a diameter of the circle above.

	Quantity A	Quantity B	
3.	The length of *AB*	The average (arithmetic mean) of the lengths of *AC* and *AD*	Ⓐ Ⓑ Ⓒ Ⓓ

Ⓐ **Quantity A is greater.**
Ⓑ **Quantity B is greater.**
Ⓒ **The two quantities are equal.**
Ⓓ **The relationship cannot be determined from the information given.**

Three consecutive integers have a sum of −84.

	Quantity A	Quantity B	
4.	The least of the three integers	−28	Ⓐ Ⓑ Ⓒ Ⓓ

In the xy-plane, the equation of line k is $3x - 2y = 0$.

	Quantity A	Quantity B	
5.	The x-intercept of line k	The y-intercept of line k	Ⓐ Ⓑ Ⓒ Ⓓ

---

n is a positive integer that is divisible by 6.

	Quantity A	Quantity B	
6.	The remainder when n is divided by 12	The remainder when n is divided by 18	Ⓐ Ⓑ Ⓒ Ⓓ

$$\frac{1-x}{x-1} = \frac{1}{x}$$

	Quantity A	Quantity B	
7.	x	$-\dfrac{1}{2}$	Ⓐ Ⓑ Ⓒ Ⓓ

GO ON TO NEXT PAGE ◣

Questions 8 to 20 have several different formats. Unless otherwise directed, select a single answer choice. For Numeric Entry questions, follow the instructions below.

Numeric Entry Questions
Enter your answer in the answer box(es) below the question.

- Your answer may be an integer, a decimal, or a fraction, and it may be negative.
- If a question asks for a fraction, there will be two boxes—one for the numerator and one for the denominator.
- Equivalent forms of the correct answer, such as 2.5 and 2.50, are all correct. Fractions do not need to be reduced to lowest terms.
- Enter the exact answer unless the question asks you to round your answer.

8. The fabric needed to make 3 curtains sells for $8.00 per yard and can be purchased only by the full yard. If the length of fabric required for each curtain is 1.6 yards and all of the fabric is purchased as a single length, what is the total cost of the fabric that needs to be purchased for the 3 curtains?

  (A) $40.00
  (B) $38.40
  (C) $24.00
  (D) $16.00
  (E) $12.80

For the following question, select all the answer choices that apply.

9. In the xy-plane, line k is a line that does <u>not</u> pass through the origin.

   Which of the following statements <u>individually</u> provide(s) sufficient additional information to conclude that the slope of line k is negative?

   Indicate <u>all</u> such statements.

   A The x-intercept of line k is twice the y-intercept of line k.

   B The product of the x-intercept and the y-intercept of line k is positive.

   C Line k passes through the points (a, b) and (r, s), where $(a - r)(b - s) < 0$.

	Distance from Centerville (miles)
Freight train	$-10t + 115$
Passenger train	$-20t + 150$

10. The expressions in the table above give the distance from Centerville to each of two trains t hours after 12:00 noon. At what time after 12:00 noon will the trains be equidistant from Centerville?

    (A) 1:30
    (B) 3:30
    (C) 5:10
    (D) 8:50
    (E) 11:30

For the following question, enter your answer in the box.

11. In the xy-plane, the point with coordinates $(-6, -7)$ is the center of circle C. The point with coordinates $(-6, 5)$ lies inside C, and the point with coordinates $(8, -7)$ lies outside C. If m is the radius of C and m is an integer, what is the value of m?

    $m = $ ☐

For the following question, select all the answer choices that apply.

12. The integer v is greater than 1. If v is the square of an integer, which of the following numbers must also be the square of an integer?

    Indicate all such numbers.

    A $81v$

    B $25v + 10\sqrt{v} + 1$

    C $4v^2 + 4\sqrt{v} + 1$

GO ON TO NEXT PAGE ◥

DISTANCE TRAVELED BY A CAR ACCORDING TO THE CAR'S SPEED
WHEN THE DRIVER IS SIGNALED TO STOP

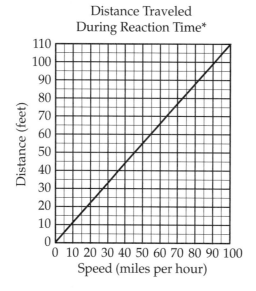

Distance Traveled
During Reaction Time*

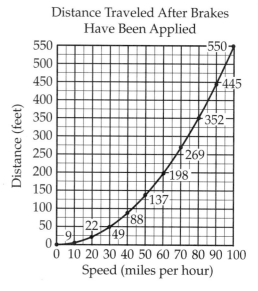

Distance Traveled After Brakes
Have Been Applied

*Reaction time is the time period that begins when the driver is signaled to stop and ends when the driver applies the brakes.

Note: Total stopping distance is the sum of the distance traveled during reaction time and the distance traveled after brakes have been applied.

13. Approximately what is the total stopping distance, in feet, if the car is traveling at a speed of 40 miles per hour when the driver is signaled to stop?

   (A)   130
   (B)   110
   (C)   90
   (D)   70
   (E)   40

14. Of the following, which is the greatest speed, in miles per hour, at which the car can travel and stop with a total stopping distance of less than 200 feet?

   (A)   50
   (B)   55
   (C)   60
   (D)   65
   (E)   70

15. The total stopping distance for the car traveling at 60 miles per hour is approximately what percent greater than the total stopping distance for the car traveling at 50 miles per hour?

    (A) 22%

    (B) 30%

    (C) 38%

    (D) 45%

    (E) 52%

16. What is the least positive integer that is <u>not</u> a factor of 25! and is <u>not</u> a prime number?

    (A) 26

    (B) 28

    (C) 36

    (D) 56

    (E) 58

17. If $0 < a < 1 < b$, which of the following is true about the reciprocals of a and b?

    (A) $1 < \dfrac{1}{a} < \dfrac{1}{b}$

    (B) $\dfrac{1}{a} < 1 < \dfrac{1}{b}$

    (C) $\dfrac{1}{a} < \dfrac{1}{b} < 1$

    (D) $\dfrac{1}{b} < 1 < \dfrac{1}{a}$

    (E) $\dfrac{1}{b} < \dfrac{1}{a} < 1$

GO ON TO NEXT PAGE ◥

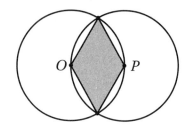

18. In the figure above, O and P are the centers of the two circles. If each circle has radius r, what is the area of the shaded region?

    Ⓐ $\dfrac{\sqrt{2}}{2}r^2$

    Ⓑ $\dfrac{\sqrt{3}}{2}r^2$

    Ⓒ $\sqrt{2}r^2$

    Ⓓ $\sqrt{3}r^2$

    Ⓔ $2\sqrt{3}r^2$

For the following question, enter your answer in the boxes.

19. Of the 20 lightbulbs in a box, 2 are defective. An inspector will select 2 lightbulbs simultaneously and at random from the box. What is the probability that neither of the lightbulbs selected will be defective?

Give your answer as a fraction.

$$\frac{\boxed{}}{\boxed{}}$$

20. What is the perimeter, in meters, of a rectangular playground 24 meters wide that has the same area as a rectangular playground 64 meters long and 48 meters wide?

    Ⓐ 112
    Ⓑ 152
    Ⓒ 224
    Ⓓ 256
    Ⓔ 304

STOP. This is the end of Section 5.

Evaluating Your Performance

Now that you have completed Practice Test 1, it is time to evaluate your performance.

Analytical Writing Measure

One way to evaluate your performance on the Analytical Writing topic you answered on this practice test is to compare your essay response to the scored sample essay responses for this topic and review the rater commentary. Scored sample essay responses and rater commentary are presented starting on page 523 for the topic presented in the Analytical Writing section of Practice Test 1. The scoring guide starts on page 23.

To better understand the analytical writing abilities characteristic of particular score levels, you should review the score level descriptions on page 25.

Verbal Reasoning and Quantitative Reasoning Measures

The tables that follow contain information to help you evaluate your performance on the Verbal Reasoning and Quantitative Reasoning measures of Practice Test 1. An answer key with the correct answers to the questions in the Verbal Reasoning and Quantitative Reasoning sections in this practice test begins on page 517. Compare your answers to the correct answers given in the table, crossing out questions you answered incorrectly or omitted. Partially correct answers should be treated as incorrect. Knowing which questions you answered incorrectly or omitted can help you identify content areas in which you need more practice or review.

The answer key contains additional information to help you evaluate your performance. With each answer, the key provides a number, the P+. The P+ is the percent of a group of actual GRE takers who were administered that same question at a previous test administration and who answered it correctly. P+ is used to gauge the relative difficulty of a test question. The higher the P+, the easier the test question. You can use the P+ to compare your performance on each test question to the performance of other test takers on that same question. For example, if the P+ for a question is 89, that means that 89 percent of GRE test takers who received this question answered it correctly. Alternatively, if the P+ for a question is 14, that means that 14 percent of GRE test takers who received this question answered it correctly. A question with a P+ of 89 may be interpreted as a relatively easy question, and a question with a P+ of 14 may be interpreted as a difficult question.

To calculate your scores on Practice Test 1:

- Add the number of correct answers in Sections 2 and 3 to obtain your raw Verbal Reasoning score.
- Add the number of correct answers in Sections 4 and 5 to obtain your raw Quantitative Reasoning score.
- Once you have calculated your raw scores, refer to the Practice Test 1 score conversion table on pages 521–522. Find the scores on the 130–170 score scales that correspond to your Verbal Reasoning and Quantitative Reasoning raw scores. Note the scaled scores provided.

Once you determine your scaled scores, you will need to evaluate your performance. To get a sense of how test takers are scoring on the Verbal Reasoning and Quantitative Reasoning measures of the actual test, you can review Verbal Reasoning and Quantitative Reasoning percentile ranks on the GRE website at **www.ets.org/gre /percentile** (PDF). A percentile rank for a score indicates the percentage of examinees who took that test and received a lower score. Updated annually in July, this table includes the Verbal Reasoning and Quantitative Reasoning scores on the 130–170 scale in one-point increments and the corresponding percentile ranks. For each score you earned on Practice Test 1, note the percent of GRE test takers who earned lower scores. This is a reasonable indication of your rank among GRE General Test examinees if you took Practice Test 1 under standard timed conditions.

Answer Key

Section 2. Verbal Reasoning

Question Number	P+	Correct Answer
1	37	**Choice A:** Some record or evidence of the thought of the *tlamatinime* is available. AND **Choice B:** For at least some Nahuatl expressions, researchers are able to trace their derivation from another ancient language.
2	59	**Sentence 6:** Of these forms, the most characteristic in Nahuatl is the juxtaposition of two words that, because they are synonyms, associated terms, or even contraries, complement each other to evoke one single idea.
3	55	**Choice B:** creations
4	67	**Choice A:** anachronistic; **Choice F:** alienated from
5	63	**Choice D:** invention
6	86	**Choice A:** Many climbers, lulled into a false sense of security, use the new equipment to attempt climbing feats of which they are not capable.
7	10	**Choice D:** sartorial
8	36	**Choice A:** undemonstrative panache; **Choice F:** deflect
9	18	**Choice C:** strategic; **Choice D:** brandish; **Choice H:** deeply felt moral code
10	56	**Choice C:** provide an example of a way in which scholarship on the history of women in photography has been unsatisfactory
11	41	**Choice C:** In addition to providing a record of certain historical events, Marion Palfi's photographs played a role in subsequent events.
12	77	**Choice A:** exaggeration
13	37	**Choice A:** antedated AND **Choice D:** preceded
14	69	**Choice B:** disparate AND **Choice C:** divergent
15	85	**Choice C:** thrilled about AND **Choice E:** elated by

Answer Key

Section 3. Verbal Reasoning

Question Number	P+	Correct Answer
1	68	**Choice B:** fleeting AND **Choice C:** momentary
2	77	**Choice A:** diversity AND **Choice C:** variety
3	51	**Choice A:** synoptic AND **Choice B:** abridged
4	68	**Choice B:** intransigent AND **Choice F:** resolute
5	33	**Choice A:** A correct understanding of how phytoplankton photosynthesis utilizes carbon dioxide AND **Choice B:** A correct prediction about how the addition of iron to iron-poor waters would affect phytoplankton growth AND **Choice C:** An incorrect prediction about how phytoplankton growth would affect the concentration of atmospheric carbon dioxide
6	33	**Choice A:** help explain why Martin's hypothesis is incorrect
7	26	**Choice E:** There are fewer traffic accidents annually in Sparva than in any of the provinces of comparable or greater population.
8	62	**Choice B:** extravagance; **Choice F:** profligate
9	37	**Choice B:** complacency; **Choice D:** embrace only a portion of the truth; **Choice G:** erroneous
10	35	**Choice D:** inform
11	43	**Choice E:** reconcile
12	56	**Choice C:** *The Quest of the Silver Fleece* has at least one feature that typically would attract the attention of literary scholars.
13	75	**Choice D:** DuBois' novels may eventually attract greater scholarly interest than they have to date
14	68	**Choice E:** The degree of consideration that has been given to DuBois' novels, including *The Quest of the Silver Fleece*
15	14	**Choice A:** undermines; **Choice E:** inimical
16	30	**Choice B:** malignant; **Choice E:** insufficient; **Choice H:** benignity
17	54	**Choice C:** such a warm Arctic Ocean would trigger the melting of massive land-based glaciers in the Arctic

Answer Key

Question Number	P+	Correct Answer
18	38	**Choice A:** Some of them offered a religious explanation for their immigration.
19	94	**Sentence 5:** When he moves beyond the principal actors, he finds that religious explanations were less frequently offered, and he concludes that most people immigrated because they were recruited by promises of material improvement.
20	68	**Choice A:** summarizing the findings of an investigation

Section 4. Quantitative Reasoning

Question Number	P+	Correct Answer
1	65	**Choice B:** Quantity B is greater.
2	62	**Choice D:** The relationship cannot be determined from the information given.
3	36	**Choice A:** Quantity A is greater.
4	26	**Choice C:** The two quantities are equal.
5	46	**Choice B:** Quantity B is greater.
6	62	**Choice D:** 8 to 9
7	51	**121**
8	52	**Choice C:** 75
9	18	**Choice C:** The sales tax was less than $0.45.
10	19	**Choice B:** Two
11	70	**Choice A:** 2.5 and 3.0
12	35	**Choice D:** 2^{24}
13	17	**Choice A:** DBC is an equilateral triangle. AND **Choice D:** The length of BC is 10.
14	51	**18**
15	34	**Choice C:** 35.0

Answer Key

Section 5. Quantitative Reasoning

Question Number	P+	Correct Answer
1	66	**Choice A:** Quantity A is greater.
2	73	**Choice D:** The relationship cannot be determined from the information given.
3	52	**Choice A:** Quantity A is greater.
4	48	**Choice B:** Quantity B is greater.
5	33	**Choice C:** The two quantities are equal.
6	40	**Choice D:** The relationship cannot be determined from the information given.
7	26	**Choice B:** Quantity B is greater.
8	67	**Choice A:** $40.00
9	10	**Choice A:** The x-intercept of line k is twice the y-intercept of line k. AND **Choice B:** The product of the x-intercept and the y-intercept of line k is positive. AND **Choice C:** Line k passes through the points (a, b) and (r, s), where $(a - r)(b - s) < 0$.
10	49	**Choice B:** 3:30
11	38	**13**
12	21	**Choice A:** $81v$ AND **Choice B:** $25v + 10\sqrt{v} + 1$
13	44	**Choice A:** 130
14	41	**Choice A:** 50
15	30	**Choice C:** 38%
16	11	**Choice E:** 58
17	58	**Choice D:** $\dfrac{1}{b} < 1 < \dfrac{1}{a}$
18	24	**Choice B:** $\dfrac{\sqrt{3}}{2} r^2$
19	15	$\dfrac{153}{190}$ (or any equivalent fraction)
20	30	**Choice E:** 304

Score Conversion Table

Raw Score	Verbal Reasoning Scaled Score	Quantitative Reasoning Scaled Score
35	170	170
34	170	170
33	170	170
32	170	170
31	170	170
30	170	169
29	169	169
28	167	168
27	166	166
26	165	165
25	164	164
24	163	163
23	162	162
22	160	161
21	159	159
20	158	158
19	157	157
18	155	156
17	154	155
16	153	153

Score Conversion Table

Raw Score	Verbal Reasoning Scaled Score	Quantitative Reasoning Scaled Score
15	151	152
14	150	151
13	148	149
12	147	148
11	145	147
10	143	145
9	141	143
8	139	141
7	136	139
6	134	137
5	131	134
4	130	131
3	130	130
2	130	130
1	130	130
0	130	130

Analytical Writing Sample Responses and Reader Commentaries

SECTION 1
Analytical Writing

ANALYTICAL WRITING TOPIC

The best way to teach is to praise positive actions and ignore negative ones.

Write a response in which you discuss the extent to which you agree or disagree with the recommendation and explain your reasoning for the position you take. In developing and supporting your position, describe specific circumstances in which adopting the recommendation would or would not be advantageous and explain how these examples shape your position.

*Score 6 Response**

The recommendation presents a view that I would agree is successful most of the time, but one that I cannot fully support due to the "all or nothing" impression it gives.

    Certainly as an educator I agree fully that the best way to elicit positive response from students is to make use of students' positive energy and then encourage actions that you would like to see repeated. It is human nature that we all want to be accepted and achieve on some level, and when people in authority provide feedback that we have done something well, the drive to repeat the action that was praised is bound to be particularly strong.

    This blanket statement would obviously pay dividends in situations in which a teacher desires to have students repeat particular behaviors. For example, if an educator is attempting to teach students proper classroom etiquette, it would be appropriate to openly praise a student who raises his or her hand when wishing to speak or address the class. In such cases, the teacher may also help shape positive behaviors by ignoring a student who is trying to interject without approval from the teacher. In fact, the decision to ignore students who are exhibiting inappropriate behaviors of this type could work very well in this situation, as the stakes are not very high and the intended outcome can likely be achieved by such a method. However, it is important to note here that this tactic would only be effective in such a "low-stakes" situation, as when a student speaks without raising her hand first. As we will discuss below, ignoring a student who hits another student, or engages in more serious misbehaviors, would not be effective or prudent.

    To expand on this point, it is important for teachers to be careful when working with the second half of this statement, only ignoring negative actions that are not serious. Take for instance a student who is misbehaving just by chatting with a fellow classmate.

---

*NOTE: All responses are reproduced exactly as written, including errors, misspellings, etc., if any.

This student might not be presenting much of a problem and may be simply seeking attention. Ignoring the student might, in fact, be the best solution. Now assume the negative action is the improper administering of chemicals in a science experiment or the bullying of a fellow student. To ignore these negative actions would be absurd and negligent. Now you are allowing a problem to persist, one that could potentially lead to much bigger and more dangerous issues. In a more serious situation, addressing the negative actions quickly and properly could stop the problem it in its tracks. It is for reasons like this that I do not advocate the idea that a teacher can be successful by simply ignoring negative actions.

I do, however, greatly support the idea that the central focus of teaching should be to build on and encourage positive actions. However, the author's all-encompasing statement leaves too many negative possibilities for the classroom. Perhaps a better way to phrase this statement would be to say, "The best way to teach is to praise positive actions and ignore negative ones that are not debilitating to class efficiency or the safety of any individual".

Thus, in the original statement, there are indeed some good intentions, and there could be a lot of merit in adopting its basic principles. Data proves that positive support can substantially increase motivation and desire in students and contribute to positive achievements. In fact, most studies of teaching efficacy indicate that praising positive actions and ignoring negative ones can create a more stable and efficient classroom. It needs to be stressed, however, that this tool is only effective at certain levels of misbehavior. As mentioned above, when the behavior is precipitated by feelings of revenge, power or total self-worthlessness, this methodology will likely not work. It is likely to be very successful, however, when the drive behind the misbehavior is simple attention seeking. In many of these instances, if the teacher demonstrates clearly that inappropriate behavior does not result in the gaining of attention, students are more likely to seek attention by behaving properly. Should the student choose this path, then the ignoring has worked and when the positive behavior is exhibited, then the teacher can utilize the first part of the theory and support or praise this behavior. Now it is much more likely to be repeated. If the student does not choose this path and instead elects to raise the actions to a higher level that presents a more serious issue, then ignorance alone cannot work and other methods must be employed.

In conclusion, one can appreciate the credo expressed in this instance, but surely we all can see the potential error of following it through to the extreme.

Reader Commentary

This response receives a 6 for its well-articulated, insightful analysis of the issue. Rather than simply rejecting or accepting the prompt, the writer argues that the recommendation made by the prompt can often be true but is too "all or nothing" to be endorsed without qualification. The writer turns this idea into an insightful position by providing examples and evidence to fully and persuasively support its nuanced argument. The response offers nicely detailed situations that provide compelling support for a claim that the recommendation can, in fact, work. At the same time, it also highlights the recommendation's limits using additional specific, detailed examples. Particularly persuasive is the fourth paragraph, in which the writer compares the impact of ignoring minor behavioral problems like talking in class to the potential costs of ignoring more serious issues like bullying. Thus, the writer recognizes that the prompt's claim, as well as his/her own, is inevitably dependent on the specific context for its success or failure. Throughout the response, the writer demonstrates the ability to convey ideas fluently and precisely, using effective vocabulary and sentence variety. This sentence demonstrates the level of language facility seen throughout the response: "It is human nature that we all want to be accepted and achieve on some level, and when people in authority provide feedback that we have done something well, the drive to repeat the action that was praised is bound to be particularly strong."

Score 5 Response

I partially agree with the statement "The best way to teach is to praise positive actions and ignore negative ones". Children should be rewarded when they perform well; however, they should not be ignored for performing sub-optimally. For purposes of this essay, the term "actions" is defined as behaviors within the classroom.

Utilizing positive reinforcements, such as tangible rewards, can be a good method to teach children. If the teacher praises children for actions that are desirable, then the children are more likely to repeat those actions. For example, a student who completes an assignment on time and does a good job is likely to want to do a good job on the next assignment if he gets positive feedback. Likewise, the children who are not currently engaging in the desirable actions may be more inclined to do so in order to recieve the positive reinforcement.

Conversely, children should not be ignored for negative actions. If a child is not exhibiting appropriate behavior in the classroom, then it is the teacher's responsibility to encourage the child to perform optimally. Ignoring something doesn't make it go away, actions and consequences do. A student who is being disruptive in class will continue to be disruptive unless the teacher does something about it. However, the teacher's actions need be appropriate.

Before the teacher attempts to modify a child's behavior, the teacher needs to try and identify the reason behind the behavior. For instance, children who leave their seat often, stare in to space, or call out of turn may be initially viewed as having poor behavior. However, the teacher may suspect that the child has an attentional problem, and request that the child be tested. If the child does have an attentional problem, then the teacher can work with a related service, such as occupational therapy, to alter the classroom environment in order to cater to the needs of the child. For instance, the teacher could remove some of the stimulating bulliten board displays to make the room more calming to the child. If the child becomes more attentive in class then the teacher was able to assist the child without scorning them or ignoring them. The teacher met the needs of the child and created an enviornment to enable the child to optimally perform in the educational setting.

On the other hand, if the child is tested, and does not have any areas of concern that may be impacting the educational performance in the classroom, then the negative behavior may strictly be due to defiance. In such a case, the teacher still should not ignore the child, because the negative actions may hinder the learning opportunity for the remaining children in the class. As a result, a child who is being disruptive to the learning process of the class should be set apart from the class so that they do not receive the positive reinforcement of peer attention.

The teacher should not ignore the student who is misbehaving, but that does not mean that the teacher just needs to punish. It is better to address the child privately and make sure the child is aware of the negative actions. Once the child is aware, then the teacher should once again try to determine the reason why the child is behaving in a negative manner. Perhaps the child's parents are in the middle of a divorce and the child is outwardly expressing his frustration in the classroom. Or the academic content of the class may not be challenging enough for the child and so he is misbehaving out of boredom. Whatever the reason behind the behavior, the key factor is that the teacher works with the child to try and identify it. Simply punnishing or ignoring the child would not solve the problem, whereas working to create a plan for success in the classroom would. Likewise, rather than punnishing and defeating the child, the teacher is working with and empowering the child; a much more positive outcome to the situation.

Reader Commentary

This strong response presents a thoughtful and well-developed analysis of the issue. In this case the writer argues that teachers need to modify their approach based on context and observation, meaning that a blanket approach cannot be successful. The writer supports this position with relevant reasons and examples that present logically sound support. Note that the task instructions ask writers to discuss circumstances in which adopting the recommendation might or might not prove advantageous, and this response does that quite clearly. In the second paragraph, the writer gives an example of a student who completes an assignment on time and receives positive feedback, showing how the recommendation could prove advantageous. Other examples show circumstances in which adopting the recommmendation would not be a good idea, and these various points are brought together to support the writer's position that teachers have to look at the context of the situation and cannot rely on simply ignoring negative actions. This response also demonstrates facility with language, using appropriate vocabulary and sentence variety. Sentences like this one demonstrate the writer's command of the conventions of standard written English: "If the child does have an attentional problem, then the teacher can work with a related service, such as occupational therapy, to alter the classroom environment in order to cater to the needs of the child." There are some minor errors, but overall the response demonstrates strong control of language. Although the response is clearly stronger than a 4, which would simply present a clear position on the issue according to the task instructions, it does not reach the level of a 6 because it does not develop its points in a way that creates a cogent and insightful position. It does, however, present a generally thoughtful and well-developed analysis of the issue, leading to a score of 5.

Score 4 Response

I absolutely agree with the first section of the statement above, but find fault with the latter half.

There is no doubt that praising positive actions is an excellent way to teach, and this method is most clearly exemplified when dealing with much younger children. When a young child is learning basic social behavior, it is imperative that he is encouraged to repeat positive actions. For example, when a child voluntarily shares his toys with another, if a teacher rewards that behavior, the child will understand that this is a good practice, and likely share again in the future.

In contrast, if a child displays negative behavior by stealing a toy away from his playmate, it would be very dangerous for the teacher to ignore this action, for then the child may never recognize that this is unacceptable. In this instance, the child has not learned from the situation at all. So what should a teacher do when faced with such a situation? Punishment is not necessarily the optimal choice, either. Rather than scolding a child for mistreating his playmates and sending him off to a corner, a teacher would be wise to demonstrate the positive alternative: to share his toys instead. In this case, rather than ignoring or punishing negative actions, the teacher could seize the opportunity to reinforce positive behavior, and further extend the child's learning experience.

In summary, positive reinforcement is certainly an excellent method for teaching new methods or behaviors, and encouraging a student to learn more. However to ignore, rather than recognize and correct negative actions, would be a disservice to the student, for he would not know what conclusion to draw from his action.

Reader Commentary

This adequate response follows the task directions and presents a clear position on the issue, supporting its main points with examples that are relevant, if only adequately developed. For instance, the discussion in the second paragraph of a teacher who reinforces the positive behavior of sharing a toy is certainly relevant and on-task (i.e., it describes a situation in which adopting the recommendation would be advantageous). However, the development of this idea does not lead to generally thoughtful or insightful analysis. Instead, it is simply presented as an example. In addition to its adequate development, this response also demonstrates sufficient control of the conventions of standard written English, and its main points are made with reasonable clarity. Some of the sentences demonstrate the syntactical variety normally seen in responses that receive higher scores (e.g., "Rather than scolding a child for mistreating his playmates and sending him off to a corner, a teacher would be wise to demonstrate the positive alternative: to share his toys instead"). However, the overall use of language in this response is merely adequate.

Score 3 Response

Praising postive actions and ignoring negative ones may be a good way to teach but not the best way. Ignoring negative actions could negate all the postive praises given to an individual, having negative actions go unchecked will lead to habits formed that would overwhelm any positive actions that are complementary to an individuals learning process.

For instance, in a classroom full of eight-year old kids; if during a lesson they are making alot of noise, having this ignored would tell the kids that it is okay to be disruptive in class. The individuals in that class would develop the habit of being distruptive hence hindering their learning process. However if the eight-year old kids were immediately told to stop the distruption then it will never become a habit.

Every action needs to have a related consequence follow in a learning environment. In the early years of education, the way they are taught becomes a lifelong habit which is hard to change in later years. If negative actions are not assigned a related consequences then teaching becomes ineffective because the students negative actions soon diminish the ability to do well in school. The way postive actions are dealt with should also be done with negative actions rather than being ignored which in turn enhance the learning environment.

Reader Commentary

Although this response has minor errors in its use of language, it receives a 3 primarily for insufficient overall clarity and for the limited development of its claims. The writer does make an attempt to follow the specific task instructions, and the response has a clear position on the issue, arguing that it is not acceptable practice to ignore negative behaviors. However, the development provided in support of that position is limited. The example of "eight-year old kids" making noise during class can be seen as a situation in which following the recommendation is not advantageous. Instead of developing that point in a logically persuasive way, however, the writer proceeds to make an unsupported assertion about the consequences of following the recommendation ("The individuals in that class would develop the habit of being disruptive hence hindering their learning process"). Another issue that keeps this response at the 3 level is a lack of clarity, particularly in the final paragraph. The final sentence demonstrates this problem with clarity: "The way postive actions are dealt with should also be done with negative actions rather than being ignored which in turn enhance the learning environment." Problems with the structure of this sentence make it difficult to determine the writer's intended meaning.

Score 2 Response

I don't agree with this afirmation, because I think is very important to praise positive actions but also is important to sign the negative ones, in some situations acording to the students level, grade, etc., could be better to put more emphasis in the positive things and if not ignore all the negative ones, do not give so much importance to them, this is particulary important in the lowest levels of education.

But in another situations you must sign the negative things, trying to avoid that the students can repeat them in the future, because I think you can also learn from the negative situations.

For this reason I believe that is important to praise positive actions but is also important no to ignore the negative ones, because in a given situation the student can have troubles recongnising what is right and what is wrong. And finally as a conclusion I think that the best way to teach is combination of praise positive things but also to sign the negative ones.

Reader Commentary

This response clearly fits several characteristics of a 2, as defined by the scoring guide. It is seriously limited in its development, organization, and focus. The response repeats itself rather than developing any of its statements, pointing to an inability to organize a response capable of supporting any specific claims with relevant reasons or examples. Additionally, serious language control problems frequently interfere with meaning. Thus, even though the writer does seem to be making an attempt to respond to the specific task instructions, the response merits a score of 2.

Score 1 Response

> Write a response in which you disuss the extent to which you agree or disagree with the recommendation and explain your reasoning for the position you take. In developing and supporting position, describe specific circumstances in which adopting the recommendation would or would not be advantageous and explain how these examples shape your position.
>
> Author says that The best way to teach is to praise positive actions and ignore negative ones. I agree to this recommendation. Explaining, I strongly believe that the best way to teach is not to praise positive action and ignore negative ones but is making everyone to be a good ones. Specific crimstances lead me which adopting the recommendation as the following:
>
> First, we will lost the good children who have negative maner if we ignore them. Children are future, not all. Praise in negative should not be, teaching to children to best way. I strongly believe adopting this recommeindation would be not advantages.
>
> second, negative ones in today may be a great people in the future. Not only ones behave do worse they are teenage. Teenage in today is not easy for all! Negative ones can not better, if only prainse positive actions, ignore negativeone. Negative ones may not positive be having, but if we praise them only, they not think they should be positive person later.
>
> conclusion, specific circumstances are which adopting the recommendation would not be advantage, I am not agree to the the recommendation. Ignore negative manor when they will not be positive behavrio in futre. But they can, if do not ignore them. we should not ignor negative person but should make them think that they can be a good man future like positive person.

Reader Commentary

This response has severe and pervasive problems in language and sentence structure that, as stated in the scoring guide, consistently interfere with meaning and result in incoherence. The response begins by repeating the prompt, but then the severe problems with language control and organization undermine any evidence of the ability to understand the prompt or to present and develop a clear position. For example, it is not clear what the writer means by the claim that the best way to teach is "makeing everyone to be a good ones." Severe problems with language control in that sentence and throughout the response prevent it from developing a coherent position on the issue or responding to the specific task instructions. Although the writer makes an attempt at organization, with points marked as first, second, and conclusion, the response actually exhibits little or no evidence of the ability to develop any potential understanding of the prompt into a logical position on the issue.

Answers and Explanations

SECTION 2
Verbal Reasoning
15 Questions with Explanations

> For each of Questions 1 to 3, select **one** answer choice unless otherwise instructed.

Questions 1 to 3 are based on the following reading passage.

Whether the languages of the ancient American peoples were used for expressing abstract universal concepts can be clearly answered in the case of Nahuatl. Nahuatl, like Greek and German, is a language that allows the formation of extensive compounds. By the combina-

line
5 tion of radicals or semantic elements, single compound words can express complex conceptual relations, often of an abstract universal character.

The *tlamatinime* (those who know) were able to use this rich stock of abstract terms to express the nuances of their thought. They also availed themselves of other forms of expression with metaphorical meaning, some probably original, some derived from Toltec coinages. Of these forms, the most characteristic in Nahuatl is the juxtaposition of two

10 words that, because they are synonyms, associated terms, or even contraries, complement each other to evoke one single idea. Used metaphorically, the juxtaposed terms connote specific or essential traits of the being they refer to, introducing a mode of poetry as an almost habitual form of expression.

Description

This passage claims that Nahuatl was used to express abstract universal concepts, by combining semantic elements, and goes on to explain that the *tlamatinime* used these terms to express subtle distinctions.

For the following question, consider each of the choices separately and select all that apply.

1. Which of the following can be inferred from the passage regarding present-day research relating to Nahuatl?

    [A] Some record or evidence of the thought of the *tlamatinime* is available.

    [B] For at least some Nahuatl expressions, researchers are able to trace their derivation from another ancient language.

    [C] Researchers believe that in Nahuatl, abstract universal concepts are always expressed metaphorically.

Explanation

Choices A and B are correct.

Choice A is correct: the *tlamatinime* are mentioned in the first sentence of the second paragraph, where it says they were able to use Nahuatl's stock of abstract terms "to express the nuances of their thought." This suggests that there is some evidence of what those thoughts were, and therefore Choice A can be inferred.

Choice B is correct: according to the next sentence, Nahuatl speakers used "forms of expression with metaphorical meaning," some of which were probably "original" and others "derived from Toltec coinages." That researchers know certain Nahuatl expressions are derived from Toltec suggests that they are able to trace the derivation of some Nahuatl expressions from another language besides Nahuatl, and therefore Choice B may be inferred.

Choice C is incorrect: the passage says that in Nahuatl there are single compound words that can express conceptual relations of an "abstract universal character" and mentions "other forms of expression with metaphorical meaning," but it does not indicate whether metaphorical words or phrases are the only way that abstract universal concepts are expressed in Nahuatl, or whether researchers believe this about Nahuatl. Therefore Choice C cannot be inferred.

2. Select the sentence in the passage in which the author introduces a specific Nahuatl mode of expression that is not identified as being shared with certain European languages.

Explanation

The passage introduces two specific Nahuatl modes of expression. One is the formation of single compound words that are capable of expressing complex conceptual relations (first paragraph); the other is the juxtaposition of two related words to evoke a single idea (second paragraph). In the formation of compounds Nahuatl is described as being "like Greek and German," but the second mode is not identified as being shared with other languages. Therefore the **sixth sentence** ("Of these forms . . . one single idea") is the best choice.

3. In the context in which it appears, "coinages" (line 9) most nearly means
    (A) adaptations
    (B) creations
    (C) idiosyncrasies
    (D) pronunciations
    (E) currencies

Explanation

"Coinage" has two senses that are represented among the answer choices: in one sense it denotes coins and currency, while in the other it denotes things—especially words—that are invented. The fifth sentence draws a contrast between linguistic expressions original to Nahuatl and those derived from Toltec. In this context of original versus derived language, "coinages" means "inventions," not "currencies." Of the answer choices given, "creations" is the nearest equivalent of "coinages" in the sense of "inventions," and therefore **Choice B** is the best answer.

For Questions 4 and 5, select one entry for each blank from the corresponding column of choices. Fill all blanks in the way that best completes the text.

---

4. In her later years, Bertha Pappenheim was an apostle of noble but already (i)_____ notions, always respected for her integrity, her energy, and her resolve but increasingly out of step and ultimately (ii)_____ even her own organization.

Blank (i)	Blank (ii)
(A) anachronistic	(D) emulated by
(B) accepted	(E) appreciated by
(C) exotic	(F) alienated from

Explanation

The sentence is clearly conveying a contrast since "but" is used twice to indicate something positive and something negative about Pappenheim. The clue to the negative aspect is in the later part of the sentence, where "out of step" leads both to "anachronistic" as the answer for the first blank and "alienated from" as the answer for the second.

Thus, the correct answer is **anachronistic** (Choice A) and **alienated from** (Choice F).

5. The reception given to Kimura's radical theory of molecular evolution shows that when _____ fights orthodoxy to a draw, then novelty has seized a good chunk of space from convention.

(A) imitation
(B) reaction
(C) dogmatism
(D) invention
(E) caution

Explanation

The sentence sets up two parallel, contrasting concepts. The word in the blank must contrast with "orthodoxy," and since "convention" in the second contrasting pair is synonymous with "orthodoxy," the correct answer should be roughly synonymous with "novelty." The word "invention" is the best choice.

Thus, the correct answer is **invention** (Choice D).

For Question 6, select one answer choice unless otherwise instructed.

Question 6 is based on the following reading passage.

In the past ten years, there have been several improvements in mountain-climbing equipment. These improvements have made the sport both safer and more enjoyable for experienced climbers. Despite these improvements, however, the rate of mountain-climbing injuries has doubled in the past ten years.

6.   Which of the following, if true, best reconciles the apparent discrepancy presented in the passage?

   (A) Many climbers, lulled into a false sense of security, use the new equipment to attempt climbing feats of which they are not capable.

   (B) Some mountain-climbing injuries are caused by unforeseeable weather conditions.

   (C) Mountain climbing, although a dangerous sport, does not normally result in injury to the experienced climber.

   (D) In the past ten years there have been improvements in mountain-climbing techniques as well as in mountain-climbing equipment.

   (E) Although the rate of mountain-climbing injuries has increased, the rate of mountain-climbing deaths has not changed.

Explanation

In this question you are asked to identify the fact that would best reconcile the apparent discrepancy that the passage presents. The discrepancy is that despite improvements in mountain climbing equipment that have made climbing safer, the incidence of mountain-climbing injuries has greatly increased. Choice A explains how this could have happened—the improvements in equipment have led climbers to attempt feats that are beyond their level of skill. Therefore, **Choice A** is the correct answer.

None of the other choices provides information that resolves the discrepancy. Neither Choice B nor Choice C relates to conditions that have changed over the relevant ten-year period. Choices D and E do relate to the relevant period. But if, as Choice D says, techniques as well as equipment have improved, that fact by itself only makes the increase in injuries more puzzling. Choice E provides more data about the consequences of climbing accidents, but doesn't suggest any explanation for the increase in injuries.

For Questions 7 to 9, select one entry for each blank from the corresponding column of choices. Fill all blanks in the way that best completes the text.

---

7.   The novelist devotes so much time to avid descriptions of his characters' clothes that the reader soon feels that such _____ concerns, although worthy of attention, have superseded any more directly literary aims.

   (A) didactic

   (B) syntactical

   (C) irrelevant

   (D) sartorial

   (E) frivolous

Explanation

The "concerns" described by the adjective that fills the blank relate to clothing, so "sartorial" fits the blank. Although these concerns could also be described as "irrelevant" or "frivolous," neither of these choices is correct because the sentence identifies the concerns as "worthy of attention."

Thus, the correct answer is **sartorial** (Choice D).

8.   Belanger dances with an (i)_____ that draws one's attention as if by seeking to (ii)_____ it; through finesse and understatement, he manages to seem at once intensely present and curiously detached.

Blank (i)	Blank (ii)
(A) undemonstrative panache	(D) focus
(B) unrestrained enthusiasm	(E) overwhelm
(C) unattractive gawkiness	(F) deflect

Explanation

The point of the sentence is to emphasize contradictory aspects of Belanger's dancing: we are told, for example, that he seems "at once intensely present and curiously detached." Looking at the second blank with this point in mind, we can see that the sentence is saying that Belanger draws attention in some way that would not normally be a means of doing so. The only choice that fits, therefore, is "deflect"; focusing or overwhelming attention would certainly be expected to draw it. And since employing "unrestrained enthusiasm" or "unattractive gawkiness" would not be ways of deflecting attention, the correct choice for the first blank is "undemonstrative panache," another paradoxical term, since "panache" means "dash or flamboyance in style."

  Thus, the correct answer is **undemonstrative panache** (Choice A) and **deflect** (Choice F).

9.   The most striking thing about the politician is how often his politics have been (i)_____ rather than ideological, as he adapts his political positions at any particular moment to the political realities that constrain him. He does not, however, piously (ii)_____ political principles only to betray them in practice. Rather, he attempts in subtle ways to balance his political self-interest with a (iii) _____, viewing himself as an instrument of some unchanging higher purpose.

Blank (i)	Blank (ii)	Blank (iii)
(A) quixotic	(D) brandish	(G) profound cynicism
(B) self-righteous	(E) flout	(H) deeply felt moral code
(C) strategic	(F) follow	(I) thoroughgoing pragmatism

Explanation

Since the politician is portrayed as adapting political positions to political realities, blank (i) should be filled with "strategic," which is also the only choice that provides the required contrast with "ideological." The second blank, *brandishing* political principles is what a politician might do piously, while *flouting* is not pious and *following* principles does not make sense when combined with "betray[ing] them in practice." The third blank requires something that would have to be balanced against "political self-interest" and that would be embraced in service of an "unchanging higher purpose," making "deeply felt moral code" the only viable choice.

  Thus, the correct answer is **strategic** (Choice C), **brandish** (Choice D), and **deeply felt moral code** (Choice H).

For each of Questions 10 to 12, select <u>one</u> answer choice unless otherwise instructed.

The condition of scholarship devoted to the history of women in photography is confounding. Recent years have witnessed the posthumous inflation of the role of the hobbyist Alice Austen into that of a pioneering documentarian while dozens of notable senior
line   figures—Marion Palfi, whose photographs of civil-rights activities in the South served as
5   early evidence of the need for protective legislation, to name one—received scant attention from scholars. And, while Naomi Rosenblum's synoptic *History of Women Photographers* covers the subject through 1920 in a generally useful fashion, once she reaches the 1920s, when the venues, forms, applications, and movements of the medium expanded exponentially, she resorts to an increasingly terse listing of unfamiliar names, with approaches and
10   careers summarized in a sentence or two.

Description

The passage expresses dismay at the current state of scholarship concerning the history of women in photography: some figures receive disproportionate attention, and past 1920 Rosenblum's book is too sketchy to be useful.

10.   The author of the passage cites Rosenblum's book most likely in order to

(A) suggest that the works documented most thoroughly by historians of women in photography often do not warrant that attention

(B) offer an explanation for the observation that not all aspects of the history of women in photography have received the same level of attention

(C) provide an example of a way in which scholarship on the history of women in photography has been unsatisfactory

(D) suggest that employing a strictly chronological approach when studying the history of women in photography may be unproductive

(E) provide support for the notion that certain personalities in women's photography have attained undue prominence

Explanation

As mentioned above, the topic of the passage is the unsatisfactory condition of scholarship devoted to the history of women in photography. Since Rosenblum's book is clearly presented as an example of this unsatisfactory scholarship, **Choice C** is the correct answer. Choice D may seem appealing, because a strictly chronological approach might be inadequate to represent the explosive growth of the field in the 1920s. However, the sentence does not develop this idea, and this is not the reason for mentioning Rosenblum.

For the following question, consider each of the choices separately and select all that apply.

11. Which of the following statements about Marion Palfi is supported by the passage?

    [A] Marion Palfi's photographs would have received greater recognition from historians had her work been done in an era when most aspects of photography were static rather than in a state of transition.

    [B] Alice Austen has achieved greater notoriety than has Marion Palfi primarily because the subjects that Austen photographed were more familiar to her contemporaries.

    [C] In addition to providing a record of certain historical events, Marion Palfi's photographs played a role in subsequent events.

Explanation

Choice C is correct.

   Choice A is incorrect: the passage does not state whether the period in which Palfi was working was an era when photography was static or in transition.

   Choice B is incorrect: the passage does not state the nature of the subjects Austen photographed, nor compare their relative familiarity to those photographed by Palfi.

   Choice C is correct: Palfi's photographs played a role in subsequent events because they served as early evidence of the need for protective legislation.

12. In the context in which it appears, "inflation" (line 2) most nearly means

    (A) exaggeration
    (B) acquisition
    (C) evaluation
    (D) distortion
    (E) attenuation

Explanation

The term "hobbyist" suggests Austen's relative lack of seriousness as a photographer when compared with "senior figures," yet her role has been elevated to that of a "pioneering documentarian" at the expense of these other figures. Choice D may be appealing in that this elevation could be considered a form of distortion, but Choice A is more specific as well as more in line with the dictionary definition of "inflated" as "expanded to an abnormal or unjustifiable volume or level." Thus, **Choice A**, "exaggeration," is the correct answer.

> For Questions 13 to 15, select the <u>two</u> answer choices that, when used to complete the sentence, fit the meaning of the sentence as a whole <u>and</u> produce completed sentences that are alike in meaning.

13. Though feminist in its implications, Yvonne Rainer's 1974 film _____ the filmmaker's active involvement in feminist politics.

   - A antedated
   - B cloaked
   - C portrayed
   - D preceded
   - E renewed
   - F represented

Explanation

The words that fill the blank must fit with the idea that Rainer's film has some feminist implications, but that those are limited compared with her other activities. From the six words offered as answer choices, the pair "antedated" and "preceded" and the pair "portrayed" and "represented" each produce sentences that are similar in meaning. However, only "antedated" and "preceded" make sense in the context of the sentence: Rainer's 1974 film exhibits feminist themes in a limited way because it came before she became active in feminist politics.

   Thus, the correct answer is **antedated** (Choice A) and **preceded** (Choice D).

14. Congress is having great difficulty developing a consensus on energy policy, primarily because the policy objectives of various members of Congress rest on such _____ assumptions.

   - A commonplace
   - B disparate
   - C divergent
   - D fundamental
   - E trite
   - F trivial

Explanation

The words that fill the blank must help explain the difficulty of developing a consensus. A lack of agreement on the assumptions that underlie Congress members' policy objectives would contribute to such a difficulty. Accordingly, "disparate" and "divergent" are the best choices because they both indicate disagreement among the members. Although the words "trite" and "trivial" are similar in meaning, triteness and triviality do not help to explain the difficulty in developing a consensus.

   Thus, the correct answer is **disparate** (Choice B) and **divergent** (Choice C).

15. Because they had expected the spacecraft Voyager 2 to be able to gather data only about the planets Jupiter and Saturn, scientists were _____ the wealth of information it sent back from Neptune twelve years after leaving Earth.

A anxious for
B confident in
C thrilled about
D keen on
E elated by
F eager for

Explanation

In the sentence, the words "expected" and "only" imply that the data received from the spacecraft exceeded scientists' expectations. Therefore, the words that fill the blank should describe a reaction to results that are better than hoped for, and the choices "thrilled about" and "elated by" both express such a reaction. The scientists may well also have been eager for, or keen on, the information, but their eagerness is not well explained by the unexpectedness of the information.

Thus, the correct answer is **thrilled about** (Choice C) and **elated by** (Choice E).

SECTION 3
Verbal Reasoning
20 Questions with Explanations

> **For Questions 1 to 4, select the <u>two</u> answer choices that, when used to complete the sentence, ft the meaning of the sentence as a whole <u>and</u> produce completed sentences that are alike in meaning.**

1. Only by ignoring decades of mismanagement and inefficiency could investors conclude that a fresh infusion of cash would provide anything other than a _____ solution to the company's financial woes.

   A complete
   B fleeting
   C momentary
   D premature
   E trivial
   F total

Explanation

The key phrases that indicate how the blank for this question should be completed are "Only by ignoring decades of mismanagement and inefficiency" and "provide anything other than." Taken together, these phrases indicate that the sentence will not envision a very beneficial or successful resolution of the "financial woes." Among the answer choices, "complete" and "total" are quite close in meaning and would clearly create two sentences very similar in meaning. But those two sentences would be internally contradictory, suggesting that doing something unwise would completely solve a problem. "Fleeting" and "momentary" suggest that the event referred to ("a fresh infusion of cash") might have some beneficial effect, but that it would ultimately not resolve the problem.

Thus, the correct answer is **fleeting** (Choice B) and **momentary** (Choice C).

2. Some scientists argue that carbon compounds play such a central role in life on Earth because of the possibility of _____ resulting from the carbon atom's ability to form an unending series of different molecules.

   A diversity
   B deviation
   C variety
   D reproduction
   E stability
   F invigoration

Explanation

The key phrase that indicates how the blank for this question should be completed is "the ability to form an unending series of different molecules." Among the answer choices, "diversity" and "variety" clearly it logically with "unending" and "different" and create two very similar sentences. No other pair of choices here would produce two sentences as similar in meaning as those created by placing "diversity" and "variety" in the blank. Thus, the correct answer is **diversity** (Choice A) and **variety** (Choice C).

3. Given the flood of information presented by the mass media, the only way for someone to keep abreast of the news is to rely on _____ accounts.
   - [A] synoptic
   - [B] abridged
   - [C] sensational
   - [D] copious
   - [E] lurid
   - [F] understated

Explanation

The key phrase that indicates how the blank for this question should be completed is "the only way for someone to keep abreast of the news." Among the answer choices, "synoptic" and "abridged," while not synonymous in the strict sense, both fit the logic of this description, "synoptic" because of its emphasis on breadth and generality as opposed to detail, and "abridged" because of its obvious focus on brevity. "Sensational" and "lurid" would create two similar sentences but do not fit the logic for completing the blank, since we would not be relying on sensational or lurid accounts in order to keep abreast of the news.

Thus, the correct answer is **synoptic** (Choice A) and **abridged** (Choice B).

4. Always circumspect, she was reluctant to make judgments, but once arriving at a conclusion, she was _____ in its defense.
   - [A] deferential
   - [B] intransigent
   - [C] lax
   - [D] negligent
   - [E] obsequious
   - [F] resolute

Explanation

The key phrases that indicate how the blank for this question should be completed are: "circumspect," "reluctant," and "but once." Taken together they point to completing the blank with something that is opposite in some way to the two cited adjectives. Among the answer choices, "intransigent" and "resolute," although not strictly synonymous, both fit the logic of the description given here for completing the blank and create sentences that are similar in meaning. "Lax" and "negligent" are clearly similar in meaning and would create sentences similar in meaning, but they continue the sentiment voiced in the initial clause rather than contrasting with it. "Deferential" and "obsequious" are also similar in meaning, but their emphasis on "politeness," while not strictly synonymous with reluctance and circumspection, like "lax" and "negligent" fail to pick up on the expected contrast.

Thus, the correct answer is **intransigent** (Choice B) and **resolute** (Choice F).

For each of Questions 5 to 7, select **one** answer choice unless otherwise instructed.

When marine organisms called phytoplankton photosynthesize, they absorb carbon dioxide dissolved in seawater, potentially causing a reduction in the concentration of atmospheric carbon dioxide, a gas that contributes to global warming. However, phytoplankton flourish only in surface waters where iron levels are sufficiently high. Martin therefore hypothesized that adding iron to iron-poor regions of the ocean could help alleviate global warming. While experiments subsequently confirmed that such a procedure increases phytoplankton growth, field tests have shown that such growth does not significantly lower atmospheric carbon dioxide. When phytoplankton utilize carbon dioxide for photosynthesis, the carbon becomes a building block for organic matter, but the carbon leaks back into the atmosphere when predators consume the phytoplankton and respire carbon dioxide.

line 5

10

Description

The paragraph presents a hypotheses about reducing global warming by adding iron to iron-poor areas of the ocean and explains why adding the iron does not have the hoped-for benefit.

For the following question, consider each of the choices separately and select all that apply.

5.   It can be inferred from the passage that Martin's hypothesis includes which of the following elements?

   A   A correct understanding of how phytoplankton photosynthesis utilizes carbon dioxide

   B   A correct prediction about how the addition of iron to iron-poor waters would affect phytoplankton growth

   C   An incorrect prediction about how phytoplankton growth would affect the concentration of atmospheric carbon dioxide

Explanation

All three choices are correct. Martin's hypothesis was that adding iron to iron-poor regions of the ocean could help alleviate global warming.

   Choice A is correct: the passage presents Martin as using the standard understanding of how phytoplankton photosynthesize as a basis for the hypothesis.

   Choice B is correct: the passage states that experiments confirmed that adding iron to iron-poor regions increases phytoplankton growth in those regions. Therefore, Martin's prediction about this was correct.

   Choice C is correct: it can be inferred that in Martin's hypothesis the means by which adding iron in certain regions could alleviate global warming is that phytoplankton increase in those regions and absorb atmospheric carbon dioxide. The passage states that predators who consume phytoplankton respire carbon dioxide, so that the carbon dioxide absorbed by phytoplankton reenters the atmosphere. Therefore, Martin's prediction about this was incorrect.

6.   It can be inferred that the author of the passage mentions predators (line 10) primarily in order to

Ⓐ help explain why Martin's hypothesis is incorrect

Ⓑ identify one effect of adding iron to iron-poor waters

Ⓒ indicate how some carbon dioxide is converted to solid organic matter

Ⓓ help account for differences in the density of phytoplankton between different regions of the ocean

Ⓔ point out a factor that was not anticipated by the scientists who conducted the field tests mentioned in the passage

Explanation

Lines 7–10 of the paragraph present the evidence against Martin's hypothesis. Lines 7–8 present field test results showing that Martin's hypothesis is incorrect, and the last sentence explains these results: the reason the increased phytoplankton resulting from the addition of iron do not reduce atmospheric carbon dioxide is that while the phytoplankton absorb carbon dioxide, the gas reenters the atmosphere when it is respired by phytoplankton predators. Therefore **Choice A** is correct: predators are mentioned to explain why Martin's hypothesis is incorrect. Choice B is not correct because while predators' consumption of phytoplankton and respiration of carbon dioxide might be considered one indirect consequence of adding iron to iron-poor waters, identifying a consequence is not the primary function of the mention of predators. Choice C is incorrect because the reference to predators is used to explain how carbon dioxide reappears as a gas, and Choice D is incorrect because no connection is suggested between predators and the distribution of phytoplankton. Choice E is not correct because it is Martin who did not anticipate this factor, rather than the scientists who conducted the field tests.

Question 7 is based on the following reading passage.

Sparva, unlike Treland's other provinces, requires automobile insurers to pay for any medical treatment sought by someone who has been involved in an accident; in the other provinces, insurers pay for nonemergency treatment only if they preapprove the treatment. Clearly, Sparva's less restrictive policy must be the explanation for the fact that altogether insurers there pay for far more treatments after accidents than insurers in other provinces, even though Sparva does not have the largest population.

Description

The passage tells us that in Sparva automobile insurers pay for far more medical treatments after accidents than they do in Treland's other provinces. The passage concludes that the explanation is to be found in the difference in legal requirements for insurers in Sparva as compared to other provinces.

7.   Which of the following, if true, most strengthens the argument?

Ⓐ Car insurance costs more in Sparva than in any other province.

Ⓑ The cost of medical care in Sparva is higher than the national average.

Ⓒ Different insurance companies have different standards for determining what constitutes emergency treatment.

Ⓓ Fewer insurance companies operate in Sparva than in any other province.

Ⓔ There are fewer traffic accidents annually in Sparva than in any of the provinces of comparable or greater population.

Explanation

The question asks you to identify among the answer choices a fact that would support the passage's argument. The explanation offered in the passage can be supported by ruling out other explanations that might, given the information presented in the passage, appear likely. One obvious explanation for there being more medical treatments in Sparva is that there are more accidents there. Choice E rules out that explanation. So **Choice E** strengthens the argument in the passage and is the correct answer. Choices A and D each present consequences that are likely results of insurers in Sparva having to pay for more medical treatments. But neither bears on the cause of insurers having to pay for more treatments. Choice B does not strengthen the argument and may weaken it. A higher cost of medical care provides additional motivation for people to seek insurance payments to cover whatever post-accident care they receive. So Choice B might weaken the argument by providing an alternative explanation for insurers paying for more medical treatments in Sparva. According to the passage, whether treatment is emergency treatment is, in other provinces, an important criterion in determining insurers' responsibility. But since this criterion does not apply in Sparva, Choice C is not directly relevant to the point that the passage is trying to establish.

For the following question, consider each of the choices separately and select all that apply.

> **For Questions 8 to 11, select one entry for each blank from the corresponding column of choices. Fill all blanks in the way that best completes the text.**

8. Ironically, the writer so wary of (i)_____ was (ii)_____ with ink and paper, his novel running to 2,500 shagreen-bound folio pages—a fortune in stationery at the time.

Blank (i)	Blank (ii)
(A) probity	(D) acquisitive
(B) extravagance	(E) illiberal
(C) disapprobation	(F) profligate

Explanation

The last part of the sentence provides most of the context needed to fill in the two blanks. The novel was extremely long and required vast amounts of paper. Among the choices for the second blank, only "profligate" matches this lack of restraint. The word "Ironically" indicates that what the writer was "wary of" was something similar to profligacy; of the choices for the first blank, "extravagance" is the closest.

Thus, the correct answer is **extravagance** (Choice B) and **profligate** (Choice F).

9. What readers most commonly remember about John Stuart Mill's classic exploration of the liberty of thought and discussion concerns the danger of (i)_____: in the absence of challenge, one's opinions, even when they are correct, grow weak and flabby. Yet Mill had another reason for encouraging the liberty of thought and discussion: the danger of partiality and incompleteness. Since one's opinions, even under the best circumstances, tend to (ii)_____, and because opinions opposed to one's own rarely turn out to be completely (iii)_____, it is crucial to supplement one's opinions with alternative points of view.

Blank (i)	Blank (ii)	Blank (iii)
(A) tendentiousness	(D) embrace only a portion of the truth	(G) erroneous
(B) complacency	(E) change over time	(H) antithetical
(C) fractiousness	(F) focus on matters close at hand	(I) immutable

Explanation

An overview of the passage suggests that the first sentence is relatively self-contained and that the blank is answerable without the succeeding sentences, where the topic shifts slightly. The colon after the first blank signals that what follows will define the word in the blank and will explain what danger Mill was concerned about. It says that without challenge, one's opinions grow "weak and flabby" and therefore one becomes *complacent*, not tendentious or fractious. A quick reading of the next two sentences suggests that the topic will be another danger that Mill described, "the danger of partiality and incompleteness." Free and open discussion needs to take place because each person's opinion tends to "embrace only a portion of the truth" and others' views are partially right, or never completely "erroneous." The other choices for the second and third blanks deal with change, immediacy, or antithesis, none of which relate to the second danger of "partiality" or "incompleteness."

Thus, the correct answer is **complacency** (Choice B), **embrace only a portion of the truth** (Choice D), and **erroneous** (Choice G).

10. Just as the authors' book on eels is often a key text for courses in marine vertebrate zoology, their ideas on animal development and phylogeny _____ teaching in this area.

(A) prevent
(B) defy
(C) replicate
(D) inform
(E) use

Explanation

The "just as" structure indicates that the second half of the sentence should somehow parallel the idea presented in the first half (i.e., the idea that the authors' book on eels is a "key text" in marine vertebrate zoology). Among the choices given, "inform" is clearly the best choice. "Prevent" and "defy" work in the opposite direction, while "use" and "replicate" would suggest that the authors' ideas are drawing upon the teaching in this area rather than the other way around. "Inform" leads to a meaning that nicely matches the first half of the sentence.

Thus, the correct answer is **inform** (Choice D).

11. Mechanisms develop whereby every successful species can _____ its innate capacity for population growth with the constraints that arise through its interactions with the natural environment.

- Ⓐ enhance
- Ⓑ replace
- Ⓒ produce
- Ⓓ surpass
- Ⓔ reconcile

Explanation

A quick overview of the sentence indicates that the blank should be filled with a verb that indicates what a successful species does with its "innate capacity for population growth" in the face of certain constraints on that growth. This analysis suggests that the correct answer will have something to do with adjusting that capacity in the face of these constraints. Of the choices given, "reconcile" is closest to that meaning. None of the other options make for a meaningful, coherent sentence. "Enhance," for example, may fit nicely with "its innate capacity," but it does not make sense with "constraints."

Thus, the correct answer is **reconcile** (Choice E).

For each of Questions 12 to 14, select **one** answer choice unless otherwise instructed.

Questions 12 to 14 are based on the following reading passage.

It would be expected that a novel by a figure as prominent as W.E.B. DuBois would attract the attention of literary critics. Additionally, when the novel subtly engages the issue of race, as DuBois' *The Quest of the Silver Fleece* (1911) does, it would be a surprise not to encounter an abundance of scholarly work about that text. But though valuable scholarship has examined DuBois' political and historical thought, his novels have received scant attention. Perhaps DuBois the novelist must wait his turn behind DuBois the philosopher, historian, and editor. But what if the truth lies elsewhere: what if his novels do not speak to current concerns?

Description

The paragraph first presents reasons for critical interest in DuBois' novels, but then goes on to explain that there has in fact been very little such interest and speculates as to why that might be.

12. Which of the following can be inferred from the passage regarding DuBois' *The Quest of the Silver Fleece*?

   (A) The lack of attention devoted to *The Quest of the Silver Fleece* can be attributed to the fact that it was DuBois' first novel.

   (B) Among DuBois' novels, *The Quest of the Silver Fleece* is unusual in that it has received scant attention from scholars.

   (C) *The Quest of the Silver Fleece* has at least one feature that typically would attract the attention of literary scholars.

   (D) *The Quest of the Silver Fleece*, given its subtle exploration of race, is probably the best novel written by DuBois.

   (E) Much of the scholarly work that has focused on *The Quest of the Silver Fleece* has been surprisingly critical of it.

Explanation

Choice C is correct. The second sentence states that *The Quest of the Silver Fleece* subtly engages the issue of race and implies that such an issue would attract the attention of literary scholars. The passage provides no information about whether *The Quest of the Silver Fleece* is DuBois' first novel (Choice A), whether it received more or less scholarly attention than his other novels (Choice B), whether it is better than any of his other novels (Choice D), nor about what scholars have said about it (Choice E).

13. In the fourth sentence ("Perhaps DuBois . . . editor."), the author of the passage is most likely suggesting that

   (A) scholars will find that DuBois' novels are more relevant to current concerns than is his work as philosopher, historian, and editor

   (B) more scholarly attention will be paid to *The Quest of the Silver Fleece* than to DuBois' other novels

   (C) DuBois' novels will come to overshadow his work as philosopher, historian, and editor

   (D) DuBois' novels may eventually attract greater scholarly interest than they have to date

   (E) it will be shown that DuBois' work as philosopher, historian, and editor had an important influence on his work as novelist

Explanation

The fourth sentence speculates that once DuBois scholars have exhausted potential avenues of research in the fields of philosophy, history, and editing, they will turn to his novels, so **Choice D** is the correct answer. None of the other choices fits the metaphor in "Perhaps DuBois the novelist must wait his turn."

14. Which of the following best describes the central issue with which the passage is concerned?

(A) The perfunctoriness of much of the critical work devoted to DuBois' novels

(B) The nature of DuBois' engagement with the issue of race in *The Quest of the Silver Fleece*

(C) Whether DuBois' novels are of high quality and relevant to current concerns

(D) The relationship between DuBois the novelist and DuBois the philosopher, historian, and editor

(E) The degree of consideration that has been given to DuBois' novels, including *The Quest of the Silver Fleece*

Explanation

The passage focuses on the scant attention given to DuBois' novels, *The Quest of the Silver Fleece* in particular. The first two sentences give reasons to expect greater attention, while the last two offer speculations about the explanation for the scant attention. Thus, **Choice E** is correct. The issues described in the other answer choices are all marginal to the passage, if they are mentioned at all.

> **For Questions 15 and 16, select one entry for each blank from the corresponding column of choices. Fill all blanks in the way that best completes the text.**

15. The activists' energetic work in the service of both woman suffrage and the temperance movement in the late nineteenth century (i)_____ the assertion that the two movements were (ii)_____.

Blank (i)	Blank (ii)
(A) undermines	(D) diffuse
(B) supports	(E) inimical
(C) underscores	(F) predominant

Explanation

The sentence is about the implications of the activists' energetic work for some assertion about the woman suffrage and temperance movements. The second blank, however, obscures the nature of that assertion. But it is clear that the "energetic work" could either support an assertion that the two movements were similar, or undermine an assertion that the two movements were opposed. "Supports" is offered as a choice for the first blank (as is the somewhat similar "underscores"), but there is no corresponding term in the second blank, nothing along the lines of "similar" or "compatible." "Undermines" and "inimical" make for the only meaningful statement.

Thus, the correct answer is **undermines** (Choice A) and **inimical** (Choice E).

16. Wills argues that certain malarial parasites are especially (i)_____ because they have more recently entered humans than other species and therefore have had (ii)_____ time to evolve toward (iii)_____. Yet there is no reliable evidence that the most harmful *Plasmodium* species has been in humans for a shorter time than less harmful species.

Blank (i)	Blank (ii)	Blank (iii)
Ⓐ populous	Ⓓ ample	Ⓖ virulence
Ⓑ malignant	Ⓔ insufficient	Ⓗ benignity
Ⓒ threatened	Ⓕ adequate	Ⓘ variability

Explanation

The "Yet" that begins the second sentence indicates that Wills' position would be supported by evidence that the newer parasites are in humans, the more harmful they are. So Wills' position must be that more recent parasites are especially harmful, implying that "malignant" is the correct choice for the first blank. What follows "therefore" is a potential explanation for the trend that Wills expects, namely an evolution toward harmlessness, implying "benignity" for the third blank, with newer species having had "insufficient" time (second blank) to evolve toward harmlessness.

Thus, the correct answer is **malignant** (Choice B), **insufficient** (Choice E), and **benignity** (Choice H).

For each of questions 17 to 20, select _one_ answer choice unless otherwise instructed.

Question 17 is based on the following reading passage.

Observations of the Arctic reveal that the Arctic Ocean is covered by less ice each summer than the previous summer. If this warming trend continues, within 50 years the Arctic Ocean will be ice free during the summer months. This occurrence would in itself have little or no effect on global sea levels, since the melting of ice floating in water does not affect the water level. However, serious consequences to sea levels would eventually result, because _____.

17. Which of the following most logically completes the passage?
    Ⓐ large masses of floating sea ice would continue to form in the wintertime
    Ⓑ significant changes in Arctic sea temperatures would be accompanied by changes in sea temperatures in more temperate parts of the world
    Ⓒ such a warm Arctic Ocean would trigger the melting of massive land-based glaciers in the Arctic
    Ⓓ an ice-free Arctic Ocean would support a very different ecosystem than it does presently
    Ⓔ in the spring, melting sea ice would cause more icebergs to be created and to drift south into shipping routes

Explanation

To logically complete the passage's open-ended "because," something is needed that will explain why the continuation of the warming trend would have serious consequences for sea levels. The passage explains that the melting of the Arctic Ocean ice will not affect sea levels because the contribution that the water contained in that ice makes to sea levels is the same whether the water is frozen or liquid. But Choice C points to a way in which increasing temperatures in the Arctic could add water to the ocean, namely by melting ice on the land. So **Choice C** logically completes the passage and is the correct answer.

Given that the passage has already explained that melting sea ice does not affect sea levels, the formation of sea ice described in Choice A does not explain why there would be consequences for sea levels.

Choices B, D, and E all describe possible consequences of increased temperatures in the Arctic, but none of these consequences suggests a mechanism by which sea levels would change. So none of these options provides a logical completion for the passage.

Questions 18 to 20 are based on the following reading passage.

In a recent study, David Cressy examines two central questions concerning English immigration to New England in the 1630s: what kinds of people immigrated and why? Using contemporary literary evidence, shipping lists, and customs records, Cressy finds that most
line
5   adult immigrants were skilled in farming or crafts, were literate, and were organized in families. Each of these characteristics sharply distinguishes the 21,000 people who left for New England in the 1630s from most of the approximately 377,000 English people who had immigrated to America by 1700.

With respect to their reasons for immigrating, Cressy does not deny the frequently noted fact that some of the immigrants of the 1630s, most notably the organizers and clergy,
10 advanced religious explanations for departure, but he finds that such explanations usually assumed primacy only in retrospect. When he moves beyond the principal actors, he finds that religious explanations were less frequently offered, and he concludes that most people immigrated because they were recruited by promises of material improvement.

Description

The passage discusses Cressy's answers to the questions posed in the first sentence. The immigrants were skilled, literate, and in families, and they apparently immigrated to have a better life materially, rather than religiously.

For the following question, consider each of the choices separately and select all that apply.

18. The passage indicates that Cressy would agree with which of the following statements about the organizers among the English immigrants to New England in the 1630s?

    A Some of them offered a religious explanation for their immigration.

    B They did not offer any reasons for their immigration until some time after they had immigrated.

    C They were more likely than the average immigrant to be motivated by material considerations.

Explanation

Choice A is correct.

Choice A is correct: the organizers are mentioned in the second paragraph, where the passage says that Cressy "does not deny" that organizers "advanced religious explanations" for leaving England and immigrating to New England in the 1630s. This suggests that Cressy would agree with the statement in choice A about the organizers.

Choice B is incorrect: in lines 10–11, the passage says that Cressy finds that religious reasons for immigration "assumed primacy" only in retrospect, but this is not the same as Cressy's concluding that no reasons were given at the time of immigration. Therefore it cannot be inferred that Cressy would agree with the statement in Choice B.

Choice C is incorrect: the passage refers in line 13 to "promises of material improvement" as a factor that in Cressy's view motivated most immigrants other than "the principal actors." This suggests that Cressy regards the principal actors, such as organizers, as having been less, not more, motivated by material considerations than average immigrants were. Therefore it cannot be inferred that Cressy would agree with the statement in Choice C.

19. Select the sentence that provides Cressy's opinion about what motivated English immigrants to go to New England in the 1630s.

Explanation

The last sentence says that Cressy "concludes that most people immigrated because they were recruited by promises of material improvement." Because this suggests that Cressy believes immigrants were motivated by these promises to go to New England, **sentence 5** ("When he . . . improvement.") is the correct choice. The preceding sentence suggests that Cressy does not believe religion was a primary motive influencing immigrants' decision to immigrate in the 1630s. Thus, although this sentence provides an opinion of Cressy's concerning some immigrants' stated reasons for immigrating, it does not say what motive he believes was actually behind the immigration, and therefore does not answer the question.

20. In the passage, the author is primarily concerned with
    (A) summarizing the findings of an investigation
    (B) analyzing a method of argument
    (C) evaluating a point of view
    (D) hypothesizing about a set of circumstances
    (E) establishing categories

Explanation

The passage is about Cressy's investigation of English immigration to New England in the 1630s, and it summarizes his findings concerning who immigrated and why. **Choice A**, "summarizing the findings of an investigation," is therefore the best description of the author's primary concern in the passage. The passage does not analyze a method of argument, so Choice B is incorrect. Choice C is incorrect because the passage is not primarily concerned with evaluating a point of view: it does not assess the merits or demerits of Cressy's viewpoint. The passage is concerned with reporting Cressy's findings, not with hypothesizing or with establishing categories, so Choices D and E are incorrect.

SECTION 4
Quantitative Reasoning
15 Questions with Explanations

For each of Questions 1 to 5, select one of the following answer choices.
- (A) Quantity A is greater.
- (B) Quantity B is greater.
- (C) The two quantities are equal.
- (D) The relationship cannot be determined from the information given.

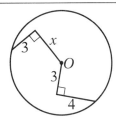

O is the center of the circle above.

Quantity A	Quantity B	

1.   *x*   5   Ⓐ Ⓑ Ⓒ Ⓓ

Explanation

In this question you are asked to compare *x* with 5, where *x* is the length of a line segment from the center of the circle to a point inside the circle. In a circle the easiest line segments to deal with are the radius and the diameter. Looking at the figure in the question, you can see that you can draw two radii, each of which "completes" a right triangle, as shown in the figure below.

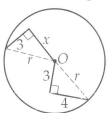

Since in one of the triangles the lengths of both legs are known, you can use that triangle to determine the length of the radius of the circle. The triangle has legs of length 3 and 4. If the length of the radius is *r*, then, using the Pythagorean theorem, you can see that

$$r^2 = 3^2 + 4^2 \text{ or}$$
$$r^2 = 9 + 16 \text{ or}$$
$$r^2 = 25, \text{ and thus, } r = 5$$

Since the length of the radius of the circle is 5 and the line segment of length *x* is clearly shorter than the radius, you know that $x < 5$, and the correct answer is **Choice B**.

You could also see that the two triangles are congruent, and so $x = 4$, again yielding **Choice B**.

This explanation uses the following strategy.
Strategy 4: Translate from a Figure to an Arithmetic or Algebraic Representation

$$x < y < z$$

Quantity A	Quantity B	
2. $\dfrac{x+y+z}{3}$	y	Ⓐ Ⓑ Ⓒ Ⓓ

Explanation

In this question you are given that $x < y < z$, and you are asked to compare $\dfrac{x+y+z}{3}$ with y.

Two approaches that you could use to solve this problem are:

    1: Search for a mathematical relationship between the two quantities.
    2: Plug in numbers for the variables.

Approach 1: Note that $\dfrac{x+y+z}{3}$ is the average of the three numbers x, y, and z and that y is the median. Is the average of 3 numbers always equal to the median? The average could equal the median, but in general they do not have to be equal. Therefore, the correct answer is **Choice D**.

Approach 2: When you plug in numbers for the variables, it is a good idea to consider what kind of numbers are appropriate to plug in and to choose numbers that are easy to work with, if possible.

Since $\dfrac{x+y+z}{3}$ is the average of the three numbers x, y, and z and you are comparing it to the median, you may want to try plugging in numbers that are evenly spaced and plugging in numbers that are not evenly spaced.

You can plug in numbers that are both evenly spaced and easy to work with. For example, you can plug in $x = 1$, $y = 2$, and $z = 3$. In this case,

$$\frac{x+y+z}{3} = \frac{1+2+3}{3} = \frac{6}{3} = 2, \text{ and so } \frac{x+y+z}{3} = y.$$

You can also plug in numbers that not are not evenly spaced and are easy to work with. For example, you can plug in $x = 3$, $y = 6$, and $z = 12$. In this case,

$$\frac{x+y+z}{3} = \frac{3+6+12}{3} = \frac{21}{3} = 7, \text{ and } \frac{x+y+z}{3} > y. \text{ Since in the first case, } \frac{x+y+z}{3}$$

is equal to y and in the second case, it is greater than y, the relationship between the two quantities $\dfrac{x+y+z}{3}$ and y cannot be determined from the information given. The correct answer is **Choice D**.

This explanation uses the following strategies.
Strategy 10: Trial and Error
Strategy 11: Divide into Cases
Strategy 12: Adapt Solutions to Related Problems
Strategy 13: Determine Whether a Conclusion Follows from the Information Given

p is the probability that event E will occur, and s is the probability that event E will <u>not</u> occur.

Quantity A	Quantity B	
3. $p + s$	ps	Ⓐ Ⓑ Ⓒ Ⓓ

Explanation

Since event E will either occur or not occur, it follows that $p + s = 1$, and the value of Quantity A is always 1. Since Quantity B is the product of the two probabilities p and s, you need to look at its value for the cases $p = 1$, $p = 0$, and $0 < p < 1$.

If $p = 1$, then $s = 0$; similarly, if $p = 0$, then $s = 1$. In both cases, ps is equal to 0.

If $0 < p < 1$, both p and s are positive and less than 1, so ps is positive and less than 1. Since Quantity A is equal to 1 and Quantity B is less than 1, the correct answer is **Choice A**.

This explanation uses the following strategy.

Strategy 11: Divide into Cases

X is the set of all integers n that satisfy the inequality $2 \le |n| \le 5$.

Quantity A	Quantity B	
4. The absolute value of the greatest integer in X	The absolute value of the least integer in X	Ⓐ Ⓑ Ⓒ Ⓓ

Explanation

When comparing these quantities, it is important to remember that a nonzero number and its negative have the same absolute value. For example, $|-2| = |2| = 2$. Keeping this in mind, you can see that the positive integers 2, 3, 4, and 5 and the negative integers -2, -3, -4, and -5 all satisfy the inequalities $2 \le |n| \le 5$, and that these are the only such integers. Thus, the set X consists of the integers -5, -4, -3, -2, 2, 3, 4, and 5. The greatest of these integers is 5, and its absolute value is 5. The least of these integers is -5, and its absolute value is also 5. Therefore, Quantity A is equal to Quantity B. The correct answer is **Choice C**.

This explanation uses the following strategy.

Strategy 1: Translate from Words to an Arithmetic or Algebraic Representation

A random variable Y is normally distributed with a mean of 200 and a standard deviation of 10.

Quantity A	Quantity B	
5. The probability of the event that the value of Y is greater than 220	$\dfrac{1}{6}$	

Explanation

This problem involves a normal distribution with mean 200 and standard deviation 10. Thus, the value of 210 is 1 standard deviation above the mean, and the value of 220 is 2 standard deviations above the mean. To compare Quantity A with Quantity B, it is not necessary to exactly determine the probability of the event that the value of Y is greater than 220. Remember that in any normal distribution, almost all of the data values, or about 95% of them, fall within 2 standard deviations on either side of the mean. This means that less than 5% of the values in this distribution will be greater than 220. Thus, the probability of the event that the value of Y is greater than 220 must be less than 5%, or $\dfrac{1}{20}$, and this is certainly less than $\dfrac{1}{6}$. The correct answer is **Choice B**.

Another approach to this problem is to draw a normal curve, or "bell-shaped curve," that represents the probability distribution of the random variable Y, as shown in the figure below.

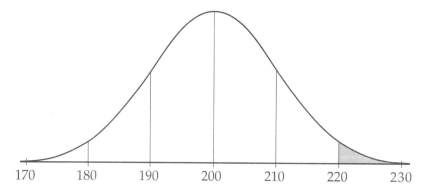

The curve is symmetric about the mean 200. The values of 210, 220, and 230 are equally spaced to the right of 200 and represent 1, 2, and 3 standard deviations, respectively, above the mean. Similarly, the values of 190, 180, and 170 are 1, 2, and 3 standard deviations, respectively, below the mean. Quantity A, the probability of the event that the value of Y is greater than 220, is equal to the area of the shaded region as a fraction of the total area under the curve.

From the figure, you can see that the area under the normal curve has been divided into 6 regions and that these regions are not equal in area. The shaded region is one of the two smallest of the 6 regions, so its area must be less than $\dfrac{1}{6}$ of the total area under the curve. The correct answer is **Choice B**.

This explanation uses the following strategies.
Strategy 2: Translate from Words to a Figure or Diagram
Strategy 8: Search for a Mathematical Relationship

6. The ratio of $\frac{1}{3}$ to $\frac{3}{8}$ is equal to the ratio of

 Ⓐ 1 to 8

 Ⓑ 8 to 1

 Ⓒ 8 to 3

 Ⓓ 8 to 9

 Ⓔ 9 to 8

Explanation

Multiplying both parts of a ratio by the same positive number produces an equivalent ratio. While you could multiply both fractions in the ratio by any number, 24 is a good number to choose because it is the least common multiple of 3 and 8. Thus, multiplying both $\frac{1}{3}$ and $\frac{3}{8}$ by 24, you get that the ratio of $\frac{1}{3}$ to $\frac{3}{8}$ is equal to the ratio of 8 to 9. The correct answer is **Choice D**.

An alternate approach to this problem is to express the ratio of $\frac{1}{3}$ to $\frac{3}{8}$ as the fraction $\dfrac{\frac{1}{3}}{\frac{3}{8}}$. This fraction is equivalent to $\left(\frac{1}{3}\right)\left(\frac{8}{3}\right)$, or $\frac{8}{9}$. The correct answer is **Choice D**.

This explanation uses the following strategy.

Strategy 5: Simplify an Arithmetic or Algebraic Representation

For the following question, enter your answer in the box.

7. In a graduating class of 236 students, 142 took algebra and 121 took chemistry. What is the greatest possible number of students that could have taken both algebra and chemistry?

 [   ] students

Explanation

This is the type of problem for which drawing a Venn diagram is usually helpful. The Venn diagram below is one you could draw to represent the information given in the question.

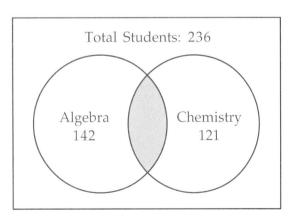

Note that the algebra and chemistry numbers given do not separate out the number of students who took both algebra and chemistry, and that this question asks for the greatest possible number of such students. It is a good idea, therefore, to redraw the Venn diagram with the number of students who took both algebra and chemistry separated out. The revised Venn diagram looks like the one below.

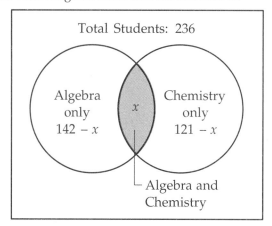

To solve this problem you want the greatest possible value of x. It is clear from the diagram that x cannot be greater than 142 nor greater than 121, otherwise $142 - x$ or $121 - x$ would be negative. Hence, x must be less than or equal to 121. Since there is no information to exclude $x = 121$, the correct answer is **121**.

This explanation uses the following strategy.

Strategy 2: Translate from Words to a Figure or Diagram

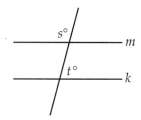

8.   In the figure above, if $m \parallel k$ and $s = t + 30$, then $t =$

   (A)   30
   (B)   60
   (C)   75
   (D)   80
   (E)   105

Explanation

When trying to solve a geometric problem, it is often helpful to add any known information to the figure. Since corresponding angles have equal measures, you could place two more angle measures on the figure, as shown below.

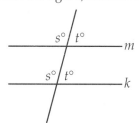

Now, from the figure, you can see that $s + t = 180$. Therefore, since it is given that $s = t + 30$, you can substitute $t + 30$ for s into the equation $s + t = 180$ and get that $(t + 30) + t = 180$, which can be simplified as follows.

$$(t + 30) + t = 180$$
$$2t = 150$$
$$t = 75$$

The correct answer is **Choice C**.

This explanation uses the following strategy.

Strategy 4: Translate from a Figure to an Arithmetic or Algebraic Representation

For the following question, select all the answer choices that apply.

9.   The total amount that Mary paid for a book was equal to the price of the book plus a sales tax that was 4 percent of the price of the book. Mary paid for the book with a $10 bill and received the correct change, which was less than $3.00. Which of the following statements must be true?

Indicate <u>all</u> such statements.

A The price of the book was less than $9.50.

B The price of the book was greater than $6.90.

C The sales tax was less than $0.45.

Explanation

For this problem you may find it helpful to translate the given information into an algebraic expression. Since the price of the book is unknown, you can call it x dollars, and then the total amount that Mary paid is x dollars plus 4% of x dollars, or $1.04x$ dollars. The problem states that Mary received some change from a $10 bill, so $1.04x$ dollars must be less than $10. Since the change was less than $3.00, the total amount Mary paid for the book must have been greater than $7.00. You can express this information algebraically by the inequality

$$7.00 < 1.04x < 10.00$$

Solving the inequality for x by dividing by 1.04, and rounding, you get

$$6.73 < x < 9.62$$

So you see that x, the price of the book, must be between $6.73 and $9.62, and each price in between is possible. With this information, you can quickly examine the first two statements. Choice A is not necessarily true because the price could be as high as $9.61, and Choice B is not necessarily true because the price could be as low as $6.74.

To examine Choice C, you could compute the tax for the greatest possible price, which would be 4% of 9.61, or $(0.04)(9.61) \approx 0.38$. Since this greatest possible tax is less than $0.45, Choice C must be true.

You can also quickly see that Choice C must be true if you note that 4% of $10.00 would only be $0.40, and since the price must be less than $10.00, the tax must be less than $0.40. The correct answer consists of **Choice C**.

This explanation uses the following strategies.

Strategy 1: Translate from Words to an Arithmetic or Algebraic Representation
Strategy 8: Search for a Mathematical Relationship

10. If $\dfrac{1}{(2^{11})(5^{17})}$ is expressed as a terminating decimal, how many nonzero digits will the decimal have?

(A) One   (B) Two   (C) Four   (D) Six   (E) Eleven

Explanation

To convert the fraction to a decimal, it is helpful to first write the fraction in powers of 10. Using the rules of exponents, you can write the following.

$$\frac{1}{(2^{11})(5^{17})} = \frac{1}{(2^{11})(5^{11+6})}$$

$$= \frac{1}{(2^{11})(5^{11})(5^{6})}$$

$$= \frac{1}{(10^{11})(5^{6})}$$

$$= \left(\frac{1}{5}\right)^{6}(10^{-11})$$

$$= (0.2)^{6}(10^{-11})$$

$$= ((2)(10)^{-1})^{6}(10^{-11})$$

$$= (2^{6})(10^{-6})(10^{-11})$$

$$= (2^{6})(10^{-17})$$

$$= (64)(10^{-17})$$

So the decimal has two nonzero digits, 6 and 4. The correct answer is **Choice B**.

This explanation uses the following strategy.

Strategy 5: Simplify an Arithmetic or Algebraic Representation

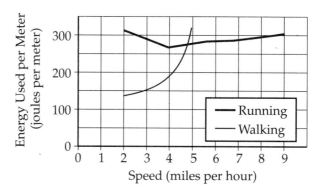

ENERGY USED PER METER VERSUS SPEED
DURING RUNNING AND WALKING

11. If s is a speed, in miles per hour, at which the energy used per meter during running is twice the energy used per meter during walking, then, according to the graph above, s is between

(A) 2.5 and 3.0

(B) 3.0 and 3.5

(C) 3.5 and 4.0

(D) 4.0 and 4.5

(E) 4.5 and 5.0

Explanation

This question is about the speed at which the energy used per meter during running is twice that used per meter during walking. Graphically, this is the speed for which the running energy is twice as high as the walking energy. Looking at the graph, you can see that for speeds greater than or equal to 3.0 miles per hour, the running energy is less than twice the walking energy, so the desired speed must be less than 3.0. In fact, the desired speed is between 2.0 (the lowest speed on the graph) and 3.0. Looking at the answer choices, you see that there is only one answer choice that is between 2.0 and 3.0; namely, Choice A, which says the desired speed is between 2.5 and 3.0. The correct answer is **Choice A**.

This explanation uses the following strategy.

Strategy 4: Translate from a Figure to an Arithmetic or Algebraic Representation

12. If $n = 2^3$, then $n^n =$

    Ⓐ 2^6

    Ⓑ 2^{11}

    Ⓒ 2^{18}

    Ⓓ 2^{24}

    Ⓔ 2^{27}

Explanation

When answering a question in which you are asked to calculate the value of an expression, it is often helpful to look at the answer choices first to see what form they are in. In this question the answer choices are all in the form 2 raised to a power, so you should try to achieve that form. It is given that $n = 2^3 = 8$. Therefore, $n^n = (2^3)^8 = 2^{24}$. The correct answer is **Choice D**.

This explanation uses the following strategy.

Strategy 5: Simplify an Arithmetic or Algebraic Representation

For the following question, select all the answer choices that apply.

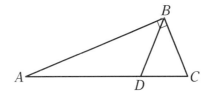

The length of AB is $10\sqrt{3}$.

13. Which of the following statements <u>individually</u> provide(s) sufficient additional information to determine the area of triangle ABC above?

Indicate <u>all</u> such statements.

    Ⓐ DBC is an equilateral triangle.

    Ⓑ ABD is an isosceles triangle.

    Ⓒ   The length of BC is equal to the length of AD.

    Ⓓ   The length of BC is 10.

    Ⓔ   The length of AD is 10.

Explanation

From the figure you know that *ABC* is a right triangle with its right angle at vertex *B*. You also know that point *D* is on the hypotenuse *AC*. You are given that the length of *AB* is $10\sqrt{3}$. However, because the figure is not necessarily drawn to scale, you don't know the lengths of *AD, DC,* and *BC*. In particular, you don't know where *D* is on *AC*.

The area of a triangle is $\frac{1}{2}$(base)(height). Thus, the area of right triangle *ABC* is equal to $\frac{1}{2}$ of the length of *AB* times the length of *BC*. You already know that the length of *AB* is $10\sqrt{3}$. Any additional information that would allow you to calculate the length of *BC* would be sufficient to find the area of triangle *ABC*. You need to consider each of the five statements individually, as follows.

Statement A: DBC is an equilateral triangle. This statement implies that angle *DCB* is a 60° angle; and therefore, triangle *ABC* is a 30°- 60°- 90° triangle. Thus the length of *BC* can be determined, and this statement provides sufficient additional information to determine the area of triangle *ABC*.

Statement B: ABD is an isosceles triangle. There is more than one way in which triangle *ABD* can be isosceles. Below are two redrawn figures showing triangle *ABD* as isosceles. In the figure on the left, the length of *AD* is equal to the length of *DB*; and in the figure on the right, the length of *AB* is equal to the length of *AD*.

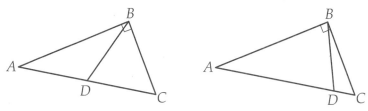

Either of the figures could have been drawn with the length of *BC* even longer. So, statement B does not provide sufficient additional information to determine the area of triangle *ABC*.

Statement C: The length of *BC* is equal to the length of *AD*. You have no way of finding the length of *AD* without making other assumptions, so statement C does not provide sufficient additional information to determine the area of triangle *ABC*.

Statement D: The length of *BC* is 10. The length of *BC* is known, so the area of triangle *ABC* can be found. Statement D provides sufficient additional information to determine the area of triangle *ABC*.

Statement E: The length of *AD* is 10. The relationship between *AD* and *BC* is not known, so statement E does not provide sufficient additional information to determine the area of triangle *ABC*.

Statements A and D individually provide sufficient additional information to determine the area of triangle *ABC*. Therefore, the correct answer consists of **Choices A and D**.

This explanation uses the following strategies.

Strategy 8: Search for a Mathematical Relationship
Strategy 14: Determine What Additional Information Is Sufficient to Solve a Problem

For the following question, enter your answer in the box.

$$a_1, a_2, a_3, \ldots, a_n, \ldots$$

14. In the sequence above, each term after the first term is equal to the preceding term plus the constant c. If $a_1 + a_3 + a_5 = 27$, what is the value of $a_2 + a_4$?

$$a_2 + a_4 = \boxed{}$$

Explanation

Note that answering this question requires information only about the first five terms of the sequence. So it is a good idea to work with the relationships among these five terms to see what is happening.

Since you are given that in this sequence each term after a_1 is c greater than the previous term, you can rewrite the first five terms of the sequence in terms of a_1 and c as follows.

$$a_2 = a_1 + c$$
$$a_3 = a_2 + c = a_1 + 2c$$
$$a_4 = a_1 + 3c$$
$$a_5 = a_1 + 4c$$

From the question, you know that $a_1 + a_3 + a_5 = 27$, and from the equations above, $a_1 + a_3 + a_5 = a_1 + (a_1 + 2c) + (a_1 + 4c) = 3a_1 + 6c$. So you can conclude that $3a_1 + 6c = 27$, or $a_1 + 2c = 9$.

To find $a_2 + a_4$, you can express a_2 and a_4 in terms of a_1 and c and simplify as follows.

$$a_2 + a_4 = (a_1 + c) + (a_1 + 3c)$$
$$= 2a_1 + 4c$$
$$= 2(a_1 + 2c)$$

But $a_1 + 2c = 9$, so $a_2 + a_4 = 2(9) = 18$. The correct answer is **18**.

This explanation uses the following strategies.

Strategy 5: Simplify an Arithmetic or Algebraic Representation
Strategy 7: Find a Pattern

15. A desert outpost has a water supply that is sufficient to last 21 days for 15 people. At the same average rate of water consumption per person, how many days would the water supply last for 9 people?

(A) 28.0
(B) 32.5
(C) 35.0
(D) 37.5
(E) 42.0

Explanation

The water supply is enough for 15 people to survive 21 days. Assuming the same average rate of water consumption per person, 1 person would have enough water to last for $(15)(21) = 315$ days. Therefore, 9 people would have enough water for $\frac{1}{9}$ of the 315 days, or 35 days. The correct answer is **Choice C**.

Another approach to solving this problem is to recognize that the water supply would last $\frac{15}{9}$ as many days for 9 people as it would for 15 people. Therefore, since the water supply would last 21 days for 15 people, it would last $\left(\frac{15}{9}\right)(21)$, or 35 days for 9 people. The correct answer is **Choice C**.

This explanation uses the following strategy.

Strategy 1: Translate from Words to an Arithmetic or Algebraic Representation

SECTION 5
Quantitative Reasoning
20 Questions with Explanations

For each of Questions 1 to 7, select one of the following answer choices.
Ⓐ **Quantity A is greater.**
Ⓑ **Quantity B is greater.**
Ⓒ **The two quantities are equal.**
Ⓓ **The relationship cannot be determined from the information given.**

Country	Value of 1 United States Dollar
Argentina	0.93 peso
Kenya	32.08 shillings

	Quantity A	Quantity B	
1.	The dollar value of 1 Argentine peso according to the table above	The dollar value of 1 Kenyan shilling according to the table above	

Explanation

When you are answering Quantitative Comparison questions, it is a good time-saving idea to see whether you can determine the relative sizes of the two quantities being compared without doing any calculations.

In the table accompanying this question, both the value of the Argentine peso and the value of the Kenyan shilling are compared to the United States dollar.

Without doing any calculations, you can see from the information given that 1 United States dollar is worth a little less than 1 Argentine peso, so 1 peso is worth more than 1 United States dollar. On the other hand, 1 United States dollar is worth 32.08 Kenyan shillings, so 1 Kenyan shilling is worth only a <u>small</u> <u>fraction</u> of 1 United States dollar. The correct answer is **Choice A**.

This explanation uses the following strategy.
Strategy 9: Estimate

---

       k is a digit in the decimal 1.3k5, and 1.3k5 is less than 1.33.

	Quantity A	Quantity B	
2.	k	1	

Explanation

In this question, you are given that k is a digit in the decimal 1.3k5 and that 1.3k5 is less than 1.33. So you can see that 1.30 < 1.3k5 < 1.33. Therefore, 1.3k5 must equal 1.305 or 1.315 or 1.325, and the digit k must be 0, 1, or 2. The correct answer is **Choice D**.

This explanation uses the following strategies.
Strategy 5: Simplify an Arithmetic or Algebraic Representation
Strategy 13: Determine Whether a Conclusion Follows from the Information Given

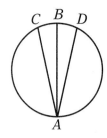

AB is a diameter of the circle above.

Quantity A	Quantity B	
3. The length of AB	The average (arithmetic mean) of the lengths of AC and AD	

Explanation

Recall that in a circle, any diameter is longer than any other chord that is not a diameter. You are given that AB is a diameter of the circle. It follows that AC and AD are chords that are not diameters, since there is only one diameter with endpoint A. Hence, AB is longer than both AC and AD. Note that the average of two numbers is always less than or equal to the greater of the two numbers. Therefore, the average of the lengths of AC and AD, which is Quantity B, must be less than the length of AB, which is Quantity A. The correct answer is **Choice A**.

This explanation uses the following strategies.

Strategy 4: Translate from a Figure to an Arithmetic or Algebraic Representation
Strategy 8: Search for a Mathematical Relationship

Three consecutive integers have a sum of −84.

Quantity A	Quantity B	
4. The least of the three integers	−28	

Explanation

Two approaches you could use to solve this problem are:

1: Translate from words to algebra.
2: Determine a mathematical relationship between the two quantities.

Approach 1: You can represent the least of the three consecutive integers by x, and then the three integers would be represented by x, $x + 1$, and $x + 2$. It is given that the sum of the three integers is −84, so $x + (x + 1) + (x + 2) = -84$. You can solve this equation for x as follows.

$$x + (x + 1) + (x + 2) = -84$$
$$3x + 3 = -84$$
$$3x = -87$$
$$x = -29$$

Since the least of the three integers, −29, is less than −28, the correct answer is **Choice B**.
Approach 2: You could ask yourself what would happen if the least of the three consecutive integers was −28. The three consecutive integers would then be −28, −27, and −26, and their sum would be −81. But you were given that the sum of the

three consecutive integers is −84, which is less than −81. Therefore, −28 is greater than the least of the three consecutive integers, and the correct answer is **Choice B**.

This explanation uses the following strategies.

Strategy 1: Translate from Words to an Arithmetic or Algebraic Representation
Strategy 8: Search for a Mathematical Relationship

In the xy-plane, the equation of line k is $3x - 2y = 0$.

Quantity A	Quantity B	
5. The x-intercept of line k	The y-intercept of line k	

Explanation

Two approaches you could use to solve this problem are:

    1: Reason algebraically.
    2: Reason geometrically.

Approach 1: To solve this problem algebraically, note that given the equation of a line in the xy-plane, the x-intercept of the line is the value of x when y equals 0, and the y-intercept of the line is the value of y when x equals 0. The equation of line k is $3x - 2y = 0$. If $y = 0$, then $x = 0$; and if $x = 0$, then $y = 0$. Therefore, both the x-intercept and y-intercept of the line are equal to 0, which means that the line passes through the origin. The correct answer is **Choice C**.

Approach 2: To solve this problem geometrically, graph the line with equation $3x - 2y = 0$ in the xy-plane. Since two points determine a straight line, you can do this by plotting two points on the line and drawing the line they determine. The points (0,0) and (2,3) lie on the line, and the graph of the line in the xy-plane is shown in the following figure.

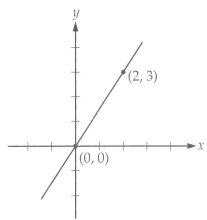

As you can see, the line passes through the origin, and so it crosses both the x-axis and the y-axis at (0,0). The correct answer is **Choice C**.

This explanation uses the following strategies.

Strategy 3: Translate from an Algebraic to a Graphical Representation
Strategy 8: Search for a Mathematical Relationship

n is a positive integer that is divisible by 6.

Quantity A	Quantity B	
6. The remainder when n is divided by 12	The remainder when n is divided by 18	

Explanation

One way to compare the two quantities is to plug in a few values of n. If you plug in $n = 36$, you find that both the remainder when n is divided by 12 and the remainder when n is divided by 18 are equal to 0, so Quantity A is equal to Quantity B. However, if you plug in $n = 18$, you find that the remainder when n is divided by 12 is 6 and the remainder when n is divided by 18 is 0, so Quantity B is greater than Quantity A. Therefore, the correct answer is **Choice D**.

Another way to compare the two quantities is to find all of the possible values of Quantity A and Quantity B. The positive integers that are divisible by 6 are 6, 12, 18, 24, 30, 36, etc. When dividing each of these integers by 12, you get a remainder of either 0 or 6, so Quantity A is either 0 or 6. When dividing each of these integers by 18, you get a remainder of either 0 or 6 or 12, so Quantity B is either 0 or 6 or 12. Note that when the value of Quantity B is 12, the value of Quantity A, 0 or 6, is less than the value of Quantity B; but when the value of Quantity B is 0, the value of Quantity A is greater than or equal to the value of Quantity B. Thus, the correct answer is **Choice D**.

This explanation uses the following strategies.

Strategy 10: Trial and Error
Strategy 13: Determine Whether a Conclusion Follows from the Information Given

$$\frac{1-x}{x-1} = \frac{1}{x}$$

Quantity A	Quantity B	
7. x	$-\dfrac{1}{2}$	Ⓐ Ⓑ Ⓒ Ⓓ

Explanation

One approach you could use to solve this problem is to solve the equation $\frac{1-x}{x-1} = \frac{1}{x}$ for x. Since fractions are defined only when the denominator is not equal to 0, the denominators of both of the fractions in the equation are nonzero. Therefore, $x \neq 0$ and $x \neq 1$.

To solve the equation for x, begin by multiplying both sides of the equation by the common denominator $x(x-1)$ to get $x(1-x) = (x-1)(1)$. Then proceed as follows.

$$x(1-x) = (x-1)(1)$$
$$x - x^2 = x - 1$$
$$x^2 = 1$$

Since $x^2 = 1$ and $x \neq 1$, it follows that $x = -1$.

Quantity A is equal to -1 and Quantity B is equal to $-\dfrac{1}{2}$. Therefore, Quantity B is greater, and the correct answer is **Choice B**.

Another approach is to notice that for all values of $x \neq 1$, the value of $\dfrac{1-x}{x-1}$ is equal to -1. You can try plugging in a few numbers for x to see that this is true. For example, if you plug in $x = 7$, you get $\dfrac{1-7}{7-1} = \dfrac{-6}{6} = -1$.

You can also show that for all values of $x \neq 1$, the value of $\dfrac{1-x}{x-1}$ is equal to -1 algebraically by rewriting $1 - x$ as $-(x-1)$. Thus, $\dfrac{1-x}{x-1} = \dfrac{-(x-1)}{(x-1)} = -1$. Because the left side of the equation $\frac{1-x}{x-1} = \frac{1}{x}$ is equal to -1, it follows that $-1 = \frac{1}{x}$, and so $x = -1$.

Therefore, Quantity A is equal to -1, which is less than Quantity B, $-\frac{1}{2}$, and the correct

answer is **Choice B**.

This explanation uses the following strategy.

Strategy 5: Simplify an Arithmetic or Algebraic Representation

8. The fabric needed to make 3 curtains sells for $8.00 per yard and can be purchased only by the full yard. If the length of fabric required for each curtain is 1.6 yards and all of the fabric is purchased as a single length, what is the total cost of the fabric that needs to be purchased for the 3 curtains?

    (A) $40.00

    (B) $38.40

    (C) $24.00

    (D) $16.00

    (E) $12.80

Explanation

Since 1.6 yards of fabric are required for each curtain, it follows that $(3)(1.6)$, or 4.8, yards of fabric are required to make the 3 curtains. The fabric can be purchased only by the full yard, so 5 yards of fabric would need to be purchased. Since the fabric sells for $8.00 per yard, the total cost of the fabric is $40.00. The correct answer is **Choice A**.

This explanation uses the following strategy.

Strategy 1: Translate from Words to an Arithmetic or Algebraic Representation

For the following question, select all the answer choices that apply.

9. In the xy-plane, line k is a line that does <u>not</u> pass through the origin. Which of the following statements <u>individually</u> provide(s) sufficient additional information to conclude that the slope of line k is negative?

    Indicate <u>all</u> such statements.

    [A] The x-intercept of line k is twice the y-intercept of line k.

    [B] The product of the x-intercept and the y-intercept of line k is positive.

    [C] Line k passes through the points (a, b) and (r, s), where
    $(a - r)(b - s) < 0$.

Explanation

For questions involving a coordinate system, it is often helpful to draw a figure to visualize the problem situation. If you draw some lines with negative slopes in the xy-plane, such as those in the figure below, you see that for each line that does not pass through the origin, the x- and y-intercepts are either both positive or both negative. Conversely, you can see that if the x- and y-intercepts of a line have the same sign then the slope of the line is negative.

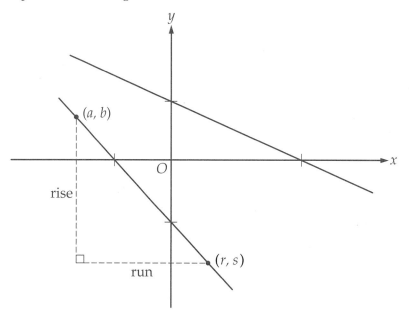

You can use this fact to examine the information given in the first two statements. Remember that you need to evaluate each statement by itself.

Choice A states that the x-intercept is twice the y-intercept, so you can conclude that both intercepts have the same sign, and thus the slope of line k is negative. So the information in Choice A is sufficient to determine that the slope of line k is negative.

Choice B states that the product of the x-intercept and the y-intercept is positive. You know that the product of two numbers is positive if both factors have the same sign. So this information is also sufficient to determine that the slope of line k is negative.

To evaluate Choice C, it is helpful to recall the definition of the slope of a line passing through two given points. You may remember it as "rise over run." If the two points are (a, b) and (r, s), then the slope is $\dfrac{b-s}{a-r}$.

Choice C states that the product of the quantities $(a - r)$ and $(b - s)$ is negative. Note that these are the denominator and the numerator, respectively, of $\dfrac{b-s}{a-r}$, the slope of line k. So you can conclude that $(a - r)$ and $(b - s)$ have opposite signs and the slope of line k is negative. The information in Choice C is sufficient to determine that the slope of line k is negative.

So each of the three statements individually provides sufficient information to conclude that the slope of line k is negative. The correct answer consists of **Choices A, B, and C**.

This explanation uses the following strategies.

Strategy 3: Translate from an Algebraic to a Graphical Representation
Strategy 14: Determine What Additional Information Is Sufficient to Solve a Problem

	Distance from Centerville (miles)
Freight train	$-10t + 115$
Passenger train	$-20t + 150$

10. The expressions in the table above give the distance from Centerville to each of two trains t hours after 12:00 noon. At what time after 12:00 noon will the trains be equidistant from Centerville?

    (A)   1:30
    (B)   3:30
    (C)   5:10
    (D)   8:50
    (E)   11:30

Explanation

The distance between the freight train and Centerville at t hours past noon is $-10t + 115$. The distance between the passenger train and Centerville at t hours past noon is $-20t + 150$. To find out at what time the distances will be the same you need to equate the two expressions and solve for t as follows.

$$-10t + 115 = -20t + 150$$
$$10t + 115 = 150$$
$$10t = 35$$
$$t = 3.5$$

Therefore, the two trains will be the same distance from Centerville at 3.5 hours past noon, or at 3:30. The correct answer is **Choice B**.

This explanation uses the following strategies.

Strategy 1: Translate from Words to an Arithmetic or Algebraic Representation
Strategy 5: Simplify an Arithmetic or Algebraic Representation

For the following question, enter your answer in the box.

11. In the xy-plane, the point with coordinates $(-6, -7)$ is the center of circle C. The point with coordinates $(-6, 5)$ lies inside C, and the point with coordinates $(8, -7)$ lies outside C. If m is the radius of C and m is an integer, what is the value of m?

$$m = \boxed{}$$

Explanation

A strategy that is often helpful in working with geometry problems is drawing a figure that represents the given information as accurately as possible.

    In this question you are given that the point with coordinates $(-6, -7)$ is the center of circle C, the point with coordinates $(-6, 5)$ lies inside circle C, and the point with coordinates $(8, -7)$ lies outside circle C, so you could draw the following figure.

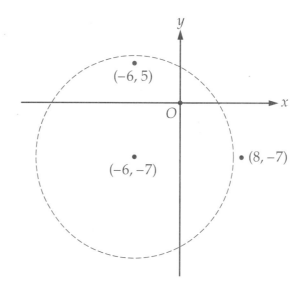

From the figure, you can see that the distance between $(-6, -7)$ and $(-6, 5)$ is $7 + 5$, or 12, and the radius of C must be greater than 12. You can also see that the distance between $(-6, -7)$ and $(8, -7)$ is $6 + 8$, or 14, and the radius of C must be less than 14. Therefore, since the radius is an integer greater than 12 and less than 14, it must be 13. The correct answer is **13**.

This explanation uses the following strategy.

Strategy 2: Translate from Words to a Figure or Diagram

For the following question, select all the answer choices that apply.

12. The integer v is greater than 1. If v is the square of an integer, which of the following numbers must also be the square of an integer?

    Indicate <u>all</u> such numbers.

    A $81v$ B $25v + 10\sqrt{v} + 1$ C $4v^2 + 4\sqrt{v} + 1$

Explanation

If v is the square of an integer, then $\sqrt{v}$ is an integer. You can use this fact, together with the fact that the product and the sum of integers are also integers, to examine the first two choices.

    Choice A: The positive square root of $81v$ is $9\sqrt{v}$, which is an integer. So $81v$ is the square of an integer.

    Choice B: $25v + 10\sqrt{v} + 1 = (5\sqrt{v} + 1)^2$ and $5\sqrt{v} + 1$ is an integer. So $25v + 10\sqrt{v} + 1$ is the square of an integer.

    Choice C: Since there is no obvious way to factor the given expression, you may suspect that it is not the square of an integer. To show that a given statement is not true, it is sufficient to find one counterexample. In this case, you need to find one value of v such that v is the square of an integer but $4v^2 + 4\sqrt{v} + 1$ is not the square of an integer. If $v = 4$, then $4v^2 + 4\sqrt{v} + 1 = 64 + 8 + 1 = 73$, which is not the square of an integer. This proves that $4v^2 + 4\sqrt{v} + 1$ does not have to be the square of an integer.

    The correct answer consists of **Choices A and B**.

This explanation uses the following strategies.

Strategy 5: Simplify an Arithmetic or Algebraic Representation
Strategy 13: Determine Whether a Conclusion Follows from the Information Given

Questions 13 to 15 are based on the following data.

DISTANCE TRAVELED BY A CAR ACCORDING TO THE CAR'S SPEED
WHEN THE DRIVER IS SIGNALED TO STOP

Distance Traveled
During Reaction Time*

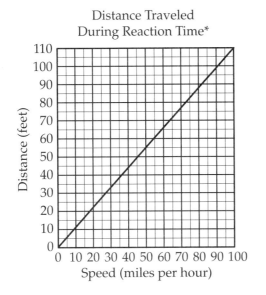

Distance Traveled After Brakes
Have Been Applied

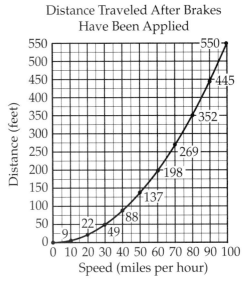

*Reaction time is the time period that begins when the driver is signaled to stop and
ends when the driver applies the brakes.

<u>Note</u>: Total stopping distance is the sum of the distance traveled during reaction time
and the distance traveled after brakes have been applied.

13.   Approximately what is the total stopping distance, in feet, if the car is traveling at
a speed of 40 miles per hour when the driver is signaled to stop?

Ⓐ 130
Ⓑ 110
Ⓒ   90
Ⓓ   70
Ⓔ   40

Explanation

Since the total stopping distance is the sum of the distance traveled during reaction time and the distance traveled after the brakes have been applied, you need
information from both graphs to answer this question. At a speed of 40 miles per
hour, the distance traveled during reaction time is a little less than 45 feet, and the
distance traveled after the brakes have been applied is 88 feet. Since 45 + 88 = 133,
the correct answer is **Choice A**.

This explanation uses the following strategies.

Strategy 4: Translate from a Figure to an Arithmetic or Algebraic Representation
Strategy 9: Estimate

14. Of the following, which is the greatest speed, in miles per hour, at which the car can travel and stop with a total stopping distance of less than 200 feet?

 (A) 50

 (B) 55

 (C) 60

 (D) 65

 (E) 70

Explanation

Since the total stopping distance is the sum of the distance traveled during reaction time and the distance traveled after the brakes have been applied, you need information from both graphs to answer this question. A good strategy for solving this problem is to calculate the total stopping distance for the speeds given in the options. For a speed of 50 miles per hour, the distance traveled during reaction time is about 55 feet, and the distance traveled after the brakes have been applied is 137 feet; therefore, the total stopping distance is about 55 + 137, or 192 feet. For a speed of 55 miles per hour, the distance traveled during reaction time is about 60 feet, and the distance traveled after the brakes have been applied is about 170 feet; therefore, the total stopping distance is about 60 + 170, or 230 feet. Since the speeds in the remaining choices are greater than 55 miles per hour and both types of stopping distances increase as the speed increases, it follows that the total stopping distances for all the remaining choices are greater than 200 feet. The correct answer is **Choice A**.

This explanation uses the following strategies.

Strategy 4: Translate from a Figure to an Arithmetic or Algebraic Representation
Strategy 9: Estimate

15. The total stopping distance for the car traveling at 60 miles per hour is approximately what percent greater than the total stopping distance for the car traveling at 50 miles per hour?

 (A) 22%   (B) 30%   (C) 38%   (D) 45%   (E) 52%

Explanation

To solve this problem you need to find the total stopping distance at 50 miles per hour and at 60 miles per hour, find their difference, and then express the difference as a percent of the shorter total stopping distance. You need to use both graphs to find the total stopping distances. At 50 miles per hour, the total stopping distance is approximately 55 + 137 = 192 feet; and at 60 miles per hour it is approximately 66 + 198 = 264 feet. The difference of 72 feet as a percent of 192 feet is $\frac{72}{192} = 0.375$, or approximately 38%. The correct answer is **Choice C**.

This explanation uses the following strategies.

Strategy 4: Translate from a Figure to an Arithmetic or Algebraic Representation
Strategy 9: Estimate

16. What is the least positive integer that is <u>not</u> a factor of 25! and is <u>not</u> a prime number?

    (A) 26   (B) 28   (C) 36   (D) 56   (E) 58

Explanation

Note that 25! is equal to the product of all positive integers from 1 to 25, inclusive. Thus, every positive integer less than or equal to 25 is a factor of 25!. Also, any integer greater than 25 that can be expressed as the product of different positive integers less than 25 is a factor of 25!. In view of this, it's reasonable to consider the next few integers greater than 25, including answer choices A and B.

Choice A, 26, is equal to (2)(13). Both 2 and 13 are factors of 25!, so 26 is also a factor of 25!. The same is true for 27, or (3)(9), and for Choice B, 28, or (4)(7). However, the next integer, 29, is a prime number greater than 25, and as such, it has no positive factors (other than 1) that are less than or equal to 25. Therefore, 29 is the least positive integer that is <u>not</u> a factor of 25!. However, the question asks for an integer that is <u>not</u> a prime number, so 29 is not the answer.

At this point, you could consider 30, 31, 32, etc., but it is quicker to look at the rest of the choices. Choice C, 36, is equal to (4)(9). Both 4 and 9 are factors of 25!, so 36 is also a factor of 25!. Choice D, 56, is equal to (4)(14). Both 4 and 14 are factors of 25!, so 56 is also a factor of 25!. Choice E, 58, is equal to (2)(29). Although 2 is a factor of 25!, the prime number 29, as noted earlier, is not a factor of 25!, and therefore 58 is not a factor of 25!. The correct answer must be **Choice E**.

The explanation above uses a process of elimination to arrive at Choice E, which is sometimes the most efficient way to find the correct answer. However, one can also show directly that the correct answer is 58. For if a positive integer n is <u>not</u> a factor of 25!, then one of the following must be true:

(i) n is a prime number greater than 25, like 29 or 31, or a multiple of such a prime number, like 58 or 62;

(ii) n is so great a multiple of some prime number less than 25, that it must be greater than 58.

To see that (i) or (ii) is true, recall that every integer greater than 1 has a unique prime factorization, and consider the prime factorization of 25!. The prime factors of 25! are 2, 3, 5, 7, 11, 13, 17, 19, and 23, some of which occur more than once in the product 25!. For example, there are 8 positive multiples of 3 less than 25, namely 3, 6, 9, 12, 15, 18, 21, and 24. The prime number 3 occurs once in each of these multiples, except for 9 and 18, in which it occurs twice. Thus, the factor 3 occurs 10 times in the prime factorization of 25!. The same reasoning can be used to find the number of times that each of the prime factors occur, yielding the prime factorization $25! = (2^{22})(3^{10})(5^{6})$ $(7^{3})(11^{2})(13)(17)(19)(23)$. Any integer whose prime factorization is a combination of one or more of the factors in the prime factorization of 25!, perhaps with lesser exponents, is a factor of 25!. Equivalently, if the positive integer n is not a factor of 25!, then, restating (i) and (ii) above, the prime factorization of n must

(i) include a prime number greater than 25; or

(ii) have a greater exponent for one of the prime numbers in the prime factorization of 25!.

For (ii), the least possibilities are 2^{23}, 3^{11}, 5^7, 7^4, 11^3, 13^2, 17^2, 19^2, and 23^2. Clearly, all of these are greater than 58. The least possibility for (i) that is not a prime number is 58, and the least possibility for (ii) is greater than 58, so **Choice E** is the correct answer.

This explanation uses the following strategies.

Strategy 8: Search for a Mathematical Relationship

Strategy 10: Trial and Error

17. If $0 < a < 1 < b$, which of the following is true about the reciprocals of a and b?

Ⓐ $1 < \dfrac{1}{a} < \dfrac{1}{b}$

Ⓑ $\dfrac{1}{a} < 1 < \dfrac{1}{b}$

Ⓒ $\dfrac{1}{a} < \dfrac{1}{b} < 1$

Ⓓ $\dfrac{1}{b} < 1 < \dfrac{1}{a}$

Ⓔ $\dfrac{1}{b} < \dfrac{1}{a} < 1$

Explanation

To answer this question, you must first look at the answer choices. Note that all of the choices are possible orderings of the quantities $\dfrac{1}{a}$, $\dfrac{1}{b}$, and 1 from least to greatest. So to answer the question, you must put the three quantities in order from least to greatest. The inequality $0 < a < 1 < b$ tells you that $0 < a < 1$ and that $b > 1$. Since a is a value between 0 and 1, the value of $\dfrac{1}{a}$ must be greater than 1. Since b is greater than 1, the value of $\dfrac{1}{b}$ must be less than 1. So you know that $\dfrac{1}{a} > 1$ and that $\dfrac{1}{b} < 1$, or combined in one expression, $\dfrac{1}{b} < 1 < \dfrac{1}{a}$, and the correct answer is **Choice D**.

This explanation uses the following strategy.

Strategy 5: Simplify an Arithmetic or Algebraic Representation

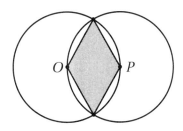

18. In the figure above, O and P are the centers of the two circles. If each circle has radius r, what is the area of the shaded region?

(A) $\dfrac{\sqrt{2}}{2}r^2$

(B) $\dfrac{\sqrt{3}}{2}r^2$

(C) $\sqrt{2}r^2$

(D) $\sqrt{3}r^2$

(E) $2\sqrt{3}r^2$

Explanation

If a geometric problem contains a figure, it can be helpful to draw additional lines and add information given in the text of the problem to the figure. For circles, the helpful additional lines are often radii or diameters. In this case, drawing radius OP will divide the shaded region into two triangles, as shown in the figure below.

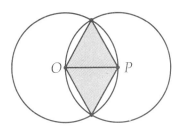

The two circles have the same radius, r. Therefore, in each of the triangles, all three sides have length r, and each of the triangles is equilateral. If you remember from geometry that the height of an equilateral triangle with sides of length r is $\dfrac{\sqrt{3}}{2}r$, you could use that fact in solving the problem. However, if you do not remember what the height is, you can use the following figure to help you find the height.

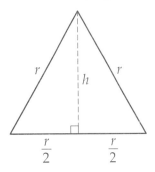

Using the Pythagorean theorem, you get

$$\left(\frac{r}{2}\right)^2 + h^2 = r^2$$

$$\frac{r^2}{4} + h^2 = r^2$$

$$h^2 = \frac{3}{4}r^2$$

$$h = \frac{\sqrt{3}}{2}r$$

So the area of the equilateral triangle is $\frac{1}{2}(\text{base})(\text{height}) = \frac{1}{2}(r)\left(\frac{\sqrt{3}}{2}r\right) = \frac{\sqrt{3}}{4}r^2$.
Since the shaded region consists of 2 equilateral triangles with sides of length r,

the area of the shaded region is $(2)\left(\frac{\sqrt{3}}{4}r^2\right) = \frac{\sqrt{3}}{2}r^2$, and the correct answer is
Choice B.

This explanation uses the following strategies.
Strategy 6: Add to a Geometric Figure
Strategy 8: Search for a Mathematical Relationship

For the following question, enter your answer in the boxes.

19. Of the 20 lightbulbs in a box, 2 are defective. An inspector will select 2 lightbulbs simultaneously and at random from the box. What is the probability that neither of the lightbulbs selected will be defective?

    Give your answer as a fraction.

Explanation
The desired probability corresponds to the fraction

$$\frac{\text{the number of ways that 2 lightbulbs, both of which are not defective, can be chosen}}{\text{the number of ways that 2 lightbulbs can be chosen}}$$

In order to calculate the desired probability, you need to calculate the values of the numerator and the denominator of this fraction.

In the box there are 20 lightbulbs, 18 of which are not defective. The numerator of the fraction is the number of ways that 2 lightbulbs can be chosen from the 18 that are not defective, also known as the number of combinations of 18 objects taken 2 at a time.

If you remember the combinations formula, you know that the number of combinations is $\frac{18!}{2!(18-2)!}$ (which is denoted symbolically as $\binom{18}{2}$ or $_{18}C_2$).
Simplifying, you get

$$\frac{18!}{2!16!} = \frac{(18)(17)(16!)}{(2)(16!)} = \frac{(18)(17)}{2} = 153$$

Similarly, the denominator of the fraction is the number of ways that 2 light-bulbs can be chosen from the 20 in the box, which is

$\binom{20}{2} = \frac{20!}{2!18!} = \frac{(20)(19)(18!)}{(2)(18!)} = \frac{(20)(19)}{2} = 190$. Therefore, the probability that neither of the lightbulbs selected will be defective is $\frac{153}{190}$. The correct answer is $\frac{153}{190}$ (or any equivalent fraction).

Another approach is to look at the selection of the two lightbulbs separately. The problem states that lightbulbs are selected simultaneously. However, the timing of the selection only ensures that the same lightbulb is not chosen twice. This is equivalent to choosing one lightbulb first and then choosing a second lightbulb without replacing the first. The probability that the first lightbulb selected will not be defective is $\frac{18}{20}$. If the first lightbulb selected is not defective, there will be 19 lightbulbs left to choose from, 17 of which are not defective. Thus, the probability that the second lightbulb selected will not be defective is $\frac{17}{19}$. The probability that both lightbulbs selected will not be defective is the product of these two probabilities. Thus, the desired probability is $\left(\frac{18}{20}\right)\left(\frac{17}{19}\right) = \frac{153}{190}$. The correct answer is $\frac{153}{190}$ (or any equivalent fraction).

This explanation uses the following strategies.

Strategy 1: Translate from Words to an Arithmetic or Algebraic Representation
Strategy 5: Simplify an Arithmetic or Algebraic Representation

20. What is the perimeter, in meters, of a rectangular playground 24 meters wide that has the same area as a rectangular playground 64 meters long and 48 meters wide?

    Ⓐ 112   Ⓑ 152   Ⓒ 224   Ⓓ 256   Ⓔ 304

Explanation

The area of the rectangular playground that is 64 meters long and 48 meters wide is $(64)(48) = 3{,}072$ square meters. The second playground, which has the same area, is 24 meters wide and $\frac{3{,}072}{24} = 128$ meters long. Therefore, the perimeter of the second playground is $(2)(24) + (2)(128) = 304$ meters. The correct answer is **Choice E**.

This explanation uses the following strategy.

Strategy 1: Translate from Words to an Arithmetic or Algebraic Representation

11

GRE
Practice Test 2

Your goals for this chapter

- Take the second full-length authentic GRE General Test under actual test time limits
- Check your answers and read explanations for every question
- Use your results to identify your strengths and weaknesses

Taking Practice Test 2

When you have taken Practice Test 1 and used the results to help you in your preparations, you can use Practice Test 2 to reassess how ready you are to take the actual GRE General Test. Practice Test 2 begins on the following pages. As with Practice Test 1, the total time that you should allow for this practice test is 2 hours and 15 minutes. The time allotted for each section appears at the beginning of that section.

Try to take Practice Test 2 under actual test conditions. Find a quiet place to work, and set aside enough time to complete the test without being disturbed. Work on only one section at a time. Use your watch or a timer to keep track of the time limit for each section.

For the Verbal Reasoning and Quantitative Reasoning portions of this practice test, mark your answers directly in this book. However, when you take the real GRE General Test on computer, you will use your mouse or keyboard to select your answer choices. For the Analytical Writing section of this test, you should type your responses.

The number of questions and time allowed per section on this practice test will give you an accurate guide to your readiness to take the test.

Following this practice test you will find an answer key. Check your answers against the key, then follow the instructions for calculating your Verbal Reasoning and Quantitative Reasoning scores and evaluating your Analytical Writing performance. You will also find explanations for each test question. Review the explanations, paying particular attention to the ones for the questions that you answered incorrectly.

Once you have worked your way through Practice Test 2, you will have a good idea of how ready you are to take the actual test. You should use the results to check whether there are any areas in which you still need improvement and whether you need to improve your test-taking speed and time management skills. Official GRE prep resources, including practice tests that simulate the real test, are available on the GRE website at **www.ets.org/gre/prepare**.

SECTION 1
Analytical Writing

30 minutes

You will be given a brief quotation that states or implies an issue of general interest and specific instructions on how to respond to that issue. You will then have 30 minutes to plan and compose a response according to the specific instructions. A response to any other issue will receive a score of zero.

Make sure that you respond according to the specific instructions and support your position on the issue with reasons and examples drawn from such areas as your reading, experience, observations, and/or academic studies.

Trained GRE readers will evaluate your response for its overall quality, based on how well you:

- Respond to the specific task instructions
- Consider the complexities of the issue
- Organize, develop, and express your ideas
- Support your ideas with relevant reasons and/or examples
- Control the elements of standard written English

Before you begin writing, you may want to think for a few minutes about the issue and the specific task instructions and then plan your response. Be sure to develop your position fully and organize it coherently, but leave time to reread what you have written and make any revisions you think are necessary.

Analytical Writing Topic

Some people believe that corporations have a responsibility to promote the well-being of the societies and environments in which they operate. Others believe that the only responsibility of corporations, provided they operate within the law, is to make as much money as possible.

Write a response in which you discuss which view more closely aligns with your own position and explain your reasoning for the position you take. In developing and supporting your position, you should address both of the views presented.

NO TEST MATERIAL ON THIS PAGE

SECTION 2
Verbal Reasoning
Time—21 Minutes
15 Questions

For questions 1 to 5, select one entry for each blank from the corresponding column of choices. Fill all blanks in the way that best completes the text.

1. The unexplained digressions into the finer points of quantum electrodynamics are so ________ that even readers with a physics degree would be wise to keep a textbook handy to make sense of them.

Ⓐ uninteresting
Ⓑ controversial
Ⓒ unsophisticated
Ⓓ frustrating
Ⓔ humorless

2. There may be a threshold below which blood pressure reductions become ________ given that a long-running study showed no decreased heart risk for drops in blood pressure below a certain point.

Ⓐ worthwhile
Ⓑ indiscernible
Ⓒ arduous
Ⓓ significant
Ⓔ superfluous

3. Unlike the problems in recent financial scandals, issues raised by the regulators in this case appear largely to pertain to unwieldy accounting rules that are open to widely divergent interpretations—not to (i)________ transactions designed to (ii)________ corporate malfeasance.

Blank (i)	Blank (ii)
Ⓐ sham	Ⓓ cloak
Ⓑ unpremeditated	Ⓔ ameliorate
Ⓒ justifiable	Ⓕ illuminate

4. Everyone has routines that govern their work. The myth is that artists are somehow different, that they reject (i)________, but of course that's not true: most artists work as the rest of us do, (ii)________, day by day, according to their own customs.

Blank (i)	Blank (ii)
Ⓐ latitude	Ⓓ impetuously
Ⓑ habit	Ⓔ ploddingly
Ⓒ materialism	Ⓕ sporadically

GO ON TO NEXT PAGE

5.	Rather than viewing the Massachusetts Bay Colony's antinomian controversy as the inevitable (i)_____ of the intransigent opposing forces of radical and (ii)_____ beliefs, male and female piety, (iii)_____ and secular power, and the like, as other critics have, Winship argues that the crisis was not "fixed and structural."

Blank (i)	Blank (ii)	Blank (iii)
(A) dissolution	(D) revolutionary	(G) clerical
(B) melding	(E) orthodox	(H) civil
(C) collision	(F) questionable	(I) cerebral

For each of questions 6 and 7, select one answer choice unless otherwise instructed.

Questions 6 and 7 are based on the following reading passage.

Arctic sea ice comes in two varieties. Seasonal ice forms in winter and then melts in summer, while perennial ice persists year-round. To the untrained eye, all sea ice looks similar, but by licking it, one can estimate how long a particular piece has been floating around.
line	When ice begins to form in seawater, it forces out salt, which has no place in the crystal
5	structure. As the ice gets thicker, the rejected salt collects in tiny pockets of brine too highly concentrated to freeze. A piece of first-year ice will taste salty. Eventually, if the ice survives, these pockets of brine drain out through fine, veinlike channels, and the ice becomes fresher; multiyear ice can even be melted and drunk.

For the following question, consider each of the choices separately and select all that apply.

6.	The passage mentions which of the following as being a characteristic of seasonal ice?
	[A] It is similar in appearance to perennial ice.
	[B] It is typically filled with fine, veinlike channels.
	[C] It tastes saltier than perennial ice.

7.	In the context in which it appears, "fine" (line 7) most nearly means
	(A) acceptable
	(B) elegant
	(C) precise
	(D) pure
	(E) small

For questions 8 to 10, select the <u>two</u> answer choices that, when used to complete the sentence, fit the meaning of the sentence as a whole <u>and</u> produce completed sentences that are alike in meaning.

8. It would have been disingenuous of the candidate to appear _____ when her opponent won the election, but she congratulated the victor nonetheless.

    A gracious
    B ecstatic
    C crestfallen
    D indifferent
    E euphoric
    F disgruntled

9. As market forces penetrate firms and bid up the value of attributes of labor that are more measurable than is the knowledge born of experience, it can be expected that trends in wages will not _____ those whose main value lies in such experiential knowledge.

    A favor
    B aid
    C affect
    D forsake
    E betray
    F differentiate

10. This is the kind of movie—stuffed with intimations of faraway strife and people in suits talking frantically on cell phones and walkie-talkies—that is conventionally described as a political thriller, but the film is as apolitical as it is _____.

    A intense
    B unprecedented
    C subtle
    D humdrum
    E refined
    F dull

For each of questions 11 to 15, select <u>one</u> answer choice unless otherwise instructed.

Questions 11 and 12 are based on the following reading passage.

Historians credit repeated locust invasions in the nineteenth century with reshaping United States agriculture west of the Mississippi River. Admonished by government entomologists, farmers began to diversify. Wheat had come to nearly monopolize the region, *line* but it was particularly vulnerable to the locusts. In 1873, just before the locusts' most with- 5 ering offensive, nearly two-thirds of Minnesota farmland was producing wheat; by the invasions' last year, that fraction had dropped to less than one-sixth. Farmers learned that peas and beans were far less vulnerable to the insects, and corn was a more robust grain than wheat. In addition to planting alternative crops, many farmers turned to dairy and beef production. Although pastures were often damaged by the locusts, these lands were 10 almost always left in better shape than the crops were.

For the following question, consider each of the choices separately and select all that apply.

11. According to the passage, before the recommendations by the government entomologists, which of the following was true about farming west of the Mississippi River?

    A Farmers focused primarily on growing wheat.

    B Peas and beans had not yet been planted in the region.

    C A relatively small portion of farmland was devoted to crops other than wheat.

12. In the context in which it appears, "robust" (line 7) most nearly means

    (A) crude

    (B) demanding

    (C) productive

    (D) vigorous

    (E) rich

Nineteenth-century architect Eugène-Emmanuel Viollet-le-Duc contended that Paris's Notre-Dame cathedral, built primarily in the late twelfth century, was supported from the very beginning by a system of flying buttresses — a series of exterior arches (flyers) and their
line
5   supports (buttresses) — which permitted the construction of taller vaulted buildings with slimmer walls and interior supports than had been possible previously. Other commentators insist, however, that Notre-Dame did not have flying buttresses until the thirteenth or fourteenth century, when they were added to update the building aesthetically and correct its structural flaws. Although post-twelfth-century modifications and renovations complicate efforts to resolve this controversy — all pre-fifteenth-century flyers have been replaced, and
10   the buttresses have been rebuilt and/or resurfaced — it is nevertheless possible to tell that both the nave and the choir, the church's two major parts, have always had flying buttresses. It is clear, now that nineteenth-century paint and plaster have been removed, that the nave's lower buttresses date from the twelfth century. Moreover, the choir's lower flyers have chevron (zigzag) decoration. Chevron decoration, which was characteristic of the second half of
15   the twelfth century and was out of favor by the fourteenth century, is entirely absent from modifications to the building that can be dated with confidence to the thirteenth century.

13.   The passage is primarily concerned with
    (A) tracing the development of a controversy
    (B) discussing obstacles to resolving a controversy
    (C) arguing in support of one side in a controversy
    (D) analyzing the assumptions underlying the claims made in a controversy
    (E) explaining why evidence relevant to a controversy has been overlooked

14.   The claim of the "other commentators" (lines 5–6) suggests that they believe which of the following about Notre-Dame?
    (A) It was the inspiration for many vaulted cathedrals built in the thirteenth and fourteenth centuries.
    (B) Its design flaws were not apparent until flying buttresses were added in the thirteenth or fourteenth century.
    (C) Its flying buttresses are embellished with decoration characteristic of the thirteenth and fourteenth centuries.
    (D) It had been modified in some respects before flying buttresses were added in the thirteenth or fourteenth century.
    (E) It was originally constructed in an architectural style that was considered outmoded by the thirteenth or fourteenth century.

GO ON TO NEXT PAGE ↘

15. The author's argument concerning Notre-Dame's flying buttresses depends on which of the following assumptions about the choir's lower flyers?

(A) They accurately reproduce the decoration on the choir's original lower flyers.

(B) They have a type of decoration used exclusively for exterior surfaces.

(C) They were the models for the choir's original upper flyers.

(D) They were the models for the nave's original lower flyers.

(E) They were constructed after the nave's flyers were constructed.

STOP. This is the end of Section 2.

SECTION 3
Verbal Reasoning
Time — 28 Minutes
20 Questions

> **For questions 1 to 6, select <u>one</u> entry for each blank from the corresponding column of choices. Fill all blanks in the way that best completes the text.**

1. Although plant and animal species that become established in ecosystems where they did not originate are sometimes referred to by the alarming term "invasive species," many such species are _____ in their new environments.

(A)	innocuous
(B)	conspicuous
(C)	robust
(D)	menacing
(E)	distinctive

2. Far from being _____ the corporate world because of cutbacks, serious researchers are playing a growing role in innovation at many firms.

(A)	lured to
(B)	enchanted with
(C)	banished from
(D)	protected by
(E)	immured in

3. The government has no choice but to (i)_____ the incessant demands for land reform, and yet any governmental action that initiated land reform without requisite attention to agrarian reform would (ii)_____ the overall goal of economic modernization.

Blank (i)		Blank (ii)	
(A)	anticipate	(D)	delineate
(B)	heed	(E)	condone
(C)	silence	(F)	compromise

4. Certain music lovers yearn for (i)_____, but when it is achieved, there is something missing; perhaps they feel uncomfortable in a world where nothing discernible is (ii)_____.

Blank (i)		Blank (ii)	
(A)	novelty	(D)	wrong
(B)	beauty	(E)	visionary
(C)	flawlessness	(F)	changed

GO ON TO NEXT PAGE ↘

5. Putting a cash value on the ecological services provided by nature—such as the water filtration "service" provided by a forested watershed—has, historically, been a (i)_____ process. Early attempts at such valuation resulted in impressive but (ii)_____ figures that were seized on by environmental advocates and then, when these figures were later (iii)_____, they were used by opponents to tar the whole idea.

Blank (i)	Blank (ii)	Blank (iii)
(A) dispassionate	(D) redundant	(G) ignored
(B) problematic	(E) unsound	(H) discredited
(C) straightforward	(F) understated	(I) confirmed

6. Only with the discovery of an ozone hole over Antarctica in 1985 did chemical companies finally relinquish their opposition to a ban on chlorofluorocarbons (CFCs), which destroy ozone. The discovery suggested that strong political action to halt production of CFCs might be (i)_____, and fortunately, the chemical industry no longer felt compelled to oppose such action: although companies had recently (ii)_____ their research into CFC substitutes, studies they had initiated years earlier had produced (iii)_____ results.

Blank (i)	Blank (ii)	Blank (iii)
(A) imminent	(D) corroborated	(G) encouraging
(B) imprudent	(E) publicized	(H) inconclusive
(C) premature	(F) curtailed	(I) unsurprising

For each of questions 7 to 10, select one answer choice unless otherwise instructed.

Questions 7 to 10 are based on the following reading passage.

Some researchers contend that sleep plays no role in the consolidation of declarative memory (i.e., memory involving factual information). These researchers note that people with impairments in rapid eye movement (REM) sleep continue to lead normal lives, and they
line
5   argue that if sleep were crucial for memory, then these individuals would have apparent memory deficits. Yet the same researchers acknowledge that the cognitive capacities of these individuals have never been systematically examined, nor have they been the subject of studies of tasks on which performance reportedly depends on sleep. Even if such studies were done, they could only clarify our understanding of the role of REM sleep, not sleep in general.

10   These researchers also claim that improvements of memory overnight can be explained by the mere passage of time, rather than attributed to sleep. But recent studies of memory performance after sleep—including one demonstrating that sleep stabilizes declarative memories from future interference caused by mental activity during wakefulness—make this claim unsustainable. Certainly there are memory-consolidation processes that occur
15   across periods of wakefulness, some of which neither depend on nor are enhanced by sleep. But when sleep is compared with wakefulness, and performance is better after sleep, then some benefit of sleep for memory must be acknowledged.

7. The primary purpose of the passage is to

    (A) present the evidence that supports a particular claim regarding REM sleep and memory

    (B) describe how various factors contribute to the effect of sleep on memory

    (C) argue against a particular position regarding sleep's role in memory

    (D) summarize the most prevalent theory regarding sleep and memory

    (E) defend the importance of the consolidation of declarative memory

8. According to the author of the passage, which of the following generalizations about memory and sleep is true?

    (A) There are some memory-consolidation processes that have nothing to do with sleep.

    (B) Sleep is more important to the consolidation of declarative memory than to the consolidation of other types of memory.

    (C) REM sleep is more important to memory consolidation than is non-REM sleep.

    (D) There are significant variations in the amount of sleep that people require for the successful consolidation of memory.

    (E) It is likely that memory is more thoroughly consolidated during wakefulness than during sleep.

9. Which of the following best describes the function of the sentence in lines 14–16 ("Certainly . . . sleep")?

    (A) It provides the reasoning behind a claim about the role of sleep in memory consolidation.

    (B) It explains why a previous claim about sleep and memory is unsustainable.

    (C) It demonstrates why wakefulness is central to the process of declarative memory consolidation.

    (D) It emphasizes the limited role sleep plays in the process of declarative memory consolidation.

    (E) It concedes that the consolidation of declarative memory does not depend entirely on one factor.

10. The importance of the study mentioned in lines 12–13 is that it

    (A) reveals the mechanism by which declarative memory is stabilized during sleep

    (B) identifies a specific function that sleep plays in the memory-consolidation process

    (C) demonstrates that some kinds of mental activity can interfere with memory consolidation

    (D) suggests that sleep and wakefulness are both important to memory consolidation

    (E) explains how the passage of time contributes to memory consolidation

GO ON TO NEXT PAGE

For questions 11 to 14, select the <u>two</u> answer choices that, when used to complete the sentence, fit the meaning of the sentence as a whole <u>and</u> produce completed sentences that are alike in meaning.

11. In American Indian art, the supposed distinction between modern and traditional was fabricated by critics, and when artists have control over interpretation of their own work, the distinction appears, happily, to have been _____ .

    (A) eliminated
    (B) reinforced
    (C) put to rest
    (D) intensified
    (E) recognized
    (F) established

12. Notwithstanding their _____ regarding other issues, township residents have consistently passed the board of education's annual budget.

    (A) accord
    (B) indecision
    (C) consensus
    (D) disagreement
    (E) divergence
    (F) enthusiasm

13. Some of the company's supporters charged that the negative report had been motivated by a broader political assault on the company that was designed to help market rivals who would like to see the company _____ .

    (A) reined in
    (B) bolstered
    (C) indemnified
    (D) propped up
    (E) manacled
    (F) lionized

14. Skeptics contend that any scheme for charging visitors to Web sites that rewards the vendor adequately would require steep prices, _____ the kind of frequent, casual use of Web sites that surfers now take for granted.

    (A) bridling
    (B) exciting
    (C) forbidding
    (D) inhibiting
    (E) provoking
    (F) reversing

For each of questions 15 to 20, select <u>one</u> answer choice unless otherwise instructed.

Question 15 is based on the following reading passage.

Astronomers found a large body orbiting close to the star Upsilon Andromedae. The standard theory of planet formation holds that no planet that large could be formed so close to a star, leading to the suggestion that the body is a companion star. A subsequent discovery puts that suggestion in doubt: two other large bodies were found orbiting close to Upsilon Andromedae, and the standard theory of companion stars allows for at most one companion star.

15. Which of the following, if true, most helps to resolve the status of the orbiting body without casting doubt on the two standard theories mentioned?

   (A) The smaller a planet orbiting a star is, and the farther away it is from the star, the less likely it is to be discovered.

   (B) If a planet's orbit is disturbed, the planet can be drawn by gravity toward the star it is orbiting.

   (C) The largest of the bodies orbiting Upsilon Andromedae is the farthest away from the star, and the smallest is the nearest.

   (D) It is likely that there are many stars, in addition to Upsilon Andromedae and the Sun, that are orbited by more than one smaller body.

   (E) In most cases of companion stars, the smaller companion is much fainter than the larger star.

Question 16 is based on the following reading passage.

In Gilavia, the number of reported workplace injuries has declined 16 percent in the last five years. However, perhaps part of the decline results from injuries going unreported: many employers have introduced safety-incentive programs, such as prize drawings for which only employees who have a perfect work-safety record are eligible. Since a workplace injury would disqualify an employee from such programs, some employees might be concealing injury, when it is feasible to do so.

16. Which of the following, if true in Gilavia, most strongly supports the proposed explanation?

   (A) In the last five years, there has been no decline in the number of workplace injuries leading to immediate admission to a hospital emergency room.

   (B) Employers generally have to pay financial compensation to employees who suffer work-related injuries.

   (C) Many injuries that happen on the job are injuries that would be impossible to conceal and yet would not be severe enough to require any change to either the employee's work schedule or the employee's job responsibilities.

   (D) A continuing shift in employment patterns has led to a decline in the percentage of the workforce that is employed in the dangerous occupations in which workplace injuries are likely.

   (E) Employers who have instituted safety-incentive programs do not in general have a lower proportion of reported workplace injuries among their employees than do employers without such programs.

GO ON TO NEXT PAGE ↘

The attribution of early-nineteenth-century English fiction is notoriously problematic. Fewer than half of new novels published in Britain between 1800 and 1829 had the author's true name printed on the title page. Most of these titles have subsequently
line been attributed, either through the author's own acknowledgment of a previously
5 anonymous or pseudonymous work, or through bibliographical research. One important tool available to researchers is the list of earlier works "by the author" often found on title pages. But such lists are as likely to create new confusion as they are to solve old problems. Title pages were generally prepared last in the publication process, often without full authorial assent, and in the last-minute rush to press, mistakes were fre-
10 quently made.

For the following question, consider each of the choices separately and select all that apply.

17. The passage suggests that which of the following factors contributes to the "notoriously problematic" (line 1) nature of authorial attribution in early-nineteenth-century English fiction?
    Ⓐ The unwillingness of any writers to acknowledge their authorship of works that were originally published anonymously or pseudonymously
    Ⓑ The possibility that the title page of a work may attribute works written by other authors to the author of that work
    Ⓒ The possibility that the author's name printed on a title page is fictitious

For the following question, consider each of the choices separately and select all that apply.

18. The passage suggests that which of the following is frequently true of the title pages of early-nineteenth-century English novels?
    Ⓐ The title page was prepared for printing in a hurried manner.
    Ⓑ Material on the title page was included without the author's knowledge or approval.
    Ⓒ Information on the title page was deliberately falsified to make the novel more marketable.

Questions 19 and 20 are based on the following reading passage.

The more definitions a given noun has, the more valuable is each one. Multiple definitions, each subtly different from all the others, convey multiple shades of meaning. They expand the uses of the word; language is enriched, thought is widened, and interpretations increase or dilate to fill the potentialities of association. The very impossibility of absoluteness in the definition of certain nouns adds to the levels of connotation they may reach. The inner life of a writer often says more than most readers can know; the mind of a reader can discover truths that go beyond the intent or perhaps even the comprehension of the writer. And all of it finds expression because a word can mean many things.

line

5

19. In the context in which it appears, "shades" (line 2) most nearly means
    (A) reminders
    (B) nuances
    (C) obscurities
    (D) coverings
    (E) degrees

20. The passage suggests that a writer's use of nouns that have multiple definitions can have which of the following effects on the relationship between writer and reader?
    (A) It can encourage the reader to consider how the writer's life might have influenced the work.
    (B) It can cause the reader to become frustrated with the writer's failure to distinguish between subtle shades of meaning.
    (C) It can allow the reader to discern in a work certain meanings that the writer did not foresee.
    (D) It allows the writer to provide the reader with clues beyond the word itself in order to avoid ambiguity.
    (E) It allows the writer to present unfamiliar ideas to the reader more efficiently.

STOP. This is the end of Section 3.

SECTION 4
Quantitative Reasoning
Time—24 Minutes
15 Questions

For each question, indicate the best answer, using the directions given.

Notes: All numbers used are real numbers.

All figures are assumed to lie in a plane unless otherwise indicated.

Geometric figures, such as lines, circles, triangles, and quadrilaterals, **are not necessarily** drawn to scale. That is, you should **not** assume that quantities such as lengths and angle measures are as they appear in a figure. You should assume, however, that lines shown as straight are actually straight, points on a line are in the order shown, and more generally, all geometric objects are in the relative positions shown. For questions with geometric figures, you should base your answers on geometric reasoning, not on estimating or comparing quantities by sight or by measurement.

Coordinate systems, such as xy-planes and number lines, **are** drawn to scale; therefore, you can read, estimate, or compare quantities in such figures by sight or by measurement.

Graphical data presentations, such as bar graphs, circle graphs, and line graphs, **are** drawn to scale; therefore, you can read, estimate, or compare data values by sight or by measurement.

For each of Questions 1 to 5, compare Quantity A and Quantity B, using additional information centered above the two quantities if such information is given. Select one of the following four answer choices and fill in the corresponding oval to the right of the question.

(A) Quantity A is greater.
(B) Quantity B is greater.
(C) The two quantities are equal.
(D) The relationship cannot be determined from the information given.

A symbol that appears more than once in a question has the same meaning throughout the question.

	Quantity A	Quantity B	Correct Answer
Example 1:	(2)(6)	2 + 6	Ⓐ Ⓑ Ⓒ Ⓓ

	Quantity A	Quantity B	Correct Answer
Example 2:	*PS*	*SR*	Ⓐ Ⓑ Ⓒ Ⓓ

(since equal lengths cannot be assumed, even though *PS* and *SR* appear equal)

> Ⓐ **Quantity A is greater.**
> Ⓑ **Quantity B is greater.**
> Ⓒ **The two quantities are equal.**
> Ⓓ **The relationship cannot be determined from the information given.**

	Quantity A	Quantity B	

1. $\dfrac{3^{-1}}{4^{-1}}$ $\dfrac{4}{3}$ Ⓐ   Ⓑ   Ⓒ   Ⓓ

The median income of a group of College *C* graduates six months after graduation was $3,000 higher than the median income of a group of College *D* graduates six months after graduation.

Quantity A   Quantity B

2.   The 75th percentile of the incomes of the group of College *C* graduates six months after graduation   The 75th percentile of the incomes of the group of College *D* graduates six months after graduation   Ⓐ   Ⓑ   Ⓒ   Ⓓ

> Ⓐ **Quantity A is greater.**
> Ⓑ **Quantity B is greater.**
> Ⓒ **The two quantities are equal.**
> Ⓓ **The relationship cannot be determined from the information given.**

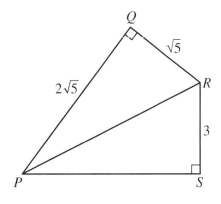

Quantity A   Quantity B

3.   The area of triangle *PQR*   The area of triangle *PSR*   Ⓐ   Ⓑ   Ⓒ   Ⓓ

GO ON TO NEXT PAGE ↘

s and t are positive integers, and $32^s = 2^t$.

Quantity A	Quantity B	
$\dfrac{s}{t}$	$\dfrac{1}{5}$	Ⓐ Ⓑ Ⓒ Ⓓ

4.

Ⓐ **Quantity A is greater.**
Ⓑ **Quantity B is greater.**
Ⓒ **The two quantities are equal.**
Ⓓ **The relationship cannot be determined from the information given.**

In a quality-control test, 50 boxes—each containing 30 machine parts—were examined for defective parts. The number of defective parts was recorded for each box, and the average (arithmetic mean) of the 50 recorded numbers of defective parts per box was 1.12. Only one error was made in recording the 50 numbers: "1" defective part in a certain box was incorrectly recorded as "10".

Quantity A	Quantity B	
5. The actual average number of defective parts per box	0.94	Ⓐ Ⓑ Ⓒ Ⓓ

Questions 6 to 15 have several different formats. Unless otherwise directed, select a single answer choice. For Numeric Entry questions, follow the instructions below.

Numeric Entry Questions
Enter your answer in the answer box(es) below the question.

- **Your answer may be an integer, a decimal, or a fraction, and it may be negative.**
- **If a question asks for a fraction, there will be two boxes—one for the numerator and one for the denominator.**
- **Equivalent forms of the correct answer, such as 2.5 and 2.50, are all correct. Fractions do not need to be reduced to lowest terms.**
- **Enter the exact answer unless the question asks you to round your answer.**

6. In year Y, the population of Colorado was approximately half that of New Jersey, and the land area of Colorado was approximately 14 times that of New Jersey. The population density (number of persons per unit of land area) of Colorado in year Y was approximately how many times the population density of New Jersey?

(A) $\dfrac{1}{28}$

(B) $\dfrac{1}{14}$

(C) $\dfrac{1}{7}$

(D) $\dfrac{1}{4}$

(E) $\dfrac{1}{2}$

For the following question, enter your answer in the box.

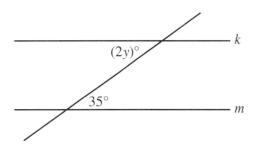

7. In the figure above, line k is parallel to line m. What is the value of y?

$$y = \boxed{}$$

8. The numbers in data set S have a standard deviation of 5. If a new data set is formed by adding 3 to each number in S, what is the standard deviation of the numbers in the new data set?

(A) 2

(B) 3

(C) 5

(D) 8

(E) 15

GO ON TO NEXT PAGE

9.   If $\dfrac{2y-3}{y} = \dfrac{3-y}{2}$, which of the following could be the value of y?

   (A) 4

   (B) 1

   (C) −1

   (D) −3

   (E) −5

For the following question, select all the answer choices that apply.

10.   List K consists of the numbers −10, −5, 0, 5, and 10. Which of the following lists of numbers have the same range as the numbers in list K?

   Indicate all such lists.

   A   −15, −1, 0, 1, 15

   B   −7, −4, −2, 1, 13

   C   0, 1, 2, 5, 8, 10

   D   2, 3, 5, 15, 19, 22

   E   4, 5, 6, 24

11.   Jacob's weekly take-home pay is n dollars. Each week he uses $\dfrac{4n}{5}$ dollars for expenses and saves the rest. At those rates, how many weeks will it take Jacob to save \$500, in terms of n?

   (A) $\dfrac{500}{n}$

   (B) $\dfrac{2,500}{n}$

   (C) $\dfrac{n}{625}$

   (D) $\dfrac{n}{2,500}$

   (E) $625n$

For the following question, select all the answer choices that apply.

12.   If $|t + 3| > 5$, which of the following could be the value of t?

Indicate <u>all</u> such values.

- [A] -9
- [B] -6
- [C] -2
- [D] 0
- [E] 2
- [F] 3

13.   The operation $\otimes$ is defined for all integers x and y as $x \otimes y = xy - y$. If x and y are positive integers, which of the following CANNOT be zero?

- (A) $x \otimes y$
- (B) $y \otimes x$
- (C) $(x - 1) \otimes y$
- (D) $(x + 1) \otimes y$
- (E) $x \otimes (y - 1)$

14.   If $x < y < 0$, which of the following inequalities must be true?

- (A) $y + 1 < x$
- (B) $y - 1 < x$
- (C) $xy^2 < x$
- (D) $xy < y^2$
- (E) $xy < x^2$

For the following question, enter your answer in the box.

15.   What is the length of a diagonal of a rectangle that has width 5 and perimeter 34?

[   ]

STOP. This is the end of Section 4.

SECTION 5
Quantitative Reasoning
Time—32 minutes
20 Questions

For each question, indicate the best answer, using the directions given.

Notes: All numbers used are real numbers.

All figures are assumed to lie in a plane unless otherwise indicated. Geometric figures, such as lines, circles, triangles, and quadrilaterals, **are not necessarily** drawn to scale. That is, you should **not** assume that quantities such as lengths and angle measures are as they appear in a figure. You should assume, however, that lines shown as straight are actually straight, points on a line are in the order shown, and more generally, all geometric objects are in the relative positions shown. For questions with geometric figures, you should base your answers on geometric reasoning, not on estimating or comparing quantities by sight or by measurement.

Coordinate systems, such as xy-planes and number lines, **are** drawn to scale; therefore, you can read, estimate, or compare quantities in such figures by sight or by measurement.

Graphical data presentations, such as bar graphs, circle graphs, and line graphs, **are** drawn to scale; therefore, you can read, estimate, or compare data values by sight or by measurement.

For each of Questions 1 to 7, compare Quantity A and Quantity B, using additional information centered above the two quantities if such information is given. Select one of the following four answer choices and fill in the corresponding oval to the right of the question.

- (A) Quantity A is greater.
- (B) Quantity B is greater.
- (C) The two quantities are equal.
- (D) The relationship cannot be determined from the information given.

A symbol that appears more than once in a question has the same meaning throughout the question.

	Quantity A	Quantity B	Correct Answer
Example 1:	(2)(6)	$2 + 6$	(A) (B) (C) (D)

	Quantity A	Quantity B	Correct Answer
Example 2:	PS	SR	(A) (B) (C) (D)

(since equal lengths cannot be assumed, even though *PS* and *SR* appear equal)

> (A) Quantity A is greater.
> (B) Quantity B is greater.
> (C) The two quantities are equal.
> (D) The relationship cannot be determined from the information given.

A circle is inscribed in a square with sides of length 5.

Quantity A	Quantity B	
1. The circumference of the circle	15	(A) (B) (C) (D)

$$2u + v = 14$$
$$uv = 0$$

Quantity A	Quantity B	
2. u	v	(A) (B) (C) (D)

Quantity A	Quantity B	
3. $950^{2,000}$	$10^{6,000}$	(A) (B) (C) (D)

Set A consists of 40 integers, and set B consists of 150 integers. The number of integers that are in both set A and set B is 20.

Quantity A	Quantity B	
4. The total number of integers that are in set A or set B, or both	170	(A) (B) (C) (D)

GO ON TO NEXT PAGE ↘

Ⓐ **Quantity A is greater.**
Ⓑ **Quantity B is greater.**
Ⓒ **The two quantities are equal.**
Ⓓ **The relationship cannot be determined from the information given.**

x is a negative integer.

	Quantity A	Quantity B	

5. 2^x 3^{x+1} Ⓐ Ⓑ Ⓒ Ⓓ

Geoff used $630 to buy a new guitar. This amount was 15 percent of his earnings last summer.

	Quantity A	Quantity B	

6. The amount of Geoff's $3,570   Ⓐ Ⓑ Ⓒ Ⓓ
   earnings last summer <u>not</u>
   used to buy the new guitar

Ⓐ **Quantity A is greater.**
Ⓑ **Quantity B is greater.**
Ⓒ **The two quantities are equal.**
Ⓓ **The relationship cannot be determined from the information given.**

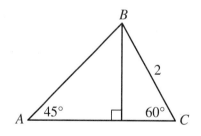

Quantity A   Quantity B

7. The length of line segment   3   Ⓐ Ⓑ Ⓒ Ⓓ
   AC

Questions 8 to 20 have several different formats. Unless otherwise directed, select a single answer choice. For Numeric Entry questions, follow the instructions below.

Numeric Entry Questions
Enter your answer in the answer box(es) below the question.

- Your answer may be an integer, a decimal, or a fraction, and it may be negative.
- If a question asks for a fraction, there will be two boxes—one for the numerator and one for the denominator.
- Equivalent forms of the correct answer, such as 2.5 and 2.50, are all correct. Fractions do not need to be reduced to lowest terms.
- Enter the exact answer unless the question asks you to round your answer.

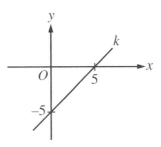

8. What is the slope of line k in the xy-plane above?

   (A) −5
   (B) −1
   (C) 0
   (D) 1
   (E) 5

For the following question, enter your answer in the box.

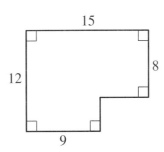

9. What is the area of the region shown above?

GO ON TO NEXT PAGE ↘

10. During a one-year study, biologists observed the number of fish in a certain pond as well as the percent of the fish that were catfish. At the beginning of the year, there were 300 fish in the pond, of which 15 percent were catfish; and at the end of the year, there were 400 fish in the pond, of which 10 percent were catfish. From the beginning of the year to the end of the year, the number of catfish in the pond

   (A) decreased by more than 5%
   (B) decreased by 5%
   (C) did not change
   (D) increased by 5%
   (E) increased by more than 5%

For the following question, enter your answer in the box.

11. On a radio tower, a red light flashes every 6 seconds and a blue light flashes every 10 seconds. If both lights flash together at a certain time, how many seconds later will both lights flash together the next time?

   ⬚ seconds

For the following question, select all the answer choices that apply.

12. If $a < b < 0$, which of the following numbers must be positive?

   Indicate <u>all</u> such numbers.

   [A] $a - b$
   [B] $a^2 - b^2$
   [C] ab
   [D] $a^2 b$
   [E] $a^2 b + ab^2$

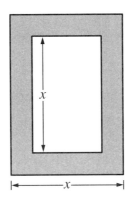

13. A flat rectangular picture, represented by the unshaded region in the figure above, is mounted in a flat rectangular frame, represented by the shaded region. The frame is 1 inch wide on all sides. For what value of x, in inches, is the area of the frame equal to the area of the picture?

    (A) 4
    (B) 5
    (C) 6
    (D) 7
    (E) 8

Questions 14 to 16 are based on the following data.

PERCENT OF THE 300 PEOPLE IN GROUP 1 AND THE 400 PEOPLE
IN GROUP 2 WHO HAVE SELECTED AILMENTS

Respiratory Ailment	Percent of People in Group 1 Who Have Ailment	Percent of People in Group 2 Who Have Ailment
Allergic sensitivity to endotoxins	14%	21%
Asthma (allergic)	3%	4%
Asthma (nonallergic)	2%	3%
Hay fever	4%	10%
Sneezing and itchy eyes	8%	11%
Wheezing (allergic)	5%	6%
Wheezing (nonallergic)	2%	5%

14. The number of people in group 2 who have hay fever is how much greater than the number of people in group 1 who have hay fever?

    (A) 37
    (B) 35
    (C) 32
    (D) 28
    (E) 24

GO ON TO NEXT PAGE

15. The number of people in group 1 who have the ailment wheezing (allergic) is what percent greater than the number of people in group 1 who have the ailment wheezing (nonallergic)?

    (A) 50%
    (B) 75%
    (C) 150%
    (D) 200%
    (E) 300%

For the following question, enter your answer in the boxes.

16. What is the ratio of the number of people in group 2 with the ailment sneezing and itchy eyes to the total number of people in both groups with the ailment sneezing and itchy eyes?

    Give your answer as a fraction.

$$\frac{\boxed{}}{\boxed{}}$$

17. Of the people in a certain survey, 58 percent were at most 40 years old and 70 percent were at most 60 years old. If 252 of the people in the survey were more than 40 years old and at most 60 years old, what was the total number of people in the survey?

    (A) 1,900
    (B) 2,100
    (C) 2,400
    (D) 2,700
    (E) 3,000

18. Alice earns d dollars and has t percent of what she earns deducted for taxes. How much of what she earns does Alice have left after taxes?

    (A) $d(1 - 100t)$ dollars
    (B) $d(1 - 10t)$ dollars
    (C) $d(1 - t)$ dollars
    (D) $d(1 - 0.1t)$ dollars
    (E) $d(1 - 0.01t)$ dollars

For the following question, select all the answer choices that apply.

19.   A student made a conjecture that for any integer n, the integer $4n + 3$ is a prime number. Which of the following values of n could be used to disprove the student's conjecture?

Indicate <u>all</u> such values.

A   1
B   3
C   4
D   6
E   7

20.   Eight points are equally spaced on a circle. If 4 of the 8 points are to be chosen at random, what is the probability that a quadrilateral having the 4 points chosen as vertices will be a square?

Ⓐ $\frac{1}{70}$

Ⓑ $\frac{1}{35}$

Ⓒ $\frac{1}{7}$

Ⓓ $\frac{1}{4}$

Ⓔ $\frac{1}{2}$

STOP. This is the end of Section 5.

Evaluating Your Performance

Now that you have completed Practice Test 2, it is time to evaluate your performance.

Analytical Writing Measure

One way to evaluate your performance on the Analytical Writing topic you answered on this practice test is to compare your essay response with the scored sample essay responses for this topic and review the rater commentary. Scored sample essay responses and rater commentary are presented starting on page 618 for the topic presented in the Analytical Writing section of Practice Test 2. The scoring guide starts on page 23.

To better understand the analytical writing abilities characteristic of particular score levels, you should review the score level descriptions on page 25.

Verbal Reasoning and Quantitative Reasoning Measures

The tables that follow contain information to help you evaluate your performance on the Verbal Reasoning and Quantitative Reasoning measures of Practice Test 2. An answer key with the correct answers to the questions in the Verbal Reasoning and Quantitative Reasoning sections in this practice test begins on page 612. Compare your answers with the correct answers given in the table, crossing out questions you answered incorrectly or omitted. Partially correct answers should be treated as incorrect. Knowing which questions you answered incorrectly or omitted can help you identify content areas in which you need more practice or review.

The answer key contains additional information to help you evaluate your performance. With each answer, the key provides a number, the P+. The P+ is the percent of a group of actual GRE takers who were administered that same question at a previous test administration and who answered it correctly. P+ is used to gauge the relative difficulty of a test question. The higher the P+, the easier the test question. You can use the P+ to compare your performance on each test question to the performance of other test takers on that same question. For example, if the P+ for a question is 89, that means that 89 percent of GRE test takers who received this question answered it correctly. Alternatively, if the P+ for a question is 14, that means that 14 percent of GRE test takers who received this question answered it correctly. A question with a P+ of 89 may be interpreted as a relatively easy question, and a question with a P+ of 14 may be interpreted as a difficult question.

To calculate your scores on Practice Test 2:

- Add the number of correct answers in Sections 2 and 3 to obtain your raw Verbal Reasoning score.
- Add the number of correct answers in Sections 4 and 5 to obtain your raw Quantitative Reasoning score.
- Once you have calculated your raw scores, refer to the Practice Test 2 score conversion table on pages 616–617. Find the scores on the 130–170 score scales that correspond to your Verbal Reasoning and Quantitative Reasoning raw scores. Note the scaled scores provided.

Once you determine your scaled scores, you will need to evaluate your performance. To get a sense of how test takers are scoring on the Verbal Reasoning and Quantitative Reasoning measures of the actual test, you can review Verbal Reasoning and Quantitative Reasoning percentile ranks on the GRE website at **www.ets.org/gre/percentile** (PDF). A percentile rank for a score indicates the percentage of examinees who took that test and received a lower score. Updated annually in July, this table includes the Verbal Reasoning and Quantitative Reasoning scores on the 130–170 scale in one-point increments and the corresponding percentile ranks. For each score you earned on Practice Test 2, note the percent of GRE test takers who earned lower scores. This is a reasonable indication of your rank among GRE General Test examinees if you took Practice Test 2 under standard timed conditions.

Answer Key

Section 2. Verbal Reasoning

Question Number	P+	Correct Answer
1	72	**Choice D:** frustrating
2	50	**Choice E:** superfluous
3	48	**Choice A:** sham; **Choice D:** cloak
4	61	**Choice B:** habit; **Choice E:** ploddingly
5	40	**Choice C:** collision; **Choice E:** orthodox; **Choice G:** clerical
6	69	**Choice A:** It is similar in appearance to perennial ice. AND **Choice C:** It tastes saltier than perennial ice.
7	93	**Choice E:** small
8	56	**Choice B:** ecstatic AND **Choice E:** euphoric
9	75	**Choice A:** favor AND **Choice B:** aid
10	59	**Choice D:** humdrum AND **Choice F:** dull
11	66	**Choice A:** Farmers focused primarily on growing wheat. AND **Choice C:** A relatively small portion of farmland was devoted to crops other than wheat.
12	44	**Choice D:** vigorous
13	46	**Choice C:** arguing in support of one side in a controversy
14	42	**Choice E:** It was originally constructed in an architectural style that was considered outmoded by the thirteenth or fourteenth century.
15	40	**Choice A:** They accurately reproduce the decoration on the choir's original lower flyers.

Answer Key

Section 3. Verbal Reasoning

Question Number	P+	Correct Answer
1	71	**Choice A:** innocuous
2	68	**Choice C:** banished from
3	74	**Choice B:** heed; **Choice F:** compromise
4	71	**Choice C:** flawlessness; **Choice D:** wrong
5	56	**Choice B:** problematic; **Choice E:** unsound; **Choice H:** discredited
6	28	**Choice A:** imminent; **Choice F:** curtailed; **Choice G:** encouraging
7	60	**Choice C:** argue against a particular position regarding sleep's role in memory
8	66	**Choice A:** There are some memory-consolidation processes that have nothing to do with sleep.
9	73	**Choice E:** It concedes that the consolidation of declarative memory does not depend entirely on one factor.
10	60	**Choice B:** identifies a specific function that sleep plays in the memory-consolidation process
11	74	**Choice A:** eliminated AND **Choice C:** put to rest
12	41	**Choice D:** disagreement AND **Choice E:** divergence
13	27	**Choice A:** reined in AND **Choice E:** manacled
14	45	**Choice A:** bridling AND **Choice D:** inhibiting
15	42	**Choice B:** If a planet's orbit is disturbed, the planet can be drawn by gravity toward the star it is orbiting.
16	35	**Choice A:** In the last five years, there has been no decline in the number of workplace injuries leading to immediate admission to a hospital emergency room.
17	52	**Choice B:** The possibility that the title page of a work may attribute works written by other authors to the author of that work AND **Choice C:** The possibility that the author's name printed on a title page is fictitious
18	83	**Choice A:** The title page was prepared for printing in a hurried manner. AND **Choice B:** Material on the title page was included without the author's knowledge or approval.
19	37	**Choice B:** nuances
20	78	**Choice C:** It can allow the reader to discern in a work certain meanings that the writer did not foresee.

Answer Key

Section 4. Quantitative Reasoning

Question Number	P+	Correct Answer
1	63	**Choice C:** The two quantities are equal.
2	46	**Choice D:** The relationship cannot be determined from the information given.
3	73	**Choice B:** Quantity B is greater.
4	59	**Choice C:** The two quantities are equal.
5	35	**Choice C:** The two quantities are equal.
6	60	**Choice A:** $\dfrac{1}{28}$
7	84	**17.5**
8	55	**Choice C:** 5
9	77	**Choice D:** -3
10	65	**Choice B:** $-7, -4, -2, 1, 13$ AND **Choice D:** $2, 3, 5, 15, 19, 22$ AND **Choice E:** $4, 5, 6, 24$
11	51	**Choice B:** $\dfrac{2,500}{n}$
12	70	**Choice A:** -9 AND **Choice F:** 3
13	42	**Choice D:** $(x + 1) \otimes y$
14	40	**Choice E:** $xy < x^2$
15	62	**13**

Answer Key

Section 5. Quantitative Reasoning

Question Number	P+	Correct Answer
1	73	**Choice A:** Quantity A is greater.
2	69	**Choice D:** The relationship cannot be determined from the information given.
3	64	**Choice B:** Quantity B is greater.
4	41	**Choice C:** The two quantities are equal.
5	36	**Choice D:** The relationship cannot be determined from the information given.
6	72	**Choice C:** The two quantities are equal.
7	36	**Choice B:** Quantity B is greater.
8	69	**Choice D:** 1
9	78	**156**
10	66	**Choice A:** decreased by more than 5%
11	72	**30**
12	58	**Choice B:** $a^2 - b^2$ AND **Choice C:** ab
13	46	**Choice C:** 6
14	90	**Choice D:** 28
15	56	**Choice C:** 150%
16	66	$\dfrac{44}{68}$ (or any equivalent fraction)
17	58	**Choice B:** 2,100
18	37	**Choice E:** $d(1 - 0.01t)$ dollars
19	53	**Choice B:** 3 AND **Choice D:** 6
20	32	**Choice B:** $\dfrac{1}{35}$

Score Conversion Table

Raw Score	Verbal Reasoning Scaled Score	Quantitative Reasoning Scaled Score
35	170	170
34	170	167
33	168	164
32	166	162
31	165	161
30	163	159
29	162	158
28	161	157
27	160	155
26	159	154
25	158	153
24	157	153
23	156	152
22	155	151
21	154	150
20	153	149
19	153	148
18	152	148
17	151	147
16	150	146
15	149	145
14	148	144
13	147	143
12	146	143
11	145	142
10	143	141
9	142	140
8	141	139
7	139	137
6	137	136
5	135	135

Raw Score	Verbal Reasoning Scaled Score	Quantitative Reasoning Scaled Score
4	133	133
3	130	131
2	130	130
1	130	130
0	130	130

Analytical Writing Sample Responses and Reader Commentaries

SECTION 1
Analytical Writing

> Some people believe that corporations have a responsibility to promote the well-being of the societies and environments in which they operate. Others believe that the only responsibility of corporations, provided they operate within the law, is to make as much money as possible.
>
> Write a response in which you discuss which view more closely aligns with your own position and explain your reasoning for the position you take. In developing and supporting your position, you should address both of the views presented.

Score 6 Response*

It is not uncommon for some to argue that, in the world in which we live, corporations have a responsibility to society and to the environment in which they operate. Proponents of this view would argue that major environmental catastrophes (e.g., the oil spill in the Gulf) are key examples of the damage that can be wrought when corporations are allowed to operate unchecked. Yet within that very statement lies a contradiction that undermines this kind of thinking—it is necessary for outside forces to check the behavior of corporations, because we do not expect corporations to behave in such a manner. In fact, the expectation is simply that corporations will follow the law, and in the course of doing so, engage in every possible tactic to their advantage in the pursuit of more and greater profit. To expect otherwise from corporations is to fail to understand their puropose and their very structure.

   The corporation arose as a model of business in which capital could be raised through the contributions of stockholders; investors purchases shares in a company, and their money is then used as the operating capital for the company. Shareholders buy stock not because they are hoping to better make the world a better place or because they have a desire to improve the quality of life but because they expect to see a return in their investment in this company. The company may itself have generally altruistic goals (perhaps it is a think tank that advises the government on how to improve relations with the Middle East, or perhaps it is a company built around finding alternative forms of energy), but the immediate expectation of the investor is that he himself will see dividends, or profits, from the investment he has made. This is even more true in the case of companies that are purely profit driven and which do not have goals that are particularly directed toward social improvement—a description that applies to the vast majority of corporations.

*NOTE: All responses are reproduced exactly as written, including errors, misspellings, etc., if any.

Is it a bad thing to have a corporation negatively affect the environment (and by extentsion, its inhabitants)? To pump noxious fumes into the atmosphere as a by-product of its manufacturing processes? Of course, and this is why agencies such as the EPA were established and why governments—federal, state, and local—are expected to monitor such companies to ensure that such practices fall within the boundaries of legal expectations. Any and all corporations should be expected to temper their pursuit of profit with the necessity of following those safeguards that have been legislated as protections. But the assumption that corporations have an inherent obligation or responsibility to go above and beyond that to actively PROMOTE the environment and the well-being of society is absurd.

Engaging in practices to adhere to legal expectations to protect society and the environment is costly to corporations. If the very purpose of a corporation is to generate profits, and the obligation to adhere to safety expectations established by law cuts into those profits, then to expect corporations to embrace such practices beyond what is required is to presume that they willingly engage in an inherently self-destructive process: the unnecessary lowering of profits. This is antithetical to the very concept of the corporation. Treehuggers everywhere should be pleased that environmental protections exist, but to expect corporations to "make the world a better place" is to embrace altruism to the point that it becomes delusion.

This is not to say that we should reject efforts to hold corporations accountable. In fact, the opposite is true—we should be vigilant with the business world and maintain our expectations that corporations do not make their profits at the EXPENSE of the well-being of society. But that role must be fulfilled by a watchdog, not the corporation itself, and those expectations must be imposed UPON the corporations, not expected FROM them.

Reader Commentary

This response receives a 6 for developing an insightful position on the issue in accordance with the assigned task, skillfully weaving a position that takes into consideration both of the statements in the prompt. Beginning in the first paragraph, the writer rejects the idea that corporations themselves "have a responsibility to promote the well-being of the societies and environments in which they operate." In the second paragraph, the writer offers compelling reasons for this rejection by discussing the purpose and structure of corporations. The writer then considers the role of government in promoting corporations' social and environmental responsibility, developing the position fully. A cogent statement of the writer's position appears at the conclusion of the response: "we should be vigilant with the business world and maintain our expectations that corporations do not make their profits at the EXPENSE of the well-being of society. But that role must be fulfilled by a watchdog, not the corporation itself." The response as a whole is logically organized, with each paragraph serving as a stepping stone in the development of the writer's position. It also demonstrates the writer's ability to convey ideas fluently and precisely, using effective vocabulary and sentence variety. This sentence demonstrates the level of language facility seen throughout the response: "If the very purpose of a corporation is to generate profits, and the obligation to adhere to safety expectations established by law cuts into those profits, then to expect corporations to embrace such practices beyond what is required is to presume that they willingly engage in an inherently self-destructive process: the unnecessary lowering of profits." Here the writer has skillfully maintained control of complex syntax and diction while making a logically compelling point. The sentence demonstrates the outstanding nature of this response.

Score 5 Response

In order to survive, corporations must make money. Successful corporations try and make as much money as possible. Yet this incentive to make money does not mean that a corporation can be a detriment to the society in which it operates. Corporations have a duty and a responsability to ensure the well being of the society in which they are a part.

Contributing to the well being of a society is actually benefical to a corporation in many cases. One of these is making sure that workers are well taken care of. Absenteeism and neglect while on duty are a big problem for corporations, as is attracting the best workers, who hopefully will lower the risks caused by absenteeism and neglect. One way that corporations can attract these workers is by offering them generous benefits. If, for example, an employer includes with employment a good health care plan, they will be able to attract better workers than one that does not, and that will aid the corporation greatly. Health care plans provided by employers mean that these people have at their disposal health coverage, which means that they have the care they need if they get sick. This also might encourage preventive care, something that has been shown to reduce the cost and risk of developing other major ailments.

Another area where corporations providing support for themselves and society is in the creation of human capital. Globalization and increased education means that employers need a better educated workforce more than ever. One way that employers can contribute to this is by sponsoring worker training programs, or paying for their employees to return to school. This creates a more educated workforce for employers, as well as may increase the loyalty of employees to an employer. An employee who received an education sponsored by an employer may be thankful for receiving that education, and may work harder for that employer. This creates a benefit for employers and employees.

The main reason that corporations have a duty to contribute to the well being of society is that they are a part of the society. Even though they have an economic desire to make a profit, corporations also should think long term about actions they take which could hurt their company. A good example of this is BP, after the recent oil spill in the gulf. Their desire to make a profit meant that they did not keep up on all of their safety regulations and standards, and the result of the then faulty equipment caused a massive spill. This cost them huge amounts of money to clean up, as well as the fines they had to pay for causing this. The biggest loss for BP however is that there brand name will be associated in the US and abroad as the company that caused this giant oil spill. As the spill was happening, many people boycotted the company, resulting in lost potential revenue. They may realize that as they lose business to people upset by the spill, that making sure a spill didn't happen in the first place was cheaper.

Another reason corporations have to ensure the well-being of a society is that by makign a society better off, a company may have more consumers. This is especially true for corporations that sell goods for middle and upper class consumers. If a corporation tries to bring people up and increase the overall economic well being of society, they may find that more and more people have to ability to afford their goods.

This could generate huge new profits for this corporation, since their pool of potential consumers has gone up considerably. Concentrating on the long term here means that corporations can increase their pool of potential consumers.

By denying responsabilty to a society, a corporation is only looking at the possible short term profits, not the potential long term ones. While in the short term it may work for a corporation to ignore their societal responsability, it is advantageous in the long term for the entire corporation to make sure society is getting better. The potential for new markets, products, production processes and other beneficial factors that come from promoting well being is quite large. This is something that corportions should be ready and willing to take advantage of, and something that society should hold them accountable for.

Reader Commentary

This strong response receives a 5 for its thoughtful, well-developed analysis of the issue. In this case, the writer argues that corporations do indeed have a responsibility to promote the well-being of the societies and environments in which they operate, offering several reasons and well-chosen examples to explain why it is in the interests of corporations to fulfill these responsibilities. The writer clearly follows the task directions by addressing the two views provided by the prompt, both explicitly in the opening paragraph and more subtly throughout the response. While the writer clearly signals at the beginning their alignment with the first position ("Corporations have a duty and a responsability to ensure the well being of the society of which they are a part"), the paragraphs that follow in fact acknowledge the writer's opening statement ("In order to survive, corporations must make money"). In areas such as employee health care and education, as well as in relation to broader issues such as the environment and the general level of prosperity in society, the writer argues that corporations should strive to meet their social obligations because in the long term, it is economically advantageous to do so. The various reasons and examples offered are brought together to support a thoughtful position that implicitly suggests that the two views are not as mutually exclusive as they might first appear. The response also demonstrates considerable facility with language. There are some minor errors, but overall the writer's control of language is strong, demonstrating sentence variety and appropriate use of vocabulary. The response lacks the superior fluency and precision of a 6 but nevertheless conveys meaning clearly and well. Discernibly stronger than the adequate level of analysis in a 4, the response has thoughtful, nuanced analysis of the issue that earns it a score of 5.

Score 4 Response

While some people may believe that corporations have a responsibility to protect society, others believe that the only purpose of a corporation is to make money. I agree that making profits is important. In the grand scheme of things, though, all companies have a responsibility to watch out for their customers. Their customers are how they make their money. If they're not watching out for their customers, they obviously will see a drop in their profits.

Consider light bulbs. This is an invention that has all kinds of potential for serious accidents. It is basically just a glass globe with electricity running through it! If a bulb gets too hot, it could potentially start a fire. Similarly, if someone removed the glass from around the tungsten wire, you'd basically have an exposed electrical wire that could hurt anyone who touched it. Makers of light bulbs know and understand all these dangers. They want consumers to purchase their products, so the first and smartest way to make that happen is to ensure that the products are safe and thus more attractive to the customer base. If everyone who used light bulbs was afraid of getting zapped profits would obviously go down and light bulbs would not be a very profitable enterprise.

This same thinking applies to all major products. The automobile is one of the most dangerous tools man uses. Tens of thousands of automobile drivers die every year in accidents. Insuring that the vehicles contain designs and parts that promote customer safety is a main focus of car manufacturers. Certain parts of of cars were built with promoting driver's well-being in mind. For instance, air bags, anti-lock braking systems, online crash reporting. These features are considered standard now, and they were all developed to increase the safety of consumers. These features were not cheap to develop, but car manufacturers improved their profits anyway because they developed products with public safety in mind, which is what customers expect. If this symbiosis relationship wasn't true, then we would still have cars without airbags or even seatbelts. Worrying about the safety and actually improving it for customers is not just a basic responsibility of corporations, but it drives their profits, too.

In conclusion, its pretty clear that a corporation's desire to make more profits is in line with a corporation's responsibility to consumers. Increasing the focus on consumers, worrying about taking care of them and the environment, can only lead to bigger profits and success for corporations in the long run.

Reader Commentary

This adequate response follows the task directions and presents a clear position on the issue. It supports and develops its position competently, using relevant examples. In accordance with the assigned task, the response addresses both of the competing positions. Specifically, its position and the examples it develops argue that businesses can care about both profits and ethical responsibility through the ways they develop products. The development of examples and ideas, while adequate, is not as thoughtful or compelling as would be needed to earn higher scores. For instance, both of the examples the response uses are about product safety; the discussion of automobile design does not advance the position much more than the prior discussion of lightbulb production. Language control in the response is also competent. It demonstrates sufficient control of the conventions of standard written English, and its main points are made with acceptable clarity. The response features a few grammatical and mechanical errors (e.g., "Certain parts of of cars..." and "symbiosis relationship") and some awkward sentences. However, for the 4 range, GRE raters allow for minor errors in responses like this one that holistically demonstrate sufficient clarity and control. Overall, then, this response demonstrates adequate development and control of language, making the score of 4 appropriate.

Score 3 Response

Corporations can be viewed as both beneficial and bad. This statement addresses both views that many people have about corporations. Views come from personal experiences and is the reason why some people like corporations and why some people do not.

Half of this argument deals with people that like the idea of corporations. Some people believe that corporations help stmiulate societies and promote the well being of society. These people are ones that have never encountered a corupt corporation. Just like in any other aspects of life, people can get images of something as being good if they only brush the outside. It isn't until they are being faced with a problem within a particular corporation where they either work for them or have just dealt with them. Also, people that are benefited from corporations are obviously going to like the idea of an corporation.

The other side of this argument is that many people believe corporations are just money hungry. This can be seen in many corporations throughout America. Many small business owners will side with this argument. The problem lies that this is corporate America and the little businesses are being taking over by larger corporations. As Mark Twain once said, "The vast amount of money is only in a couple of hands". This statement still lies true today. In addition, corporations are large and with that being said they lead to more lines of coruption. In small buisnesses, the owners can oversee their store entirely. Can these corporation owners really oversee everything that is going on? Ask any employee at a corporate office if they believe their workplace is being ran how they think the corporation would want it. One is likely to find the answer that it is not.

Just like any other issue there are two sides to the story. The problem with this issue is that most will agree that corporations are only there to make money. They don't care about the people that are helping them make money. They only care at the end of the day how much money they made.

Reader Commentary

This response receives a score of 3 primarily because it is limited in focus. Rather than addressing the conflicting views of corporate responsibility given in the prompt, the response instead incorrectly casts the two positions as "people that like the idea of corporations" and people who "believe corporations are just money hungry." The writer proceeds to develop an explanation of these two positions, citing the various qualities that lead each group of people to their beliefs, but the response concludes by declaring that "there are two sides to the story" without adopting any position of its own. This highlights another limitation of the response, the fact that it does not completely address the specific task directions. Although the response does discuss the two opposing positions, it never discusses which view more closely aligns with the writer's own. The response does contain adequate organization, and the writing demonstrates a sufficient control of language. Sentences such as "Just like in any other aspects of life, people can get images of something as being good if they only brush the outside" are typical of the writing in this response and, despite the presence of some errors, demonstrate a sufficient control of the conventions of standard written English. However, even though the response demonstrates some qualities of a 4, its problems with focus and its failure to develop a clear position on the issue in accordance with the assigned task mean that it merits a score of 3.

Score 2 Response

I think corporations have a responsibility to not only follow the law but also work with the societies and enviroments they are in. Our societies and environments in this age are affected by corporations' operations. An example of this is BP's accident in the Gulf of Mexico—they might have been following the law and regulations, but once an accident happens, our societies and environments are affected. Many fishermen and businesses around the area have been affected by the accident. Now BP faces so many liabilities and needs to pay money. As a result, they are loosing more than they made in the past.

It is also important that corporations makes as much as money possible. If they do well, there might be more employment opportunities for people and more taxes for the city, states and federal which help our country's economy better.

However, there are always choices that corporations can take and they can make money by promoting the well-being of the societies and environments. It might cost them more but it will also help to save thier expenses.

Reader Commentary

This seriously flawed response attempts to address the task directions by considering both of the views presented in the prompt. The first paragraph seems to embrace the first view given in the prompt when it asserts that "corporations have a responsibility to...work with the societies and environments they are in." The writer uses the example of the BP oil spill in the Gulf of Mexico to demonstrate that "our societies and environments in this age are affected by corporations' operations," but, apart from restating these same claims, the paragraph provides no real support for this position. Instead, the writer moves on to a discussion of the financial implications of the oil spill for BP. The second paragraph then makes an abrupt transition to a discussion of the prompt's second view and again seems to embrace this position when it claims that "it is also important that corporations makes as much as money possible." This position is supported with a single relevant but undeveloped reason. Although the writer attempts to reconcile the two positions in the last paragraph by arguing that "there are always choices that corporations can take and they can make money by promoting the well-being of the societies and environments," the response provides no support for this position beyond its unsupported and contradictory claim that "it might cost them more but it will also help to save their expenses." Overall, then, this response provides few examples in support of its claims. The response's poor focus and its very limited support, then, warrant a score of 2.

Score 1 Response

It is certainly true that some people believe that corporations have a responsibility to promote the well being of societies and environments. On the other hand, some other people argue that the only responsibility of corporations, provided they operate within the law, is to make as much money as possible. It is easy to see why it would be difficult for some people to decide between these two positions.

The responsibility of all citizens of a society, including corporate citizens, is ultimately to further the well being of the society as a whole. It takes little more than examining the recent United States financial crisis to see the ill effects suffered by society at large when corporations focus on maximizing profits.

Reader Commentary

This response earns a score of 1 because it provides little evidence of the ability to develop an organized response. The first paragraph begins with a nearly word-for-word restatement of the prompt, which increases the length of the response but does not demonstrate the ability to develop a position on the issue in relation to the specific task instructions. The final sentence in the first paragraph is analytically empty in that it could be applied to any prompt that asks writers to discuss two competing positions. The writer does nothing to relate that sentence to this specific prompt. The second paragraph, then, is all that the writer has provided in terms of original analysis of the issue. Although it does demonstrate understanding of the issue, it fits the "extremely brief" description from the scoring guide description of a 1. Because of the extreme brevity of its analysis, then, this response merits a score of 1.

Answers and Explanations

SECTION 2
Verbal Reasoning
15 Questions with Explanations

For questions 1 to 5, select <u>one</u> entry for each blank from the corresponding column of choices. Fill all blanks in the way that best completes the text.

---

1. The unexplained digressions into the finer points of quantum electrodynamics are so _____ that even readers with a physics degree would be wise to keep a textbook handy to make sense of them.

Ⓐ	uninteresting
Ⓑ	controversial
Ⓒ	unsophisticated
Ⓓ	frustrating
Ⓔ	humorless

Explanation

An initial reading of this sentence might suggest that the blank should be filled with a word like "complex" that indicates how hard it is to "make sense of" the digressions. However, there is no such word among the answer choices. Focusing on the second half of the sentence suggests a different interpretation. According to the sentence, it would be "wise to" make sense of the digressions, and a textbook would help the reader to do so. If the digressions are "uninteresting," "unsophisticated," or "humorless," the sentence provides no reason to think it would be wise to make sense of them, and if they are "controversial," it provides no reason to think that a textbook would help. Only if the digressions are "frustrating" does the sentence make a coherent whole.

    Thus, the correct answer is **frustrating** (Choice D).

2. There may be a threshold below which blood pressure reductions become _____ given that a long-running study showed no decreased heart risk for drops in blood pressure below a certain point.

Ⓐ	worthwhile
Ⓑ	indiscernible
Ⓒ	arduous
Ⓓ	significant
Ⓔ	superfluous

Explanation

The portion of the sentence that begins with "given that" provides a reason for a conclusion reached in the first part of the sentence. Since the study "showed no decreased heart risk for drops in blood pressure below a certain point," that point may be a threshold below which reductions in blood pressure provide no benefit; that is, they may be "superfluous."

    Thus, the correct answer is **superfluous** (Choice E).

3. Unlike the problems in recent financial scandals, issues raised by the regulators
    in this case appear largely to pertain to unwieldy accounting rules that are open
    to widely divergent interpretations—not to (i)_____ transactions designed to
    (ii)_____ corporate malfeasance.

Blank (i)	Blank (ii)
(A) sham	(D) cloak
(B) unpremeditated	(E) ameliorate
(C) justifiable	(F) illuminate

Explanation

The "Unlike" at the beginning of the sentence and the "not to" that follows the dash set
up a contrast between the relatively innocent problems in the current case and the
issues involved in the "recent financial scandals." Clearly, these latter issues must have
involved wrongdoing. Looking at the second blank, only transactions designed to "cloak"
corporate malfeasance would qualify: both ameliorating and illuminating malfeasance
are positive actions. For the first blank, only "sham" fits; "unpremeditated" or "justifiable"
transactions could not be designed to cloak malfeasance.

Thus, the correct answer is **sham** (Choice A) and **cloak** (Choice D).

4. Everyone has routines that govern their work. The myth is that artists are somehow
    different, that they reject (i)_____ , but of course that's not true: most artists work
    as the rest of us do, (ii)_____ , day by day, according to their own customs.

Blank (i)	Blank (ii)
(A) latitude	(D) impetuously
(B) habit	(E) ploddingly
(C) materialism	(F) sporadically

Explanation

The passage conveys the sense that artists are like everyone else in that they have "routines that govern their work." This view is contrasted with a myth that artists are "somehow different." In the first blank, only "habit" is something whose rejection presents a contrast with being governed by work routines. Rejecting "latitude" might well match being governed by work routines, and though "materialism" is sometimes rejected by artists, it is not relevant to having work routines. The second blank describes how artists "work as the rest of us do"; only "ploddingly" is consistent with the emphasis on routines and "day by day" work.

Thus, the correct answer is **habit** (Choice B) and **ploddingly** (Choice E).

5. Rather than viewing the Massachusetts Bay Colony's antinomian controversy as the inevitable (i)_____ of the intransigent opposing forces of radical and (ii)_____ beliefs, male and female piety, (iii)_____ and secular power, and the like, as other critics have, Winship argues that the crisis was not "fixed and structural."

Blank (i)	Blank (ii)	Blank (iii)
Ⓐ dissolution	Ⓓ revolutionary	Ⓖ clerical
Ⓑ melding	Ⓔ orthodox	Ⓗ civil
Ⓒ collision	Ⓕ questionable	Ⓘ cerebral

Explanation

The words "Rather than" indicate that the other critics, unlike Winship, think of the controversy as "fixed and structural." Since both "dissolution" and "melding" of "intransigent opposing forces" would tend to lessen the controversy, only "collision" (Choice C) fits the first blank. The second and third blanks appear in a series of examples of such opposing forces; only "orthodox" contrasts with "radical" in the second blank and only "clerical" contrasts with "secular" in the third blank.

Thus, the correct answer is **collision** (Choice C), **orthodox** (Choice E), and **clerical** (Choice G).

For each of questions 6 and 7, select <u>one</u> answer choice unless otherwise instructed.

Questions 6 and 7 are based on the following reading passage.

Arctic sea ice comes in two varieties. Seasonal ice forms in winter and then melts in summer, while perennial ice persists year-round. To the untrained eye, all sea ice looks similar, but by licking it, one can estimate how long a particular piece has been floating around.
line   When ice begins to form in seawater, it forces out salt, which has no place in the crystal
5   structure. As the ice gets thicker, the rejected salt collects in tiny pockets of brine too highly concentrated to freeze. A piece of first-year ice will taste salty. Eventually, if the ice survives, these pockets of brine drain out through fine, veinlike channels, and the ice becomes fresher; multiyear ice can even be melted and drunk.

Description

The passage describes two varieties of Arctic sea ice and explains how the freezing process causes seasonal ice to taste much saltier than perennial ice.

For the following question, consider each of the choices separately and select all that apply.

6. The passage mentions which of the following as being a characteristic of seasonal ice?
    A It is similar in appearance to perennial ice.
    B It is typically filled with fine, veinlike channels.
    C It tastes saltier than perennial ice.

Explanation

Choices A and C are correct.

Choice A is correct: the passage states that "to the untrained eye, all sea ice looks similar" (line 2).

Choice B is incorrect: it is clear that perennial ice contains fine, veinlike channels, but the passage does not mention whether seasonal ice contains them.

Choice C is correct: in lines 6–8, the passage establishes that first-year ice tastes salty but eventually gets fresher if the ice survives.

7.   In the context in which it appears, "fine" (line 7) most nearly means

   (A) acceptable
   (B) elegant
   (C) precise
   (D) pure
   (E) small

Explanation

"Fine" appears in the context of an explanation of how the brine drains out; in such a context, it must be being used to describe a physical characteristic of the channels. In addition, the word "Eventually" implies that the draining is a slow process. Only **Choice E**, "small," helps to explain why the process is slow and is therefore the best choice. None of the other choices contributes to the explanation.

> For questions 8 to 10, select the <u>two</u> answer choices that, when used to complete the sentence, fit the meaning of the sentence as a whole <u>and</u> produce completed sentences that are alike in meaning.

8.   It would have been disingenuous of the candidate to appear _____ when her opponent won the election, but she congratulated the victor nonetheless.

   [A] gracious
   [B] ecstatic
   [C] crestfallen
   [D] indifferent
   [E] euphoric
   [F] disgruntled

Explanation

To answer the question, one must understand what sort of reaction on the part of a losing candidate would appear "disingenuous." Certainly "ecstatic" and "euphoric" reactions would be highly disingenuous or insincere. "Gracious" also fits the blank, but there is no other word offered that is nearly alike in meaning.

   Thus, the correct answer is **ecstatic** (Choice B) and **euphoric** (Choice E).

9. As market forces penetrate firms and bid up the value of attributes of labor that are more measurable than is the knowledge born of experience, it can be expected that trends in wages will not _____ those whose main value lies in such experiential knowledge.

    A favor
    B aid
    C affect
    D forsake
    E betray
    F differentiate

Explanation

The sentence states that market forces are bidding up the value of certain attributes of labor that are "more measurable than is the knowledge born of experience." The blank has to do with trends in wages for those whose main value in the labor force lies in "experiential knowledge." Since experiential knowledge appears to be losing value in the bidding war for labor, the blank needs to be filled in a way that leads to something negative. Given the "not" that precedes the blank, "favor" and "aid" make for such an outcome and result in sentences alike in meaning.

Thus, the correct answer is **favor** (Choice A) and **aid** (Choice B).

10. This is the kind of movie—stuffed with intimations of faraway strife and people in suits talking frantically on cell phones and walkie-talkies—that is conventionally described as a political thriller, but the film is as apolitical as it is _____.

    A intense
    B unprecedented
    C subtle
    D humdrum
    E refined
    F dull

Explanation

The sentence suggests that the film is not well described by the conventional term "political thriller." The film is not political but rather apolitical, and the phrase "as apolitical as it is…" sets up a parallel between "apolitical" and the blanked word; therefore, the blanked word should go against the term "political thriller" in the same way that "apolitical" does. "Humdrum" and "dull" are the opposite of "thrilling" and are therefore the best choices.

Thus, the correct answer is **humdrum** (Choice D) and **dull** (Choice F).

For each of questions 11 to 15, select <u>one</u> answer choice unless otherwise instructed.

Historians credit repeated locust invasions in the nineteenth century with reshaping United States agriculture west of the Mississippi River. Admonished by government entomologists, farmers began to diversify. Wheat had come to nearly monopolize the region, but it was particularly vulnerable to the locusts. In 1873, just before the locusts' most withering offensive, nearly two-thirds of Minnesota farmland was producing wheat; by the invasions' last year, that fraction had dropped to less than one-sixth. Farmers learned that peas and beans were far less vulnerable to the insects, and corn was a more robust grain than wheat. In addition to planting alternative crops, many farmers turned to dairy and beef production. Although pastures were often damaged by the locusts, these lands were almost always left in better shape than the crops were.

line
5

10

Description

The passage explains how the damage caused by repeated invasions of locusts in the nineteenth century caused farmers west of the Mississippi River to diversify. Since wheat, the dominant crop in the region, was especially susceptible to damage from locusts, it made sense for farmers to lower their wheat production and raise their production of other crops and animals less vulnerable to locust invasions.

For the following question, consider each of the choices separately and select all that apply.

11. According to the passage, before the recommendations by the government entomologists, which of the following was true about farming west of the Mississippi River?

    [A] Farmers focused primarily on growing wheat.

    [B] Peas and beans had not yet been planted in the region.

    [C] A relatively small portion of farmland was devoted to crops other than wheat.

Explanation

Choices A and C are correct.

    Choice A is correct: according to the passage, "wheat had come to nearly monopolize the region" prior to the recommendations of government entomologists.

    Choice B is incorrect: although wheat was the dominant crop, there is no indication that peas and beans had not been planted in the region prior to the admonishments of government entomologists.

    Choice C is correct: given that wheat was the dominant crop, only a relatively small portion of farmland could have been devoted to other crops.

12. In the context in which it appears, "robust" (line 7) most nearly means

(A) crude

(B) demanding

(C) productive

(D) vigorous

(E) rich

Explanation

In discussing the advantages of less vulnerable crops, the author describes corn as "robust." Of the choices presented, "vigorous" is most similar in meaning to "robust." Neither "crude" nor "demanding" is an advantage, and although being "productive" or "rich" might be desirable, neither matches the meaning of "robust" in this context. Therefore, **Choice D** is the correct answer.

Questions 13 to 15 are based on the following reading passage.

Nineteenth-century architect Eugène-Emmanuel Viollet-le-Duc contended that Paris's Notre-Dame cathedral, built primarily in the late twelfth century, was supported from the very beginning by a system of flying buttresses—a series of exterior arches (flyers) and their supports (buttresses)—which permitted the construction of taller vaulted buildings with slimmer walls and interior supports than had been possible previously. Other commentators insist, however, that Notre-Dame did not have flying buttresses until the thirteenth or fourteenth century, when they were added to update the building aesthetically and correct its structural flaws. Although post-twelfth-century modifications and renovations complicate efforts to resolve this controversy—all pre-fifteenth-century flyers have been replaced, and the buttresses have been rebuilt and/or resurfaced—it is nevertheless possible to tell that both the nave and the choir, the church's two major parts, have always had flying buttresses. It is clear, now that nineteenth-century paint and plaster have been removed, that the nave's lower buttresses date from the twelfth century. Moreover, the choir's lower flyers have chevron (zigzag) decoration. Chevron decoration, which was characteristic of the second half of the twelfth century and was out of favor by the fourteenth century, is entirely absent from modifications to the building that can be dated with confidence to the thirteenth century.

line 5

10

15

Description

The passage describes a disagreement about when Notre-Dame cathedral was supported by flying buttresses, with Viollet-le-Duc arguing that buttresses were present from the cathedral's construction in the late twelfth century and others claiming the buttresses were built later. The author of the passage goes on to present evidence that suggests that Viollet-le-Duc's argument is correct.

13. The passage is primarily concerned with

(A) tracing the development of a controversy

(B) discussing obstacles to resolving a controversy

(C) arguing in support of one side in a controversy

(D) analyzing the assumptions underlying the claims made in a controversy

(E) explaining why evidence relevant to a controversy has been overlooked

Explanation

As the preceding description indicates, **Choice C** is correct: the passage supports one side in a controversy. Choice A is incorrect because while the passage describes a controversy, it makes no mention of how that controversy developed. The passage also does not discuss any obstacles to resolving the controversy, any assumptions underlying the claims in the controversy, or any reasons why pertinent evidence may have been overlooked, so Choice B, Choice D, and Choice E are all incorrect.

14. The claim of the "other commentators" (line 6) suggests that they believe which of the following about Notre-Dame?

    (A) It was the inspiration for many vaulted cathedrals built in the thirteenth and fourteenth centuries.

    (B) Its design flaws were not apparent until flying buttresses were added in the thirteenth or fourteenth century.

    (C) Its flying buttresses are embellished with decoration characteristic of the thirteenth and fourteenth centuries.

    (D) It had been modified in some respects before flying buttresses were added in the thirteenth or fourteenth century.

    (E) It was originally constructed in an architectural style that was considered outmoded by the thirteenth or fourteenth century.

Explanation

The passage states that the "other commentators" claim that Notre-Dame first received flying buttresses when it was updated for aesthetic and structural reasons in the thirteenth or fourteenth century. This claim thus suggests that the aesthetics of Notre-Dame were then seen as out of date, making **Choice E** correct. Choice A is incorrect because the passage does not include any information about other cathedrals, let alone attribute a view of them to the other commentators. While the other commentators do suggest that the design of Notre-Dame was seen as flawed in the thirteenth or fourteenth century, they say that flying buttresses were added to correct these flaws, not that the flaws became apparent after the addition of the flying buttresses, which makes Choice B incorrect. Choice C is incorrect because the passage does not attribute any views of the embellishments on the flying buttresses to the other commentators; similarly, Choice D is incorrect because the passage does not describe the other commentators as discussing any modifications prior to the thirteenth or fourteenth century.

15. The author's argument concerning Notre-Dame's flying buttresses depends on which of the following assumptions about the choir's lower flyers?

    (A) They accurately reproduce the decoration on the choir's original lower flyers.

    (B) They have a type of decoration used exclusively for exterior surfaces.

    (C) They were the models for the choir's original upper flyers.

    (D) They were the models for the nave's original lower flyers.

    (E) They were constructed after the nave's flyers were constructed.

Explanation

The author supports the claim that flying buttresses were present on Notre-Dame from the twelfth century by noting that the choir's lower flyers feature a chevron decoration that was characteristic of the twelfth century. But since all flyers constructed prior to the fifteenth century have been replaced, the chevron decorations can indicate only that flyers were present in the twelfth century if those decorations accurately reproduce the decorations that existed on the original flyers. Thus, **Choice A** is the correct answer.

Choice B is incorrect: whether chevron decorations are used only on the exterior is not a point of dispute in the passage. Choices C, D, and E are all incorrect: no part of the argument turns on any claim about the choir's upper flyers, the nave's lower flyers, or the sequence in which the choir's and the nave's flyers were constructed.

SECTION 3
Verbal Reasoning
20 Questions with Explanations

> **For questions 1 to 6, select <u>one</u> entry for each blank from the corresponding column of choices. Fill all blanks in the way that best completes the text.**

1. Although plant and animal species that become established in ecosystems where they did not originate are sometimes referred to by the alarming term "invasive species," many such species are _____ in their new environments.

(A) innocuous
(B) conspicuous
(C) robust
(D) menacing
(E) distinctive

Explanation

The sentence begins with "Although," indicating that the correct answer will contrast in tone with the "alarming term 'invasive species.'" The only answer choice that provides the necessary contrast is "innocuous." All the other choices are consistent with being alarming.

   Thus, the correct answer is **innocuous** (Choice A).

2. Far from being _____ the corporate world because of cutbacks, serious researchers are playing a growing role in innovation at many firms.

(A) lured to
(B) enchanted with
(C) banished from
(D) protected by
(E) immured in

Explanation

The words "Far from being" and the mention of "cutbacks" imply that the correct answer will create a contrast with the idea that "serious researchers are playing a growing role in innovation." Being "banished from" the corporate world and playing a growing role in it are strongly contrasted. Choices A, B, D, and E do not create any such contrast.

   Thus, the correct answer is **banished from** (Choice C).

3. The government has no choice but to (i)_____ the incessant demands for land reform, and yet any governmental action that initiated land reform without requisite attention to agrarian reform would (ii)_____ the overall goal of economic modernization.

Blank (i)	Blank (ii)
(A) anticipate	(D) delineate
(B) heed	(E) condone
(C) silence	(F) compromise

Explanation

The sentence informs us that the government has an "overall goal," and the use of "and yet" indicates that initiating land reform without attending to agrarian reform would have some negative consequence for that goal. Thus, the only answer choice that fits the second blank is "compromise." The use of "and yet" also implies that the government's response to the demands for land reform must be in line with initiating such reform, so Choice C, "silence," is incorrect. The description of the demands as "incessant" implies that the demands already exist, so "anticipate" is incorrect. Only "heed" describes an appropriate response.

Thus, the correct answer is **heed** (Choice B) and **compromise** (Choice F).

4. Certain music lovers yearn for (i)_____, but when it is achieved, there is something missing; perhaps they feel uncomfortable in a world where nothing discernible is (ii)_____.

Blank (i)	Blank (ii)
(A) novelty	(D) wrong
(B) beauty	(E) visionary
(C) flawlessness	(F) changed

Explanation

The structure of the sentence alerts us that it will describe a kind of contradiction or paradox: music lovers want something, but when they get what they want, they discover some cause for dissatisfaction. Among the answer choices, the only two words that produce such a paradox are "flawlessness" and "wrong"—the music lovers long for flawlessness but are unsatisfied with a world in which nothing is wrong.

Thus, the correct answer is **flawlessness** (Choice C) and **wrong** (Choice D).

5. Putting a cash value on the ecological services provided by nature—such as the water filtration "service" provided by a forested watershed—has, historically, been a (i)_____ process. Early attempts at such valuation resulted in impressive but (ii)_____ figures that were seized on by environmental advocates, and then, when these figures were later (iii)_____, they were used by opponents to tar the whole idea.

Blank (i)	Blank (ii)	Blank (iii)
(A) dispassionate	(D) redundant	(G) ignored
(B) problematic	(E) unsound	(H) discredited
(C) straightforward	(F) understated	(I) confirmed

Explanation

The correct response for the first blank cannot be determined without considering the second sentence. The correct choice for the second blank, however, can be determined more readily. Neither Choice D, "redundant," nor Choice F, "understated," makes sense when coupled with the preceding "impressive but." Since the figures were "used by opponents to tar the whole idea," Choice E, "unsound," is the word that makes the most sense in this context.

Once "unsound" is selected for the second blank, it follows that "confirmed" cannot be correct for the third blank. And if the figures were "used by opponents," then they cannot have been "ignored." Since the figures were unsound, it is natural that they would later be "discredited."

Now that the figures have been characterized as unsound and discredited, it is possible to identify the correct response for the first blank. From the second sentence it is clear that the process of putting a cash value on the ecological services provided by nature is neither "dispassionate" nor "straightforward." It is instead "problematic."

Thus, the correct answer is **problematic** (Choice B); **unsound** (Choice E); and **discredited** (Choice H).

6.   Only with the discovery of an ozone hole over Antarctica in 1985 did chemical companies finally relinquish their opposition to a ban on chlorofluorocarbons (CFCs), which destroy ozone. The discovery suggested that strong political action to halt production of CFCs might be (i)_____, and fortunately, the chemical industry no longer felt compelled to oppose such action: although companies had recently (ii)_____ their research into CFC substitutes, studies they had initiated years earlier had produced (iii)_____ results.

Blank (i)	Blank (ii)	Blank (iii)
Ⓐ imminent	Ⓓ corroborated	Ⓖ encouraging
Ⓑ imprudent	Ⓔ publicized	Ⓗ inconclusive
Ⓒ premature	Ⓕ curtailed	Ⓘ unsurprising

Explanation

According to the first sentence, chemical companies opposed a ban on CFCs and then changed their stance in 1985 with the discovery of an ozone hole.

In the first blank, only "imminent" is compatible with the discovery of an ozone hole linked to CFCs: such a discovery would suggest that "strong political action" is required, not that it is "imprudent" or "premature."

What follows the colon in the second sentence explains why the chemical industry "no longer felt compelled to oppose" a ban on CFCs. In order for the industry to drop its opposition, the outcome of the studies into CFC substitutes must have been positive. Among the choices for the third blank, only "encouraging" has a sufficiently positive connotation.

Finally, the word "although" after the colon indicates that the second blank should contrast with the third blank in some way. Since the completed third blank now indicates that studies of CFC substitutes have been successful, "curtailed" makes the most sense in the second blank. "Corroborated" and "publicized" do not contrast appropriately with the success of the studies.

Thus, the correct answer is **imminent** (Choice A); **curtailed** (Choice F); and **encouraging** (Choice G).

For each of questions 7 to 10, select <u>one</u> answer choice unless otherwise instructed.

Some researchers contend that sleep plays no role in the consolidation of declarative memory (i.e., memory involving factual information). These researchers note that people with impairments in rapid eye movement (REM) sleep continue to lead normal lives, and they argue that if sleep were crucial for memory, then these individuals would have apparent memory deficits. Yet the same researchers acknowledge that the cognitive capacities of these individuals have never been systematically examined, nor have they been the subject of studies of tasks on which performance reportedly depends on sleep. Even if such studies were done, they could only clarify our understanding of the role of REM sleep, not sleep in general.

These researchers also claim that improvements of memory overnight can be explained by the mere passage of time, rather than attributed to sleep. But recent studies of memory performance after sleep—including one demonstrating that sleep stabilizes declarative memories from future interference caused by mental activity during wakefulness—make this claim unsustainable. Certainly there are memory consolidation processes that occur across periods of wakefulness, some of which neither depend on nor are enhanced by sleep. But when sleep is compared with wakefulness, and performance is better after sleep, then some benefit of sleep for memory must be acknowledged.

line 5
10
15

Description

The passage presents and then rebuts two arguments made by researchers who question the contribution of sleep to the consolidation of declarative memory (memory involving factual information). The first argument is that people with impairments to REM sleep continue to lead normal lives. In response, the passage says that these researchers themselves acknowledge the absence of systematic study of such individuals' cognitive abilities, study that would be necessary in order to fully support the researchers' claim. The passage also points out that the researchers' claim applies only to REM sleep rather than to sleep in general. The second claim is that improvements of memory that occur overnight might be explained merely by the passage of time. In response, the passage cites research findings that demonstrate the role of sleep in stabilizing declarative memory.

7. The primary purpose of the passage is to
    (A) present the evidence that supports a particular claim regarding REM sleep and memory
    (B) describe how various factors contribute to the effect of sleep on memory
    (C) argue against a particular position regarding sleep's role in memory
    (D) summarize the most prevalent theory regarding sleep and memory
    (E) defend the importance of the consolidation of declarative memory

Explanation

As described, the purpose of the passage as a whole is to argue against the view held by some researchers that sleep plays no role in the consolidation of declarative memory. Therefore, **Choice C** is correct. Choice A is incorrect: the passage does mention REM sleep twice in the first paragraph, but its primary purpose is not to examine REM sleep in particular, and it does not present evidence related to REM sleep. Choice B is incorrect: the passage is concerned with the effect of sleep on memory, but not with any factors that contribute to that effect. Choice D is incorrect: the passage does not summarize a theory. Instead, it cites a claim and then assesses and rejects that claim. Choice E is incorrect: although the passage is about the consolidation of declarative memory, it does nothing to defend its importance.

8. According to the author of the passage, which of the following generalizations about memory and sleep is true?

    (A) There are some memory-consolidation processes that have nothing to do with sleep.

    (B) Sleep is more important to the consolidation of declarative memory than to the consolidation of other types of memory.

    (C) REM sleep is more important to memory consolidation than is non-REM sleep.

    (D) There are significant variations in the amount of sleep that people require for the successful consolidation of memory.

    (E) It is likely that memory is more thoroughly consolidated during wakefulness than during sleep.

Explanation

The passage states that "there are memory-consolidation processes that occur across periods of wakefulness." Accordingly, **Choice A** is correct. Choices B, C, and D are incorrect: the passage does not discuss types of memory other than consolidative memory, the relative importance to consolidative memory of REM and non-REM sleep, or differences among individuals in the amount of sleep they require. Choice E is also incorrect: the passage suggests that the truth is the opposite of what this answer choice states. The last sentence of the passage indicates that performance on memory tasks has been found to be better after sleep than after periods of wakefulness.

9. Which of the following best describes the function of the sentence in lines 14–16 ("Certainly...sleep")?

    (A) It provides the reasoning behind a claim about the role of sleep in memory consolidation.

    (B) It explains why a previous claim about sleep and memory is unsustainable.

    (C) It demonstrates why wakefulness is central to the process of declarative memory consolidation.

    (D) It emphasizes the limited role sleep plays in the process of declarative memory consolidation.

    (E) It concedes that the consolidation of declarative memory does not depend entirely on one factor.

Explanation

The cited sentence begins with the word "Certainly," a clue that the sentence will concede that the researchers are not entirely wrong: in this instance, they are not wrong about memory consolidation occurring during periods of wakefulness. Thus, **Choice E** is correct. Choice A is incorrect: the sentence deals with memory consolidation during wakefulness, not with the role of sleep in memory consolidation. Choice B is incorrect:

the sentence does follow an assertion that the researchers' claim is unsustainable, but it does not explain why it is unsustainable. Choice C is incorrect: the sentence does not demonstrate anything. It acknowledges that memory consolidation occurs during wakeful periods but does not identify wakefulness as central to the process. Choice D is incorrect: while the sentence does acknowledge that some memory-consolidation processes are not dependent on sleep, it does not go so far as to claim that sleep plays a limited role in memory consolidation generally.

10. The importance of the study mentioned in lines 12–14 is that it
    - (A) reveals the mechanism by which declarative memory is stabilized during sleep
    - (B) identifies a specific function that sleep plays in the memory-consolidation process
    - (C) demonstrates that some kinds of mental activity can interfere with memory consolidation
    - (D) suggests that sleep and wakefulness are both important to memory consolidation
    - (E) explains how the passage of time contributes to memory consolidation

Explanation

The question asks what "the importance of the study mentioned in lines 12–14" is. The study is described as having shown that sleep stabilizes declarative memory from future interference caused by mental activity during wakefulness. This protection of memory from interference is the "specific function" played by sleep mentioned in Choice B. Therefore, **Choice B** is correct. Choice A is incorrect: there is no description of any mechanism, or specific process, by which declarative memory is stabilized. Although Choices C, D, and E each involve issues connected with the study, those connections are all tangential.

> For questions 11 to 14, select the <u>two</u> answer choices that, when used to complete the sentence, fit the meaning of the sentence as a whole <u>and</u> produce completed sentences that are alike in meaning.

11. In American Indian art, the supposed distinction between modern and traditional was fabricated by critics, and when artists have control over interpretation of their own work, the distinction appears, happily, to have been _____.
    - A eliminated
    - B reinforced
    - C put to rest
    - D intensified
    - E recognized
    - F established

Explanation

By characterizing the distinction as "supposed" and "fabricated," the sentence indicates that the distinction has no basis in reality. Accordingly, when the sentence reports a happy outcome, this must mean that the distinction has been abandoned or rejected. Only "eliminated" and "put to rest" convey that sense; all the other answer choices suggest that the distinction is maintained, or even strengthened.

Thus, the correct answer is **eliminated** (Choice A) and **put to rest** (Choice C).

12. Notwithstanding their _____ regarding other issues, township residents have consistently passed the board of education's annual budget.

A accord
B indecision
C consensus
D disagreement
E divergence
F enthusiasm

Explanation

By using the word "Notwithstanding," the sentence sets up a contrast between the township residents' behavior regarding the "other issues" and their behavior regarding the board's annual budget, which they have "consistently passed." "Accord" and "consensus" are similar in meaning but do not provide the required contrast. Only "disagreement" and "divergence" provide the necessary contrast and lead to two sentences nearly alike in meaning. "Indecision" fits the context, but there is no other word among the possible choices that matches it closely.

Thus, the correct answer is **disagreement** (Choice D) and **divergence** (Choice E).

13. Some of the company's supporters charged that the negative report had been motivated by a broader political assault on the company that was designed to help market rivals who would like to see the company _____.

A reined in
B bolstered
C indemnified
D propped up
E manacled
F lionized

Explanation

The "market rivals" would clearly like to see the company experience some negative outcome. Only "reined in" and "manacled" describe such an outcome; the other choices all describe positive results for the company.

Thus, the correct answer is **reined in** (Choice A) and **manacled** (Choice E).

14. Skeptics contend that any scheme for charging visitors to Web sites that rewards the vendor adequately would require steep prices, _____ the kind of frequent, casual use of Web sites that surfers now take for granted.

   [A] bridling
   [B] exciting
   [C] forbidding
   [D] inhibiting
   [E] provoking
   [F] reversing

Explanation

The sentence concerns skeptics' reaction to a plan to generate revenue by charging visitors to Web sites. To justify the skeptics' reaction, the "steep prices" must be associated with a decrease in visitor volume. Only "bridling" and "inhibiting" are consistent with this logic and result in sentences nearly alike in meaning. "Forbidding" is too strong: steep prices might dissuade a casual visitor, but they would not forbid one. Although "exciting" and "provoking" can be similar in meaning, they do not fit the logic of the sentence.

   Thus, the correct answer is **bridling** (Choice A) and **inhibiting** (Choice D).

For each of questions 15 to 20, select <u>one</u> answer choice unless otherwise instructed.

Question 15 is based on the following reading passage.

Astronomers found a large body orbiting close to the star Upsilon Andromedae. The standard theory of planet formation holds that no planet that large could be formed so close to a star, leading to the suggestion that the body is a companion star. A subsequent discovery puts that suggestion in doubt: two other large bodies were found orbiting close to Upsilon Andromedae, and the standard theory of companion stars allows for at most one companion star.

15. Which of the following, if true, most helps to resolve the status of the orbiting body without casting doubt on the two standard theories mentioned?

   (A) The smaller a planet orbiting a star is, and the farther away it is from the star, the less likely it is to be discovered.

   (B) If a planet's orbit is disturbed, the planet can be drawn by gravity toward the star it is orbiting.

   (C) The largest of the bodies orbiting Upsilon Andromedae is the farthest away from the star, and the smallest is the nearest.

   (D) It is likely that there are many stars, in addition to Upsilon Andromedae and the Sun, that are orbited by more than one smaller body.

   (E) In most cases of companion stars, the smaller companion is much fainter than the larger star.

Explanation

The passage outlines a conflict between two standard theories—one of planet formation, the other of companion stars—and observations of one large body, and later two others, orbiting close to a star. The question asks what would resolve this conflict without casting doubt on either one of the theories.

Choice B is correct: if, as it asserts, it is possible for a planet to be formed relatively far from a star and later move closer to it, then the observed large bodies found close to Upsilon Andromedae can be planets without casting doubt on the standard theory of planet formation. This explanation also leaves the standard theory of companion stars intact.

Choice A is incorrect because it describes difficulties with discovering a small planet far from a star, not anything pertaining to a large body near a star. Choice C is incorrect as well, since whatever the relative size and position of the three bodies may be, all three appear to be too close according to the standard theories. Choice D is incorrect because the pervasiveness of stars with multiple orbiting bodies has nothing to do with the status of the large bodies discussed in the passage. Choice E is similarly irrelevant and thus incorrect: information about the brightness of a star relative to its companion star does not help clarify the status of the large bodies discussed in the passage.

Question 16 is based on the following reading passage.

In Gilavia, the number of reported workplace injuries has declined 16 percent in the last five years. However, perhaps part of the decline results from injuries going unreported: many employers have introduced safety-incentive programs, such as prize drawings for which only employees who have a perfect work-safety record are eligible. Since a workplace injury would disqualify an employee from such programs, some employees might be concealing injury, when it is feasible to do so.

16. Which of the following, if true in Gilavia, most strongly supports the proposed explanation?

(A) In the last five years, there has been no decline in the number of workplace injuries leading to immediate admission to a hospital emergency room.

(B) Employers generally have to pay financial compensation to employees who suffer work-related injuries.

(C) Many injuries that happen on the job are injuries that would be impossible to conceal and yet would not be severe enough to require any change to either the employee's work schedule or the employee's job responsibilities.

(D) A continuing shift in employment patterns has led to a decline in the percentage of the workforce that is employed in the dangerous occupations in which workplace injuries are likely.

(E) Employers who have instituted safety-incentive programs do not in general have a lower proportion of reported workplace injuries among their employees than do employers without such programs.

Explanation

The question asks what would support the claim that the decline in reported workplace injuries in Gilavia may be the result of incentives for workers to not report those injuries that they can conceal. If the number of injuries that cannot be concealed—such as injuries requiring immediate emergency care—has not declined in the same period, that could help bolster the claim that the decline in overall reported injuries may be a result of concealable injuries going unreported rather than an actual decline in workplace injuries in general, so **Choice A** is correct.

If employers have to provide financial compensation to employees injured on the job, employees would have an incentive to report injuries. More reported injuries would not support the author's argument, making Choice B incorrect. Choice C is incorrect because the fact that some injuries that cannot be concealed do not result in lost time or changed responsibilities has nothing to do with whether concealable injuries are going unreported. While a decline in dangerous occupations could well result in a decrease in workplace injuries, this fact would challenge the author's argument, not support it, so Choice D is incorrect. Similarly, if employers with safety-incentive programs do not see any drop in reported injuries compared to employers without such programs, the author's argument would be weakened, not supported, making Choice E incorrect.

Questions 17 and 18 are based on the following reading passage.

The attribution of early-nineteenth-century English fiction is notoriously problematic. Fewer than half of new novels published in Britain between 1800 and 1829 had the author's true name printed on the title page. Most of these titles have subsequently

line
5   been attributed, either through the author's own acknowledgment of a previously anonymous or pseudonymous work or through bibliographical research. One important tool available to researchers is the list of earlier works "by the author" often found on title pages. But such lists are as likely to create new confusion as they are to solve old problems. Title pages were generally prepared last in the publication process, often without full authorial assent, and in the last-minute rush to press, mistakes were fre-

10   quently made.

Description

The passage discusses the reasons why identifying the authors of early-nineteenth-century British fiction poses significant challenges. The passage explains that few authors during this period used their real names and goes on to describe how title pages can facilitate—but also hamper—efforts to attribute these works.

For the following question, consider each of the choices separately and select all that apply.

17. The passage suggests that which of the following factors contributes to the "notoriously problematic" (line 1) nature of authorial attribution in early-nineteenth-century English fiction?

    A The unwillingness of any writers to acknowledge their authorship of works that were originally published anonymously or pseudonymously

    B The possibility that the title page of a work may attribute works written by other authors to the author of that work

    C The possibility that the author's name printed on a title page is fictitious

Explanation

Choices B and C are correct.

    Choice A is incorrect: the passage mentions that the attribution of early-nineteenth-century fiction was sometimes achieved when the author came forward to acknowledge a previously anonymous work (lines 4–5), so Choice A can be eliminated.

    Choice B is correct: in lines 5–7, the passage mentions that "one important tool available to researchers is the list of earlier works 'by the author' often found on title pages," but goes on to say that these title pages were prepared hastily and "frequently" contained mistakes (lines 8–10). Since the mistake most likely to "create new confusion" would be the inclusion of works not written by the author, Choice B may be inferred.

Choice C is correct: in lines 2–3, the passage states, "Fewer than half of the new novels published in Britain…had the author's true name printed on the title page." Line 5 suggests that pseudonyms—fictitious names—were commonly used. Hence, Choice C may be inferred.

For the following question, consider each of the choices separately and select all that apply.

18. The passage suggests that which of the following is frequently true of the title pages of early-nineteenth-century English novels?

   A The title page was prepared for printing in a hurried manner.

   B Material on the title page was included without the author's knowledge or approval.

   C Information on the title page was deliberately falsified to make the novel more marketable.

Explanation

Choices A and B are correct.

   Choice A is correct: the passage mentions that title pages were prepared last and that mistakes often occurred "in the last-minute rush to press" (line 9). This indicates that title pages were often prepared for printing in a hurried manner; hence, Choice A can be inferred.

   Choice B is correct: the passage includes the detail that title pages were often prepared for printing "without full authorial assent" (line 9); hence, Choice B can be inferred.

   Choice C is incorrect: nowhere does the passage speculate about commercial motives for falsifying information on title pages. Choice C, therefore, cannot be inferred.

Questions 19 and 20 are based on the following reading passage.

The more definitions a given noun has, the more valuable is each one. Multiple definitions, each subtly different from all the others, convey multiple shades of meaning. They expand the uses of the word; language is enriched, thought is widened, and interpretations
line increase or dilate to fill the potentialities of association. The very impossibility of absolute
5 ness in the definition of certain nouns adds to the levels of connotation they may reach. The inner life of a writer often says more than most readers can know; the mind of a reader can discover truths that go beyond the intent or perhaps even the comprehension of the writer. And all of it finds expression because a word can mean many things.

Description

The passage claims that the capacity of words to have multiple meanings can greatly enhance the resources of a language. The passage describes how this increases possibilities for interpretation and the expression of ideas, thus enriching the relationship between readers and writers.

19. In the context in which it appears, "shades" (line 2) most nearly means

   (A) reminders
   (B) nuances
   (C) obscurities
   (D) coverings
   (E) degrees

Explanation

In the context in which it appears, "shades" is used to refer to the subtle distinctions in meaning that are made possible by "multiple definitions, each subtly different from all the others." Since the sentence deals with multiple definitions conveying meaning, Choice C ("obscurities") and the more literal Choice D ("coverings") may be eliminated. In deciding between Choice B and Choice E, one should bear in mind that the sentence focuses on subtle differences in meaning as opposed to different degrees of emphasis for the same meaning. **Choice B**, "nuances," best captures this sense of slight variations in meaning and is therefore the correct answer.

20. The passage suggests that a writer's use of nouns that have multiple definitions can have which of the following effects on the relationship between writer and reader?

   (A) It can encourage the reader to consider how the writer's life might have influenced the work.

   (B) It can cause the reader to become frustrated with the writer's failure to distinguish between subtle shades of meaning.

   (C) It can allow the reader to discern in a work certain meanings that the writer did not foresee.

   (D) It allows the writer to provide the reader with clues beyond the word itself in order to avoid ambiguity.

   (E) It allows the writer to present unfamiliar ideas to the reader more efficiently.

Explanation

Line 7 clearly indicates that multiple meanings of words enable readers to "discover truths that go beyond the intent or perhaps even the comprehension of the writer"; hence, **Choice C** is the correct answer. Choices A, B, D, and E all deal with topics that are not mentioned in the passage: the writer's life, the reader's frustration, the avoidance of ambiguity, and the question of how efficiently multiple definitions can aid in the presentation of unfamiliar ideas.

SECTION 4
Quantitative Reasoning
15 Questions with Explanations

> **For each of Questions 1 to 5, select one of the following answer choices.**
> Ⓐ **Quantity A is greater.**
> Ⓑ **Quantity B is greater.**
> Ⓒ **The two quantities are equal.**
> Ⓓ **The relationship cannot be determined from the information given.**

Quantity A	Quantity B	
1. $\dfrac{3^{-1}}{4^{-1}}$	$\dfrac{4}{3}$	Ⓐ Ⓑ Ⓒ Ⓓ

Explanation

In this question, you are asked to compare $\dfrac{3^{-1}}{4^{-1}}$ with $\dfrac{4}{3}$. Recall that if a is a

nonzero number, then $a^{-1} = \dfrac{1}{a}$ and $\dfrac{1}{a^{-1}} = a$. Using these rules of exponents, you can see that

$$\frac{3^{-1}}{4^{-1}} = (3^{-1})\left(\frac{1}{4^{-1}}\right) = \left(\frac{1}{3}\right)(4) = \frac{4}{3}$$

Thus, $\dfrac{3^{-1}}{4^{-1}} = \dfrac{4}{3}$, and the correct answer is **Choice C**.

This explanation uses the following strategy.

Strategy 5: Simplify an Arithmetic or Algebraic Representation

> The median income of a group of College C graduates six months after graduation was $3,000 higher than the median income of a group of College D graduates six months after graduation.

	Quantity A	Quantity B	
2.	The 75th percentile of the incomes of the group of College C graduates six months after graduation	The 75th percentile of the incomes of the group of College D graduates six months after graduation	Ⓐ Ⓑ Ⓒ Ⓓ

Explanation

In this question, you are asked to compare the 75th percentiles of the incomes of two groups of college graduates six months after graduation. The only information you are given is that the median income of the group in Quantity A is $3,000 greater than the median income of the group in Quantity B.

Recall that the median of a group of numbers is the middle number (or the average of the two middle numbers) when the numbers are listed from least to greatest. The median is also equal to the 50th percentile. The median does not indicate anything about the spread of the numbers in the group. In particular, for each group of incomes, you do not know how much greater than the median the 75th percentile of the group of incomes is, nor do you know the relationship between the 75th percentiles of the two groups. Since the relationship between Quantity A and Quantity B cannot be determined, the correct answer is **Choice D**.

This explanation uses the following strategies.
Strategy 8: Search for a Mathematical Relationship
Strategy 13: Determine Whether a Conclusion Follows from the Information Given

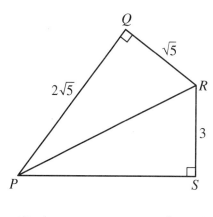

Quantity A	Quantity B	
3. The area of triangle *PQR*	The area of triangle *PSR*	Ⓐ Ⓑ Ⓒ Ⓓ

Explanation

In this question, you are asked to compare the area of triangle *PQR* with the area of triangle *PSR*. Note that both triangles are right triangles and that line segment *PR* is the hypotenuse of both triangles. Recall that the area of a triangle is equal to one-half the product of a base and the height corresponding to the base. Also, for any right triangle, the lengths of the two legs of the triangle are a base and the corresponding height.

The area of triangle PQR: In the figure, it is given that the length of leg *PQ* is $2\sqrt{5}$ and the length of leg *QR* is $\sqrt{5}$. Therefore, you can conclude that the area of triangle *PQR* is $\frac{1}{2}(2\sqrt{5})(\sqrt{5})$, or 5.

The area of triangle PSR: To calculate the area of triangle *PSR*, you need to know the lengths of the legs *PS* and *RS*. From the figure, you know that the length of *RS* is 3, but you do not know the length of *PS*. How can you determine the length of *PS*? If, in addition to the length of *RS*, you knew the length of hypotenuse *PR*, you could use the Pythagorean theorem to determine the length of *PS*. So, to find the length of *PS*, you first need to find the length of hypotenuse *PR*.

Recall that *PR* is also the hypotenuse of triangle *PQR*. The lengths of legs *PQ* and *QR* of triangle *PQR* are $2\sqrt{5}$ and $\sqrt{5}$, respectively. By the Pythagorean theorem,

$$(PR)^2 = (PQ)^2 + (QR)^2$$
$$= (2\sqrt{5})^2 + (\sqrt{5})^2$$
$$= 20 + 5$$
$$= 25$$

Thus, the length of *PR* is $\sqrt{25}$, or 5.

Returning to triangle *PSR*, you now know that the length of hypotenuse *PR* is 5 and the length of leg *RS* is 3. Therefore, by the Pythagorean theorem,

$$3^2 + (PS)^2 = 5^2$$
$$9 + (PS)^2 = 25$$
$$(PS)^2 = 25 - 9$$
$$(PS)^2 = 16$$

and the length of *PS* is 4.

Since legs *PS* and *RS* have lengths 4 and 3, respectively, the area of triangle *PSR* is $\frac{1}{2}(4)(3)$, or 6. Recall that you have already determined that the area of triangle *PQR* is 5. So Quantity B, the area of triangle *PSR*, is greater than Quantity A, the area of triangle *PQR*, and the correct answer is **Choice B**.

This explanation uses the following strategies.
Strategy 4: Translate from a Figure to an Arithmetic or Algebraic Representation
Strategy 8: Search for a Mathematical Relationship

s and *t* are positive integers, and $32^s = 2^t$.

	Quantity A	Quantity B	
4.	$\dfrac{s}{t}$	$\dfrac{1}{5}$	Ⓐ Ⓑ Ⓒ Ⓓ

Explanation

In this question, you are given that *s* and *t* are positive integers and that $32^s = 2^t$, and you are asked to compare $\frac{s}{t}$ with $\frac{1}{5}$. Since the expression $\frac{s}{t}$ involves the variables *s* and *t*, you need to look for a relationship between *s* and *t* using the equation $32^s = 2^t$.

If the two bases in this equation were equal, then the exponents would be equal. However, one of the bases is 32 and the other is 2. This suggests making the two bases equal by rewriting 32 as a power of 2 if it is possible to do so. In fact, $32 = 2^5$. Therefore, $32^s = (2^5)^s = 2^{5s}$, and the equation $32^s = 2^t$ can be rewritten as $2^{5s} = 2^t$. In the rewritten equation, the bases are equal, so you can conclude that $5s = t$.

Since $5s = t$, it follows that $\frac{s}{t} = \frac{1}{5}$. Quantity A is equal to Quantity B, and the correct answer is **Choice C**.

This explanation uses the following strategy.
Strategy 5: Simplify an Arithmetic or Algebraic Representation

In a quality-control test, 50 boxes—each containing 30 machine parts—were examined for defective parts. The number of defective parts was recorded for each box, and the average (arithmetic mean) of the 50 recorded numbers of defective parts per box was 1.12. Only one error was made in recording the 50 numbers: "1" defective part in a certain box was incorrectly recorded as "10."

Quantity A	Quantity B
5. The actual average number of defective parts per box	0.94

Ⓐ Ⓑ Ⓒ Ⓓ

Explanation

In this question, you are given that the number of defective parts in each of 50 boxes was recorded and that the average of the 50 recorded numbers was 1.12. You are also given that an error was made in recording one of the 50 numbers—the number 10 was recorded instead of the number 1—so the actual number of defective parts in this box is 9 less than the recorded number. Then you are asked to compare the actual average number of defective parts per box with 0.94.

To determine the actual average number of defective parts per box, first note that the sum of the 50 recorded numbers equals the average of the 50 recorded numbers times 50—that is, (1.12)(50), or 56.

Now you know that for 49 of the 50 boxes, the actual number of defective parts is equal to the recorded number; and for one box, the actual number is 9 less than the recorded number. From this you can conclude that the sum of the 50 actual numbers is equal to the sum of the 50 recorded numbers minus 9. So the sum of the actual numbers of defective parts is 56 – 9, or 47.

Therefore, the actual average number of defective parts per box is $\frac{47}{50}$, or 0.94.

Quantity A is equal to Quantity B, and the correct answer is **Choice C**.

This explanation uses the following strategy.

Strategy 1: Translate from Words to an Arithmetic or Algebraic Representation

6. In year Y, the population of Colorado was approximately half that of New Jersey, and the land area of Colorado was approximately 14 times that of New Jersey. The population density (number of persons per unit of land area) of Colorado in year Y was approximately how many times the population density of New Jersey?

Ⓐ $\frac{1}{28}$ Ⓑ $\frac{1}{14}$ Ⓒ $\frac{1}{7}$ Ⓓ $\frac{1}{4}$ Ⓔ $\frac{1}{2}$

Explanation

The information given in the question can be rewritten algebraically as follows.

$$\text{population of Colorado} \approx \left(\frac{1}{2}\right) \times (\text{population of New Jersey})$$
$$\text{land area of Colorado} \approx (14) \times (\text{land area of New Jersey})$$

Using the information given and the fact that population density is the number of persons per unit of land area, you can express the population density of Colorado in terms of the population density of New Jersey as follows.

$$\text{population density of Colorado} = \frac{\text{population of Colorado}}{\text{land area of Colorado}}$$

$$\approx \frac{\left(\frac{1}{2}\right) \times (\text{population of New Jersey})}{(14) \times (\text{land area of New Jersey})}$$

$$\approx \left(\frac{1}{2}\right) \times \frac{1}{14} \times \frac{\text{population of New Jersey}}{\text{land area of New Jersey}}$$

$$\approx \left(\frac{1}{28}\right) \times (\text{population density of New Jersey})$$

Thus, the population density of Colorado was approximately $\frac{1}{28}$ times the population density of New Jersey. The correct answer is **Choice A**.

This explanation uses the following strategy.
Strategy 1: Translate from Words to an Arithmetic or Algebraic Representation

For the following question, enter your answer in the box.

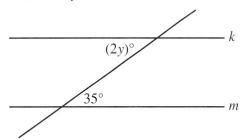

7.   In the figure above, line k is parallel to line m. What is the value of y?

$$y = \boxed{}$$

Explanation
In the figure, the angles with measures $(2y)°$ and $35°$ are between parallel lines k and m, and they are on opposite sides of the line that crosses k and m. Therefore, you can conclude that these two angles are congruent. So $2y = 35$, and $y = \frac{35}{2} = 17.5$. The correct answer is **17.5**.

This explanation uses the following strategy.
Strategy 4: Translate from a Figure to an Arithmetic or Algebraic Representation

8. The numbers in data set S have a standard deviation of 5. If a new data set is formed by adding 3 to each number in S, what is the standard deviation of the numbers in the new data set?

(A) 2

(B) 3

(C) 5

(D) 8

(E) 15

Explanation

Recall that the standard deviation of the numbers in a data set is a measure of the spread of the numbers about the mean of the numbers. The new data set is formed by adding the <u>same</u> number, 3, to <u>each</u> number in data set S. Thus, the mean of the numbers in the new data set is 3 more than the mean of the numbers in S, but the spread of the numbers in the new data set about the mean of the numbers in the new data set is the same as the spread of the numbers in S about the mean of the numbers in S. Because the standard deviation of the numbers in S is 5, the standard deviation of the numbers in the new data set is also 5. The correct answer is **Choice C**.

This explanation uses the following strategy.

Strategy 8: Search for a Mathematical Relationship

9. If $\dfrac{2y-3}{y} = \dfrac{3-y}{2}$, which of the following could be the value of y?

(A) 4

(B) 1

(C) −1

(D) −3

(E) −5

Explanation

One approach to answer the question is to solve the equation for y as follows.

$$2(2y-3) = y(3-y)$$
$$4y-6 = 3y-y^2$$
$$y^2 + y - 6 = 0$$
$$(y+3)(y-2) = 0$$

Since a product equals 0 only if at least one of the factors equals 0,

$$y+3 = 0 \quad \text{or} \quad y-2 = 0$$
$$y = -3 \quad \text{or} \quad y = 2$$

Thus, there are two values of y that satisfy the equation, −3 and 2. The value −3 is Choice D, and the value 2 is not among the answer choices. The correct answer is **Choice D**.

Another approach is to determine, for each answer choice, whether the equation holds. To do this, you can substitute the answer choice for y in the equation $\frac{2y-3}{y} = \frac{3-y}{2}$, replace the equals sign in the equation by the place-holder symbol $\overset{?}{=}$, and then simplify to see whether the two expressions are in fact equal.

For Choice A, substituting $y = 4$ in the equation $\frac{2y-3}{y} = \frac{3-y}{2}$ and replacing the equals sign = with the placeholder symbol $\overset{?}{=}$ yields the relationship $\frac{2(4)-3}{4} \overset{?}{=} \frac{3-4}{2}$, which can be simplified as follows.

$$\frac{2(4)-3}{4} \overset{?}{=} \frac{3-4}{2}$$
$$\frac{8-3}{4} \overset{?}{=} \frac{-1}{2}$$
$$\frac{5}{4} \overset{?}{=} -\frac{1}{2}$$

Since $\frac{5}{4} \neq -\frac{1}{2}$, you can conclude that the placeholder symbol does not represent equality, and therefore the equation does not hold for $y = 4$.

If you continue evaluating the answer choices, you will find that the correct answer is **Choice D**, −3. To see that the equation $\frac{2y-3}{y} = \frac{3-y}{2}$ is true when $y = -3$, substitute $y = -3$ in the equation and replace the equals sign = with the placeholder symbol $\overset{?}{=}$. This yields the relationship $\frac{2(-3)-3}{-3} \overset{?}{=} \frac{3-(-3)}{2}$. This relationship can be simplified as follows.

$$\frac{2(-3)-3}{-3} \overset{?}{=} \frac{3-(-3)}{2}$$
$$\frac{-6-3}{-3} \overset{?}{=} \frac{3+3}{2}$$
$$\frac{-9}{-3} \overset{?}{=} \frac{6}{2}$$
$$3 \overset{?}{=} 3$$

Since $3 = 3$, you can conclude that the placeholder symbol represents equality, and therefore the equation holds for $y = -3$. The correct answer is **Choice D**.

This explanation uses the following strategy.

Strategy 5: Simplify an Arithmetic or Algebraic Representation

For the following question, select all the answer choices that apply.

10. List K consists of the numbers −10, −5, 0, 5, and 10. Which of the following lists of numbers have the same range as the numbers in list K?

    Indicate <u>all</u> such lists.

    A −15, −1, 0, 1, 15   D 2, 3, 5, 15, 19, 22

    B −7, −4, −2, 1, 13   E 4, 5, 6, 24

    C 0, 1, 2, 5, 8, 10

Explanation

Recall that the range of a list of numbers is defined as the difference between the greatest number and the least number in the list. The greatest number in list K is 10 and the least number is -10. Therefore, the range of the numbers in list K is $10 - (-10) = 10 + 10 = 20$. So, to answer the question, you need to consider each list of numbers given in the choices and determine whether that list of numbers has a range of 20.

Note that in each of the choices, the numbers are listed in order from least to greatest. Therefore, you need to look only at the first number and last number in each list to determine which lists have a range of 20. The ranges can be calculated quickly as follows.

Choice A: The greatest number is 15 and the least number is -15; therefore, the range is $15 - (-15) = 15 + 15 = 30$.

Choice B: The greatest number is 13 and the least number is -7; therefore, the range is $13 - (-7) = 13 + 7 = 20$.

Choice C: The greatest number is 10 and the least number is 0; therefore, the range is $10 - 0 = 10$.

Choice D: The greatest number is 22 and the least number is 2; therefore, the range is $22 - 2 = 20$.

Choice E: The greatest number is 24 and the least number is 4; therefore, the range is $24 - 4 = 20$.

In each of Choices B, D, and E, the range is 20. The correct answer consists of **Choices B, D, and E**.

This explanation uses the following strategy.

Strategy 8: Search for a Mathematical Relationship

11.   Jacob's weekly take-home pay is n dollars. Each week he uses $\frac{4n}{5}$ dollars for expenses and saves the rest. At those rates, how many weeks will it take Jacob to save \$500, in terms of n?

    (A) $\dfrac{500}{n}$

    (B) $\dfrac{2,500}{n}$

    (C) $\dfrac{n}{625}$

    (D) $\dfrac{n}{2,500}$

    (E) $625n$

Explanation

It may be helpful to consider how you would determine the number of weeks it would take Jacob to save \$500 if you knew how much he saved each week. For example, suppose Jacob saved \$25 each week. At that rate, it is easy to see that it would take him $500 \div 25$, or 20, weeks to save \$500. Using this example, you can see that the number of weeks it will take Jacob to save \$500 is equal to 500 divided by the amount he saves each week.

Now use the information given in the question to determine an algebraic expression representing the amount Jacob saved each week. In the question, you are given that Jacob's weekly expenses are $\frac{4n}{5}$ dollars. Therefore, the amount he saves each week is equal to his weekly take-home pay minus his weekly expenses, or

$$n - \frac{4n}{5} = \frac{5n}{5} - \frac{4n}{5} = \frac{5n-4n}{5} = \frac{n}{5} \text{ dollars.}$$

Recall that you had already concluded that the number of weeks it will take Jacob to save \$500 is equal to 500 divided by the amount he saves each week. So the number of weeks it will take Jacob to save \$500 is

$$500 \div \frac{n}{5} = 500 \times \frac{5}{n} = \frac{2,500}{n}. \text{ The correct answer is } \textbf{Choice B.}$$

This explanation uses the following strategy.

Strategy 1: Translate from Words to an Arithmetic or Algebraic Representation

For the following question, select all the answer choices that apply.

12. If $|t + 3| > 5$, which of the following could be the value of t?

Indicate <u>all</u> such values.

- [A] −9
- [B] −6
- [C] −2
- [D] 0
- [E] 2
- [F] 3

Explanation

One way to approach this question is to substitute each of the answer choices into the inequality and determine which ones satisfy the inequality. If you do this, you will see that Choice A, −9, and Choice F, 3, satisfy the inequality, but the other answer choices do not. The correct answer consists of **Choices A and F.**

An algebraic approach to the question is to note that the inequality $|t + 3| > 5$ is satisfied whenever $t + 3 > 5$ or $t + 3 < -5$, that is, whenever $t > 2$ or $t < -8$. Therefore, all values of t greater than 2 or less than −8 satisfy the inequality $|t + 3| > 5$. The only answer choices that meet those conditions are −9, Choice A, and 3, Choice F. The correct answer consists of **Choices A and F.**

This explanation uses the following strategy.

Strategy 5: Simplify an Arithmetic or Algebraic Representation

13. The operation $\otimes$ is defined for all integers x and y as $x \otimes y = xy - y$. If x and y are positive integers, which of the following CANNOT be zero?

    (A) $x \otimes y$

    (B) $y \otimes x$

    (C) $(x - 1) \otimes y$

    (D) $(x + 1) \otimes y$

    (E) $x \otimes (y - 1)$

Explanation

In the formula $x \otimes y = xy - y$, the variables x and y are placeholders that can be replaced by integers or by expressions representing integers. Here are two examples.

If x is replaced by 3 and y is replaced by 4, then the formula gives

$$3 \otimes 4 = (3)(4) - 4 = 12 - 4 = 8$$

If x is replaced by $x - 1$ and y is replaced by 2, then the formula gives

$$(x - 1) \otimes 2 = ((x - 1)(2)) - 2 = 2x - 2 - 2 = 2x - 4$$

Scanning the answer choices, you can see that all of them are of the form

"first expression" $\otimes$ "second expression"

For each answer choice, you must determine whether the answer choice can be equal to 0 for some positive integers x and y. Are there positive integers x and y for which the answer choice is equal to 0? If not, then that answer choice is the correct answer.

    Choice A: $x \otimes y$. Using the formula, try to find positive integers x and y for which $x \otimes y = 0$, that is, for which $xy - y = 0$. To solve this equation, note that factoring y out of the left-hand side of the equation $xy - y = 0$ gives the equation $(x - 1)y = 0$. So now you must find positive integers x and y such that the product of the two numbers $x - 1$ and y is 0. Since the product of two numbers is 0 only if at least one of the numbers is 0, it follows that the product of $x - 1$ and y will be 0 if $x = 1$, no matter what the value of y is. For example, if $x = 1$ and $y = 2$, then $x \otimes y = 1 \otimes 2 = (1)(2) - 2 = 0$, and both x and y are positive integers. Therefore, Choice A is not correct, since there are positive integers x and y for which $x \otimes y = 0$.

    Choice B: $y \otimes x$. This is similar to Choice A, except the x and y are interchanged. Therefore, you might try the example in Choice A but with the values of x and y interchanged: $y = 1$ and $x = 2$. Using the formula, $y \otimes x = yx - x = (1)(2) - 2 = 0$. Therefore, Choice B is not correct, since there are positive integers x and y for which $y \otimes x = 0$.

    Choice C: $(x - 1) \otimes y$. Using the formula, try to find positive integers x and y for which $(x - 1) \otimes y = 0$, that is, for which $(x - 1)y - y = 0$. Factoring y out of the left-hand side of the equation $(x - 1)y - y = 0$ yields $(x - 1 - 1)y = (x - 2)y = 0$. Here the product of the two numbers $x - 2$ and y is 0. So the product will be 0 if $x = 2$, no matter what the value of y is. For example, if $x = 2$ and $y = 10$, then $(x - 1) \otimes y = (2 - 1) \otimes 10 = 1 \otimes 10 = (1)(10) - 10 = 0$, and both x and y are positive integers. Therefore, Choice C is not correct, since there are positive integers x and y for which $(x - 1) \otimes y = 0$.

Choice D: $(x + 1) \otimes y$. Using the formula, try to find positive integers x and y for which $(x + 1) \otimes y = 0$, that is, for which $(x + 1)y - y = 0$. Factoring y out of the left-hand side of the equation $(x + 1)y - y = 0$ yields $(x + 1 - 1)y = xy = 0$. Here the product of x and y is 0, so $x = 0$ or $y = 0$. Since both x and y must be positive but 0 is not positive, it follows that there are no positive integers x and y for which $(x + 1) \otimes y = 0$. The correct answer is **Choice D**.

Choice E: $x \otimes (y - 1)$ cannot be correct, since Choice D is correct, but Choice E is considered here for completeness. Using the formula, try to find positive integers x and y for which $x \otimes (y - 1) = 0$, that is, for which $x(y - 1) - (y - 1) = 0$. Factoring $y - 1$ out of the left-hand side of the equation $x(y - 1) - (y - 1) = 0$ yields $(x - 1)$ $(y - 1) = 0$. Here the product of the two numbers $x - 1$ and $y - 1$ is 0. So the product will be 0 if $x = 1$ or $y = 1$, no matter what the value of the other variable is. For example, if $x = 20$ and $y = 1$, then $x \otimes (y - 1) = 20 \otimes (1 - 1) = 20 \otimes 0 = (20)(0) - 0 = 0$, and both x and y are positive integers. Therefore, Choice E is not correct, since there are positive integers x and y for which $x \otimes (y - 1) = 0$.

This explanation uses the following strategies.

Strategy 5: Simplify an Arithmetic or Algebraic Representation
Strategy 10: Trial and Error
Strategy 11: Divide into Cases
Strategy 13: Determine Whether a Conclusion Follows from the Information Given

14. If $x < y < 0$, which of the following inequalities must be true?

   (A) $y + 1 < x$
   (B) $y - 1 < x$
   (C) $xy^2 < x$
   (D) $xy < y^2$
   (E) $xy < x^2$

Explanation

The conditions stated in the question, $x < y < 0$, tell you that x and y are negative numbers and that y is greater than x. Keep this in mind as you evaluate each of the inequalities in the answer choices, to see whether the inequality must be true.

Choice A: $y + 1 < x$. According to the conditions given in the question, y is greater than x. Since y is greater than x and $y + 1$ is greater than y, it follows that $y + 1$ is greater than x. So it cannot be true that $y + 1 < x$. Therefore, Choice A is not the correct answer.

Choice B: $y - 1 < x$. While it is true that both x and $y - 1$ are less than y, it may not be true that $y - 1 < x$. Consider what happens if $y = -2$ and $x = -7$. In this case, the inequality $y - 1 < x$ becomes $-3 < -7$, which is false. Therefore, Choice B is not the correct answer.

Choice C: $xy^2 < x$. Note that y^2 is positive and x is negative, so xy^2 is negative. Is the negative number xy^2 less than the negative number x? It depends on whether $y^2 > 1$ or $y^2 < 1$. Consider what happens if $x = -4$ and $y = -\frac{1}{2}$, where $y^2 < 1$. In this case, the inequality $xy^2 < x$ becomes $-1 < -4$, which is false. Therefore, Choice C is not the correct answer.

Choice D: xy < y². Since *y* is a negative number, multiplying both sides of the inequality *x* < *y* by *y* reverses the inequality, resulting in the inequality *xy* > *y²*. So it cannot be true that *xy* < *y²*. Therefore, Choice D is not the correct answer.

Since Choices A through D have been eliminated, the correct answer is Choice E.

Choice E: You can show that the inequality in Choice E, *xy* < *x²*, must be true as follows: Multiply both sides of the given inequality *x* < *y* by *x* to obtain the inequality *x²* > *xy*, reversing the direction of the inequality because *x* is negative. Therefore, the inequality *xy* < *x²* must be true, and the correct answer is **Choice E**.

This explanation uses the following strategies.

Strategy 5: Simplify an Arithmetic or Algebraic Representation
Strategy 10: Trial and Error
Strategy 11: Divide into Cases
Strategy 13: Determine Whether a Conclusion Follows from the Information Given

For the following question, enter your answer in the box.

15. What is the length of a diagonal of a rectangle that has width 5 and perimeter 34?

        ┌─────────────┐
        │   │
        └─────────────┘

Explanation

In this question, you are given that a rectangle has width 5 and perimeter 34, and you are asked to find the length of a diagonal of the rectangle. Let L and W represent the length and width of the rectangle, respectively, and let D represent the length of a diagonal. Note that you are not given L but you are given that $W = 5$ and that the perimeter is 34. Because the perimeter is equal to $L + L + W + W$, or $2(L + W)$, you can determine L as follows.

$$2(L + 5) = 34$$
$$L + 5 = 17$$
$$L = 12$$

The following figure shows a rectangle of length 12, width 5, and diagonal of length D.

From the figure, you can see that the diagonal is the hypotenuse of a right triangle with legs of length 5 and 12. Therefore, by the Pythagorean theorem,

$$5^2 + 12^2 = D^2$$
$$25 + 144 = D^2$$
$$169 = D^2$$
$$13 = D$$

The length of the diagonal is 13, so the correct answer is **13**.

This explanation uses the following strategies.
Strategy 2: Translate from Words to a Figure or Diagram
Strategy 8: Search for a Mathematical Relationship

SECTION 5
Quantitative Reasoning
20 Questions with Explanations

For each of Questions 1 to 9, select one of the following answer choices.
- (A) Quantity A is greater.
- (B) Quantity B is greater.
- (C) The two quantities are equal.
- (D) The relationship cannot be determined from the information given.

A circle is inscribed in a square with sides of length 5.

Quantity A	Quantity B	
1. The circumference of the circle	15	(A) (B) (C) (D)

Explanation

In this question, you are given that a circle is inscribed in a square with sides of length 5 and are asked to compare the circumference of the circle with 15. Since the circle is inscribed in the square, the diameter of the circle is equal to the length of a side of the square, or 5. Thus, the circumference of the circle is 5v. Because v is greater than 3, it follows that 5v is greater than 15. Therefore, Quantity A is greater than Quantity B, and the correct answer is **Choice A**.

This explanation uses the following strategy.

Strategy 1: Translate from Words to an Arithmetic or Algebraic Representation

$$2u + v = 14$$
$$uv = 0$$

Quantity A	Quantity B	
2. u	v	(A) (B) (C) (D)

Explanation

In this question, you are asked to compare u with v, given that $2u + v = 14$ and $uv = 0$.

Consider the equation $uv = 0$. Since a product can equal 0 only if at least one of the factors in the product equals 0, you know that $u = 0$ or $v = 0$, or both. But since you are also given that $2u + v = 14$, it follows that u and v cannot both equal 0.

Knowing that either $u = 0$ or $v = 0$, you can substitute 0 into the equation $2u + v = 14$ for either u or v in order to determine the relationship between u and v if it is possible to do so from the information given. If $u = 0$, then $2u + v = 14$ simplifies to $v = 14$. In this case, u is less than v. However, if $v = 0$, then $2u + v = 14$ simplifies to $2u = 14$, or $u = 7$. And in this case, u is greater than v.

In the first case, $u < v$, and in the second case, $u > v$. Therefore, the relationship between the two quantities u and v cannot be determined from the information given, and the correct answer is **Choice D**.

This explanation uses the following strategies.

Strategy 5: Simplify an Arithmetic or Algebraic Representation
Strategy 13: Determine Whether a Conclusion Follows from the Information Given

	Quantity A	Quantity B	
3.	$950^{2,000}$	$10^{6,000}$	Ⓐ Ⓑ Ⓒ Ⓓ

Explanation

In this question, you are asked to compare the quantity $950^{2,000}$ with the quantity $10^{6,000}$. Note that both quantities are written in the form "base to a power." If the bases were equal, you would be able to compare the quantities by comparing the powers. Because powers of 10 are easier to work with than powers of 950, it is reasonable to try to compare the quantities by rewriting the quantity $950^{2,000}$ as a power of 10. Unfortunately, there is no obvious way to do that. However, if you can approximate 950 by a power of 10, you may then be able to use the approximation to compare the quantity $950^{2,000}$ with the quantity $10^{6,000}$.

Note that 950 is close to, but a little less than, 1,000, or 10^3. Raising both sides of the inequality $950 < 10^3$ to the power 2,000 gives the inequality $950^{2,000} < (10^3)^{2,000}$. Since $(10^3)^{2,000} = 10^{6,000}$, you can conclude that $950^{2,000} < 10^{6,000}$. Thus, Quantity A is less than Quantity B, and the correct answer is **Choice B**.

This explanation uses the following strategies.
Strategy 5: Simplify an Arithmetic or Algebraic Representation
Strategy 9: Estimate

Set A consists of 40 integers, and set B consists of 150 integers. The number of integers that are in both set A and set B is 20.

	Quantity A	Quantity B	
4. The total number of integers that are in set A or set B, or both		170	Ⓐ Ⓑ Ⓒ Ⓓ

Explanation

In this question, you are given that the number of integers in set A is 40, the number of integers in set B is 150, and the number of integers that are in both A and B is 20. You are asked to compare the total number of integers that are in set A or set B, or both, with 170.

This is the type of question for which a Venn diagram is usually helpful to represent the information given. The following Venn diagram is a representation of the integers in sets A and B.

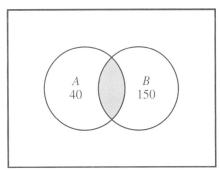

Note that there is no number in the shaded region of the diagram—the region representing the integers in both A and B. In fact, the number of integers in both A and B is included in both the number of integers in A and the number of integers in B. It is a good idea, therefore, to redraw the Venn diagram so that the numbers are separated into three categories: the integers in A only, the integers in B only, and the integers in both A and B. The revised Venn diagram follows.

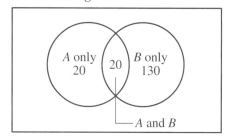

Observe that summing the numbers of integers in set A only, set B only, and both A and B yields the total number of integers that are in set A or set B, or both. Therefore, Quantity A is $20 + 130 + 20$, or 170, and the correct answer is **Choice C**.

Another approach is to realize that if you listed the integers in set A and the integers in set B, you would have listed the integers that are in both A and B twice and all of the other integers once. So the total number of integers in set A or set B, or both, is equal to

(number in set A) + (number in set B) − (number in both sets)

Thus, the number of integers in set A or set B, or both, is $40 + 150 − 20$, or 170, and the correct answer is **Choice C**.

This explanation uses the following strategies.
Strategy 2: Translate from Words to a Figure or Diagram
Strategy 8: Search for a Mathematical Relationship

x is a negative integer.

Quantity A	Quantity B	
5. $\quad\quad 2^x$	3^{x+1}	Ⓐ Ⓑ Ⓒ Ⓓ

Explanation

In this question, you are asked to compare 2^x with 3^{x+1}, given that x is a negative integer. One way to approach this problem is to plug a value of x in both expressions and compare the results.

You are given that x is a negative integer, so the greatest integer you can plug in for x is -1.

For $x = -1$, it follows that $2^x = 2^{-1} = \dfrac{1}{2}$ and $3^{x+1} = 3^{-1+1} = 3^0 = 1$.

In this case, 2^x is less than 3^{x+1}. However, to conclude that Quantity B is greater, it is not sufficient for 2^x to be less than 3^{x+1} for one particular value of x; the relationship would need to be true for <u>all</u> negative integer values of x. To analyze this relationship further, plug in another value of x, for example, -2.

For $x = -2$, it follows that $2^x = 2^{-2} = \dfrac{1}{2^2} = \dfrac{1}{4}$ and $3^{x+1} = 3^{-2+1} = 3^{-1} = \dfrac{1}{3}$.

Again, 2^x is less than 3^{x+1}, but note that these values are closer together than the previous values of 2^x and 3^{x+1}. It appears that the relationship between the quantities may differ for smaller values of x, so now try plugging in -3 for x.

For $x = -3$, it follows that $2^x = 2^{-3} = \dfrac{1}{2^3} = \dfrac{1}{8}$ and $3^{x+1} = 3^{-3+1} = 3^{-2} = \dfrac{1}{3^2} = \dfrac{1}{9}$.

In this case, 2^x is greater than 3^{x+1}.

Since 2^x is less than 3^{x+1} for $x = -1$ and 2^x is greater than 3^{x+1} for $x = -3$, the relationship between these two quantities cannot be determined from the information given. The correct answer is **Choice D**.

Since both quantities are algebraic expressions, another way to approach the comparison is to set up a placeholder relationship, denoted by $\boxed{?}$, between the two quantities and then to simplify to see what conclusions you can draw. As you simplify and draw conclusions, keep in mind that x is a negative integer.

$$2^x \ \boxed{?} \ 3^{x+1}$$
$$2^x \ \boxed{?} \ 3(3^x)$$
$$\frac{2^x}{3^x} \ \boxed{?} \ 3$$
$$\left(\frac{2}{3}\right)^x \ \boxed{?} \ 3$$

For any value of x (including negative integer values of x), the value of 3^x is positive, so dividing by 3^x does not affect any inequality that might be represented by the placeholder. Since each step in this simplification is reversible, the simplification reduces the problem to comparing $\left(\frac{2}{3}\right)^x$ with 3, given that x is a negative integer. Note that $\left(\frac{2}{3}\right)^x = \left(\frac{3}{2}\right)^n$, where $n = -x$; so the problem can be reduced further to comparing $\left(\frac{3}{2}\right)^n$ with 3, given that n is a positive integer.

Because $\frac{3}{2}$ is greater than 1, the value of $\left(\frac{3}{2}\right)^n$ becomes greater as n becomes larger. For small values of n, $\left(\frac{3}{2}\right)^n$ is less than 3, but for large values of n, $\left(\frac{3}{2}\right)^n$ is greater than 3. Therefore, the relationship between Quantity A and Quantity B cannot be determined from the given information, and the correct answer is **Choice D**.

This explanation uses the following strategies.

Strategy 10: Trial and Error
Strategy 13: Determine Whether a Conclusion Follows from the Information Given

Geoff used $630 to buy a new guitar. This amount was 15 percent of his earnings last summer.

Quantity A	Quantity B	
6. The amount of Geoff's earnings last summer <u>not</u> used to buy the new guitar	$3,570	Ⓐ Ⓑ Ⓒ Ⓓ

Explanation

In this question, you are asked to compare the amount of Geoff's earnings last summer <u>not</u> used to buy a new guitar with the amount $3,570. You are given that Geoff used 15% of his earnings last summer, or $630, to buy the new guitar. So the relationship between Geoff's earnings last summer and the amount he spent to buy the guitar can be expressed by the equation

$$(0.15) \times (\text{Geoff's earnings last summer}) = \$630$$

Therefore, you can conclude that Geoff's earnings last summer totaled $\frac{\$630}{0.15}$, or $\$4,200$. Since Geoff earned $\$4,200$ last summer and spent $\$630$ of his earnings to buy the guitar, the amount he did <u>not</u> spend to buy the guitar was $\$4,200 - \$630$, or $\$3,570$. Therefore, Quantity A is equal to Quantity B, and the correct answer is **Choice C**.

This explanation uses the following strategy.

Strategy 1: Translate from Words to an Arithmetic or Algebraic Representation

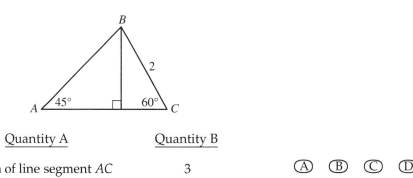

Quantity A	Quantity B	
7. The length of line segment *AC*	3	Ⓐ Ⓑ Ⓒ Ⓓ

Explanation

In this question, you are asked to compare the length of line segment *AC* with 3.

Note that in the figure, the vertical line segment divides triangle *ABC* into two right triangles. Based on the fact that the sum of the measures of the angles in a triangle is $180°$, you can conclude that the triangle to the left of the vertical line is a $45°–45°–90°$ right triangle and the triangle to the right of the vertical line is a $30°–60°–90°$ right triangle. The following figure shows all of these angle measures, along with a new label *D* at the vertex of the right angles.

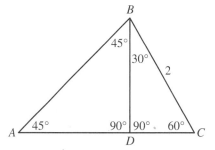

Note that the length of *AC* is equal to the length of *AD* plus the length of *DC*. Also note that *AD* is a leg of the $45°–45°–90°$ triangle and *DC* is a leg of the $30°–60°–90°$ triangle.

In the figure, you are given that the length of *BC*, the hypotenuse of the $30°–60°–90°$ triangle, is 2. No other lengths are given. Recall that if the length of the hypotenuse of a $30°–60°–90°$ triangle is 2, then the length of the side opposite the $30°$ angle is 1, and the length of the side opposite the $60°$ angle is $\sqrt{3}$. So, in the $30°–60°–90°$ triangle *BDC*, the length of *DC* (the side opposite the $30°$ angle) is 1, and the length of *BD* (the side opposite the $60°$ angle) is $\sqrt{3}$.

Now consider the $45°–45°–90°$ triangle *ABD*. Since this is an isosceles right triangle, its legs, *AD* and *BD*, have equal length. Since the length of *BD* is $\sqrt{3}$, the length of *AD* is also $\sqrt{3}$.

As noted above, the length of AC is equal to the length of AD plus the length of DC. Since the length of AD is $\sqrt{3}$ and the length of DC is 1, it follows that the length of AC is equal to $\sqrt{3}+1$.

Recall that in the question you were asked to compare the length of AC with 3. Because $\sqrt{3}$ is less than 2, it follows that the length of AC, which is equal to $\sqrt{3}+1$, is less than $2+1$, or 3. Hence, Quantity B is greater than Quantity A, and the correct answer is **Choice B**.

This explanation uses the following strategies.

Strategy 6: Add to a Geometric Figure
Strategy 8: Search for a Mathematical Relationship

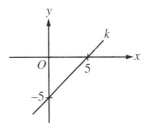

8. What is the slope of line k in the xy-plane above?

(A) –5   (B) 1

(C) –1   (D) 5

(E) 0

Explanation

Recall that if a line passes through the points with coordinates (x_1, y_1) and (x_2, y_2), where $x_1 \neq x_2$, then the slope of the line is

$$\frac{y_2 - y_1}{x_2 - x_1}$$

From the graph of line k in the xy-plane, you can conclude that the x-intercept of line k has coordinates $(5, 0)$ and the y-intercept of line k has coordinates $(0, -5)$. Thus, the slope of line k is

$$\frac{-5-0}{0-5} = \frac{-5}{-5} = 1$$

The correct answer is **Choice D**.

This explanation uses the following strategy.

Strategy 4: Translate from a Figure to an Arithmetic or Algebraic Representation

For the following question, enter your answer in the box.

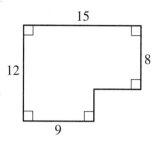

9.   What is the area of the region shown above?

Explanation

In this question, you are asked to determine the area of the given region. One approach to solving this problem is to split the region into two rectangles, rectangle R and rectangle S, as follows.

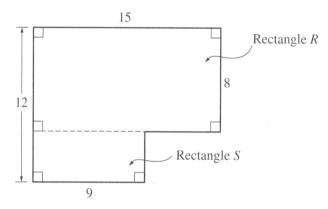

The area of the region is the sum of the areas of the two rectangles. The area of rectangle R is $(15)(8)$, or 120. Since the width of rectangle S is $12 - 8$, or 4, the area of rectangle S is $(9)(4)$, or 36. Thus, the area of the region is $120 + 36$, or 156. The correct answer is **156**.

  Another approach to solving this problem is to form the region by removing a small rectangle from a rectangle with length 15 and width 12, as follows.

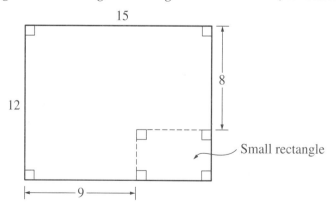

The area of the region is the area of the rectangle with length 15 and width 12 minus the area of the small rectangle. The area of the rectangle with length 15 and width 12 is

(15)(12), or 180. Since the length of the small rectangle is 15 – 9, or 6, and the width of the small rectangle is 12 – 8, or 4, the area of the small rectangle is (6)(4), or 24. Thus, the area of the region is 180 – 24, or 156. The correct answer is **156**.

This explanation uses the following strategies.
Strategy 6: Add to a Geometric Figure
Strategy 8: Search for a Mathematical Relationship

10. During a one-year study, biologists observed the number of fish in a certain pond as well as the percent of the fish that were catfish. At the beginning of the year, there were 300 fish in the pond, of which 15 percent were catfish; at the end of the year, there were 400 fish in the pond, of which 10 percent were catfish. From the beginning of the year to the end of the year, the number of catfish in the pond

    (A) decreased by more than 5%   (D) increased by 5%
    (B) decreased by 5%   (E) increased by more than 5%
    (C) did not change

Explanation

The answer choices indicate that the question is asking about the percent change in the number of catfish. The number of catfish in the pond at the beginning of the year was 15% of 300, or (0.15)(300), which is 45. The number of catfish in the pond at the end of the year was 10% of 400, or (0.10)(400), which is 40. Thus, the number of catfish decreased by 5.

The percent by which the number of catfish decreased from the beginning of the year to the end of the year is

$$\frac{\text{the decrease in the number of catfish over the year}}{\text{the number of catfish at the beginning of the year}} \times (100\%) = \left(\frac{5}{45}\right)(100\%) \approx 11\%$$

Thus, the number of catfish decreased by about 11%. This is a decrease of more than 5%, so the correct answer is **Choice A**.

This explanation uses the following strategy.
Strategy 1: Translate from Words to an Arithmetic or Algebraic Representation

For the following question, enter your answer in the box.

11. On a radio tower, a red light flashes every 6 seconds and a blue light flashes every 10 seconds. If both lights flash together at a certain time, how many seconds later will both lights flash together the next time?

             [   ] seconds

Explanation

One way to approach this question is to look at the "flash times" for both lights to see what times they have in common. The following lists show the flash times for both lights as the numbers of seconds after the time at which both lights flashed together.

    Red light: 6, 12, 18, 24, 30, 36, 42, 48, 54, 60, . . .
    Blue light: 10, 20, 30, 40, 50, 60, 70, 80, 90, . . .

Note that 30 is the first number that is common to both lists. Therefore, if both lights flash together, they will flash together again 30 seconds later. The correct answer is **30**.

Alternatively, you may realize that if the lights flash together, the number of seconds that will elapse before they flash together the next time is the least common multiple of 6 and 10. To find the least common multiple of 6 and 10, begin by writing each integer as the product of its prime factors.

$$6 = (2)(3)$$
$$10 = (2)(5)$$

Since 2 is a factor in both products, but 3 and 5 are factors of only one of the products, the least common multiple of 6 and 10 is $(2)(3)(5)$, or 30. Therefore, if both lights flash together, the next time they will flash together is 30 seconds later. The correct answer is **30**.

This explanation uses the following strategies.

Strategy 1: Translate from Words to an Arithmetic or Algebraic Representation
Strategy 7: Find a Pattern

For the following question, select all the answer choices that apply.

12.   If $a < b < 0$, which of the following numbers must be positive?

Indicate <u>all</u> such numbers.

- [A] $a - b$
- [B] $a^2 - b^2$
- [C] ab
- [D] $a^2 b$
- [E] $a^2 b + ab^2$

Explanation

In this question, you are given that $a < b < 0$ and are asked to determine which of the answer choices must be positive. Note that the condition $a < b < 0$ means that a and b are negative and that $a < b$.

Choice A: $a - b$. In the question, it is given that $a < b$. Subtracting b from both sides of the inequality $a < b$ gives the inequality $a - b < 0$. Therefore, $a - b$ must be negative.

Choice B: $a^2 - b^2$. Since a and b are negative, you can square both sides of the inequality $a < b$ to get the inequality $a^2 > b^2$. Then you can subtract b^2 from both sides of the inequality $a^2 > b^2$ to conclude that $a^2 - b^2 > 0$. So $a^2 - b^2$ must be positive. Alternatively, note that $a^2 - b^2$ can be factored as $(a - b)(a + b)$. The factor $a - b$ is Choice A, which must be negative, and the factor $a + b$ is the sum of two negative numbers, which also must be negative. Thus, $a^2 - b^2$ is the product of two negative numbers, so it must be positive.

Choice C: ab. Because a and b are negative, you can conclude that their product ab must be positive.

Choice D: $a^2 b$. Because $a^2 b$ can be written as $(a)(a)(b)$, which is the product of three negative numbers, you can conclude that $a^2 b$ must be negative.

Choice E: $a^2 b + ab^2$. By the reasoning in the explanation of Choice D, Choice E is the sum of two negative numbers. Therefore, you can conclude that $a^2 b + ab^2$ must be negative.

Choices B and C must be positive, and Choices A, D, and E must be negative. The correct answer consists of **Choices B and C**.

This explanation uses the following strategies.
Strategy 5: Simplify an Arithmetic or Algebraic Representation
Strategy 13: Determine Whether a Conclusion Follows from the Information Given

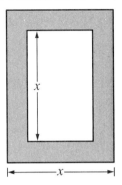

13. A flat rectangular picture, represented by the unshaded region in the figure above, is mounted in a flat rectangular frame, represented by the shaded region. The frame is 1 inch wide on all sides. For what value of x, in inches, is the area of the frame equal to the area of the picture?

(A) 4

(B) 5

(C) 6

(D) 7

(E) 8

Explanation

In this question, you are asked to determine the value of x for which the area of the frame is equal to the area of the picture. To do this, you need to express both the area of the frame and the area of the picture in terms of x and then find the value of x for which the two expressions are equal.

The area of the picture is the area of the inner rectangle, and the area of the frame is the area of the outer rectangle minus the area of the inner rectangle. Since the area of a rectangle is the length times the width, you need to know the length and width of the inner and outer rectangles.

In the figure, you are given that the length of the inner rectangle is x inches, but the width is not given. However, since you know that the width of the frame is 1 inch, it follows that the width of the inner rectangle is equal to the width of the outer rectangle minus 2 inches, or $x - 2$ inches. Thus, the area of the inner rectangle is $x(x - 2)$ square inches.

In the figure, you are given that the width of the outer rectangle is x inches, but the length is not given. However, since you know that the width of the frame is 1 inch, it follows that the length of the outer rectangle is equal to the length of the inner rectangle plus 2 inches, or $x + 2$ inches. Thus, the area of the outer rectangle is $x(x + 2)$ square inches.

Since the area of the frame is the area of the outer rectangle minus the area of the inner rectangle, the area of the frame is $x(x + 2) - x(x - 2) = x^2 + 2x - x^2 + 2x = 4x$ square inches.

Now you are ready to set up the equation. Set the expression for the area of the picture equal to the expression for the area of the frame and solve the resulting equation for x, as follows.

$$x(x - 2) = 4x$$
$$x^2 - 2x = 4x$$
$$x^2 - 6x = 0$$
$$x(x - 6) = 0$$

There are two solutions to the equation, $x = 0$ and $x = 6$. Since x represents the length of a picture, in inches, the solution $x = 0$ does not make sense in this context. Therefore, when $x = 6$, the area of the picture equals the area of the frame. The correct answer is **Choice C**.

This explanation uses the following strategies.

Strategy 4: Translate from a Figure to an Arithmetic or Algebraic Representation
Strategy 5: Simplify an Arithmetic or Algebraic Representation

Questions 14 to 16 are based on the following data.

PERCENT OF THE 300 PEOPLE IN GROUP 1 AND THE 400 PEOPLE
IN GROUP 2 WHO HAVE SELECTED AILMENTS

Respiratory Ailment	Percent of People in Group 1 Who Have Ailment	Percent of People in Group 2 Who Have Ailment
Allergic sensitivity to endotoxins	14%	21%
Asthma (allergic)	3%	4%
Asthma (nonallergic)	2%	3%
Hay fever	4%	10%
Sneezing and itchy eyes	8%	11%
Wheezing (allergic)	5%	6%
Wheezing (nonallergic)	2%	5%

14. The number of people in group 2 who have hay fever is how much greater than the number of people in group 1 who have hay fever?

Ⓐ 37
Ⓑ 35
Ⓒ 32
Ⓓ 28
Ⓔ 24

Explanation

In group 1, there are 300 people, 4% of whom have hay fever. Therefore, in group 1, there are $(0.04)(300)$ people, or 12 people, who have hay fever. In group 2, there are

400 people, 10% of whom have hay fever. Therefore, in group 2, there are (0.10)(400) people, or 40 people, who have hay fever. Since 40 − 12 = 28, it follows that there are 28 more people in group 2 who have hay fever than there are in group 1. The correct answer is **Choice D**.

This explanation uses the following strategy.

Strategy 4: Translate from a Figure to an Arithmetic or Algebraic Representation

15. The number of people in group 1 who have the ailment wheezing (allergic) is what percent greater than the number of people in group 1 who have the ailment wheezing (nonallergic)?

   (A) 50%   (D) 200%
   (B) 75%   (E) 300%
   (C) 150%

Explanation

In group 1, there are 300 people, 5% of whom have allergic wheezing and 2% of whom have nonallergic wheezing. That is, (0.05)(300) people, or 15 people, have allergic wheezing and (0.02)(300) people, or 6 people, have nonallergic wheezing. Therefore, in group 1, the number of people who have allergic wheezing exceeds the number who have nonallergic wheezing by 9, which is $\left(\dfrac{9}{6}\right)$ (100%) greater than 6, or 150% greater than 6. The correct answer is **Choice C**.

This explanation uses the following strategy.

Strategy 4: Translate from a Figure to an Arithmetic or Algebraic Representation

For the following question, enter your answer in the boxes.

16. What is the ratio of the number of people in group 2 with the ailment sneezing and itchy eyes to the total number of people in both groups with the ailment sneezing and itchy eyes?

   Give your answer as a fraction.

   $$\frac{\boxed{}}{\boxed{}}$$

Explanation

In group 2, there are 400 people, 11% of whom have sneezing and itchy eyes. Therefore, in group 2, there are (0.11)(400) people, or 44 people, who have sneezing and itchy eyes. In group 1, there are 300 people, 8% of whom have sneezing and itchy eyes. Therefore, in group 1, there are (0.08)(300) people, or 24 people, who have sneezing and itchy eyes. So the total number of people in both groups who have sneezing and itchy eyes is 24 + 44, or 68. Thus, the ratio of the number of people in group 2 who have sneezing and itchy eyes to the total number of people in both groups who have sneezing and itchy eyes is $\dfrac{44}{68}$. The correct answer is $\dfrac{44}{68}$ (or any equivalent fraction).

This explanation uses the following strategies.

Strategy 4: Translate from a Figure to an Arithmetic or Algebraic Representation
Strategy 5: Simplify an Arithmetic or Algebraic Representation

17. Of the people in a certain survey, 58 percent were at most 40 years old and 70 percent were at most 60 years old. If 252 of the people in the survey were more than 40 years old and at most 60 years old, what was the total number of people in the survey?

   Ⓐ 1,900
   Ⓑ 2,100
   Ⓒ 2,400
   Ⓓ 2,700
   Ⓔ 3,000

Explanation

In this question, it is given that of the people surveyed, 58% were at most 40 years old and 70% were at most 60 years old. Therefore, 70% − 58%, or 12%, of the people surveyed were more than 40 years old and at most 60 years old, and you are given that 252 people are in this group. Let x be the total number of people in the survey. Then 12% of x is 252, that is, $0.12x = 252$, and so $x = \dfrac{252}{0.12} = 2{,}100$. Therefore, the total number of people in the survey was 2,100, and the correct answer is **Choice B**.

This explanation uses the following strategies.

Strategy 1: Translate from Words to an Arithmetic or Algebraic Representation
Strategy 8: Search for a Mathematical Relationship

18. Alice earns d dollars and has t percent of what she earns deducted for taxes. How much of what she earns does Alice have left after taxes?

   Ⓐ $d(1 - 100t)$ dollars
   Ⓑ $d(1 - 10t)$ dollars
   Ⓒ $d(1 - t)$ dollars
   Ⓓ $d(1 - 0.1t)$ dollars
   Ⓔ $d(1 - 0.01t)$ dollars

Explanation

Recall that t percent can be expressed as $\dfrac{t}{100}$, or $0.01t$. Therefore, the amount that Alice has deducted for taxes, which is t percent of d dollars, can be expressed as $0.01td$ dollars. The amount that Alice has left after taxes is the amount that she earns minus the amount that she has deducted for taxes, or $d - 0.01td$ dollars. Note that $d - 0.01td$ is an algebraic expression with two terms, each containing d as a factor. Factoring out d from each term results in the algebraic expression $d(1 - 0.01t)$. The correct answer is **Choice E**.

This explanation uses the following strategy.

Strategy 1: Translate from Words to an Arithmetic or Algebraic Representation

For the following question, select all the answer choices that apply.

19.   A student made a conjecture that for any integer n, the integer $4n + 3$ is a prime number. Which of the following values of n could be used to disprove the student's conjecture?

Indicate <u>all</u> such values.

[A]   1

[B]   3

[C]   4

[D]   6

[E]   7

Explanation

Recall that a prime number is an integer greater than 1 that has no positive divisors other than 1 and itself.

The answer choices for this question are integer values of n. Any of the answer choices for which the integer $4n + 3$ is <u>not</u> a prime number could be used to disprove the conjecture that for any integer n, the integer $4n + 3$ is a prime number.

To answer this question, you must determine for each of the answer choices whether the integer $4n + 3$ is a prime number. The evaluations are as follows:

Choice A: For $n = 1$, the integer $4n + 3$ is $4(1) + 3$, or 7, which is a prime number.

Choice B: For $n = 3$, the integer $4n + 3$ is $4(3) + 3$, or 15, which is not a prime number.

Choice C: For $n = 4$, the integer $4n + 3$ is $4(4) + 3$, or 19, which is a prime number.

Choice D: For $n = 6$, the integer $4n + 3$ is $4(6) + 3$, or 27, which is not a prime number.

Choice E: For $n = 7$, the integer $4n + 3$ is $4(7) + 3$, or 31, which is a prime number.

Therefore, of the answer choices, only Choices B and D, that is, $n = 3$ and $n = 6$, result in integers $4n + 3$ that are not prime numbers. Thus, the correct answer consists of **Choices B and D**.

This explanation uses the following strategies.

Strategy 10: Trial and Error
Strategy 13: Determine Whether a Conclusion Follows from the Information Given

20. Eight points are equally spaced on a circle. If 4 of the 8 points are to be chosen at random, what is the probability that a quadrilateral having the 4 points chosen as vertices will be a square?

(A) $\frac{1}{70}$

(B) $\frac{1}{35}$

(C) $\frac{1}{7}$

(D) $\frac{1}{4}$

(E) $\frac{1}{2}$

Explanation

For questions involving geometry, it is often helpful to draw a figure representing the information in the question as accurately as possible. The figure below shows a circle with 8 equally spaced points, labeled A through H, and quadrilateral $BCDH$, which is one of the many quadrilaterals that have 4 of the 8 equally spaced points as vertices.

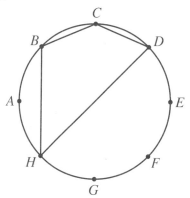

The probability that a quadrilateral having the 4 points chosen as vertices will be a square is equal to the following fraction.

$$\frac{\text{the number of squares that can be drawn using 4 of the 8 points as vertices}}{\text{the number of quadrilaterals that can be drawn using 4 of the 8 points as vertices}}$$

To calculate the desired probability, you need to determine the number of squares and the number of quadrilaterals that can be drawn using 4 of the 8 points as vertices.

To determine the number of quadrilaterals, first note that since the 8 points lie on a circle, every subset of 4 of the 8 points determines a unique quadrilateral. Therefore, the number of quadrilaterals that can be drawn using 4 of the 8 points as vertices is equal to the number of ways of choosing 4 points from the 8 points shown. The number of ways of choosing 4 points from the 8 points shown (also called the number of combinations of 8 objects taken 4 at a time) is equal to $\dfrac{8!}{4!\,(8-4)!}$. You can calculate the value of this expression as follows.

$$\dfrac{8!}{4!\,(8-4)!} = \dfrac{(8)(7)(6)(5)(4!)}{(4)(3)(2)(1)(4!)}$$

$$= \dfrac{(8)(7)(6)(5)}{(4)(3)(2)}$$

$$= 70$$

Thus, there are 70 quadrilaterals that can be drawn using 4 of the 8 points as vertices.

Because the points are equally spaced around the circle, there are only 2 squares that can be drawn using 4 of the 8 points as vertices, namely *ACEG* and *BDFH*, as shown in the following figures.

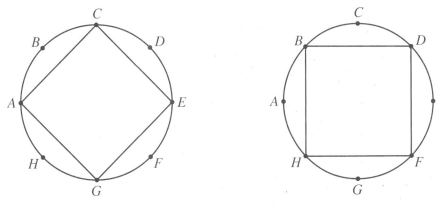

Therefore, the probability that the quadrilateral will be a square is $\dfrac{2}{70}$, or $\dfrac{1}{35}$, and the correct answer is **Choice B**.

This explanation uses the following strategies.
Strategy 2: Translate from Words to a Figure or Diagram
Strategy 8: Search for a Mathematical Relationship

NOTES